The American Jewish Woman:

A DOCUMENTARY HISTORY

by JACOB R. MARCUS

KTAV PUBLISHING HOUSE, INC.
New York, New York

AMERICAN JEWISH ARCHIVES
Cincinnati, Ohio
1981

Library of Congress Cataloging in Publication Data
Main entry under title:

The American Jewish woman : a documentary history

"Intended as a supplement to Jacob R. Marcus, The
American Jewish woman, 1654-1980."—Pref.
  Bibliography: p.
  Includes index.
  1. Women, Jewish—United States—History—Sources.
2. Jews—United States—History—Sources. 3. Women—
United States—History—Sources. 4. United States—
Ethnic relations—Sources. I. Marcus, Jacob Rader,
1896-
HQ1172.M37 suppl   305.4'8   81-1966
ISBN 0-87068-752-2   AACR2

Manufactured in the United States of America

To
Nettie and Merle

CONTENTS

LIST OF ILLUSTRATIONS

PREFACE

This documentary has been compiled for a number of reasons. It is intended as a supplement to Jacob R. Marcus, *The American Jewish Woman, 1654–1980*. It serves as a support, an amplification, of the statements made in the above narrative. In a larger sense these documents speak for themselves and permit every reader to be his/her own historian. The Marcus narrative, *The American Jewish Woman, 1654–1980*, is inevitably subjective, although the author has made a determined attempt to be thoroughly objective, schooled as he is in the rigid, impersonal tradition of the critical school. Documents are less subjective than posteventum narratives. They offer a "control" for the opinions, the conclusions, the divagations of the writer of history. Even though the documents in the following collection must be evaluated in the light of the critical method, nevertheless they do reflect the actual thinking, the behavior, the manners, the doings of many Jewish women for the years 1737 to 1980. For the purpose of this compilation any woman has been accepted as a Jewess who was born of a Jewish father and mother, or even of one Jewish parent. There are no other criteria. Thus this work includes documents on Lubavitcher female Hasidim and on the anti-religious, atheistic Emma Goldman.

This collection has not been angled. Every effort has been made to include documents of importance and interest that reflect the psyche, the activity, the social, economic, political, and religious struggles, the influence, and certainly the growing self-awareness of the American Jewish woman. It is the editor's hope that he has assembled a well-balanced collection. The only limitation or possible distortion would lie in the fact that the compiler is dependent on extant materials. He must use what he finds. The culture pattern of typical housewives finds expression very infrequently in literary works. In a few instances the editor has been frustrated in reprinting documents by the refusal of the copyright holders to permit republication. It is the conviction of the compiler that this documentary is indeed a realistic one. It tends, however, to reproduce data on the American Jewess as a Jew rather than as an American, though to be sure some documents will mirror the activities of the woman in both areas. Excluded are the writings of American Jewish poets, women, who have written only in the general field, who have evinced no interest in Jews or their culture.

The editorial rules observed are few and simple. Documents are reproduced as they were written; spelling and capitalization of nouns are not altered. Words are retained as they were misspelled! There is no form of bowdlerization. Punctuation and paragraphing have been changed in order to ensure clarity, for the prime purpose of the editor is not to attempt to reproduce a facsimile which in many cases would only confuse the reader. Clarity is deemed an imperative. Though Hebrew and Yiddish words abound, no glossary has been appended. Each non-English term is explained as it occurs, and the same translation is repeated as often as necessary. Hebrew and Yiddish words which are accepted as English and included in *Webster's Third New International Dictionary* (Merriam-Webster) are frequently not translated. Words that appear in the text in Hebrew type are transliterated and italicized; the system of transliteration employed is a modified form of one used in the *Jewish Encyclopedia* (see the introductory pages). In transliterating Yiddish words, I have adapted them to the German equivalents; transliterations, however, that appear in the documents themselves are not altered.

I wish to acknowledge my gratitude to the Freudenthal Foundation of Trinidad, Colorado. The trustees, dear friends of mine, have never failed to evince an interest in my work. Their generosity has helped make this volume possible. My colleagues in the Alumni Association of the Hebrew Union College–Jewish Institute of Religion, devoted disciples and affectionate friends, have given me a substantial grant in order that this volume might see the light of day. To them and "the saving remnant in Trinidad," my most heartfelt thanks. And finally I find it difficult to express adequately my thanks to the many who have helped me prepare this documentary. Individuals and institutions have been most gracious in their assistance. The Acknowledgment pages will of course list those publishers and authors who have generously permitted me to reproduce documents whose copyright they hold. I am grateful to all of them. I have leaned very heavily on Professor Herbert C. Zafren and his staff in the Hebrew Union College Library in Cincinnati. They have been a tower of strength and exceedingly patient with me as I have harassed them with innumerable requests for their most treasured possessions. The authorities of the Cincinnati Public Library, and especially Mr. Jacob Epstein, have afforded me special courtesies. Their many kindnesses have lightened my task immeasurably. My staff at the American Jewish Archives have indeed made this compilation possible. I am indebted to them, especially to my colleague Abraham J. Peck, the Associate Director of the American Jewish Archives. He has constantly evinced interest in my work and has never failed to help me when I turned to him. My good friend, Professor Stanley F. Chyet, Dean of the Graduate School of the Hebrew Union College–Jewish Institute of Religion, Los Angeles, California, and professor of American Jewish history, has sacrificially spent many hours "vetting" this manuscript as he has other works of mine. I cannot begin to say how grateful I am. My colleague, Professor Jonathan Sarna, has read this typescript and has made a number of helpful suggestions. Rabbi Kurt Stone and Faedra Lazar Weiss of the Hebrew Union College–Jewish Institute of Religion, Cincinnati, have most carefully checked these documents to guarantee accuracy. This was an arduous labor for which I am deeply appreciative. I would be remiss if I did not mention my copy editors Mr. and Mrs. Robert J. Milch for their expertise and unremitted efforts. For their concern and interest I am grateful. My personal secretary, Mrs. Etheljane Callner, not only typed and retyped my manuscripts but offered me sage advice in the inclusion of borderline materials. Thank you, Mrs. Callner, for your devotion and for your prodding when the road was rough.

Jacob R. Marcus

American Jewish Archives
On the campus of the Hebrew Union College–
Jewish Institute of Religion, Cincinnati, Ohio
January 1981

ABIGAIL FRANKS, NEW YORK, WRITES TO HER SON, HEARTSEY, IN LONDON
1737–1743

Abigail Bilhah Levy Franks (1696–1756) was married to Jacob Franks (1698–1769), one of the most important merchants and army suppliers in eighteenth-century North America. Abigail was a woman of culture with a good knowledge of English literature and an appreciation of the fine things of life. Her spelling, like that of many of her contemporaries, left much to be desired. She was an observant Jewess and maintained a kosher home, but was critical of some of the Jewish rituals, which she looked upon as superstitions. She and her husband sent two of their sons to London in order to integrate them into the business empire of the Franks brothers, an empire which was international in scope. Undoubtedly she hoped also that in London the boys would find Jewish mates. They did. With justice she feared that if they remained in New York they would marry out. Of the children who did remain at home, two intermarried; the others, it would seem, remained single.

Ashkenazi in ancestry, Abigail seems to have kept her Sephardi congregation—most of whose members were, like the Frankses, also of Central and East European provenance—at arm's length. Culturally she was superior to most of them; the Portuguese minority in town tended to keep to themselves; they looked down on the Ashkenazim.

Abigail wrote many letters to her son Naphtali (1715–1796) in London. His middle name was Herz or, in English, Hart, but she called him Heartsey. Two of her numerous letters to this beloved son are reproduced in part here. The first, dating from 1737, deals with the death of her brother-in-law Isaac Franks. The second, written in 1743, describes her shock at discovering that her daughter Phila had secretly married Oliver DeLancey. The Protestant DeLanceys were one of the colonies' most distinguished families, but that circumstance offered Abigail no comfort. Like most eighteenth-century Jews, the Franks were bitterly opposed to intermarriage.

A

[New York, June the 5th, 1737.]

Dear Heartsey:

I have three of your letters answered. The first of them brought us the melancholly acco[un]'t of the death of that worthy and good man Mr. Is[aac]. Franks, wich truly was a very great shock, especialy to your father who for a long while had bin very uneasy on acc't of his [brother's] indisposision, and, as he very justly fear'd, you had not given him a true information how ill he was. Sam. Myers brought a letter wich Uncle Asher's [Levy] had inclosed to him and befor he opened it tould him the sorrowfull contents. Y[ou]'r father seemed imoveable for some time. At last he broake out in a flood of tears. He was very melancholly for a long time, but now begins to be more setled.

For my part when I find a person has soe great a cause for greife I can say but little by way of releife, knowing nature has its call opon these occassions and nothing but time and reasson to aswage the dolor. You tell me I may geuss the concern you laboured under at the loss of soe tender a parent [your future father-in-law] and friend. I truly sampathized with you, but under that great misfourtune you had the satisfaction of imploying y[ou]'r indefatigable endeavours in discharg[in]'g you last dutys to him in such a manner as procoured you the commendations of all his freinds. And I hope you still make it your endeavour in a strickt preserverance of regard and duty to his remains, for that is all wee have left to show our gratitude to the memory of soe kind a benefactor. He was but a very young man, "but in the grave there is noe inquissition wether a man be ten, twenty, or a hundred years ould." All the difference after death is a man's works here on earth, for that never dyes, and one that has left soe great and good a name may be said to have lived full of days and dyed in a good ould age.

I hope soe great an example of worth may be an emulation, to all those that have the happyness to be his relations, to follow his steps in dischargeing theire duty to God an man in the severall stages of life it shall please the Allmighty to set them in.

I hope this may find you in company of all freinds in a happy state of health, and that happyness and long life may allways attend them. My best respects to Mr. Aaron Franks [your uncle] and Mrs. Franks, her son and daughter I sallute with my love. . . .

I have endeavoured by a sort of medly to make a long letter for wich I'll make noe excuse, but would have you take it as a testimony of the pleassure I take in saying something to you, and lett this assure you that I am, dear child,

Your most affectionate mother,
Abigaill Franks. . . .

B

Flatt bush, June 7th, 1743.

Dear Heartsey:

My wishes for your felicity are as great as the joy I have to hear you are happyly married. May the smiles of Providence waite allways on y'r inclinations and your dear [wife] Phila's whome I salute with tender affections, pray'g kind Heaven to be propitious to your wishes in makeing her a happy mother. I shall think the time teadious untill I shall have that happy information, for I don't expect to hear it by the return of these ships, and therefore must injoyn your care in writting by the first oppertunity (after the birth of wathever it shall please God to bless you with) either by via Carrolina, Barbadoz, or any other.

I am now retired from town and would from my self (if it where possiable to have some peace of mind) from the severe affliction I am under on the conduct of that unhappy girle [your sister Phila]. Good God, wath a shock it was when they acquainted me she had left the house and had bin married six months. I can hardly hold my pen whilst I am a writting it. Itt's wath I never could have imagined, especialy afffter wath I heard her soe often say, that noe consideration in life should ever induce her to disoblige such good parents.

I had heard the report of her goeing to be married to Oliver Delancey, but as such reports had offten bin off either off your sisters [Phila and Richa], I gave noe heed to it further than a generall caution of her conduct wich has allways bin unblemish'd, and is soe still in the eye of the Christians whoe allow she had disobliged us but has in noe way bin dishonorable, being married to a man of worth and charector.

My spirits was for some time soe depresst that it was a pain to me to speak or see any one. I have over come it soe far as not to make my concern soe conspicuous but I shall never have that serenity nor peace within I have soe happyly had hittherto. My house has bin my prisson ever since. I had not heart enough to goe near the street door. Its a pain to me to think off goeing again to town, and if your father's buissness would permit him to live out of it I never would goe near it again. I wish it was in my power to leave this part of the world, I would come away in the first man of war that went to London.

Oliver has sent many times to beg leave to see me, but I never would tho' now he sent word that he will come here [to Flatbush]. I dread seeing him and how to avoid I know noe way, neither if he comes can I use him rudly. I may make him some reproaches but I know my self soe well that I shall at last be civill, tho' I never will give him leave to come to my house in town, and as for his wife, I am determined I never will see nor lett none of the family goe near her.

He intends to write to you and my brother Isaac [Levy] to endeavour a reconciliation. I would have you answer his letter, if you don't hers, for I must be soe ingenious to conffess nature is very strong and it would give me a great concern if she should live unhappy, tho' its a concern she does not meritt. . . .

Wath you say abouth y'r sister's [Richa] comeing to England, I shall very readly agree to it, and the sooner the better, if it was only a means of her not seeing the other [Phila], wich she will hardly be able to avoid unless she intirely excludes her self from all company, wich she has don for this three months past, tho' Phila has not bin in town since she left us but has (wathever I have forbid) found means to send messages, for as they lived very affectionately it subsists still, and I am sure she will find all the means she can to see Richa. . . .

My spirets is too depresst to write. It is with reluctancy I doe write to any one at pr'st, therefore whoever I omit you must excuse me to them. I think I've spun this to a considerable length and shall conclude with the repetition of my prayers for your health and happyness. I am, my dear son,

Your affectionate mother,
Abigaill Franks. . . .

2

ANCHOVIES AND WENCHES
1762

Among the customers of Michael Gratz (1740–1811), a Philadelphia merchant, was Meyer Josephson, a German Jewish immigrant who had settled in the German district of Pennsylvania during the early years of the French and Indian War. By 1761, Josephson was married and busy raising a family in Reading, where he had a country store.

As we see from the following letter to Michael (Yehiel) Gratz, originally written in Yiddish, Josephson's relations with his coreligionists, who were also his suppliers, were close and intimate. If our interpretation is correct, the first part of the letter indicates that the Gratzes were thinking of leaving the city for an indefinite period. Apparently Michael and his brother Barnard were not doing so well in those early days.

The second part of the letter deals with the problem of domestics. Female help was scarce in colonial times; women servants were at a premium. Enticing maids to leave their employers and to take jobs with others was by no means uncommon in those days. People made shift with indentured servants and Negro slaves. We know that slavery was no bed of roses for the enslaved; but judging from this letter at least, it is obvious that the slaveowners, too, had their problems. If one misses a humanitarian approach, let it be borne in mind that slaves in the colonies were almost universally deemed a commodity. Only too often Jews reflect the zeitgeist, as is the case here.

Reading (with the help of God, may
God protect it herein),
Sunday, 5 Ab, 5522 [July 25, 1762].

Peace to my beloved friend, the honorable Mr. Yehiel. May the Lord protect him, and may this letter find his entire household at peace.

Your letter came at a propitious moment, also the books and bills of exchange [?] and one jar [?] of anchovies which was very important and which my wife, may she live long, has already eaten. Of course, I helped her somewhat. So if I could obtain another jar of this kind, will you send it to me, because it is the best I ever saw.

Also, I was very sorry to see from your letter that you, my special good patron, intend to leave Philadelphia, which I had not expected at this time. However, if you think that it is not to your best interest to remain, I cannot blame you. One must do many things for the sake of a livelihood. I wish it were in my power to advise you what is best for you to do and arrange that you would not leave Philadelphia, because your brother, may he be blessed, intends at present to go to London, and you, sir, will leave also, and I'll be a stranger when I come to Philadelphia. I really don't know where I can go!

If you come here for the coming Sabbath Nachmu [the Sabbath of Consolation]—may it come at an auspicious moment!—it would please me very much, because we are presently very lonesome on the Sabbath. And if you could stay here with us for eight days, it would be still better.

I also inform you that I may again sell my nigger wench at a profit. So if a ship with niggers should arrive, or a ship with [indentured] Germans, you will let me know, because I cannot manage without a servant. The wench I now have has two virtues, both bad ones. First, she is drunk all day, when she can get it, and second, she is mean, so that my wife cannot say a word to her. She is afraid of her. How did all this happen? A free nigger here wants to court her and to buy her from me. I don't want to give her away for less than 110 pounds, with her bastard, because I bought the bastard too. At present she costs me 90 pounds. So if

I can make out with her, I think it is best to let her go and get another. So if you should have occasion to hear of a good nigger wench, or of a good servant, you will inform me.

I am,

> Your affectionate friend, the humble
> Meir, son of Joseph from Yever,
> scholar, of blessed memory

[Postscript in English]
My spouse gives hear [her] complements to you and very much oblige to you for your coucumers.

3

MIRIAM GRATZ KEEPS IN TOUCH WITH THE FAMILY
1769–1777

The two Gratz brothers, Barnard (1738–1801) and Michael, were Silesians who had come as teenagers to Philadelphia, where they went into business, attained a modest degree of success, and married American girls. Barnard, the older, took as his wife Richea Myers-Cohen, an in-law of Joseph Simon, a Lancaster businessman noted for his prominence in the Indian trade. Michael, the younger, married Simon's daughter, Miriam. Richea had apparently died in 1769, for when Barnard went to England on a business trip that year, he left his only child, Rachel, with Miriam and Michael. A letter which Miriam sent to Barnard in London tells us all about Rachel, at that time less than five years of age (A).

By the year 1777, in the midst of the Revolution, with its perils of war and inflation, Miriam was safely ensconced in Lancaster, living with her father, Joseph Simon, the fur entrepreneur and rifle manufacturer. As a town in the Pennsylvania interior, Lancaster was safe from British raids. Miriam's husband, Michael, was in Fredericksburgh, Virginia, where he had business interests. As a good Jewish wife who knew something about business, Miriam did not fail to describe the galloping inflation. Her spelling had not improved. Let it be said, as an excuse for her, that illiteracy among women at that time was high (B).

A

Philadelphia, August 26th, 1769.

My dear Brother:

As I have just Now heard of this opportunity, Do myself the pleasure of Dedicating a few lines to you and hope to be Excus'd For not Dooing my Duty before, but can ashure you that it was not Neglected . . . For the wante of regard to My Dear Brother. Therefore, as I [k]Now your goodness, I Neede not Make anny further Opoligys.

I have the happiness of acquainting You that our Family Injoys perfect health. Dear Little Rachel [your daughter] has Escapt the Small pox and is Extreamly hartey. Often taulks of hear Dear Littel Daddy and Whishes to see him, as indeade we all do the same. But how could it be otherways when A person whome we all Love and Esteame is at so great a distant from us. Would that It Was spring, then should We be in Expectation of a new happiness [I expect a baby]. But alass A Long Winter is before it. Though can ashure you that thare is nothing wanting To make us Compleatly Happy but your preasence. I have a Dear good and kind husband And a Dear Little pratling Niese [Rachel] which is a great comforte.

I pray that the Almighty May prosper you in all your undertakings, and conduct you safe Over the Wide Oashan to your Dear frinds hear. I hope you'l make yourself interely Easy aboute Rachel, and be ashur'd that she is as well takin care of by us all As she posibally can be. Beckey [the nurse?] is the same kind body she always was. She Desir'd me to Rember her kindly to you and to let you know that she is much Pleas'd of Living as she dose. I can ashure I do all in my power to Render Every thing Agreabell to her.

Rachell gives her Love to you and hopes that you Wonte forget her London Doll as she caules it. I hope after the recipt of this I Shall [be] favour'd with a few Lines from you as could not expect it before, as it Was my place to wright furst. My Dear Michel joynes with me in Love to You. Must Conclude whishing you Every Felicitey this world can afford,

From Your Ever Loving and Affisionate Sister
Miriam Gratz

P.S. I Shall be much Oblig'd to you if you would be kind Enough to make my kind Love Exceptebell to my Aunts and to My New Couzen, Mr. Solomon Henry.

You must make haste home. This is Rachel wrighting as she beg me to let her write. I was oblig'd to gide her hand to please her.

Rachel Gratz

B

Lancaster, June 2nd, 1777.

My dear Micheal:

I had the pleasur of receaving your severel Agreable Favours From Baltimore which Afforded me great Satisfation to hear that you was well and Harty, which I sincarly pray may Continue so whith Every Other Blessing this world can afford.

I thank you my Dear for your good Advise in advising Me to be contented and happy in your Absenc. I Ashure you I Shall Endeavour to be as much so As possible, tho' you very well know it's Impossible that I should be truly so When I have so meany ancxious thoughts about you, tho' you can remove them in a great degree by Letting me heare from you a[s] often as is convenent. And you may be ashur'd I Shall be as puntiall in wrighting as I can. I Waite Impatiently To heare from you which I hope will be in a few days.

In regard to News, Nothing New has Occur'd worth commun'cting. All quiet; God knows how Long it will continue so.

Mr. Moses and Family has removed from this [Lancaster] in hopes of Living in safty at Chessnut hill this Summer. I sencarly Whish thay may, for Thay seam'd Extreamly happy to Leave this place. Barnet [your brother] Leaves this [place] in a few days. He tells me that he expects that you will pay us a visit shortly after he arrives at Verjiney. Perhaps he only flatters me [with your speedy return]. But I Will hope for it. I shall [hope] however Longer then the jenarality of People Dose [remain when they make a visit].

I sopose you desir'd me to Lett you know the prises of goods. It's a thing imposile; Every thing excecve high and changable. Every day is some Altration in the prices. Lofe Suger 10 Shil. pr pound and Every thing Elce in propotion. . . .

Our Dear little Comforts is thank God well and gives thar Love to you and hopes to see you soon. [Miriam had four little ones already.] I think I have wrote a Long letter and for fear of Encroaching on your patienc will conclud, my dare Michel,

Your Ever Loving and Aff' wife
Miriam Gratz

P.S. Dadys fam'y is thank God well and desire thare Love to you and so does Rechel Gratz. [Nurse?] Beck'y comp[limen]'t to you.

Pleas to make my Best Respects Exceptable to our Worthy Frind Sol. Myer and thank him for his Letter which I shall answer by some privet opper'ty, as this is to goe by post. Donte forget your promess in getting me a Gegro [Negro] boy or girl if to be had, as servents is very [scarce?].

ESTHER HART WRITES A FRIENDLY NOTE TO AMERICAN JEWRY'S LEADING TYCOON
1773

In general, Jewish girls were not only taught to write but to write well. Good letter-writing was deemed an art in the eighteenth century. The following pleasant note was written by Esther (Hetty, Hester) Hart, of Charlestown, South Carolina, to Aaron Lopez, an enterprising Newport merchant-shipper. Esther's father, Joshua, was a Charlestown businessman of modest means.

Charles Town, 3d Sept., 1773.

Mr. Aaron Lopez,
Sir:

Your much esteem'd favour came safe to hand with the assurances of your kind wishes towards my papa and mama and family, which you have our greatfull acknowledgements in return for them. If my papa was presant he would with a great deal of pleasur answare his worthy friend's esteem'd favour, but as he [is] not, is deprived of that satisfaction, as [he] is gone to Philadelphia for the benefit of his helth, for he has been very much indisposed this summer.

My papa had thoughts of paying your place also a visit if he found himself better, which I hope kind providence will grant him. I hope my friend will excuse the liberty I have taken in addressing him with this scrall, but as papa being absent was the reason of my being so bold.

My mama joines with me in congratulating you and my dear Mrs. Lopez on her safe delivery. It also renders us happy to think she is so brave with all your dear branches [children]. A continuance of that blessing we sincerly wish you all.

Good sir, you will pleas to make mama and selff respects acceptab[l]e to Mrs. Lopez and Mrs. Mendez [your daughter], and Miss Ester [Lopez], and the rest of the family. You will pleas to accept the same from one that subscribes herself,

Your obliged humble serv't,
Esther Hart.

REBECCA FRANKS HAS A MARVELOUS TIME
1778–1781

Rebecca Franks (1760–1823), a granddaughter of Abigail and Jacob Franks, was the daughter of David Franks, of Philadelphia. Franks, who remained Jewish to the end despite his marriage to a Christian, was one of America's outstanding merchants and army purveyors. As a Loyalist, hostile to a secessionist America, he was constantly under surveillance by the Continental Congress. His uncertain position was certainly not made easier for him by the fact that his daughter Rebecca was notoriously a partisan of the British. When the British took Philadelphia, the Franks home, like many of the best homes in the city, was opened to the British officers. Rebecca was a charming, brilliant girl, one of the wits of her generation, and a great favorite of the English, who were very much drawn to the attractive young lady.

There is no record of her baptism, but it is safe to assume that she was reared by her mother as a Christian. Unlike her father, she appears to have had no interest whatsoever in Jews and Judaism, yet she was constantly referred to as the "Jewess"; in the mind of the average Gentile, a person is a "Jew" until the fact of Jewish origin is no longer known.

One of Rebecca's good friends was Anne Harrison, of Wye Island, Maryland, who had married the patriot William Paca, a signer of the Declaration of Independence. Paca was considerably older than Anne, who was his second wife. Loyalist Rebecca kept up a correspondence with Nancy, as she called her, even though Nancy was the wife of a delegate to the Congress. Rebecca even asked General Sir William Howe, then in command at Philadelphia, for permission to send Nancy a little gift through the lines and prepared to make arrangements to have her come to visit her. Evidently her political prejudices did not extend to her patriot friends—nor theirs to her. The following letter to Nancy, selection A, gives us an excellent picture of social life in the occupied city as seen through the eyes of an eighteen-year-old girl.

The Loyalist David Franks, exiled from Philadelphia by the Whigs in 1780, was accompanied by his daughter Rebecca when he went to British-occupied New York. His other daughter, Abigail (Mrs. Andrew) Hamilton, remained behind in Philadelphia with her family.

Rebecca kept in constant touch with both patriot and Tory friends back home through letters. Her father's tribulations did not lessen her frivolous chatter, and her letters retailed the choicest Gotham gossip. During the hot summer days, there were parties with the British officers. A captain's barge, she wrote, was ready down at the wharf to carry guests to General Robertson's summer home. They were always chaperoned, for in New York no unmarried girl of good breeding went out without an older woman to accompany her. In Philadelphia, of course, all this was unnecessary: "We Philadelphians, knowing no harm, fear'd none." There was an ample supply of attractive officers eager to dance attendance, the handsome Captain Montague, for instance—"Such eyes!" In her more quiet moments, Rebecca went to church or yearned for her sister and the familiar scenes at home or at Woodlands, the Hamilton estate. But she could never quite keep the men out of her thoughts, and the choicest blessing she could conjure up for sister Abigail's girls back home was their choice of the wealthy titled suitors who were floating about: three Honorables, one with £26,000 a year!

One of Rebecca's long, chatty letters, selection B, was sent to Abigail from the Flatbush country estate of the Van Horns. It gives us an excellent opportunity to study social life in aristocratic Loyalist New York during the Revolution.

In 1782, Rebecca married Henry Johnson, a British officer, and made her home in England, where the Frankses, her uncles, were notable entrepreneurs and active members of London's metropolitan Jewish community.

A

[Philadelphia, 1778.]

Dear Nancy:

You can have no idea of the life of continued amusement I live in. I can scarce have a moment to myself. I have stole this while everybody is retired to dress for dinner. I am but just come from under Mr. J. Black's hands, and most elegantly am I dressed for a ball this evening at Smith's where we have one every Thursday. You would not know the room, 'tis so much improv'd.

I wish to Heaven you were going with us this evening to judge for yourself. I spent Tuesday evening at Sir Wm. Howes, where we had a concert and dance. I asked his leave to send you a handkerchief to show the fashions. He very politely gave me permission to send anything you wanted, tho' I told him you were a delegate's lady. I want to get a pair of buckles for your brother, Joe. If I can't, tell him, to be in the fashion, he must get a pair of harness ones.

The dress [I am wearing] is more ridiculous and pretty than anything that ever I saw: great quantity of different coloured feathers on the head at a time, besides a thousand other things; the hair dress'd very high in the shape [the Wilmington beauty] Miss Vining's was the night we returned from Smiths. The hat we found in your mother's closet wou'd be of a proper size. I have an afternoon cap with one wing, tho' I assure you I go less in the fashion than most of the ladies, no[t] being dress'd without a hoop. B[ecky]. Bond makes her first appearance tonight at the rooms.

No loss for partners, even I am engaged to [dance with] seven different gentlemen, for you must know 'tis a fix'd rule never to dance but two dances at a time with the same person. Oh, how I wish Mr. P[aca]. wou'd let you come in for a week or two. Tell him I'll answer for your being let to return. I know you are as fond of a gay life as myself. You'd have an opportunity of rakeing [having a good time] as much as you choose, either at plays, balls, concerts, or assemblys. I've been but three evenings alone since we mov'd to town. I begin now to be almost tired.

Tell Mrs. Harrison [your mother] she has got a gentleman in her house who promises me not to let a single thing in it be hurt, and I'm sure he'll keep his word. The family she left in it still remain. I had a long conversation about you the other evening with John Saunders. He is just the same as when you knew him. Two or three more of your old acquaintances are in town such as Prideaux and Jock DeLancy [my cousin]. They often ask after you.

Is Mrs. White with you? I long to hear all that concerns you. Do pray try to get an opportunity [to send a letter]. The clock is now striking four, and Moses [my brother] is just going out to dinner, quite the Congress hours. Moses wrote to your mother about her house six weeks ago. Did she get the letter? All your Philadelphia friends well, and desire their loves; mine to all in Maryland. When you see the Miss Tilghmans, tell them I never hear a new song or piece of music that I don't wish them to have it. I must go finish dressing as I'm engaged out to tea.

God bless you,
B[ecky]. F[ranks].

Thursday,
Feb'y 26, '78.

I send some of the most fashionable ribbon and gauze; have tried to get Joe's buckles in all the best shops, but in vain. B[ecky]. Redman is here and sends her love.

B

Flat Bush, Saturday, 10 o'c[lock]., August 10th, [17]'81.
My dear Abby:

The night before last I receiv'd y'r letter by *Comfort* [the messenger]. I wish I had been in town to have answer'd it and sent the things out, but I fancy eer [ere] I cou'd have receiv'd y'rs, he must have left E[lizabeth]. Town. And a few days ago I got y'rs and the chicks [my nieces], all of which I thank you and them for. If I have time this morning I'll answer them and the girls' letters.

You will think I have taken up my abode for the summer at Mrs. V[an]. Horn's, but this day I return to the disagreeable hot town much against my will and the inclinations of this family, but I cannot bear papa's being so much alone; nor will he be persuaded to quit it, tho' I am sure he can have no business to keep him. Two nights he staid with us, which is all I've seen of him since I left home. I am quite angry with him.

I have wrote you several times with in these two weeks; you can have no cause to complain, with out it is of being too often troubled with my nonsense. Those [letters] you mention'd sending by P[olly]. R[edman]. have not yet come to hand. The ham is safe; the cracker's haven't as yet made their appearance. I fear they never will tho' I heard they were safe on S[taten]. Island. I fancy the person to whose care they were sent thought them too good to part with. The *person* who sent them and the ham, I beg you'll *give* my sincere thanks to.

You ask a description of the Miss V[an]. Horn that was with me, Cornelia. She is in disposition as fine a girl as ever you saw, a great deal of good humour and good sense. Her person is too large for a beauty, in my opinion (and yet I am not partial to a *little* woman). Her complection, eyes, and teeth are very good, and a great quantity of light brown hair (*Entre nous*, the girls of New York excell us Phil[adelphi]'ans in that particular and in their form), a sweet countinance and agreeable smile. Her feet, as you desire, I'll say nothing about; they are V[an]. Horn's and what you'd call Willings. [The Willings, who evidently had big feet, were partners of Robert Morris.]. But her sister Kitty is the belle of the family, I think, tho' some give the preference to Betsy. You'll ask how many thousand there are, only *five*. Kitty's form is much in the stile of our admir'd Mrs. Gallwey [Galloway], but rather taller and larger, her complection very fine, and the finest hair I ever saw. Her teeth are beginning to decay, which is the case of most N[ew]. Y[ork]. girls after eighteen—and a great deal of elegance of manners.

By the by, few N. York ladies know how to entertain company in their own houses unless they introduce the card tables, except this family (who are remarkable for their good sense and ease). I don't know a woman or girl that can chat above half an hour, and that's on the form of a cap, the colour of a ribbon, or the set of a hoop stay or *jupon* [petticoat]. I will do our ladies, that is Phila'ans, the justice to say they have more cleverness in the turn of an eye than the N. Y. girls have in their whole composition. With what ease, have I seen a Chew, a Penn, Oswald, Allen, and a thousand others entertain a large circle of both sexes, and the conversation without the aid of cards not flag or seem the least strain'd of [or] stupid.

Here, or more properly speaking in N. Y., you enter the room with a formal set curtesy and after the how do's, 'tis a fine or a bad day, and those triffling nothings are finish'd, [then] all's a dead calm 'till the cards are introduc'd when you see pleasure dancing in the eyes of all the matrons, and they seem to gain new life. The misses, if they have a fav'rite swain, frequently decline playing for the pleasure of making love, for to all appearances 'tis the ladies and not the gentlemen that shew a preference now adays. 'Tis here, I fancy, allways leap year. For my part that am us'd to quite an other mode of behaviour, cannot help shewing my surprize, perhaps they call it ignorance, when I see a lady single out her *pet* to lean all most in his arms at an assembly or play house (which I give my honor I have too often seen both in married and single), and to hear a lady confess a partiality for a man who perhaps she has not seen three times. [These women say] "Well, I declare, such a gentleman is a delightfull creature, and I could love him for my husband," or "I could marry such or such a person." And scandle sais [with respect to] most who have been married, the advances have first come from the ladies side. Or she has got a male friend to introduce him and puff her off. 'Tis really the case, and with me they loose half their charms; and I fancy there wou'd be more marriage was an other mode adopted. But they've made the men so saucy that I sincerely believe the lowest ensign thinks 'tis but ask and have; a red coat and smart epaulet is sufficient to secure a female heart. . . .

And now, my d'r Abby, I am going to tell you a piece of news that you'll dislike as much as I do. What do you think of Moses [our brother in London] coming out with a cockcade [an officer's insignia]! He writes to papa and me 'tis his serious resolve, and we must not be surpriz'd if we see him this summer. The idea of ent'ring an ensign at his time of life [he was probably close to thirty] distresses [me] more then any thing I've met with since I left you. All the comfort I have is that his Uncle M[oses]. will not allow him. I have not had an oppor[tuni]'ty of asking papa's opinion of it, as I receiv'd the letters since I've been here, but I am certain he must disapprove of it as much as I do. Was he ten or twelve years younger, I should not have the smallest objection, but 'tis too late for him to enter into such a life, and after the indulgence he's ever been us'd to he'll never brook being commanded from post to pillow by ev'ry brat of [or] boy who may chance to be longer in the service. Tomorrow I shall write to him and make use of ev'ry argument I am misstress of to disuade him from so mad a project, which I hope will arrive in time to prevent it, for if he once enters I wou'd be the first to oppose his quiting it, as I ever lov'd a steady character. The danger of the war I have in a measure reconcil'd myself to. 'Tis only his age I object to and the disagreeable idea of his being sent the L[or]'d knows where. If he does enter (which I hope to God he may not), I wish he may join the 17th, or els get into the dragoons; the latter I think he'll prefer on account of his lameness. He has not, I believe, wrote to you by this oppor[tuni]'ty; Aunt [Moses?] Franks and Aunt Richa [father's sister], I believe, have. . . .

Nanny VaHorn and self employ'd yesterday morn'g in trying to dress a rag baby [doll] in the fashion, but cou'd not succeed. It shall however go, as 'twill in some degree give you an idea of the fashion as to the jacket and pinning on of the handkerchief.

Yesterday the granadiers had a race at the Flatlands [Long Island], and in the afternoon this house swarm'd with beaus and some very smart ones. How the girls wou'd have envy'd me cou'd they have peep'd and seen how I was surrounded, and yet I shou'd have [felt] as happy if not much more to have spent the afternoon with the Thursday Party at the W[oo]'dlands. I am happy to hear you'r out there as the town must be dreadfull this hot summer. N. Y. is bad enough tho' I do not think 'tis as warm as Phil'a. . . .

Well, this is sufficiently long; love to everybody.

Y[ou]'rs,
[R. F.]

1. Zipporah Levy Seixas

6

ISAAC SEIXAS ARRANGES FOR THE MARRIAGE
OF HIS SON, BENJAMIN
1778

Isaac Seixas, a Sephardi immigrant from England in the 1730's, was a shopkeeper, although from all indications not a very successful one. During the Revolution, the Seixas clan fled from the British and settled in Stratford, Connecticut. Among Isaac's several children were Gershom and Benjamin. Gershom was the "rabbi" of the New York Jewish community; Benjamin, a freeman of the city, was a saddler with a shop of his own. When the British occupied New York City in 1776, Benjamin accompanied his kin as they went into exile.

When the Seixas family assembled in Stratford, Isaac found a pleasant task to perform for Benjamin—he asked his friend Hayman Levy on Benjamin's behalf for the hand of his daughter Zipporah in marriage. The prospective groom was thirty; the bride eighteen. Hayman Levy, one of New York's leading fur traders and merchants, had moved to Philadelphia with the coming of the enemy. The stilted tone of Isaac's letter hides the fact that the Seixases and the Levys knew each other well. Propriety, however, demanded that they address each other on this subject in formal fashion.

Ben married Zipporah the following January; undoubtedly, brother Gershom made a special trip to Philadelphia to officiate. It was a very successful marriage, certainly in one respect—they had twenty-one children. Ben Seixas stayed on in Philadelphia until the war was over. He returned to New York about the same time as Gershom. In later years Ben became one of New York's distinguished Jewish citizens, a founder of the New York Stock Exchange, and a president of the synagogue.

Stratford, Novemb. 13, 1778

Mr. Hayman Levy,
S'r:

It is at the request of my son Ben. Seixas that I presume to trouble you with this, to acquaint you that he has inform'd his mother and my self that he has a very great regard for y'r daughter, Miss Zipporah Levy, and shou'd think himself very happy if he cou'd obtain your consent and approbation, as well as your amiable spouse's, and all others connected with the young lady, in permitting him soon to be joined to her in the sacred bonds of matrimony.

We have no manner of objection thereto, and most sincerely wish it may meet with your parental approbation, and that it may prove a source of joy and happiness to all our families. I hope this may find you, good Mrs. Levy, all the children and conexions enjoying perfect health. Mrs. Seixas and all our family join with me in our most respectfull salutations, and I remain, s'r,

Your most obedient and humble servitor,
Isaac Seixas

7

RACHEL GRATZ WRITES TO HER DEAR DADDY
1779–1791

Barnard Gratz's only surviving child was his daughter Rachel, who grew up to marry Solomon Etting of Baltimore, an important member of the notable Etting clan. When Rachel was seven or eight years of age, her "honored farther" showed her how much he loved her. He and Uncle Michael wrote William Murray telling him that an agent was bringing out a shipment of goods to the Illinois country. Among the supplies was a small package of jewelry which Murray was to sell, the profits to go to Rachel and two other Gratz youngsters. This was Rachel's first "adventure" in business, and Murray was asked to watch the account and remit the profits separately.

As she grew up, her father lavished all his love on her. She, too, was very fond of her "dear little daddy" and missed him very much when he left on a long trip to England or crossed the mountains into the dark forests. For safety's sake, during the Revolution, Barnard sent his only child to relatives in the Pennsylvania hinterland.

Although Rachel was in her teens in 1779, she was apparently getting her first formal instruction in arithmetic—rather late, to be sure—but then all sorts of things happen in wartime. However, she had already learned to write, as the following letter, selection A, testifies. Barnard received it from her while he was away from Lancaster. He was probably at his business in Philadelphia at the time.

On November 13, 1791, about three weeks after Rachel married Solomon Etting (dear Solly), she wrote her father asking him to visit her in Baltimore (B). She mentioned the kindness of Mrs. Benjamin Levy. The Levys, originally of New York, Philadelphia, and Baltimore, were pioneers and aristocrats. When the Gratz brothers landed at Philadelphia in the 1750's, the Levys were the dominant Jewish family in town. Since then they had come down in the world; the Gratz-Ettings were on the way up and were now socially acceptable, salonfaehig.

A

Lancaster, August 3, 1779.

Hon[ore]'d Farther:

I cannot let slip this favorable opportunity after my long silence to let you know that I am in good health, thank God, as *I* hope this may find you in the same. You mention in your letter about my minding my schooling, which shall do my endeavors to learn as I know it is my dear daddy's desire. I have just begun to cipher and I am very much delighted at it. I am in averdepois weight and now can cast up anything. I should be very much obliged to my good daddy if you see a pretty fan to get it for me, as they are very dear in this place. Today I was at a French colonel's funeral who was buried with all the honors of war. The day before that he was buried but it was not regular; so they took him up again. Today was the finishing.

I must conclude, hon'd father, with wishing you every earthly felicity this world can afford.

Your ever-loving and obedient daughter,
Rachel Gratz

Aunt [Miriam Gratz?] and all the children desire their love to you. Aunt Bush desires to be remembered to you. Becky's [the nurse?] compliments to you. Please to remember me to Moses.

My d[ea]'r daddy, I have one favor to beg of you, not to forget to get me a lining for my cloak and some lace. Becky begs of you the favor to get her three yards of linsey, please.

B

Baltimore, November 13th, 1791.

My ever hon'd parent:

I was made very happy on Fryday last, on the receipt of your welcome letter. As an assurance of the welfare of my dearest father is the first wish of my heart, continue to favour me frequent, there by affording much satisfaction to me, and [I] flatter my self with the pleasure of soon embraceing you and convinceing you verbally, how very happy I am situated, and the wish of entertaining my dear father is the most earnest of my solicitations. Do not disappoint me, my best of paren[ts]; tho[ugh]t of your not accompanying me was painful; [I] therefore entreat you will not prolong your stay, but hasten to make perfectly happy your grateful daughter.

I this morning was favoured with a visit from Mrs. Levy, who was very pressing in her invitations to me. Amidst the many I have received from the people here who have called on me, one of the number was an old acquaintance of yours, a Mrs. Hunter, who was very particular in her enquiries about you and wishes much to see you. From what little I have seen of this place, think I shall like it very much, as it far exceeds my expectations.

My dear Solly [Etting] is well and intends writeing to you. Mrs. [Elijah] Etting [my mother-in-law] and family beg their best respects to you, as does Mrs. Salomons. It is now late and am fearful of missing the oppertunity [of sending this]. Must conclude, with my most ardent wish for your health and contentment.

[I] remain your most affectionate and dutiful daughter,

Rachel Etting

Please to present my best regards to Mrs. and Mr. Josephson, Mrs. and Mr. Cohen, with all other friends.

8

ABIGAIL MINIS, GEORGIA WHIG, GOES INTO EXILE
1779

Accompanied by his wife, Abigail, Abraham Minis landed in Savannah, Georgia, just about five months after Colonel Oglethorpe's arrival with the first group of colonists. Abraham died in 1757, leaving his horses to his three sons, Joseph, Minis, and Phillip, his cattle to his five daughters, and the rest of the estate and his business to the sturdy Abigail.

When, in September 1779, the American troops and their French allies landed on the Georgia coast and attempted to recapture Savannah from the British, they needed supplies and provisions. Among those to whom they turned was the vigorous Abby Minis, then a woman of about eighty, but still active in business. She did not disappoint those who turned to her, but after the disaster which overtook the allied expedition she found it difficult to remain in town. Charges were preferred against her as a Whig, and no doubt measures were also taken to confiscate her property. Under the circumstances, she found it advisable to go to nearby Charlestown. Accordingly, she and her five daughters sent the following petition, in October 1779, to Governor Wright and the Royal Council. The governor and his cabinet approved of her request, promised not to confiscate her property, and permitted her to leave for South Carolina. Obviously, she must have had influential friends in high places.

[Oct. 1779.]

To His Excellency Sir James Wright . . .

The humble petition of Abigail Minis of Savannah in the said province, widow, and her daughters, Leah, Hester, Judy, Hannah, and Sarah Minis, sheweth that your petitioner Abigail Minis is seized and possessed in her own right of a small plantation near the town of Savannah and of a house in said town, some Negroes and other personal property. And your other petitioners are seized and possessed of some lots of land and premises in said town and personal property,

That some prosecution of late has been entered against your petitioners, [who] are desirous the same may be withdrawn, and [they] be permitted to go to Charlestown, South Carolina, to reside for some time, and carry with them their personal property,

That your petitioners desire permission to appoint one or more attorneys or attorney to rent out or otherwise manage their said real property in Georgia for their sole use and benefit,

That your petitioners hope by means of removing to Charlestown the same will not be deemed or looked upon as forfeiture of any part of their said real property,

Your petitioners therefore most humbly pray your Excellency and Your Honorable Board will be pleased to grant them the several matters stated and set forth in this their petition, and that you will be further pleased to grant or order a proper vessel to carry them and their personal property with a flag [of truce boat] by water to Charlestown.

And your petitioners as in duty bound will ever pray.

Abigail Minis, Leah Minis, Esther Minis,
Judy Minis, Anna Minis, Sally Minis

9

FRANCES SHEFTALL, WIFE OF MORDECAI
SHEFTALL, PRISONER OF WAR
1780

In December 1778, Mordecai Sheftall, a leading Georgia Whig, and his teenage son, Sheftall Sheftall, were captured by the British. They were not exchanged until the summer of 1780. During Mordecai's detention by the British on Antigua in the West Indies, his wife Frances (Fanny) Hart Sheftall (1740–1820) wrote him.

In the letter, selection A, she described her efforts to help the two and, because they were hungry for news, regaled them with gossip; she was in business, she wrote, and doing well. All this, however, may have been a device on her part to keep their spirits up. Perla, their seventeen-year-old daughter, served as Frances' scribe.

About June 1780, Mordecai and his son were paroled by the British and went on to Philadelphia, the capital of the new country, the center of its commercial life, and at the time the home of its largest Jewish community. Fanny and the younger children were obliged to remain in Charlestown, South Carolina, then in British hands. In July, Fanny wrote to her husband in Philadelphia, describing what had happened to her and the children and their friends when Charlestown was besieged in the early months of the year (B).

A

Charls Town, March 3th, 1780.

My dear Sheftall:

I had the pleasure to receive your laste letter, with my son's, by Mr. Coshman Polack by the way of North Carolina, and was glad to here [hear] that you and my son injoyed your healths, a continuance of which I sincerely whish you. But [I] was verry miserable to hear that you and my dear child was in so much distress. I would have endeavoured to have sent something for your reliefe, but the enemy now lay off of the bar, so that it is not in my power to do any thing for you at present, but the first safe

28

oppertunity you may depend on my sending you whatever is in my power.

Their is a Jew gentleman gone from here to North Carolina, by the name of Mr. Levy. He has promised me to buy up six halfe johanases [gold coins] theare [there] and to send them to you with a letter, as thay are much cheaper thare than [they] are here.

I had not the pleasur off seeing Mrs. Walton, as the vessel she came in was obliged to put in to North Carolina. Mr. Coshman Polack has been to St. Eustatia and was passenger with Mrs. Walton, since whitch he has arrived here. He likewhise told us that he wrote to you, but that he never received an answer. Your brother [Levi] has shewn your letter to Genaral [Benjamin] Lincoln, and he has assured him that he will do all in his power in your behalfe as soon as times is a little more settled here.

You must tell my son that I would have answered his letter in full, but it is Friday afternoon and very late. [Writing is not permitted on the Sabbath.] But he may depend that I will whrite him by the next oppertunity. Our friend Mrs. Whrite is here and has been with me some time. She sincerely wishes to see you. Our old friend, Miss Sally Martin, is dead, and likwhise poor Mrs. Brady. Old Mrs. Mines [Abigail Minis] is here with all her family and is settled here. They all desire to be kindly remembered to you. I hav the pleasure to inform you that your brother's wife is safely delivered off a fine son and he is called Isaac. Mr. Jacobs and wife, in company with Mr. Cohen and wife, desire to be kindly remembered to you. Mr. Cohen's family is likely to increas shortly. I can assure you that Mr. Jacobs is been a father to your children and a great friend to me. I had like to [I almost] forgot to mention to you that I have received the 2 thousand pounds of Mr. Cape, with which I make exceeding well out by doing a little business. Your children all go to school. I have no more at present, but that I and all the children are in good health, and am, my dear Sheftall,

Your loving wife,
Frances Sheftall

Pearla begs that you will excuse this scrool, as she has wrote it in great haste and our Sabbeth is coming on so fast.

The children all desire their love to their brothe[r] and their duty to you. They all long for to see you.

B

Charls Town, July 20th, 1780.

My dear Sheftall:

I have now the pleasure to inform you that I received your letter on the 19 instn., dated May the 5, and sincerly congratulate you and my dear childe on your enlargement [prospective release], hoping that we may once more meet again in a great deal of pleasure, for I can assure you that we have been strangers to that for some time past. But I still hope that our troubles will now be soon at an end.

I make not the least doubt, but ere thise comes to hand that you have herd that thise place was given over to the British troops on May 12th by a caputalation after three longe months sige. During that time I retier'd into the country with my family, and a great many of our people ware at the same place. During the sige thare was scarce a woman to be see[n] in the streets. The balls flew like haile during the cannonading.

After the town was given over, I returned to town and have hierd a house in St. Michael's Alley belonging to Mrs. Stephens at the rate of fifty pounds sterlinge a year. And whear the money is to come from God only knows, for their is nothing but hard money goes here, and that, I can assure you, is hard enough to be got.

I am obliged to take in needle worke to make a living for my family, so I leave you to judge what a livinge that must be.

Our Negroes have every one been at the point of death, so that they have been of no use to me for thise six weeks past. But, thankes be to God, they are all getting the better of it except poor little Billey, he died with the yellow fever on the 3 of July.

The children have all got safe over the small pox. They had it so favourable that Perla had the most and had but thirty. How I shall be able to pay the doctor's bill and house rent, God only knowes. But I still trust to Providence knowing that the Almighty never sends trouble but he sends some relife.

As to our Adam [a free servant?], he is so great a gentleman that was it to please God to put it in your power to send for us, I do thinke that he would come with us.

I wrote to you about three weeks agoe by way of St. Austatia [Eustatius] to Antigua, whare I mention every particular to you, but must now refer it untill it shall pleas God that we see you again. You[r] brother Levy went out of town during the sige toward the northward and has not returned as yet. Thise day his youngest baby, Isaac, was buried. The poor baby was sicke for about three weeks and then died.

We have had no less than six Jew children buried since the sige, and poor Mrs. Cardosar [Cardozo], Miss Leah Toras that was, died last week with the small pox. Mr. DeLyon has lost his two grand children. Mrs. Mordecai has lost her child. Mrs. Myers Moses had the misfortune to have her youngest daughter, Miss Rachel, killed with the nurse by a cannon ball during the sige.

Perla begs that you will excuse her not whriting by thise oppertunity as she has been with her Aunt Sally for several nights and is very much fatigued, and the flag [of truce ship] goes immediately, but hopes that she will be the bearrer of the next [letter] herselfe. But havinge so favourable an oppertunity as the flag [I] was willing to let you no [know] some little of our family affairs.

I have nothing more at present but wish to hear from you by the first oppertunity.

The children joine me in love to you and their brother, and I remain

Your loving wife,
Frances Sheftall

10

RACHEL MYERS, A LOYALIST, APPEALS FOR HELP
1781

While Newport, Rhode Island, was held by the British (1776–79), the Loyalists were secure enough, but when the French forces commanded by the Comte de Rochambeau arrived in 1780, many of them found it advisable to leave.

Among the refugees was the widow Rachel Myers, one of whose sons, Benjamin, had been an active Loyalist. Taking her large brood of children with her, Mrs. Myers went to New York City, which had been under British occupation since 1776. Lacking means of support there, she appealed for aid to Sir Henry Clinton, the Commander in Chief of the British forces in North America.

After the British evacuation of New York in 1783, the widow and her family were once again forced to flee. They spent some time in Canada, and then, when the acerbities engendered by the war had been dulled by the passage of time, they returned to the United States. One of the boys, Mordecai, served as an American officer in the War of 1812.

To His Excellency, Sir Henry Clinton, Knight of the Most Honorable Order of the Bath, General and Commander in Chief, etc., etc., etc.

The petition of Rachel Myers, late of Newport, widow, humbly sheweth:

That your petitioner was for many years an inhabitant of Newport where she supported by her industry a large family of children;

That from the decissive part her son, Benjamin Myers, took with the associated refugees and other loyalists at Rhode Island, she was obliged to leave that place after it was evacuated by his Majesty's troops and come to this city in a flag of truce [ship] with all her family, consisting of nine children;

That she has in the maintenance of her family struggled with many difficulties and, from the assistance she has derived from a few benevolent friends hitherto been able to support, tho indifferently, her children. But all her industry is not now sufficient to afford them the necessaries of life, which constrains her to implore your Excellency to extend her some relief from government, by permitting her to receive for her family such rations of provisions, etc., as may be thought necessary.

And your petitioner, as in duty bound, shall ever pray.

Rachel Myers

New York, April 3, 1781.

11

MANUEL JOSEPHSON PETITIONS THE PHILADELPHIA CONGREGATION TO BUILD A RITUAL BATHHOUSE

1784

Manuel Josephson (ca. 1729–1796), an emigrant from Germany, was one of the best-educated men in the Philadelphia congregation. A sometime sutler during the French and Indian War, Josephson became a merchant in New York and finally settled in Philadelphia. He was a good Hebraist and was interested in general culture; in religious matters he was a fervent traditionalist.

In 1784, Josephson presented the following petition to the board of Mikveh Israel, asking that a ritual bathhouse (mikvah) be built for the women of the congregation. His motivation is classical in its orthodoxy: inasmuch as the American Jew had been blessed with desirable privileges, it was incumbent upon him to thank God by scrupulously observing the Divine Law. If he failed to do so, all the curses threatened in Holy Writ would descend upon the transgressor.

By 1786, the ritual bathhouse had been erected and placed under the supervision of the zealous Josephson.

[1784]

It having pleased the Almighty God of Israel to appoint our lot in this country, the rulers whereof he has inspired with wisdom and a benevolent disposition toward us as a nation, whereby we enjoy every desireable priviledge and great preeminence far beyond many of our brethren dispersed in different countries and governments,

And in order to manifest our gratitude for those peculiar favors and blessings, we ought, in a very sincere manner, observe a strict and close adherence to those laws and commandments ordained by Him and delivered to our master Moses, of blessed memory, which have been handed down to us in a regular succession to the present time, wherein we are told [Exod. 19:5 "Ye shall be a peculiar treasure unto me above all people"] that the Almighty has made choice of our nation in preference of all others, on condition (*ibid.*, "If ye obey my voice and keep my covenant") that we hearken unto his voice and observe his covenants; and on the other hand, if we neglect our duty, He has denounced [Lev. 26:14, etc., etc.] severe and tremendious sentences against us, to avoid which we should endeavour with all our might to regulate our conduct in every respect conformable to His Holy Law, rectify every deviation therefrom, and supply every omission so far as in our power.

In order thereto, we, the subscribers, having taken these matters to heart and duly reflected on the many defects this congregation called Mikve Israel in Philadelphia labours under, and to our great regret and sorrow we find one in particular, which strikes us most forcibly and cannot but affect with astonishment and horror every judicious and truly religious mind. This is the want of a proper *mikve* or batheing place, according to our Law and institution, for the purification of married women at certain periods. The necessity of having and using such place will readily appear from the text [Lev. 20:18] where a transgression of this ordinance is highly criminal to both husband and wife. Nor does it rest with them only, but the very children born from so unlawful cohabitation are deemed *bene niddot* [children conceived during the menstrual period], which makes this offence the more hoeinous [heinous] and detestable, in as much as it effects not only the parents, but their posterity for generations to come. And should it be known in the congregations abroad that we had been thus neglectful of so important a matter, they would not only pronounce heavy anathemas against us, but interdict and avoid intermarriages with us, equal as with [a] different nation or sect, to our great shame and mortification.

Now, therefore, in full consideration of the foregoing, we have unanimously agreed that a proper *mikve* or batheing place for the sole use of our congregation be forthwith built, and that no delay may be made in accomplishing so necessary and laudable a work. We do hereby, each of us for himself, most solemnly and religiously engage and promise to pay such sum of money as is annexed to our respective names, without any hesitation or demur whatever, unto such person or persons as shall hereafter be nominated for the purpose of receiveing the said subscription money and to see the said work carried on and compleated. And we flatter ourselves that evry married man will use the most persuasive and evry other means to induce his wife to a strict compliance with that duty so incumbent upon them, that so the Almighty may look down in mercy upon us and send the Redeemer to Zion in our days. Amen, so be it.

Philadelphia, 21st May, 1784.

Rosh Hodesh Sivan (the first of Sivan), 5544.

A JEWISH MARRIAGE CEREMONY
1787

A good description of a Jewish marriage ceremony in early America is afforded by Dr. Benjamin Rush in a letter to his wife. Rush, in his day the best-known physician in the United States, had been invited by the Jonas Phillipses to attend the ceremony uniting their daughter Rachel with a Virginian named Michael Levy. In 1792, Rachel gave birth to a son whom the couple named Uriah Phillips Levy. The child was destined to have a fabulous career. He ran away to sea at the age of ten, joined the United States Navy during the War of 1812, and finally, in the days before the Civil War, became the "Commodore" of the American squadron in the Mediterranean. Uriah's was a stormy life, for he faced boards of inquiry twice and courts-martial six times. Many of his troubles may be ascribed to the circumstance that he was a Jew in an age when Jews were not welcome in the Navy; nor was his road made any easier by the fact that, in addition to being a successful businessman, he was nothing if not "hard-boiled." He lavished a great deal of time and energy on the effort to abolish flogging in the Navy, and his tombstone in Cypress Hill Cemetery bears the inscription: "Father of the law for the abolition of the barbarous practice of corporal punishment in the Navy of the United States."

Philadelphia, June 27, 1787.

My dear Julia,

Being called a few days ago to attend in the family of Jonas Phillips, I was honored this morning with an invitation to attend the marriage of his daughter to a young man of the name of Levy from Virginia. I accepted the invitation with great pleasure, for you know I love to be in the way of adding to my stock of ideas upon all subjects.

At one o'clock the company, consisting of sixty or forty men, assembled in Mr. Phillips' common parlor, which was accommodated with benches for the purpose. The ceremony began with prayers in the Hebrew language, which were chaunted by an old rabbi and in which he was followed by the whole company. As I did not understand a word except now and then an Amen or Hallelujah, my attention was directed to the haste with which they covered their heads with their hats as soon as the prayers began, and to the freedom with which some of them conversed with each other during the whole time of this part of their worship. As soon as these prayers were ended, which took up about twenty minutes, a small piece of parchment was produced, written in Hebrew, which contained a deed of settlement and which the groom subscribed in the presence of four witnesses. In this deed he conveyed a part of his fortune to his bride, by which she was provided for after his death in case she survived him.

This ceremony was followed by the erection of a beautiful canopy composed of white and red silk in the middle of the floor. It was supported by four young men (by means of four poles), who put on white gloves for the purpose. As soon as this canopy was fixed, the bride, accompanied with her mother, sister, and a long train of female relations, came downstairs. Her face was covered with a veil which reached halfways down her body. She was handsome at all times, but the occasion and her dress rendered her in a peculiar manner a most lovely and affecting object. I gazed with delight upon her. Innocence, modesty, fear, respect, and devotion appeared all at once in her countenance. She was led by her two bridesmaids under the canopy. Two young men led the bridegroom after her and placed him, not by her side, but directly opposite to her. The priest now began again to chaunt an Hebrew prayer, in which he was followed by part of the company. After this he gave to the groom and bride a glass full of wine, from which they each sipped about a teaspoonful. Another prayer followed this act, after which he took a ring and directed the groom to place it upon the finger of his bride in the same manner as is practised in the marriage service of the Church of England.

This ceremony was followed by handing the wine to the father of the bride and then a second time to the bride and groom. The groom after sipping the wine took the glass in his hand and threw it upon a large pewter dish which was suddenly placed at his feet. Upon its breaking into a number of small pieces, there was a general shout of joy and a declaration that the ceremony was over. The groom now saluted his bride, and kisses and congratulations became general through the room. I asked the meaning, after the ceremony was over, of the canopy and of the drinking of the wine and breaking of the glass. I was told by one of the company that in Europe they generally marry in the open air, and that the canopy was introduced to defend the bride and groom from the action of the sun and from rain. Their mutually partaking of the same glass of wine was intended to denote the mutuality of their goods, and the breaking of the glass at the conclusion of the business was designed to teach them the brittleness and uncertainty of human life and the certainty of death, and thereby to temper and moderate their present joys.

Mr. Phillips pressed me to stay and dine with the company, but business . . . forbade it. I stayed, however, to eat some wedding cake and to drink a glass of wine with the guests. Upon going into one of the rooms upstairs to ask how Mrs. Phillips did, who had fainted downstairs under the pressure of the heat (for she was weak from a previous indisposition), I discovered the bride and groom supping a bowl of broth together. Mrs. Phillips apologized for them by telling me they had eaten nothing (agreeably to the custom prescribed by their religion) since the night before.

Upon my taking leave of the company, Mrs. Phillips put a large piece of cake into my pocket for you, which she begged I would present to you with her best compliments. She says you are an old New York acquaintance of hers.

During the whole of this new and curious scene my mind was not idle. I was carried back to the ancient world and was led to contemplate the passovers, the sacrifices, the jubilees, and other ceremonies of the Jewish Church. After this, I was led forward into futurity and anticipated the time foretold by the prophets when this once-beloved race of men shall again be restored to the divine favor and when they shall unite with Christians with one heart and one voice in celebrating the praises of a common and universal Saviour. . . .

Adieu. With love to your mama, sisters, and brothers, and to our dear children, I am your affectionate husband,

B. Rush

· 13 ·

SALOMON RAFFELD (RAPHAEL) ASKS FOR
PERMISSION TO BE MARRIED
1788

*American Jewish congregations of the eighteenth century required a couple
to submit a formal request to the president before the marriage could be
solemnized by the hazzan or minister. By granting or withholding
approval, the community leaders attempted to control intermarriage,
inevitable in sparsely settled countries where young Jewish women were
scarce.*

*A typical example of such a request is the following petition, which
Salomon Raffeld addressed to Levy Phillips in October 1788. This Raffeld
is identical with Solomon Raphael, a merchant and auctioneer, who at
various times did business in Philadelphia, Baltimore, and Richmond.*

*Unfortunately, Raffeld's letter does not speak for itself. Because its
English is almost unintelligible, it is followed by a paraphrase.*

To the anerable, the presedent and the genthelman jauntay:
 Weer as I have pramis mie selleff in matteri mony whit one gall,
the dogter of Mr. Barent Jacob, in the Norderen Libberthes in
Philladelpia; and I would bie werry happay that jour anerable
budday would order to Mr. Jacob Kohon as gasan of the
congragashis of Mikvy Israel to give mie goupa and kadousin
agins Dousday. Ther for, genttelman, I pray one ansver of jour
shentel man to mourow . . . the 12 day of Tisri at 11 o'clok and,
by soo douing, your pertisnar will eiver pray.
                                        Froom jour omble sarwint,
                                                    Salomon Raffeld
To Mr. Levy Phillip, President of the K.K. Mikvy Israel,
Philadelphia, Sonday, the 11 day of Tisri, 5549.
To the honorable, the president and the gentlemen [of the board]
junta
 Whereas I have promised myself in matrimony with one [a]
girl, the daughter of Mr. Barent Jacob, in the Northern Liberties

40

[section] in Philadelphia, I would be very happy if your honorable body would order Mr. Jacob Cohen, as hazzan [cantor] at the congregation of Mikveh Israel, to give me *huppah* and *kiddushin* [a legal and ritually proper Jewish marriage] against [next] Tuesday. Therefore, gentlemen, I pray one [an] answer from you gentlemen tomorrow, the 12th day of Tishri at eleven o'clock and, by so doing, your petitioner will ever pray.

From your humble servant,

Salomon Raffeld

To Mr. Levy Phillips, President of the Holy Congregation Mikveh Israel, Philadelphia, Sunday, 11th day of Tishri, 5549 [October 13, 1788].

· 14 ·
AN OBSERVANT JEWESS LOOKS AT AMERICA
1791

Hyman Samuel, who married Rebecca Alexander, was a silversmith and a watchmaker, living in Petersburg, Virginia, Baltimore, and Charleston, South Carolina. During the last decade of the eighteenth century, Rebecca described Jewish life in Petersburg in two letters to her parents, who were then living in Hamburg, Germany. The Samuels, who were probably of German stock, had apparently spent some time in England, and looked with contempt upon the uncouth German Jews they found in the United States.

Rebecca Samuel's letters are among the most significant that we possess for this period, inasmuch as they touch, albeit lightly, on the vital questions of anti-Jewish prejudice, acculturation, the religious education of children, the separation of church and state, the absence of craft guild restrictions, and the larger opportunities available in this country for the common man.

Rebecca Samuel's two letters, printed below, were written in Yiddish. The first, selection A, is unfortunately incomplete. The second, selection B, though undated, was probably written within the same decade, for we know that the Samuels were still in Petersburg in 1792. By 1796, they had moved to Richmond.

A

Petersburg, January 12, 1791,
Wednesday, 8th [7th?] Shebat, 5551.

Dear and Worthy Parents:

I received your dear letter with much pleasure and therefrom understand that you are in good health, thank God, and that made us especially happy. The same is not lacking with us—may we live to be a hundred years. Amen.

Dear parents, you complain that you do not receive any letters from us, and my mother-in-law writes the same. I don't know what's going on. I have written more letters than I have received from you. Whenever I can and have an opportunity, I give letters to take along, and I send letters by post when I do not have any other opportunity. It is already six months since we received letters from you and from London. The last letter you sent was through Sender [Alexander], and it was the beginning of the month of Ab [July, 1790] when we received it. Now you can realize that we too have been somewhat worried. We are completely isolated here. We do not have any friends, and when we do not hear from you for any length of time, it is enough to make us sick. I hope that I will get to see some of my family. That will give me some satisfaction.

You write me that Mr. Jacob Renner's son Reuben is in Philadelphia and that he will come to us. People will not advise him to come to Virginia. When the Jews of Philadelphia or New York hear the name Virginia, they get nasty. And they are not wrong! It won't do for a Jew. In the first place it is an unhealthful district, and we are only human. God forbid, if anything should happen to us, where would we be thrown? There is no cemetery in the whole of Virginia. In Richmond, which is twenty-two miles from here, there is a Jewish community consisting of two quorums [twenty men], and the two cannot muster a quarter [quorum when needed?].

You cannot imagine what kind of Jews they have here [in Virginia]. They were all German itinerants who made a living by begging in Germany. They came to America during the war, as soldiers, and now they can't recognize themselves.

One can make a good living here, and all live at peace. Anyone can do what he wants. There is no rabbi in all of America to excommunicate anyone. This is a blessing here. Jew and Gentile are as one. There is no galut ["exile," rejection of Jews] here. In New York and Philadelphia there is more galut. The reason is that there are too many German Gentiles and Jews there. The German Gentiles cannot forsake their anti-Jewish prejudice, and the German Jews cannot forsake their disgraceful conduct, and that's what makes the galut.

[Rebecca Samuel]

B

Dear Parents:

I hope my letter will ease your mind. You can now be reassured and send me one of the family to Charleston, South Carolina. This is the place to which, with God's help, we will go after Passover. The whole reason why we are leaving this place is because of [its lack of] Yehudishkeit [Jewishness].

Dear parents, I know quite well you will not want me to bring up my children like Gentiles. Here they cannot become anything else. Jewishness is pushed aside here. There are here [in Petersburg] ten or twelve Jews, and they are not worthy of being called Jews. We have a shohet [slaughterer of animals and poultry] here who goes to market and buys terefah [nonkosher] meat and then brings it home. On Rosh Ha-Shanah [New Year] and on Yom Kippur [the Day of Atonement] the people worshipped here without one sefer torah [Scroll of the Law], and not one of them wore the tallit [a large prayer shawl worn in the synagogue] or the arba kanfot [the small set of fringes worn on the body], except Hyman and my Sammy's godfather. The latter is an old man of sixty, a man from Holland. He has been in America for thirty years already; for twenty years he was in Charleston, and he has been living here for four years. He does not want to remain here any longer and will go with us to Charleston. In that place there is a blessed community of three hundred Jews.

You can believe me that I crave to see a synagogue to which I can go. The way we live now is no life at all. We do not know what the Sabbath and the holidays are. On the Sabbath all the Jewish shops are open, and they do business on that day as they do throughout the whole week. But ours we do not allow to open. With us there is still some Sabbath. You must believe me that in our house we all live as Jews as much as we can.

As for the Gentiles [?], we have nothing to complain about. For the sake of a livelihood we do not have to leave here. Nor do we have to leave because of debts. I believe ever since Hyman has grown up that he has not had it so good. You cannot know what a wonderful country this is for the common man. One can live here peacefully. Hyman made a clock that goes very accurately, just like the one in the Buchenstrasse in Hamburg. Now you can imagine what honors Hyman has been getting here. In all Virginia there is no clock [like this one], and Virginia is the greatest province in the whole of America, and America is the largest section of the world. Now you know what sort of a country this is. It is not too long since Virginia was discovered. It is a young country. And it is amazing to see the business they do in this little Petersburg. At times as many as a thousand hogsheads of tobacco arrive at one time, and each hogshead contains 1,000 and sometimes 1,200 pounds of tobacco. The tobacco is shipped from here to the whole world.

When Judah [my brother?] comes here, he can become a watchmaker and a goldsmith, if he so desires. Here it is not like Germany where a watchmaker is not permitted to sell silverware. [The contrary is true in this country.] They do not know otherwise here. They expect a watchmaker to be a silversmith here. Hyman has more to do in making silverware than with watchmaking. He has a journeyman, a silversmith, a very good artisan, and he, Hyman, takes care of the watches. This work is well paid here, but in Charleston, it pays even better.

All the people who hear that we are leaving give us their blessings. They say that it is sinful that such blessed children should be brought up here in Petersburg. My children cannot learn anything here, nothing Jewish, nothing of general culture. My Schoene [my daughter], God bless her, is already three years old; I think it is time that she should learn something, and she has a good head to learn. I have taught her the bedtime prayers and grace after meals in just two lessons. I believe that no one among the Jews here can do as well as she. And my Sammy [born in 1790], God bless him, is already beginning to talk.

I could write more. However, I do not have any more paper.

I remain, your devoted daughter and servant,

Rebecca, the wife of Hayyim, the son of Samuel the Levite

I send my family, my . . . [mother-in-law?] and all my friends and good friends, my regards.

[Postscript of Hyman Samuel, the husband:]

I, Hayyim, send my regards to you both and all my good friends. I do not have any time to write much. We shall, however, write another letter to you soon. We received letters from. . . . I should write to Raphael and my nephew. In the first place, they defamed me innocently, and if they don't write to me first, I can assure them they will receive none from me; they will perhaps say they are not interested in me. I say the same thing. Further, I remain your devoted son,

The humble Hayyim, the son of Samuel, of blessed memory.

[A sentence scratched out.]

[Additional postscript of Rebecca:]

Hayyim wanted to write impudence, so I crossed it out.

[Additional postscript of Hyman Samuel:]

You can note my son's pretty fingers in the letter. If you want to write us direct to Charleston, my address there will be: Hyman Samuel. Watch and Clock, Charleston, South Carolina.

You will see and hear that we are leaving Petersburg honorably. I will send you a newspaper from which you will see that I am not writing you any lies.

To Mr. Aaron Alexander,

On the New . . .

Hamburg.

· 15 ·
ADVICE ON THE RIGHT MAN AND THE RIGHT WOMAN
1791–1793

Joseph Simon, the Lancaster trader, had a large family. Shinah, one of his daughters, married Dr. Nicholas Schuyler, of Troy, New York. Although she became a Christian when she married out of the faith, Shinah appears to have been happy. Both she and her husband maintained good relations with the Simons after an initial period of rejection. Shinah's sister Miriam married Michael Gratz, the Philadelphia merchant. Two of the Gratz children, Richea and Frances, became favorites of their childless Aunt Shinah. In the following gossipy letter, selection A, Aunt Shinah, writing probably from Troy or Lansingburgh, expressed herself on the selection of a husband.

When Aunt Shinah Simon Schuyler wrote to her nieces Richea, seventeen, and Frances, twenty, in 1791, she told them to wait a few years before marrying. Richea took her suggestion to heart. Two years later she was engaged to Samuel Hays, a member of a well-known family active in the New York synagogue. One of the first things that Richea did was to write the good news to an older brother, Simon (Simmy), then living in Lancaster, where in all likelihood he worked for Grandpa Simon. Simmy, out of the fullness of his wisdom and inexperience—he was all of twenty years of age—wrote nineteen-year-old Richea a pompous letter, selection B, telling her how she was to conduct herself as a matron. Obviously the ideal woman he conjured up was the then common concept of what a wife should be. Apparently, however, he failed to find her in his own Jewish circle, for he was to marry out of the faith.

A

December 17th, 1791.

Miss Richea Gratz,
Lancaster.

I received my dear Richea's two aggreeable letters with inexperssable [inexpressible] pleasure. . . . My dear Richea, I sincerly thank [you] for all the news. Why, my dear, your information was quite from the matrimonal budget. . . .

And when, pray, do you enter the list of matrimony? Seriously, my love, I must be your confident; however, my dear Fanny [Frances] must enter her claim first. You have my most cordial prayers for both your happiness whenever that happy period arrives. I would advise you not to be too percipitate, unless an extraordinary and worthy man solicits that honor, and your heart can accompany the gift. Never, my lovely girls (for I address you both), alter your situation but by uniting your selves to a worthy man and one you can love and esteem. Should even adversity be your lot, their will be a consolation experienced which your marrying for wealth will never yeild [yield] you, and compleat your misery with an undeserving man. Let esteem for virtueous principles be the first basis for love, and then your happiness will be perminant. That both of you, my dear girls, may marry agreeable to your parents, and each have a worthy husband, I sincerely wish, tho' I would still advise you to continue single. Your both young, and two or three years more will be suffcent for to think of altering your situation.

I am in exceeding good health and spirits; indeed, few have less reason to complain. I have a very dear, good husband. I think few, very few, can say they live happier, and, thank God, he's exceedingly hearty and has constant employ in either writing or visiting his patience [patients] and chatting to his little wife, for, you know, I will have some attention paid to me.

Well, Richea, where do you spend your winter? I hope you'll attend the Lancaster [dancing] assemblys. We have refused subscribeng to the Albany assemblys as it will interfear too much with the doctor's business, but he seems a strenious advocate for having them here; if so, I must attend, tho' to speak truth, I would rather not this winter. We have some very elegant women in this place, and they dress too much for my indolent disposition, for I have an utter aversion to dress unless it's to be clean and neat.

I wish you was here, my dear; I long to see you. Let me hear from you soon. How are my dear mamy's eyes? I hope both my dear parents enjoy their health. My most affectionate love to my dear sister [your mother]. Tell her I wish she lived near me.

I once lived in the same town with my dear [sister] Bell [Mrs. Solomon M. Cohen], tho' I was deprived of her society. [The sister probably ignored Shinah, because she had married a Gentile and had become a convert to Christianity.] Believe me, my dear, at this moment my eyes are filled at the bear [bare] recollection. I think if she had not a heart of stone she would have stole to see me when their [there], tho' I forgive her. Pray let me know how she does and what her situation is. I would write to my dear sister [Miriam] but as I write to you, my dear Richea, it will answer every purpose.

Do write by the post. I shall expect you will, as it will be impossible to convey a letter in any other manner. The river will be closed shortly [because of the ice]. Write long letters. The postage is the same if you inclose two letters so that it don't appear, which may easely be done by folding them exactly of a size. I have wrote so fast that my fingers are perfectly crampt. God bless you, my dearest girl. May you enjoy an [un]interrupted serees [series] of happiness is the sincere prayers of your affectionate friend and aunt,

Shinah Schuyler

My love to my dear sister, Fanny, Simon, etc., etc. My dear old man desires his best love may be acceptable to you. We both join in compliments to the Mr. Gratzes.

I insist on your writing by the post. Could you have them conveyed and put in the [post] office in New York? If not, put them in the Lancaster or Philadelphia office. It's impossible to send by private conveyances, and I am very an[xious] to hear from you often. Write long letters an[d the ne]ws; every circumstance of my family [and] friends will be agreeable. Tell my dear sister

[Miriam] to write likewise. Don't laugh at my long poscript. God bless you, my dearest girl, and grant you every laudable wish of your little heart.

B

Lancaster, August 5th, 1793.

Miss Richea Gratz,
Philadelphia.
The letter of the 1st instant from my dear sister I now seat myself to accknowledge. Its contents I duly note. The subject it treats on is of the most interesting nature, and I hope my dear sister gave it the consideration due.

You are now about to enter into a state wherein I hope and pray you may experiance nothing to give you pain but, on the contrary, enjoy perfect happiness and tranquility. But, my dear, you must remember that to ensure to yourself and to the man you love a lasting continuance of happiness, you must ever make it your constant duty and study to please. In short, copy our amiable and virtuous mother; act as she does, and you will ensure to yourself and to all about you contentment. But as a preliminary to all happiness, lett a due sence of relegion, and a proper attention to the precepts and commands of the great God always actuate you, and place your sole confidence and trust in him.

Be pleased to remember me affectionately to Mr. Hays. I shall be down at Philadelphia immediately after the [Jewish] hollow-days, and shall then spend some time with you. Grandpa [Joseph Simon] desires his love to you and begs you would write and inform him how Aunt Leah [his daughter] is, as his greatful son-in law, Mr. [Levi] Phillips, has not thought proper to write him a line this 5 months.

I shall write to you again shortly, but in the intrem, belive me to be with constant prayers of your happiness,

Your ever affectionate brother and well wisher,
Simon Gratz

Hyman [our brother] desires his love to you and can't write this week.

INTERMARRIAGE AND CONVERSION TO JUDAISM
1793–1794

Intermarriage was a problem in the colonies from almost the first day. Communities were small, individuals lived in the countryside, social relations were easy and natural, and intermarriage was inevitable. The typical Jewish settler wanted a home and children, and when there were no Jewish women, he married a Gentile.

The fact that a Jew married out of the faith did not necessarily mean that he himself deserted the religion of his fathers. There can be no doubt that on numerous occasions the Jewish village merchant held to his ancestral faith to his dying day and would gladly have brought his Gentile wife into town for conversion had he been given any encouragement by the Jewish community, but conversion was frowned upon by the congregations.

As early as 1763, Shearith Israel in New York passed a law forbidding the acceptance of proselytes or marriage with a proselyte. It is not too difficult to understand the motivations of these early Jews. They may have maintained—in defense of their attitude—that they did not have the proper religious authorization to admit converts; they may have argued, with some cogency, that English Jewry had promised the civil authorities not to engage in proselytizing and that they were merely following current English synagogal practice, but all this was certainly a rationalization. Underlying the taboos was the desire on the part of the struggling young community to maintain itself in the face of powerful assimilatory influences. Once they let down the bars, they knew or believed that they would be lost as a Jewish group. Back of it all was their grim and almost fanatical determination to survive as a distinct religious entity.

In 1793, a member of the Philadelphia community, Moses Nathans, brought his problem of intermarriage before the congregation. He and the Gentile mother of his children had never been married according to Jewish law. However, she was willing to become a Jewess and sought the privilege of conversion and of Jewish marriage. The husband's friends were sympathetic to the request. Nevertheless, they felt that they could do nothing on their own account and referred the matter to the ecclesiastical court of the Spanish-Portuguese synagogue in London. Accordingly, the president, Benjamin Nones, sent the following letter, selection A, to the British capital. Very likely a similar note was dispatched to the Great Synagogue (Ashkenazi) in the same city. In the meantime, the man concerned—a member of the board!—was, from the point of view of synagogal ritual, looked upon as unmarried.

The hazzan's records show that he married the woman in 1794 in accordance with Jewish ritual. It was in the same year that the board of Mikveh Israel received a petition, item B, from Anna Barnett asking to be accepted as a convert. In all probability she was either married to a Jew or hoped to be married to one. Very few Gentiles converted to Judaism out of love for the faith.

A

To the *Beth Din* [court] of K. K. [the holy congregation] Shagnar a Shamaïm of London, whom God augment.

Philadelphia, Aug't 7th, 1793.

Gent'n:

We the *parnass* [the president] and *adjuntas* [board members] of K. K. Mickvey Israel of this city have the honor to address your respectable board on business of importance to Jewdaïsme at large and to our young and rising congregation in particular; and, we flatter ourself you will, as soon as it may be convenient, favor this congregation with your answer and advice.

The case is this: a *yahid* [member] of this congregation has lived in a public way with a *goyah* [Gentile] woman who has kept house for him about [eig]ht years and has had by her three children, two of which are boys, which he had *nimolim* [circumcised] at the eighth day.

The same person now applies to us, with the consent of the woman, to make her a *giyyoret* [proselyte], as also to grant him permission to marry said woman with *hupah u-kiddushin* [according to the Jewish ritual]. We must say in favor of the above *yahid* that he has and does keep up, as far as we know, to our rules, and contributes toward the support of our cong'on, as others do.

We have represented to the best of our knowlidge the case and conduct of the person, and therefore request your opinion on the subject, and what we have to do.

Your answer will much oblidge this congregation in whose behalf, we are, gent'n,

Your most obed't, h'ble serv'ts,

Benjamin Nones Esq., Parnass.

B

Philadelphia, November 13, 1794.

Gentlemen:

Permit one, who has not the happiness to be born a Jewess and favoured imediatly from the God of Israll as you are, to request your attention to my perticalar case and trust that nothing has been or shall be wanting on my part to render me worthy of being admitted in associate of your congregat'on and to become a Jewiss. This I ask not as a favour, but as a right, feeling as I do the [need] of living up to the divine precepts of the Bible. I am ready and willing to submit to such ceremonies as are necessary to optain this my demand, the greattest of all my worldly wishes, and may the God of Abraham, Isaac, and Jacob take you under his holy protection and instill into your minds to do what is just and right in his sight, and grant a speedy answer to this the petition of your humble friend,

Anna Barnett

17

JACOB MORDECAI WRITES TO TWO LITTLE GIRLS
1797

Colonial America suffered a high rate of infantile mortality. About 40 percent of all children died in infancy; only the heartiest survived. This new and rugged land was hard on women too, for many a mother died in childbirth and left her bereft husband with a handful of tots. One of those widowed fathers was Jacob Mordecai, a shopkeeper in the North Carolina village of Warrenton. When Judith Myers, his wife, died, she left him with six little ones, and because he could not rear all of them, he sent some of them to live with his kinfolk in Richmond. He kept in touch with little Rachel and Ellen—they were then all of eight and seven years of age—by writing them and telling them what to do and how to behave. By our standards, most of his letters to the children were heavy, pedantic, and stodgy. He addressed them as if they were mature women. In one letter, however, he forgot his mannered pedantry and wrote like a father and a human being—even by twentieth-century standards.

In his emphasis on reading and studying and in his dogged devotion to the intellectual development of his children, including his girls, he was not typical of the Jews of his generation.

[1797]

My dear Rachel and Ellen:

You don't know how much I was pleased when your Uncle Samy [Myers] came to see me and told me you were very good girls and attended to the advise he and your uncles Moses [Mears Myers] and Samson [Mears Myers] give you, that they all love you very much, and you in return, I am sure, love them so well that whenever you are told of any thing you do amiss, you will not do so again.

You must write to me very soon and tell me how your grand mama [Joyce Mears Myers] and Aunt Richa [Myers] were when you left them, for I suppose you will be in Petersburg very soon after Uncle Samy gets home. Your dear brothers and little Caroline send a great deal of love to you and want to see you very much. Little Solly [age five] and Caroline [age three] call for you every day and they all love you both very much. Uncle Samy will give you the chest of drawers I forgot to send with your other toys.

Be good girls, mind your reading and writing, that you may be able to send me letters often, for I love you so dearly that I shall always be pleased when you can write to me. God bless you, my dear children. Love each other and mind your dear uncles and then you will always afford pleasure to your papa.

I participate with you at this remote distance in the pleasure that will attend the recet [receipt] of these few lines which will be delivered by your belovd brother Moses. He will give you all the news and every information respecting your brothers, who are in health and both send an abundance of love to you. Solly says he is going to Petersburg next week to see his sisters and has several horses in readiness.

I hope my dear Rachel has received the book I sent to the care of Uncle Samson some time past. The bearer has another in charge from me, with some other trifles which you will accept as a mark of my love for you, my dear girls. Tell Ellen my lips have not diminished in consequence of the kisses she gave me, and that I long to press her to my heart.

You are all equally dear to me and shall never know an abatement of my affection while you continue to merit my tenderness, and that, I am sure, will be as lasting as your lives.

God bless you, my dear children, and preserve you from every ill, is the wish of

Your affectionate father,
J.M.

Kiss dear Caroline for me whenever you visit her.
September 4th, 1797.

18

REBECCA FRANKS WRITES TO A LONG-LOST BROTHER
1799

The Frankses, of London, came from Germany in the latter part of the seventeenth century. Some time after 1700 one of the sons, Jacob, came to New York, followed by members of other branches of the family. Judging from the recurrence of the same common given names (Abraham, Isaac, Jacob, David, John, Moses, Rebecca, etc.), most of the Jewish Frankses were related, although there is no positive proof to that effect.

The following letter was sent by a Rebecca Franks, of Philadelphia, to her brother John, then in Montreal. (The writer is not to be confused with her famous namesake, the brilliant if somewhat flighty daughter of David Franks, the Philadelphia Loyalist.) Her father may have been a John Franks who did business with Halifax in the 1750's. Evidently the family moved to Canada while Rebecca was very young. Two of her brothers, John Jr. and Moses, went with her, but Moses ultimately returned to Philadelphia, where he made a home for himself and his sister. It is very likely that he was the Moses Franks who, after the siege of Boston in 1776, was one of the three men selected by John Hancock and the Continental Congress to convey $250,000 in coin to General Washington.

John remained in Canada and became a merchant of some stature. In 1784 he joined a group of Canadians petitioning for a representative government based "on fixed and liberal principles," and later he became the first chief of the Quebec fire brigade.

At the time Rebecca wrote to John, her other brother, Moses, who had sailed to the West Indies, had been gone for almost two years, leaving his sister alone in Philadelphia. It must have seemed a miracle to Rebecca to receive word from John, whom she had given up for dead, saying that he was in Canada. His promise to send some money was particularly welcome news in her present straits.

Rebecca's letter is interesting because it emphasizes an aspect of American life only too frequently ignored or overlooked: the hard lot of the woman in the early American economy. True, there was little comparison between the lot of the woman on a pioneer clearing, bowed down under the yoke of work and a brood of children, and the fate of a mother, sister, or wife in Philadelphia, the country's largest city, enjoying the comforts and luxuries of a thriving metropolis. Still, the life of the woman in a merchant's family was by no means an untroubled one, for the man she loved was often away from home for months or even years, braving the dangers of the Indian trail, the threat of pirates, or the devastating power of Caribbean storms.

Philadelphia, February 5th, 1799.

My Dear Brother:

I realy am at a loss to find words to express my joy in addressing my long lost Brother. Be assur'd I never had the most distant Idea of ever hearing from you, for I had long thought you had gone to that bourn from whence no traveller returns, but thank God I have been most agreeably surpris'd.

Oh! Brother, it is many Years since we have been with each other. I suppose you have no recollection of me and I am sure I have none of you. I have gone through many scenes since I was in Canady. I was a very young adventurer, as I may say am still, but I trust in God. . . . that [I] Shall shortly be settled with or near you, for at present I feel friendless and desert'd without parents, without connection, for my Brother Moses is never with me. If he was, my situation would be far more agreeable, but he is sometimes gone for 2 years when he tells me it [is] probable he will be back in the course of 6 or 8 months and in that time he never writes one line to know where he is. I some times by chance hear. This last Voyage he has nearly been gone two years and has never wrote once to me.

My feelings are sensibly wound'd, for he knows my sole dependance is on his bounty. I have been under the disagreeable necessity of applying to a friend of his for Money to pay my board and get necessaries for I am oblig'd to appear genteel. I cannot think his slight is for want of affection but the whant of thought, for untill now he has ever been kind and attentive. I have wrote twice lately but have receiv'd no answer. Had I done any thing to cause his displeasure I should not be surpris'd, but thank God I have never done any thing to occasion a blush in either of my Brothers' faces. It would be a very great happiness to me was I capable of doing something for my self but I am not, therefore I must be content.

I pay at the rate of five dollars pr Week for my board, and is as cheap as I can get it. I am with a very worthy couple who are adva[nced] in life without Children. They do all they can to make me comfortable, but you know that is not like being with or near our own relations. Their is but three of us left, and I think it a very great pity that we could not all be to gather, but instead of that you are in Canada, my Brother Moses in the West Indies, and poor me in Philadelphia.

It would have been a very great gratification to me had I seen Mr. Levy, but I immagine he must have been here at the time of the dreadfull [yellow fever] malady, and every person at that time where [were] oblig'd to fly for their lives which will be the case again this Summer, for we have many instances of it now. It is plain to be seen that the c[old weather?] has only check'd it, that as soon as the warm commences it [will return?] with as much violence as ever, but I have not heard the [news?] of Mr. Levy's being hear.

I will not fatigue you by [writing?] too long a letter. I will accept of your generous offer. You [may be?] assur'd I never want'd it more then at present, for the little I had is nearly spent and I have no person that I can apply to, for the Gentleman who advanc'd me the last sum Said that he could not think of doing it again as he had not receiv'd orders from my Brother. I have been very particular in telling you every thing, mayby more so then I ought to be. All [I can?] say is to request you to write soon as you can [to me?] for I am very anxious to hear from you.

May every wish'd for[tune] attend. This is the sincere wish of [your?]

Affectionate Sister
[Rebecca]

Direct to Philadelphia, South Second Stree[t], between C[hestnut and?] Walnut at Mr. Blackburns. *Do pray write soon.*

19

JOYCE MYERS RETAILS THE GOSSIP TO HER DAUGHTER BECKY
1800–1805

Joyce Mears Myers (1737–1824) was the widow of the famous silversmith Myer Myers (d. 1795), who with equal broad-mindedness had fashioned collection plates for the Presbyterian church and little tinkling bells for the Torah scrolls of the Sephardic synagogue. He left his widow some money, which was probably supplemented by her sons. She lived in New York except for a brief period when she moved to Newport, a resort city where she had family and where she hoped living would be cheaper. She was disappointed and soon moved back to the metropolis. At night, tired after her housework or a day's visiting, she would wile away the long, lonely hours by writing to her beloved daughter Rebecca in Richmond, beguiling her with the gossip she had picked up. Here are excerpts from four letters to her "beloved Becky." One might have expected better spelling from a woman whose family had lived for three generations under the British flag, but few people in those days spelled correctly and consistently.

Her Becky was the wife of Jacob Mordecai (d. 1838), a scholarly businessman who later opened a girls' school in Warrenton, North Carolina. Rebecca Mordecai's family was numerous, for she had inherited a large brood from Jacob's first wife and was to give birth to many children of her own. There was no problem with the stepchildren; the first wife had been Becky's sister.

Joyce Myers' letters are important because she was no notable; she was a housewife and, in many respects, a typical Jewess of the late eighteenth and early nineteenth centuries.

A

New York, June 23d, 1800.

Not a moment can my loved Becky detach from her domestick concerns to tell her anxious mother that she, her good man, and

children are enjoying health with the blessings of the season. . . .
There is quite a new scene opened in your Aunt Rachel's
[Isaacks] family. I believe I mentioned their removal to Princess
Street. That was were [your brother] Samson keeps a custom
house, broker's office, besides being clerk in the same. He is in
good reput. Hetty [Isaacks] was married last Wednesday to a Mr.
Isaac Moses of S[outh]. C[arolina]. You must remember the man
that lodged at J. Jacobs some years ago. The stigma he then
labour'd under is quite taken off as your Aunt would not accede to
his [pro]posels till she knew her son Ab'm['s] opinion which was
approved by him.

I was at the [wedding] celibration which was as decent and
private as posible. She was dressed elegantly neat as her brid-
groom has fitted her for the place he resides in. She was married in
what they call a sattin muslem, trimed with ribbon and lace
tucker and veil; her hair in the fashionable way, ful curled with a
string of pereal passing between; white kid shos; silk stockings,
and gloves; diminity [dimity] peticoats of the best quality; her
linnen equaly so, not only one but many changes of garments. He
has her and his own minature taken. His and her picture is to be
drawn and left with her mother. . . . This day terminates the
visiting which commenced Saturday. Three days is now the
ton[e].

The 4th ins't I was at the [wedding] of Mr. J[oshua]. Isaac's
daughter Fanny who is married to [Mr. Harmon] Hendricks
between the hours of five and six. Their was a select few which
partook of a good supper. Her dress was similar to the fore
mentioned, only trimed with lace instead of ribbon. They had
plumb and plain cake. Hetty's was the latter [plain cake!] and no
supper. They seem to have got in the spirit of matrimony. Its
talk[ed] Minky I'[saa]cs is to be the next, to Mr. Gotchalkson. . . .

Interesting as this subject may be to my beloved Becky, it must
convince her no task so irksom that I would not under take to
shew the desire I have of amuseing her, if only for a moment. The
employment of the pen is of all others the most fatiguing to me.
You know I would rather make my bed, sweep my room, wash
my hankerchiefs and caps, and iron my clothes—the former I do
every day, the latter once a fortnight—then be thus scribling.

The only pleasure resulting from it is that it conveys to my Becky the love, the blessing, the thoughts, and affection of her mother.

Joyce Myers

My affectionate love of your own dear Joseph [Jacob!]

B

Newport, Aug. 26, 1801.

My dear beloved Becky must have rece'd my letter at the time hers came to hand of the 14th ulto., previous to my quiting N.Y., which was the first ins't, between the hours of twelve and one, and [I] arrived here the next day at the same time. Therefore the [sea] sickniss I experienced was short and light. Consequently an agreable passage, especially having my good son Samson with me, whose endeavors have been indefatigueable to place me comfortable, or as much so as circumstanced as I am will admit.

On our arrival here we were conducted to [Mrs. Hiam Levy] your Aunt Grace's house were I found her and her daughter Judy in good health and extreemly glad to see a sister who had been separated from her only thirty-five years. You may then judge wether we could appear to each other the identical persons as when we parted. We have since recounted over many sad and pleasurable [things] in the laps of time. The latter [the pleasurable] we keep most in view to inliven the vale we are now met in. She and Judy have enjoined me to mention them in the most affectionate terms as I can assure you they desire to be.

I expect by Novem'r to reside in the same house with her, as the people's time will expire by then that now occupys thos appartments that I am to have independent of hers. Between this and then I shall move from the rooms I am now in. . . . too extravagant to pay four and half dollars pr. week for rooms consisting one to sit in, a bed room, and kitchen, a table, and few chairs which she calls furniture is all I have for the price. To live at this rate frustrates the design for which I came hither. I am in hopes when the strangers, that at this season resorts here, depart, provisions will fall, the price which in my opinion are equal to N. York, and not so easily procured. I have a young white girl [as a servant] of whom I cannot complain.

C

New York, Nov. 30th 1802.

I daily experience His all merciful goodness towards my self in granting me a perfect state of health and unimpaired faculties which enables me to be patient and perservering throughout my many past and present vicissitudes. And what is yet to come I hope to bare with becoming fortitude which is at present put to the test by the late melancholy accounts from Charleston which has been a place of graves for my truly beloved and much regreted sister Becky and almost all her devoted family. In the space of one month Miss Judith Isaaccks, the dear angel of a woman, your aunt and her daughter Josey now swallowed up in death. The subject is heart rending to me and must be painful to my dear child; therefore [I] shall not dwell longer on it than to say such an assemblage of virtues blended in her character seldom is it be met with in us frail mortals. From her infantine state to the day of her death such was my angelic sister whose soul is now enjoying that bliss which the righteous can never doubt. This is and this must be the firm belief of her connexions or my grief would know no bounds. The 30th of Sept. was the date of the dear departed's last letter giving me an account of her sister Judith's death with every kind and feeling affection such a human heart could dictate and every wish that could constitute our happiness here or hereafter which she desired I would extend to my beloved children. And ere this most affectionate letter came to hand her extince was terminated as was her daughters. Wether her other two discosolate girls is yet in being is almost a matter of doubt for their dear mother was the very vital breath they drew. If they yet survive, Heaven I hope will endow them with his manyfold blessings in giving a heart and a protecting hand to their surviving brother. Write to me soon my ever dear daughter and such tidings I hope to receive as may alliviate the spirits or disperse the gloom that now pervades the mind of your mother which as soon as a decent time will permit I shall endeavor to dissipate by going more generaly among my acquaintinces who have all been frequently to visit us.

D

New York, March 21, 1805.

Dull times here for the girls not a young fellow to wait upon them on an evening visit. Samson Simson [the bachelor lawyer] can't find a leasure moment . . . to gallant any girls. Our congregation is very unsocial indeed. Abby Phillips is here upon a visit to her parents. Her mother [Mrs. Benjamin Seixas] has not yet been abroad since she had given birth to her seventeenth child which is a daughter called Leah [d. 1886]. They have almost gone through the names of the Bible and I think I have come to the end of my paper and as there is nothing more interesting for my dear Becky to know then I am in perfect health and that my home is the mansion of peace.

20

AN APOSTROPHE TO WOMEN
1806

The Hebrew Orphan Society of Charleston, South Carolina, is the oldest Jewish child-care agency in the United States. Its clients, impoverished widows with young children, were given grants so as to insure the continuity of family life; the children were not institutionalized, though they were often clothed and given special schooling, particularly in Hebrew. Like all charities, this one, too, was dependent on the largesse of its sponsors and friends. Interest in its work was stimulated by what was probably an annual address.

In 1806, the orator for the occasion was young Myer Moses (1779– 1833), a Charlestonian destined to become a distinguished South Carolinian. In later years he served in the state legislature, was elected to high office in the militia, furthered the new public school system, and accepted election to the board of the Planters' and Mechanics' Bank. Several years before his death, he moved on to New York, the city of the future, and there, in 1831, he was called upon by the Tammany Society to deliver the annual anniversary address.

In 1806, when Moses spoke to the Hebrew Orphan Society, Charleston sheltered the largest and most cultured Jewish community in the United States. The following apostrophe to women, whose help he solicited, is in the best tradition of Southern chivalry.

I should conceive myself wanting in my duty, and ungrateful to this society, did I pass unnoticed the manifest loss we have sustained by the scythe of death having mowed down some of our ripe stock, and some that were but just shooting forth their many excellencies . . . When I calculate on the loss we have sustained in the former, and the satisfaction we expect to derive from the latter, I cannot but pronounce, that in its then truly infant state, the death of an aged and highly respected gentleman, added to the premature dissolution of two younger though not less honorable members, proved a manifest injury to the then anticipated advancement of this society. However, if to their departed souls it will afford gratification to know that the goodly work which they commenced is quick progressing, and that although they are translated to another, and a better world, they have left behind them those who will never tarnish that fair name, which was intended should be preserved pure and inviolate. Yes, if it were possible to hold converse with the dead I would say to them your children are and will be its guardians. . . . They will watch over it as does the anxious mother over the safety of her child, who, although its infant cheek blooms with ruddy health, still is she not less watchful of its fate, less by contagion and disease she may be deprived of that so near her soul's content. . . . To the one of you I would say, your brother did guide this tender barque through a two years voyage, with skill, care, and discretion . . . Then to the other would I address myself and speak, was the helm resigned to your son, who, with equal caution and as anxious solicitude has this day closed his journal, making the fifth year since the launching of this tender barque, and to your departed souls receive this grateful tiding, that as far as depends on prudent and skilful management so never shall the helm be guided but by virtue. Then may you rest in peace, satisfied we will reach the haven of prosperity.

At best I am poor in language, I am doubly poor when my duty and feelings prompt me to address you, thou fairer part of God's creation . . . Hail woman! . . . hail though [thou] bright benignant star! a star, which shoots forth to all mankind, the most lovely, the most resplendent virtues; a star, which can shine upon, and brighten the gloomy object of its care, and afford to its disconsolate partner the hope of better prospects; a star, whose sympathizing qualities can quell the troubled and distressed feelings of the soul, and speak to man in the soft and persuasive language of woman . . . If I have made you the last theme of my subject it is but from a wish to leave the more recent recollection of the high estimation that I hold you in . . . From the moment that we are ushered into the world, we owe to you the debt of our existence, and here the obligation but commences, for if here you left us " 'twere to be born but to die" . . . With parental fondness does the anxious mother afford to her infant that source of nourishment requisite for its existence when it has so advanced into life as to render unnecessary this food of nature, "then, by degrees does she bring it to the general use of the common sustenance so requisite for existence" . . . But this does not lessen the ever anxious solicitude of the mother, with the growth of her child grows her affection; her eye beams forth joy when in her offspring she beholds the bloom of health, and as with its years it ripens into virtue, or degenerates into vice, so does she become either blessed or miserable . . . When by a reciprocity of love and affection we become united to lovely woman, and partake of all the happiness resulting from the enjoyment of such union, for me to endeavour to pourtray the high sense that I entertain of it, is a task far beyond my reach, suffice it to say, that prosperity gives to man no such opportunities to know the excellencies of woman as does adversity . . . For to the distresses of the mind there exists no cure more potent than the kind affection and persuasive language of woman, with which there is ever accompanied a conduct as gentle and as mild as is their nature.

If the picture which I have endeavoured to draw of your sex, has been guided only by the pencil of truth and justice, surely then I need not speak to you in behalf of the orphan and helpless child; neither will I point out to you how necessary it is to walk in the path which leads to virtue . . . I will not occupy your time in saying, watch over your children, particularly your daughters . . . Let not the whitened stock become blasted, and loose that on which it should build its name, virtue. . . . If the foul tongue of slander from appearances is warranted and lays hold of the character of your sex, 'tis forever gone and past redemption; nay, though even the object, be as chaste and pure as innocence itself. Then continue lovely woman to tread the path of virtue; teach to your children early lessons of piety and religion, so will you insure to yourselves the satisfaction of having done your duty, and, to them, the happiness resulting from an inculcation of such principles.

POLLY AND L. E. MILLER, BOND SERVANTS, WANT TO BE REDEEMED
1807

Many impoverished immigrants, Jews among them, managed to finance their transatlantic crossing by selling themselves as redemptioners. They bound themselves to serve for years in payment for their passage to this country. In effect, they were slaves for a limited number of years.

The following document is an appeal by two Jewish servants, a man and his wife, to be redeemed from Gentile bondage by fellow-Jews. They were willing to work for coreligionists in whose households Judaism was practiced. The congregation, however, found it "inexpedient to purchase the time of Mr. Miller and his wife."

———————

[February 15, 1807.]

To the Parnass [president] and Gentlemen Trustees of Kall Kadosh Beth [the Holy Community of the House of] Shearith Israel [of New York]:

The petition of L. E. Miller and Polly his wife humbly sheweth:

That your petitioners came to New York as redemptioners, they being sold for their passage to Mr. J. Jackson, where the said Miller has to serve four years and his wife Polly five years for the amount they were sold for, being one hundred and fifty dollars.

Your petitioners being in a very deplorable situation amongst Goyim [Gentiles], they humbly wish if there could be any means obtained for them for their releif they would be happy to serve with any Yehuda [Jew] for any length of time till they are freed from bondage, as they wish to keep up to their profession [of religion].

A YOUNG JEWESS IN A SMALL SOUTHERN TOWN
1807

Rachel Mordecai, eighteen years old in 1807, kept in touch with brother Samuel in Richmond. Samuel, age twenty-one, was learning to be a businessman; there was no future for him in Warrenton, a village. At this time he was probably in the employ of Jacob I. Cohen, a prominent businessman who had formerly lived in Richmond, but was now active in Philadelphia.

These letters of Rachel, all addressed to Samuel, throw light on the cultural background of a Jewish girl and family in an early-nineteenth-century Southern town where they were almost completely enveloped, both spiritually and intellectually, by Protestant Christianity. It is, therefore, not surprising that in spite of the fact that the father, Jacob, was an observant Jew, Rachel and her siblings manifested little interest in Judaism, or that a number of the Mordecai children intermarried and either lived as Christians or became converts to the dominant faith.

A

Warrenton, April 21, 1807.

My dear Samuel:

We ate the bread of affliction [unleavened bread] in the true sense of the word, for this week past, for our box [of Passover supplies] is not yet arrived. I hardly think our predecessors were more rejoiced at leaving Egypt than we all were this evening at having a loaf of wheat bread set before us. What added to our penance was the temptation of having it constantly before our eyes. However it is now past and I believe we are all very willing to forget it. . . .

On Thursday week there is to be a grand ball here given to the two new married pairs: Mr. and Mrs. Jones and Mr. and Mrs.

2. Rachel Mordecai's Home, Warrenton, North Carolina

Courtesy, Robert Neal, The Press Publishing Co., Warrenton, N.C.

George [the teacher], on which occasion I expect all our little world will be assembled.

Moses [our brother] has some idea of visiting your great city to be present at the trial of Mr. [Aaron] Burr [for treason]. Papa wishes him very much to go but he is not yet determined. I had the superlative felicity of beholding the head of Mr. [Thomas Abthorpe] Cooper's horses as he [America's greatest actor] passed through, but that was all. . . .

Believe me, now and ever
Yours,
R.

B

Warrenton, May 9th, 1807.

Did you know the extent of the loss you have sustained by the miscarriage of my letter, I am sure, you would mourn in sack cloth and ashes. If it should happen to reach, and be opened at the general post office, it will afford its readers a *literary treat*. I expect to see it published in all the Northern papers as a model for all future scribes, and in such a case I am sure you have too much *republicanism* [Jeffersonism] in your composition, not to give up, without repining, the pleasure you have been deprived of when you find it so conducive to the general good, as that will undoubtedly be. Plenty of *nonsense*, I hear you say, but permit me to tell you, my dear brother, that I am in a most nonsensical humour tonight, and must either be indulged to fill at least one half my letter with *nothings*, or lay down my pen, which as yet I feel not the smallest inclination to do.

We had the storm you mention here, but it was not so severe as with you, and did very little injury to any thing. Moses said that a hail stone came down his chimney and rolled with such force as to overset a table on which he was studying [the *Commentaries of the Laws of England* of] Blackstone, and, extinguishing his candle, left him in utter darkness. Having with some difficulty *reenlightened* himself, he searched for the stone which had occasioned the disaster, when, wonderful to relate, he found it no larger than a common sized *turkey* egg!! How it could do so much mischief I leave it to you and Mr. Jefferson [our scientific minded President] (if you transmit an account of the transaction to him) to determine. I can only inform you further, that by a newly discovered philosophical process, Moses kept the wonderful stone untill the next day in warm water! Thus goes the story. I will not pledge my veracity as to the truth of it.

Moses has, I believe, given up all thoughts of a visit to Richmond and cannot even accept your terms, as the unfortunate *hail stone* carried his stenographic pen into a rat's hole from whence he has not been able to recover it. You must, however, write to Mr. Cohen [the Richmond-Philadelphia merchant, Jacob I. Cohen?] and make your arrangements in such a manner as to be with us by the 4th of June when our races commence. . . . You know not how much mortified we shall be if you disappoint us, therefore be a *good boy* and come by the last day of May at any rate. . . .

So farewell, you know, I am

Ever yours,
R.

P.S. In lieu of beaux, I will take half an ounce of floss thread, not very fine, and a box of Adelphi cotton.

C

Warrenton, October 11th, 1807.

The ball which I mentioned in my last is over, and our highly raised expectations were completely gratified by the elegance and taste displayed in the decorations and the excellence of the supper itself. For the ballroom I cannot say much. The walls were plentifully and variously adorned with advertisements of different kinds, the [tavern] bar being removed to one side served as a raised seat for the married ladies, and the seats which have hitherto been occupied either by the proud dispensers of justice to our county or some itinerant brawling preacher, were now humbled or exalted, whichever you please to term it, or if neither, altered, into an orchestra. The evening was very pleasant, and we contrived (notwithstanding a few trifling hills and dales in the floor which occasionally impeded the evenness of our motions in rigadoon, etc., etc.,) to dance very agreeably until after twelve, when we retired soberly and in good order to our respective homes and willingly resigned ourselves to the dominion of Morpheus, who failed not to renew in our dreams the pleasures which the evening's *amusement* had afforded us. . . .

Farewell, thou knowest I am thy very

Affectionate sister,

R.

I wish you could copy and send me a reciept which Uncle Moses [Myers] can give you for washing silk lace.

GRACE NATHAN, THE FIRST OF HER CLAN
1810–1827

Grace Nathan (1752–1831), the wife of Simon Nathan, a Revolutionary War businessman, was the sister of the minister Gershom Seixas. Her education was probably limited to the elementary schooling given the girls of her pre-Revolutionary generation. Nonetheless, Grace developed literary interests and wrote poetry and an ethical letter to her son. Two of her poems and her "ethical will" are printed below. Her cultural leanings and talents were reborn in her descendants, who include Emma Lazarus, Maud Nathan, Annie Nathan Myer, Robert Nathan, and Benjamin Nathan Cardozo.

Like her brother Gershom, she was pious and devoted to her faith. Possibly even more so than Gershom, she was ardently public-spirited. It was during the War of 1812 that she wrote:

I cannot for the life of me feel terrified. Besides I am so true an American, so warm a patriot, that I hold these mighty armies and their proud, arrogant, presumtious, and over-powering nation [Great Britain] as beings that we *have conquered and* shall *conquer again.*

A

Written on a geranium plant which a severe frost blasted. Jan'y 1810.

> Oh how keenly the sharp air has blown;
> It has stript my fair plant of its bloom,
> And its life with its beauty has flown,
> Ere yet it had reached to its noon.
> I had raised it from infancy's bud;
> I had made it a daily delight,
> Yet a breath that was piercing rude
> Destroyed my fair plant in a night.

Now withered and blasted to view,
I behold it with anguish severe.
I recall both its fragrance and hue,
And I pensively shed the sad tear.
I received the fair plant from a friend,
And I would not have lost it so soon,
For I said when my being should end,
I would have it placed nigh to my tomb.
Like the cypress it there might have grown
And marked out the sod(?) for my head,
For sweet friendship was ever my own.
And I would still embrace it when dead.

B

I had a bud so very sweet—its fragrance reached the skies.
The angels joined in holy league—and seized it as their prize.
They bore it to their realms of bliss—where it will ever bloom,
For in the bosom of their God they placed my rich perfume.

Written on the death of my grandchild, Jan'y 19th, 1819.

C

To My Son

This effort will speak to you from the tomb. Years of infirmities lead to the reflection that we must soon part. I am perfectly resigned to meet the last earthly event, grateful to God for the blessings he has given me.

I *die* in the *full faith* of my *religion*. I leave you in the bosom of a virtuous wife, surrounded by a numerous offspring, who give promise of comfort.

Long may they live to shew *you* the same filial duties that I have uninterruptedly received from you. Now in this solemn moment when I am taking an eternal earthly farewell let me express my full approbation of your deportment toward me. It has been exemplary, as you have devoted your kindnesses so may be your great reward; more I could not say. Need I exhort you to the cultivation of your endearing children and give them a just idea of their religious and moral principles, these being the corner stones of all *good*, and on which the basis of life here and hereafter may be supported. You my son will live in peace and bear a kind manner to those who have shown it to me; by this they will cherish my memory; and I shall live.

Now thou my son who wast the joy of my younger days and the balm of my declining age, let me thrice bless you and say may peace rest with you forever and ever. Amen.

Your mother Grace Nathan

Keep the seven days of mourning and no more; for that time *only* you will keep your beard.

Began, November 1827

· 24 ·
EPITAPHS AND THE CULT OF TRUE WOMANHOOD
1811–1868

It was Shakespeare who said: "Our life . . . finds . . . sermons in stones and good in every thing." There are sermons to be found in epitaphs—and history too. The following epitaphs, which graced the tombs of Charleston's female dead, eloquently portray Jewry's concept of the cult of true womanhood. The good Jewess is kind, amiable, charitable, and above all else pious. The span of life, it is worthy to note, was shorter than it is now; medicine has made remarkable strides since the mid-nineteenth century.

Sacred to the Memory of
ELIZA,

Daughter of Mordecai and Leah Cohen.
Her dawning virtues and beauty, her innocent and amiable manners were the pride of her parents, the delight of her friends. She lived innocent and died beloved, October 7th 1811, aged 11 years.

"In mildest morning of thy day,
By angels thou wert borne away;
While kindred cherubs from above,
Greet thee to realms of purest love."

SARAH C. MOISE,

Who departed this life on the 1st day of March, 1828, in the 37th. year of her age. By this mournful dispensation, a fond husband was bereft of an inestimable companion and her children of a devoted and affectionate parent. But their bereaved hearts will find a consolatory resource in fondly cherishing her precious memory, and although she has been removed in the bloom of her existence, the recollection of her sincere piety and social virtues inspires in their bosoms the sustaining hope that Heaven has already smiled upon her and that in dying, she has happily exchanged the evanescent pleasures of this world for those of a blissful immortality.

> "Always prepared to answer God's decree,
>   Earth's tender ties alone would stay her flight—
> Worthy, we hope, that bright Heaven to see,
>   She now is heir of its eternal light."

Sacred to the Memory of
MISS CECILIA MORDECAI,

Who departed this life on the 7th. November 1833, in the 21st year of her age. Brief as was her pilgrimage on this earth, yet it served to display the many excellencies of a truly feminine character; her virtues, in deed, form her most enduring monument and will dwell in the memories of her survivors long after this perishable memorial shall have crumbled into dust. This tomb is erected by an affectionate brother, who loved her in life and lamented her in death.

Sacred to the Memory of
MRS. JANE SIMPSON,

Relict of Michael Simpson, who departed this life 17th March, 1843, aged 54.

Kind, generous, and benevolent, she was a tender and indulgent parent, devoting her entire energies to the happiness of her offspring and endeavoring through an eventful life to instil into their minds and hearts a firm and constant reliance upon divine providence. With a heart chilled by the fatal shafts of adversity, yet with an abiding confidence in the Author of all good, she with resignation departed this life. As a slight memorial of their love and reverence this stone is erected by her attached children.

Sacred to the Memory of
MRS ABIGAIL REBECCA ANCKER,

Consort of Gustavus V. Ancker, who departed this life July 25th, 1844, aged 21 years and 21 days. In the discharge of the important and varied duties of life, she was truly happy, as a Jewess, pure and zealous, as a wife, ardent and affectionate, as a parent fond and devoted. She passed from time to eternity with the fullest assurance of a blessed immortality beyond the grave.

To her, death has lost its sting, the grave its victory.

The Mortal Remains of
SARAH CARDOZO,

Relict of David N. Cardozo repose beneath this slab. Born 12th. June, 1766 and departed this life 25th. October, 1853. Aged 87 years, 3 months and 25 days. An affectionate parent and fond wife, of unbounded charity and social disposition. She was a model of the household virtues, uniting to these the qualities that are most valued in the domestic sphere. In her long life she was a continued example of kind manners and a humane heart.

Sacred to the Memory of
MRS. FANNY MANTOUE, nee JACOB,

Born at Paris, France, died at Charleston, S. C., on the 15th April, 1868, in the 23rd year of her age.

"A last smile to her husband,
A single kiss to her infant,
A prayer for both to the Lord,
His angels carried her soul to Heaven."

25

AN OLDER SISTER WRITES A CODE OF ETHICS FOR A YOUNGER BROTHER
1815

Levi Cohen (1800–1868) was the son of a German Jewish immigrant who had settled in the British colonies during the 1760's. When Levi was fifteen years old, his father sent him to London to learn the stationer's trade under a half-brother, Solomon. Before sailing for England, Levi's older sister Judith gave him an ethical letter to serve as spiritual fare for the road. Such ethical statements, wills, wall tablets, and moral essays have their roots in the biblical gnomic literature, the books of Proverbs and Ecclesiastes.

Judith's injunctions form an interesting mixture of Jewish piety and common sense. Levi returned to his native America, settled in New York City, and, as Lewis J. Cohen, became a successful stationer.

RULES

FOR LEVI COHEN'S PERUSAL WHEN HE HAS LEISURE

Fear God and keep His commandments, and He will ever protect and guard you from evil. Honor your superiors and they will love you. Be particular in keeping the Law you were brought up to. Keep truth in all your doings and you will never be brought to shame. Let your actions be such that you will always deserve praise without pride. Keep no vicious company. If you can not keep company with your superiors or equals, keep none at all. And be sure when, please God, you arrive at Liverpool to inquire for one of your own persuasion, and go to them, or him; tell without falsehood your story. Ask the Captain's permission as soon as you arrive to let you go ashore, and be care-ful of your cloaths, and do not be too communicative to inquisitive people.

The first house you get to, be sure to write to your brother [in London] and wait for an answer to know how you are to come to him. Be grateful to your benefactors, and treat them with that respect that is due to their reverence.

Do not forget the aged parent you have left behind, but keep in your memory the many troubles he has undergone for you, the anxiety he will be in untill he hears of your arrival.

Do not forget to write to us by the first opportunity; make yourself as agreeable to your shipmates as you can be, and do anything in your power to oblige them.

Let virtue be your guide, and remember these are the sentiments of your affectionate sister.

April 20th, 1815   Judith Cohen

26

RACHEL MORDECAI LAZARUS WRITES TO MARIA EDGEWORTH ON JUDEOPHOBIA AND AMERICAN SLAVERY
1815–1838

In 1815, Rachel Mordecai (1788–1838), a Warrenton, North Carolina, schoolteacher, wrote to the Anglo-Irish novelist Maria Edgeworth protesting against the portrayal of a villainous Jew in Miss Edgeworth's novel, The Absentee *(selection A). This was the beginning of a transatlantic correspondence which continued till Rachel's death. In 1827, Rachel, now married to Aaron Lazarus of Wilmington, North Carolina, wrote to her friend Maria on the subject of slavery (B); in 1831, Rachel dispatched a note to a brother on the same subject (C); in a letter she sent Maria in 1836, Rachel's anger was directed against Northern abolitionists, who she thought were advocating emancipation through violence (D); in 1838, the North Carolina matron turned again to the subject of slavery in the United States (E). Rachel had never recovered from the shock of the 1831 Nat Turner rebellion, in which dozens of Whites lost their lives. Wilmington, her hometown, was also not spared. Apparently, she was not distressed by the massive White retaliation, although she constantly deplored the "peculiar institution" of the South.*

On the basis of published and manuscript material now available, it appears that no Jewess in pre–Civil War America was Rachel's superior or equal intellectually. On her deathbed she embraced Christianity—a conversion which may have been a revolt against her observant father.

A

Warrenton, North Carolina,
U. S. of America,
August 7th, 1815.

[Rachel to Maria]

Relying on the good sense and candour of Miss Edgeworth I would ask, how it can be that she, who on all other subjects shows such justice and liberality, should on one alone appear biased by prejudice: should even instill that prejudice into the minds of youth! Can my allusion be mistaken? It is to the species of character which wherever a *Jew* is introduced is invariably attached to him. Can it be believed that this race of men are by nature mean, avaricious, and unprincipled? Forbid it, mercy. Yet this is more than insinuated by the stigma usually affixed to the *name*. In those parts of the world where these people are oppressed and made continually the subject of scorn and derision, they may in many instances deserve censure; but in this happy country, where religious distinctions are scarcely known, where character and talents are all sufficient to attain advancement, we find the Jews to form a respectable part of the community. They are in most instances liberally educated, many following the honourable professions of the Law, and Physick, with credit and ability, and associating with the best society our country affords. The penetration of Miss Edgeworth has already conjectured that it is a Jewess who addresses her; it is so, but one who thinks she does not flatter herself in believing that were she not, her opinion on this subject would be exactly what it is now. Living in a small village, her father's the only family of Israelites who reside in or near it, all her juvenile friendships and attachments have been formed with those of persuasions different from her own; yet each has looked upon the variations of the other as things of course— differences which take place in every society.

B

Wilmington, January 6th, 1827.

[Rachel to Maria] My dear Madam:
The more I learn of the actual state of Ireland, the more am I inclined to wonder at the mistaken policy of a wise and enlightened government in pursuing a system so glaringly oppressive, and, I should say, injurious to their own interests. Much has been humanely urged in the British Parliament on the subject of Negro slavery; yet is the condition of the Irish poor incomparably worse than that of the slave, either here, or as far as I am informed, in the Islands. I do not mean to defend the Slave System, of which I feel and acknowledge all the evils; but where is the consistency of practising, without even a similar shadow of apology, a system which wants but the name to render it more than equally odious?

C

Wilmington, October 6th, 1831.

[Rachel Mordecai to George W. Mordecai, Raleigh]
I can readily conceive the alarm and anxiety which must have been excited in your mind by the shocking reports of us which were so groundlessly circulated far and wide. During the period of the first and greatest commotion among our townsfolk, I thought the accounts (as they eventually proved) so vague that I felt merely a state of discomfort from the scene of indefinable terror and confusion around me without realizing sufficiently to partake of them, and as [our brother] Washington no doubt informed you, we remained quietly at home during the day and night (a very inclement one), when many were exposing themselves in the streets or crowding into the bank and other houses on the front street. The horrible disclosures which have subsequently been made have made a total change in my feelings, and I view the condition of the Southern states as one of the most unenviable that can be conceived. To be necessarily surrounded

by those in whom we cannot permit ourselves to feel confidence, to know that unremitted vigilance is our only safeguard, and that soon or late we or our descendants will become the certain victims of a band of lawless wretches who will deem murder and outrage just retribution is deplorable in the extreme. The United States government might possibly find a remedy by rendering some equivalent to slave owners and exporting the slaves in as large numbers as practicable to Africa. But I do not know whether if such a plan were proposed it would be acceded to by any considerable majority; people are too short sighted, too unwilling to relinquish present convenience from the fear of future ill or for the prospect of future good. Mr. L[azarus] regrets holding so much property here, and if not actually tied down to the place, would gladly remove to the north, and I cannot help hoping that we may at some period be enabled to do so.

D

Wilmington, January 10th, 1836.

[Rachel to Maria]
If you see our papers you must have remarked the efforts that are making for the Abolition of Slavery, an end to be desired by all, tho' the means too inconsiderately adopted are in every point of view unjustifiable. The excellent, the Philanthropick [William] Wilberforce [the English abolitionist] who spent his best years in the advancement of this labour of love viewed the subject with wisdom and humanity. But what can be said of men who blindly, madly urge the slave to seek his freedom through a sea of blood, who promise to aid him in the commission of crime, without even glancing at the too-certain consequences, and who, while pledging themselves in the cause of suffering humanity, would spread horror and devastation among their brethren and over one half of their mother land? Their mischievous purposes will I trust in Heaven be averted, and the removal of this mighty evil, of which we of the South are not insensible, be left to our own legislators whose wisdom will find means gradually but surely to effect the end.

E

Wilmington, March 18th, 1838.

[Rachel to Maria]

Now to turn to the slave question. I and very many others agree with you and Miss Martineau on the inconsistency of slavery with American liberty, [Harriet Martineau, the English writer, was opposed to slavery.] but before we condemn in toto we must attend to the arrangement of historical facts. Was it the American states proud of their freedom and boasting of their rights who employed slave ships to go to Africa and bring to them hewers of wood and drawers of water? No it was English Colonies planted in America under grants from the king of Great Britain who entailed this curse upon our land. In process of time these colonies, being denied what they deemed their rights by the mother country, laboured successfully to throw off her government, and declared themselves an Independent people. They were free from the rule of any other nation and they set about forming a government of their own. Could they at that time have loved liberty for itself alone and looked with an equally humane and philosophic eye on the miseries of the Slave and the Slave holder, all had now been well, but such ideas had not then entered into the mind even of a Wilberforce, and it would have been expecting too much from poor human nature that a people, an infant people, impoverished by war, uncertain of the issue of a newly formed constitution and employing all their faculties to maintain the advantages so hardly gained, should say, the South to the North, we would be wholly free, give us half the worth of our slaves and we will relinquish the other half and labour and till the ground with our own hands (a Utopian supposition), but the North must have replied, we are ourselves bankrupt, our continental money is worse than blank paper and our common country has no treasury and is involved in debt; we cannot assist you nor can you relinquish the only medium by which your shattered fortunes can hope to be repaired.

Will you not allow that this true statement does in part excuse the inconsistency? That the system is an evil, that by it are produced a host of minor evils, is a point readily conceded; whether it is criminal in us to retain our slaves is yet to be considered, and to proceed reasonably and deliberately I would ask what would be their condition were they to be freed tomorrow? Ignorant and inconsiderate as they are, they would for the most part be unable to support or take care of themselves; they would be most uncomfortable as well as a burden to the community. Miss Martineau presents a true picture in the note which she extracts from a Southern publication in which the lady is described as giving medicines to her servants and dressing their wounds with her own hands. There are few of them who will perform these offices of kindness for each other, tho' without compulsion they will, I scarce know why, shew an inclination to attend on the whites under similar circumstances.

But to return, those who are most earnest on the subject of abolition cannot point out the necessary means for its accomplishment; it would not surely be by rendering slaves discontented and instigating them to rise up in arms against their masters. They must then be exterminated in self defence. Yet this has been the means, Miss Martineau's assertion notwithstanding, by which many of those mistaken enthusiasts at the North sought to irritate the minds of our slaves. Eastern pedlars were commissioned to carry pamphlets to distribute among them filled with prints of slaves suffering under the lash and degraded in various ways with which they themselves were unacquainted. These tracts were of a most mischievous nature and calculated only to do harm. It was after the insurrection at Southampton, Virginia [the 1831 Nat Turner revolt], and at a time when both North and South Carolina were similarly threatened that the outrage was committed on the post office in Charleston [when a mob burned abolitionist newspapers]. That it was an outrage all admit, that it was sanctioned by circumstances some will argue, that its being approved by a member of the state council was an unprecedented stretch of authority none will deny. You are mistaken in supposing that this was an effort to conceal the existing evil or the possible danger from ourselves; aware of its existence the effort was made to avert or at least to prevent its being accelerated.

I do hope that means will be adopted for the gradual and judicious emancipation of slaves. The Legislature of Kentucky, a wealthy slave holding state west of and adjoining Virginia, have a bill for considering means for this purpose now under consideration; the result will be important to all its sister states. I have long averred that I would willingly undergo the hardship and inconvenience of waiting on myself were that the only alternative, to be freed from the charge and responsibility of living in a slave state. Miss Martineau has I think been deceived in many of her statements, at least they were as new and strange to me and to all with whom I have conversed on the subject as they could be to you, and some of her negro anecdotes I might venture to pronounce absolutely false, so little do they concur with our knowledge and experience of facts. I marked many passages in her book intending to note them in my reply to your letter but I believe it would be useless; your own excellent discrimination has doubtless enabled you to detect errors and contradictions which are to my mind palpable and self-evident. I have written truly and candidly as you desire, and though you may think my views too lenient, you will at least be possessed of the facts on which they are grounded, and I know you will say how far you think I may be blinded by habit or early prejudice.

3. Rebecca Gratz

27

REBECCA GRATZ, AMERICA'S OUTSTANDING AFFILIATED JEWESS
1819–1869

Antebellum American Jewry looked upon Rebecca Gratz (1781–1869), of Philadelphia, as the country's most distinguished Jewess. Actually the best-known Jewish woman in the country was Ernestine Rose, but Mrs. Rose had no affiliation with the Jewish community nor did she exhibit the slightest interest in the Jewish religion. Mrs. Rose was an intellectual; Miss Gratz, though highly intelligent, never assumed an intellectual stance. Undoubtedly her parents had seen to it that she was sent to good schools; it is probable, too, that she was given some tutorial instruction. She made the most of her training by reading widely, especially in English literature. She was a cultured person in every sense of the term, a clever, perceptive woman, but always careful to observe the amenities; dignity was almost a fetish with her. In the democratic generation of Thomas Jefferson, she bemoaned the lack of interest in George Washington. Rebecca was recognized and respected by her fellow-Jews because of her old-line family, her devotion to Judaism, her superior educational qualifications, and the fact that she was accepted in the highest echelons of Christian society. She was incontestably the leading Jewish social worker of her day—American Jewry's proto-clubwoman.

Miss Gratz was opposed to intermarriage, and in a note to a dear friend, a Christian, expressed herself unequivocally on this subject. She was moved to declare where she stood because her brother Ben was about to marry a Gentile, Maria Gist (selection A).

Rebecca was active in Philadelphia's nondenominational philanthropic associations. In all probability, it was she who took the lead in 1819–1820 in establishing Philadelphia's Female Hebrew Benevolent Society. This Jewish women's charity, the first of its kind in the United States, documents the initial stirring of the Jewish female consciousness. The newly established society limited its help to the "respectable" poor, and then only after careful investigation. It offered the services of Jewish physicians and access to dispensaries, the latter through the courtesy of the men's sick-care association established by Philadelphia Jewry in 1813. The sick were also attended in their last moments by salaried helpers. An employment bureau of sorts for seamstresses was envisaged. Extracts from the 1819 constitution of the Female Hebrew Benevolent Society of Philadelphia are reprinted below (item B).

Though an ardent Orthodox Jew, Miss Gratz seems to have nursed no prejudice against other religionists, as is eloquently documented in item C, a letter to her sister-in-law, Maria Gist Gratz. Rebecca was an indefatigable letterwriter to her family, whose members were scattered as far south as Savannah, Georgia, and as far west as Lexington, Kentucky. It is literally true that hundreds of her letters are still available for research; they were preserved because her correspondents loved, respected, and even venerated her.

As Rebecca's welfare and social work testified, she was a humanitarian, yet strange to say, she had scant sympathy for trade unions, as item D testifies. Letter E reflects her interest in the traditional celebration of the Jewish holidays. It is important to note in this item that Rebecca's brother Ben and his Christian wife observed the Festival of Booths in the age-old fashion by actually building a booth during the harvest festival and eating in it.

Rebecca Gratz became a legend in her own day. Her niece, Sarah (Sara) Ann Hays (1805–1894), had a "crush" on her "sainted" Aunt Rebecca. Hence Sarah Ann's published recollections of Rebecca are highly subjective and sentimental, but basically accurate (F).

In selection G, Rebecca expressed her horror when an orphan of five was sent to a House of Refuge among convicts; her criminological approach is comparatively modern. Rebecca Gratz's indignant reaction to the Reform-ist anti-traditional utterances of the Charleston synagogue's hazzan is mirrored in excerpt H. Letter I reflects the social-minded thinking of the writer at her best; the 1844 internecine war between Catholics and Protestants in Philadelphia dismayed her. The final excerpt, J, reflects her attitude toward the Mexican War, which she saw as a cruel, unnecessary, unjust attack on a neighbor. No doubt her anger was exacerbated by the knowledge that the war had the wholehearted support of the Southern pro-slavery forces. Though no abolitionist, she had no sympathy for slavery, and no desire for its extension.

A

Rebecca Gratz to Maria Fenno Hoffman, October 31, 1819.
I do not know whether you, my dearest friend, can comprehend my feelings on this subject. Yet you know my opinions and have witnessed their influence on my conduct thro' life. I hope mine is not a narrow creed. My most cherished friends and the companions of my choice have generally been worshipers of a different faith from mine—and I have not loved them less on that account. But in a family connection I have always thought conformity of religious opinions essential, and therefore could not approve my brother's election. In other respects, Miss Gist is a woman any family might be proud to receive. And as they have resolved to blend their fate, I most sincerely hope they may find the means to worship God faithfully and without offence to each other.

B

1819
PREAMBLE, &c.

In all communities, the means of alleviating the sufferings of the poor are considered of high importance by the benevolent and humane. The ladies of the Hebrew Congregation of Philadelphia, sensible to the calls which have occasionally been made in their small society, and desirous of rendering themselves useful to their indigent sisters of the house of Israel, agree to establish a charitable Society; and in order to make the benefit permanent, adopt the following
CONSTITUTION.

ARTICLE I.

The society shall be established and known by the title of the Female Hebrew Benevolent Society of Philadelphia.

ARTICLE II.

Every lady subscribing the sum of two dollars annually shall be considered a member; and every person paying thirty dollars shall be a member for life.

ARTICLE III.

The society shall be regulated by a board, consisting of thirteen managers, to be annually elected by the society, out of which number shall be chosen a first and second directress, a treasurer, and a secretary.

ARTICLE IV.

The first meeting shall be held on the 24th day of November, 1819, for the purpose of organizing the society and appointing officers.

ARTICLE V.

There shall be two general meetings of the society in the year; the fourth Wednesday of November, and the fourth Wednesday in April. The meeting in November shall be considered its anniversary, when subscriptions become due, and a board of managers are appointed. At the semi-annual meeting in April, the board of managers shall report to the society the effects of the charity, amount of expenditures, and all other concerns of the institution.

ARTICLE VI.

All life subscriptions, legacies, and donations, exceeding ten dollars, shall be invested in some productive property, to form a permanent fund, the interest arising from which shall be added to the amount of annual collections for general expenditure.

RULES AND REGULATIONS

For the Government of the Female Hebrew Benevolent Society of Philadelphia. . . .

Visiting Committee.

A committee of managers shall be appointed monthly, to investigate the situation of applicants, and administer to their relief. They shall visit the pensioners, make inquiries respecting their characters and conditions, and in all cases provide them with necessaries, rather than with money.

Pensioners.

The pensioners of the society shall be Israelites, residents of the city or county of Philadelphia, of good moral character. Assistance may also be given to sojourning Israelites, in clothing or small sums of money.

To educate the children of indigent families, will be a desirable object of the society, when their funds will permit. . . .

REPORT . . .

From the organization of the society in November until the present meeting, the board have met once a fortnight, and every application for assistance has been attended to by the visiting committee. One or two cases may have been attended with disappointment to the applicants, as upon investigation it was thought necessary to reject one altogether, and to give but little to another. The board would not trouble the society with these particulars, but they are desirous to explain the principles on which they act. The funds elicited by charity they consider a sacred trust, to be distributed only where the purposes of charity can be effected. They could not, consistently with this, bestow upon the idle and improvident, although their poverty may excite to pity. An indigent family, who are frugal, industrious and grateful, have been assisted during the winter. They bless the Society for many comforts, which had else been strangers to their dreary habitation.

It is to modest worth, pining in obscurity; to the indigent who are "ashamed to beg"; to the sick, and to the infirm, that the assistance of this society will be most freely given. And that every delicacy may be secured to those who have "seen better days," a select committee will be formed at the next session, through whose hands relief may be secretly bestowed on reduced families, should such unhappily be found in our congregation.

The board likewise desirous of establishing a reciprocal service to the industrious and the infirm, propose that persons willing to attend on the sick or to assist in performing the last charitable offices for the deceased, should leave their names with the president of the society; that when occasions among our poor occur, they may be called on and remunerated by the society. Females who wish employment as seamstresses, and those who want them, may also make application to the president, who will keep a register for their accommodation. The board have the pleasure to state, they have received and accepted the offer of professional services from Drs. [Manuel] Phillips and [Isaac] Hays, for the sick among the pensioners, and also the use of the Hebra's [the 1813 men's sick-care society] contributions to the city and Northern Liberties dispensaries. They have expended by the visiting committee forty-one dollars and thirty cents, and deposited in the savings bank three hundred dollars until a purchase of United States six per cent stock can be made on favourable terms, reserving at the disposal of the board, fifty-four dollars and seventy cents for present purposes.

In making this first communication to their patrons [1820?] the board are duly impressed with the importance of the trust reposed in them; and feeling the deepest interest in the success of the institution, they pray that the God of Israel may give them understanding equal to their zeal, so to conduct its concerns as to benefit the distressed and do credit to those who have "stretched forth their hands to the poor and needy."

C

Rebecca Gratz to Maria Gist Gratz, 1832.

I had my philosophy a little tried the other day by some good Christians, and as I dare not complain about it to anybody else (for I hate to set the subject in its true light at home), I must make you my confidante. You know I promised our friend Mrs. Furness to apply for a little girl out of the Asylum for her. Well there is a good little girl I have kept my eye on and she is ready for a place, and my application is rejected because it is for a Unitarian. But "Ladies," said I, "there are many children under my special direction; you all know my creed; suppose I should want one to bring up in my family?" "You may have one," said a church woman, "because the Jews do not think it a duty to convert." "But," said a presbyterian, "I should not consent to her being put under the influence of a Unitarian." And so, my dear, after putting the question to vote, I could get nothing. And when the meeting broke up, had a mischievous pleasure in telling one of the most blue of the board that I construed their silence into consent, for only one lady voted in the affirmative, and they were all ashamed to vote no. But I do not mean to let Mrs. F. know how she is proscribed, Because notwithstanding my own position, I am ashamed of such an illiberal spirit. I got into a long discussion on the subject of religion with a lady after the meeting and though we have been more than twenty years acquainted, I expect she will look shy on me for the rest of our lives. What a pity that the best and holiest gift of God to his most favoured creatures should be perverted into a subject of strife, and that to seek to know and love the most High should not be the end and aim of all—without a jealous or persecuting feeling towards each other.

D

Rebecca Gratz to Maria Gist Gratz, January 7, 1837.

I do not know what is to become of the poor, unless they see the folly of these "trade unions" which seem to forget the wholesome old adage "half a loaf is better than no bread" and hold out for high wages or no work. In your plentiful country they might go out and plant corn and hemp, and produce enough to feed & cover themselves & families, but here they must either crowd our poor houses or beg, since they are bound in honor not to work.

E

Rebecca Gratz to Maria Gist Gratz, Novr 5th 1837.

You may be sure, My dear Maria, necessity alone prevented my answering your interesting letter as soon as it was received, particularly as you had experienced uneasiness at my long silence, but I have been sick & spiritless and therefore such a bad companion that I thought it more kindness to keep quiet and leave our brothers correspondence to suffice, for [my brother] Jo told me several times that he had written. I am glad you were kind enough to find an excuse for me and kept the Tabernacle celebration, in scenes so naturally appropriate to the season. For My own part I was only once under the shelter of its roof, and partook no further of the feast spread before me than a little bread & salt, tho' I enjoyed the sight of goodly fruit & wine distributed in plenty and listened to a hymn of thanksgiving that we were permitted to meet at the sanctification of this festival & view the emblems of former rejoicing. The palm & branches of goodly trees, mentioned in scripture as taken by the youths & damsels as they went out after the ingathering of the blessings of the year, to dwell in booths and rejoice before the Lord, has always had a great charm in my imagination.

I like the idea of cheerful gratitude and combining religious worship with heartfelt thankfulness in scenes where they had just reaped the benefits of their labor and praying that God would enable them to use his gifts for their good and the benefit of the poor. This is making religion one of our daily duties, a habit of our lives, and the commemoration annually of some National event in our history, which at this period of the world is called "supersticious" observances, has to me such a different bearing that I can hardly understand how a Jew can consider them oppressive or consent to forget them. Ben has told you of [Joseph Simon of Lancaster] our Grandfather's patriarchal habit of living, of his hospitalities to his brethren, and his amiable disposition. He has told you too, how liberally and justly he dealt with all mankind, and how he was beloved by his neighbours & the poor who were within reach of his bounty. I remember & feel a yearning to view the old Lancaster homestead, and felt offended that it should have fallen into strange hands as long as one of his children survived who might have been sheltered by its roof. But dissensions crept in and when the good old man was gathered to his fathers [1804], there was no son to reign in his stead. The last day I spent in Lancaster I visited his tomb. The fence was broken, cows were grazing among the high grass & weeds that covered it, and I came away sorrowful.

F

Recollections of Sarah Ann Hays, 1838–1869

How well I remember her eightieth birthday [1861]! Draped in a handsome silk dress and new cap, she was seated in her comfortable, warm chair to receive her friends and her relations on this memorable day. She appeared to be fully aware of the great event, and her face was draped in smiles, and each gift and good wish she received with loving pride and affection. She had cakes and flowers, pincushions and little mats, the handiwork of her nieces, and everyone brought some little offering. She would rise and accept the gift with smiles and thanks, and, quite overpowered, exclaim: "You make me feel so humble with your gifts. I am not worthy of all this." . . .

SHE WAS SUCH AN ELEGANT WOMAN

When I was young I used to hear all my young friends and their mothers admire my aunt, "Miss Gratz." She was such an "elegant woman, so handsome, so refined." "She graced the ball last night. She and her brother, Mr. Hyman Gratz, were the handsomest people in the room." As a child I was flattered at this notice of my aunt, whom my beloved mother always taught me to revere, but it was not until after years that the greatness, and I may say nobleness, of her character dawned upon me. An acquaintance with the world taught me how far superior she was to those I mingled with, how quiet and unobtrusive in all her elegance, how modest when referred to and admired. How beautiful in thought and feeling her letters can only show, as they often did to all her relations, for to them she was always a ministering angel. Coming to them in sorrow, with affection in one hand and religion in the other, she always healed the wound she came to bind. Her soothing words came to comfort me once at the death of a little child, which I lost after a short illness. Her words soothed me more than any other; they appeared to reach the right place and give me ease. Words at that time appeared useless, but hers were inspired to me and I felt them. . . .

It has been said that women had less education in those days, perhaps less in the "ologies," but my aunt was conversant with Burns, and Pope, and Milton, and even to her last days would repeat the "Universal Prayer" [by Alexander Pope], "Edwin and Angelina" [by Oliver Goldsmith], Scott's Ellen in the *Lady of the Lake*, and many other poems. She also repeated beautiful snatches of poetry and would say: "Where is that from, do you know?" And I had often to confess myself at fault. One verse she particularly dwelt upon. One day she repeated it so often that I retained it:

> Let me, like Israel, hope in God;
> This name alone implore,
> Both now and ever trust in Him
> Who lives for evermore. . . .

My aunt was alway efficient, no matter where placed or by whom called upon. A board of twenty-four ladies, of whom she was one, were the founders of the Asylum for Orphans in Philadelphia [1815], and for forty years she acted as secretary and member of the purchasing committee. Those who have read her annual reports may see the beauty of her language and the simplicity of her style. Every succeeding year her reports were read with interest, and each one differed from the other, and all were alike beautiful to my mind. I have never read such beautiful language as hers. Her letters, and she had many correspondents, are unparalleled—the flow of her language so easy, her ideas new and brilliant, her words natural, affectionate. Of all the famous letter writers whose letters have been published, not one can compare to her.

She was always accustomed, from her childhood, to the best society, and, when a girl, the Ogdens, Go[u]verneurs, Hoffmans, Fennos, Washington Irving, James Paulding, Sam. Ewing, the choicest wits of the time, were her intimates, and all admired and appreciated her. She and her two beautiful sisters were the toast of the club and of the day, as "The Graces," slightly altering "The Gratzes." They were beautiful women, as two miniatures I have copies of by Malbone, which he took when they were about twenty years old, can testify; and they were good as well as beautiful. . . .

My aunt, Rebecca Gratz, was an old maid, at least in the common acceptance of the term. True, she never married, but she was a mother to the orphan and destitute, to the friendless and oppressed, to those in poverty and want, and to the sinner and contrite.

LABORS OF LOVE

But it was among her own people she shone most conspicuously. There her labors were truly of love. She saw the young of her people growing up in ignorance of their faith, and she conceived and executed the idea of a "Sunday school," to be held in some room where the children would assemble to hear the word of God, to learn his commandments, and receive instruction in the religion of Israel. She, with other ladies, founded the institution [1838], and for years she was its president and head.

Every Sunday her steps were bent to the room appointed. Her majestic figure rose high above all there collected, a hundred scholars or more, to hear her mild and firm voice read a chapter of the Holy Bible, and then they, in unison, repeated a prayer written for them by herself, which combined "all prayer." She appointed and arranged all the teachers, and conducted the school with a dignity and modesty which pervaded all her works. The children looked up to her with reverence and admiration, their parents with gratitude and love. . . .

Her good works did not cease here. The [Female] Hebrew Benevolent Society [1819] was the work of her hands. She reared and fostered it, and cared and toiled for it and made it what it is, a society doing good to all our people, clothing the naked, feeding the hungry, and giving them assistance in every way.

The [Ladies' Hebrew] Sewing Society had its first impulse from her hands [1838]. The Fuel Society [1841] was also encouraged and benefited by her substantial aid, and, in truth, she assisted them all, not only by head and heart, but in more substantial ways.

Nor must I forget the Foster Home, for poor Hebrew children. She began [1855] and fostered that institution; she wrote its code and bylaws; she was its head and director, its manager for years. She gave the managers the experience of a life of usefulness, and they accepted her as a chief who would guide them with her knowledge and ability, and they delighted to follow where she led. It is surprising to think how many institutions she managed at the same time, and all with ability and energy. She was always an active member of all these societies, and her opinion was met with deference by all the ladies of the board. . . .

I went with her the year before I was married, in June, 1835, to visit her brother Ben, in Kentucky. There her reputation had preceded her, and on our first day Henry Clay, the hero of Ashland, came to see her and invited her to dine at Ashland. I went with her to that dinner party and saw the honors paid to her. Mr. Clay had invited a party to meet us, but he it was who took Rebecca Gratz in to dinner and placed her by his side, talked to her as great men talk, and after dinner gave her his arm and conducted her to see his farm, his sheep and his cattle, his dairy and his chickens.

From all the high men and women in Kentucky she received ovations of respect and attention; from all men and women of her day she was admired and praised; no matter how great expectation rose, no one was ever disappointed when they saw her; the beauty of her face and dignity of her form, the grace and ease of her manners, won all admirers.

I never shall forget when Washington Irving returned from Spain [1832], after an absence of fifteen [seventeen] years from his native country. I most fortunately was at Aunt Becky's when he called, immediately after his arrival, to see his old friend, Rebecca, and, with the familiarity of an old friend, she called him "Washington." He told her all about the book he was then publishing, *Tales of the Alhambra*. He spoke of the Alhambra with warmth and delight, expatiated on its courts and baths and wondrous splendors, said that Matio, who flourishes in his book, was a real character, and what struck me afterwards in reading his book was that he wrote precisely as he talked. I could hear his voice talking as I read. He dined the next day after his visit at aunt's, and I had the happiness to be invited to dine with him and sat next to him. . . .

Last Days

It may not be out of place in this little sketch of my dear Aunt Rebecca to mention that during her life that unfortunate Civil War occurred, which shook this continent to its centre and almost dissolved these United States. She, like a true woman, stood firm and true to her country; as she had followed one true God, so she could know but one united country. She knew, as Mr. Webster said, "no North, no South, no East, no West"; all the United States were her country, and she could not divide them during the four years of bloodshed. She never doubted but that the government would be successful and never allowed herself to believe to the contrary. She was true to her country as to her religion, and in both was true to herself. . . .

Her latter days were feeble, and the time came when "the grasshopper was a burden," and the health which had sustained her in all her labors gave way. A slight paralysis of the throat made swallowing at times difficult, but when the attack was off she would forget it and ever welcome her friends with a smile of affection, and when you asked her how she was, "I'm well, thank God." . . .

Her family surrounded her in her last illness, her only surviving brother from Kentucky, the three nieces to whom she had acted a mother's part, and her nephew Horace [Moses], who was a son to her. One day I went in to see her and found her very sick; she was sitting up in bed, and after saying "good morning," I found her suffering. I asked her if she wanted anything. She looked around her; seeing Becky Nathan at the foot of the bed and Miriam Cohen on the other side, she bowed gracefully to me and, pointing to each of the girls, she replied: "What could I want, so surrounded?" . . .

Her last will and testament in this world began with these beautiful words: "I, Rebecca Gratz, of Philadelphia, being in sound health of body and mind, advanced in the vale of years, declaim this to be my last will and testament. I commit my spirit to the God who gave it, relying on her mercy and redeeming love, and believing with a firm and perfect faith in the religion of my fathers: 'Hear, O Israel, the Lord our God is one Lord.' "

This was the heading of her will, and so she remained ever steadfast to her God and her religion. Hers was truly a *noble* life; and may she rest in peace with all the daughters of Israel, and let us say, "Amen."

G

Rebecca Gratz to Maria Gist Gratz, 1841.

I have just been called away on a business that interests me very much. Application was made for the admission of a boy into the Orphan Asylum, by a person who had received him from his dying mother, had indentured him to be adopted as his own son, to change his name, educate & give him a trade. At this period the child was three years old. He is now five, and they brought him to me with such evil reports of his character that I thought it necessary to get the consent of the Board. This was obtained but thinking the man who had taken him with such promises ought to pay some consideration, he was told so, and while I supposed he was making preparations to relinquish the child, found he had (perhaps to save the fee) placed him in the house of Refuge. A child 5 yrs old to be brought up among convicts!! This appears so shocking that we intend to get him out and take him to the Asylum. It is impossible that such an infant can deserve to be punished to such a degree, and if not, what must he become living among old offenders? You shall know the result if we succeed and make him a good boy; if not it will be time enough to place him in the prison after the experiment has been tried.

H

Rebecca Gratz to Miriam Gratz Cohen, March 29, 1841.

I have not seen the paper you sent containing an account of the Charleston Congregation but have heard some passages quoted that are certainly unorthodox. 'This is *our* temple, this *our* city this *our* Palestine.' Is it possible a Jew can write or speak so? Then where is the truth of prophesy? Where the fulfillment of promises? What is the hope of Israel? Of what does the scattered people bear witness? Alas we may hang our harps on the willow and weep for the spiritual destruction of Jerusalem when her own children are content to sing the songs of Zion in a strange land and deny the words of God so often repeated by the prophets. I am afraid the good people of Charleston are paying too much for their organ and allow more important objects to be sacrificed. Certainly the greatest enemies of the Jews never have denied their claims on the country inherited from their fathers, or doubted they would be restored to it in the time God shall appoint. How then can the Charleston congregation sell their birth right for a mess of pottage? But I beg your pardon, as I said before, I speak from hearsay and would fain hope there are (?) watchmen at their posts, scattered among the people who will warn them when they are in danger of falling into error by the spirit of innovation which has been the vice of ages among other religious denominations.

I

Rebecca Gratz to Benjamin Gratz, July 11, 1844.

The present outbreak is an attack on the Catholic Church, and there is so much violent animosity between that sect and the Protestants that unless the strong arm of power is raised to sustain the provisions of the Constitution of the U.S., securing to every citizen the privilege of worshiping God according to his own conscience, America will be no longer the happy asylum of the oppressed, and the secure dwelling place of religion.

Intolerance has been too prevalent of late, and many of the clergy of different denominations are chargable with its growth. The whole spirit & office of religion is to make men, merciful & humble & just. If such teaching was preached by the pastors to their own congregations and the charge of others left to their own clergy, God would be better served, and human society governed more in accordance to *His* holy commandments. But this is not what I intended to say to you, my dear brother. I thought you would like to hear something from *the scene of war*, and sat down merely to tell you that we were safe. St. John's, one of the threatened [?] chapels and our very near neighbour, is still standing and we depend on the measures now taking to secure it.

J

Rebecca Gratz to Ann Boswell Gratz, July 22, 1847.

My dear Ann:

. . . We have heard of Horaces arrival at Pensacola, I cannot tell you how glad I am he has left Mexico. I feel so much more sorrow & disgust, than heroism in this war, that I could not bear to think of his being in any way connected with it. When we were obliged to fight for our liberty and rights, there was motive & glory in the strife, but to invade a country and slaughter its inhabitants, to fight for boundary, or political supremacy, is altogether against my principles & feelings and I shall be most happy when it is over, tho many bleeding hearts will be left over losses of their dearest & most beloved victims. . . .

28

THE SPIRITUAL AGONY OF A CONVERT TO JUDAISM
1821

Some Gentile women who married Jews retained the faith in which they had been reared; others became Jews formally or by accepting the Jewish way of life. Undoubtedly some of the Christians who embraced the religion of their Jewish husbands had their moments of regret. A case in point, a pathetic one, is [Sarah?] Jane Picken (Mrs. A. H. Cohen), the daughter of a Presbyterian minister. She was a woman of culture and a poetess of quality. Abraham Hyam Cohen, the son of the minister Jacob R. Cohen, of Philadelphia, was alternately a businessman and a religious functionary. For years he served as the hazzan of Mikveh Israel in Philadelphia and Beth Shalome in Richmond. As spiritual leader of the Richmond Sephardic congregation in 1840, he evidenced qualities of leadership when the community protested against the persecution of the Jews in Damascus. He had met Miss Picken in 1806, fallen in love with her, and married her after she accepted Judaism and was formally converted. In 1821, she rejected her adopted faith, although for her husband's sake she made no public pronouncement of her return to Christianity. Ten years later, in 1831, she and her husband separated. In the following pages, Mrs. Cohen describes the circumstances accompanying her rechristianization.

During our residence in Baltimore, I made the acquaintance of the Rev. Mr. Brooke, a Baptist minister, and his most excellent wife. He was an exemplary Christian and a very intelligent man. I enjoyed many of his agreeable and instructive conversations, for he took deep interest in me; and especially in regard to my connection with the Jewish people, in whose history he had made deep research. But I was not long permitted to enjoy the society of this valuable friend, who was far advanced in consumption, and died soon after our acquaintance commenced, leaving his lovely wife and interesting little daughter to mourn his early loss, and, as is frequently the case with clergymen's widows, but scantily provided for in the future; so that she wisely concluded to open a school which yielded ample support to her and her little daughter. And we were now the more closely drawn together by the sympathy I felt for her in this sad bereavement; and that which had been but an agreeable interchange of feeling between us now ripened into friendship—a deep, undying friendship—that burns on the altar of my heart even now. For I loved her with a devotedness unfelt for any other female friend and this love was returned by her with all the ardor of an affectionate heart. This dear friend is now living in Winchester, Va.

In the year 1821, I took my dear children in the country to pass the summer months, and invited my friend, Mrs. Brooke, to spend her weeks of vacation with me, which she accepted; and I shall never forget that summer. Our time was spent most pleasantly in reading, conversation, and rambling over hill and dale; for our tastes were so congenial in all things that she seldom left my side; and to her I unfolded my heart's deep sorrow; and she breathed into my spirit a new life, by her sympathy and love. When mingling our tears together she ofttimes enfolded me in her arms, with this ejaculation: "Oh! my dear friend, that you could be buried with me in Christ." Would I could see her now, this dear friend, who wept with me in sorrow and stood by me in the hour of trial and sickness; for she well knew the inward workings of this sad heart, and the chains that bound me. But those chains were to be loosened at last, and the glory of God made manifest.

It was now the month of September, and my friend would resume the duties of her school, whilst I made preparation to return to the city. The mornings and evenings were cool, chills and fever prevalent, and on the morning of Sept. 3d, all being ready, the carriage drove up to the door, when, on going into the open air, I exclaimed, "I'm so cold," and folding my wrappings more closely around me told the driver on seating myself to drive quickly, that I was very sick. The journey of two or three miles was soon accomplished, and on reaching my house in town I retired at once to my chamber, and sent for Dr. B———, our family physician, who soon came, and finding me in a high fever prescribed accordingly and left me saying he thought I would be better in the morning. But this sickness was to be a serious one.

The malady increased, assuming different forms alternately, baffling the skill of our kind and good physician, and week succeeded week, and no change for the better. At length, our good doctor seemed at a loss how to proceed, and taking my dear husband aside questioned him in regard to the state of my mind; "For," said he, "there's something preying on the mind of your wife and may be termed a disease of the mind. I have done all I can. If you wish other advice, I approve of your having it, for Mrs. Cohen is very ill."

I had then been confined to my bed seven weeks, was covered with jaundice and deeply salivated; and, oh! the agony of suffering I endured; mind and body, heart and soul, all involved, I feared, in one eternal ruin! These, these were my feelings at this juncture and I thought I must die, all unprepared as I was to meet the king of terrors, and I cried out in agony, "Save me, Lord, save me!"

Day after day passed on, and my agony increased; for it was the agony of a soul on the verge of eternity. "Lost, lost!" I exclaimed, "I grope in darkness; what shall I do to be saved?" [cf. Acts 26:30] This was uttered aloud, involuntarily, and the good doctor was present. He said I looked at him as if I would pierce his inmost thought, and he took my trembling hands in his—they were icy cold, and a shudder ran through my frame with long-continued cold shiverings. And when, by the use of restoratives I was a little composed, the good doctor said: "How long, my dear Mrs. Cohen, has your mind been thus exercised?" "Some weeks," I replied; "but not so intensely as now. Pray for me, doctor; I'm lost, lost, and cannot pray for myself." And that dear old saint—he is in heaven now—knelt at my bedside and breathed the sweetest, soul-inspiring prayer, and I felt for the time as if lifted up from the bed of death to life everlasting; but those happy feelings were of short duration. Again I was beset with those gloomy presages of my lost state. The tempter was near and "no redemption" was ringing in my ears continually, and I could not be comforted. This was the third day of that extreme suffering I had endured.

I sent for my friend, Mrs. Brooke, who came and sat by me, talked and read to me, and wept over me; for she, too, thought I could not live until the setting sun, and she remained with me until the close of evening when she was obliged to return to her dear little girl, and she left me with my young friends who had come to watch with me during the night, and this dear friend took her farewell of me nor dreamed I could live until the morning. She therefore embraced me in the most affectionate manner at parting and pointed to the cross of Christ. "Look," she said, "there you will find comfort; for all who come, even at the eleventh hour, 'I will in no wise cast out.' 'Seek, and ye shall find, knock, and it shall be opened unto you.' " [John 6:37 and Matt. 7:7.] These were the comforting words of this dear friend. "Farewell! and if we never meet again, my dear friend, on this earth, may God in his infinite mercy receive your spirit. Once more, farewell."

She then left me—that dear friend left me alone to my God, and to him I carried a lacerated and bleeding heart and laid it at the foot of the cross as an atonement for the multiplied sins I had committed, whether of ignorance or wilfulness. And how shall I proceed to portray the heartfelt agonies of that night preceding my deliverance from the shafts of Satan? Oh! this weight, this load of sin, this burden, so intolerable that it crushed me to the earth; for this was a dark hour with me, the darkest; and I lay calm to all appearance but with cold perspiration drenching me, nor could I close my eyes; and these words again smote my ear, No redemption, no redemption. And the tempter came inviting me with all his blandishment and power, to follow him to his court of pleasure. My eyes were open; I certainly saw him, dressed in the most fantastic shape. This was no illusion; for he soon assumed the appearance of one of the gay throng I had mingled with in former days and beckoned me to follow.

I was awake and seemed to lie on the brink of a chasm and spirits were dancing around me, and I made some slight outcry and those dear girls watching with me came to me and looked at me. They said I looked at them but could not speak, and they moistened my lips, and said I was nearly gone; then I whispered and they came and looked at me again but would not disturb me. It was well they did not; for the power of God was over me, and angels were around me and whispering spirits near, and I whispered in sweet communion with them as they surrounded me, and pointing to the throne of grace said, "Behold;" and I felt that the glory of God was about to manifest itself; for a shout, as if a choir of angels had tuned their golden harps, burst forth in, "Glory to God on high," and died away in softest strains of melody.

I lifted up my eyes to heaven, and there, so near as to be almost within my reach, the brightest vision of our Lord and Saviour stood before me enveloped with a light, ethereal mist, so bright and yet transparent that his divine figure could be seen distinctly, and my eyes were riveted upon him. For this bright vision seemed to touch my bed, standing at the foot, so near, and he stretched forth his left hand toward me whilst with the right one he pointed to the throne of grace, and a voice came to me, saying: "Blessed are they who can see God; arise, take up thy cross and follow me; for though thy sins be as scarlet they shall be white as wool." And with my eyes fixed on that bright vision I saw from the hand stretched toward me great drops of blood as if from each finger; for his blessed hand was spread open as if in prayer, and those drops fell distinctly as if upon the earth; and a misty light encircled me. And a voice again said: "Take up *thy* cross and follow me; for though thy sins be as scarlet they shall be white as wool." And angels were all around me and I saw the throne of heaven. And oh! the sweet calm that stole over my senses. It must have been a foretaste of heavenly bliss. How long I lay after this beautiful vision I know not; but when I opened my eyes it was early dawn, and I felt so happy and well. My young friends pressed around my bedside, to know how I felt, and I said: "I am well and so happy." They then said I was whispering with some one in my dreams all night. I told them angels were with me; that I was not asleep and I had sweet communion with them and would soon be well.

Early in the day, my dear friend, Mrs. Brooke came to see me, having sent to know how I was and hearing I was better; but when I began to rejoice and tell her of the night, she laid her hand upon my mouth, saying: "Not now, my dear friend, you must be quiet—you are very weak." But I longed to break forth in praises to God; for I was a new being. My load of sin was gone, gone. I was lifted up by the wonderful power of God. And that beautiful vision stands before me now, as on that bright and glorious night when the power of Satan was driven back and my soul redeemed from death—eternal death! And this was conversion—deep and heartfelt conversion—such as baffles the pen of description; for language can give no idea of it; and such as can only be experienced once in our lives—a change of heart, a pure and holy offering to God. We may sin and repent a thousand times, perhaps, but never more than once enjoy that sweet manifestation of the pardoning blood that I experienced on that glorious night.

And from that time I regained my strength rapidly and was soon able to rise from that bed to which I had been confined for nine weeks. My eldest daughter, then about eleven years of age, was my companion and nurse during my convalescent state. She had heard something of the exercises of my mind, and possessing more mature sensibility than children of her age generally, I was induced to communicate to her the sufferings I had endured and the manifestation of the goodness and glory of God. In the recital she became perfectly enthusiastic, and said: "O ma! do be a Christian and I'll be one, too." Alas! this dear child little knew what I had to encounter; for this bright light which had shone upon me unto the perfect day was not to be hid under a bushel; nor could I quench the Spirit, and longed to burst forth in praises to God.

But my dear husband—how was I to break this subject to him, he a rabbi at the head of the Jewish Church? But it was to be done, and I summoned all the fortitude I could command for the occasion and told him as briefly as possible of the sufferings I had endured and the beautiful vision I had seen. This he would not listen to but rent his clothes and called it blasphemy declaring if I adhered to such belief he would cast me off forever. Deeply painful was the scene, and the language too heart-rending to repeat; for now the cold grave is closed over him—he sleeps in peace. He was not to blame—in his religion he would have died the death of a martyr; and he left for the time being saying if I did not recant we would never meet more as man and wife. Oh! the agony of heart, I will not further refer to it and hardly dare think of it.

This state of matters continued for nearly one month, and a relapse occasioned by the distress of my mind was the result. Again with difficulty I was restored; but continued for a long time so weak that I could not sit up without support, and I sent for my dear husband to come up and see me. He did so and was so touched by my appearance that he at once resolved to compromise this serious affair, and prefaced the matter thus: "My still dear wife, in consideration that you have descended from Christian parents, who in early life instructed you in the Christian religion, and for the sake of our dear children, I must try and reconcile these things so very repugnant to my feelings, and so in opposition to the tenets of that blessed religion to which by birth I am entitled and grafted more firmly by the force of education; let us see then what can be done to ameliorate the condition of each, for we both suffer. I cannot acknowledge a Christian wife before the world who are looking to me for a precedent to the rising generation; but provided you will keep these things within your own breast, locked up from the world, our society [the Jewish community], and our dear children, we may yet be happy. If otherwise, and you cannot consent to this, we must separate, painful as the trial may be. This is my resolve. Think of it and when properly reflected on let me hear from you." "As to the world," I promptly replied, "I care not; it is a dead letter—a blank. I could brave ten thousand such, for I have seen a better one in the eternal heavens, and this cannot be obliterated; but, my dear husband, I will, in as far as practicable, conform to that you desire, and when I can no longer do so I will honestly confess it to you, and this not only in consideration of your position, but for the sake of our dear, dear children; but even all this will not induce me to play the hypocrite. I may be called an apostate but never a hypocrite."

Thus matters rested for the time in an amicable manner; but it was a great trial to quench the Spirit that invited me forth. I could at that time have spoken in public, in highways, or byways; for my whole spirit was dissolved and I was like a little child. But peace was once more restored to our dwelling; and this to my aching heart and feeble state of health was a comfort I had long been denied, and I tried to be happy, if not satisfied, and looked back to the night of my conversion, and a voice again cried out: "Take up thy cross and follow me." And I said, "I will," and I then felt strengthened.

4. Sally Etting

4. Sally Eiring

29

AUNT SALLY ETTING, BUSINESSWOMAN, AFTER A FASHION
1825

Sally Etting, of Baltimore, was descended from a notable colonial family of German origin which came to British North America in the 1730's. The Gratzes and the Ettings became kinsmen through marriage. The Philadelphia merchant Benjamin Etting (1795–1875) was a nephew of Rebecca Gratz and Sally Etting. Most of the Ettings were proud Jews; Sally—like Miss Gratz—never married. Two of her sister took Christian husbands. The following letter indicates quite clearly that Aunt Sal was dabbling in trade.

Balt., May the 19th, 1825.

Mr dear Ben:

With pleasure I heard from the girls you are about to make us a visit, my dear son, and we shall expect you every day untill we see you. I wrote a few lines Monday by Miss Alexander to your dear parents. I hope they rec'd it. Mr. Cohen was *kind* enough when he was on his way to the boat to call and say he was just going. Too late for any one to write a line by him.

Have you sold all your goods, and have you done well by them? I want to know all your concerns for I believe no one takes a more sincere interest for you than your poor old Aunt Sal. Have you many chests of tea such as my brother [Solomon] got from you, and what is the price? He tells me he don't know as the chest was a present from you to Rachel [Gratz Etting, Solomon's wife]. If they are not too high I think it likely I could dispose of them.

You have not yet let us know what we owe you on the china. 'Tis very beautifull, and every time I look at it I see something new to admire. My dear Ben, bring down a little black tea, for we cannot get such as you have been drinking, and I wish you to be fed as well here as at home. 'Tis a high joke to invite company and request them to find their own provisions.

Do you think it possible to find out the person that makes mint lozenges? I should be very glad if you can get me two pound. Please pay for them and forward them by first opportunity. The crape [crepe] and them I will settle with you for.

Our little garden looks beautifull. Tell your dear father it is worth while to come down and see it. I am writing at a window surrounded by roses. How often do we wish to have him and your dear mother [Fanny Gratz Etting] with us. Your Uncle [Solomon] talks of moving next week. I have no news to tell you, for in the literal translation of the word I am a very homely girl [she stays home].

To all friends give my love. The girls all send theirs to our dear brother, sister, and the children. God bless and protect you all prays

Your affectionate friend,
Sally Etting

Mrs. Caton requested me to ask you the price of the first quality silk damask in Canton.

30

THE WILL (AND COMFORTS) OF A MIDDLE-CLASS MAIDEN LADY
1828

Esther Sheftall (b. 1771) was the daughter of the Savannah Whig, Colonel Mordecai Sheftall. In 1828, this spinster signed a will distributing her holdings. It is interesting to note that it does not begin with the stereotyped pious phrases which characterized contemporary wills. In this testamentary instrument, she disposes of her lands, the goods in her little shop, her silver, linens, furniture, cattle, and Negroes. This document is important for the light it casts on the standard of living of a middle-class, third-generation Southern Jewess.

State of Georgia,
County of Chatham.

This is the last Will and Testament of Esther Sheftall of the City of Savannah.

First. Whereas I am entitled to and own one undivided third part of the Lot of Land and building in Savannah, known as Lot Number (7) seven Heathcote Tything, Decker Ward, and also hold a Mortgage or written lien on the said Lots for the sum of Five Hundred Dollars which bear date the tenth day of April, 1820, Eighteen Hundred and twenty, and is under the hands and seal of Sheftall Sheftall, Moses Sheftall, and Perla Sheftall, I give, devise, and bequeath the said undivided third part of said Lot and buildings as follows, to wit, unto my Executors in Trust for the use of my brother Sheftall Sheftall during the time of his natural life. . . .

Second. I order and direct that my Negro woman Caty be sold by my Executors at private or public sale, and the proceeds of the sale to go toward the payment of my debts and the erection of a Stone over mine and my late sister Perla's grave. The surplus if any to be divided between my brothers Sheftall and Moses.

Third. I give and bequeath unto my Grand niece, Rosaline Cohen, daughter of Isaac and Rebecca Cohen, my small Negro girl Matilda with her future issue. Said Negro Matilda to be delivered to the mother of the said Rosaline immediately after my death.

Fourth. I dispose of all the rest of my Negro slaves as follows. I give and bequeath my Negro man Isaac to my brother Sheftall, to hold for and during the term of his natural life, and after his death unto Mrs. Rebecca B. Cohen, wife of Isaac Cohen, to her sole and separate use, not subject to the debt of her present or any future husband. I give and bequeath the rest of my Negroes unto my Brothers Sheftall and Moses to hold as Joint tenants during life only, and at the death of the survivor to be equally divided between Mrs. Nelly Sheftall and my three nieces Rebecca, Frances, and Perla, but Isaac, above given to Rebecca, shall be valued and form a part of said Rebecca's share in the whole. When the division takes place, the share of each Niece is to be held by her to her sole and separate use notwithstanding any present or future coverture [marital status].

Fifth. I give, devise, and bequeath the undivided third part of the Tract of Land left by my late mother unto my brothers Sheftall and Moses, their heirs and assigns forever. My third of the stock of cattle to be used by my Brothers Sheftall and Moses and at the death of my brother Sheftall to go to my Nephew Moses Sheftall forever. [The Sheftalls also grazed cattle; they were ranchers as well as shopkeepers.]

Sixth. I give my household and kitchen furniture, beds, bedsteads, bedding, and house linen (except such particular articles as are hereinafter specifically bequeathed) unto my brother Sheftall for life and afterwards to my Brother Moses forever.

Seventh. To each of the daughters of Mr. A. Jacobs of New York, to wit, Sarah, Frances, Georgina, Rachael, now Mrs. Barnett, and Richea, a mourning Breast pin of the value of Five dollars.

Eighth. I give the larger of my two Table-cloths to my Niece Frances Sheftall and the smaller one to my Niece Perla Sheftall, a sextagon bed spread marked with my mother's name and age to Frances Sheftall, my china bed spread with the fringe to Mrs.

Rebecca B. Cohen, the unfinished sextagon bed quilt to my niece, Perla Sheftall, the Bed spread made of a number of small stars, to my Brother Sheftall, it having been made for him by my Mother. The residue of my Bed spreads to my Brother Moses, my Father's miniature picture with chain etc. to my niece Frances Sheftall; my mother's miniature and with it a strand of gold beads to my niece Mrs. Rebecca B. Cohen, the mourning ring, which is in the case with my Mother's miniature, to my Niece Perla Sheftall; the diamond ring in the same case to my Niece Frances Sheftall. My Mother's wedding girdle, buckles, and the Silver girdle belonging thereto to my said Niece Frances. At the decease of my Brother Sheftall, the table china together with the Pitcher, Basin, and three Baskets attached to it, the brass andirons, shovel, and tongs to my said Niece Frances; the smallest sized silver Milk Pot together with eight silver teaspoons, sugar tongs, and tea strainer to my said niece Frances; the largest sized flowered milk pot with five silver teaspoons to my said niece Perla; all that portion of my Grand Father's plate which was willed to me by my sister Perla, consisting of a silver ladle, silver spice boxes, a plain silver salt cellar, two small silver shovels, and a plain silver milk pot to my brother Sheftall; my sett of chimney Jars to Perla Sheftall; the sett of Tea-china used in the Passover is the property of my Brother Sheftall.

I also give to my Niece Rebecca B. Cohen the largest sized china bowl together with two painted glass mugs; to my great Niece Laura Malvina Cohen a pair of gold bracelets, together with a small gold clasp; to my great niece Rosaline Cohen, the small sized paste [artificial gem] earings, to Perla Sheftall two paste, long and one steele pin. Frances and Perla shall throw [dice] for my real Mother of Pearl box, and I give it to the winner. After the death of my brother Sheftall, I direct that my Bureau and Toilette Glass be given to my Great Niece Rachael Cohen. I give to my Brother Sheftall Two Cordial bottles cut glass, five wine glasses figured with stars, five cordial cut glasses, two china mugs usually left on the mantle piece, a small sized china bowl, and seventeen tea china plates, to be by him left to either of his three nieces as he may see proper. I also give him the large and small silver shoe buckles. I give my two diamond cut glass pint pitchers or milk pots and butter cup and stand, which came from my sister Perla, to my niece Perla Sheftall.

My Mother's suit of wedding brocade to my niece Frances Sheftall with a wish that should she ever marry, she may be married in it, having the same altered to suit the fashion of the times, my lead coloured shawl of Canton Crape to my sister in Law, Mrs. Nelly Sheftall, my long claret coloured scarf with a brocade border to my niece Frances, also an unfinished dove coloured spotted silk, my two white silk dresses, one of which is white satin trimmed with white, the other a white spotted silk, to my niece Perla; a dark rich spotted silk trimmed with satin to go to Rebecca B. Cohen; the blue silk frock to Perla Sheftall, my Masarine blue levantine pelisse to Frances Sheftall, my rich levantine silk pelisse (lead coloured) and the trimming belonging to it, which are now off, to my Niece Perla; the rest of my wearing apparel to be divided between Mrs. Nelly Sheftall and her two daughters Frances and Perla. I give one cut glass tumbler with a medallion in it to my great nephew Moses Sheftall Cohen.

Ninth. I order that the goods in my shop be sold by my Executors at private or public sale, and from the proceeds to pay my Brother Sheftall one hundred dollars, being a legacy left him by my late mother, the surplus, if any, also to be paid him. I give to my said Brother Sheftall the real odoriferous aromatic amulet beads and Bracelets to be by him disposed of to either of his three nieces or his great niece Rachael Cohen. The Pier Glass now at my Brother Moses Sheftalls, I give to my Brother Sheftall during life and after his death to my said Brother Moses. I give one half golden eagle to Frances, and one to Perla Sheftall, to be by them kept as pocket pieces; my work box usually kept in my Bureau together with a silver scissors sheath, to go to Rebecca B. Cohen; my silver tweaser case to Perla Sheftall; a small piece of gold called a dollar to Rosaline Cohen; at the death of Sheftall Sheftall the silver ladle and all the silver marked M. S. I give to my nephew Moses Sheftall, also a pair of gold sleeve buttons marked M. S. The plate without mark I give to my Brother Sheftall for life and then to my Brother Moses. The China Bust of Bonaparte, the small gold sleeve buttons, and the silver bells belong to my Brother Sheftall.

Tenth. I give the gold mourning ring which is marked with the age and time of decease of my Grand Father Benjamin Sheftall to my Brother Sheftall for life and after his death to my Brother Moses; any other articles of plate or jewels not enumerated to go to Sheftall Sheftall with the right to dispose of it to either of his nieces. The profiles of myself, Mother, Sister and Nephew Mordecai, I give to my Niece Rebecca Cohen.

Eleventh. I give, devise, and bequeath all the rest, residue and remainder of my estate, real and personal, to my Brother Sheftall during his life and after his death to my Brother Moses Sheftall, his heirs and assigns. I give all my Hebrew and English Prayer Books to my Brother Moses Sheftall.

Twelfth. I give the silver Snuff Box to Sheftall Sheftall during his life and after his death to Moses Sheftall my Brother. I give my large silver Coffee Pot unto my Brother Moses for his life; at his death, the same is to be thrown or drawn for by my two nieces Frances and Perla and held by the winner.

Thirteenth. I appoint Sheftall Sheftall, Moses Sheftall, and Isaac Cohen Executors of this my will.

In witness whereof I have hereunto set my hand and seal this Sixth day of June, one thousand eight hundred and twenty eight.

Esther Sheftall

Signed, sealed, published, pronounced, and declared by the Testatrix as and for her last Will and Testament in the presence of us who in her presence and in the presence of each other have hereunto set our hand as *witnesses*

Ed. Harden

M. C. Daniell

H. Hudson

31

ISAAC GOMEZ, JR., WRITES A LOVE LETTER TO HIS WIFE
1829

Isaac Gomez, Jr. (1768–1831), a descendant of one of the most distinguished Sephardi families in New York City, sat down in 1829 and wrote his wife a love letter. This pillar of the Sephardi Jewish community was well-educated, editor of an anthology of prose and verse, and himself a poet of sorts. He was a happy husband and a devoted son. When his beloved mother passed away, he made this notation: "May her soul enjoy the felicity of an angel before the throne of her God whom she at all times worshipped with sincerity."

Yet, from all indications, his life had not been an easy one; we know that he experienced financial reverses. A fire had destroyed his home and his place of business. Prior to that, he had lost three infants. Years later—in 1828—when Congregation Shearith Israel offered him $2,000 to renounce any claims he might have to the Chatham Street Cemetery (he was the last survivor of one of the original deedholders), he was glad to accept the money.

Yet, despite all the difficulties with which life had confronted him, he was happy in his surviving family of seven children, a number of grandchildren, and his dearly beloved wife, Abby, a daughter of the Rhode Island merchant Aaron Lopez. Now, in 1829, when the following letter was written, he was sixty-one years old and in the thirty-ninth year of what had been a very happy marriage. Abby was still the cherished wife of his youth whom he had wed when but a young man of twenty-two, and he was eager, after all these years, to give her an unusual gift, which would truly be his own. What would be more fitting than a manuscript prayer book. He applied himself and spent long, weary hours copying a volume of David Levi's English translation of the Hebrew prayer book according to the Sephardi rite. When he was done with this labor of love, he bound it in leather, marbled its edges, and handed it to her with the following letter, which served as a preface.

[New York, 1829.]

Mrs. Abby Gomez,
My Angelic Wife:
   Permit me to request your kind acceptance of this book. Having written it for your use, I flatter myself you will use it with pleasure, it being the work of him who has the honour of having been your loving husband for upwards of Nine and Thirty years, during which time it's a pleasant thing to know that domestic happiness has been our lot, and I make no doubt but it will continue during our journey through life. And I feel the happiness so great that I may say with truth, "That I thank my God for having created thee for me and me for thee." And may we be permitted by "The Great Monarch of the Universe" to be together for many years yet to come of uninterrupted felicity, is my sincear wish.

   And I trust you are well convinced that did I possess the riches of Peru, my greatest happiness would be to lay them at your feet.

   With those sentiments sincearly expressed, I take lieve to say that I am truly

Your devoted and loving husband,
Isaac Gomez, Jun'r.

32

AFFAIRS OF THE HEART
1830–1840

In eighteenth-century America, it was the parents of the prospective bride and groom who arranged marriages, at least pro forma. By 1830, Moses Nathans, in love with Benveneda Valentina Solis, negotiated directly with the bride's father (selection A). The English of Nathans' letter is a trifle baffling, but his intent is clear. It is gratifying to record that his suit was favored and he married the girl in 1831.

Five years later, Alfred Mordecai (1804–1887) wrote to Samuel Hays asking for permission to marry his daughter Sara Ann. Mordecai, son of Jacob and brother of Rachel Mordecai Lazarus, was at the time a captain in the Ordnance Department of the United States Army. He had graduated first in his class at West Point in 1823. By 1836, he was the commander of the arsenal at Frankford, Pennsylvania, and thus had an opportunity to meet Sara Ann. Like Nathans, Mordecai wrote directly to his prospective father-in-law. People had begun to disregard the formalities of the eighteenth century. On April 17, 1836, he sent Mr. Hays a note asking for permission to marry his daughter (item B); only after the permission was granted did Alfred write to his father, Jacob, seeking his blessing. In later years, Mordecai became one of the most distinguished ordnance experts in antebellum America. Alfred was the only one of Jacob's sons to marry a Jewess.

The English of Alfred Mordecai's letter to Samuel Hays is impeccable. Mordecai, the author of numerous books and articles of a technical nature, had received a good grounding in classical and modern languages. By the second quarter of the century, most native American Jews of middle-class status wrote well. They were usually people of some education and culture. These qualities certainly typified the Charlestonians, as is reflected in the letter which Rachel Hart of that city wrote to her prospective daughter-in-law Hetty Maria Gomez (selection C). Mrs. Hart's letter was in answer to a message of consolation sent to her by Hetty Maria; Rachel Hart's husband, Nathan, had just passed away.

A

Philadelphia, November 14th, 1830.

Dear Sir:

I can no longer do so great violence to my own inclinations as to retain in my own breast a passion which has pray'd on my Spirits for a long time, and I flatter myself that the Integrity of my Intentions will excuse the fredom of these few lines whereby I am to acquaint you of the great value and affection I have for your amiable daughter whome I have had the hononour [sic] of being acquainted with for Some time.

I would not, Sir, attempt any Indirect address that should have the least appearance of Inconsistency with her duty to you and my honourable views to her. Choosing, by your Influence, If I may approve myself to your worthy of that honour, to commend myself to her approbation.

If I might have the honour of your Countenance, Sir, on this occasion I would open myself and Circumstances to you in that Frank and Honest Manner which should convince you of the Sincerity of my affections for your daughter and at the same time of the honourableness of my Intentions.

Sir, of my Reputation or Capability I will say nothing, But am ready to make appear to your Satisfaction.

This, Sir, I thought But Fair and honest to acquaint you with, that you might Know Something of a person who sues you for your Countenance in an affair that I hope may one day prove the greatest happiness of my life, as it must be, if I can be bless'd with that of your daughter's approbation.

And the Favour of a line, I take the Liberty to subscribe myself,

Your Ob't and Humble S't
Moses Nathans

B

Frankford Arsenal,
April 17th, 1836.

My dear Sir:

I am about to make a request the magnitude of which might well deter me from proferring it, if I were not reassured by the very kind & friendly manner in which I have always been received by your family; it is to ask your sanction to my union with your daughter, Sara Ann, whose consent I have been happy enough to obtain.

Dependent as I am solely on my commission in the army for a support, my circumstances, in a pecuniary point of view, must be too well known to you to make it necessary for me to say anything further on that subject. But moderate as my appointments are, I venture to hope that in yeilding to our wishes you will have no cause to regret having allowed your daughter to secure the happiness of

Your friend and servant

A. Mordecai

To Saml. Hays, Esqr.

C

Charleston, October 2, 1840.

My dear Miss Gomez:

With mingled feelings of pleasure and pain I am seated to acknowledge your very kindly sympathizing and affetionate letter. How can I but feel deeply grieved when my congratulations and warmest approval cannot be associated with those of a devoted Father, of one who ever considered the happiness of his Family as the highest object of his ambition.

The deeply afflictive event which has thus suddenly deprived me of one of the kindest of Husband[s], his children of a most affectionate Parent, alone has delayed the expression of those joyful feelings which a mother must experience at so important a crisis in the life of a worthy son [Hyman N. Hart]. Whilst I now indulge in such feelings the pangs of sorrow are alas rendered more keen, associated as they are with the reflection How much joy his dear Father would have felt at this consummation of his son's fondest Hopes, but it has pleased an All Wise God to decree otherwise.

It was ever the advice of my deceased Husband, I may say the very basis of his approval, ever to regard the respectability of a Family of the highest consideration in the selection of a companion for life. Altho I have not the pleasure of a personal acquaintance with your's, they are known to me by reputation and cannot but feel gratified that my son has thus evinced[?] a proper filial regard to the counsel of his deceased father.

I feel no delicacy in saying to you, my dear Miss Gomez, tho' the feelings of a mother may prompt too much, that He to whom your Heart is given is richly worthy of it. He has ever been to me an affectionate son and I feel sure that your happiness will be ever dear to him. As to myself let me assure you I shall cherish you with the feelings of a Mother and will receive you into the bosom of my Family as a Daughter.

Oblige me and present my kind regard[s] to your parents, and believe me,

Yours very truly
Rachel Hart

PENINA MOÏSE, POET
1833

Penina Moïse (1797–1880) was probably the first American Jew to publish a volume of poetry. Her volume, Fancy's Sketch Book, *appeared at Charleston in 1833. Penina, the child of French refugees who had fled from Haiti after the slave insurrection of the 1790's, was born in Charleston, where she spent most of her life. After her father's death, she went to work at the age of twelve making lace and embroidery. Many of her eighty-three years were spent in genteel poverty. Hardship and deprivation were as common among the antebellum Jews as they were later among the East European émigrés. Penina was self-taught and through her reading became a person of education and culture. To support herself after the Civil War, she, along with a sister and a niece, conducted a small private school; the "trio" barely eked out a living. Penina was blind the last twenty years of her life, a misfortune exacerbated by neuralgia. She paid her respects to this torture by defining it as follows:*

Neuralgia, a fugitive from purgatory, who having served as an apprentice in Lucifer's penal laboratory, acquired such proficiency in the art of torturing that, having excited the jealousy of her master, quitted the Satanic institute, and established a patent rack and screw factory, distancing all nerve-racking competitors—not excepting the familiars of the Inquisition.

Penina Moïse was a person of exemplary character and integrity, a devout religionist who was concerned with and troubled by the sufferings of her people in Europe and Asia. She was a warm, sympathetic, magnificent human being. If for no other reason, she deserves to be remembered. Though her verses were published in a number of America's outstanding women's periodicals, she was not a great poet—maybe not even a good poet—but some of her stanzas are touched by the divine spark. Her light verse is often amusing. Because Penina's generation admired and loved her, they tended to exaggerate her poetic gifts.

Item A is a verse from a poem dedicated to persecuted foreigners; it

5. Penina Moïse

5. Penina Moïse

appeared after the 1819 riots in Germany, when Jews were beaten and robbed. The verses of selections B, C, and D show Penina in her lighter moods. Item E is a hymn. Penina was a prolific hymn writer; some of them are still sung today. Congregation Beth Elohim published her hymnal in 1856; it went through four printings. The stanzas in item F show her in a sober, reflective moment; G, "A Farewell Message to All Friends," was composed shortly before her death.

A

If thou art one of that oppressed race,
Whose name's a proverb, and whose lot's disgrace,
Brave the Atlantic—Hope's broad anchor weigh,
A Western Sun will gild your future day.

B

STANZAS.

> Oh! hide those eyes of violet hue,
> Wild passion they inspire;
> They beam too fiercely to be blue,
> Their dew is lost in fire.

> Yet in thine heart eternal snow
> The torch of Love destroys;
> Long have I felt affection's woe,
> But never felt its joys.

> I saw thee cull a lovely rose
> And place it near thy heart;
> I knew its languid leaves would close,
> Its fragrance would depart.

> In sorry I behold the flower
> On thy cold bosom lie;

I knew 'twould languish there an hour,
I knew it then would die!

I traced my doom reflected here,
My bloom is fading fast;
I live but in thy beauty's glare,
I'll die in it at last!

C

EPIGRAM.

The following coincident actually occurred:

And am I no longer betrothed, dear mother?
Oh Cupid! suppose I should ne'er get another?
And must I return his perfumed billet-deux
And the gold heart, that loveliest little bijou?

Weep no more, dearest daughter, for such a deserter
I protest that your sorrows exceed those of Werther
And deeply it grieves me your feelings to shock
But he must be made to surrender your lock.
Oh! would that were all of my delicate task.
To resign is more difficult far than to ask,
For indeed softly whispered the yet sobbing girl,
My own hair is innocent—'twas a false curl!

The gentleman on hearing the above, returned the lock with
the following couplet:

How false the foundation on which both have built,
If your hair was spurious—my heart was gilt.

D

IMPROMPTU.

On hearing that Gas Light was introduced into a house just as an intellectual lady had made it her abode.

Mrs. C. M. M.

"Two stars held not their zenith in one sphere"—
Thus saith old England's gifted Will Shakespeare.
In our blessed land quite the reverse is seen;
And in full view of our college campus green
There *Two* bright lights together forth have burst—
So lustrous both, 'tis hard to rank the first,
Save that the one shines brightest far by night,
While from the other beams perpetual light.
November 22, 1848.

E

SUBMISSION TO THE WILL OF GOD.

God Supreme! to Thee I pray.
Let my lips be taught to say,
Whether good or ill may flow,
Hallelujah, be it so!

What Thy wisdom may dictate
Let Thy servant vindicate;
Though it may my hopes o'erthrow.
Hallelujah, be it so!

Friends may falsify my trust.
Kindred also prove unjust,
Wound my heart and chill its glow,—
Hallelujah, be it so!

Health and comfort may decline,
Why at this should I repine?
Both to Thee, my God, I owe,
Hallelujah, be it so!

When by disappointment stung,
Hard it is for human tongue
Still to say, though tears may flow,
Hallelujah, be it so!

Yet, from Mercy's aid shall spring
Strength of spirit still to sing
'Mid bereavement, pain, and woe.
Hallelujah, be it so!

F

But wherefore, man, in thy serenest mood,
    When joy upon thee flashes,
Still minglest thou with songs of gratitude
    Sad thoughts of dust and ashes?
Wilt thou no hint from frailer natures take?
    From flowers, that at eve appear to die,
Yet 'neath the canopy of heaven wake
    To greet God's morning messenger on high?

G

But why should I not wish to linger here?
Do I not dwell in Friendship's atmosphere?
Where generous souls such balmy tribute bring,
As makes my wintry age so like to spring
That scarce the blind recluse, amid its snows,
Detects the absence of the vernal rose.

· 34 ·
HOW TO EDUCATE JEWISH GIRLS
1835

On June 2, 1835, Isaac Leeser, the hazzan of Philadelphia's prestigious Sephardi congregation, preached on religious education. A substantial portion of his very long sermon, excerpted below, was devoted to the education of women. This discourse of his is important because he was then the most articulate Jewish preacher in the country; his talk was printed twice, and when it appeared the second time in 1866–67, he was the country's outstanding Jewish clergyman. His philosophy of education for women makes interesting reading. He was preaching a cult of true Jewish womanhood, one based on the Bible and morality, meekness and modesty, and above all, piety. In all probability his system of ideas does not accurately reflect the views of the typical Jewish papa or mama of the 1830's; Leeser was too far over on the right. He was then a bachelor, all of twenty-nine years of age, a very sérieux high-minded minister. What was he trying to prove?

_____

How then is the child to become religious? How is he to read the Bible understandingly if instruction upon the most essential subject of life is to be withheld from him? Some however may say: "That they will admit, that male children should be carefully instructed, that it is perfectly reasonable that those who are to become, as it is called, 'the lords of creation' should be qualified for their stations by practical training, that their morals should be carefully attended to and their mental culture strictly watched over. But females, they aver, need not that knowledge; theirs being a more dependent lot it is immaterial whether they are high-learned in sacred literature or versed in the holy tongue. In short for them superficial reading is enough, for them it will be sufficient if the lighter branches of elegant learning are cultivated by them." As usual, this reasoning contains with some sprinkling of soundness a great share of fallacy which will be apparent upon a slight review of the question. It is not to be denied that it is almost entirely useless for the female to become learned in the strictest sense of the word; it would indeed unsex her, if she were to study the legal profession; if she were to step abroad as a physician; if she, forgetful of feminine decorum, would lay on the harness of war and wage a mortal combat with the enemy. Well has it been commanded: "There shall not be man's apparel upon a woman" [Deut. 22:5]; for the female's sphere is not the highway, not the public streets, not the embattled field, not the public halls.

But her home should be the place of her actions; there her influence should be felt, to soothe, to calm, to sanctify, to render happy the rugged career of a father, a brother, a husband, or a child. Yet, how is she to become qualified for this holy, for this noble task, if you leave her mind a blank—a barren waste—open to the evil seed which the world's corruption is but too apt to scatter? Behold this woman, watch her well, and then decide upon her claims to your regard and affections. She is proud, vain, frivolous, ignorant, vicious, and you despise her; she is no doubt undeserving of your regard; but the fault is hardly hers, it is her parents and teachers that are to blame. God has given her beauty, a mind alive to the charms of nature; a soul delighting in the romantic and the affectionate; wealth also has not been denied her, since her father has all which a covetous world might desire.

Now mark how this girl is educated. Before she can lisp she hears her charms praised; her will is almost law to the dependents of the family; the rod of correction she never is made to feel no matter what her faults may be; the word of reproof even is but sparingly administered. Her schooling, next, is not of the highly morally elevated, but again the frivolous, the showy—grant it be elegant; but her soul is all the time uncultivated because that is never regarded as of the least importance to her; her beauty is to win admiration; her accomplishments are to captivate and her wit is to dazzle. And lo! the bashful girl grows into the lovely woman: flatterers crowd round her in greater number; menials in larger swarms now await her commands; she has perhaps rivals to encounter upon the path of conquest which she has chalked out for herself, or which fond, foolish parents have bidden her to tread, and what can you expect should be the result, but that she should be proud, vain, frivolous, ignorant, vicious, revengeful, and perhaps at last morally depraved? This indeed is but a fancy picture of a spoiled beautiful heiress; but does it not apply almost to every female in a greater or less degree who has the advantage or rather the curse of an elegant education and a fashionable parentage? At the same time the daughters of the commonly so-called lower classes are in many respects but little better circumstanced; since moral culture is with them also much neglected at the expense of wordly and vain acquirements.

I do not wish to say, that my observations hold universally true but their general correctness cannot be gainsayed. All this must tend to prove that between the two extremes, between un-feminine learning and useless acquirements, the true course should be sought for. Our daughters then should learn early, even whilst yet infants, that they as well as the other sex are creatures and dependents of God; they too should be early told of the greatness, the mercy and the unending goodness of the Almighty; they should be taught to direct their hopes in affliction and their confidence in prosperity to the Giver of all good. They should be informed that beauty is perishable, wealth is fleeting, joy evanes-cent, and wisdom fallacious; they should be impressed with the conviction that flattery is a pernicious gift dangerous to the receiver; that the world will crouch and cringe to the prosperous and turn away with disgust and loathing the confiding one whom they themselves have corrupted. Above all the father should betimes commence to teach his daughter the way she should go; he should, so to say, be her guide on the road to eternal life; he should bid her look into the sacred page to gather wisdom and hope from the undying words of Holy Writ; and he should admonish her to cull the antidote to affliction from those records where it is taught to us that the virtuous are never forsaken. Especially however he should inform her how becoming is meekness and how lovely is modesty in the beautiful woman, how much more commanding her loveliness must be if she bears it as a gift of Heaven, not as some gaudy jewel of which the wearer may be proud.

Think you that an education based upon such principles can be otherwise than beneficial? Even if the time consumed in this training should preclude the acquisition of accomplishment; still far better will it be that our daughters grow up religious women and excellent housewives than that they be elegant musicians, skilful painters, graceful dancers or pretenders to sciences which to the great majority of females must be quite useless. If time is left, if the parent's means will permit it, then some of the more showy branches might with advantage be added; but care should always be taken that they be viewed as secondary and that religious instruction and useful solid information should be the first, the most important pursuit.

Whilst on the subject I cannot dismiss it without adding a few words as to the books which are generally considered fit for female reading. I allude to the whole class of fictitious writings, by which I mean romances, novels, and dramas. That some are good, others harmless, is not to be denied; but the majority of them contain false views of morality; a perverted philosophy, and a mawkish sensibility are generally their chief pervading characteristics; and, when, as it is often the case, the young mind has not been stored with sound religious knowledge, this kind of literature destroys almost entirely all sound principles, and it may well-nigh reduce one to the awful state on which the prophet pronounced the curse: "Wo to those who say to the good evil, and to the evil good." [Isa. 5:20].

It were therefore far better, if the whole of such works were banished or set out of the reach of the young; but if this cannot be done, at least do teach the females, at least prepare them with that kind of information which may act as the antidote to the poison they so plentifully imbibe. In this manner then let us proceed in the education of our children: let religion form the basis both for males and females on which the superstructure of useful and ornamental knowledge can afterwards be profitably built; for without the former, as has been shown, the latter can never produce good and wholesome fruits.

35

THE ETHICAL WILL OF DEBORAH MOSES
1837

Deborah Moses (1776–1848) was the daughter of Hazzan Jacob R. Cohen, of Philadelphia's Mikveh Israel, and the sister of Abraham Hyam Cohen, who officiated for a time in his father's post and later at Beth Shalome in Richmond. Deborah's son was Major Raphael J. Moses, who served with distinction in the Confederate Army. Deborah's will is reproduced here in part because of its final injunctions to her husband and son. Wills with ethical prescriptions are relatively common in Jewry; prototypes go back to pre-Christian times. This will was signed in 1837; the testatrix died in 1848 at St. Joseph, Florida.

THE STATE OF SOUTH CAROLINA. In the name of God, Amen. I, Deborah Moses of the city of Charleston and State aforesaid, being deeply impressed with the conviction that the Almighty had blessed me beyond my deserts, I feel bound in humble gratitude to avail myself of the full possession of all my faculties to regulate and dispose of my worldly effects in a way that I deem most advantageous to those exclusively dear to my heart, and who claim both from nature and affection every effort on my part to secure my property which I hold and have possessed as a free dealer, to them and for their interest and future welfare should the will of God so ordain (which with humility of spirit I hope may be the case) that they should survive me. . . .

I request that no pomp or parade whatever may be exhibited over my last remains. A plain coffin of the most simple materials, and in due time a wooden head and foot post without any inscription whatever are all that I require. The wisdom of God has mingled us indistinctly with the earth; why then shall we take from the living to arrogantly perpetuate an ephemeral name. To be forgotten is the lot of all. I therefore require no mark of outward woe. Lay the earth quietly and with respect on me; I leave the rest to conscience, feeling, and duty. Mourn not beyond the hour sanctified by nature and true grief; the tears which spring from the heart are the only dews the grave should be moistened with. The dead receive sufficient honor in being called to face their God . . .

Witness my hand and Seal this fourteenth day of November, One thousand eight hundred and thirty seven.

Deborah Moses

36

REBECCA GRATZ AND AMERICA'S FIRST JEWISH SUNDAY SCHOOL
1838

Together with some of her friends in Philadelphia's Congregation Mikveh Israel and in the Female Hebrew Benevolent Society, Rebecca Gratz established the first Jewish Sunday school in 1838. It was long overdue, for the Philadelphia Christians had opened their first school in 1790; by 1838, there were in the United States at least 7,000 such institutions and a host of textbooks and religious magazines for Christian children. The Jews may well have hesitated because Sunday schools seemed so typically Christian. Rebecca may have been influenced by the work of Hannah More, an English protagonist of this type of education. Rebecca was well aware of the religious and philanthropic work of this famous woman. More to the point, German Jews had by then begun arriving in the United States in increasing numbers. The children of these humble newcomers had to be saved for Judaism. Efforts were even made to teach the youngsters to read English. In a very modest way, the nineteenth-century schools Miss Gratz advocated were proto-settlement houses. The Sunday school was the most important Jewish children's educational innovation in the nineteenth century; it was created and staffed, for the most part, by women.

The following sober and realistic account of the early Philadelphia Sunday schools was written by Rosa Mordecai (1839–1936), the daughter of Captain Alfred Mordecai and herself a kinswoman of Miss Gratz.

THE ZANE STREET SUNDAY SCHOOL

My first distinct impression of going to the Hebrew Sunday school was some years after it was organized by my great-aunt, Miss Rebecca Gratz, and while she was still its moving spirit (some time, I think, in the early fifties). The room which the school then occupied was on Zane Street (now Filbert Street) above Seventh Street, over the Phoenix Hose Company. This was prior to the days of the paid fire department. Before mounting the stairs, I would linger, as many of the girls and all the boys did, to admire the beautifully-kept machines, with the gentlemanly loungers, who never wearied of answering our questions. The sons of our most "worthy and respected" citizens ran after the Phoenix in those days. But I catch a glimpse of Miss Gratz approaching, and we all scatter as she says: "Time for school, children!"

The room in which we assembled was a large one with four long windows at the end. Between the centre windows was a raised platform with a smaller one upon which stood a table and a chair. On the table was a much worn Bible containing both the Old and the New Testaments (Rev. Isaac Leeser's valuable edition of the Hebrew Bible had not then been published), a hand-bell, Watts's Hymns, and a penny contribution box "for the poor of Jerusalem." [Leeser's Hebrew Bible was published in 1848; the English translation, in 1853.]

Here Miss Gratz presided. A stately commanding figure, always neatly dressed in plain black, with thin white collar and cuffs, close-fitting bonnet over her curled front, which time never touched with grey; giving her, even in her most advanced years, a youthful appearance. Her eyes would pierce every part of the hall and often detect mischief which escaped the notice of the teachers.

The only punishment I can recall was for the delinquent to be marched through the school and seated upon the little platform, before mentioned, under the table. Sometimes this stand would be quite full, and I was rather disposed to envy those children who had no lessons to say. But, her duties over, Miss Gratz would call them by name to stand before her for reproof, which, apparently mild, was so soul-stirring that even the most hardened sinner would quail before it. She was extremely particular to instill neatness and cleanliness. A soiled dress, crooked collar, or sticky hands never escaped her penetrating glance, and the reproof or remedy was instantaneous.

The benches held about ten children each. They were painted bright yellow, with an arm at each end; on the board across the back were beautiful medallions of mills, streams, farmhouses, etc., etc.

The instruction must have been principally oral in those primitive days. Miss Gratz always began school with the prayer, opening with "Come ye children, hearken unto me, and I will teach you the fear of the Lord." This was followed by a prayer of her own composition, which she read verse by verse, and the whole school repeated after her. Then she read a chapter of the Bible, in a clear and distinct voice, without any elocution, and this could be heard and understood all over the room. The closing exercises were equally simple: a Hebrew hymn sung by the children, then one of Watts's simple verses, whose rhythm the smallest child could easily catch as all repeated: "Send me the voice that Samuel heard," etc., etc.

Many old scholars can still recall the question: "Who formed you, child, and made you live?" and the answer: "God did my life and spirit give"—the first lines of that admirable Pyke's *Catechism*, which long held its place in the Sunday school, and was, I believe, the first book printed for it. The Scripture lessons were taught from a little illustrated work published by the Christian Sunday School Union. Many a long summer's day have I spent pasting pieces of paper over answers unsuitable for Jewish children, and many were the fruitless efforts of those children to read through, over, or under the hidden lines. . . .

THE ANNUAL EXAMINATION

The Sunday school was removed in 1854 from Zane Street to the lower floor of the building of the Hebrew Education Society, then situated on Seventh Street, below Callowhill. This kindness has never been withdrawn, and the Sunday school has ever since enjoyed the free use of the rooms of the Society, wherever located.

Miss Gratz was still superintendent, president, treasurer and secretary—the powerful and most capable factotum. I, with many others, was soon promoted from the ranks of the scholars to the dignity of teacher, owing to the great increase of very young children. The room was by no means as suitable as the old one, having a very low ceiling and small windows, affording insufficient light and air in summer, while two large stoves at the entrance heated only a small area on a cold winter's day. But economy was most strictly observed by Miss Gratz in all her dealings, and it was very necessary in the management of such a limited revenue as the school has always possessed. The saving of rent, however, enabled her to spend more liberally for the growing wants of the school.

The benches were low and semicircular; the teacher, sitting in much closer contact with the pupils, was thus supposed to be able to maintain better order, and little restless feet were not so often seen dangling under the superintendent's table. The platform was much larger and had a kind of alcove behind, in which were seated the pupils of the graduating class, taught by Miss Sim'ha C. Peixotto, who struggled with the difficulties of Johlson's catechism [translated in 1830] until Mr. Leeser wrote his valuable *Catechism* [1839] for the school, and dedicated it to Miss Gratz. The articles on the table were also slightly changed; a handsome copy of Rev. Isaac Leeser's large edition of the Holy Scriptures replaced the old King James's version.

A roll book was added, and a fine gong bell rang for order, instead of the little tinkling one of the old schoolroom. Maps of Palestine, the Ten Commandments, and other more appropriate emblems adorned the walls, and resolutions of the members of the Phoenix Hose Company.

A few changes had also crept into the weekly routine. The psalm read one Sunday was repeated the next week by the older classes, a certain number of verses being assigned to each scholar. It sometimes happened that the succession would be broken by the absence of one or two pupils, but good marks, pretty cards, and a general desire to improve or get a prize made attendance very regular.

There were various devices used to amuse the very young children before Miss Rebecca Moss started her infants' class, attended with such marked success. Both Hebrew and English primers were resorted to, in the vain attempt to teach reading, but if the least progress was made one Sunday, it would be entirely forgotten before the next lesson; particularly as the books were not allowed to be taken home. . . .

About this time Miss Sim'ha C. Peixotto, of grateful memory, saved us the trouble of pasting over objectionable passages, by undertaking to write the scriptural questions, and published the first volume of her excellent catechism [1840], which held its well-deserved place in the school for many years.

Pyke's *Catechism* was freely distributed, and instead of being taught, parrot-fashion, by the teacher, the tiny green books went home to many Jewish households, with a penalty of five cents attached if injured or lost; and this fee was strictly exacted by the young librarian, who was a great disciplinarian. Books were not very often allowed by him to be taken home, but were read, after the lessons were recited by the scholars, or aloud by the teacher, if it so happened that all her class studied in the same book, or the same lesson. Generally, however, owing to private reasons, kinship, or popularity, a class would be composed of eight or ten boys and girls of different ages and ability, and consequently these were taught out of several books, or even different parts of the same book.

Both Rev. Isaac Leeser and the Rev. Dr. (then Mr. [Sabato]) Morais were constant visitors. The former, with his strongly [pock-]marked face, gold spectacles and inexhaustible fund of ever-ready information, was a most welcome sight to the young teachers, puzzled by the questions of their big, clever scholars. He knew every child and teacher, called each by name, and nothing was too trivial or too intricate to claim his clear explanation.

Mr. Morais was then young, active, and full of enthusiasm, always ready to lead the Hebrew hymns or take the class of an absent teacher. Tradition says it was in Sunday school that he was first attracted to his beautiful young wife [Clara E. Weil], who was one of the most beloved teachers. Be that as it may, most certainly courting was openly encouraged both by Miss Gratz and Miss [Louisa B.] Hart, who, having never tasted the delights of matrimony, naturally wished all their young charges to enjoy connubial bliss. My own teacher has often told me since, how her husband was first drawn towards her by her gentle manners to her young pupils. Other successful and unsuccessful lovers will always retain pleasant memories of the old Sunday school, and of their walks to and from it.

The annual examination was held about Purim time [February-March]. Why at that time, I never could find out, as the work of the class had to be immediately recommenced, unless it was a sort of anniversary, as the school was first opened March 4th, which, by a curious coincidence, was Miss Gratz's birthday.

Can any of you recall the dear old Cherry Street Synagogue, on those March Sundays [when the annual examination was held]? I can see it so distinctly with its circular benches and deep gallery facing the large open space between the *Tebah* and the *Hechal* [the reading desk and the Ark], with its broad steps and light doors that raised like a window. It was with something like awe that on these anniversaries we women took possession of the ground floor. [Women were not allowed to sit with the men at the regular services.] A small table was placed in front of the reading desk for Miss Gratz. The classes were all arranged in the men's seats and were called up to stand and recite by Mr. Abraham Hart [the famous publisher], who presided at the desk, his own clever children invariably making the best recitations and carrying off the prizes. The classes were arranged in a semicircle, according to the part of the book they studied, the pupils returning to their seats when the limit of their lessons had been reached. One teacher stood in the centre, giving the questions, or, if the classes were numerous, walked gradually around the circle. Thus every child was really examined, and each book recited in whole or in part.

The monotony was varied by monologues and dialogues; then came the distribution of prizes, which were called out by Mr. Hart, giving the name of the teacher with the three best scholars. The first prize was always a Bible; or, rather, a Bible and two books were given to each class. These books were most carefully selected by Miss Gratz herself, and handed by her to each child with a kind, encouraging word, often with a written line on the flyleaf. As the happy children went out orderly by class, through the back door, each was given an orange and a pretzel.

Simple days of our youth, where are you now?

No More Oranges and Pretzels

In 1857, before the Jewish Foster Home was removed to its present handsome building in Germantown, the older children came to the Sunday school for instruction. I had in my class, together with children of my own personal friends and relatives, many of these bright boys and girls. It was a real pleasure to teach them from [H. Loeb's 1864] *The Road to Faith*, the best work for the purpose. May I be pardoned for saying that I retain a personal interest in all the members of that class and that each boy and girl (most of them now with children of their own) has done credit to my instruction?

In 1858, Miss Gratz, after twenty years of untiring energy and admirable management of the school, though her "sight was not dim, nor her natural force abated," took Jethro's admirable advice to Moses by appointing "officers to assist her in her work"; so The Hebrew Sunday School Society was incorporated, with Miss Gratz as its first president. She was then seventy-seven years old, but she continued her weekly attendance several years longer until in 1864, when increasing infirmities gradually made the duties no longer possible, she resigned the presidency in favor of her devoted friend, Miss Louisa B. Hart.

Miss Hart's aim in carrying on the school was to maintain in every particular the high standard of her predecessor, and to continue as "Miss Gratz would have done" was her final decision in all matters. She entered heart and soul into her work, and was universally beloved by both pupils and teachers, whom she encouraged to meet every Saturday evening and on other occasions at her house on Lombard Street, and subsequently on Clinton Street. Those hours of innocent mirth, good cheer, and unstinted hospitality must still linger in the memory of her numerous "young friends," as she delighted to call them.

In 1871, Miss Ellen Phillips, a lady of much intelligence, kindly ways, and attractive manners, became the third superintendent of the Sunday school. She had been one of the original teachers and had served faithfully under both Miss Gratz and Miss Hart. She saw plainly that with the great increase of the foreign [immigrant] element, the school could no longer be conducted on its old basis. Changes and improvements were introduced, and in the following year the school was divided into Northern and Southern schools, and Miss Gratz's great-niece [my sister], Miss Laura Mordecai, inaugurated, at Twelfth and Chestnut Streets, the first radical change to a "Mission School."

About this time, cards with the thirteen articles of the Jewish creed were printed for the school, and others with the picture of Moses holding the Tables of the Law and the Commandments in rhyme beneath. The reciting of the psalm was discontinued. The superintendent read a chapter from the Holy Bible which was carefully explained on the following Sunday by the Rev. Dr. S. Morais, who never allowed inclement weather or other duties to interfere with this self-imposed task. Miss Hart and Miss Phillips both relied on Dr. Morais in many ways, and he always proved himself more than equal to their constant demands upon his time and great erudition, in explaining each holy festival, as it occurred, conducting the examinations, etc., etc. His devotion to the interests of the school has never flagged, and has become one of the many ways by which he has gained what the poet tells us should be the crown of old age, "honor, love, obedience, troops of friends."

Now, besides a religious school attached to every synagogue and temple in Philadelphia, the Sunday school has four large schools, each consisting of many hundred[s of] scholars, as you may read in *The Hebrew Watchword*, but which, I am ashamed to say, I have never visited, and must therefore leave to others to describe the good work done in them. At the time of the branching out of the schools, classes were arranged in accordance with the capacities of the pupils, and the lessons for each Sunday were clearly defined and explained in teachers' meetings after school, when "Work, work, work" took [the] place of "The Voice that Samuel heard"; when oranges and pretzels were superseded by theatrical performances and tableaux. I had already ceased to be a teacher in the Sunday school, thinking myself, even then, too old to learn new ways; but I am young again, in recalling for the benefit of the rising generation incidents which will make them smile at the changes which time has wrought.

I must say a few words to the teachers, as well as to the pupils, upon the birth, growth, and extent of the school, established in 1838. Miss Gratz was then fifty-seven, an age which most people would consider too advanced to attempt a new undertaking. Yet she lived to see it increase from a handful—fifty children and seven teachers, mostly of her own family and all of the Mickveh Israel Congregation—until, when she handed it over to her successor twenty-six years later, there were scholars from every congregation in this city, besides many foreigners among the 200 pupils.

Nor was all the good work done by this little "acorn." The "tall oak" whose branches extend near and far over our crowded streets and alleys into every corner of Penn's "Faire Towne" has yet stretched further, until at present, in almost every part of this vast country, South, North, East, West, the example first set by the Hebrew Sunday school of Philadelphia has been taken up, and Jewish religious schools are planted wherever there exists a settled Jewish community.

REBECCA COHEN LOSES HER BABY
1838

Rebecca Phillips, who married Jacob Cohen, Jr., in 1836, was the daughter of Zalegman Phillips, a very successful Philadelphia lawyer and leader of the local Jewish community. Zalegman was the son of Jonas, a Revolutionary War merchant and militiaman. Rebecca seems to have been an unusually attractive girl, for she had a number of beaux; she finally decided on Jacob Cohen, Jr., a member of a notable Charleston family and a veteran of the Seminole War of 1836.
The following letter describes her anguish at the death of an infant girl. Two years later Rebecca herself died; she was not yet thirty-three.

Charleston, Sept. 19th, 1838.

My dear Father:

I would have written to you ere this had I been able, but my feelings would not let me, and I requested my dear husband to write which he did about a week since. I am now, thank God, quite well, a little weak, but when able to take exercise will be entirely renewed. I do not go out on account of the [yellow fever] sickness it being more prudent to remain entirely within doors. The fever does not rage as violently as represented in the Northern papers; it is greatly on the decrease and only the intemperate and those exposed to the sun and night airs are victims. The doctors understand the treatment of it and few die who have medical advice in time.

Doubtless, dear Father, you have heard how I have been afflicted ('tho not one word from home has been rec'd since my loss). I can scarcely bring my feelings to write to you, how heavily I have felt the blow, 'tho to submit is our lot. This is the second time I have been unfortunate and this time more heavily than the last, for the dear angel was with me for only eight days and the feeling she had created was so delightful a nature that to be deprived of it I was not prepared for. Had you have seen her you would have pronounced her an angel; she was perfectly beautiful, small, well-made, and had she been spared to us you would have been proud of her. We had already from the hour of her birth named her, 'tho at the end of the month she would have been named in snoga [synagogue]. I had called her after my sainted Mother and had promised myself she would have resembled her in all her virtues, but as God wills all for the best I must not or ought not to murmur.

I hope, my dear Father, this may meet you and all of the family well, and my congratulations to you on the birth of your grandson. Love to Frances [my sister-in-law] and hope she and the child are well. As this is the first time I have taken pen in hand it will not be prudent for me to write much, but as our New Year is approaching let me, my dear Father, wish it may be to you and all I love a propitious one, and that all your wishes may be gratified, and a complete restoration of your health prays

Your affectionate
daughter,
Rebecca

Z. Phillips, Esqr.
   Philad'a

P.S. I suppose ere this [brother] Naph has arrived; it was fortunate he left as he could not avoid exposure. Love to [my brothers and sisters] Henry, Alt[amount], Ellen, Emily, Aunt S. and R., and all in which my dear husband unites. Write soon. R.C.

· 38 ·
RACHEL COHEN GOES OFF TO SCHOOL
1840

On June 25, 1840, Mrs. Benjamin I. Cohen, of Baltimore, sent her daughter Rachel (1825–1913) off to boarding school in Burlington, New Jersey. She gave Rachel some "food for the journey"—detailed instructions on how she was to conduct herself. These parental admonitions are interesting, for they mirror the mores of a cultured, wealthy banking family. The Cohens of Baltimore were the outstanding Jewish clan in town, highly respected, and politically influential. That very year the Misses Pallache opened a Jewish girls' boarding school in New York City, but the Cohens preferred to send their daughter to a Gentile institution. It is very likely that Rachel attended St. Mary's Hall, an Episcopal school for girls. The Cohens were loyal Jews, but their associations were Gentile; they moved in the highest Christian social circles.

There is no evidence that any school catering to the public at this time limited the number of Jewish applicants; the Jewish population in antebellum America was simply too small to inspire any wish for a Jewish quota.

A few words of parental advice for my Daughter Rachel on her first absence from home—Balt. June 25th, 1840.

Make it your habit no matter what may [be] the habits of others to *rise early;* enquire the hours of Breakfast, Dinner etc., and be sure that in *this and in all other respects you conform to the ways of the house.* Let the family of which you are an inmate be thereby not inconvenienced else their time and y'r own is rendered unpleasant and your absence will be desired.

Let me again inculcate as I could wish to do most urgently: *cleanliness* in *appearance* and *in fact.* Keep your body pure, the surface of your skin free of blemish; use (during the summer season especially) *water* freely on *rising* and on *retiring;* besides the good which in all respects is the result of such habit, health is vastly promoted.

You are to recollect after y'r arrival in Burlington that you are under Mrs. Emory's guidance and responsible to her for all your actions. Nothing must be done without her knowledge and *consent*, and let all your movements be dictated by a strict sense of propriety.

If at any time whether at home or abroad you meet with *disappointment*, bear it with patience and without murmur, *no pouting;* reflect that 'tis for the best and that exhibitions of temper (which I regret to say I have seen latterly rather too much of) do not mend the matter. Patience under good government is evidence of a kindly disposition and of sound sense.

In your intercourse with society recollect your youth; with the youthful be animated and say as you please; in the presence of mature age do not be prominent; *converse* when y'r conversation is sought, and when had let it be in moderate tone, not so loud as to annoy those who may be near and do not desire to hear.

Your host or hostess must not be put to expense on y'r account without return. I refer of course now to the *direct* expenses, that is to say, for instance, for *postage*, porterage etc. Make it y'r business always in such cases to repay the amount expended for you *no matter how small the amount.* The greater y'r attention to small matters the more do you evidence your conscience of propriety.

A REPENTANT APOSTATE
1841

Rather unusual is the authentic story of a Jewess in Charleston, South Carolina, who left her religion and then returned to it, repentant, several years later.

This women fell in love with a Gentile and accepted his faith, either because he demanded it or because she believed that conversion to Christianity would make for a happier home. Unfortunately, she was disappointed in her expectations and finally broke with her lover or husband; the details are not given. In 1841, twelve years after her apostasy, she wrote to the board of trustees of Charleston's Congregation Beth Elohim ("The House of God") asking them to receive her back into the synagogue.

The repentant sinner was brought before the board of the congregation, where she again affirmed her desire to be restored to her people, and informed the trustees that in her opinion "she felt perfectly satisfied that no person born in the Jewish faith can reconcile himself to any other." The following Saturday she appeared before the whole congregation, made a public proclamation of her error, and was then accepted back into the synagogue, to which she remained a loyal and devoted adherent until her death.

1841, Oct'r 17

Mr. Sol Moses stated that Miss Mary Ann Suares, who had some Years ago abandoned her religion, and Joined a Christian Church, does now reprent of the act committed, and was desirous of returning in the bosom of our Holy Religion, and that a Letter from her to that effect shall be laid before the Board at their next Meeting; it was on motion Resolved, that a committee be appointed to conferr with the Rev'd Mr. Poznanski and to ascertain what was necessary and proper on the occasion, and report to the Board the result. . . .

1841, Oct'r 18th

At a Special Meeting of the Board of Trustees, the Presid't stated he convened the Board to submit the Report of the committee in the case of Miss Mary Ann Suares, having conferred with the Rev'd Mr. Poznanski on the subject.

The committee appointed to confer with the Rev'd Mr. Poznanski on the application of Miss Mary Ann Suares, beg leave to report the following requisitions.

First. That the applicant do appear in the Synagogue before the Minister and Trustees on a convenient day, and there declare her sincere regret at having embraced the Christian Religion, and also her earnest determination to return to the religion of her forefathers.

Second. That the above declaration be proclaimed by the Secretary in the Synagogue on the Succeeding Sabbath.

Third. That the applicant publish the following Card in the Journals of the City:

A CARD

The undersigned is happy to inform her friends, and all whom it may concern, that on the   day of   she appeared before the Minister and Elders of the Hebrew Congregation Beth Elohim of this City, assembled in the Synagogue, and there with a sincere and repentent heart expressed her deep regret at having abandoned the Jewish faith, and also her earnest desire to return to the religion of her forefathers. [The Board later voted against the necessity of such a card.]. . . .

Ordered that the Secr'ty inform Miss Suares of these proceedings, and that she would appoint a day most convenient for her to attend when the Board would be ready to receive her to carry out the foregoing proceedings. . . .

Letter from Miss Mary Ann Suares on the application referred to at a Meeting 17th inst.:

To the Board of Trustees of KKBE [The Holy Congregation Beth Elohim]

Gent'n:

Relying on your generous sympathy with one, who though she committed a great error, appears now before You a penitent, I take the Libery to request Your aid in reinstating me in the religion of my forefathers. You are aware Gen.[tlemen] that some 12 Years ago, I abandoned the religion of my forefathers and became a Christian. I was then young and inexperienced, living entirely among a Christian community, all of which overcame my understanding and I took the step, of which I have for the last 6 years deeply repented. I am convinced of the truth of our holy religion, and it is my utmost desire again to worship with You at the same altar, at which Your and my ancestors worshipped, and am willing to undergo any penalty you may feel inclined to inflict. As the representatives of a Congregation who are Israelites, and who believe in that Sacred Law of Moses, which commands Kindness and Charity to all mankind, in the name of that God who revealed himself to his chosen people, I conjure You not to dismiss a penitent, but to receive her as one who went astray and is anxious to return to her flock.

With my best relyance on your generous sympathy, I remain Yr

(Sig'd) Mary Ann Suares

1841, Octb'r 21

At a special Meeting of the Board of Trustees, held this day within the Synagogue. . . .

The Rev'd Mr. Poznanski was present by request of the Board to aid with his consel on this important occasion.

Miss Mary Ann Suares appeared agreable to appointment, accompanied by her Mother and Sister, and again stated her desire to become a Jewess, and her repentance of the step taken in having embraced Christianity.

The Secr'ty read all the proceeding of the Board to Miss Suares, who again repeated her firm determination to return to our Holy religion, adding she felt perfectly satisfied that no person born in the Jewish faith can reconcile himself to believe in any other. She also stated she wished her return to the Jewish religion should be publicly known, and that she would be glad if the Synagogue was filled with Christians on Saturday next, to he[a]r the proceeding read, and that if any One should state in the Journals of the City that she had not returned to the religion of her forefathers, she would promptly in the same contradict it, and with tearful eyes again expressed her desire to become a Jewess.

Miss Suares replied to all Questions promptly and the Presd't then informed her that after Saturday next, when the proceeding shall have been read in the Synagogue, she would be considered as a Jewess and entitled to her former priveleges.

Miss Suares then withdrew, when the Rev'd Mr. Poznanski addressed the Board, and stated his regret that the Board had, at the request of Miss Suares, rejected the publishing of the Card recommended by the Committee, as in his opinion it was highly requisite on so important an occasion.

The Secr'ty then read the proceeding which are to be publicly read by him on Saturday next, which were approved of and then adj'd

(signed) S Valentine
Secr'ty.

· 40 ·

AN APOSTROPHE TO WOMEN BY A SOUTHERN GENTLEMAN
1842

On February 8, 1842, Nathaniel Levin, of Charleston, delivered an address before the Society for the Instruction of Jewish Youth. It appears that this was the women's organization which established and led the local Jewish Sunday school, patterned on the one Rebecca Gratz had founded in 1838 at Philadelphia. In the course of his oration—and it was that— Levin took time out to praise womanhood in general: "What woman is, man will forever be, for man cannot be other than depressed where woman is not exalted." It was his firm belief that women were "on an equality with man in this happy land." America's feminists, who were to issue their own Declaration of Independence in 1848, would have vehemently disagreed with him.

Levin (1816–1899) was well-known in mid-nineteenth-century Charleston. As a federal customs inspector and civil servant, he could not excel as a philanthropist, but he was a Mason of high degree, a staunch defender of Orthodoxy against the onslaught of the Jewish Reformers, and an actor or elocutionist of considerable talent: Levin once played Othello to Edwin Booth's Iago. It was he who wrote the first history of the Charleston Jewish community. The Charleston Jewish intellectuals had made their city the Jewish Athens of America in the decades before the Civil War. The cultured and eloquent Levin was one of the last of that company.

It has been frequently and truly said, that the influence of woman upon society is one of the most powerful and efficient causes of its progress in refinement and civilization. In every age and nation in which she has been permitted to occupy the position allotted to her by nature, reason, and religion, she has exerted a power of an almost unlimited force and extent, and this with the most happy consequences. Delicate in her constitution, mild and beneficent in her disposition, warm in her affections, and lovely in all her actions, she has ever been (where her worth was properly appreciated) the guardian and the ornament of the social compact. Her domestic virtues confer on home all its comforts and allurements; her presence in society humanizes law and imparts a more lofty honour and a more refined state of morals to the civil relations; her connection with *our* country adds strength to its institutions, and her graceful and softening manners give order and beauty to its political fabric. In countries where her true charms are unknown, and where her sphere of action is circumscribed within the narrow circle of household labours, or the more degrading limits of unintellectual pleasures, man rises but little above the level of animal organization, and despotism and injustice mark the operations of government.

There is not, nor can there be, such a thing as that community of friendship and interchange of good offices which bind mankind together without her interposition. What woman is, man will for ever be; for man cannot be other than depressed, where woman is not exalted. Patriotism would be little more than a blind devotion to the soil but for her presence in society; and the devotion displayed at the family shrine would be scarcely more than idolatry if she did not preside at the altar and mould the sacrificial rites into the forms of holy religion. Wisely and bountifully has the supreme Creator fashioned the female heart in all the richness of its faith and affections; wisely did He ordain that she should be a *companion* to man; and bountifully has He supplied her with every requisite for a companionship, both attractive and agreeable.

Man, naturally hardy in constitution, and rugged and boisterous in temper, turns to her from native impulse, to seek relief from his conflicts and his own oppressive strength, and finds not only the repose he covets but a refining tenderness, a cheering confidence, and a consoling faith which awaken the noble emotions of his soul and excite him to the generous and lofty pursuits of patriotism and philanthropy. She makes him forget that he is an individual by teaching him to love and by surrounding him with the enchantments of home she fixes him in his sphere in society, and invests him with the reciprocally agreeable relationships, immunities and duties of husband, father, friend, and citizen.

"Who that would ask a heart to dulness wed,
The waveless calm, the slumber of the dead?
No! the wild bliss of nature needs alloy,
And fear and sorrow fan the fire of joy!
And say, without our hopes, without our fears,
Without the home that plighted love endears,
Without the smile from partial beauty won,
Oh! what were man?—a world without a sun!"

The influence of woman has ever been celebrated in song, marked by deeds of chivalry, and acknowledged so fully and so often that it would be in vain now to attempt to impress it more thoroughly upon the public mind. All admit that her influence is great in the accomplishment of good, and while they make the admission, they must freely own, too, that it is irresistible; for come in what shape she may, whether as mother, sister, wife or friend, she ever meets a sincere welcome from the feeling heart, and as she never approaches to encourage but with a smile, nor to move our mercy but with a tear, she invariably wins us to her cause, as we would not, if we could, repulse her.

In this enlightened age and country she deservedly ranks among the highest. On an equality with man in this happy land, she shows herself worthy of her station by emulating him in every good enterprise in which she can properly embark and by taking a prominent, though modest part, in his moral reformation and intellectual improvement. Indeed, so accustomed has the American citizen become to the co-operation of woman in undertakings which affect the community in its social aspect, that he seldom ventures far in his labours, whether they be of a moral, religious, or charitable character, without first obtaining her sanction or at least her advice. This is alike creditable to her and to him. It proves that her power and influence depend not so much upon the beauty of a perishable outward form as the possession of intrinsic excellence; and it also shows that while he can, and does, admire the graces of her person, he is not insensible to her higher endowments of mind and heart.

The Jewish female, enjoying all the blessings and privileges that emanate from a free and republican government, does not wait to be *led* into schemes of benevolence; she does not merely accompany man in the promulgation of useful principles or the performance of popular charities. Like an angel of light she points the way herself and is often among the foremost in missions of mercy. I might easily enumerate many instances in proof of this but shall content myself with merely referring to the institution of this society, the anniversary of which we have assembled to honour. It is exclusively the work of woman's hand. Her benevolence prompted its foundation; her labour, patience, and devotion have raised the superstructure to what it now is. Not our faithful ancestors restoring the temple of God, surrounded by enemies, *with arms by their side*, whilst progressing with their allotted labour, were engaged in a more hallowed task than you are now, beloved friends; for ye are upholding the *temple* of the *Jewish mind*, and giving perpetuity to that faith which threw the majesty of Heaven from the harp of David, and which wrapped Isaiah's hallowed soul in fire.

This institution is one of those which, without making any pretensions to notoriety, is calculated to produce results of the utmost importance to us and to the community at large. In a country like ours, depending for its stability upon the intelligence and virtue of the people, it becomes our duty to educate our children so that they may fully understand their civil rights, and at the same time teach them to cling to *that*, which we can prove to have been *before all human charters*, the *"first born"* of the rights of man, the indefeasible inheritance of every genuine worshipper of the God of Abraham, of Isaac and of Jacob. Over the internal operations of the Jewish mind a dominion is reserved which it belongs not to man to assume. There the arm of flesh has no power; thither the *fiat* of sovereignty carries with it no terrors, and the formalities of law recoil from the mission on which tyranny would array them. "Secure within her winding citadel" the intellect holds her sway, and not even the united powers of earth can shake, for one instant, *that* "sceptre" from "the sons of Judah."

The chief object of your institution is to disseminate such principles and knowledge among those for whose advantage it was formed, as will afford them the best guides in their future connection in this world, and place them in that bright path which finally leads to the throne of the one, omniscient, eternal God. You, its founders, knew how much depended upon the culture of the tender mind; you knew that early impressions are the last to fade from the memory; you knew that the character, the permanency and the happiness of the state are formed and influenced chiefly by the manner in which its children are educated; and you felt that your power and position required you to unite in the noble task of superintending the development of that mind, of forming those impressions, and of supplying that education to the full extent and compass of your ability. The purity of your motives must be apparent even to the casual observer, while the wisdom of your design is manifesting itself daily. Already has abundant evidence of the usefulness of your institution been given, and, by the blessing of Providence and the aid of the good, its founders will soon see their brightest anticipations realized, their hopes crowned with success, and the harvest of their labours gathered up in mental wealth and moral worth.

Such objects are in true accordance with the character, the influence, and the power of woman. Men seldom attempt such works, although they frequently claim and receive a share of the honours which belong to them. In many respects they possess a larger degree of universal influence and collective strength, and are, from circumstances, her superiors in knowledge and the reasoning faculties; but they lack her patience under difficulties, her devotion under opposition, her unwavering constancy of purpose under all circumstances; and they but partially know the great secret, which she possesses intuitively, of exercising power and influence with the certainty of success.

41

A WEDDING ADDRESS
1851

On April 2, 1851, Isaac Leeser united a couple in marriage at Philadelphia. They were Mr. Wolf Steppacher, of Pontotoc, Mississippi, and Miss Caroline Meyers, of Philadelphia. Leeser had been a clergyman for twenty-two years, but reported that the wedding address he delivered on that occasion was his first. Obviously, homilies of this type were not customary in those days. Leeser's talk to the couple is of interest because in it he clearly outlines his concept of the role which the man and the woman are expected to accept in a Jewish marriage. Equally unequivocal is his conviction that it was incumbent upon the wife to acquiesce in all that the husband suggested. She could rightfully defy him only if he departed from traditional Jewish religious practice.

Beloved Friends:

You are about to enter the state of marriage in which each of you assumes new relations both to each other and society, which are to endure during all your life, as long as the Lord of all spirits permits you to dwell on earth. Hitherto both of you were free to choose another mate from the rest of the world; but henceforth you vow to be to each other friends in joy and in sorrow and to travel the round of earthly existence hand in hand and heart linked to heart. Think, therefore, well of the nature of the engagement which you are going to assume, and do not esteem lightly the weight of the obligation which will rest upon you from this moment. I will not admonish you to love one another, since it is for this very reason that you cherish the kindest mutual affection, that you have invoked the aid of our holy religion to bless your union in the assembly of Israelites, who like yourselves avow love and fealty to the sole God who rules all in heaven and earth. Reflect, then, that it is before the Searcher of hearts you avow fidelity to each other, to be true and faithful on all occasions and to bear together the trials which will in the course of nature assail even the happiest. Imagine not that the joy of this hour will last for ever; think not that the vigour of youth will always impart strength to your limbs, or that sickness and sorrow will never reach you. To expect this would be to suppose that the common lot of mankind is not to be yours; and sure I am, that you have told this already to yourselves in the recesses of your soul, though perhaps your lips have not given utterance to your apprehensions.

But, even in the ordinary calm and in the highest prosperity which our existence is capable of, there are constant occasions for the exercise of domestic virtues, which when observed will render the married state one of happiness, but which neglected will envelope it with the clouds of sorrow. The husband must consult his wife's wishes; she must obey his directions in the government of the family, he must be indulgent, she yielding; he should counsel with mildness and moderation; she acquiesce in all his opinions even if she occasionally fancies that her views are the best, and look upon him in all things as the one she ought to obey; excepting only when it regards the higher obligation which she owes to her God, in which no husband's injunctions can be an excuse for transgressing the requirements of religion. In short, husband and wife must not only be loving and affectionate when strangers are there to observe them, but in the retirement also of their domestic fireside, when no eye save that of the All-seeing is upon them, should they be like one soul dwelling in two bodies. God created our first mother that she should be a help suitable to her spouse whose existence preceded hers in the order of creation; and thus her daughters should seek their highest happiness in the marriage state by helping their husbands in all things, by assisting them with advice, by assuaging them with a pleasant reception on their return home from the cares which business or harassing occupations so often inflict, and to be to them an unwavering friend though all the rest of mankind should forsake them.

Reflect, also, that it is not merely to gratify the feelings of love which now animate you both that you have a right to invoke the name of the Lord to hallow your union. For if this were all, the civil law of the land could declare you man and wife no less than the servant of your faith. But such a marriage, you justly think, would lack the sanction of religion, religion, the soother of our sorrows and the only source whence the pleasures of life derive their highest value. You then wish to be united not as mere citizens of the commonwealth but as followers of the Law of Moses, and you, bridegroom, are going to espouse this your bride after the ancestral manner by means of a golden ring in the presence of Jewish witnesses, according to the law of Moses and Israel, not alone the written word of the Bible but also the institutions of our people under which we have always administered the precepts which the Scriptures contain. As a son, therefore, of Israel you claim this daughter of Jacob as your chosen wife, and as such she accepts from your hands the token of union by which she pledges herself to be yours, and yours only, in feeling, no less than in person, till death severs the link which now is to make you one. Do you understand, both of you, the importance of this public declaration? Perhaps you do; still bear with me a little while whilst I endeavour to illustrate it in your presence, and I trust that you will respond to it inwardly with a sincere affirmation. You stand, then, now in the presence of God to make a covenant with one another, to love and cherish each other mutually, to bear together whatever mishaps or pleasures may be decreed to you, and to contribute all that is possible to promote each other's happiness. But you avow this as Israelites, in the name of God whose aid you hope for to guide you aright and securely in the perilous and slippery path of life, and without whose blessing all your striving would be in vain. Know then, that to obtain this last, you must deserve his love and approbation by a thorough religious conduct.

Our wise men teach us "that three obtain a forgiveness of their sins: a gentile who embraces our religion, a person who is raised to a high dignity, and a man who espouses a wife." [This is a rabbinic interpretation based on Gen. 36:3.] Hence has sprung the good old custom for the parties to fast on their nuptial day in order to make it a day of atonement and serious reflection and repentance for themselves. But a day of forgiveness of sin it only can be when, as the annual period of atonement, the wrong is sincerely repented of and a resolution is adopted to sin no more. No man passes through the active turmoil of life without transgression; the best, therefore, has a necessity of being forgiven and must humble himself before God to entreat a remission of iniquity. If, however, a new life is commenced with the day of marriage; if it is really the beginning of a renewed love of God in our hearts, we may justly regard it as a means of reconciliation with our heavenly Father, whom in the wantonness of youthful feeling we may have often forgotten in the hours of our joys or neglected in not seeking his aid when darkness rested on our souls. Resolve, then, to let your future days be distinguished by an active love of the Creator and a sincere endeavour to observe his precepts.

Should your union be blessed with children, regard them not as exclusively your own but as pledges entrusted to you by the Supreme for you to watch over, to see that they grow up in his fear and his service. Instil early into their minds that as Jews you were born, that as Jews you were married, and that as such you devote them to the same faith for which our nation has laboured so long, has suffered so much. Speak yourselves of the pleasant concerns of everlasting life in their presence, and show them, by a careful heeding of all your duties that the religion of God is the highest good in your estimation. In this manner alone can your future offspring "rise up and call you happy" [Prov. 31:28] to use the words of the philosopher King of Israel, and thus only can you accomplish the obligation you assume in being united according to the law of Moses and Israel.

In whatever situation you may be, remember that you are of the children of Jacob; wherever your future walk may be, honour your religion by a uniform holy life and a bold avowal of its principles. It has all the sources of consolation which man requires in his earthly existence; it refers all to God who is ever near us to aid and assist us in all times of trouble and affliction; and never for a moment think to hide your faith as something to be ashamed of from the eyes of strangers. Should your brothers in hope be assailed, defend them; should they be ill-used, protect them; should they require assistance, aid them; should they be misguided, instruct them; and do in your own persons whatever is required to magnify the name of God and increase the respect which the world at large will ultimately feel for our heaven-born law.

As regards your conduct towards each other, I need say but little, for this has, without question, been long since impressed on your mind. But I may still exhort you, bridegroom, to cherish an unbroken attachment for your chosen companion, in the words of the Bible, . . . "Let thy fountain be blessed, and rejoice with the wife of thy youth" (Prov. V, 18). Her honour should be your honour, and never in thought even be for a moment unfaithful to her who should be the joy and ornament of your house. There may be dark moments which may overshadow the peace of your domestic circle; but if this should ever unfortunately be, fly to your God for aid to assist you in the trial, and light will again chase away the darkness, and the brilliance of renewed affection will again illumine your dwelling.

And you, beloved bride, reflect well that . . . "Grace is deceitful, and beauty is vain; the woman only that feareth the Lord will be praised" (Prov. XXXI, 30). The heyday of youth will pass away ere many years will have elapsed, and approaching age will rob your cheek of its bloom and your eye of its lustre. What will then chain to you the husband who is no longer the ardent lover? Nothing but the cheerfulness of the mature matron, the God-fearing wife, who labours in all "the walks of the house," to make his life happy and to render easy for him the toils and hardships inseparable from our mortal state.

If you both act thus towards God, your fellow-men, and yourselves, you may joyously look forward to the future; all is well; all will be well; this earth may then fade away from your sight but reunited will you stand before the mercy-seat of the Lord to receive your reward; and in the mean time your days will glide along in tranquillity, whether you are wealthy or of narrow means, for peace will dwell in your hearts and God's blessing will surround you. That this may be your lot is my sincere prayer; and now let us pronounce the blessings before this congregation by which you may be united in that bond which God has ordained for his children as the happiest lot on earth.

42

ERNESTINE L. ROSE, SOCIAL REFORMER
1851–1853

Ernestine Louise Siismondi Powtowski Rose (1810–1892) was undoubt-edly the most famous Jewess in the United States during the mid-nineteenth century. She was not affiliated with the Jewish community, although she never in any sense denied her origins or disguised her sympathy for her people. She resented and sharply rebuffed any attack on Jews as Jews. She referred to herself as a "Child of Israel."

Ernestine Rose was a native of Russian Poland; her father is said to have been a rabbi and to have seen to it that she received an excellent Jewish education. Such concern for the religious education of Jewish girls was not usual in Eastern Europe. Details of her early life smack of the mythical, although the Hebrew Union College historian, Gotthard Deutsch, always warned his critical students: "The fact that data may be true is no reason why they are not true." At all events, while still a teenager, she broke with her father and with Orthodoxy, left home, traveled about Europe for some years, and finally settled in England, where she became a follower of Robert Owen, the Utopian Socialist. Before long, she was widely known as a radical social reformer. In 1836 she married William E. Rose, a non-Jew, and accompanied him to the United States. Ernestine remained here till 1869, when she returned to England.

By the 1840's she was one of the leading reformers and feminists in this country. There were few social causes that were foreign to her. As a freethinker and an atheist, she was concerned with the right of the individual to accept or reject religion; she was a temperance advocate; she fought for women's suffrage and for the right of all females to hold and control property in their own name. Women were not to be treated as chattel; they were entitled to complete equality in every sense of the term. On October 15–16, 1851, she attended the second national Woman's Rights Convention in Worcester, and on September 8–10, 1852, a similar meeting in Syracuse. Excerpts from her addresses at both conventions are reprinted below (items A and B).

Like most reformers of her day, she was an ardent abolitionist. On August 4, 1853, she made an address at Flushing, Long Island,

6. Ernestine L. Rose

celebrating the anniversary of the emancipation in 1834 of the slaves in the British West Indies. (It is an interesting coincidence that in 1657, the freemen of Flushing, in a "Remonstrance" directed at the intolerant Dutch of New Netherland, insisted on freedom of conscience for every human being.) When Mrs. Rose spoke in 1853, slavery was still in full force in this country; there were about 1,700,000 men, women, and children in bondage. This speech of hers is reproduced in large part below (C).

Mrs. Rose was a brilliant speaker, witty, sarcastic, incisive. Her talks were characterized by a Talmud-like acuity and were frequently punctuated by applause. In a way she was a prototype of the radical East European Jewesses who would come to America at the turn of the century.

A

1851

Even here, in this far-famed land of freedom, under a Republic that has inscribed on its banner the great truth that all men are created free and equal, and endowed with inalienable rights to life, liberty, and the pursuit of happiness—a declaration borne, like the vision of hope, on wings of light to the remotest parts of the earth, an omen of freedom to the oppressed and downtrodden children of man— . . . even here, in the very face of this eternal truth, woman, the mockingly so called "better half" of man, has yet to plead for her rights, nay, for her life; for what is life without liberty, and what is liberty without equality of rights? And as for the pursuit of happiness, she is not allowed to pursue any line of life that might promote it; she has only thankfully to accept what man in his magnanimity decides as best for her to do, and this is what he does not choose to do himself. Is she then not included in that declaration? Answer, ye wise men of the nation, and answer truly; add not hypocrisy to oppression! Say that she is not created free and equal, and therefore (for the sequence follows on the premises) that she is not entitled to life, liberty, and the pursuit of happiness. But with all the audacity arising from an assumed superiority, you dare not so libel and insult humanity as to say, that she is not included in that declaration; and if she is, then what right has man, except that of might, to deprive woman of the rights and privileges he claims for himself? And why, in the name of reason and justice, why should she not have the same rights? Because she is woman? Humanity recognizes no sex—virtue recognizes no sex—mind recognizes no sex—life and death, pleasure and pain, happiness and misery recognize no sex. Like man, woman comes involuntarily into existence; like him she possesses physical and mental and moral powers, on the proper cultivation of which depends her happiness; like him she is subject to all the vicissitudes of life; like him she has to pay the penalty for disobeying nature's laws, and far greater penalties has she to suffer from ignorance of her far more complicated nature than he; like him she enjoys or suffers with her country. Yet she is not recognized as his equal!

In the laws of the land she has no rights, in government she has no voice. And in spite of another principle, recognized in this Republic, namely, that "taxation without representation is tyranny," yet she is taxed without being represented. Her property may be consumed by taxes to defray the expenses of that unholy, unrighteous custom called war, yet she has no power to give her veto against it. From the cradle to the grave she is subject to the power and control of man. Father, guardian, or husband, one conveys her like some piece of merchandise over to the other. At marriage she loses her entire identity, and her being is said to have become merged in her husband. Has nature thus merged it? Has she ceased to exist and feel pleasure and pain? When she violates the laws of her being, does her husband pay the penalty? When she breaks the moral laws, does he suffer the punishment? When he supplies his wants, is it enough to satisfy her nature? And when at his nightly orgies, in the grog-shop and the oyster cellar, or at the gaming-table, he squanders the means she helped by her coöperation and economy to accumulate, and she awakens to penury and destitution, will it supply the wants of her children to tell them, that owing to the superiority of man she had no redress by law; and that as her being was merged in his, so also ought theirs to be? What an inconsistency, that from the moment she enters that compact, in which she assumes the high responsibility of wife and mother, she ceases legally to exist, and becomes a purely submissive being. Blind submission in woman is considered a virtue, while submission to wrong is itself wrong, and resistance to wrong is virtue alike in woman as in man.

B

1852

Ernestine L. Rose, being introduced as a Polish lady, and educated in the Jewish faith, said—

It is of very little importance in what geographical position a person is born, but it is important whether his ideas are based upon facts that can stand the test of reason, and his acts are conducive to the happiness of society. Yet, being a foreigner, I hope you will have some charity on account of speaking in a foreign language. Yes, I am an example of the universality of our claims; for not American women only, but a daughter of poor, crushed Poland, and the down-trodden and persecuted people called the Jews, "a child of Israel," pleads for the equal rights of her sex. I perfectly agree with the resolution, that if woman is insensible to her wrongs, it proves the depth of her degradation. It is a melancholy fact, that woman has worn her chains so long that they have almost become necessary to her nature—like the poor inebriate, whose system is so diseased that he cannot do without the intoxicating draft, or those who are guilty of the pernicious and ungentlemanly practice of using tobacco until they cannot dispense with the injurious stimulant. Woman is in a torpid condition, whose nerves have become so paralyzed that she knows not she is sick, she feels no pain, and if this proves the depth of her degradation, it also proves the great wrong and violence done to her nature. . . .

Woman is a slave, from the cradle to the grave. Father, guardian, husband—master still. One conveys her, like a piece of property, over to the other. She is said to have been created only for man's benefit, not for her own. This falsehood is the main cause of her inferior education and position. Man has arrogated to himself the right to her person, her property, and her children; and so vitiated is public opinion, that if a husband is rational and just enough to acknowledge the influence of his wife, he is called "hen-pecked." The term is not very elegant, but it is not of my coining; it is yours, and I suppose you know what it means; I don't. But it is high time these irrationalities are done away, for the whole race suffers by it. In claiming our rights, we claim the rights of humanity: it is not for the interest of woman only, but for the interest of all. The interest of the sexes cannot be separated—together they must enjoy or suffer—both are one in the race.

C

1853

I love to attend . . . anniversaries; I think the effect is very beneficial . . . there are . . . anniversaries kept in this country, one of which I presume you all love to celebrate; and that is the anniversary of the Declaration of Independence. That great and glorious day did not create, but gave the world a great truth—that all men are born free and equal, and are therefore entitled to life, liberty, and the pursuit of happiness. My heart always rejoices in that day, and I shall never forget the emotions I felt when I first witnessed its celebration in this country. . . . All my feelings and principles are republican; I may say I am a republican by nature; but in comparison to the liberation of 800,000 [West Indian] slaves, the Declaration of Independence falls into utter insignificance. . . . It falls short, just as theory falls short of practice. . . . There is almost an immeasurable distance between the two. The one was the utterance of a great truth that will last forever; the other was a practical application of it. How different the results! the Declaration of Independence—has it yet abolished Slavery? But the great act of emancipation of 800,000 human beings has shown to the world that the African race are not only capable of taking care of themselves, but are capable of enjoying peacefully as much liberty and as much freedom as the white men. Thus it has done far more towards the cause of freedom—towards emancipation from all kinds of slavery—than the Declaration of Independence did. For in spite of that

Declaration—in sadness and sorrow do I say it—the United States of America are guilty of outrage and recreancy to their own principles in retaining slavery; while Great Britain, without that Declaration, having yet a great deal of oppression and tyranny in her midst, has shown a noble example to the world in emancipating all her chattel slaves.

It is utterly impossible for us, as finite beings, with the utmost stretch of the imagination, to conceive the depth and immensity of the horrors of slavery. I would that, instead of speaking and listening to-day, we could all sit down in perfect silence, and each and every one of us ask ourselves what is it to be a slave? What is it to emancipate eight hundred thousand slaves? We have the evil among us; we see it daily and hourly before us; we have become accustomed to it: we talk about it; but do we comprehend it—do we realize it—do we feel it? What is it to be a slave? Not to be your own, bodily, mentally, or morally—that is to be a slave. Ay, even if slaveholders treated their slaves with the utmost kindness and charity; if I were told they kept them sitting on a sofa all day and fed them with the best of the land, it is none the less slavery; . . . for what does slavery mean? To work hard, to fare ill, to suffer hardship, that is not slavery; for many of us white men and women have to work hard, have to fare ill, have to suffer hardship, and yet we are not slaves. Slavery is not to belong to yourself—to be robbed of yourself. There is nothing that I so much abhor as that single thing—to be robbed of one's self. We are our own legitimate masters. Nature has not created masters and slaves; nature has created man free as the air of heaven. The black man and the white man are equally the children of nature. The same mother earth has created us all; the same life pervades all; the same spirit ought to animate all. Slavery deprives us of ourselves. The slave has no power to say, 'I will go here, or I will go yonder.' The slave cannot say, 'My wife, my husband, or my child.' He does not belong to himself, and of course cannot claim anything whatever as his own. This is the great abomination of slavery, that it deprives a man of the common rights of humanity, stamped upon him by his Maker. . . .

I go for emancipation of all kinds—white and black, man and woman. Humanity's children are, in my estimation, all one and the same family, inheriting the same earth; therefore there should be no slaves of any kind among them. There are ties that bind man to man far stronger than the ties of nation—than the political and commercial ties—ay, even stronger than the ties of relationship; and these are the ties of humanity. Humanity, the great mother of all, has thrown around us ties, sympathies and feelings which are more endearing, more effectual, and more noble, than any other that have ever bound man to man.

Our friend who has addressed you to-day [William Lloyd Garrison] has mentioned the fact that the opposers of emancipation are fearful that the South will not trade with the North. No greater folly was ever conceived. The South forsake the North! What will they do? Six years ago, I was in Columbia, S.C. A senator, returning from Washington, made a speech there in which he talked a great deal about Abolitionists and Disunionists of the North. A young lawyer, who boarded at the same hotel where I stopped, came home full of these ideas and commenced a conversation with me on the subject of slavery; and he was so full, that he could scarcely find time to express his indignation. 'We don't want the North,' said he—'we are independent of the North, and we can afford to dissolve the Union to-day.' I let him go on for some time for I knew he would run himself out . . . After he had done so, I told him I did not wish to have the Union dissolved; I would like to stick to you, because you need us. . . . I then asked him, 'Wherein could you be independent of the North? Who are your teachers and professors? Northern men. Who weaves your cloth and bedecks you? Northern laborers. Who grows much of the food that nourishes you? Northern men. (Indeed, so greatly impoverished is the land in the South that it is a positive fact, that I once saw a cow held up while she was fed.) . . . 'Just remember, my dear Sir,' said I, 'that from your head to your feet, you were manufactured at the North; directly or indirectly. From him who first taught you your alphabet, to the professor who gave the finish to your education, and taught you to make black appear white, they were all Northern men. Nevertheless, I don't want to see the Union dissolved; for as long as we are united, we have an influence over you; indeed, you stand so greatly in need of us that I should be very sorry to leave you. . . .'

It has always appeared to me to be the greatest error and absurdity to suppose that the South is ever going to forsake the North. Where are they to go? It was a sheer political trick, raised for the purpose of making political capital, when our politicians in 1850 raised the cry—which . . . of course the newspapers had to echo. . . —that the Union was in danger. There was not a man of sound sense in the South, I venture to say—and there are many such—that believed it for a moment. It was got up by political gamblers of both sections for the purpose of making capital. If you could only estimate the immense injury that slavery does, not only to the South, but to the North—in fact, the whole world— you would say, 'Leave us, if you will; we will willingly give you a passport, if you will rid us of this incumbrance. . . .'

Yes, every act brings its own reward or its own punishment. Every good act produces its own corresponding reward and every bad act its corresponding punishment. How, then, must not only the South but the North be punished in consequence of that great, immeasurable wrong of slavery? Oh, the shame and outrage that, for one single moment, that great blot should be suffered to remain on the otherwise beautiful escutcheon of this republic!

But permit me to say that the slaves of the South are not the only people that are in bondage. All women are excluded from the enjoyment of that liberty which your Declaration of Independence asserts to be the inalienable right of all. The same right to life, liberty, and the pursuit of happiness, that pertains to man, pertains to woman also. For what is life without liberty? Which of you here before me would not willingly risk his or her life, if in danger of being made a slave? Emancipation from every kind of bondage is my principle. I go for the recognition of human rights, without distinction of sect, party, sex, or color.

43

GROWING UP IN AMERICA
1851–1864

*The following memoir of Emily Fechheimer Seasongood (1851–1941)
provides an excellent introduction to the social background, home life,
educational practices, and leisure-time activities of a young mid-
nineteenth-century Jewish girl, the child of German immigrant parents.
By the 1850's, Emily's father, Marcus Fechheimer, was already a
successful businessman. He was active in Cincinnati's young congregation, Bene Yeshurun—indeed its president—when Isaac M. Wise was
elected rabbi. Emily married Bavarian-born Alfred Seasongood, who
became a wealthy clothing manufacturer. Their son Murray (b. 1878)
studied law at Harvard, was elected reform mayor of Cincinnati in 1926,
and was responsible in large measure for the good government which has
distinguished the Queen City of the West for two generations.*

In 1854, when I was three years old, I can remember the time
Dr. Isaac M. Wise visited our city, Cincinnati, to officiate as a
candidate for minister to the K.K.B.Y. [*Kehillah Kedosha Bene
Yeshurun*] Temple. My father (of blessed memory) was the
president of the congregation and had invited Dr. Wise to be his
guest. It was the first event in my life that I remember at that age.
I mention this fact, as I can recall his taking me on his knee and
petting me. My dear parents' home was always a very hospitable
one, and all strangers were very welcome, and I can distinctly
remember how pleased my dear father was when he saw the table
extended and many seated around it, and my dear mother busy
preparing the food and serving it to the guests.

When I was older, I enjoyed watching my dear mother in her
various duties around the house. She had great artistic talent,
designed and sewed dresses, and I often wanted to assist her, and
she would give me bits of goods (calico in those days) and a needle.
My dear mother was a very refined, intelligent, accomplished
woman, and her circle of acquaintances was of like manner. The

7. Emily Seasongood

circle was not large, as at the present time, and entertainments not as extravagent nor on so large a scale. The ladies met at each other's homes, sewed and discussed literature, and the like, but not much gossiping took place. Children were never allowed in the room except to say "good day," and when there was an entertainment, it was furnished by the school children and was considered a great event. Many children came before the footlights, bowed, and had to repeat a sentence many times over before being able to finish reciting the poem or whatever part might have been assigned to them, but the parents, nevertheless, enjoyed it and thought them wonderful. . . .

My dear mother was very progressive, and had private tutors for me and my sainted sister, Rosa, when we were a little older. My dear sister was compelled to take me with her wherever she went, even though there were fourteen months' difference in our ages, and she was always much older in her ways than I, and her companions also. But my dear mother would say: *"Nimm es mit"* ("Take her with you"), meaning me, and so I trotted along, much to her regret. My sister and I were always dressed alike. I presume it was easier to buy enough of one piece of goods to make two dresses and cut them out of the same piece, than be choosing another kind. Besides, the stock was not as large in the shops then as in the present day. Every week my sister and I received one penny together, for which we were allowed to buy candy, which was of the purest and simplest production. Two sticks or cakes of molasses cocoanut candy could be purchased for that sum, and we would share it with our little friends.

We had a highly educated maid of excellent family, who often took us out with her to see her friends, and I remember distinctly how one of them one day offered us some peaches. As I was always very shy, I refused them, but oh, so wished I had not done so, as they were not passed the second time, and after that I never refused if I cared for anything which was offered, and which was the custom in those days when visiting. . . .

I had a lovely pet, a white poodle, which was given to me by a friend of my father's. My sister had one too, and we took great pleasure in bathing them and placing them in a large basket before the lovely grate fire to dry after their bath. We always kept them on our laps when our tutor, Mr. Shoenbrun, came to teach us German, and as I was rather mischievous, when he dictated a sentence to me after which he said *Komma* ["comma"] (when the sentence required it), I would write it out in full. He was so incensed that he told my father we would never learn if we kept the poodles. So, to my sister's and my regret, we had to part with them.

We always sat around the grate fire in the evening, and while my dear father read, I would take great pleasure in playing with his silvery, soft hair, and I often wondered how he could stand my foolish pranks. But he was so lenient, kind, and good, and very patient with us. My dear mother, too, was of that temperament. My sister and I were supplied with all sorts of games, and I did enjoy the Friday nights and holidays when we were allowed to play them. Black Peter and Dressderla were my favorite games, old maid, etc., likewise. We had a large bowl of choice apples, nuts, and salted peas on a table, which we could partake of after finishing our games. One of the most interesting toys we possessed was a picture show which was on a stand and looked somewhat like a circus tent, and had to be twirled to show the pictures in the inside of it; the pictures were changed every little while. . . .

Our tutor, Mr. Shoenbrun, had a sister who was a wonderful musician and a fine pianist. She taught us piano, which we detested, as she always came at an unearthly hour in the morning, and we were supposed to be ready for her. Neither of us cared to be the first to come downstairs, as it was so early, and my sister always insisted upon my coming down first, and sometimes hurried me so that I came down in my nightgown, as she was not ready and the teacher would become impatient.

Later we had a teacher in drawing, Mr. Knopf, who was very gruff to most of his pupils but kind to us. He was an artist and taught us the first rudiments of drawing and took us out for sketching. Our first [sketch of a] bunch of flowers was sent to our grandparents, Amalia and Abraham Thurnauer, in Germany, Burgkundstadt, Bavaria, which pleased them greatly. For my dear parents, I drew a large eagle carrying a diploma on which it said: "This is a specimen of my first efforts." Every feather of the bird was finely drawn and looked like an etching, and both they and I felt quite proud of my work. My dear mother taught us needlework, and when we were older had us go to a sewing school, where a Mrs. Baurittle taught us cross-stitch, and we worked our first samples [samplers].

We also went to a gymnasium, which we thoroughly enjoyed, especially the jumping of the bucks, swinging rings, turning-poles, etc. We also took dancing lessons from a Mr. Graeser, who taught us calisthenics, and gave some of the most beautiful exhibitions, on the stage of a large hall, which was always well-attended by the parents of the children. . . .

A schoolhouse was in the annex of the synagogue which most all of the children of the members of the congregation attended. We were taught English and Hebrew. The *Chumish* ["Pen-tateuch"] I could not understand, and told my beloved father I could not see why it was taught us [in Hebrew] and please to have the teachers do away with it. As he was president of the congregation then, he brought it before the board, who quite agreed with me, and I was very happy after it was removed from our studies. Our teachers in English were Mrs. Rau [Rauh?] and Mr. Bryan. Dr. Dessauer and Mr. Buttenwieser taught us German and Hebrew. Dr. Dessauer had a small cabinet in the corner of his room in which he always placed the stumps of his cigars, when he entered the room, and which he always smoked the following day.

Mr. Buttenwieser was a very small man and wore eyeglasses. He always called the pupils by their last name first when calling the roll. My cousin Betty Fechheimer was quite mischievous and would make him repeat her name until he became tired. He then took his rattan in his hand and said: "For that, Fechheimer Betty, come out before the class and receive your punishment." So she went to where he stood, took hold of the rattan, and danced him around the room. As he was nearsighted, he did not know she was close to him, and this was much to the amusement of all the class. . . .

I attended a private school after that, Miss Appleton's, and was taught Roman history, algebra, etc. Then I went to public school until I graduated from the second intermediate. We had lovely teachers there: the Misses Johnson, Walters, McAvoy, McCormick, and Professor Smith. My favorite studies were grammar, geography, and elocution. We always had a little prayer said before school opened, and then the class sang. I played the accompanyment on a piano, which was placed on a raised platform. We often had school exhibitions; Milton Hoffheimer and Freddie Forchheimer (in later years known as the great and renowned Dr. Forchheimer [professor of medicine at the University of Cincinnati]) played the violin, while my sister and I played piano duets. We had much fun at our house when we used to practice for these performances. . . .

I was always very orderly, and at night before retiring would arrange my bureau drawers. In some I kept the trinkets I brought from Europe, which I prized highly. My sister was a great reader and would read in bed, and, on the sly, would often pretend to read, but watched me place my various treasures, and while I went to the bathroom to finish my toilet for the night, she would muss my drawers and take cakes or chocolate I had also saved, and there was great commotion.

Many of our summers were spent in Rogersville, Ky., where my Uncle Sam Fechheimer had a large plantation and he and his family lived for many years. He owned many slaves, as this was before the Civil War. The neighbors lived quite a distance from one another; they were very hospitable and would spend the day together. We children always rode on horseback, sometimes three of us on one horse, and had to pass many fields incased in wooden fences, of which many slats were taken out by us to get through, and how we did enjoy jumping the fences and stiles! Our parents rode in buggies.

Many log cabins, in which the colored help (slaves) lived, were built side by side some distance from my Uncle Sam's home, and we enjoyed going there and watching the little pickaninnies play and their mammies comb and wash them. They were quite musical and some had very excellent voices.

In one log cabin banjos, guitars, etc., were strung along the wall. In this cabin lived a handsome young darkey who was my uncle's valet, and was quite out of the ordinary; he used to sing and play most divinely. The mammies were called aunts, and I remember one especially, very black and fleshy, but the dearest, most affectionate woman. Her name was Aunt Tobithy; she would sing the oddest little songs to us, and while I sat on her knee, taught me many. One was "Buzza Buzza Sitting on a Yoe. . . ." My dear Aunt Caroline had great patience with all the help and taught them cooking, sewing, etc., and my Aunt Delia would often bring some of the black babies into the house and comb, wash, and dress them by the open grate fire.

One rainy, dismal day my Cousin Delia asked me how I would like to put on an old coat of her brother's and a slouch hat, that she would do likewise, and we would ride up the pasture on horseback to the store, which we did. The store was about a mile from the house; it was a general merchandise one. My Uncle Sam was the postmaster of the village. . . . All the backwoods men, usually carrying long knives and pistols in their belts [who] would shoot a man at the slightest provocation, and the other men of the neighborhood would . . . congregate there. Their principal occupation was chewing tobacco and relating stories. My dear uncle was amazed when he saw us gallop up to the store and made us turn right back in all the rain.

We then went to the garden which was back of the log cabin, gathered some watermelons, and sat in Aunt Tobithy's kitchen eating them with some hoe cakes, a specialty of hers, made of corn meal and baked on the coals. She was an excellent cook. Her fried chicken and corn bread could not be excelled. Hoop skirts were worn in those days and my Cousin Delia was quite jealous of those we wore, as she had none. So my mother took one hoop out [of] each of ours and made a skirt for her out of them, and she was very proud to be the possessor of it.

Many young gentlemen living in that district would call on us. . . . In those days, it was quite customary for young men to serenade the young ladies, and which they often did. We were very angry at a Mr. Barnet, who lived at my uncle's house and was a clerk in his store, as he invariably threw his heavy boots down to make a noise when the young men came to serenade us. This Mr. Barnet was a great character and often entertained us by juggling, etc. He would pretend to swallow very large knives, and although they would skillfully go up his sleeve, it seemed as though he had really swallowed them. . . .

We rode in stagecoaches to get to and fro to Kentucky, and had to cross the river in a ferryboat. When the Civil War broke out in 1863[1], we could not go to Kentucky again to spend our summers, as my uncle soon moved away from Rogersville after that. The slaves were all set free, and there were trying times, as most of the Southern people were so dependent upon them and were unable to do things for themselves. Many young ladies were helpless. . . . Many slaves who had kind masters refused to be set free and wanted to remain with them. . . .

The ladies sewed and knit garments and made lint for the soldiers. My mother used to send coffee and edibles to the soldiers stationed in the park [in Cincinnati]. Sanitary [soldiers' aid] fairs were also held, and the proceeds given to alleviate the suffering. These fairs were also social events, and the young ladies were escorted by the young men after assisting at the various booths. It was an intensely cold winter and the snow was very deep. Automobiles were unknown in those days, and other vehicles being very limited, we were compelled to walk. We bundled up good and warm and went through the deep snow to our destinations. . . .

When I was thirteen years of age and my sister fourteen, we were confirmed at the Lodge Street Synagogue by Dr. [Isaac M.] Wise, and I remember the poem I recited. Each child was assigned one and said it aloud. It was a very large class, I think about twenty-eight or thirty children, boys and girls. And after the service, we walked home together, where usually on this occasion friends called to offer congratulations, and tables were laden with edibles for them; and the confirmants' presents, which they received from relatives and friends, were displayed in the parlor. I received a beautiful, silver filigree bouquet holder with a silver chain and ring attached, in which I carried my bouquet. I also received many other beautiful gifts. Every girl confirmant carried a bouquet while walking up the aisle and placed it on the pulpit as an offering, but which we were allowed to take up again before the service was over.

I had a good voice, and my mother had it cultivated by Madam Rivé, who was the most noted teacher at that time, and who taught by the Italian method. She was one of the most lovable characters, patient and kind. She was the mother of the famous Julia Rivé King, who never had any other teacher but her mother, and when she played Liszt's rhapsody was highly praised. I was soon able to sing difficult songs, and was also taught dramatic music. My voice had a peculiar range, from the lower C to the higher one, and Madam Rivé trained it into an alto, although I could sing high notes also, as in the aria from *Freischütz*, etc. She gave some voice recitals to which our parents and friends were invited. One was at the Town Hall in Clifton, one of our suburbs, where many of our best families lived. I sang "I Waited for the Lord" with Henrietta Sneider (Mrs. Billings), and also some other solos. The Gibsons, who lived next door to the hall, sent me some tea and sandwiches, as we left home early and had partaken of no supper.

44

DEVOTIONAL EXERCISES FOR WOMEN
1852

In 1852, Morris J. Raphall, one of America's leading rabbis, translated a volume of devotional exercises for the use of the Daughters of Israel. The prayers were taken from the German works of three Europeans. Thus it is clear that the original manuals were intended to edify German-reading Jewesses. Two exercises are reprinted below. The first selection offers the reflections of a bride before the marriage ceremony; the second is the plaint of a wife who is unhappily married. In selection A, a woman complaisantly agrees to play a secondary role in the marriage partnership; she desires nothing else than to be a good housewife. In B, the abused wife is ready to believe that she is in some measure the cause of her own misfortunes. In its emotionalism, this prayer verges on the maudlin and self-flagellating. One wonders how acceptable such spiritual exercises were to an American girl in the 1850's. The original works from which Raphall chose his material went through numerous editions in Germany. Women there, it appears, accepted and enjoyed these pious lucubrations; Raphall's anthology here did not survive its first edition.

A

REFLECTIONS OF A BRIDE (BEFORE THE MARRIAGE CEREMONY).

I will greatly rejoice in the Lord, my soul shall exult in my God. For he hath clothed me in the garments of salvation; in the robe of virtue he hath wrapped me. Like a bridegroom, with jewels he adorns me like a bride with her gems all bedecked [Isa. 61:10].

Lord of Life, Director Supreme of the fate and fortunes of human kind: With thee I seek refuge from the busy, noisy throng of the festive circle in order that I may in solitude and without interruption give vent to my pent-up feelings, and pour forth my throbbing heart to thee, my God! And thus duly prepare my mind for the most decisive and important step of my life and invoke thy blessing thereon.

From thy mild hand, O my heavenly Father, I have received life and health, protection and prosperity. Thee I have to thank for the development and cultivation of my bodily and mental powers; and from the day of my birth until the present moment thy loving-kindness has been richly and unceasingly extended to me. Parents who love me, friends and relations, most kind and affectionate to me, did thy paternal goodness bestow on me: In the truth of thy faith thou did'st permit me to be educated; in the light of thy law thou didst graciously let me walk; and as thy crowning mercy thou dost allow me to be united to the man of my choice. O that I had more than tears and words to offer to thee in token of my gratitude. O that my future life and conduct may prove me not altogether ungrateful for thy abundant goodness.

I stand now at the close of the first period of my young life. I cease to be a girl or even a young woman. I become a wedded wife. I, a creature, feeble, inexperienced, and gifted with but slender intelligence; I am now to quit my parents dear whom thou gavest me to be thy representatives on earth; I am to leave the loving circle of brothers and sisters and to give my hand to the man, whose companion for life thou hast appointed me to be. O grant that I may enter into this covenant for life and death, for adversity and prosperity, for grief and joy; grant, I pray thee, that I may enter into this covenant pure, free from sin, and hallowed by thy blessing. Father! bless, I beseech thee, our union, that to both of us it may prove a covenant of grace and of happiness, of bliss and of sanctification. Grant me understanding, intelligence, strength, and ability, that I may act and manage his household in a manner becoming an affectionate and faithful wife; that I may do my duty cheerfully and truly; and that thus I may acquire his love and affectionate regard.

Incline both our hearts to forbearance and meekness, so that in loving acquiescence we may bear with the failings and infirmities of each other, while gentle compliance acts as the conciliating mediator of our homestead. Grant that spite and scorn, ill-temper and stubbornness, may never kindle the flames of discord between us and destroy the harmless quiet of our domestic peace.

Inspire my mind with unassuming contentedness so that I indulge in no vain and absurd pretensions, nor exact from my husband that the hard-earned fruits of *his* industry should be wasted to gratify *my* luxury or ostentation. Root out from my heart any tendency it may harbour towards profusion, idle enjoyments, and showy appearance; so that I may meekly rest content with the humble lot, which at the side of my husband, thou hast meted out for me, nor ever murmur or repine at thy inscrutable will, or at the trials thou mayest visit us withal. O let my heart be filled with ardent, affectionate, and undivided sympathy with, and participation in, his feelings: So that I may rejoice and be glad when he is joyful, that I may weep and mourn when he is grieved; that I be delighted with his prosperity, and participate in his adversity—to avert which from his beloved head is my unceasing prayer to thee, my God.

Bless us, Father! that we may become as one soul; that we may long live with and for each other in undisturbed harmony and prosperity, to give peace and glory unto thy holy name evermore. Amen.

B

Exercise for a Wife Who is Unhappily Married.

For as a woman forsaken and grieved in spirit the Lord hath called thee, and like a youthful wife who is cast off [Isa. 54:6].

Almighty God! who inclinest thine ear to the heart-stricken and art a stay and support unto the mind of the afflicted; thou who sendest them relief that they despond not and sink not under their despair. O hear me, I beseech thee: Graciously give ear unto my supplications while I pour forth my anguished heart before thee and give vent to the plaint which before earthly ears I must not utter.

The burden of thy chastisement weighs heavily upon me; the intensity of my misery crushes me to the dust. Poignant grief gnaws on my heart, mortification and suffering embitter the fairest days of my life. My inward anguish preys upon my health and spirits until my cheek is grown pallid, and my appearance haggard and ghastly, whilst briny tears dim my eye. My fate, so dismal, troubles every hour of my existence, and my destiny, so cruel, leaves me not a moment's rest. With whom can I seek refuge, save with thee, my God! Thou who hast ever been my supreme benefactor, do not forsake me in my utmost need. From thee alone can I ask and obtain help, for thou art All-mighty and All-merciful! To thee I confide my sorrows and my sufferings. Father of mercies have pity on thy child.

Lord! peace is fled from my dwelling; concord has forsaken my home. The man to whom thou gavest me, my husband, to whom in thy name and before thine altar I gave my hand and devoted my heart in love and affection for life; his heart is become turned away from me. He who should have been my stay and my protector, forsakes me and treats me with dislike and aversion, so that the blessing of the marriage state is to me become a curse. Demolished is the structure of my domestic bliss, broken the pillars of my earthly joy, undermined and destroyed my happiness. Rancour, ill-temper, strife, and hatred, have superseded the devoted love and tender affection that should unite husband and wife in harmony of will and of soul. And thus I spend my days in grief, my nights in agony, whilst tears and lamentations are all that remain to me, save prayers to thee, my God, and appeals to thy pity.

I know and feel, Lord, most just and merciful, that no chastisement proceeds from thy hand, unless called forth by our errors and our sins, that no punishment visits us except what we have provoked by our own wrong. I confess before thee, Lord! that it is not thy will that has estranged my husband's affections from me, that my own thoughtless and unhappy temper are, in a great measure, the cause of my present misery. But thou, Lord, art gracious and long-suffering, pardoning sin and iniquity! Pardon me, Lord! be gracious unto me, Father in heaven!

O thou Most High and Holy! have pity on me! Thou who, according to thy Supreme will, inclinest the hearts and minds of all that liveth, incline the heart of my husband towards me. Restore to me his love and affection. Call back unto us the first bright and happy days of our wedded life. Teach him to govern his temper that he subdue his irritability and give less sway to his censoriousness and his overbearing ways. Teach me to subdue my stubborn disposition that I may be able to meet his censures with meekness, his reproofs with submission, his ill-temper with kindness, and that thus I regain his love and undivided affection. Then our domestic happiness will revive; the blessing of conjugal love and fidelity will once more descend and rest upon us in thy grace, Lord! who vouchsafest to hear and have mercy on me, thy servant, now and evermore. Amen.

· 45 ·
REBEKAH HYNEMAN, POET
1853

Rebekah Gumpert Hyneman, of Philadelphia (1812–1875), was the daughter of an intermarried couple, a Jewish father and a Gentile mother. She was not reared as a Jew, but when she grew up she turned to Judaism and became a most ardent and zealous devotee. Like many other Jewish women of her day who nursed literary aspirations, she was self-taught; through her reading, she became a person of some learning and even knew enough French and German to translate from those languages.

Hers was not a happy life. She married a man named Benjamin Hyneman, but he disappeared after some five years of married life. One of her sons died young; another, a cavalryman in the Union Army, was captured by the Confederates and died in Georgia's notorious Andersonville Prison; she herself was plagued with disease. Rebekah wrote prose, essays, stories for young children, but her forte was poetry. A volume of her verse, The Leper and Other Poems, *appeared in 1853. Three selections from this collection are printed below. The "Sarah" to whom Rebekah pays tribute is, of course, the wife of the patriarch Abraham.*

183

SARAH.

Room for that queenly one!
    Room for the peerless gem—
Place on her form the regal robe,
    On her brow the diadem.

And hail her as the queen
    Of a high and noble race;
Proud mother of a princely line,
    Radiant in every grace.

She comes, a husband's pride,
    Protected by his arms;
And haughty kings and princes bend
    In homage to her charms.

From her our race hath sprung—
    She has given us a dower
More dear than gems or robes of price,
    Or the pomp of earthly power.

Then blest, forever blest!
    Be she, who thus hath given
Unto her weary, earth-born sons,
    A heritage in heaven.

LIKE SOME LONE BIRD.

Like some lone bird whose wailing note
    Tells of its grief o'er wood and plain;
Whose melancholy warblings float
    O'er scenes of sorrow, care and pain—
        Even such am I.

Or, like a flower all crushed and pale,
   Torn by the wind, its bed upriven,
Its leaflets scattered to the gale,
   Careering wild by tempests driven,
     Even such am I.

No mate to list that bird's sad lay,
   No hand to raise that drooping flower;
The song must float unheard away,
   The bud still bear the whirlwind's power,
     And helpless lie!

ON THE DEATH OF A CHILD.

Thy life's brief day has passed and gone;
   Never shall winter, stern and dread,
Nor fervid heat of summer sun,
   Disturb thy lonely, quiet bed.

Freed from all the ills of life,
   No heavy sins to be forgiven,
Rest thee from thy mortal strife,
   Frail child of earth, high heir of heaven.

46

WOMEN AND THE CEREMONY OF
CONFIRMATION
1854

In 1854, the following article appeared in the Asmonean *of New York emphasizing the importance of confirmation for girls. Bar mitzvah is a male ceremony; confirmation is a ritual for all Jews, both boys and girls. Confirmation for girls was first initiated in Germany no later than the second decade of the nineteenth century; it was carried to North America in the 1840's. It is important, because it recognizes and even emphasizes the equality of women in Judaism; it is a departure from the traditional norm.*

This particular article was signed by "W," the abbreviation adopted by Rabbi Isaac M. Wise of Albany, New York, a contributing editor of the Asmonean. *Wise, a liberal religionist, had established a Reformist synagogue in Albany in 1850. No doubt his plea for confirmation owed something to his close friend Rabbi Max Lilienthal, who had introduced this ritual in New York City in 1846.*

THE CONFIRMATION AND THE BAR MITZVAH

It is well known to our readers that our ecclesiastical code considers a boy of thirteen years and a girl aged twelve years of full age in religious matters. Our fathers have done well in adopting some ceremonial wherewith to impress upon the mind of the young son of Israel that he has reached the age of reflection and responsibility; but as in many other respects they forgot all about our daughters who are not introduced in the Synagogue until married, as if the connection between God and the female heart was conditional upon her having a male associate in this life. But no blame can be attached to our fathers, for those views are of an oriental origin and were the product of a bye-gone age. Then and in the East particularly, an unmarried woman could not leave the house or harem without giving offence to common decency; it would not do for her, of course, under such circumstances to show herself in the Synagogue, or in any other public place. We have dispensed with those oriental notions; they have been extinguished by the onward march of western civilization, and therefore that class of our people who progress with the time consider it the duty of the Synagogue to extend its benevolent influence over the daughters of Israel, as well as the sons. The act of confirmation is for the young of both sexes while the ceremonies of the *Bar Mitzvah* is for lads only. We leave it to the reader to decide whether this reform was right and good or uncalled for. At the same time we cannot restrain ourselves from entering our complaint on behalf of our female friends. Is it not an insolence that men say in their morning prayers, "Blessed art thou &c., that thou hast not made me a woman." Is not this offensive to their mothers, wives, sisters, and daughters? And if it should not be said, why is it printed in the prayer books? Is it not a rudeness of the meanest kind that a female is considered as nobody in respect to person in religious affairs not only in the Synagogue, but even at the table in the family circle? This is one of the "established" absurdities—this is evidently the mildest name we could find for it—which serves as arms in the hands of our opponents and which deprives the Synagogue of its most devout friends, the most sensible of its devotees. If it was a custom among us that a man with his wife and children should go to the Synagogue and occupy their seats together, the whole would be improved, decorum and devotion would be gained, and a ready attendance would be secured. . . .

Let us see the benefit of all this. Suppose man knows the whole law concerning tephilin [phylacteries] does he know why he is a Jew and what duties he has to perform? No! If he can read the whole of the Law and the Prophets in the manner as those lads were instructed (they were not taught to understand, but merely to read a section with the ancient accents), is he aware of his duties and obligations, or has his mind or heart been the least improved, or is the imperfect knowledge he has, of any imaginable use? No! Therefore it was found necessary that the lad should be instructed in catechism, and that he should pass a public examination therein. This is the first part of the preliminary of a modern confirmation. The Rabbi or Preacher, twice weekly (from Hanukah, December, to Shebuoth, June), attends to a class of boys and girls who have reached the proper age and instructs them in the duties and doctrines of Judaism. Those pupils who are able to pass a public examination are admitted to the confirmation and the rest must wait till next year. So far no objection can be made, and we say ministers who neglect to establish and instruct such a class fail in their duty. . . .

The modern confirmation is entirely the opposite of this old and modernized Bar Mitzvah. The first day of Shebuoth, the day of the revelation on Mount Sinai, is appointed for this purpose in almost all modern Synagogues. No day could be better appropriated to this end. On the anniversary of that epoch when our fathers received the law from the Almighty, we transmit it to our sons and daughters; when the covenant between God and Israel was renewed, we receive our sons and daughters into the same covenant. This is a profound theme on which the preacher may enlarge, and interest both his pupils and his congregation. Under the songs of the choir the young aspirants are brought into the Synagogue by the officers of the Synagogue and the parents. Arrived at the pulpit, the minister receives them with a benediction and prays with them. After all have taken their seats the young aspirants being ranged on each side of the minister, after an appropriate hymn, the preacher addresses the congregation on the subject; he then turns to his pupils and reviews the principles and doctrines of Judaism. Then all of them rise and pass an examination, after which they declare their consent to live in accordance with those precepts. Then the congregation rises to witness the act of confirmation; the minister lays his hands upon the heads of his pupils and blesses them two by two. Then the choir sings the biblical blessing of the priest (Yevorechecho, etc. [Num. 6:24–26]), while the pupils go to receive the blessing of their parents. Having returned to the pulpit, the minister prays with them and the choir sings a concluding psalm. . . .

We have often witnessed the solemn scene of a confirmation and we have never heard or seen any one who was not instructed and edified; it always gave general satisfaction. Still, strange enough, this improvement has found numerous adversaries; our modern men with olden views object to it because they do not know what it is; they never saw it, had only heard the word "confirmation," and know that their fathers did not know anything of it. Others object to a confirmation, we believe, from motives of laziness; it gives so much trouble to instruct the young. And, again, others make objections because they have no minister who could undertake it.   W.

47

FRONTIER DAYS ON THE UPPER MISSISSIPPI
1855

Amelia Ullmann, the author of St. Paul Forty Years Ago, *written in Europe in 1896, was a native of the Rhineland who came to America in 1852, ignorant of the English language. She soon acquired an unusual mastery of the tongue and, in her reminiscences, manifested a literary skill unmatched by most of her Jewish contemporaries. Her husband-to-be, Joseph Ullmann, had also emigrated to the United States in 1852, and after brief sojourns in New York, Havana, New Orleans, Louisville, and New Albany, Indiana, moved on to St. Louis, where he pursued the liquor trade. In 1854, he moved north, settling at the frontier post of St. Paul, Minnesota.*

It was in St. Louis, in 1853, that he met and married Amelia, a woman of cultural capacity with a mind of her own. The year after Joseph's trip to St. Paul, she followed her husband on a steamboat. In her reminiscences, she tells of her attempted adjustment to the rigors of life on the Northwest frontier of the fifties and sixties. This is a woman's story of the problems confronting a young mother in a small town on the edge of civilization. Life was indeed hard, but Mrs. Ullmann never realized, or, if she did, failed to admit, that it was harder still for a lone woman on the bleak prairie striving to wrest a livelihood from the stubborn hard soil.

In her autobiography, excerpted below, Mrs. Ullmann occupies the center of attention at all times. Her husband remains a vague figure in the background, darting in and out of her pages, never emerging as the striking person he was. It is unfortunate that Joseph Ullmann, the real hero of the family, left no memoirs, for he had a story to tell. Within the span of a few short years, he abandoned his liquor and grocery store, and turned to the more remunerative fur trade. By the time of his death, early in the twentieth century, he had established one of the world's great fur and hide companies. The firm which Ullmann founded grew into an enterprise whose branches and agents reached from St. Paul to Shanghai.

8. Amelia Ullmann

On the Way to the End of the World

"St. Paul is a new and thriving town and has for us decided advantages as a place of business. I shall remain here and hope that you will start as soon as possible that we may begin our home life in this young Northwest." So read the letter that I received from my husband, May 2, 1855.

I was then in St. Louis. My husband had gone, early in April, up the Mississippi in order to take advantage of the passage of the first steamboat over Lake Pepin whose surface, frozen long after the river above and below was open, offered a serious impediment to spring navigation.

As I had been directed, I went to the levee to arrange for passage to St. Paul. . . .

The friends that came to see me started seemed to think that I was going to [a] strange land and a new life, and I parted from them with a feeling of sadness. . . .

I remembered, then, that when my husband had asked me before our marriage what dowry my father would give me, I told him: "I know not how much he has; but I do know that I shall take nothing from him as he has a large family to care for. In America, though, anyone who will work and be economical can earn money for themselves. We are young and in order that we may not be in want in old age and that we may honestly earn a competence, I shall go with you to the end of the world." But when we started up the river at noon on that bright May day, I did not think that the time to go to "the end of the world" had come so soon. . . .

First Impressions of St. Paul

At daybreak the boat was dragged off the bar and we steamed up to the landing. On the left hand, the land rose slightly from the river's edge and then rolled in gentle undulations towards the west. There were no houses nor cultivated fields to be seen, only the prairie with the early spring verdu[r]e and wild flowers. A low marshy tract lay upon the right, covered over with tall swamp grass and now and then ponds coated with green scum. The land rose back of this, and about a quarter of a mile above the sandbar a steep bluff ran inland. This ridge of high land curved around and, further up the river, ended in another bluff. Within the elevated space between these two ridges was St. Paul.

A few wooden shanties were scattered along the foot of the side that we passed, and upon the higher land further on were the more pretentious buildings that made up the town. The landing was the river bank leveled for a hundred feet or more and the swamp, filled in with piles driven into the water at the edge to fasten the boat ropes. Stacks of merchandise were piled upon the river bank, and a crowd of people were lounging about awaiting the arrival of the boat. The boat's whistle was to St. Paul then, as to most of the towns on the river, a signal for a general rush to the landing. It being Sunday, the crowd was larger than on the working days of the week. Many of the men greeted my husband and showed a kindly interest in my arrival. New residents were much sought for the struggling new towns, and anyone who came with the intention of becoming a settler was sure of a hearty welcome.

We went in a wagon up the only street that led from the landing to the town. It was scarcely more than a rough, unpaved country road, but, as a sort of continuation of one of the principal streets of the new place, was called Lower Third Street. Near the landing upon the right were several brick or stone warehouses and, at irregular intervals, roughly built wooden shanties. At the junction of this street with Third was the first building which I had passed that was large enough to be called a house. It was the Merchants' Hotel, a two-story, plainly built frame structure. Turning into Third Street, which was then the principal thoroughfare, we were driven along the inner side of the bluff that rose steep from the river.

"This is the principal business part of the city," said my husband with a wave of the hand. I saw one or two good-sized brick buildings and a collection of rough, unpainted, frame shanties, any one of the greater part of which could have been conveniently put into the parlor of an ordinary dwelling house. The door and windows were all closed. There were only a few persons upon the street and most of these were tall, erect, wild-looking creatures, wrapped up in colored blankets and having feathers braided in their long black hair. The impression was not at all favorable for a place of either business or residence.

"The principal business part of the city," I repeated. "Where? There appears to be no business and no people except those wild creatures."

"But today is Sunday; wait until tomorrow, and you will see life enough," was the reply.

My husband then explained that the "wild creatures" were Indian[s], many of whom lived near St. Paul and whom I should very often meet upon the street. They were the first red men that I had ever seen, and I shall never forget the impression that they made upon me. . . .

Housing and Food Problems

Only a consciencious housewife, only a devoted mother who had lived in St. Paul in those days know[s] all the inconveniences and miseries that I was forced to endure in my efforts to do what I felt to be my duty. No servants, no house help of any kind was to be obtained. Every drop of water used had to be carried across the prairie from a well in a livery stable back of the American Hotel; and to get this, it was necessary to crowd in among drivers and rough men from the prairies. My child was ill much of the time and from lack of proper nourishment; for good, wholesome food was difficult to obtain. Fresh vegitable[s] and fruit were unknown. These things being brought up from St. Louis by the boats, they were often in such a condition upon their arrival at St. Paul that their use would have been deleterious to health.

Weary of bacon, potatoes, and tea, I went one day to my poor neighbors and asked if there be a market in St. Paul. There was, they said, and directed me to the market house that was across the prairie at some distance from my home. By making many inquiries I found the place of the market, a two-story, almost square brick building without anything that would identify it as a place where food was sold. There were no stands nor market wagons in the space around the building. The interior would have been entirely empty but for two stands where butchers were endeavoring to dispose of a poor quality of meat at a high price. As I came out of the building, I met a woman carrying some butter and cheese; and, when I found that she had these for sale, I greeted her as if she were an old friend. The woman said that she was the owner of the only cow in town and agreed to furnish me weekly with milk and butter, which, however, she failed to do even for the first week.

In the apartment to which we had moved were left several pieces of furniture that the former occupants generously placed to our use. The first night made clear the reason of their removal and also of their generosity. Everything was so alive with those terrors to good housekeeping, bedbugs, that it was not only impossible to sleep but even to exist in the same room with such a myriad of earlier claimants. We retreated before the swarm to an appartment on the first floor a few days afterwards. This was somewhat better, but when one of my neighbors confided to me that the previous summer five persons had died in the house from cholera, I determined to get away from it, cost whatever inconvenience it might.

In the meantime, my husband had by chance secured a storeroom on Jackson Street, and into a little room back of the salesroom we made the third change of residence within two weeks. From rough pine boards my husband built a little addition that we used as a kitchen, and later on we were given the use of one of the rooms on an upper floor as a sleeping room. Even though our quarters here were limited and lacked most of the conveniences and many of the comforts, yet they possessed some of the elements of a home. The experiences, too, that I had already gone through had taught me, as it had many another woman who has left the comforts of civilization to go into the new lands of the Great West, that many vexations and privations must be nobly born[e]. I thus found myself becoming more contented with the conditions as I found them. . . .

WINTER IN ST. PAUL, ENTERTAINMENT

We dwellers in St. Paul, from being thrown so much upon our own resources for entertainment, became as one big family living under different roofs. Among us there was a geniality and a cordiality that was most agreeable. Whatever viciousness there may have been seemed to have been so gently modified that it did not become obtrusive enough to be burdensome upon the community. That every one had his or her intimates, that there were circles and cliques, was natural; but these special friendships were not permitted to become so selfish as to exclude an interest in the general society of the town. The inhabitants were as a whole an earnest, enterprising people; there were not many young children nor aged persons, and the women were a small percentage of the entire population. The majority were young or middle-aged men who were able and fitted to build well and firmly the foundation of a new city.

The means of amusements were few. There were no theatres; and, except the entertainments given at some of the churches, there were no attempts at amateur performances of plays or operas. People came often together at church meetings or the circles that were formed among the members. Men appeared to find some pleasure in conversing in the barrooms of the hotels or in attendance upon the sessions of the lodges, for already there were branches in St. Paul. Both the Freemasons and Odd Fellows were, I think, established here at this time. The Sons of Malta, which was then so popular throughout the East, had a number of adherents here among the businessmen; the meeting place was in the third story of the Coulter [Colter] Building.

Several balls were given at either the Market House hall or the Portgesa [Pottgieser] hall. They were attended by members of the best families and were enjoyable social affairs. In St. Paul there were not a few pretty girls and good-looking women who dressed with good taste; the young men, too, were not niggardly in the matter of expenditures, and, while their money might not have purchased clothes that shewed the skill or fashion of eastern tailors, hatters, or haberdashers, yet they were the best that could be got in St. Paul. Sometimes, too, there was a certain degree of brilliancy added by the presence of officers from the garrison at Fort Snelling. Dancing would continue until three or four o'clock in the morning with an intermission of an hour or more for supper at midnight. A few private parties were given at homes of some of the residents.

In this dearth of public entertainment the family life developed. There were many house[s] in which the evenings were spent as at our own modest home in Jackson Street. To two young men whom unsuccessful business ventures had landed penniless upon the street, we gave shelter and food. They, as were also we, were fond of reading and thus developed among ourselves a reading circle that eagerly devoured all the books that could be obtained in St. Paul. Seated before a bright wood fire and around an oil lamp, we took turns reading from a favorite book, and lived in the warmth of the sunshine or in the bustle of a great city while the wind howled and the snow drifted in blinding clouds over our buried settlement in the far Northwest.

Letters and newspapers, that were brought twice a week by the mail sledge over the prairie from Dubuque, were eagerly read and discussed. One evening, I remember, we read with the keenest interest of the bur[n]ing of a ferry boat on the Delaware River between Camden, N.J., and Philadelphia. We were moved with sympathy by the description of the agony and suffering of the hundreds of passengers afloat upon the burning hulk in the icy current. It was days after the catastrophe happened that we read of it, and it was still many days later that I received a letter from my husband, then in the East, telling me that he had been aboard the burning boat and had narrowly escaped with his life.

The cold increased in the months of January and February. It was that dry, piercing cold that nipped an exposed ear or finger before one was aware. Buffalo hides were plentiful and not costly, and men and women wrapped themselves up in garments made from them whenever they went out of their houses. Every day we were told of persons maimed for life or even killed by the rigor of the climate. The driver of the St. Anthony coach, in spite of the heavy furs, was sometimes taken off his box unconscious from the cold and had to be resuscitate[d] by stimulants. Not unfrequently was an adventur[e] some teamster overtaken in a blizzard on the prairie, and his team dragged home his body frozen stiff in the wagon. The melting snows of spring often solved the mystery of a sudden disappearance in the dead of winter by disclosing a team and driver caught in the cold embraces of a snow drift and left there to perish. . . .

SPRINGTIME BROUGHT THE INDIANS

One day in the spring, I walked up to the level tract that lay on St. Anthony's Hill and was struck by the peculiar sight that I saw. Several hundred men of dark complexions, with long black hair and black eyes, a collection of carts made entirely from wood, and scraggy Indian ponies or long-horned oxen had possession of the hill. They were the half-breeds, as we called them, who had come from the Red River country and beyond to St. Paul to sell their furs. The men, with their tall, straight figures clothed in furs or rough cloth, were lounging around their rude two-wheeled carts, in the construction of which no iron, not even a nail, had been used, and displaying the furs that they had brought. They had started as soon as the melting snow and ice would permit and with their crude carts and heavy burdens had consumed three or four months on the way. After they had made the purchase of such necessaries as they wished to take back with them, they silently disappeared. For several years they continued to make these business pilgrimages and encamped upon St. Anthony Hill, but later, when the country was opened up to settlement and the fur dealers sent their agents there to buy furs, this peculiar feature of St. Paul life became only a reminiscence.

These people, although considered by us as very primitive and almost uncivilized, were very different from the neighboring Indian tribes, representations of which we saw every day upon the streets. The men were tall and erect; few had adopted the clothes of the white man but wrapped themselves in government blankets. The squaws were in striking contrast; they were small and almost childlike in appearance. . . . Their costume was a skirt that came to their knees, buckskin leggings that were sometimes artistically embroidered, a colored waist, and a shawl for their shoulders. Their papooses they carried crosswise on their backs, the little one's stolid face peeping over the mother' left shoulder. The burdens that they often lugged at the bidding of their husbands excited our sympathy, for they appeared sometimes sufficient to crush the little creatures. . . .

BY SLEIGH, WAGON, BOAT, AND TRAIN TO CHICAGO

The enterprising St. Paul merchant started sometimes as early as February for St. Louis or the East to lay in his stock of summer goods. The river not being navigable, the first part of the journey as far as Dubuque, must be made in sledges over the prairie. At Dunleith, across the Mississippi, was the western terminus of railroad line to Chicago. In these days of improved means of travel, the hardships of such a journey can be scarcely realized

My husband look[ed] aghast when I proposed in 1857 to accompany him to St. Louis. "It is impossible for a woman to make such a trip," he said, "and men undertake it with fear and dread."

"I am younger than you and equally as strong," was my concluding and decisive argument. So, in spite of advice and of even the offer of $100 for a new fur cloak from my husband, I determined to go.

At nine o'clock on St. Patrick's Day we . . . were ready for the start. The conveyance was from a courtesy that had extended over from the summer months called the mail coach; it was however, two sledge runners with a wooden bed crossed by board seats. The sledge bed was filled with straw, and a robe was furnished each traveler; but sad, indeed, would have been his plight should he not have supplied himself well with wraps and furs. The team was two horses, useful more because they were hardened to the severe climate than that they were speedy. Besides ourselves, the passengers were two St. Paul merchants and we were all booked through to Dubuque. . . .

Scarcely were we under way than a snow storm, of a severity such as I had never before experienced in the Northwest, closed in around us. The wind blew with a terrific velocity over the open prairie, and the frozen snow beat down with such cruel force that one dared not expose his face or hands. I tried to balance upon my lap a bandbox in which I was carrying some feminine finery. In an unguarded moment the wind lifted up the box and strewed its contents in shreds far out over the prairie. The men in the front seats attempted to protect themselves with umbrellas; the wind and snow riddled the covers as if they were paper.

All day long we faced this terrible pelting fire of frozen snow. I was so weak and exhausted by the exposure that, when the last stopping place for the day was reached, I could not walk unsupported from the sled to the inn. Strawberry Point was the name given to this station on the route. Why, no one appeared to know. "Perhaps because it is not a point," our hostess suggested, "and because such a thing as a strawberry never grew here." . . .

At four o'clock in the afternoon we were rejoiced to see Dubuque. The thirty hours' continuous riding in the cramped, uncomfortable position, and the bruises and battering from the jolting and tossing of the wagon made me so stiff and weak that I could move only with great pain when we at last stopped before the door of the St. Julian Hotel [Julien House].

The warmth of the room at the St. Julian was at first grateful; but, as the cold that had accumulated in my body from the long journey began thawing the sensation was most unpleasant. Every joint ached, every muscle pained, and my face was as if afire. I seemed to be living over all the miseries of the journey.

When dressing for dinner the next day, I saw for the first time after leaving St. Paul my face in a mirror. The part which had not been protected by my hood was the hue of an Indian; it looked as if a reddish brown oval had been painted around my eyes and nose. The appearance was so grotesque that in spite of the pain I had to laugh. . . .

Independant of the four days' rest which were absolutely necessary, the journey from St. Paul to Chicago had consumed five days and one night. Of the great contrast between the comforts of modern travel and the discomforts of earlier days, I thought a few years ago when in the station at St. Paul I retired to a berth in a palace car and slept through uninterrupted until [I] awoke the next morning at Chicago.

Chicago was in the throes of the spring thaw and rain. Of this western metropolis, there was then nothing, not even the streets, that would be today a landmark. Its appearance was that of a big village stuck down in the mud. The impression was less favorable than that of St. Paul. Sidewalks were in course of construction along several streets; they were not yet finished all the way on Lake Street where was situated the hotel at which we stayed. After wading out for a short distance in the mud I abandoned a shopping expedition and returned in disgust to the hotel.

48

OCTAVIA HARBY MOSES: A DAUGHTER OF THE OLD SOUTH
1856

A founding father of the liberal Jewish religious movement in the United States was a scholarly, brilliant Charlestonian, Isaac Harby (d. 1828). His daughter Octavia (1823–1904) was encouraged to pursue learning, and by the time she was thirteen was already writing poetry. All this was in the best Charleston intellectual tradition. Two days after her sixteenth birthday, Octavia married Andrew Jackson Moses, and after a brief stay in Cheraw moved on to Sumter, South Carolina, where she spent the rest of her life. Seventeen children were born to her; fourteen survived. Five of her sons fought in the Confederate Army; one of them was only fourteen years of age; the oldest boy was shot down by Northern troops after he had surrendered. No wonder Mrs. Moses was fervently attached to the Lost Cause. In later years, she served as president of the committee which erected a war monument in Sumter to commemorate the county's soldiers who had fallen in that unhappy call to arms.

Octavia Moses was a kind, dignified person, an idealist, and a truly pious woman. It was her custom to gather the family in her home on Sabbaths and holidays and conduct services for them. Something of a disciplinarian, she insisted in later years that the grandchildren come to her home every afternoon to prepare their schoolwork under her guidance.

When her daughter Rebecca (1841–1918) was fifteen, Octavia wrote a poem dedicated to this beloved child. It is reprinted below.

TO MY DAUGHTER REBECCA ON HER 15TH BIRTHDAY.
(Feb. 10th, 1856.)

Fifteen to-day! With magic power
    Remembrance sweeps the past away,
And leads me back to that sweet hour,
    When I too said, fifteen to-day!
In that fresh season all was glad,
    Young hope, gay visions brought to view,
While joy in rosy vestments clad,
    Lent to each hour her own bright hue.

My heart swelled high with hopes of fame,
    I'd breathe in song, my soul of fire,
And I would win a glorious name,
    As mistress of the tuneful lyre!
Little recked I of coming care,
    Little I knew of life's stern strife,
Or thought the lapse of one short year,
    Would bring the thrice blessed name of wife.

Say dearest, are such visions thine?
    Do bright conceits thy fancy fill,
Forgetful that the Fates will twine,
    A mingled web of good and ill?
To-day perchance thou bid'st adieu,
    To childhood's pure and simple pleasures,
While opening girlhood brings to view,
    Far higher, richer, dearer treasures.

And deem them not mere earthly gems,
    The ruby's glow, the sapphire's sheen,
The light the changeful opal lends,
    Not these the charms of sweet fifteen.
No, richer, rarer gems are thine,
    The loving, true, unselfish heart,
The soul serene, the unsullied mind,
    Where every virtue has a part.

Dearest, thy charms are all God-given,
   Then turn thy grateful gaze above,
And humbly bless the bounteous Heaven,
   That showered on thee, these gifts of love.
And oh, my child, when years and cares,
   Have left their impress on thy brow,
Still turn to heaven thy grateful gaze,
   Still bless as fervently as now.

Then shalt thou feel, within thy heart,
   When waves of woe, have o'er it rolled,
Earth in thy treasures has no part,
   She gives not, nor can she withhold.
Dearest, on this thy natal morn,
   Thy mother breathes the heart-felt prayer—
Long may such gems, my child adorn,
   And make her more than passing fair!

49

HEBREW LADIES' BENEVOLENT SOCIETIES
1857–1912

It is no exaggeration to maintain that the "ladies' society" was the most important women's organization in the Jewish community. Indeed, it was an essential part of the structure, of the very being, of the entire Jewish group in any town. If no male Hebrew benevolent society had been established, then the female organization would serve as Jewry's social-welfare arm. Its functions were manifold. Very often it was a mutual-aid society helping the local Jewish poor, especially impoverished women. The organization also operated as the community's synagogal auxiliary, providing funds for its physical maintenance and its aesthetic improvement. Though dedicated to charity and synagogal aid, it was at the same time the social club for the town's Jewish women; the associative importance of such organizations cannot be overstressed. The Ladies' Benevolent Society, like the men's Hebrew Benevolent Society, maintained itself, often vigorously and successfully, till shunted aside by the coming and ultimate dominance of professional social workers. Once the women could no longer engage in philanthropy, they limited themselves to synagogal work; they became "sisterhoods." But whatever the guise, the members persisted in emphasizing their identity as women.

Something of a cross-section of the women's eleemosynary activity in the United States is revealed in the following five selections. They include the Deborah Society of Hartford, Connecticut (1857), the Ladies' Hebrew Benevolent Society of Anniston, Alabama (1890), the Ladies' Hebrew Benevolent Society of Portsmouth, Ohio (1891), the Ladies' Hebrew Benevolent Society of Galveston, Texas (1903), and the sisterhood of Philadelphia's Keneseth Israel (1912). The Deborah Society, item A, began as a Frauen Verein (Ladies' Society) in the early 1850's; by 1854, it called itself the Deborah Society; in 1857, it was reorganized when, in all probability, the bylaws reprinted here were adopted. Around the year 1880, it continued its work as the Hebrew Ladies' Benevolent Society. In the early days, its meetings are likely to have been conducted in German; most of its members had been born abroad. The extant minutes indicate that, though a mutual-aid society, these women not only made provision for themselves but also busied themselves with the town's Jewish poor and with its sick, dying, and dead. They reached out to help others; they supplied layettes to impoverished mothers and sewed clothes for the needy. The garments they made and collected were distributed both to Jews and to non-Jews. The social and fund-raising needs of these women were satisfied by masquerades, a variety of parties, trolley-car excursions, coffee get-togethers, and the collection and distribution of recipes.

The Ladies' Hebrew Benevolent Society of Anniston, Alabama, launched in 1890, may lay claim to a fascinating record of organization and accomplishment (selection B). The solo sung at the dedication, "Consider the Lilies," is a New Testament theme (Matt. 6:28). Music of Christian origin was frequently sung in Reform synagogues; for the most part, congregants were not aware of the provenance of the music that enraptured them.

The Portsmouth Ladies' Hebrew Benevolent Society, selection C, was established in 1860; by 1891 it probably had a membership of about twenty-five. The Ladies' Hebrew Benevolent Society of Galveston was founded in 1870. Galveston was at the time a very important town, sheltering the largest Jewish community in the state. The society's constitution of 1903, item D, reveals the workings of a somewhat sophisticated social-service institution. The mutual-aid dimension had been reduced to a minimum; there was even provision for an employment committee.

Document E illustrates the tendency of the new type of sisterhood to serve primarily as a synagogal auxiliary. The following extracts from the 1912 constitution of Philadelphia's Keneseth Israel sisterhood show that this women's organization was geared almost entirely to the religious needs of the congregation, although the sick were still visited and the poor still given garments by an allied sewing circle.

A

1857(?)
ART. IV.—BENEFITS.

SEC. 1. Each member, after 1 month's membership, is entitled, in case of sickness, to receive the services of a physician and to get the prescribed medicines from a druggist, who are employed at the expense of the society. Members who leave Hartford to reside elsewhere, lose their right of benefit. Should such persons return though within 3 years and desire to be members again, they shall be reinstated without ballot, provided a committee of inquiry finds their moral character satisfactory; such reinstated members have to pay again the initiation fee according to their age, and if more than 40 years old, the highest fee of $7.00.

SEC. 2. In case of death of a member, 8 members shall be designated in the order of their membership, to attend the funeral in two carriages, which are to be paid from the treasury. If a child of a member dies, the President shall designate 4 members to attend the funeral and the carriage used for that purpose is also paid from the treasury.

SEC. 3. Every member is entitled to draw $25 from the treasury in case of the death of the husband.

SEC. 4. One person is paid for out of the treasury for watching the corpse of a member.

Washing and dressing the corpse is to be done by the members, on information by the society's messenger.

SEC. 5. Members in childbed are, in case of sickness, not entitled to benefits of physician and medicines until 14 days after confinement.

SEC. 6. Donations shall be kept in a separate fund and shall be used for extraordinary benevolent purposes, as the society may decide.

ART. V.

SEC. 1. If a member becomes sick, she shall report the fact to the President or Secretary.

SEC. 2. The Secretary shall then designate a visiting committee, consisting of the President, Vice-President, Cashier and 3 members in their order, who shall visit the sick for 1 month.

If the visiting committee or the physician finds a nurse necessary, the President shall employ one.

The expenses shall be paid from the treasury, until they are taxed on the members, which tax shall be collected with the regular dues.

SEC. 3. Only members shall have the benefit of visitors and nurses, and are not extended to other members of the family.

SEC. 4. The committee of visitors are in duty bound to visit the sick member on the day assigned to them.

In case of a contagious sickness the committee is dispensed from visits, but shall try to find out the state of the patient and report.

ART. VI.

SEC. 3. Meetings shall be opened at the latest 15 minutes after specified time.

SEC. 4. At the opening of the meeting every member shall be in her seat, and stop every private conversation.

ART. VII.—PENALTIES AND DISMISSALS.

SEC. 1. Every officer shall be present at the opening of a meeting, unless excused for sufficient reasons.

SEC. 2. Any member not minding a call to order or not behaving properly, shall be fined 25 cts.

SEC. 3. Absence from general meetings without sufficient reasons for excuse shall be fined 25 cts.

SEC. 4. Should a member neglect to pay monthly dues, the

privilege of benefits shall be withheld until payment is made. Non-payment for 6 months dismisses from the roll of membership.

SEC. 5. An excuse for non-attendance of orders or duties is only acceptable for reasons of sickness or absence.

SEC. 6. The doings at the meetings shall be kept strictly secret. Any communications to non-members shall at the first offence be punished by a suspension of rights of membership for 3 months, the second time for 6 months, and the third time by expulsion from the society.

B

THE LADIES' HEBREW BENEVOLENT SOCIETY, ANNISTON, ALABAMA.

1890

[Paper read by Mrs. Leon Ullman at the "Get together" meeting of the Sisterhood, Feb., 1917.]

Ladies: I was asked by the chairman of this committee to tell of the early history and struggles of the Ladies' Hebrew Benevolent Society. I will endeavor to give you a summary of those days. I cannot relate the history of that time without mentioning the names of those two well beloved people of sainted memory, Mr. and Mrs. Anselm Sterne, for their deeds are so interwoven with our past that it would be an utter impossibility to do otherwise. About 27 years ago there were a number of Jewish families in our city. The spirit of Judaism prevailed among them as now. During the great fall holidays of Rosh Hashonah and Yom Kippur, services were held usually in a hall, occasionally in a home. Our divine services were none the less sublime under these conditions, for it stimulated a desire to hold those days sacred, and it turned our hearts to tender memories of our dear ones in their far off homes.

Usually a layman officiated at these services. From the coming of our revered Mr. Sterne—he was our leader—his impulses were consistent with the welfare of our Jewish community. One day almost all of our ladies received a message from our friends, Mr. and Mrs. Sterne, stating that if we felt interested in organizing a Ladies' Hebrew Benevolent Society we were invited to their home to discuss the matter with them. All responded to the call. There were about twelve ladies present. I believe not one had ever been members of an organization before. After a cordial welcome from our hosts, we were seated. Standing before us were that imposing couple. They made the most inspiring addresses, letting us know of the beauties and duties of a Jewish benevolent society. We became enthused to the highest pitch, and all expressed a willingness to give their time and effort to the work that had been outlined to them. That was the beginning of our Society, later to be known as the Ladies' Hebrew Benevolent Society. Our object: to promote Judaism in our midst and aid our co-religionist in distress. Our aim: to build a temple, a Beth El [a House of God].

Officers were elected on that occasion. Our own beloved Mrs. Sterne became our president, which office she graced as long as life lasted. Of course there was a vice-president, and the offices of secretary and treasurer were combined. At another meeting by-laws were drafted. We held most rigorously to our constitution. Our members were fined for tardiness and absence but that was a rare occurence. All were so interested and came so eagerly, and no one ever appealed to us for aid in vain. Now, in order to achieve our aim, to build a temple, we had to have funds, and to procure these funds it was decided a bazaar should be held. As you can imagine and as some present know, for I see some charter members here, we worked faithfully. We gave our time and of our substance. We met at the homes of the members weekly at half past two in the afternoon. Light refreshments were served for which a small sum, ten cents, was required. That money, together with an extra dollar given by each member, was used as a needle work fund. Our initiation fees and dues, the same as now, were kept separate. I believe our [synagogal] windows were bought with that money. We bought our material for [the sewing] work out of this fund, besides giving material very often ourselves.

Suffice it to say, our little band accomplished much. Some

really beautiful pieces of embroidery and fancy articles were made. We were enthused and wanted to accomplish our exalted purpose. After a winter of work and really pleasant meetings, we decided the time had come to hold our bazaar. Our vice-president thought it would be a good move to enlist the outside support of our husbands and other members of the congregation in our work. So we asked them to write to the firms they had "biz" dealings with for aid in our cause. Nearly all responded generously. We actually received merchandise and money amounting to over a thousand dollars. That was a busy time for a small number of willing workers, for not alone did we rely on the fancy articles we had to sell, but we served dinner and supper for three days to the public, besides replacing articles we saw there was a demand for. Of course there was raffling, and other means of chance were resorted to. After three days of arduous labor our bazaar was closed. We had the means on hand wherewith to build a sanctuary. The ladies turned the money over to the congregation. The congregation appointed Mr. Sterne chairman of the building committee. Our revered leader was indeed a pillar of strength to us and a wise counsellor. I don't know what we would have done without his cooperation.

Now, before we could build, a lot had to be secured to build on. A committee of ladies were appointed, consisting of the officers of the Society, to visit the Anniston City Land Co. with the purpose of purchasing a lot. We were shown the greatest courtesy by the late Col. Wm. H. McKleroy, president of the company. He gave us every encouragement. After days of looking around we bought our lot, Col. McKleroy immediately writing out a check for $25.00, a donation from himself, and advising us to write to the Land company in New York, as they were co-religionists, for a donation. This was done and they answered they could not send us money but pledged us their moral support. A fine sentiment but not far-reaching! We made terms to pay for our lot in yearly installments; our money on hand would not cover this expence. Also there was interest to be paid on each installment which Col. McKleroy voluntarily deducted each year. That again made more work for the ladies, paying for the lot. The oyster suppers and the strawberry festivals that were held—and the donations that we made again! Really, I can't take any more of your time for further details. The lot became ours. We presented 100 feet of it to the congregation on which to build the temple. We still own 90 feet.

After a few months of waiting, our temple was completed. Thanks to the efficiency of our building committee all details were well-looked after. Then came our hour of triumph—the culmination of our hopes—our building was to be dedicated to our God. I must mention, though, the building was completed, but not furnished. We had no pews; chairs were used. An organ was bought from the proceeds of a raffle. But now all looked forward to the beautiful dedication services of the Jewish faith. It was agreed upon that that consecrated man, Dr. Max Heller of New Orleans, should be our officiating rabbi. I want to mention he is the father of Dr. James Heller who officiated at our fall holidays two years ago.

That dedication was the most wonderful and inspiring scene imaginable. The carrying of the Ark around the temple, led by the rabbi, and then came the president carrying a Torah, and then other officers in the temple following. I believe they walked around the temple twice, the rabbi offering prayers. Then the handing over of the keys of the temple by a child, and the scholarly address of our rabbi! Oh, we wept tears of joy at it all—it was sublime! I cannot refrain from mentioning the music on that occasion—it was truly operatic. Mrs. Joseph Aderhold of our city rendered a wonderful solo, "Consider the Lilies," with an exquisite charm. The devotional music for the occasion was arranged by our learned Mr. Sterne and all of this, ladies, was made possible by the untiring efforts of a small band of women.

On Dr. Heller's return to New Orleans, he sent the beautiful Bible, which rests on our reading desk, to the congregation as a mark of esteem and appreciative record of what had been done to the glory of God in a small community. In acknowledgement of this, at the request of our president, two of the members of the L.H.B.S. embroidered and made lace for a beautiful linen center piece which was sent by our society to the wife of our esteemed Dr. Heller in appreciation of his beautiful dedication services.

After that, there was yet the furnishings to be worked for, the pews, the pulpit furniture, the chandeliers, the fencing around the temple, the trees, and the lawn. Only the members of those days know the amount of money and work it took to establish that lawn. It was a matter of such pride with us that our lawn should be in harmony with our temple. It was the fruit of our handiwork. Our cornerstone tells the story. It reads: "Erected by Ladies' Hebrew Benevolent Society." It is dated 1893. In our hearts we feel that our temple stands as a monument to the memory of that revered couple who inspired us and led us in the achievement of this great work.

And now, ladies, our organization has need of you, as we had of our fellow-members years ago, to meet with us each month, and by your presence be an encouragement to lead us to accomplish other things of equal importance that may manifest themselves as time progresses, for it behooves us to give personal services in the cause of Judaism. I trust that at our next meeting, and others to follow, we will have all of you with us as earnest workers, ripe with suggestions for the good of the Society.

C

CONSTITUTION

1891
TITLE

1. This Society shall be known as the "Ladies' Hebrew Benevolent Society" of Portsmouth, Ohio.

OBJECTS

2. This Society shall be a Mutual Aid Society. The purpose of this Society is to visit sick members and to render such aid as the constitution of this Society proscribes. Another purpose of the Society is to practice charity at home or abroad.

Officers

3. The officers of this Society shall be a president, vice-president, secretary, treasurer, and a sick committee, consisting of two members. . . .

Amendments. . . .

6. c) A woman whose husband, father or brother is a member of our congregation may become a member of our Society. . . .

By-Laws. . . .

1. b) Should this Society ever be disbanded, the money on hand shall revert to the synagogue or in case none exists, to some charitable institution.

2. All business is to be transacted in the English language. . . .

Monthly Dues. . . .

4. The monthly dues of this Society shall be ten cents (10 c'ts).

Fines

5. A fine of 25 c'ts shall be imposed on any absent officer, and a fine of 10 c'ts on any absent member, unless excused on account of illness, or abscence from the city. . . .

7. Members accepting a nomination and after election refusing to serve, then or any time during their term of office, shall be fined five dollars ($5).

Presidential Duties

8. a) The president is at liberty to expend not more than five dollars without assembling the members of the Society.

b) A manual should be kept by the president in order to appoint nurses and those who watch the dead, in rotation. . . .

11. A find of $1.50 shall be imposed on all members refusing to act in the capacity of nurse or to sit up with the dead.

12. It is the duty of all members of this Society to assist in the making of shrouds for our co-religionists.

Mortuary Benefits

13. a) This Society furnishes a carriage to be occupied by members of the Society in the funeral cortege of a member deceased.

b) Resolutions of Respect are to be published in the *American Israelite* and in the local papers.

Duties of the Sick-Committee

The duties of the sick committee are to investigate all cases of illness, or those in need of monetary assistance, and thereafter to confer with the president as to the best means for alleviation.

In case of non-fulfillment of duty they are to be fined $2.

Duties of Floral Committee

The floral committee attend to the decorating of the temple on all holidays. . . .

AMENDMENTS TO THE BY-LAWS. . . .

Article 13(a) shall be amended as follows:
This society furnishes a floral gift for any deceased member (anulling the hire of a carriage).
Article 13(b) be amended as follows:
Resolutions of Respect are to be published in the local papers (not in the "American Israelite" as heretofore). . . .

MEETING OF JULI 2ND, 1893. . . .

One of the members made a motion to render pecuniary aid to a very needy and worthy Hebrew family. After a heated discussion it was decided to purchase provisions for the family to be paid out of the [immigrant] Russian Fund, and if that was insufficient, to be supplemented by funds from the L.H.A.S. treasury.

The treasurer's report showed an expenditure of thirteen dollars and twenty-five cents for repairs and cleansing the synagogue, for decorating the same, one dollar, which leaves a balance of twenty-one dollars and five cents. . . .

MEETING OF JAN. 9TH, '94. . . .

A motion was then made to have the Sunday school room cleaned and papered and that the Society should appropriate a certain Sum for that purpose, the sum of ten dollars was neamed; the same was voted upon and carried. A committee of three was then appointed to superintend the cleaning. . . .

MINUITS OF REGULAR MEETING OF OCT. 7TH['94]. . . .

Dues and fines collected amounted to $5.20. Expenses since last meeting were $3.20 for cleaning and decorating sinagogue for Schavuoth, and $2.00 given to two poor men amounting to $5.20. Balance in [hands of] treasurer, $32.20.
As there was no more business, adjourned. . . .

JAN. 5, 1896. . . .

A motion was made and carried that the organ, which is badly in need of repairs, be put in order, and Mrs. Ike Levi and Mrs. Clara Wise were appointed as a committee to attend to it.

The President appointed Mrs. Felix Haas and Mrs. Ike Levi to consult with some of the officers of the Congregation to see if they are willing and able to do anything towards improving the appearance of the temple, as it is in need of a new coat of paint. They are to hand in a report. . . .

JAN. 27, 1897. . . .

A motion was made and seconded to supply a poor Jewish family with 10 cents worth of meat daily, for two weeks; Mrs. Fanny Labold being appointed to attend to this matter. Another motion made and carried that another poor family be given $5.00. . . .

PORTSMOUTH, O. JAN. 30th, '98. . . .

Balance on hand $27.18. A motion was made and carried that in case the gentlemen's benevolent society were short of funds, that our society would assist the above society to the extent of $5.00.

A motion was made and lost to buy new chairs for the Synogogue. . . .

PORTSMOUTH, O. AUG. 25TH, 1898.
RESOLUTIONS OF CONDOLENCE

Whereas our Heavenly Father has removed from our midst one of our respected and honored therefore be it

Resolved that in the death of sister Barbera Weisel, The Hebrew Ladies' Benevolent Society looses a most faithful and most charitable member and that the many noble deeds of our associate shall never be forgotten.

Be it further

Resolved, that we mourn with her relatives, and especially with sister Amelia Schloss in their bereavement, and that these resolutions be published in one of the city papers and a copy be sent to the relatives of the deceased.

Respectfully submitted,
Laura Horchau
Mrs. H. Atlas
Mrs. Max Wise. . . .

PORTSMOUTH, OHIO JAN. 22ND, '99. . . .

The treasurer reported $5.00 expended since last meeting for charity. Rev. Schapiro came before the meeting with an appeal to aid the Wisconsin Jewish farmers, and to contribute to the National Monument. After listening to the appeal the society allowed $5.00 for both causes. . . .

D

CONSTITUTION

1903

ARTICLE I.

NAME.

The name of this Society shall be "The Ladies Hebrew Benevolent Society of Galveston, Texas."

ARTICLE II.

PURPOSE.

The purposes of this Society are to assist women of the Jewish faith; to perform such duty to dead Jewesses as ought to be done by women only, and generally to act in harmony with the Hebrew Benevolent Society of this city. . . .

ARTICLE IV.
COMMITTEES.

The President shall appoint the following Standing Committees:

(1) COMMITTEE ON MEMBERSHIP.—To consist of six members including the President, whose duty it shall be to increase the membership of the Society.

(2) VISITING COMMITTEE.—To consist of five members, including the President, whose duty it shall be to visit the indigent, the infirm and the sick women of the Jewish faith and make report thereof to the President.

(3) EMPLOYMENT COMMITTEE.—To consist of seven members, including the President, whose duty it shall be to find work for the unemployed.

(4) DISTRIBUTING COMMITTEE.—To consist of two members, including the President, whose duty it shall be to receive and distribute among the poor all clothing and wearing apparel sent to them for that purpose, and to solicit such donations.

ARTICLE V.
MEMBERS.

SECTION 1. Any Jewess, having attained the age of 17 years, shall be eligible to membership.

SEC. 2. Applications for membership must be in writing, endorsed by two members of the Society in good standing, and handed to the Secretary, who shall present the same to the Society at the first ensuing regular meeting.

SEC. 3. Each applicant shall be voted upon by the members at a regular meeting of the Society, and will become a member provided that not more than two votes are cast against her.

SEC. 4. The Society may elect honorary members.

ARTICLE VI.

DUES.

SECTION 1. The monthly dues shall be fifty cents, payable quarterly as the same accrue. . . .

ARTICLE VIII.

RELIEF, DONATIONS, ETC.

SECTION 1. Indigent, infirm, or sick Jewesses shall be assisted by the Society by donation of money or by expending for their benefit such sum or sums as may be appropriated for the purpose.

SEC. 2. In cases of sickness, the President may, at her discretion, secure medical attendance, nurses, etc.

SEC. 3. Upon the death of a Jewess, the President shall designate five members of this Society to prepare the body for burial according to Jewish custom.

SEC. 4. It having heretofore been necessary, and as it may hereafter be necessary, to send poor women and children from Galveston to eleemosynary institutions, the Society may, from time to time, send donations to such institutions.

SEC. 5. No appropriation or expenditure of an amount exceeding twenty dollars shall be made in any one case (except under Section 2 of this Article) unless first authorized by the Society; but the President, Vice President, Secretary and Treasurer, or any three of them, may expend not exceeding fifty dollars in any one case; and the President alone may expend at her discretion, not exceeding ten dollars in any one case for relief or for any other purpose provided for in this Article. . . .

E

1912

CONSTITUTION

ARTICLE I.
Name and Object.

SECTION 1.   This association shall be known as THE SISTER-HOOD OF KENESETH ISRAEL.

SEC 2.   The objects of this association shall be to further the religious and educational usefulness of Temple Keneseth Israel, and to promote social intercourse among its members.

BY-LAWS

ARTICLE I.
Membership.

SECTION 1.   Any woman in sympathy with the work of this organization is eligible for membership.

SEC. 2.   The dues of this association shall be one dollar annually, payable at the April meeting.

SEC. 3.   Members in good standing only shall have the right to vote. . . .

DUTIES OF COMMITTEES

1.   *Committee on Religion.*—It shall be the duty of this committee to further attendance upon divine worship and participation in worship; to foster religious services in the home; to invite and welcome strangers to the Temple; to assist in spreading knowledge concerning the Jew and Judaism, by dissemination of printed discourses of the pulpit of Keneseth Israel among Jews and non-Jews. It shall devise ways and means looking toward an

eventual establishment of Reform services and Reform religious schools in the congested centers of the city and in its outlying districts. It shall encourage, through the medium of classes, lectures and readings, the study of the Jewish religion, history, literature and kindred subjects.

2. *Committee on Religious School.*—It shall be the duty of this committee to bring about close co-operation between the religious school and the home; to get in touch with parents whose children are of age to be enrolled as pupils of the school; to encourage the organization of post-confirmation classes; to provide, with the aid of teachers, suitable celebrations for the children on festal occasions.

3. *Committee on Music.*—The duties of the Music Committee shall be to strengthen, in every way possible, the effectiveness of the Temple choir; to arrange a choral society for the purpose of fostering and encouraging congregational singing and to aid every effort made to train the religious school for participation in the music of the services. The Music Committee shall also prepare all musical programs for the entertainment of the monthly meetings of the Sisterhood, the school entertainments, the annual meetings of the congregation and other occasions that may arise.

4. *Committee on Alumni.*—The Alumni Committee shall be composed only of alumni of the religious school. Its duties shall be to exercise superintendence over the Alumni Building; to popularize the facilities of the Alumni Building for purposes of revenue and to cooperate with the Alumni in its dinners and public social affairs.

5. *Committee on Membership.*—It shall be the duty of this committee to increase the membership of the Sisterhood, the Congregation, the Alumni and the Library.

6. *Committee on Visiting.*—The duties of this committee shall be to visit the sick, the mourning, new members of the Sisterhood and the Congregation, and to inform the Rabbis of sickness and trouble in the families of members of the Sisterhood and Congregation.

7. *Committee on Sociability.*—The duties of this committee shall be to promote good fellowship among the members of this association during the social half-hour following monthly meet-

ings, at receptions, Congregational dinners, and all other social affairs of the Sisterhood and Congregation.

8. *Committee on Hospitality.*—The duties of this committee shall be to arrange the refreshments at the social half-hour of the monthly meetings, the collations, receptions and all other social affairs that may require their services.

9. *Committee on Program.*—It shall be the duty of this Committee on Program to furnish all entertainment, excepting musical, at the monthly meetings and all other social affairs of the Sisterhood or Congregation.

10. *Committee on Property.*—The duties of this committee shall be to provide and care for all the property belonging to the Sisterhood, such as silverware, china, etc.

11. *Committee on Floral Decorations.*—It shall be the duty of this committee to continue the work of the present Floral Committee—*i. e.*, to decorate the pulpit and Temple for divine worship, on Sabbaths, holidays, special and festal occasions, and to raise the means therefor.

12. *Committee on Sewing.*—It shall be the duty of this committee to continue and enhance the work of the present Temple Sewing Circle—*i.e.*, to collect material, sew and distribute garments for the poor, and to raise the means therefor.

13. *Committee on Ways and Means.*—It shall be the duty of this committee to provide ways and means for raising funds for the furtherance of the work of the Sisterhood, of the Congregation, of the religious school and the Alumni, excepting in such cases where committees will undertake to raise their own funds.

Note.—At the discretion of the President of the association, work other than here enumerated may be assigned to these committees.

Members of the Sisterhood shall keep the various committees informed of work that falls within their respective spheres of activity.

50

ANNA MARKS ALLEN WRITES TO A BAR MITZVAH BOY
1858

On June 28, 1858, Anna Marks Allen, of Philadelphia, wrote to a nephew, Lewis Arnold (b. 1845), and congratulated him on the occasion of his becoming bar mitzvah. Her letter merits publication, not only because she was a prominent social worker, but because it reflects in detail the religious beliefs of a pious Jewess who also knew some Hebrew.

Anna Marks (1800–1888), scion of a Revolutionary War family, was born in Sing Sing, New York, but at an early age moved with her parents to Philadelphia. There, in the course of time, she became one of the city's most highly respected matrons for her work in the Jewish charities. Her record in the Jewish community was an enviable one: she was a pillar of the Female Hebrew Benevolent Society, a cofounder with Rebecca Gratz of the Sunday school, and finally, in 1855, a founder and first president of the Jewish Foster Home, an orphan asylum.

In 1823, Anna married Lewis Allen, a merchant, who in 1834 became president of Mikveh Israel and remained at the helm of that prestigious Sephardi synagogue till his death in 1841.

Phila., June 28, 1858.

My dear Lewis,

Accompanying these few lines, you will receive articles suitable for a Boy soon to become *bar mitzvah*, and with them accept the love and Blessing of your aunt who sincerely congratulates you on your attaining so important an Epoch in your life.

May you live to be a credit to yourself, a comfort and Blessing to your dear parents and the Pride and protector of your sisters. As your God Mother, my dear Lewis, I may be allowed the privilege, perhaps, of speaking to you of the Many *Duties* and *Responsibilities* which every *Day* and *Hour* of your life encreases and assumes a more important Character.

In the first place, my dear Boy, let the duties you owe your

Maker ever predominate over every other. Diligently study our *Holy* laws and Ordinances, so that when you look upon the Sacred Emblem Of *Faith* (the Tzitzith) [prayer fringes] you may be reminded that *no Temtation* that the world can offer may induce you to forsake your God. And when you Bind upon your Body the *Tephillin* [phylacteries], you Must remember that it is not *only* intended to Commemmorate the Chief Commandment of the Mosaic Religion [love of God], but that we Must *Obey* and *do* them, so that the Mantle [the prayer shawl] that Envelopes you when in the House of God may not prove a Covering for *vain thoughts* and Evil *Imaginations*.

Next comes, my dear Lewis, your *duty* to your parents. I cannot point out a more impressive and beautifull passage by which to Govern your actions than that contained in the fifth Commandment: "Honor thy Father and Mother." What a vast amount of Duties do these Emphatic words contain! To Define them, my dear Nephew, would take a more able pen than mine, but let us hope as you advance in Youth and Manhood that the Instruction you Receive from your dear parents and Teachers, and your own good sense, may develop them. And may the *Holy One* of *Isreal Enlighten* your *Eyes* and impress them on your *Heart* that you may "do *always* that which is Right in *His* Sight"

is the prayer of your
Aunt Anna

51

THE AMERICAN JEWESS
1859–1862

*In 1862, there appeared in Hannover, Germany, a two-volume work,
Drei Jahre in Amerika, 1859–1862 ("Three Years in America"). A
man of positive opinions, the author, Israel Joseph Benjamin II, could not
refrain from paying his respects to the American Jewess, especially the
teenagers. His presentation, which follows in part, is anything but
complimentary. Though fully conscious of the demands of modernism and
in no sense an obscurantist, Benjamin looked askance at an American
Jewry which pampered its women. Benjamin was a world traveler. Before
he landed in the United States in the summer of 1859, he had already
visited many Jewish communities in Asia and North Africa. His notes and
comments on those communities were published in the 1850's in French,
German, and Hebrew.*

Of all the inflexible demands which his religion and his duty
make on each Israelite, the first and foremost is to give his child a
good education, to equip it for the journey through life and give it
the means to find its way. The American schools, of which we are
about to speak, certainly guarantee this in part; but it is much to
be regretted that, because they exclude all religion and confessions of faith—not with an unwise purpose—I must say with the
deepest regret that the study of the Holy Scriptures, particularly,
is much neglected among the daughters of Israel.

Jewish boys after a fashion—for that is the established way—
are instructed in their religion, as is also the case with the sons and
daughters of Christians. The Jewish boys attend some Hebrew
school or other, or are instructed privately; but in this respect,
what does the situation look like for the daughters of Israel? What
a great difference! How sad is the provision for the religious
instruction of these Jewish housewives and mothers of the future!
How little do they learn of their duties towards God and man!
What do they know of what our faith requires and of the

commandments that they must obey as daughters of Israel? Should not those who are to perform the holiest religious duties be thoroughly prepared for such performance? These duties are indeed many and noble and it is with regret and astonishment that one learns that half of the American Jewesses are at present unable to undertake and fulfil worthily the place in life for which they are intended; nevertheless, it is unfortunately all too true. And why? The reason for this lies in their neglected education.

To throw more light on this statement and confirm the truth of it, let us describe the upbringing that the American Jewish women of today receive, and then let us proceed to show how the evil may and should be remedied.

The mother of a little girl, a good-hearted, rather well-to-do woman, let us say, will try to impress on the young spirit of her child as much good instruction as ever she can. This private care lasts until the child is five. Then the child, it is obvious, must be sent to a public school or, what is more respectable, to a so-called "institute." Accepted by the "institute," the child begins the usual course of studies, makes the acquaintance of girls of other religions and has friends among them, and may well, without any objection or even realization of its significance, kneel during morning prayers which are arranged for those of other faiths, before classes begin. After school, she studies her lessons for the next day or, like all children, plays. Upon going to bed or arising in the morning, she may very likely recite for her mother some Hebrew or English prayers; but as for Judaism, the child experiences nothing and knows nothing.

In this manner the girl continues to be brought up until she is fifteen, except for the unimportant difference that in time she leaves the institute to attend a high-school or college. On her fifteenth birthday a new life begins; the longed-for day arrives at last; Papa and Mamma have promised her that on this day she shall be free and shall leave school, and she "graduates," to her great joy. What useful knowledge has she gained during this time? Extremely little in fact. She has spent ten years of her precious life among all kinds of books, and, with all that, she has not advanced in the least; the time is lost, indeed, forever. What she has learned is of no use to her and of no profit. She does not know how to sew, has no knowledge of household affairs, and still less of higher things. Ask her who has created her, who clothes her, who gives her her daily bread; and she may have the correct answer—perhaps, but it is more likely that she will say: "That was not in my book."

Her good parents have increased their wealth during these ten years and have taken the commendable resolution that their daughter should not forget all that she has learnt. Accordingly, they provide her—to complete her education—with a music-teacher, a singing-teacher, a drawing-teacher, and a governess to continue the practice of French; the latter also teaches her how to sew, knit and the like; and, to give it all a final touch, they assign a teacher to give her Hebrew lessons. He must make her acquainted with the alphabet of a language in which, as a child, she should have lisped the name of God. She will find this last teacher, as is only to be expected, a bore. She will find Hebrew too dull and also too difficult; she will weep over her lessons so that her yielding parents, who will be touched by her tears and moved to pity, will give the teacher notice—he whom they should have engaged first and dismissed last. But they took the opposite course, out of their own lack of true religious feeling, and so they engaged him last, and, again, dismissed him first.

Since, in this manner, the girl has come to the end of her religious upbringing, she continues to recite in English the few prayers which she has learnt from her mother. Should she, quite by accident, attend synagogue, she takes a book in the same language. Her other teachers soon share the same fate as her former Hebrew teacher. Because of the parties, balls, soirées, and so on, which have now become the important questions of the day for her, and at which she remains until the last, the girl becomes full of whims, her mind is distracted. She listens to the chatter of young men and all thought of study and the desire for it is gone. The young lady—she will no longer permit herself to be called a girl—believes that her upbringing is now completed in every respect, considers herself qualified to take her place in the world, able to make a man happy and to become a Jewish mother. I must remark that unfortunately, this can serve as an example for a thousand cases that occur in this land with only slight variations.

Who is to blame for this completely inadequate upbringing? The girl with her whims or her over-indulgent parents? I answer neither. The girl is like all other children; the parents are doing all in their power to give their child the best upbringing: they would give their wealth, their energies, their time, yes, even their lives to provide her with the highest possible education; and they imagine, without doubt, that they have done so. But, alas! To their horror, they will soon discover their mistake—and it will be too late.

I blame neither the young woman nor her parents; rather are all those who are members of the Jewish religious community to blame: as a body, as is the case in England, France and Germany, they should have supplied the general need and have founded a "Jewish school" for girls as well as for boys. There girls would be provided, from their early years, with a thoroughly good upbringing that would make them familiar with their duties towards their Creator. This is the most urgent need; for I am quite convinced that such an arrangement would have as beneficial an effect on the generations to come as any other that might be hit upon.

Napoleon the First, the greatest benefactor that France ever had, understood very well the value of schools for the daughters of the land and of the influence of mothers, well brought up, upon future generations. When he came to power, one of the first acts which he pursued, energetically, was to establish institutions for the education of women. He himself visited them often and distributed very valuable prizes among the outstanding students in the various institutions. To this I most certainly ascribe the wonderful ability and the cleverness of the present generation of French women in the sphere of their activities. It would be well to consider the example of Napoleon the Great and to establish a "Jewish school" in America: the blessings of such an institution would be innumerable.

52

CINCINNATI IN BYGONE DAYS
1870's

In 1976, Sarah M. Wartcki, descendant of a family which had come to Cincinnati in the 1830's, published some of the stories handed down to her by her mother, Julia Cohen Wartcki. These oral reminiscences date back to the 1860's and 1870's.

They are of historical value, for they throw light on the religious practices and social life of the German Jews who came to this country in antebellum days. The traditional folkways described here are not exceptional; most Central European immigrants made every effort to transfer and reconstruct here the same religious style that had nurtured them in the old homeland. Reform Judaism was certainly not widespread in nineteenth-century Germany.

The German cited here by Miss Wartcki in her narrative is reproduced as printed; the numerous errors are not corrected. Despite the fact that the public schools of that day taught German, most children were not at home in that language.

GRANDMA LENA AUER

My mother was only two-and-a-half years old when her grandfather, Zachariah Auer, died and his widow, Lena Auer, came to live with the family of her only child, Sarah Cohen. Therefore, little Julie Cohen (my mother) could not remember her childhood home before it was dominated by Grandma Auer's Orthodox Jewish rules.

From Friday dusk until Saturday evening, no one of the Cohen family was allowed to do any work—"work" including sewing, cutting, tearing, writing, lighting a match, or a fire, or a lamp, touching money, carring a burden (even a handkerchief in a pocket) riding a horse or in a conveyance or even walking farther than a certain allowed distance.

Fortunately, however for the Cohen children, the household employed two "shiksas", Minnie Miller and Tillie Taylor, who being gentile, were not prevented from carring the heavy scuttles of coal up the three flights of stairs to keep the open grate fires, with which the house was heated in winter, blazing, the lamps and candles lighted, the kitchen stove hot and the Saturday meals well-cooked.

Grandma Auer had consented to the marriage of her daughter, Sarah, to Wolf Cohen, who was a non-observing Jew, only when he gave a solemn promise that he would not work on the Sabbath and would always close his tailorshop at five o'clock Friday afternoon until the same time Saturday evening.

Wolf Cohen kept his promise not to work on Saturday but he did not go to the synagogue. He had a Gentile friend who was a judge who held court on Saturday morning and Wolf Cohen joined this friend on the bench and my mother told me her father gained a more lenient sentence for many a "good Jewish boy" who was in trouble with the police.

Little Julia (my mother) was very proud of her grandmother, and she was especially proud of grandma's false teeth. For these teeth, of pure porcelain, were set in glistening gums of shining yellow gold.

"My teeth are just like those made for George Washington," Grandma Auer would explain and would add proudly, "the gums are 24 carat, pure gold."

One afternoon Grandma Auer was peeling apples for the little children, sitting before the open grate fire in the dining room. She was dressed in her good black wool skirt and over it she wore a plaid silk apron and, as she peeled an apple for each little girl, she dropped the peelings in her apron. Then she put a slice of apple in her own mouth, but, too bad, found the apple too firm to chew with her false teeth without feeling pain. So she took out her dentures and dropped them, also, in the lap of her apron. Then she dozed off in the warmth of the grate fire, awakened with a start, saw the apple skins in her good apron and, still only half awake, stood up and shook the contents of her apron into the blazing fire. Only then did she remember that her expensive gold dentures had been, also, in the lap of her apron and that they were now in among the red-hot burning coals.

Yes, the gums of the dentures were truly of pure, 24-carat gold.

The fire proved it by quickly forming the pure, soft, easily melted metal into a shapeless mass.

Little Julia was also proud of Grandma Auer's beautiful black Sabbath "scheitel", the wig that all Orthodox Jewish married women wore constantly to cover their natural hair. For Grandma Auer had both an everyday wig and a Sabbath wig which she would comb every Friday morning on its wig stand and adorn with a delicate black lace cap with modish ribbon rosettes over the ears. For Grandma Auer was too "frum" (religious) to comb her wig on the Sabbath.

But the thing that fascinated the four little Cohen girls about Grandma Auer's bedroom was the large wooden box that stood on the dresser. It was about two feet long and a foot deep and a foot-and-a half high, made of polished dark mahogany, bound on all the edges with bands of etched brass. It also had a brass padlock hanging from the lid and was kept securely locked. No one had ever seen Grandma Auer use the key. Grandma had brought the box with her from her native village in Bavaria, Germany.

The little girls knew that Grandma opened the box sometimes because every month or so, if any of the children were with her in her bedroom, she would say, "Now, my child, go back into the nursery. I am going to open my box." Then she would lock her bedroom door.

The four little girls were intensely curious to know what was in Grandma's box. (There were only four Cohen sisters then because the two younger girls had not yet been born. Rose was six years younger than Julia, and Retta was thirteen years younger.)

The two oldest of the sisters, Belle and Delia, who were in their early 'teens, were inclined to be romantic and thought Grandma Auer might be keeping the love letters she received from Grandpa Auer when he was courting her. For hadn't she taught them the German love ballad (for Grandma Auer forgot her English, which she had learned upon coming to Cincinnati at the age of thirty-one, and spoke only German) as follows:

> Kommt ein fogel geflogen
> Sitz sich nieder auf mein fusz.

Had ein brieflein in Snabel,
von meine Schatzchen einen Gruz.

(A bird comes winging
And perches down on my foot.
It has a little letter in its bill,
A greeting from my sweetheart.)

Mamie, who was four years younger and very practical-minded, thought the box was probably full of gold-pieces like the gold dollars brought from California by their father's sister. And little Julia, by two years more junior, hoped that the box might be full of German chocolate and that Grandma Auer would open the box soon and give them all some.

But Julia, at least, never learned what was in the box until the eve before her wedding. Then Grandma Auer took a large brass key from a dresser, unlocked the box and removed a large envelope.

"Here, Julia," she said. "This is my wedding present for you. Open it."

Julia opened the envelope and saw that it held some paper money. There were ten one-hundred dollar bills—a thousand dollars. So though Grandma Auer was saving and thrifty, never wasting anything, she could be generous.

For certainly Grandma Auer did not approve of what she considered foolish extravagance. When my father was courting my mother, he sent her on Valentine's Day a large heart made of fresh red roses set upon a gilt easel. Of course Julia was delighted but Grandma Auer gave the expensive but useless gift a sour look and said:

"Das kann Mann nicht essen!" ("You can't eat that!" In other words "What a waste of good money."). . . .

Delia's Pranks

My mother remembered her oldest sister, Delia, who was six years her senior, as perhaps the liveliest of the little Cohen girls, but certainly not the brightest in school.

The school day was divided into two parts: German studies in the morning and English in the afternoon. So Delia spent the mornings paying not the slightest attention to what Herr Damas was trying to teach (the little boys in the class changed the teacher's name to the English Mr. Damn Ass) and muttering when she thought the teacher could not hear, the German school-boy rhyme:

> Lehrer mit ein basensteil,
> Klopft die Kinder gar zu fiel,
> "Gar—zu—fiel" is ungezunt.
> Lehrer is ein Dumkopf!

> (Teacher with a broomstick,
> Hits the children entirely too much.
> "Too—much" is unhealthy.
> Teacher is a dunce!)

Of course Herr Damas knew what she was saying, only pretending not to notice, but it did not serve to make him more kindly in his attitude to this inattentive student of his language lessons.

Then one day he noticed that Delia had opened the German newspaper in front of her face as if she were hiding something. He marched angrily down the aisle and snatched the paper away and there Delia was revealed. Instead of studying the paper she was using it to hide the fact that she was breaking the strict rule against eating in class, for she had peeled and was eating a large soft banana.

Herr Damas was completely outraged. He pulled Delia out from her desk, grasped the soft banana and, as it turned into a shapeless mass in his hands, rubbed it into the little girl's hair. Then he sent her home.

This incident made Grandma Cohen (Delia's mother) decide to send Delia to a private school. The school she chose was a Catholic girls' school, but my mother did not remember which one. She only knew that Delia was the only one of the children to go to a private school. This was a hundred years ago and at that time many Sisters' schools specialized in fine needlework. So

Delia was taught to do cross-stitch on canvas. Each little student was assigned a holy picture to complete during the term. The Catholic girls were given representations of the various events in the life of the Virgin Mary, but the Sisters, very kindly and wisely, gave the little Jewish girl, Delia, a Jewish scene from the Old Testament. It was "Moses in the Bulrushes." (I myself, often saw the framed two-foot-by-three-foot piece of needlework, when I visited my aunt in her later years.) The embroidered picture showed the blue Nile, with lush green foliage on its banks and large brown bulrushes in the stream. The sky was blue, also, and on the left-hand bank of the Nile stood Pharoah's daughter and two of her maidens in bright-colored robes, while on the right-hand bank, Miriam, older sister of Moses, was half-hidden, as she watched over the floating cradle that held the baby, Moses.

All the above parts of the picture were worked in a large cross-stitch, in wool, but the hands and faces of the women and the baby's body were worked in a much smaller stitch in flesh-colored silk. Also, Pharoah's daughter had a necklace of tiny gold beads about her neck.

My mother always said that Delia did the coarse wool cross-stitch, but she knew the Sisters must have done the delicate silk work on hands and faces.

I am sure that "Moses in the Bulrushes" still exists somewhere. Amy Leiser treasured it and had it hanging in her bedroom until she passed away.

The year my mother was eight years old and Delia was fourteen, Delia decided to go out begging on Purim evening, for the Purim Festival is celebrated by children by masquerading and collecting presents. But Delia decided to do an almost unheard of thing. She blackened her face and dressed up in a pair of her father's pants, although for a woman to go out in the street in pants was, a hundred years ago, considered more indecent and shocking than "streaking" is now. But Delia was well-camouflaged by the too-large pants and her blackened face. She went about the neighborhood holding out her hands and saying

> Gut Purim, gut Purim, mein leibe Leut.
> Vissen Sie niche vas Purim bedeut?

"Purim" bedeut ein lange leben.
Unt vollen Sie mir ein bissel Gelt geben?

(Good Purim, good Purim, my dear people.
Do you not know what Purim means?
"Purim" means a long life.
And will you please give me a little money?)

It was the little German verse Grandma Auer had taught the Cohen children.

Delia was having a good time and she was sure no one would recognize her. But, just at this time, Wolf Cohen, her father, was returning from a lodge meeting. He noticed the masked figure in the pants, but had no idea it could possibly be one of his young-lady daughters. Yet something about it seemed familiar. All at once, he realized it was the pants. They were made of a woolen material with a peculiar design and they certainly had to be the very pair he had tailored for himself of that very material, because none of his customers had liked the cloth, so that he decided to use it himself. At first Wolf Cohen thought someone had stolen his pants and then, looking closer, he saw that it was his oldest daughter who was wearing them.

My mother told me her father was so angry with Delia "he almost killed her," and I really think it was this incident that influenced him to move from his house on Vine Street near Eighth to a quieter neighborhood and build another house on Richmond Street. Because he realized the "night life" of Vine Street made it an improper place to bring up his six daughters.

53

SOPHIA HELLER GOLDSMITH: COURTSHIP AND MARRIAGE
1861–1865

Sophia Heller Goldsmith was a babe in arms, less than a year old, when her parents brought her to this country in the late 1840's. Her father, a cattle dealer, had been compelled to leave his Bohemian village home because of personal enmities and costly litigation. The family settled down in pioneer Milwaukee in the days when Indians still camped in the nearby hills.

When Sophia was only thirteen years old, she met the young immigrant destined to become her husband. He was Phillip Goldsmith, a handsome "man with a black mole on his back." She fell in love with him, and four years later they were married.

The recollections of the later business adventures of the family are a record of bitter hardship, constant struggle, and an indomitable desire to make good. Sophia stood shoulder to shoulder with her husband, reared a large family, and though almost crushed by constant illness and disease, worked in store and factory with him to help him attain the success that was finally his.

By 1878, the Goldsmiths had crossed the Ohio at Cincinnati and settled in Covington, Kentucky, where they manufactured doll bodies, toys, and baseballs. Between rearing and burying children, Sophia dressed dolls and sewed baseballs in the factory. But by 1885 they were on their feet, and when Phillip was drowned in 1894, the Goldsmiths were wealthy. Years later, the boys, carrying on the family business, built it into one of the great sporting-goods manufacturing concerns of the country: MacGregor Sports Products, Inc.

These memoirs were written in 1908 and continued in 1918. Despite the fact that at birth she was "as small as a doll" and weighed but a pound and a half, Sophia reached the ripe old age of eighty-one, surrounded by a large and affectionate family. She was in all truth "a woman of valor," and well might "her children have risen up to call her blessed."

9. Sophia Heller

Milwaukee: Indians Were Many

I was brought into the world with a nervous system, weighing one pound and a half, as small as a doll. I was wrapped in cotton for many months, and it was marvelous that I could live. I was born Nov. 16, to [in] Zitov [Citow], Bohemia, 1848. Many a time mother related how she feared, during the six-weeks' voyage on a sailing vessel, that I would die. But it seemed the little being was to live for some purpose, nursing the grief from [a] mother who had been raised in wealth, coming to such trials [which] were sad for her, and I had to suffer for it, as my constitution was poisoned by such nourishment. Poor mother did not know then but [in] later years, often, she spoke of it why I was so nervous.

June 1848 [1849], we landed in Milwaukee, then a city four or five years old. Indians were many, and I remember my parents dealt with them. Toil and labor and much suffering and hardship was their [my parents'] lot; with 25¢ in their pocket. . . .

In 1858 a larger temple was erected. I was then about ten years of age. Dr. I. M. Wise was asked to dedicate the temple. The Jewish community was in one excitement to have such a learned man come from Cincinnati to our city. He was invited to our house and his stay was a short one. He only called, and how well I remember him as a young man. Two girls and myself were the happy children robed in white with baskets of flowers. We walked in front of Dr. Wise as he carried the *Safratorah* ["Scroll of the Law"] around in the temple. We strewed flowers in front of him.

Mother had presented the temple with a *Shulchendeck* now called the alter [cloth]. Same was made of red silk velvet and embroidered in gold. Father had bought the best seat in the temple. How big I felt! It was quite an honor to see my parents so prosperous. About seven years later I was married in the same temple.

I grew to be a tall girl but slender. Between twelve and thirteen I went to swimming school. In 1861, one summer day, not being able to take the usual hour at seven in the morning, which was our usual hour for instruction for girls, a friend and I went in the afternoon till four o'clock for girls. We rushed through dressing as it was time for the boys' turn. [I was] standing on the platform waiting for my friend as she came towards me, saying: "Sophia, look at that handsome fellow." Of course, I was not slow in doing same. I saw the back and profile of the young man with a black mole on his back. I answered: "O, Amelia, isn't he handsome?" He had turned so I could see his rosy face. We spoke about him on our way home and after that he was forgotten.

A few weeks later Mr. and Mrs. [Nathan?] Pereles, old friends of ours, with their three boys (they never went without them), Franklin, Madison, and Jefferson, named after our Presidents, this family stopped at our house to ask if mother would join them at the swimming school. Behold, who was with them but the handsome young fellow with the mole on his back. My heart gave a bound. He was introduced to us as their nephew Phillip Goldsmith. He had come from the old country. That I could see in his clothes. We met occasionally after that going to the swimming school.

Did Not My Heart Give a Bound!

Time past [passed]. I never saw him again. Winter came. As my brother Adolph enjoyed dancing, he was a very big boy at the age of sixteen, therefore [he] joined the Saturday-evening class. I was a natural-born dancer and would rather have danced than eaten. In the winter, 1861, mother, brother, and myself attended Saturday-evening class at Mr. Vesie's dancing school, Milwaukee. Previous to that I occasionally went on Wednesday afternoon and took lessons for fancy dancing and made use of that knowledge on several occasions.

At those times children gave ballads [ballets] in private charity balls. On one of these Saturday evenings, as before mentioned, I was as usual sitting next to mother opposite the door. The door opened opposite us and Uncle Pereles' wife and sons entered and, behold, my Phillip likewise. How happy I was! If he only could and would dance with me, were my thoughts. After their wraps were taken off they joined us. Mr. Goldsmith asked me to dance.

I assure you he was a fine dancer. He and I enjoyed dancing together. For week after week we met every Saturday evening. I thought him handsomer every time I saw him. I was too young to realize anything else but his pretty face. In those days there were no letter carriers so I used to go to the post office. One day I met Mr. Goldsmith with a large tin notion box in one hand and a large heavy bundle of dry goods tied in a striped ticking on one shoulder, peddling. We were both embarrased.

One year passed. Then he took sick in a hotel with no one to care for him. He upbraided me because I did not call. The rich Uncle and Aunt Pereles had forgotten him. . . . The second year of our acquaintance came around; I went to school. Mr. Goldsmith gave up peddling.

I always made excuses that the bridge was open when I came home late from school. Instead I had to get a glimpse of my handsome friend and walked squares to pass the store he clerked in. I stopped school at age of thirteen without sufficient education. What I learned later was through my own effort and ambition. A self-made woman.

By this time people commenced to talk we would be a couple, and so on. My parents took me to a masquerade ball. I wore a handsome satin costume and represented the goddess of liberty, for which I got a prize. Mr. G. was there but did not dance as often as usual with me. I was offended, and [in] later years he told me it was on account of the people's talk. My pride suffered. I was distant toward him when we met after that. In the meantime I saw no more of Mr. G. He had left the city, and clerked at Mr. Stein's in Waukashaw [Waukesha, Wisconsin], the former Judge [Philip] Stein of Chicago's brother. . . .

One summer evening . . . about 6:30 P.M., I happened to look across the street. Behold, who did I see but Mr. Goldsmith. Well, did not my heart give a bound! With all that, I had not forgotten how he had slighted me. Instead of going his way, he turned around about halfway; crossed over to speak to me. I treated him cooly yet I was glad to see him, but he never knew it. After that I saw him occasionally. He again disappeared from my sight. Time passed. . . .

Father Said: "Kiss Each Other."

As I came to my brother's store [in Chicago] he told me he gave Mr. Goldsmith permission to take me for a drive. Mr. Alex Goldsmith, his wife, and young baby in one buggy, and I in another with Mr. G. We drove ten miles to the Insane Asylumn which was also [a] home for old folks where Mrs. A. G. had a grandmother. That evening I went with Mr. Goldsmith to German theatre. During the acts he took out of his pocket an unusual large apple which he cut in two. In those days it was customary to do that and also to bring knitting. . . .

That evening Mr. Goldsmith took me to my first English performance. I was very nervous, as I had gone without my parents' knowledge, as in those days children always went with their parents' consent. I left for Milwaukee next day.

Mr. G. requested me to correspond with him. I told him he would have to get permission from my parents first. It would be wiser if children nowadays showed so much regard for their parents' opinion; there would not be so many mistakes in marriages and other unhappy affairs of the present century.

The following Sunday, Oct. 30, 1864, my brother Albert was married in the Temple Benyeshurum [B'ne Jeshurun], Milwaukee. Three months had elapsed, and I was sent to Chicago again to assist my sister-in-law to sew little clothes, as well as assist in the store, as they could not afford help. Brother had a friend by the name of Wetzler who was in love with me. Many years later Mr. Cairo, our former traveling man, met him as a well-to-do businessman in Missouri. Mr. Wetzler told Mr. Cairo how much he had loved me and that he had proposed and was refused.

I was busy one day and who should come to see me but Mr. P. G. There was a great deal of rivalry between the two men. Time passed and I left for home. Mother came to Chicago and much attention was paid her by Mr. Alex G. Her consent was given for us to correspond.

Finally I was sent on again [to Chicago] to be an assistant, as my sister-in-law was not in the best of health. Mr. G. had opened a dry goods store next to my brother's with his brother Alex as partner.

We saw a great deal of one another. Mr. G. heard I was in the city, and it happened during the time Pres. Lincoln was assassinated, April 14, 1865. He lay in state in the courthouse. I can't dwell on the crowds that went to see him but one thing I want to mention. Mr. G. insisted that I take his arm as the crowd was so large, but I was so timid I halfway refused but finally had to consent in order not to be separated. In those days if a girl was seen on the arm of a gentleman she was considered to be an engaged girl and, as usual, his sister-in-law had to see us. She had other views for him with her sister.

Mr. G. proposed. I would not give definite answer until my parents were consulted. As I was determined not to break the vow made years ago, I put Mr. G. off from time to time with my excuse that I was too young, as I was little over fifteen years of age. At that time a girl of twenty was considered an old maid. Early marriages was the custom. . . .

After a lengthy correspondence with my parents, Mr. G. at last received their consent to our engagement. Mr. G. could not leave his business at the time. Father came on to Chicago to give us his blessing. That evening my father, brother Albert, and his wife went to Mr. Alex Goldsmith's home, which was over their store. Brother Albert had but a few rooms, so could not have the celebration there. As we arrived a Mr. Lehman, his young wife, a very rich fur dealer, were there, also a devoted friend, Mr. Adolph Stumas, and a few friends of A. Goldsmith. A swell supper was served at papa's expense. Champagne was served, which was quite scarce at that time.

We were all seated. I was quite embarrassed, like a schoolgirl, so shy. Father asked Mr. G. if he would have me for his future wife before everybody; then asked me if I would have Mr. G. I turned all colors, not expecting this. After answering, my father said: "Kiss each other." This was quite embarassing. Mr. P. G. placed a ring, rather three rings in one, "two hands over two hearts and same was closed," it was the emblem of love on my finger, and he kissed me.

At a very late hour we broke the gathering up. Mr. Stumas, the intimate friend of P. G., took us home at two-thirty in the morning from this celebration. On the way he took two hands full of silver coins and threw it in the air for the luck of the young couple. . . .

My dear Phillip and I saw each other at least a couple of hours each day, after his store was closed. The parting came again. Weeks passed. Mother and I left Chicago. My parents consented to let the marriage take place, as we two children were lonesome for want of seeing each other. Your father was then only twenty-one, and I sixteen years and nine months on the wedding day. After three months' engagement our marriage took place August 27th, 1865, in the Temple Beneyeshurum on Fourth Street, Milwaukee, Wis., on a beautiful Sunday at 2:00 P.M. The sky was blue and silvery. Arriving at the temple, we found it filled to its capacity. I little realized the step I was taking, and when the choir began to sing, the tears rolled down my cheeks and I did not know whyfore. At home the table was set for fifty guests. Rabbi Faulk [S. Falk] was the minister and my former teacher. The following Tuesday, Aug. 29th, 1865, papa [Phillip Goldsmith] and I left for Chicago, where he had rented a large four-room flat for $25 per month, on State near Harrison, at that time a fashionable street.

My parents gave me a $300 check as a present, for which we bought furniture consisting of haircloth parlor set, bedroom furniture, and kitchen, and woolen, damask-upholstered chairs, and etc. And a piano and sundries were given me as a present on my following birthday, Nov. 16th. Wednesday, the thirtieth of Aug., papa [my husband] took me to my future home, expecting many of our cases, etc. As I looked under the sink in the kitchen I was surprised to find a mother cat with five little ones. I was as happy as a child to play with them. Our first dinner in our home was ice cream and cake. I started housekeeping with $3 a week. Our house was gradually put in order, arranged prettily, and we were two happy children.

54

CIVIL WAR RELIEF ASSOCIATIONS
1861–1863

On December 25, 1860, a number of German Jewesses created a general relief society which came to be known as the Ladies' Hebrew Relief Sewing Association of Philadelphia. Before a year had passed, the Civil War erupted, and these women not only continued their family welfare work—primarily the distribution of clothing—but also began making lint and bandages for the wounded. Dr. Jacob Solis Cohen (1838–1927) was the Association's volunteer physician. Before another year had passed, the good doctor himself had joined the army and was soon appointed an assistant surgeon. Postbellum years would see him become one of the country's most distinguished laryngologists. In 1862, the Association's secretary, Isaac M. Long, resigned to enter the armed forces. These German women, mostly immigrants, not only had a male secretary, but also a male board of advisers. Societal administration was still foreign to them; they sought guidance from experienced men.

Encouraged by the Reverend Sabato Morais of Mikveh Israel, a group of Philadelphia women, natives and older settlers for the most part, created the Ladies' Hebrew Association for the Relief of Sick and Wounded Union Soldiers. This was in May 1863. The new organization, affiliated with the nondenominational, semi-official Sanitary Commission, worked primarily to succor veterans and their destitute families. Soldiers in the hospitals were supplied with clothing, food, stationery, and tobacco.

Document A is a copy of the first annual report of the Ladies' Hebrew Relief Sewing Association; document B is a June 1863 newspaper account of the Ladies' Hebrew Association for the Relief of Sick and Wounded Union Soldiers.

A

1861

LADIES' HEBREW RELIEF SEWING ASSOCIATION OF PHILADELPHIA. . . .

To the Hon. President and the Members of the Ladies' Hebrew Relief Sewing Association:

The following report is most respectfully submitted:

Our Association has passed the first year of its existence. We are assembled for purposes concerning its welfare, and I am pleased to announce the triumphant success which our organization has attained, especially as we have labored under many difficulties. The year which has just ended is without parallel in the history of want and suffering, and the worst of calamities, a civil war, pervades our land; it has thrown distress and want in our midst, and we have experienced a wide field in which to spread the welcome hand of aid and comfort. Our co-religionists have also increased largely, and among them distress has left a bitter mark.

You who enjoy pleasant homes and cheerful firesides cannot realize the existing want and suffering which surround you. The earth is like a sea, many being thrown upon the tumultous billows of life without a mite for their comfort. To be kind and charitable are attributes of our national [Jewish] character; thus inspired were all those who so cheerfully responded to the call for the formation of our society, and beyond expectations have we been successful.

Our weekly meetings have been invariably well attended, while a spirit of ardor and cheerfulness prevailed. A large amount of work had been prepared—the same distributed to the deserving poor by competent visiting committees. Patriotism has also found its way among us. Having kind remembrances for those brave ones who have sacrificed all for their country's honor, extra meetings have been held and a large quantity of lint and bandages manufactured for the sick and wounded of those regiments which have been the recipients of the same.

Especially would I call your attention to the untiring efforts of the "Committee on Donations" who spared no pains in accumulating as large an amount as possible, which in these stringent times has been a fact bordering on impossibility. We reside in a country where religious persecution is unknown, and thankful to those who have lent us a helping hand, even persons not of our persuasion, have received what aid we found it in our power to bestow.

Your board of directors have used every effort for the promotion and welfare of the society. Several vacancies having occured by resignations, the same have been filled by regular elections; and in all particulars the utmost discretion has been adopted. Nothing has been done conflicting with similar institutions, but a spirit of co-operation has always been advised with the kindred feeling that in union there is power.

The resignation of the President, Mrs. S. STERNBERGER, is to be regretted. It is evident that it was her desire to see the society prosper, and to that end she exerted herself with a zeal seldom manifested. She well merits the kindest wishes and thanks of the association.

The Association, under the supervision of your Board of Directors, have distributed the following to the deserving poor of the city:—856 finished Garments, 150 pairs of Shoes, 75 pairs of Hose, 20 heavy Blankets, 2,283 yards of Calico, Flannel &c., and 12 entire suits of Boys' Clothes.

This will be found a very flattering result for a Society having but just reached the end of the first year. It is also proper to state that the greatest care has been taken, in order to avoid any deception on the part of applicants while at the same time all who were actually in need, received plentifully.

Dr. J. SOLIS COHEN kindly tendered his professional services; he attended to many poor invalids. He deserves the hearty thanks and approbation of the Association. The receipts for regular dues have reached the amount of $551—this would have been somewhat more had not several delinquencies occured on the part of members failing to pay their regular dues.

The amount of Donations received in cash was $455, besides a large amount of Merchandise. This, it is evident, has been a helping hand to our Association, and it is to be hoped, that the success will be equally as great in the forthcoming year.

The entire outlay during the year has been $844.55, leaving a balance on hand of $151.45.

Our members at present number three hundred and nine. The accessions to the roll have been quite numerous during the year, and it is to be hoped that the same will not be diminished. All should exert themselves to the utmost, and in no instance should the payment of dues be neglected. It is to be hoped that every member will assist in increasing the numerical strength of our Association.

Compare your happy homes and cheerful firesides, to the dreary and unprotected homes of the poor. You, who have not witnessed the ravages of that stern agent "want," cannot realize the horrors of destitution. The object of our Association is a noble one—"*to alleviate in part the suffering surrounding us.*" We should be infinitely thankful to an almighty power, for placing in our hands the means of doing good. We have been successful, and our labors have merited the most flattering results. How many homes (for years the scene of poverty and degradation) have been revived and made cheerful through our agency. After witnessing such scenes can any one hesitate in offering up his mite on the great altar of charity! We must obey a high ordeal, let us do it cheerfully.

Our Association is about to enter a new period of its existence. Let us hope that success may light its path, and that it may yet rank first among the Jewish Charitable Institutions of the country.

ISAAC M. LONG,
Recording Secretary.

B

JUNE 26, 1863

A Charitable and Praiseworthy Organization.—A short time since, a number of Jewish ladies of this City conceived the idea of forming a society from among their own number for the relief of the sick and wounded soldiers irrespective to religious creed. They held their first meeting on the 18th of this month, and again convened last evening having in the interim obtained the names of two hundred and fifty to be placed on the roll as members. The title of the society as now formed, is "The Ladies Hebrew Association for the Relief of Sick and Wounded Union Soldiers." By the payment of fifty cents any lady or gentleman can become an annual contributing member. The President is Miss Celia Myers.

The object of the society is to obviate the sufferings of the brave soldiers, by providing them with delicacies and clothing while they lie in the army hospitals. Appeal is made to the patriotic and benevolent to aid them. This can be done in many ways. Anything adapted to the wants of the soldiers will be very acceptable. The society's board of managers will meet every month, and their executive committee every week, or oftener if it be necessary. The annual meetings will convene on the 4th of July.

55

THE MATRON OF CHIMBORAZO
1862–1863

One of the daughters of Jacob C. Levy, of Charleston and Savannah, was Phoebe Yates Levy, who in 1856, at the age of thirty-three, married a Gentile, Thomas Noyes Pember, of Boston. Pember died five years later, and when Phoebe Pember appeared on the scene in 1861, she was already a widow.

Jacob C. Levy had done a good job in educating his children. Certainly his daughters, Eugenia and Phoebe, wrote beautifully; Samuel Yates Levy, his son, was something of a poet, and the father himself was the author of a very interesting apologia for Judaism, still in manuscript. Forced by need to support herself, Phoebe Pember became a matron of the Chimborazo Hospital in Richmond, a complex of wards that sheltered about 7,000 sick and wounded soldiers.

From her autobiography and her extant letters, it is abundantly clear that Phoebe had few social contacts with the "new" German Jews— immigrants—who were to be found everywhere in the South. It is interesting to note that while she dropped the family name Levy, she did retain the name—Yates—of her maternal Anglo-Jewish forebears. Her associates were nearly all Gentiles, and she moved in the highest social circles in the Confederacy. Among her closest friends were Confederate Secretary of War George W. Randolph and his wife, with whom she lived for some time in wartime Richmond; Mrs. Randolph was responsible for Mrs. Pember's appointment as matron at the Chimborazo Hospital.

Judging from her writings—and, of course, from her own marriage—Mrs. Pember had no objection whatsoever to intermarriage; yet, as her father's daughter, she was conscious, if not proud. of her ancestral faith—of her "church."

The following excerpts from her autobiography recount her experiences as matron at Chimborazo.

10. Phoebe Yates Pember

Courtesy, McCowat-Mercer Press, Jackson, Tennessee

. . . Pleasant episodes often occurred to vary disappointments and lighten duties.

"Kin you writ me a letter?" drawled a whining voice from a bed in one of the wards, a cold day in '62.

The speaker was an up-country Georgian, one of the kind called "Goubers" [peanuts] by the soldiers generally; lean, yellow, attennuated, with wispy strands of hair hanging over his high, thin cheek-bones. He put out a hand to detain me and the nails were like claws.

"Why do you not let the nurse cut your nails?"

"Because I aren't got any spoon, and I use them instead."

"Will you let me have your hair cut then? You can't get well with all that dirty hair hanging about your eyes and ears."

"No, I can't git my hear cut, kase as how I promised my mammy that I would let it grow till the war be over. Oh, it's onlucky to cut it!"

"Then I can't write any letter for you. Do what I wish you to do, and then I will oblige you."

This was plain talking. The hair was cut (I left the nails for another day), my portfolio brought, and sitting by the side of his bed I waited for further orders. They came with a formal introduction: for Mrs. Marthy Brown.

My dear Mammy:

I hope this finds you well, as it leaves me well, and I hope that I shall git a furlough Christmas and come and see you, and I hope that you will keep well, and all the folks be well by that time, as I hopes to be well myself. This leaves me in good health as I hope it finds you and—

But here I paused, as his mind seemed to be going round in a circle, and asked him a few questions about his home, his position during the last summer's campaign, how he got sick, and where his brigade was at that time. Thus furnished with some material to work upon, the letter proceeded rapidly. Four sides were conscientiously filled, for no soldier would think a letter worth sending home that showed any blank paper. Transcribing his name, the number of his ward and proper address, so that an answer might reach him—the composition was read to him. Gradually his pale face brightened, a sitting posture was assumed with difficulty (for, in spite of his determined effort in his letter "to be well," he was far from convalescence). As I folded and directed it, contributed the expected five-cent stamp, and handed it to him, he gazed cautiously around to be sure there were no listeners.

"Did you writ all that?" he asked, whispering, but with great emphasis.

"Yes."

"Did *I* say all that?"

"I think you did."

A long pause of undoubted admiration—astonishment ensued. What was working in that poor mind? Could it be that Psyche had stirred one of the delicate plumes of her wing and touched that dormant soul?

"Are you married?" The harsh voice dropped very low.

"I am not. At least, I am a widow."

He rose still higher in bed. He pushed away desperately the tangled hay on his brow. A faint color fluttered over the hollow cheek, and stretching out a long piece of bone with a talon attached, he gently touched my arm and with constrained voice whispered mysteriously:

"You wait!"

And readers, I *am* waiting still; and I here caution the male portion of creation who may adore through their mental powers to respect my confidence, and not seek to shake my constancy. . . .

At intervals the lower wards, unused except in times of great need, for they were unfurnished with any comforts, would be filled with rough soldiers from camp sent to recuperate after field service, who may not have seen a female face for months; and though generally too much occupied to notice them much, their partly concealed but determined regard would become embarrassing. One day while directing arrangements with a ward-master, my attention was attracted by the pertinacious staring of a rough-looking Texan. He walked round and round me in rapidly narrowing circles, examing every detail of my dress, face, and figure; his eye never fixing upon any particular part for a moment but traveling incessantly all over me. It seemed the wonder of the mind at the sight of a new creation. I moved my position; he shifted his to suit the new arrangement—again a change was made, so obviously to get out of his range of vision, that with a delicacy of feeling that the roughest men always treated me with, he desisted from his inspection so far, that though his person made no movement, his neck twisted round to accommodate his eyes, till I supposed some progenitor of his family had been an owl. The men began to titter, and my patience became exhausted.

"What is the matter, my man? Did you never see a woman before?"

"Jerusalem!" he ejaculated, not making the slightest motion towards withdrawing his determined notice, "I never did see such a nice one. Why, you's as pretty as a pair of red shoes with green strings."

These were the two compliments laid upon the shrine of my vanity during four years' contact with thousands of patients, and commit them to paper to stand as a visionary portrait, to prove to my readers that a woman with attractions similar to a pair of red shoes with green strings must have some claim to the apple of Paris [in the Homeric epic].

Scenes of pathos occurred daily—scenes that wrung the heart and forced the dew of pity from the eyes; but feeling that enervated the mind and relaxed the body was a sentimental luxury that was not to be indulged in. There was too much work to be done, too much active exertion required, to allow the mental or physical powers to succumb. They were severely taxed each day. Perhaps they balanced, and so kept each other from sinking. There was, indeed, but little leisure to sentimentalize, the necessity for action being ever present.

After the battle of Fredericksburg [where the Union sustained a defeat in December, 1862], while giving small doses of brandy to a dying man, a low, pleasant voice said, "Madam." It came from a youth not over eighteen years of age, seeming very ill, but so placid, with that earnest, far-away gaze, so common to the eyes of those who are looking their last on this world. Does God in his mercy give a glimpse of coming peace, past understanding, that we see reflected in the dying eyes into which we look with such strong yearning to fathom what they see? He shook his head in negative to all offers of food or drink or suggestions of softer pillows and lighter covering.

"I want Perry," was his only wish.

On inquiry I found that Perry was the friend and companion who marched by his side in the field and slept next to him in camp, but of whose whereabouts I was ignorant. Armed with a requisition from our surgeon, I sought him among the sick and wounded at all the other hospitals. I found him at Camp Jackson put him in my ambulance, and on arrival at my own hospital found my patient had dropped asleep. A bed was brought and placed at his side, and Perry, only slightly wounded, laid upon it. Just then the sick boy awoke wearily, turned over, and the half-unconscious eye fixed itself. He must have been dreaming of the meeting, for he still distrusted the reality. Illness had spiritualized the youthful face; the transparent forehead, the delicate brow so clearly defined, belonged more to heaven than earth. As he recognized his comrade the wan and expressionless lips curved into the happiest smile—the angel of death had brought the light of summer skies to that pale face. "Perry!" he cried, "Perry!" and not another word, but with one last effort he threw himself into his friend's arms, the radiant eyes closed, but the smile still remained—he was dead.

Feminine sympathy being much more demonstrative than masculine, particularly when compared with a surgeon's unresponsiveness, who, inured to the aspects of suffering, has more control over his professional feelings, the nurses often summoned me when only the surgeon was needed. One very cold night . . . [in] 1863, when sleeping at my hospital rooms, an answer was made to my demand as to who was knocking and what was wanted. The nurse from the nearest ward said something was wrong with Fisher. Instructing him to find the doctor immediately and hastily getting on some clothing I hurried to the scene, for Fisher was an especial favorite. He was quite a young man, of about twenty years of age, who had been wounded ten months previously very severely, high up on the leg near the hip, and who by dint of hard nursing, good food, and plenty of stimulant had been given a fair chance for recovery. The bones of the broken leg had slipped together, then lapped, and nature, anxious as she always is to help herself, had thrown a ligature across, uniting the severed parts; but after some time the side curved out, and the wounded leg was many inches shorter than its fellow. He had been the object of sedulous care on the part of all—surgeons, ward-master, nurse, and matron, and the last effort made to assist him was by the construction of an open cylinder of pasteboard, made in my kitchen, of many sheets of coarse brown paper, cemented together with very stiff paste, and baked around the stove-pipe. This was to clasp by its own prepared curve the deformed hip, and be a support for it when he was able to use his crutches.

He had remained through all his trials stout, fresh, and hearty, interesting in appearance, and so gentle-mannered and uncomplaining that we all loved him. Supported on his crutches, he had walked up and down his ward for the first time since he was wounded, and seemed almost restored. That same night he turned over and uttered an exclamation of pain.

Following the nurse to his bed and turning down the covering, a small jet of blood spurted up. The sharp edge of the splintered bone must have severed an artery. I instantly put my finger on the little orifice and awaited the surgeon. He soon came—took a long look and shook his head. The explanation was easy; the artery was imbedded in the fleshy part of the thigh and could not be taken up. No earthly power could save him.

There was no object in detaining Dr. ———. He required his time and his strength, and long I sat by the boy, unconscious himself that any serious trouble was apprehended. The hardest trial of my duty was laid upon me; the necessity of telling a man in the prime of life and fullness of strength that there was no hope for him.

It was done at last and the verdict received patiently and courageously, some directions given by which his mother would be informed of his death, and then he turned his questioning eyes upon my face.

"How long can I live?"

"Only as long as I keep my finger upon this artery." A pause ensued. God alone knew what thoughts hurried through that heart and brain, called so unexpectedly from all earthly hopes and ties. He broke the silence at last.

"You can let go."

But I could not. Not if my own life had trembled in the balance. Hot tears rushed to my eyes, a surging sound to my ears, and a deathly coldness to my lips. The pang of obeying him was spared me and for the first and last time during the trials that surrounded me for four years, I fainted away.

56

CLARA L. MOSES: WAR DAYS IN OLD NATCHEZ
1863–1865

In 1929, Mrs. Clara Lowenburg Moses (1865–1951), a native of Natchez, Mississippi, published a collection of memoirs and stories for her nieces and nephews. She had no children of her own, and after the death of her husband, Abram Moses, lived with relatives. The children called her Aunt Sister. In the following excerpt, Aunt Mellie's story, Clara Moses portrayed the fortunes of her grandparents, the John Mayers, as told to her by Aunt Melanie Mayer Frank. This account gives us an intimate, romantic picture of life in a Mississippi town during the Civil War period.

AUNT MELLIE'S STORY OF THE WAR BETWEEN THE STATES

In the beginning of the year 1800, one of your great-great-grandparents, dear children, lived in Landau, France. His name was Simon Levy, and he and his wife, Jeanette Rachel Mayer, were comfortable and happy with their three sons and one daughter. But one of the boys was dissatisfied at home, and so ran away and settled in Paris where he apprenticed himself to a shoemaker and became a master of his trade. He was so afraid his father would find him and make him come home that he changed his name from Mayer Levy to Jacob Mayer. But his life in Paris during the 1820's was anything but pleasant and he soon decided to embark for America.

One bright morning in October, 1833, a sailing vessel, hailing from Havre de Grace, landed at Nouvelle Orléans [New Orleans], after a most unpleasant voyage of ninety days, during which time the provisions and water became so scarce that each person aboard ship received only a small portion daily.

Among the passengers was Jeanette Reis, a beautiful French girl of fifteen years, who with her parents, sisters, and brother had come to the New World believing that there Dame Fortune would be kinder to them than she had been in Obernai or

Auperney, France. Jacob Mayer, now a young man of twenty-seven, was also one of the many passengers. During the voyage, he had often been attracted by the grace and beauty of the young French girl, and before the end of the journey had discovered that an affinity of souls existed between them. It seemed to be a work of destiny in the lives of these two emigrants to a foreign land, for as each became a resident of Nouvelle Orléans their friendship became strengthened, and gradually ripened into a love companionship for life. On the twenty-fifth of April, 1835, Jeanette Reis and Jacob Mayer were married, and they, dear children, are your great-grandparents.

During the first five years of a most happy union, while still living in Nouvelle Orléans, two sons and a daughter, Maurice, Emma, and Simon, were born to them.

Shortly after, in 1841, they moved to Natchez, Mississippi, and the other children who came to bless and enliven their home were Caroline, Ophelia, your grandmother, Henry, Clementine, Melanie (myself), Adelaide, Theresa, John Jr., Benjamin, Eleanor Louisa, and Joseph Eggleston Johnston.

John, as he was now called, worked diligently at his trade and eventually built up a fine business in which the elder sons were able to assist. The daughters, beautiful and lovely girls, attracted many friends, and life seemed only made for fun and gayety, music, dancing, and songs. . . .

After the fall of Vicksburg, in July, 1863, the Yankees took possession of Natchez. At this time Henry Frank, Isaac Lowenburg, and John Hill came into our family life and helped to make its history. They were in the commissary department of the Union Army. They had visited our father at his store, the two former making themselves known as Jews, and father, the president of the Hebrew [*Hebra*] *Kadusha* ["Holy Brotherhood"] Congregation, invited them to attend the services during the Holy Days. We had no temple nor weekly services, but during Roshashona and Yom Kippur ["New Year" and "Day of Atonement"] some of the members officiated at services held upstairs in the old engine house on North Union Street.

Father invited these new acquaintances to visit his family, and, being cordially received, they became frequent visitors. Many were the heated discussions between these Yankees and our rebel family, until mother forbade political wrangling, but encouraged social affinity, prompted by her usual tact and good sense, to say nothing of her clever foresight, for two of these hated Yankees became loved and loving sons to our dear parents.

Once during the war the soldier boys had written home that they needed boots, shoes, socks, shirts, trousers, everything, it seemed, but how could such contraband goods be sent to Confederate soldiers? A fine scheme was planned. Our friend, Henry Frank, promised to get passes for mother, Emma, and Carrie to pass through the Union guards at the city limits, where friends living in the country would meet them and forward the clothes. Fortunately, the women in those days wore great hoop skirts, and under these, around their waists, mother, Emma, and Carrie hung all the needed articles. Thus laden, they were helped into the carriage and were driven to the city limits where the passes had to be examined. With fear and trembling Emma handed the guard the papers. Imagine her delight when she noticed that he was trying to read them upside down! "Any contraband goods?" and all being fair in love and war, they answered "No." "Drive on then and have a nice day with your friends," was the pleasant rejoinder of the ignorant unsuspecting guard. . . .

Shortly after the surrender at Vicksburg of Pemberton's Confederate Army to General Grant, General [T. E. G.] Ransom with his brigade was sent to take possession of Natchez. His headquarters were in the beautiful Wilson home overlooking the river. Natchez was under martial law. General Ransom was a gentleman, considerate of the humiliation of a conquered people, and soon won the favor and esteem of the citizens, but after several months he was ordered to take charge of some other post, and General [Mason] Brayman placed in his command at Natchez. Not content to occupy the same headquarters used by General Ransom, he chose the stately home of George Malen Davis, later occupied by Stanton College. General Brayman was a true type of the selfish conqueror: he had not the courage to be strong and firm yet kind to the subdued; he rejoiced in the distress which the cruel war brought to our fair Southland, and to its noble men and women. He resorted to the basest means to make them feel that they would eventually be overcome. Through the medium of well-paid spies, he learned that many of our young women were in constant correspondence with their soldier boy friends in the Confederate Army.

On one certain day one of his female spies, whose name I prefer not to give you, dear children, delivered a large batch of letters to him. Among them was one written by my sister Ophelia, your dear grandmother, in which she wrote of the removal of General Ransom and said: "In his place we have a miserable tyrant, Brayman, in command here." These words were thought very rebellious, and as each of the letters contained expressions of hatred and enmity against General Brayman, before sunset, Ophelia and twenty other women were arrested and placed in confinement in the City Hall, near the market, which building is still standing and in use for the meetings of the mayor and board of aldermen. Through the kind intervention of Henry Frank and Isaac Lowenburg, who knew Lieutenant Marble, the officer of that day, brother Henry was permitted to remain with her that night. Next day, being in a highly nervous condition with much fever, she was allowed to be taken home, through the kindness of Lieutenant Parker, the officer of that day and a personal acquaintance of our good friends Henry Frank and Isaac Lowenburg.

Our home was surrounded by guards; no one was permitted to leave the house for three days. Father's store was closed, and all the merchandise, as well as the home with all its effects, would have been confiscated had not our good Yankee friends used their influence to the contrary. Ophelia's spirit was not subdued, but her health became much affected. Mr. Tillman, who nicknamed her "Old Kentuck," admired her for her spunk in writing the truth about the meanness of General Brayman. He once offered to buy her a French calico dress costing at that time $1.50 per yard if she would make and wear a blue cotton dress, such as the slaves wore, and walk down Main Street. She accepted the dare, and was soon on Main Street again dressed in her fine French calico.

She had many admirers, but none so ardent as Isaac Lowenburg. She had refused his attentions and his frequent proposals for her hand in marriage, for she believed him to be a Yankee and against the sentiment of the Southerners, since he came with the

Federal Army. But when she learned to know him as a man of sterling worth, she realized that in him she would find congeniality of spirit for the rights to which she had been so loyal, a sincere protector and true defender. A final proposal was received and sanctioned by our parents, and on the fourth of January, 1865, they were married by Judge Thacher, a neighbor and close friend of our family. . . . Our parents . . . invited several of the officers of the Federal Army who had been kind to Ophelia and to the family during the trying ordeal of the days of the imprisonment.

Father [Jacob Mayer] lived to be seventy-five years of age, respected and honored for an upright, high-principled man, and mother lived only a year and a half longer. She died at the age of sixty-five, a woman of high ideals, who spared no pain or trouble in doing kindness to others. Intelligent, sympathetic, light-hearted and happy, she made her home, even in the darkest days, a haven of peace and pleasantness. She was a director in the Protestant Orphanage in Natchez and a friend to all the sorrowful. Her house was, as she often said every house should be, "as large as its mistress' heart," and there was always room for some homeless one. She was a fine nurse and during the terrible yellow fever epidemic organized a regular nursing corps and joined the brave men and women who daily offered their lives in the cause of humanity. She was one of the women who began the planting of trees and the beautifying of the city cemetery in 1865. Her home was the center of all Jewish festivities, and at the long dining table (which had been bought from Judge Thacher and at which George Washington had once dined) there were often seated as many as thirty-five guests on Passover Eve, the feast of Seder, which was always celebrated with much pomp and ceremony.

Her stories were really wonderful and many of them have never been forgotten; the children who heard them adored her, and she in her pureness of heart was like a little child with sympathy for their troubles and sorrows.

So to the end every one who knew her even casually felt the great influence of her noble soul. This is an ancestress of whom to be proud.

57

ELEANOR H. COHEN, CHAMPION OF THE LOST CAUSE
1865–1866

The following diary—of which a copy is found in the American Jewish Archives—covers about fourteen months in the life of a young woman, Eleanor H. Cohen.

She was living in Columbia, South Carolina, when she started her journal on the last day of February 1865. Eleanor was then twenty-six years of age.

Two themes characterize the diary: Eleanor's love for the South and a personal love affair. Her sweetheart was B. M. Seixas, a member of the New York family whose best-known scion was the Revolutionary patriot, the Reverend Gershom Seixas, minister of Congregation Shearith Israel. B. M. Seixas had come south and gone into business in Charleston. For a time, during the Civil War, he was a soldier in the Twentieth Regiment, South Carolina Volunteers.

Eleanor Cohen's diary is an intense, personal, human document, the outpourings of a highly emotional young woman during the last year of the dying Confederacy. She was a passionate adherent of the Lost Cause. Today her romantic devotion to the South seems exotic, unreal, almost ludicrous; in her own generation, such euphoric enthusiasm was typical of the cultured, aristocratic women of her state. Her diary is of particular significance because of the many insights it offers into the psyche of a Confederate patriot in the last days of the war.

As we shall see in the following pages, Eleanor married her beloved Mr. Seixas. What her diary does not tell us is that she had four children who survived her, and that she, unfortunately, died at the age of thirty-five. What a pity this vibrant woman died so young!

PROLOGUE

Columbia, February 28th, 1865: I have been in the habit of keeping a journal for ten years, from the time of girlish beatitude, "sweet sixteen," up to the mature age I have reached, twenty-six! All the labors of years, all the records of my girlish triumphs, of my first love, all have been destroyed, and yet I am determined to recommence the labors, to rebuild from the ashes of dispair a new record, and enthrone blue-eyed hope as the presiding deity. . . .

At sixteen I fancied, if I was unmarried at twenty-five, I would surely be an old maid and feel inclined to resign all gayety. Now I have reached twenty-six. I feel nearly as young [as] I did then, and wonder if it is possibly true that I am so old. I am rather small, have a good figure, rather pretty, dark complexion, black eyes, and a quantity of straight, black hair of which I am rather proud, [and] small hands and feet, with a bright expression. I am well educated, have read a good deal, and am called intelligent.

I have had several beaux and love affairs, and was privately engaged to be married at sixteen to one I thought the perfection of a man. Now, with increased years and maturity of judgment, I bless God I did not marry him. I am quick-tempered, but warm and loving. He is jealous, passionate, dictatorial, and harsh, and, had I married him, my life would have been an endless quarrel, or I would have sunk into being a slave! But God kindly spared me, and tho' at the time I suffered, as every woman must when she sees her idol shattered, yet I now [bless] and have for years blessed God, that I did not marry my first love.

MR. SEIXAS

Dear Journal, I suppose you think, as I am still Miss Cohen and twenty-six, that I am an old maid. No, for next month was to have smiled on my wedding, now *indefinitely* postponed. But I am betrothed, and to one who loves me truly, fondly, and with his whole heart, and I return his love. Yes, my noble, precious, darling, come what may, my heart is yours. I have been engaged six months to Mr. B. M. Seixas. He is very good-looking, gentlemanly, good-hearted, liberal, honest, and upright, and devotedly attached to me. My precious love, what would I not give for a glance at your dear face! . . .

I was to be married in April [1865]; father was going to housekeeping [for himself] all was bright before me. Mr. Seixas left here on [the] seventh of February [for Charleston], promising to come again in March and in April to come to claim his promised bride. Vain hope! When he left me, I felt a foreboding of evil and begged him to remain here. I made him reiterate again and again and tell me repeatedly of his love, and vow again and again that nothing should wean his heart from me.

April 16th: Joy is mine, dear Journal. I have had a letter from my most precious love. He is well and doing well, is doing business in Charleston, in dear old King St. He expects us down, but says if Pa don't come, he will come for me and be married. Oh, happy I am to be reassured of his love, to read his fond letter, and know he loves me as fondly as ever! And yet there is a sad struggle in my heart, if [whether] to leave my dear parents in their time of trouble, our cause and country in her darkest hours, to follow him, or to allow him to come for his wife and find her unwilling to return with him. I do not yet clearly see my duty. . . . I fear I don't see clearly, for the path of duty is seldom adorned with flowers. Father, mother, and all here think I should go. I am getting ready the few things I have to do. Oh, it is sad to see what my trusseau now will be and compare it with what it might have been! But my love loves me not for fine clothes.

April 20st: A dark, heavy cloud dims the brightness that has illumed my life since I received Mr. S.'s letters. Father call[ed] me and told me a friend had told him that there was much bad feeling excited towards Mr. S., owing to his intimacy with the Yankees, and some even declared he was in their *pay*, and [that Mr. Seixas] had pointed out Rebel property, and that his life was not safe if he came up. Father said he wished to write him not to come up for the present. Farewell to all my hopes of a speedy marriage, and, saddest of all, he may come up and be arrested. Oh, God, have pity on me! I have suffered *greatly;* spare me *this*. . . .

THE SOUTHERNER AND THE YANKEE

April 30th: Politically I have much to say. No peace yet agreed upon, but negociations are being carried on, and people generally think peace will follow. Abram Lincoln was assassinated in the Washington theatre by a man [John Wilkes Booth] who exclaimed: "Death to traitors; Virginia is avenged!" So our worst enemy is laid low, and [Secretary of State William H.] Seward, the arch fiend, was also stabbed, and today we hear the glorious tidings that the Yankee Congress had a row and [Vice President] Andy Jonson [Johnson] was killed. God grant so may all our foes perish! I had a short letter today from Mr. S., but it told me he was well, and loved me; so I am happy.

June 2d: I cannot but blame myself for my long neglect of this dear old book, but really I have lived in such a whirl that I entirely forgot to note events, important as they are. Peace has come, but, oh, God, what a different peace to the one we prayed for! We are conquered by superior numbers. Sherman and Johns[t]on declared an armistice; since then, the war is over, we know not on what terms.

Slavery is done away with. Our noble [Confederate President] Jeff Davis, as well as all of our great men, are prisoners; even the governors of the several states have been arrested. Confederate money is worthless and greenbacks rule the day. Columbia and all the principal [cities] are garrisoned by Yankees. How it makes my Southern blood boil to see them in our streets! Yes, we are again in the hated Union, and over us again floats the banner that is now a sign of tyranny and oppression. [Andrew] Johnson was not killed and is now President. Sad, sad is the change since the days of [President George] Washington. My brothers are all home after fearful deprivations and hardships. Thank God, they are spared. Poor Josh Moses, the flower of our circle, was killed at Blakely [Alabama, April, 1865]. He was a noble man, another martyr to our glorious cause. . . .

Oh, God, my trials *this year* have been great. Grant, I beseech thee, they may soon end! Another source of trouble to me is that Mr. S. wants to go North. This is natural, for his family are there, but, oh, I don't want to go. My feelings are yet *too bitter* to go among them. I cannot so soon forget Sherman, and, while I hope to love Mr. S.'s family, I fear some remark may call forth my Southern blood, and it would be truly disagreeable to have any dispute. Besides, father's loss is so great he can't give me a trusseau, and I do dislike going among *total* strangers who will value me for my dress, destitute as I am of so many things. Besides, if Mr. S. is poor, it will be a great expense, and I think we ought to study economy. Mr. S. does not write satisfactorily. He speaks of buying furniture, and I think it far more pleasant and economical to board at first. He is also not very attentive in writing and, though *I don't doubt* his love, it makes me very unhappy.

Our servants, born and reared in our hands, hitherto devoted to us, freed by Lincoln, left us today. It is a severe trial to mother, and quite a loss to me. Among them went Lavinia, a girl given to me by my grandmother, very handy, and who had promised always to remain with [me] and, when I was married, to go with me. Mr. S. was so pleased; he wrote me to tell her, if she proved faithful, he would take her North and show her [off] as one faithful servant. But she went. She behaved better than most of them; she offered to come to me in town and do anything. She gave me notice and showed regret at parting. This is one of the fruits of war. I, who believe in the institution of slavery, regret deeply its being abolished. I am accustomed to have them to wait on me, and I dislike white servants very much. . . .

Mrs. Seixas

July 26th: Grand news, dear old book! I guess this is the last entry Eleanor Cohen will ever make in this book, for next Wednesday, God willing, I will become Mrs. B. M. Seixas. This event, long, long, looked [for] is at hand, and yet I hardly realize it. I don't yet feel either scarry or nervous, though my whole being is pervaded by a kind of serious strain of thought, and I feel fully that I am leaving the love that is tried and true, going to the love untried and new. I have ever been an indulged, petted daughter. [I] had my own way considerably and, now entering on new duties, I feel that perchance I will have to give all this up. I know Mr. S. loves me, and I love him with my whole heart. [I] am willing to make sacrifices for him, and all I ask is that he will continue to love me, to be patient with my high temper, and, above all, be *just*. I had a telegram yesterday. [I] look for him every day. 'Tis six months since I have seen him, and my heart yearns for him. God grant me strength to be a *good, true* wife, show me the clear line of duty!

I expect to be married next Wednesday at four o'clock, leave at five for Winnsboro, to go North. It seems to me to be very hard to go away among those who were so lately our enemies and, as my heart is filled with Southern fire, I fear I may, by look or word, say things that I ought not to; but I will try to learn to keep quiet. Truly I fear the change from deathlike quiet of Columbia to the whirl and confusion of gay New York will almost set me wild. I am calmly, quietly happy. . . .

August 2d, 1865: My wedding day, can it be, long thought of, long hoped for, here at last? I am very, very happy, fully satisfied of Mr. Seixas' love, yet feeling a shade of deep pain at the severing of old ties, leaving my darling parents [to] go among new relations. Today I cease to be a girl, a woman, and enter on the duty of a wife. God grant me strength to act correctly, to make him happy and, above all, to live in the fear and love of God! Can it be that today maidenhood ceases? Oh, this getting married is no trifle, but a[n] event that gives rise to *grave, serious* thought. . . .

Entry number one of Mrs. B. M. Seixas, Richmond, August 6th, 1865: Yes, I am a bride, a wife, four days married, but I must start at the beginning. The sun shone clearly, brightly, while I was married. All said I looked better than I ever did before, and I feel I did look well. I was very plainly dressed. White Swiss muslin, high [neck] and long sleeves, trimmed with Valienciene lace, a lace barbe [scarf] at my throat, my hair beautifully braided, a white illusion that enveloped me, and a few natural flowers. All passed of[f] well. The glass broke [underfoot, according to Jewish custom]; the ring was on my finger, and from every side I received kisses and congratulations for Mrs. Seixas. Mr. S. was very nicely dressed. He wore a suit of black except [for] a very handsome, white vest. He looked remarkably well. He was serious and felt fully the responsibility of his position. My cake was splendid, and, after eating it and drinking my health, I hastened to my room and donned my travelling dress.

We arrived after six days' travel in New York City. We met Mr. Seixas' father at the wharf. They greeted me very kindly, put us in a carriage, and drove us up to the house, 129 West Thirty-eighth. It is a large, four-story house. Imagine my feelings in going to see perfect strangers! His mother wept over us, and all greeted me with affection. I was taken to my room, a nice, large one, all ready for me, and I love them all already. Vic [Mrs. Meyer Seixas] is very kind to me. She has three lovely children and the prospect of a fourth.

My experience of married life is that there is no true happiness in single life, yet marriage without love must be intolerable. Only deep, pure, holy love can ever fit a woman for what she has to undergo. My dear husband is kind and affectionate. Of course he has faults, as have I, but I will try to cure mine, and bear with his. His greatest fault is that he never thinks seriously. He is always lighthearted, and life is not made of sunshine *alone*, as we all know.

He has determined to stay in New York, and this has pained me much, for I don't like this place to live in. It is too grand, too large, too gay and fashionable to suit poor me, and I wanted to live with my beloved family. The separation from them is too hard, but as a true wife I try to reconcile myself to my husband's will. I have visited theatres, ice cream saloons, etc., and I am forcibly struck by the contrast between the prosperous North and our poor, desolate South, yet is she [the South] dearer to me in her desolation than this gay, heartless country.

I have not been well and have yearned for home and ma. The first year, all say, is hard. I am obeying my husband. My honeymoon is over; a glorious one it has been. I have had crowds of calls. . . .

January 1st, 1866: I feel very much ashamed of myself to think I have allowed so long a time to pass, but now, at the new year, I must take a retrospective glance at the past, present, and future.

My husband will live in New York, and I have reconciled myself to it, for he is so good, so kind. I must be happy; my marriage life is a truly happy one, and I can't feel grateful enough to God for the blessing he has given me in my precious husband. His business is as good as we could expect, and life looks brightly to me. My parents expect daily to go to Charleston, and I will go home in two months to stay three [months].

Dear old Journal, let me whisper to you that a woman's crowning glory will, with God's blessing, be mine this year. I will become a mother. Oh, how my heart thrills at the word! Yes, please God, in May I will have a pledge of love given me in *our baby*, as we love to call it, the blessed assurance of my husband's love. I can hardly believe it, that I will be a mother. My dear husband has liberally supplied me with materials, and I am busy making up a baby wardrobe.

Epilogue

Charleston: Home again, tho' not to me the home of old, for, since the war, everything is changed. . . .

They are all devoted to me, and, save that I am separated from my dear husband, I am perfectly happy. All my baby things are done, washed, and in their place, and, as I look on them, I cannot but be thankful to the best of husbands for his generosity to me in giving me such nice things and in such abundance. He has truly made me happy. He has sent me several boxes and writes often sweet, loving letters. My time of trouble approaches rapidly. God be with me, and grant *our baby*, as he loves to call it, may be well and perfect. . . .

May will be an *important* month for both of us, for she [my cousin Isabel] will become a *wife*, and I, a mother, during its course. Oh, God, grant all my excitement may not injure the tender luck under my heart, but that it may be a *perfect*, well-formed, healthy babe, one calculated to render its father and myself happy! I have not heard often of late from my husband; hope to hear today.

58

MAUD NATHAN: SEPHARDIC ARISTOCRAT
ca. 1867

Maud Nathan (1862–1946) was a member of the Daughters of the American Revolution; her husband, a cousin, was a member of the Sons of the American Revolution. She was born a Nathan and was related to both the Seixases and the Cardozos. Emma Lazarus was a member of her widely ramified clan. She was reared as an Orthodox Sephardi and accepted the tenets of these traditionalists, though not without some reservation. Her Jewish sympathies and her strong sense of noblesse oblige prompted her to serve on the board of the Mt. Sinai Training School for Nurses, to support a kindergarten on the Lower East Side, to accept the presidency of the first sisterhood of Congregation Shearith Israel, and to play an important part in the New York section of the National Council of Jewish Women. By the late 1890's, she had already been invited to "preach" at Temple Beth-El. She was a clubwoman, a voluntary social worker, and a brilliant speaker.

Yet, though closely tied to her synagogue and her ancestral religious heritage, she achieved recognition as a notable American because of her solid, constructive work in the Woman's Exchange, in the Consumers' League, in the fight for women's rights. In leaving the narrow confines of her Sephardi world to engage in social work dedicated to the advancement of impoverished and underprivileged women, she was but following in the footsteps of Rebecca Gratz, who had begun her career in a nondenominational charity. Maud Nathan's significance lies in the fact that she built a world for herself in which she harmonized her loyalty to religious Orthodoxy and her determination to ease the lot of oppressed women in commerce, industry, and politics. Unlike other turn-of-the-century Jewish clubwomen, she did not find it difficult to live comfortably in the two worlds of religious tradition and socioeconomic reform. Maud Nathan was a good Jewess, an exemplary social reformer. Yet it behooves the historian to point out that in her later years she had no sympathy for Franklin D. Roosevelt's New Deal; no woman, no human being is all of one piece. The following excerpts are taken from Mrs. Nathan's autobiographical recollections.

We always said our prayers at night at our mother's knee. These prayers were said partly in Hebrew and partly in English. When my mother and father were going out to dinner, we said our prayers a little earlier. When my parents went to Niagara Falls without me, I said my prayers to "Mammy" [my Christian nurse]. It was then that I missed my mother most. I missed her maternal blessing; she always placed her hand gently on my head and blessed me; then she always embraced me tenderly, while I, with my arms clasped around her neck, would hug her closely. My mother was a beautiful and brilliant woman. I know she was the recipient of much genuine admiration, but I doubt whether she ever had any greater admirer than her own little daughter. I was a very proud little girl of five years of age the Saturday that my mother took me for the first time to Sabbath service at the synagogue. The building at that time was on Nineteenth Street, just west of Fifth Avenue. We were brought up to keep the Sabbath day holy, according to the literal rendering of the Commandments. Therefore, we walked to and fro, in order that no horse should be compelled to work for us. I was dressed in my blue Irish poplin dress (a dress which has become historically important in my memory, because I also wore it to my first matinée: *The Black Crook*).

In our orthodox synagogue, the women according to oriental custom are relegated to the gallery, while the men sit below. My mother and I toiled up the high flights of stairs and I was told to sit on the steps of the aisle, next to my mother's seat. And here my memories carry me twenty-three years ahead of my story when I took my own little girl to synagogue for the first time.

My little girl was following with rapt attention the same service I had followed so many years before. She sat on the steps of the aisle right next to me, and as I watched her it seemed as though I were looking at myself and living through once more my childish experiences. After my little girl's first service, we lunched with an aunt who asked the child how she liked "shule." My little daughter replied, "Oh, it was very nice, but I like the circus better."

To go back to my own childhood impressions, I was much interested in watching the services conducted by Rabbi [Jacques

Judah] Lyons, my aunt's husband (who was rabbi over a period of fifty years), dressed in his long black gown, with a wide "talith" (praying shawl) over his shoulders and a high silk hat on his head. The chanting in Hebrew was melodious and I was able, in my childish piping voice, to join in the singing of the familiar hymns. After service, the boys, who sat below with the men, were blessed by their fathers and by the rabbi. Then we all met in the vestibule and Sabbath greetings were exchanged. The most interesting synagogue service for us children was that of "Succoth," when the annual celebration of the harvest occurs. This harvest festival of thanksgiving antedates by many centuries the New England Thanksgiving festival. In memory of the days of the Exodus, when the children of Israel dwelt in booths, a booth is erected in the court between the synagogue and the vestry house, decorated with foliage, flowers, and the fruits of the harvest.

A short service in this booth follows the regular service in the synagogue and the participants break bread, eat olives and fruit, and drink the juice of the grape—this wine being sent from Palestine. How well I remember my impatience at being obliged to sit through the long service in the synagogue, with the many repetitions of prayers and the slow, measured responses in Hebrew, when I was anxious to get into the fairylike booth fragrant with flowers and heavily scented with luscious fruit. The bread—small twisted crisp rolls, covered with poppy seeds—always tasted better than any bread served at home. The olives were more juicy and the Palestinian wine had a flavor all its own. It was only at Succoth and Passover seasons that we children were permitted to sip wine and it was nectar to us.

The Passover service was distinctly a home ceremony. We invariably held the "Hagodah" [the narrative prayers for the Passover supper] service on the eve of the holy day in our own dining room. My father would chant the prayers in Hebrew and we all made the responses together and sang the hymns and psalms in unison. This home service was specially adapted for children. There were questions which the oldest son and the youngest son were supposed to ask their father, and his replies explained all the symbols used.

The "matzoths"—the unleavened bread—which we ate during Passover were, to us children, the most delicate and appetizing of all crackers. It was no hardship for us to be denied bread through Passover week. We often begged to be allowed to continue substituting matzoths for bread after the week had passed. The only hardship for us lay in the fact that Good Friday usually fell in Passover week, so we could not eat the hot cross buns which our playmates ate with so much gusto.

There were other hardships which seemed to differentiate us from our little playmates. My mother was very strict as to Sabbath observance; we were not allowed to attend parties on a Friday night (our Sabbath Eve) or go to matinées on a Saturday. These deprivations may have strengthened our characters, but they were a great source of annoyance at the time. For all our companions, outside of the large family circle of cousins, were Christians. The small group of Sephardic Jews who had settled in the United States in the seventeenth and eighteenth centuries had intermarried from generation to generation, because they did not wish to give up their faith. But the business and social fabric of their lives had been interwoven with their Christian neighbors—as they had hoped for—and their friendly inter-course was but natural. They were actively participating in the civic and national life and had become a strong power in the community.

On Sunday mornings, my older brother and I were sent to Sunday school, where we were taught the history and principles of our religion and were also taught to read Hebrew. All this training in Jewish ritual, Jewish principles, and Jewish traditions has formed the background of my spiritual life. I can well remember how irksome at that time seemed these religious observances. The long walk back and forth from synagogue, instead of riding, the being debarred from social functions other than family gatherings on Friday nights and Saturdays; the insistence upon the rigidity of certain dietary laws, all seemed to me, at the time, so unnecessary. I longed to live the same life as my playmates. Although I secretly resented these little things, which made me seem different in the eyes of my playmates, it never occurred to me to rebel. In this feeling of resentment I can now see the sense of group consciousness, the desire to be part of the dominant group, rather than of the minority group. I felt particularly resentful because we were debarred from joining in the festivities of Christmas and Easter.

We children not only learned the traditions and principles of our own religion, but we were also taught to respect the customs and conventions of other religions. We were not permitted to practice our exercises on the piano on Sundays—out of consideration for our neighbors. In the country we were not permitted to play croquet on Sundays.

In the light of the present, I can now appreciate the value of this training. If I have been able to express in my life, standards, ideals, a code of ethics, that have spelled helpfulness to others, has it not been because the roots were laid in a distinctive religious background? Does it make any difference whether our youth have, as a religious background, Jewish principles, Christian principles, or the principles of any of the great religions of the East? Is not the essential thing that they have a real spiritual background upon which to build character? It is possible to be moral, ethical, without having a spiritual background; but mere morals, and a code of ethics, cannot, by themselves, develop a certain fineness of feeling, the lack of which is felt by those who have spiritual tentacles.

11. Adah Isaacs Menken

59

ADAH ISAACS MENKEN, UNHAPPY POET
1868

Adah Isaacs Menken (ca. 1835–1868), actress and poet, may have been a Jewess by birth; her origins are clouded in obscurity. Her first husband was a Cincinnati Jew; spiritually, emotionally, she was devoted to Judaism, its traditions and aspirations, though there is scant evidence that she was observant or conformed to the imperatives of the faith she avowed. Three of her husbands were non-Jews. Menken was no Sarah Bernhardt, but she did achieve recognition in New York and San Francisco, in London, Paris, and Vienna, because she appeared in flesh-colored tights while playing the title role in Mazeppa. *For a time she was probably the theatre's highest-paid actress. In a Victorian age which preached—and paid lip service to —austerity, her sensationalism made her famous. "Lo, this is she that was the World's delight"; she was the "naked lady." She died at Paris a young woman in her early thirties and now lies in the Jewish section of the Montparnasse cemetery.*

It was only about a week after her death that a thin, modest volume of her poems appeared. Its title, Infelicia *("The Unhappy One"), reflects the woman she was, but it is equally true that as a poet she was gifted, possibly the most talented of all the nineteenth-century Jewesses who laid their offerings on the altar of the muses. In an age of repression, hers was a soul that yearned to breathe free. Feminism is a drive as old as Lilith, a consort of the primeval Adam.*

The following selections are typical of her genius. It is not improbable that she was influenced by Walt Whitman, whom she knew.

JUDITH.

"Repent, or I will come unto thee quickly, and will fight thee with the sword of my mouth."—REVELATION ii. 16.

I.

Ashkelon is not cut off with the remnant of a valley.

Baldness dwells not upon Gaza.

The field of the valley is mine, and it is clothed in verdure.

The steepness of Baal-perazim is mine;

And the Philistines spread themselves in the valley of Rephaim.

They shall yet be delivered into my hands.

For the God of Battles has gone before me!

The sword of the mouth shall smite them to dust.

I have slept in the darkness—

But the seventh angel woke me, and giving me a sword of flame, points to the blood-ribbed cloud, that lifts his reeking head above the mountain.

Thus am I the prophet.

I see the dawn that heralds to my waiting soul the advent of power.

> Power that will unseal the thunders!
> Power that will give voice to graves!

> Graves of the living;
> Graves of the dying;
> Graves of the sinning;
> Graves of the loving;
> Graves of despairing;

And oh! graves of the deserted!

These shall speak, each as their voices shall be loosed.

And the day is dawning.

II.

Stand back, ye Philistines!

Practice what ye preach to me;

I heed ye not, for I know ye all.

Ye are living burning lies, and profanation to the garments which with stately steps ye sweep your marble palaces.

Your palaces of Sin, around which the damning evidence of guilt hangs like a reeking vapor.

Stand back!

I would pass up the golden road of the world.

A place in the ranks awaits me.

I know that ye are hedged on the borders of my path.

Lie and tremble, for ye well know that I hold with iron grasp the battle axe.

Creep back to your dark tents in the valley.

Slouch back to your haunts of crime.

Ye do not know me, neither do ye see me.

But the sword of the mouth is unsealed, and ye coil yourselves in slime and bitterness at my feet.

I mix your jeweled heads, and your gleaming eyes, and your hissing tongues with the dust.

My garments shall bear no mark of ye.

When I shall return this sword to the angel, your foul blood will not stain its edge.

It will glimmer with the light of truth, and the strong arm shall rest.

III.

Stand back!

I am no Magdalene waiting to kiss the hem of your garment.

It is mid-day.

See ye not what is written on my forehead?

I am Judith!

I wait for the head of my Holofernes!

Ere the last tremble of the conscious death-agony shall have shuddered, I will show it to ye with the long black hair clinging to the glazed eyes, and the great mouth opened in search of voice, and the strong throat all hot and reeking with blood, that will thrill me with wild unspeakable joy as it courses down my bare body and dabbles my cold feet!

My sensuous soul will quake with the burden of so much bliss.

Oh, what wild passionate kisses will I draw up from that bleeding mouth!

I will strangle this pallid throat of mine on the sweet blood!

I will revel in my passion.

At midnight I will feast on it in the darkness.

For it was that which thrilled its crimson tides of reckless passion through the blue veins of my life, and made them leap up in the wild sweetness of Love and agony of Revenge!

I am starving for this feast.

Oh forget not that I am Judith!

And I know where sleeps Holofernes.

MYSELF.

"La patience est amère; mais le fruit en est doux?"

I.

Away down into the shadowy depths of the Real I once lived.

I thought that to seem was to be.

But the waters of Marah were beautiful, yet they were bitter.

I waited, and hoped, and prayed;

Counting the heart-throbs and the tears that answered them.

Through my earnest pleadings for the True, I learned that the mildest mercy of life was a smiling sneer;

And that the business of the world was to lash with vengeance all who dared to be what their God had made them.

Smother back tears to the red blood of the heart!

Crush out things called souls!

No room for them here!

II.

Now I gloss my pale face with laughter, and sail my voice on with the tide.

Decked in jewels and lace, I laugh beneath the gaslight's glare, and quaff the purple wine.

But the minor-keyed soul is standing naked and hungry upon one of Heaven's high hills of light.

Standing and waiting for the blood of the feast!

Starving for one poor word!

Waiting for God to launch out some beacon on the boundless shores of this Night.

Shivering for the uprising of some soft wing under which it may creep, lizard-like, to warmth and rest.

Waiting! Starving and shivering!

III.

Still I trim my white bosom with crimson roses; for none shall see the thorns.

I bind my aching brow with a jeweled crown, that none shall see the iron one beneath.

My silver-sandaled feet keep impatient time to the music, because I cannot be calm.

I laugh at earth's passion-fever of Love; yet I know that God is near to the soul on the hill, and hears the ceaseless ebb and flow of a hopeless love, through all my laughter.

But if I can cheat my heart with the old comfort, that love can be forgotten, is it not better?

After all, living is but to play a part!

The poorest worm would be a jewel-headed snake if she could!

IV.

All this grandeur of glare and glitter has its nighttime.

The pallid eyelids must shut out smiles and daylight.

Then I fold my cold hands, and look down at the restless rivers of a love that rushes through my life.

Unseen and unknown they tide on over black rocks and chasms of Death.

Oh, for one sweet word to bridge their terrible depths!

O jealous soul! why wilt thou crave and yearn for what thou canst not have?

And life is so long—so long.

V.

With the daylight comes the business of living.

The prayers that I sent trembling up the golden thread of hope all come back to me.

I lock them close in my bosom, far under the velvet and roses of the world.

For I know that stronger than these torrents of passion is the soul that hath lifted itself up to the hill.

What care I for his careless laugh?

I do not sigh; but I know that God hears the life-blood dripping as I, too, laugh.

I would not be thought a foolish rose, that flaunts her red heart out to the sun.

Loving is not living!

VI.

Yet through all this I know that night will roll back from the still, gray plain of heaven, and that my triumph shall rise sweet with the dawn!

When these mortal mists shall unclothe the world, then shall I be known as I am!

When I dare be dead and buried behind a wall of wings, then shall he know me!

When this world shall fall, like some old ghost, wrapped in the black skirts of the wind, down into the fathomless eternity of fire, then shall souls uprise!

When God shall lift the frozen seal from struggling voices, then shall we speak!

When the purple-and-gold of our inner natures shall be lighted up in the Eternity of Truth, then will love be mine!
I can wait.

DRIFTS THAT BAR MY DOOR.

I.

O Angels! will ye never sweep the drifts from my door?
Will ye never wipe the gathering rust from the hinges?
How long must I plead and cry in vain?
Lift back the iron bars, and lead me hence.
Is there not a land of peace beyond my door?
Oh, lead me to it—give me rest—release me from this unequal strife.
Heaven can attest that I fought bravely when the heavy blows fell fast.
Was it my sin that strength failed?
Was it my sin that the battle was in vain?
Was it my sin that I lost the prize? I do not sorrow for all the bitter pain and blood it cost me.
Why do ye stand sobbing in the sunshine?
I cannot weep.
There is no sunlight in this dark cell. I am starving for light.
O angels! sweep the drifts away—unbar my door!

II.

Oh, is this all?
Is there nothing more of life?
See how dark and cold my cell.
The pictures on the walls are covered with mould.
The earth-floor is slimy with my wasting blood.
The embers are smouldering in the ashes.

The lamp is dimly flickering, and will soon starve for oil in this horrid gloom.

My wild eyes paint shadows on the walls.

And I hear the poor ghost of my lost love moaning and sobbing without.

Shrieks of my unhappiness are borne to me on the wings of the wind.

I sit cowering in fear, with my tattered garments close around my choking throat.

I move my pale lips to pray; but my soul has lost her wonted power.

Faith is weak.

Hope has laid her whitened corse upon my bosom.

The lamp sinks lower and lower. O angels! sweep the drifts away—unbar my door!

III.

Angels, is this my reward?

Is this the crown ye promised to set down on the foreheads of the loving—the suffering—the deserted?

Where are the sheaves I toiled for?

Where the golden grain ye promised?

These are but withered leaves.

Oh, is this all?

Meekly I have toiled and spun the fleece.

All the work ye assigned, my willing hands have accomplished.

See how thin they are, and how they bleed.

Ah me! what meagre pay, e'en when the task is over!

My fainting child, whose golden head graces e'en this dungeon, looks up to me and pleads for life.

O God! my heart is breaking!

Despair and Death have forced their skeleton forms through the grated window of my cell, and stand clamoring for their prey.

The lamp is almost burnt out.

Angels, sweep the drifts away—unbar my door!

IV.

Life is a lie, and Love a cheat.

There is a graveyard in my poor heart—dark, heaped-up graves, from which no flowers spring.

The walls are so high, that the trembling wings of birds do break ere they reach the summit, and they fall, wounded, and die in my bosom.

I wander 'mid the gray old tombs, and talk with the ghosts of my buried hopes.

They tell me of my Eros, and how they fluttered around him, bearing sweet messages of my love, until one day, with his strong arm, he struck them dead at his feet.

Since then, these poor lonely ghosts have haunted me night and day, for it was I who decked them in my crimson heart-tides, and sent them forth in chariots of fire.

Every breath of wind bears me their shrieks and groans.

I hasten to their graves, and tear back folds and folds of their shrouds, and try to pour into their cold, nerveless veins the quickening tide of life once more.

Too late—too late!

Despair hath driven back Death, and clasps me in his black arms.

And the lamp! See, the lamp is dying out!

O angels! sweep the drifts from my door!—lift up the bars!

V.

Oh, let me sleep.

I close my weary eyes to think—to dream.

Is this what dreams are woven of?

I stand on the brink of a precipice, with my shivering child strained to my bare bosom.

A yawning chasm lies below. My trembling feet are on the brink.

I hear again *his* voice; but he reacheth not out his hand to save me.

Why can I not move my lips to pray?
They are cold.
My soul is dumb, too.
Death hath conquered!
I feel his icy fingers moving slowly along my heartstrings.
How cold and stiff!
The ghosts of my dead hopes are closing around me.
They stifle me.
They whisper that Eros has come back to me.
But I only see a skeleton wrapped in blood-stained cerements.
There are no lips to kiss me back to life.
O ghosts of Love, move back—give me air!
Ye smell of the dusty grave.
Ye have pressed your cold hands upon my eyes until they are eclipsed.
The lamp has burnt out.
O angels! be quick! Sweep the drifts away!—unbar my door!
Oh, light! light!

HEAR, O ISRAEL!
(From the Hebrew.)
"And they shall be my people, and I will be their
God."—JEREMIAH xxxii. 38.

I.

Hear, O Israel! and plead my cause against the ungodly nation!
'Midst the terrible conflict of Love and Peace, I departed from thee, my people, and spread my tent of many colors in the land of Egypt.
In their crimson and fine linen I girded my white form.
Sapphires gleamed their purple light from out the darkness of my hair.
The silver folds of their temple foot-cloth was spread beneath my sandaled feet.
Thus I slumbered through the daylight.

Slumbered 'midst the vapor of sin,
Slumbered 'midst the battle and din,
Wakened 'midst the strangle of breath,
Wakened 'midst the struggle of death!

II.

Hear, O Israel! my people—to thy goodly tents do I return with unstained hands.

Like as the harts for the water-brooks, in thirst, do pant and bray, so pants and cries my longing soul for the house of Jacob.

My tears have unto me been meat, both in night and day:

And the crimson and fine linen moulders in the dark tents of the enemy.

With bare feet and covered head do I return to thee, O Israel!

With sackcloth have I bound the hem of my garments.

With olive leaves have I trimmed the border of my bosom.

The breaking waves did pass o'er me; yea, were mighty in their strength—

Strength of the foe's oppression.

My soul was cast out upon the waters of Sin: but it has come back to me.

My transgressions have vanished like a cloud.

The curse of Balaam hath turned to a blessing;

And the doors of Jacob turn not on their hinges against me.

Rise up, O Israel! for it is I who passed through the fiery furnace seven times, and come forth unscathed, to redeem thee from slavery, O my nation! and lead thee back to God.

III.

Brothers mine, fling out your white banners over this Red Sea of wrath!

Hear ye not the Death-cry of a thousand burning, bleeding wrongs?

Against the enemy lift thy sword of fire, even thou, O Israel! whose prophet I am.

For I, of all thy race, with these tear-blinded eyes, still see the watch-fire leaping up its blood-red flame from the ramparts of our Jerusalem!

And my heart alone beats and palpitates, rises and falls with the glimmering and the gleaming of the golden beacon flame, by whose light I shall lead thee, O my people! back to freedom!

Give me time—oh give me time to strike from your brows the shadow-crowns of Wrong!

On the anvil of my heart will I rend the chains that bind ye.

Look upon me—oh look upon me, as I turn from the world—from love, and passion, to lead thee, thou Chosen of God, back to the pastures of Right and Life!

Fear me not; for the best blood that heaves this heart now runs for thee, thou Lonely Nation!

Why wear ye not the crown of eternal royalty, that God set down upon your heads?

Back, tyrants of the red hands!

Slouch back to your ungodly tents, and hide the Cainbrand on your foreheads!

Life for life, blood for blood, is the lesson ye teach us.

We, the Children of Israel, will not creep to the kennel graves ye are scooping out with iron hands, like scourged hounds!

Israel! rouse ye from the slumber of ages, and, though Hell welters at your feet, carve a road through these tyrants!

The promised dawn-light is here; and God—O the God of our nation is calling!

Press on—press on!

IV.

Ye, who are kings, princes, priests, and prophets. Ye men of Judah and bards of Jerusalem, hearken unto my voice, and I will speak thy name, O Israel!

Fear not; for God hath at last let loose His thinkers, and their voices now tremble in the mighty depths of this old world!

Rise up from thy blood-stained pillows!

Cast down to dust the hideous, galling chains that bind thy strong hearts down to silence!

Wear ye the badge of slaves?

See ye not the watch-fire?

Look aloft, from thy wilderness of thought!

Come forth with the signs and wonders, and thy strong hands, and stretched-out arms, even as thou didst from Egypt!

Courage, courage! trampled hearts!

Look at these pale hands and frail arms, that have rent asunder the welded chains that an army of the Philistines bound about me!

But the God of all Israel set His seal of fire on my breast, and lighted up, with inspiration, the soul that pants for the Freedom of a nation!

With eager wings she fluttered above the blood-stained bayonet-points of the millions, who are trampling upon the strong throats of God's people.

Rise up, brave hearts!

The sentry cries: "All's well!" from Hope's tower!

Fling out your banners of Right!

The watch fire grows brighter!

All's well! All's well!

Courage! Courage!

The Lord of Hosts is in the field,

The God of Jacob is our shield!

60

THE BEGINNINGS OF THE RELIGIOUS EMANCIPATION OF WOMEN IN AMERICAN JEWRY THE PHILADELPHIA RABBINICAL CONFERENCE 1869

As the following excerpts demonstrate, a group of liberal American rabbis met in Philadelphia in November 1869, and proceeded to recommend abrogation of biblical and rabbinical laws which subordinated women in marriage and divorce. The conference was important as a public denial of the binding character of Jewish law; it was a break with Orthodoxy; it marked in a way the formal ideological beginnings of American Jewish Reform. Some European rabbis and laymen had already met as a synod in Leipzig, Germany, in June and July of that year, and had taken cognizance of disabling Jewish marriage laws, but had accomplished nothing. Little could be done in authoritarian Europe; Jews were free to take action only in a land where the state exercised little or no authority in religious matters. The synod that assembled at Augsburg, Germany, in 1871, and made recommendations with respect to marriage, was probably influenced by the action taken in 1869 at Philadelphia.

MARRIAGE LAWS

(a) Marriage

1. At the solemnisation of marriages the bride shall no longer play a passive role, but there shall be reciprocal vows on the part of the bridegroom and the bride by the utterance of the same marriage formula combined with the reciprocal offering of wedding rings.

2. The marriage formula reads: "Be thou consecrated unto me as wife (husband) according to the law of God".

3. The customary [betrothal] benedictions *birkat erusin* should be replaced by one which expresses as divinely ordained the

matrimonial union in its full ethical sense, emphasising the Biblical idea of *vehayu levassar echad* ["and they shall be one flesh," Gen. 2:24], the fusion of the spouses into one personality, and forbidding extra-marital sexual relations.

4. Polygamy contradicts the conception of marriage as described. The marriage of a man already married to another woman can therefore neither take place nor have religious validity, equally the marriage of an already married woman to another man, and must be regarded as null and void.

5. The priestly marriage laws, which presumed the greater holiness of the sons of Aaron, have lost all meaning since the destruction of the Temple and the extinction of the old sacrificial cult, and should therefore no longer be observed.

(b) Divorce

6. From the Mosaic and rabbinic point of view, divorce is a purely civil matter which has never received religious consecration. It should therefore be recognised as an act emanating solely from the judicial authorities of the State. On the other hand, the so-called ritual *get* [divorce] is declared ineffectual in all situations.

7. The dissolution of a marriage pronounced by a civil court has full validity in Judaism also, if the judicial documents show that both parties to the marriage accepted the divorce. Where, on the contrary, the civil court decrees a divorce compulsorily against one or other party, Judaism on its part acknowledges the divorce as valid only if, on examination of the grounds for the judicial divorce, they are deemed sufficient according to the spirit of the Jewish religion. It is recommended, however, that in coming to a decision the rabbi obtain the assent of experts.

8. The decision of the question whether a husband or wife should be declared "presumed dead" (or missing) in doubtful cases should be left to the laws of the country. [The Jewish law forbids remarriage unless it is absolutely certain a missing husband is dead.]

(c) Levirate Marriage and Chalitzah

The rule to enter into levirate marriage and, if occasion should arise, *chalitzah*, has lost all sense, significance, and binding force for us. [The levirate marriage is the sometimes compulsory marriage of a widow by a brother of her deceased husband. Chalitzah is a biblical ceremony prescribed for the man who refuses to marry his brother's childless widow.]

61

OUR GIRLS: ARE THEY EDUCATED?
1875

In January 1875, the American Israelite *ran a series of letters from young men and women in which they discussed the intellectual world of teenage Jewesses. One correspondent, "Hyacinthia," maintained that the new crop had no interest in anything but marriage (A); another, "Minnie," affirmed stoutly that the girls did read, that it was the young men who lacked intellectual curiosity (B). It is not possible to determine the accuracy of the statements made by these letter-writers. One thing is clear, however: some of the young women expressed themselves beautifully; they were obviously well-educated and highly intelligent.*

A

[January 8, 1875.]

ABOUT OUR GIRLS

It is surely strange that in none of our Jewish papers does one find anything addressed to our women.

Is there nothing that can be said that will cause our girls to emulate their Gentile sisters in their ambition for education? None need be told that to elevate our sex is to elevate the race, for from uncultivated uneducated women cannot spring cultivated educated men; hence it follows the education of one means the education of the other. The writer has been told there is not a Jewish girl at Vassar College, and let any one go through the streets of any of our large cities when the young ladies are going to or returning from school, and how lamentable it looks—at least to the writer's eyes—to see so very few Jewish young ladies among them; how common it is to see Gentile girls from sixteen to nineteen with their school books under their arm, but how many Jewish girls go to school after fifteen?

Fashion, dress, operas, theatres, are their topics of conversation; study and elevating influences such as solid reading cannot hold their place in the same minds with first named topics; one must make room for the other. How often we read and hear of Gentile women who write books and for papers, and the writer has conversed with many Gentile girls who had read Macaule[a]y's *Essays*, all of Dickens, and like standard works.

If one would listen to the conversation of ninety-nine out of one hundred Jewish girls, they would hear, besides the before mentioned topics, the soul absorbing theme of—"who is engaged to be married," and it is evident to the most superficial observer that all of them are anxious to be in that enviable position.

We would not, for one moment, say that love, theatres, and the like were not very well in their place, but if a young lady would have none of them in her head, until she had gone through a thorough course of school training, and the refining, and intellectual improvement derived from reading the thoughts of the wise, together with the domestic culture so necessary to human happiness, she would not so plainly let the world see that her whole ambition is to marry, but would be more particular whom she marries, which I am afraid is not now the case, as long as the important individual is not poor. . . .

To a man coming home weary from labor . . . fresh, original thoughts cannot but entertain him better than whining complaints of servants and other petty cares.

If one half the time was spent in mental improvement that is wasted in trying to learn the piano (which so very many have not the least talent for), how fit a mate it would make a girl for many an intelligent man who inwardly laughs at the badly played waltz or polka.

The subject is an almost exhaustless one, but time and space limit the theme.

All that has been said, the writer prays shall be taken in the spirit it was written by one who wishes to see our Jewish women second to none in intelligence, as they are second to none in goodness and virtue.

Hyacinthia

B

Our Girls

Charleston, S.C., Jan. 16, 1875.

To the Editors of the *American Israelite*

Having perused in your excellent journal an article reflecting on the intelligence and capacity of Jewish ladies, relative to their not being conversant on literary topics, I can not let this slur upon my sex be passed over without comment.

Your correspondent intimates that the Jewish young ladies are unfamiliar with Dickens and other authors. Now, Mr. Editor, of course I can only speak for myself and the ladies of this city; they are perfectly conversant with the works of Shakespeare, Scott, Lamb, and, above all, that greatest of all novelists, Charles Dickens; his works are proverbial with us.

Your correspondent does not speak of the ignorance of the Jewish young men. To them lay the whole blame, for if they would show an appreciation for literary ideas we, of course, would use our utmost endeavors to cultivate a taste for literature; but instead of this if you commence a conversation with the least reflection on science, the fine arts, etc., you are met with a blank stare of surprise, as their conversation generally consists of plenty of stupid compliments, interspersed with the smallest of small talk; then why should we "waste our sweetness on the desert air?"—or, in other words, converse on subjects that our hearers can not understand?

It may be the custom out West for children to leave school and enter society at the age of fifteen. I am extremely sorry to see that parents take such little interest in the education of their daughters. Allow me to assure you that it is not the style down here, as no young lady leaves school before eighteen.

I regret exceedingly that your correspondent should be so unfortunate as to reside among so many ignorant girls.

In conclusion allow me to invite your correspondent, in the name of the Jewesses of Charleston, to pay us a visit and judge of our conversational powers.

Minnie

62

THE RELIGIOUS EMANCIPATION OF THE AMERICAN JEWESS
1876–1923

It was as early as 1846, the year that he landed and served as rabbi in Albany, New York, that Isaac Mayer Wise began his Reformist innovations. His first departure was to allow girls to sing in the choir. Years later in Cincinnati, in his German-language magazine Die Deborah, *of March 22, 1867, he wrote at some length on "The Jewish Woman," presenting his whole program for the religious advancement of the Jewess. Women had to be accepted as members of congregations and elected to office. They had much to offer; they were devoted religionists, cultured, diplomatic, and gifted with administrative skills. They were certainly as wise as the men who thought of themselves, by divine grace, as Lords of All Creation. Women were needed because men were too busy in their shops or at the gaming tables. Jews, he urged, should take as models those Christians who had granted equality to women in their churches. There is, however, no record that women in Wise's Cincinnati synagogue were elected to office during his lifetime.*

In 1876, Isaac M. Wise repeated in his English-language American Israelite *what he had already made clear in the* Deborah *(selection A). In 1880, the "Conservative"—at the time this meant Modern Orthodox—B'nai Jeshurun of New York announced that it was ready to accept women as members of the synagogue (item B). During the 1890's, Rosa Sonneschein, editor of the* American Jewess, *angrily contended that the ladies were still not being granted membership in any Jewish house of worship (selection C). In 1897, Germany's* Allgemeine Zeitung des Judenthums *announced that a woman had been elected president of the congregation in Corsicana, Texas. This may or may not have been true, but by the 1890's there is no question that the Jewish woman was beginning to secure a degree of recognition in the Jewish religious community. Finally, in 1923, the Council of the Union of American Hebrew Congregations declared women eligible for membership on the Executive Board (Item D).*

A

1876
WOMAN IN THE SYNAGOGUE

Moses, the great teacher of God's will, made no distinction in the duties of man to his God, to himself, to his fellow-man, and to his other fellow creatures, between the sons and daughters of Israel. According to Moses, God made man, male and female, and both in his own image, without any difference in regard to duties, rights, claims and hopes. . . .

The rabbis made a law placing women, children, and slaves in one category in regard to legal testimony, perhaps in order to protect women against the probable indecencies of criminal courts; and also in regard to the observation of such commandatory laws, which depend on a fixed time . . . which relieved woman of certain ceremonial laws, she might not be able, under certain circumstances, to perform. But neither of these rabbinical enactments lowered woman in her position; and the woman of the Hebrew poetry, like the Sulamite of the royal bard, always remained the queen of the heart, the house, and the private society. But up to 1000 A.C., all Jewish laws and customs were made in Persia and imported into Europe. The influence of oriental society and the Koran gradually excluded woman from all public affairs of the synagogue and the congregation, so that we found her in a garret in the synagogue, isolated like an abomination, shunned like a dangerous demon, and declared unfit in all religious observances. To call a woman to the Thorah in the synagogue, or let her have any of the honors, would have appeared preposterous, and would to-day be considered a desecration of the Orthodox synagogue. Those people are brutally pious and stupidly faithful to what they call ancient custom, whatever an abuse may be.

It was our first business in America to take female singers in the synagogal choir, and to make the girls attend the place of worship. The Orthodoxy cried horror, but we proceeded. Next we confirmed boys and girls together on Penta[e]cost during divine worship. The orthodoxy felt enraged therefore we let girls read the Thorah publicly on that occasion. Raising at our heels the mad-dog cry of heresy, we introduced family pews in the temple, against which all protested who had left some Orthodox sentiment; therefore we advanced, if a man may marry his deceased wife's sister, a woman may marry her deceased husband's brother; and we did it, in spite of all protests and remonstrances simply in order to emancipate the Jewish woman.

Now the mothers and daughters in Israel are in the temple, and with them came again order, decorum, and devotion. A hundred abuses have fallen down to the ground dead in our houses of public worship, since woman occupies again her place in the temple, as she did in the temple of Jerusalem. But we can not stop here, the reform is not complete yet. You must enfranchise woman in your congregations, she must be a member, must have a voice and a vote in your assemblies. We need women in the congregational meetings to bring there [their] heart, soul, piety and mutual respect, in order to expel forever from those meetings the old demons commonly called *Die Ungezogenheit* ["rudeness"] and *Kahl's Gewaltsmann* ["congregational tyrant"]. We must have women among the Boards for the sake of principle, and to rouse in them an interest for congregational affairs. We must have women in the school-boards, to visit the Sabbath-schools, and to bring there their influence. We must have women in the choir board or committee, because they understand more of music than their husbands, and are not as lazy as their liege lords. We must have woman's influence in every department of the congregation, in order to infuse life into the dead bones. But aside of all these considerations, the position of women in the congregation must be improved; they are in the temple while not unfrequently their husbands are at the lunch houses, at the gambling tables, napping at the counting rooms, or talking nonsense at some place or another. The principle, the advancement of the cause, justice to woman, and the law of God inherent in every human being, require that woman be made a member of the congregation, of equal rights with any man; that her religious feelings be given full scope to develop, and she be fully attached to the sacred cause of Israel. All laws contrary to this principle, on any statute book of a congregation, should be wiped out as reminiscences of barbarism and degrading to the cause of religion.

We are ready to appear before any congregation in behalf of any woman wishing to become a member thereof, and to plead her cause. We are not afraid to batter down any wall of abuse, and to remove the debris out of sight. Whenever one will show us in what particular woman is less entitled to any privileges of the synagogue than man, or where her duty is less important to her salvation than to man's, we will debate this question with him. Till then, we maintain that women must become active members of the congregation, for their own sake, for the sake of their right, and for the benefit of Israel's sacred cause.

B

1880
WOMAN SUFFRAGE IN THE SYNAGOGUE

Messrs. Editors:

I have read with considerable pleasure of the efforts you are making to have the Jewess represented in synagogue school boards, etc., thus interesting her in congregational work. It may be new to your readers to learn that the question of woman suffrage was raised in my synagogue last year. It seems that in the by-laws all members are entitled to vote. A member died, and the question came up for debate whether his widow, who continued paying for his pew, was to be considered a member and entitled to vote. After a spirited debate, it was finally carried that the widow was a member and entitled to vote—of which privilege she has not yet availed herself. But the principle has been recognized, and I hope that other congregations will follow the example of

B'nai Jeshurun.

New York, Sept. 2, 1881.

[We trust that at approaching synagogue meetings the subject will receive discussion. If our congregations were prudent they would speedily devise an effective method of interesting the educated Jewess in the affairs of the synagogue. We are living in America and in the nineteenth century.—Eds.]

C

1895

Recently we have had occasion to read the membership list of 102 Jewish congregations, coming from every section of this country, and representing every shade of our ancestral belief. They contained of radical reformers, conservative and ultra orthodox Jews altogether more than 20,000 names. The lists varied in size and importance, each containing different names. But in one respect they were all alike. No matter where the list came from, no matter how the name sounded, it was prefaced by the simple *Mr.* Not even the most radical congregation on record put before its members' names *Mr. and Mrs.* ————.

The fact stares us plainly in the face that in Jewish congregations married women are still debarred from membership. This ought not to be. Our girls receive the same religious instructions as our boys, most of our congregations are governed by laws equally well understood by women and men and morally and materially supported by both. Would it therefore not be befitting the spirit of our time to record as members of a Jewish congregation Mr. and Mrs. So-and-So? A great deal could be said on this subject but we prefer deeds to words. Which will be the first congregation to combine justice with dignity? Which will be the first to record our names?

D

1923
REPORT OF COMMITTEE ON LEGISLATION

To the Twenty-Eighth Council of the Union of American Hebrew Congregations:

Gentlemen: Your Committee on Legislation, to which has

)een referred certain resolutions offered upon the floor of the
:onvention, having given due consideration to the same, begs to
·eport as follows:

A. Election of Women to Executive Board of the Union
Resolution was duly offered as follows:

Whereas, women, by their loyalty, cooperation and devotion
o the best interest of the synagogue, have been elected on the
Board of Trustees of numerous congregations throughout the
:ountry, and

Whereas, the National Federation of Temple Sisterhoods has
;hown the same devotion and loyalty and cooperation to the
nterests of the Union of American Hebrew Congregations,
herefore, be it

Resolved, That the National Federation of Temple Sister-
100ds recommends that the Executive Board of the Union of
American Hebrew Congregations grant the same privilege and
:onsideration to the representatives of the National Federation of
Temple Sisterhoods as shown by other organizations.

Referring to the above resolution, reference is hereby made to
Sections 6 and 9 of the constitution, which read as follows
·espectively:

Section 6. Each congregation, in such manner as it may deem
)roper, shall appoint one representative to the Council, and one
additional representative for every twenty-five contributing mem-
)ers above twenty-five. It is provided, however, that such
·epresentative or representatives shall be members in good
;tanding of a congregation affiliated with the Union.

Wives of members and the rabbi of the congregation shall, for
he purpose of such representation, be considered members.

Section 9. The Council shall elect fifty members (nine of
vhom shall constitute a quorum) to be styled the Executive
Board, whose office shall be in Cincinnati, Ohio. The term of
)ffice shall be four years and until their successors are elected.
Twenty-five members shall be elected by each Council.

It is pointed out by your Committee that these sections can be
nterpreted only to mean that women are already by law eligible
o membership on the Executive Board of the Union, and in view
of the increasing number of women elected to represent congre-

gations your Committee believes that this fact needs emphasis before the Council, as indicative of its complete sympathy with the law of the Union which gives equality to women who have been serving the various functions of the Union so effectively.

On motion duly made and carried, the recommendation of the Committee on Legislation was adopted.

63

THE LADIES HELP SUPPORT THE STUDENTS OF THE HEBREW UNION COLLEGE
1877

When the Hebrew Union College was founded in 1875, it needed money not only for its salaried staff—one man—but also to support the students. Following a tradition already decades old, the women were expected to come to the rescue. They did. At the request of Moritz Loth, the first president of the College's sponsoring organization, the Union of American Hebrew Congregations, "Ladies' Educational Aid Societies" were established in the late 1870's. The following is the appeal for funds which the Union published.

To the Women in Israel:

Since the historical days when Miriam led in music and song to the glory of God, when Deborah arose as a mother in Israel and by her counsel and courage rescued her country from the hands of the enemies of Israel—from those remote days to these, the women in Israel have always been the guiding spirit in the preservation of the Laws of Moses and that glorious peace which the observance of those laws secures to every family, in whatever land it may dwell.

In order to perpetuate those teachings and expound them in befitting language, the Hebrew Union College has been established for the education of ministers and teachers, and, as many of the students are either orphans or children of parents who are unable to provide them with the necessaries of life while they pass through their collegiate course, and in order to enable the Board of Governors of the College to admit all the applicants for a Hebrew and classical education, the Executive Board of the Union of American Hebrew Congregations make this appeal to the women in Israel to organize in every town and city Ladies' Educational Aid Societies, each member thereof to contribute one dollar annually as dues for the support of indigent students of the Hebrew Union College. To facilitate the organization of said societies, and to preserve the names of all who may join them, the Board has adopted a uniform subscription list, called "The Roll of Honor," and as soon as the list is complete it is to be returned to the Secretary of the Union of American Hebrew Congregations who, after duly recording its receipt, will hand it to the Board of Governors of the College, among whose archives it shall perpetually remain, and be accessible to all the visitors of the College.

Forms of these lists will be forwarded on application, or as the judgment of the officers of the Union may deem best.

By order of the Executive Board,

M. Loth, President
Lipman Levy, Secretary

64

MARRIAGE À LA MODE
1879–1880

One sometimes suspects that nineteenth-century Jewish families tended to emphasize the social aspects of marriage much more than their sophisticated twentieth-century descendants.

Two marriages are described here. The one in Cincinnati, selection A, celebrated the nuptials of an upper-middle-class family; the other marriage, in Philadelphia, item B, marked the union of two families whose roots went back to colonial times. The parties in the Philadelphia marriage were Charles Joseph Cohen and Clotilda Florance Cohen—no relative. Charles J. Cohen (1847–1927) was a highly respected Philadelphia stationer and envelope manufacturer. Rebecca Gratz was his godmother. He was to guide Mikveh Israel as its president and to accept election also as the head of the Young Men's Hebrew Association. In the community at large, Cohen served as president of an art association and of the Chamber of Commerce. One of his sisters was a sculptor and painter; another was a clubwoman who founded a Browning Society.

A

1879
An Elegant Wedding

January 1, 1879, at 7 p.m., a wedding ceremony was performed in Eureka Hall by Rev. Dr. I. M. Wise uniting Mr. Sigmund Haas and Miss Jennie Levi, daughter of Herman Levi, Esq.

After the ceremony about two hundred guests, mostly relatives of the groom and bride, were escorted by the attentive managers to the grand dining hall where a most sumptuous repast was furnished, after which toasts were announced.

"The Bride and Groom—Happy they! The happiest of the kind, whom gentle stars unite, and in one fate their hearts, their fortunes, and their beings blend." Response by Rev. Dr. I. M. Wise, in humorous and very enjoyable remarks.

The second toast, "Woman! Formed to bless the heart of restless man, to chase his care, and charm existence by her loveliness."

Responded to by Mr. M. Loth, who said: "It is universally acknowledged that God's best gift to man is woman. With that gift man receives that which is the loveliest and the most precious that exists; it is the life-giving and the life-preserving angel on earth. Woman is the promoter of peace and good will; she is the unfaltering friend of religion and of education. Women is the patron of industry, of art, of music, of song, and all that which refines nature and makes happy homes, creates great states and powerful empires. Woman is to mankind what the sun is to the vegetable kingdom, and the man who marries brings the sun of happiness and prosperity nearer to his home, and makes it possible to become a father of great men, who by their wisdom shape the destiny of nations, and thus leave foot-prints behind them in the sands of time. Gentlemen, let us drink to the health, prosperity, and happiness of woman, who is the poetical creation of the great Spirit whose glory fills the universe, and in which women are the shining and guiding stars to humanity. May their splendor never diminish." . . .

The bride looked truly beautiful and very happy, in which her parents, Mr. and Mrs. Herman Levi, and their numerous sons, fully shared.

The toilets of the ladies were superb and brilliant beyond description. The most stately were those of Mrs. M. Haas, the mother of the happy groom, who wore a rich black velvet dress, trimmed with the rarest laces, and adorned with diamonds. Mrs. Mina Weiss, her sister, was also elegantly attired, and as usual, escorted by her devoted son, Bernhard, who is happy in his mother's happiness, a worthy example to every son.

Among the noted guests was Mrs. Joseph Loth, of New York, the very personification of a true mother in Israel, who greatly enjoyed the festivities, being surrounded by hosts of her relatives in the "Queen City of the West." Mrs. Seligman, of Saginaw,

Mich., wore one of the most artistically made dresses of the evening; it was a combination of art.

What pleased us most about this wedding was that the groom, at the dawn of the morning of his wedding day, handed to one of the trustees of the congregation fifty dollars to be divided among the needy. We commend this act, as one worthy of example to every groom and bride that is able to act in the same spirit. This is one of the old customs in Israel and ought to be kept up.

May the couple be always as happy as they were on the day of their wedding, and surrounded by as many well-wishing friends.

B

1880
A HEBREW WEDDING

The brilliant scene at Mikveh Israel Synagogue

A Fashionable Gathering Witnesses the Nuptial of Charles Joseph Cohen and Clotilda Florance Cohen

One of the most fashionable Hebrew weddings which has taken place in the city for many years was solemnized yesterday afternoon at the synagogue Mikveh Israel, on Seventh, above Arch street. The high contracting parties were Mr. Charles Joseph Cohen, of 1828 Locust street, and Miss Clotilda Florance Cohen, daughter of Andrew J. Cohen, Esq., of 2219 St. James place, and granddaughter of the late Jacob L. Florance. Both parties move in the elite of Philadelphia society, and the event had been looked forward to in upper-ten circles for many months. The groom is President of the Mikveh Israel congregation, a prominent member of the Young Men's Hebrew Association, and is noted for his liberality toward Jewish institutions and movements. Nearly one thousand invitations had been issued, and a large number of friends of the family came on from New York, Montreal, Canada, and Savannah, Georgia, to participate in the happy occasion.

Four o'clock was the time fixed for the ceremony. Soon after three, however, every seat was occupied, and the late comers could not find even standing room. The aisles were crowded and the galleries jammed, not less than 1,800 people being crowded into a space which would not comfortably hold more than three-fourths that number. The gentlemen and a majority of the ladies were in full dress, and the rich costumes, combined with the flashing of diamonds from nearly every nook and corner, made the scene a brilliant one. On the floor in the centre of the edifice stood a magnificent "Chuppa" or canopy, of white silk, with embroidered hangings of the same material. This had been made expressly for the occasion. The steps leading to the ark were covered with exotic and choice growing plants, while the space usually occupied by the reading desk was filled with the choicest gems of the hothouse, which sent their fragrance throughout the building. On the west side a temporary orchestra had been erected for the accommodation of Hassler's Band, which gave some suitable selections before and after the ceremony. This was the first time that the strains of music had ever been heard inside of the synagogue. According to the customs of this congregation no musical instruments are allowed to be used in the religious exercises, and the innovation of yesterday was intended as a recognition of the relation of the groom to the church and congregation.

The buzz of voices was suddenly hushed when the doors were thrown open for the bridal party. Eight groomsmen led the way. These were followed by a similar number of bridesmaids, each attired in white cashmere costumes, elaborately trimmed with swan's down, and white felt hats adorned with an ostrich feather. Behind, leaning on the arms of their sons, came the mothers of the bride and groom, the one wearing a plum-colored velvet costume trimmed with point lace, and the other a heavy black silk. Rabbi Morais, in a sombre black gown, came next, and the two whose lives were to be linked together brought up the rear. The bridal costume was of white gros grain silk, short sleeves, low corsage and adorned with point lace, the whole being entirely covered with a tulle veil. The couple took their places under the canopy, the bride standing between her mother and future mother-in-law, facing west, and the groom confronting her, while the groomsmen and bridesmaids ranged themselves in a circle. Then the shoulders of the groom were covered with an embroidered "tallith", or scarf, and the ceremony was commenced after the old Portuguese orthodox style. Rabbi Morais first delivered a short address in English, in which he dwelt upon the high and noble aims of the married state, and then chanted a blessing in Hebrew. Then a glass of wine was handed to the bride to sip, and the groom, after following suit, placed the wedding ring upon her finger; another blessing was chanted, another glass of wine sipped and then the glass having been placed on the floor the newly-made husband planted his foot upon it and crushed it into fragments. This is a Jewish custom which signifies that the bond of union cannot be more easily broken than the glass can be made whole. After this the nuptial kiss was exchanged and the ceremony was at an end. In the evening the wedding banquet was given at the residence of the bride's mother, and later the happy couple left town for their honeymoon.

65

JOSEPHINE SARAH MARCUS EARP, A LAWMAN'S CONSORT
1880's

Josephine Sarah Marcus Earp (1861–1944), daughter of Mr. and Mrs. Hyman (Henry) Marcus, of San Francisco, was the common-law wife of Wyatt B. S. Earp (1848–1929), one of the West's most famous—or, if one prefers, most notorious—gunfighters. Some writers glorify Earp as a frontier hero; others deem him little better than a gangster. Sam Aaron, an Arizona Jewish businessman, thought that he was a criminal; Josie protested that her husband had been much maligned. She loved him.

The following excerpts describe her life with Earp in the 1880's, although she lived with him and shared his trials and successes for almost fifty years as they traveled through the West and into distant Alaska, where Earp pursued his career of armed guard, entrepreneur, gambler, mine owner, and sportsman. When Earp died in 1929, he was buried in a Jewish cemetery in the Marcus plot.

Josie or Sarah—Sadie, the Earps called her—what manner of woman was she? She was vivacious, intelligent, courageous, adventuresome, and shrewish. In her early days, Sadie was certainly no lady, but as the years passed, she became a very proper, decorous matron. Not all Jewish girls pursued the cult of "true womanhood."

The need to write this story has seemed to grow greater with each passing year after the death of my husband Wyatt Earp. It is, if not an attempt to vindicate, at least an attempt to explain him. And in such an enterprise I need take a backseat to no one. I lived with him for almost half a century. That should be time enough to understand something about the man I loved—and still love, for that matter. . . .

I guess what people ask me most is, "How did you and Wyatt meet?" To make it short and sweet, we were introduced by my fiancé at that time, Johnny Behan [a peace officer and businessman]. It happened in Tombstone in 1880. I have to laugh at

12. Josephine Sarah Marcus (Earp)

the response that answer usually gets. If the questioner knows who Johnny Behan was, I generally see his jaw drop.

For those who don't know, I guess you'd call Johnny Behan Wyatt's arch enemy in Tombstone. He was surely as much the author of most of the Earp trouble as anyone. And no one was in a better position to know that than I was. Plans to marry Johnny were what brought me to Tombstone in the first place. [Actually Josephine lived with Behan as his wife.] At that time Johnny and Wyatt were on friendly enough terms. Both had been lawmen, so they had something in common.

The first Earp I was to meet was not Wyatt, however. It was his brother Morgan. Morg was riding shotgun guard on the stagecoach between Tombstone and the railroad at Benson some twenty miles north. He was the guard on the stage that first took me into Tombstone. I don't hesitate to say that I noticed him because he was a very handsome man. He greatly resembled Wyatt. In fact they were sometimes mistaken for each other.

In my opinion, an even better question than those I'm usually asked is, "What was a strictly raised girl not yet nineteen and from a prosperous German Jewish family doing putting her dainty feet down from a train in a place like Benson?"

Southeastern Arizona was only a few years away from being a howling wilderness. It was still the stamping ground of the Apache. People, I soon discovered, were sometimes picked off by stray renegade bands within a few miles of Tombstone. Wandering from the beaten path unarmed was simply asking for it; I had a close call a little later myself.

But back to why I was getting off a train at Benson, all ready to board a stage to Tombstone to marry Johnny Behan. A girl raised as I was would normally never be allowed to meet a man like Johnny, much less one like Wyatt. They were both frontiersmen who had seen hard sights. Both were boomers, which means they were the kind that gravitated from one boom camp to the next, whichever was then the big news in mining. Wyatt was more of a mining man and speculator than Johnny. Johnny was a sure-thing gambler. He always managed to wangle some sort of political appointment or other.

I liked the traveling sort of man better than the kind that sat back in one town all his life and wrote down little rows of figures all day or hustled dry goods or groceries and that sort of thing. I can see the need for solid citizens such as those, but they were never my type for a husband. My blood demanded excitement, variety, and change. I sensed that fact before I was very old. In the late 1860s my parents had brought me and my two sisters, Edna and Henrietta, from Brooklyn to San Francisco to make our home there. I must have been about seven. We came by way of the Isthmus then went up the coast by ship. When my young feet touched the well-known San Francisco Embarcadero, I wanted to investigate everything about this glamorous new place. The gold rush was not yet twenty years past. San Francisco was still a miners' town above all else. Between stampedes the boomers fell back to San Francisco to wait for the next big excitement to break. That's how we heard of Tombstone. The name may seem strange to some people, but it didn't seem that way to me, being familiar with others equally unique, such as Hangtown, Shoot-Em-Up, and the like.

I don't know where I got the adventure in my blood. Certainly not from my parents who were the soul of middle-class, solid respectability. My upbringing was all directed toward taking my place some day as a proper matron in a middle-class setting. I probably would have fulfilled this destiny if it hadn't been for Gilbert and Sullivan.

In 1879 the *H.M.S. Pinafore* craze swept the country. Tunes from the Gilbert and Sullivan operetta were sung, hummed, and whistled everywhere. The sailor's hornpipe became a dance familiar to almost everyone. I don't know how many times I sneaked off with some girlfriend to see the *Pinafore*. In my room I secretly practiced the sailor's hornpipe and could do it very well, if I do say so myself. I was then eighteen, and was I ever stage-struck!

My downfall came because of two girlfriends, Dora Hirsch, daughter of my music teacher, and a music pupil named Agnes. Somehow Agnes had landed a part in the Pauline Markham *Pinafore* troupe then playing at the Adelphi Theater in San Francisco. She persuaded Dora to run away from home and join them when the group went on the road. I suppose this was because some regular member of the cast didn't want to leave San Francisco. Pretty soon that's all Dora could talk about. She had been practically my inseparable friend for years. The prospect of life in San Francisco without her appeared to me then as a pretty lonely outlook. We had, of course, always confided in one another.

Apparently Dora was thinking somewhat along the same lines. Maybe she needed moral support. At any rate, one night when I stopped at her mother's for my music lesson she met me on the porch all excited. "Josie, you've got to come with me!" she insisted.

I knew where she meant. The thought wasn't a new one to me. Envy over the seeming luck of Dora and Agnes had fairly eaten me up. But I couldn't act or sing very well, a fact I was quick to point out. "What will I do?" I protested, but not very strongly.

"You can dance," Dora said. "They need someone to play the cabin boy, Tommy Tucker."

I did a lot of moralizing with myself over what I was about to do. But I always wanted my own way. The thought of hurting my family was not as compelling as the thought of missing out on a chance for adventure and applause. You can guess what I did.

I left home one morning, carrying my books just as though going to school as usual. My mother may have wondered at the fervent kiss I gave her, rather than a dutiful peck. Tears were very close, but I fought them back.

I can remember exactly how I was dressed, in a plaid worsted dress, a blue Normandy cap, and my raincoat. My hair was in two braids wound Dutch-fashion around my head and fastened over the ears with plaid ribbon bows. I have kept one of the ribbons to this day.

It rained all day and was pouring when we boarded the boat for Santa Barbara. Dora and I went to our cabin and immediately fell into each others arms crying. We were pretty scared but also happily excited. We were on our own with no families to shelter us. Soon enough we found out what that could mean.

Our itinerary from Santa Barbara had us scheduled for a few days in Los Angeles, a one-night stand in San Bernardino, then a stint in Prescott, Arizona, and finally a few performances in

Tombstone, which was then the big news in mining boom towns. We had two stagecoaches for the members of the troupe and a heavy transport wagon for the stage props and luggage. There were twenty-six of us in all. . . .

Unfortunately for our young plans [my marriage to Johnny Behan], the first morning we were in Prescott I was greeted by a message that a Mr. Jacob Marks [a pioneer Jewish liquor dealer] wanted to see me. I couldn't imagine who in the world he was. The name wasn't at all familiar. I soon found out. Al Sieber [the army scout] had wired my sister. Her husband wired back to Mr. Marks, one of his business associates, to tell me that my folks and Dora's wanted us to return home. I was actually a little relieved. So was Dora. We both recognized we'd got in over our heads. In a couple of days Mrs. Marks was accompanying us back to San Francisco.

Before I left, Johnny promised to come and win my folks over to our plans. He told me to write him as soon as I felt the time was ripe.

Fate threw another monkey wrench into our plans, however. I got a case of Saint Vitus dance. Maybe the strain of all the things I had just experienced was too much for my nerves. At any rate, I burned with impatience to recover so I could have Johnny come meet my folks. As soon as I was well I wrote him.

He came at once. Between his persuasiveness and my wheedling he won my parents' consent to our eventual marriage. They were both real softies; they could never say no to anything their daughters really wanted. I'm afraid I took unmerciful advantage of them.

Our plan remained the same: as soon as Johnny was securely prospering in Tombstone, I would join him and we would get married. My parents wanted the wedding to be in San Francisco, but Johnny argued that while he was just getting started in the community his business wouldn't permit him to leave. My businessman father could see the sense in that, even if my mother couldn't. Johnny's new enterprise was to be a livery stable.

Looking back on these events, I can see that my father must have had serious misgivings about the whole thing. But he was wise enough to know me, and, recognizing that I could learn only by sad experience, he hoped for the best.

Johnny gave me a diamond engagement ring before he left. There was now no question in my mind that I'd answer his call to come to Arizona to marry him. All in all, I thought his long journey to ask for my hand was the most romantic thing that had ever happened to a girl my age. Little did I know!

But the fat still wasn't out of the fire. My mother was sure I'd be prey to either Indians or desperados. Happily Johnny found just the right person to convey the word that he was ready for me to join him. This was Kitty Jones, who soon became one of my best friends. She was married to a young Tombstone lawyer, Harry Jones, and was visiting her folks in San Francisco. Her white lie assuring my parents that Tombstone was by now a budding metropolis smoothed over my mother's misgivings. Kitty promised to accompany me to the boom town and give me a home until the wedding.

So now I was on my way to Arizona again, and that's how my "dainty" feet stepped down from the train at Benson. It was the railroad's point of deposit nearest Tombstone, where one changed to the stagecoach. When I had traveled the route on my first trip, the railroad had hardly touched Arizona, and the *Pinafore* troupe had had to make the whole trip by stage. Now nearly a year had passed since that exciting adventure. Soon I would be nineteen, and I thought of myself as rather grown up and worldly. . . .

Wandering With Wyatt

Wyatt and I were discovering new things about each other each day, just as all new couples do. One of the first things we realized we had in common was an insatiable desire to travel—to see new people and places. . . .

In El Paso we met Lou Rickabaugh, one of Wyatt's former partners from the Oriental Clubrooms in Tombstone. He now had a clubroom in El Paso. (Clubroom, of course, was a polite term for a gambling parlor.) He wanted Wyatt to stay, but my husband said he "had some other fish to fry" just then. While we were in El Paso a smart aleck drunken trouble-maker tried to pick a fight with Wyatt. His name was Raynor. Before he got into serious trouble with Wyatt someone else obligingly shot him to death.

We made a stop in Fort Worth for several days to see [the gambler and gunfighter] Luke Short, who by now had an interest in a restaurant and clubrooms there, also, by coincidence, called the White Elephant. He mainly concerned himself with the gambling which took place in the upstairs clubrooms. Wyatt and I had our evening meals in the restaurant below which offered a menu as good as that in any large-city eatery. I suppose Fort Worth must have had twenty-five or thirty thousand population at that time. Wyatt would escort me back to our room at the Mansion House just a few doors up the street, then return to gamble. He struck a winning streak, and we were several thousand dollars richer when we left Fort Worth than when we came.

It may seem like a strange, lonely life for a woman, but I saw more of my husband than most women ever do. When alone there was always plenty to occupy me. Reading has always been one of my vices, and I read voraciously. There were always new people to meet too, and new things to see. Even the small things in life served to amuse me. At the Mansion House in the evenings when the street lights were lit, I used to watch the city urchins playing around the street, perhaps following the ice wagon returning from its daily route and leaping on the rear step to snitch a small sliver of ice to suck on.

Wyatt always returned by 1:00 or 2:00 A.M., and I usually waited up for him, since our days consisted of the same hours, rising around 10:00 or 11:00 A.M. In this way we took the midday and evenings meals together and spent our afternoons carefree as honeymooners, gadding about seeing the sights and doing the shops. Our third meal, if we had one, was a snack before bed, sometimes in an all-night restaurant if the town we were in had one. We did this every place we went, so, contrary to what one may think, it was actually a happy life for me.

Our next stop after Forth Worth was Austin. All this time Wyatt was still working on a case, and gambling was an ideal cover, since gamblers moved around on a regular circuit. But Wyatt would tell me, jokingly, "You're my cover. Who would expect a man-hunter to take along his wife?"

We found it hard in those days, as it is in these, to find a good place to eat in a new and strange town. In Austin the year before we'd been lucky enough to find a place where they served fine steaks. We immediately looked it up to see if it was still operating. It was. As we were waiting for our food we talked of an encounter we'd had there on our first trip to Austin, the year before. One day as we had seated ourselves a man called out to my husband, "Well I'll be jiggered if it isn't Wyatt Earp!" I could see as he came over to our table that he was short, heavy set, and slightly bald. I took him to be some sort of drummer or other. Wyatt introduced him as Mr. Thompson, but called him Ben.

"Ben and I knew each other in the Kansas days," Wyatt explained for my benefit. I was a little surprised to hear that he was the town marshal. Later someone told me he was a famous gunman and killer. I found that hard to believe. He'd impressed me as a gentleman and good company. Ben Thompson didn't look like he'd harm a fly, regardless of what they say about him. They probably made most of it up anyhow just as they have about Wyatt.

We next went to San Antonio, where we were joined by Bat Masterson [peace officer and sports writer] and two of his associates. From there we went to Laredo, Texas, on the Rio Grande. It lies across the river from the Mexican town of Nuevo Laredo. Whether we went over to the Mexican town for sight-seeing or in the interest of Wells Fargo business, I cannot remember, but I went along as usual. I had never been in Mexico before and was anxious to see how the Mexicans lived in their own land.

It was fiesta time. The men of our party found plenty of games of chance in progress, for the Mexicans love gambling. Monte was the game of chief interest as I recall. You'll laugh when I tell you what happened to Wyatt. He was wearing the expensive watch that had been given him by [the California publisher and mine owner] Senator George Hearst in Tombstone. One evening when he was playing monte he got so interested in the play he forgot to keep his eye on the watch. When he left the table Bat glanced at him. "Your chain's hanging, Wyatt!" he exclaimed. "Where's your watch?"

Wyatt clapped his hand to his watch pocket. "My God!" he said, "They've touched me!"

He never got the watch back. Reporting it to the Mexican police was a waste of time.

66

THE JEWISH WOMAN, THE JEWISH HOME, THE IDEAL ACHIEVED
1880's

In 1931, Mrs. Henry (Jennie Rosenfeld) Gerstley (1859–1937) sat down to write her memoirs so that her children might know the rock whence they were hewn. She was a remarkable woman; one quite untypical of her generation. She had begun her career as a schoolteacher and, as she grew older, devoted herself to social work in the general and the Jewish community. In 1882, while still young, she had founded a Young Ladies' Aid Society, a group dedicated to hospital visiting. The Society was to become the Chicago Woman's Aid, a Jewish women's civic and welfare association that reached out into the general community. In a way it was a precursor of the National Council of Jewish Women. Mrs. Gerstley was a founder of the Maxwell Street Settlement, of a Red Cross auxiliary, of summer recreational centers and kindergartens. She was a woman of high intelligence, an intellectual with a capacity for clear and vigorous expression. In an address she made in 1915 before the plenum of the Union of American Hebrew Congregations, she spoke of feminism: "The feminist movement is in its incipiency. . . . As we gain momentum, women will press their way into every line of activity."

The following pages from her manuscript memoirs are presented here to give the reader an insight into the Jewish home, the family life, at its best. Unwittingly, Jennie Gerstley wrote a beautiful apostrophe to herself and to the American Jewess of the last two decades of the nineteenth century.

I cannot bring this screed to a close without speaking of the deepest and most sacred memories of my life.

Uncle [Max Mayer Gerstley (1812–1893), a Chicago merchant], my more than father—who held out his hand to my mother when my father died—in her helplessness. He took us three fatherless children and gave us a home, clothed us, fed us. Much more, he gave us the best schooling available at that time because there was no university, and only one high school miles away. Still more, we were the intangible gainers thru the conversations of the learned men who were always at our house. I had a better schooling than most of my friends, although compared to what is offered to-day it was simple indeed.

I think in time Uncle grew fond and rather proud of us. We used to go out with him and passed as his daughters. I was always addressed as Miss Gerstley. As I grew older, there was a silent friendship between us. He was so wise I used to ask his advice when I was faced with problems; and he liked it I know.

It is a great comfort to remember that my turn came when he was old and ailing and needed care himself. He was never robust physically, altho' his strong character and self-control made him a tower of strength to those who sought his counsel and his aid. He was often a sufferer and confined to his bed. Henry [his son, my husband] and I took turns watching him during the night. I would be with him until midnight; then Henry would stay until morning. My mother and I were at his bed-side during the day. He was always a silent man, outwardly stern, inwardly tender. Twice, as he was lying on the sofa, half asleep, half awake, he murmured, "There is nothing like a woman." They were words that I cherish to-day, because I know that in a faint way I had returned a little of his kindness. He was always tender toward the weak or the poor, and "The Aid" [the Chicago Women's Aid] is his monument.

When the end came, the congregation [Anshe Ma'ariv] he had led for 32 years [1859–1891] asked to have the services from the Temple. So far as I know he was the first man to receive that honor. I am told that among the extreme Orthodox it is the custom for a funeral to pass the Temple, but I have never seen it done. Uncle gave us shelter and opportunity; we gave him unquestioning and complete gratitude.

Aunt Sophie. She and my mother left the old world as young girls. They never returned. For two months they were on a sailing vessel, and when they reached America, Aunt Sophie went with Uncle to Chicago, while my mother was left in an uncongenial home with Uncle Morris in Philadelphia. Our own good uncle in his frequent visits east saw she was unhappy and brought her to Chicago. She and Aunt Sophie were both simple and guileless, good to their souls, and I am glad that for the rest of their lives, they had one another. My mother was a great invalid, and her devoted sister came every day. It must have meant all the world to them to be together.

Her gratitude and devotion to Uncle were immeasurable. She gave her whole life to him. I used to see her when I was a young girl, lying on the floor beside Uncle's bed, when he was ill, so that no movement he made would escape her. It was my privilege to care for her. I felt sorry that Carrie, who had moved to Phila., couldn't have that comfort.

What can one say of a mother? And can I ever forget Aunt Sophie's simple kindness? I was with them both very much and I thought as much of Aunt Sophie as I did of my own mother. She turned to me a great deal toward the last.

Henry [my future husband, Uncle's son]. There never was a minute of my life he didn't share. When I was a tiny little girl, hardly of school age, I was conscious of his comings and goings. Our house was very unpretentious, and he used the side door. He came in with a smile and a happy word, and the room became bright; he left with a laugh and a jest that lingered till he came again. He was always wonderful. Later when I was older, I appreciated him more: his clean life, his scintillating wit, his wise judgment, his patience, his unfailing, comprehending goodness. No words were necessary between us; a look was enough. Our companionship was perfect. We shared the joy of parenthood to-gether; we shared the darker days of sorrow and anxiety. I wish our children had been old enough to really know what their father was, a man of clean hands and a pure heart. To have known him was a blessing.

And my sister, Carrie, whom I adored all my life. She was so entirely lovable, so sunny, so winning as a child, so gay; and, in the dark days that came later, so womanly, so brave, so devoted, so strong in spirit. She had wonderful, innate charm, and in every relation of life she might have been a model. She was much brighter than I, much quicker and keener, and tho' I was two years older, I knew her judgment was good, and she always influenced me. To be near her was to be content. She and Henry always joked while I, who was always heavy, listened in admiration, because I'm not witty at all. If I had loved her less, I would have been jealous, but I was always proud and happy when people loved her. What she was to me, no words can express, the best half of myself. I remember a tombstone in our cemetery that used to amuse me. A lady lost a grown-up son, and his monument described him as the brightest gem in her diadem. I understand her grief better to-day. It is truth to say that Carrie was the light that shone upon my life and warmed me. There was a strange union between us, almost an uncanny one; we were so entirely united and understanding and devoted. My children loved her but never could gauge her goodness. It was their unrealized loss when fate took her to Philadelphia.

The night before she died I dreamed of her. I saw simply a dense, dark cloud, but in the middle I saw her face clearly. Her eyes were bright, her glance straight, but her look different. It was no longer suffering; it was in a way commanding. I can't define it; it was so clear. When I woke . . . I knew the end was near. It was like a farewell. She died the next day—my sister— in my arms, as she had wished. She used to say I was more mother to her than sister, but to me she was the world with all its loveliness. I followed her while she lived, and I draw a sort of strength from the dream since life parted us. It comes to me nightly. It seems to me I'm sort of mute since she left me.

I think my love for all these was not selfish. There was too much to do, to think of myself. Uncle and my mother were ailing so many years; there were the children and the big house to manage, everything to keep me occupied. It was life to work and to give. With Simon, my best of brothers, it was different. He lived with me; he did everything for me. He was gentle and very warm-hearted and helpful. He was always doing kind things in a quiet unobtrusive way. He took me to dancing school and to lectures, took my friends home at night, tied my bundles, helped move the chairs when there was company. It was so natural; I was so used to it that I took it all for granted and didn't realize how devoted he was, in his quiet way.

On the rare occasions when I was ill it was he who made the coffee and toast for me, who brought the magazines, a flower or a bit of choice fruit. As I depended on Carrie, he depended on me. It was only when he and I were the only ones living that I understood the depth of his devotion. He was in the hospital five months, and it was my turn to bring the coffee from the hotel to him. I visited him every day, and his face brightened when I came. He was lonely, I was lonely, and we drew closer to one another. I am glad to recall the affection between us. I know it meant much to us both, until the final summons came for him.

And little Frankie, the little curly-headed baby whom I loved so deeply. I had no shoulder on which to lean, and he filled my empty arms.

My eyes are blurred as I write; they all meant so very, very much to me. My heart cries out to them, beloved.

I have a strange feeling that I have been alone in a darkened theatre; it seems as if the curtain rose on a play that was about people who lived and things that happened long ago, a play that bore me into the past. It seems as if when the curtain descended I rose, a little unsteadily, because I was deeply moved and with the illusion of living in the past still gripping me; I groped my way along the dim aisle until I reached the door and passed into the shining light of the Present.

The Present; yes, it is shining. For here are Jesse [my son] and Adelaide, and Margaret [my daughter] and Claude, my children and my children's children!

I should like my children to know that I have loved them devotedly, and I tried with all that in me lay to lead them to cherish what was fine and good and to seek to be worthy of the good name they inherited. I should like them to know that their love and kindness have filled and sweetened these declining years of my life.

They have asked for my memories. Memories, memories, what are they but the unacknowledged history of one's life? [As Henry Austin Dobson says:]

> Times go, you say? Ah, no!
> Alas! Time stays, *we* go;
>   Or else, were this not so,

What need to chain the hours,
For youth were always ours?
    Time goes, you say?—Ah, no!

How far, how far, the past lies behind our feet.

· 67 ·

A RABBI EVALUATES WOMEN OBJECTIVELY
1880's

*In the 1870's, or at the latest the early 1880's, Liebman Adler
(1812–1892) delivered a sermonette in the course of which he addressed
himself to women. Adler, a well-trained teacher who had taught at Jewish
schools in Germany for many years, came to this country in 1854. After
ministering to Detroit Jewry for several years, he moved on to Chicago,
where he remained for the rest of his life. There he served but one
congregation, The Men of the West (Anshe Ma'ariv), to whom he
preached simple homilies in German.*

*The following sermon demonstrates Adler's approach to women:
respectful, yet realistic. He could not disavow his German heritage. This
man was no worshiper at the altar of the feminine mystique and its
Christian-tinged romanticism. His objection to women in politics makes
interesting reading; women, he felt, were too good to descend into the
political arena, where they would have to expose themselves irretrievably
to slander and calumny. In many respects his views of women reflect the
thinking of the intelligent, middle-class German immigrant, who dominated American Jewish life until the turn of the century.*

According to the first account [of creation in the Bible] man was
created first. But when it was found that it was not well for man to
be alone, woman was given to him as a companion. The man was
called Adam and his wife Eve—for "she was the mother of all
living." [Gen. 2:18, 3:20.] According to this account, woman's
place in creation would be but as the complement of man; she is
valuable only as the mother of future generations; for her own
sake her existence would not be justified. This, indeed, do we find
the position of woman to be in uncivilized lands and ages; she is
but her husband's beast of burden. The social and domestic
position of woman keeps pace with culture.

In the second account of the creation, we are told, "Male and
female created he them; and blessed them, and called their name

Adam" [Gen. 1:27–28]. Here woman is created not merely as a helpmate to man, as a supplement, as it were; she is valued not only as Eve, the mother of men, but she exists independently and for her own sake. . . .

There always have been men and women who exaggerate virtue and piety into a very caricature, and so cause them to be decried. We find the same tendency illustrated in the relation of the sexes to each other. The calm sensible prose of our text would read that man and woman were created equals, and so every just, enlightened code of laws endeavors to give to woman equal rights with man. Whereas the poetical conception of the story of the creation of the "natural man" degrades woman to the level of a mere convenience to man, the romantic literature of civilized countries goes to the other extreme and deifies and beatifies the "eternally feminine" *(das Ewig-Weibliche)*. It depicts the world as one of flowers and sunshine, of homage and adoration, and oftentimes are girls and young women embittered for life, unhappy and discontented with their lot because they fancy themselves wronged, because, in real life, in the world of reality, they find that in the long run men and women alike are valued according to their services. Their eyes are opened to the fact that the demands of the home upon the housewife, of the family upon the mother, and finally the husband's assertion of *his* rights, prove to be very different from the hazy pictures of romantic literature.

Yet the charming conceits of romantic literature possess at least the merit of having given great pleasure to the world. Who can count the hours of enjoyment that such reading has bestowed or the number of hearts that it has softened? Who would deny that it has been invaluable in awakening, fostering, and cultivating the aesthetic sense in the majority of its readers? If we had to continue the Bible, who knows but that the influence of romantic literature might impel us to add a third account of the creation of woman to the two already existing? In the first, she is man's inferior; in the second, his equal; in the third, she would be a higher aesthetic being, which neither knits nor weaves nor spins, but charmingly arrayed, like the lilies of the field, would beautify our lives, and "weave heavenly roses into our earthly life." And then because it were not good for woman to be alone—for who would weave and spin and take care of things?—we would have God create man to serve her.

But exaggeration ceases to be pleasing; indeed, it becomes offensive when it introduces woman into the arena of political strife, and transports her from the peace and purity of domestic life to the noise and mire of publicity. She has a right to enter upon this life, certainly, just as the dove has a right to mingle with eagles, but the exercise of the privilege would prove fatal to the poor dove. Instinct teaches the animal to keep out of danger. Is there not enough of abuse, slander, fraud, and even bloody strife in connection with elections and politics in general among the politically-privileged sex, without casting the other and purer half of humanity into this whirlpool? Men, in their political contests, may calumniate and cast the mire of slander upon one another. A blot on a man's character is easily obliterated, and even his real shortcomings are leniently judged. But the faintest tinge upon a woman's character robs her forever of her reputation and tarnishes her name and being. Woman, more delicate and sensitive, and when good possessing a nobility of soul which even the best among men cannot approach, would not retain her equanimity as man does in the pitiless strife of politics. She would leave the field of battle hurt, deeply pained, and wounded, whereas men of opposing factions cordially shake hands after the battle, as if no unkind word had been spoken. But the cultured, patriotic woman is not debarred from exerting political influence; her spirit may guide husbands and sons in the noblest direction, and kindle them to the noblest deeds. Cornelia did not go into the Forum, but she was the mother of the Gracchi. . . .

The tendency of culture is to place the weak on an equal footing with the strong. And thus Israel [World Jewry], like woman, has been the gainer by the advance of culture. It is weak in numbers, and has been further weakened by prejudice. Look about you in the different countries of the earth. Wherever you find woman oppressed, her claims disregarded, there Israel likewise does not lie upon a bed of roses; and where woman succeeds in asserting her rights, Israel also is permitted to grow in dignity. In no land upon earth is woman held in higher esteem than in our blessed United States. Here, too, the Israelite may enjoy every privilege.

This is the best evidence that the country takes first rank, in point of culture, among the nations of the earth. May it ever remain upon this pinnacle, and be guarded from the pitfalls of exaggeration!

13. Emma Lazarus

68

EMMA LAZARUS, POET
1880's

Henrietta Szold, writing the article on Emma Lazarus in the turn-of-the-century Jewish Encyclopedia, *said that she was "the most distinguished literary figure produced by American Jewry." This is high praise. Who was this woman? Miss Lazarus was the daughter of a wealthy sugar refiner, who was identified with New York's congregation Shearith Israel. At a very early age, eleven to be exact, she began writing; by seventeen her first volume of verse had been privately published. It was not until the Russian pogrom victims came here in the early 1880's that she became deeply involved in the fate of her people. Then it was that she became an ardent Jewess and a pre-Herzlian Zionist. Her new interests were reflected in her poetry. Prior to this time, she had not been primarily concerned with Jews or Judaism, though she had written poems of Jewish interest and import. By 1881, she was already accepted as a poet of quality, albeit a minor one. She began seriously studying Hebrew and the history of her forebears. Her warm and responsive essays in defense of Jewry were, like her poems, accepted in some of the country's best periodicals; much of her verse and many articles on Jewish themes were published in the* American Hebrew. *Her prose was as good or better than her poetry.*

In 1883, she was asked to write a poem to be sold at a literary auction. The funds raised were intended to help build a pedestal for the gigantic Bartholdi statue, "Liberty Enlightening the World." In answer to the appeal, Miss Lazarus wrote a sonnet entitled "The New Colossus." In 1903, long after her death, the poem, cast in bronze, was hung in the interior of the pedestal. Since then it has been read by millions; it is the most famous, the most frequently quoted, of all her writings.

Why is Emma Lazarus so acclaimed today? People pitied her for her untimely death of a dread disease. She was a Zionist, a friend and protagonist of the East European refugees whose sons and daughters today dominate American Jewish life numerically and spiritually. American Jews admire her sonnet; it is indeed beautiful and touching. Implicitly, of course, her lines flatter America's present-day affluent Jewry, children of the huddled masses who came to these shores homeless, impoverished, tempest-tost. The Jewish Nobel Prize winners of East European origin are no longer the wretched refuse of Europe's teeming shore.

Her sonnet and two other poems follow; they were written during her "Jewish" period.

THE CROWING OF THE RED COCK.

Across the Eastern sky has glowed
    The flicker of a blood-red dawn,
Once more the clarion cock has crowed,
    Once more the sword of Christ is drawn.
A million burning rooftrees light
The world-wide path of Israel's flight.

Where is the Hebrew's fatherland?
    The folk of Christ is sore bestead;
The Son of Man is bruised and banned,
    Nor finds whereon to lay his head.
His cup is gall, his meat is tears,
His passion lasts a thousand years.

Each crime that wakes in man the beast,
    Is visited upon his kind.
The lust of mobs, the greed of priest,
    The tyranny of kings, combined
To root his seed from earth again,
His record is one cry of pain.

When the long roll of Christian guilt
    Against his sires and kin is known,
The flood of tears, the life-blood spilt,
    The agony of ages shown,
What oceans can the stain remove,
From Christian law and Christian love?

Nay, close the book; not now, not here,
  The hideous tale of sin narrate,
Reëchoing in the martyr's ear,
  Even he might nurse revengeful hate,
Even he might turn in wrath sublime,
With blood for blood and crime for crime.

Coward? Not he, who faces death,
  Who singly against worlds has fought,
For what? A name he may not breathe,
  For liberty of prayer and thought.
The angry sword he will not whet,
His nobler task is—to forget.

THE NEW EZEKIEL.

What, can these dead bones live, whose sap is
      dried
  By twenty scorching centuries of wrong?
Is this the House of Israel, whose pride
  Is as a tale that's told, an ancient song?
Are these ignoble relics all that live
  Of psalmist, priest, and prophet? Can the
      breath
Of very heaven bid these bones revive,
  Open the graves and clothe the ribs of death?

Yea, Prophesy, the Lord hath said. Again
  Say to the wind, Come forth and breathe
      afresh,
Even that they may live upon these slain,
  And bone to bone shall leap, and flesh to flesh.

The Spirit is not dead, proclaim the word,
  Where lay dead bones, a host of armed men
      stand!

I ope your graves, my people, saith the Lord,
  And I shall place you living in your land.

THE NEW COLOSSUS.

Not like the brazen giant of Greek fame,
With conquering limbs astride from land to land;
Here at our sea-washed, sunset gates shall stand
A mighty woman with a torch, whose flame
Is the imprisoned lightning, and her name
Mother of Exiles. From her beacon-hand
Glows world-wide welcome; her mild eyes command
The air-bridged harbor that twin cities frame.

"Keep, ancient lands, your storied pomp!" cries she
With silent lips. "Give me your tired, your poor,
Your huddled masses yearning to breathe free,
The wretched refuse of your teeming shore.
Send these, the homeless, tempest-tost to me.
I lift my lamp beside the golden door!"

69

GROWING UP IN A GERMAN-JEWISH AMERICAN HOME
1880's–1890's

Irma Levy (Mrs. Norvin Rudolf) Lindheim (1886–1978) grew up in a middle-class German-American Jewish home. The influences impinging on the child Irma were both acculturative and ethnoreligious. The following account describes her home life in some detail. When she was about thirty-two, she became a Zionist and began studying the history and literature of her people. For the next fifteen years, she threw herself heart and soul into the Zionist movement and rose to leadership in the Zionist Organization of America, Hadassah, and the United Palestine Appeal. In 1933, she settled in Palestine in a collective settlement.

I was born into an unexceptional family, began my life in a period in which only change was exceptional, and grew in an unexceptional environment.

Ours was a middle-class existence, well to do, well behaved, complacent. When I was born, in the last month of 1886, our house was brownstone, with a high stoop, on Ninety-fourth Street near Lexington Avenue in New York City. It was a great pleasure to me as a child to watch, from our front windows, a family of goats and their kids frisking over a patch of rocks the size of a square city block.

Twice a year my sisters and I were taken by horsecar for shopping expeditions in the big stores on Thirty-fourth Street, or farther south on Fourteenth Street. After a spree of buying we ate our lunch in a public restaurant, an adventure so unimaginably satisfying that we felt no need to envy Marco Polo or even Hannibal with all his elephants.

My father, Robert Levy, born in Hesse-Cassel, Germany, of German-Jewish parents who died in their own country without my ever knowing them, was an importer of nettings and veilings, who climbed slowly but steadily to affluence in this country.

To his family he was first and foremost a businessman, virtually a slave to his success in pursuit of security for his family. In the rare instances when he tore himself away from success, to relax and be friendly with his wife and children, he showed himself invariably to be a man of superb charm. But there was little time, really, for learning to know his children, or we him.

His America was an America of expansion, a solid, planned, conservative world, demanding the closest attention, where opportunity was unlimited for those who had energy and the industriousness to grasp it. The only kind of man considered worthwhile carefully conserved what he acquired, and built on it what he wanted for the future. Cash in the bank, or invested in the business, was the acid test of a man's value. Our father had the prejudice of many men of German-Jewish origin against Jews born "east of Berlin." I can only speculate on his feelings, had he lived to see—when German-Jews sought refuge in Palestine—that it was the Russian and the Polish Jews who were first to welcome them with open hearts and hospitality, doing everything humanly possible to ease their difficult adjustment to a new home. I can imagine only too well how he would have felt when, in time, I was to choose as my dearest friends and closest associates, people who stemmed from the very background he abhorred.

It was his fixed and unalterable belief that neither politics nor religion were fit subjects for family conversation. Even so important a topic as the Dreyfus case was proscribed, as a dinner table incident showed. It took place the evening of his arrival from a business trip in Europe.

With rage and indignation he described rioting he had seen in Paris, and how he had barely been rescued from the hands of a mob yelling "Down with Dreyfus! Down with the Jews!" While an attack on my father was too unbelievable to be real, what I could not comprehend at all was that, suddenly in the middle of a sentence, he put his finger to his lips with the sharp exclamation, "Hush!" when the Irish maids came in to change the plates.

Was the word "Jew" something not to be mentioned in front of servants? I did not understand. All I knew was the distressing shame and embarrassment I felt for something incomprehensible in my father who, I always told myself, could do no wrong.

The only other time I remember seeing him give vent to fury in connection with politics was at the time William Jennings Bryan delivered his startling "Cross of Gold" speech, at the Democratic National Convention in 1896. When the full force of Mr. Bryan's ideas struck him, my father shouted, "Why, that shameful demagogue!"

My feelings about my father were ambivalent. I dearly loved him, and he was not really the tyrant he appeared at times to be. With me he was downright indulgent—my middle sister said overindulgent—perhaps because his "baby" was the only one in the family with no fear of him. And yet often his authority and domination affected me in ways exactly opposite to his wishes or expectations. In time I came to see, for all I loved him, that I learned from him more of what I wanted *not* to be and do, than *to* be and do.

My mother had no interest whatever outside her husband, her children, and her home, and was completely content for it to be so. Not all women, eternally doing for their loved ones, are able at the same time, to create an atmosphere of tranquillity. Giving herself up solely and completely to the needs and wants of her family, she crowned it all with unity and peace.

Her parents had emigrated to Pittsburgh from Nuremburg, Germany. Our maternal grandparents Morganstern prospered until their sons, educated beyond such mundane practicality, took over the family's thriving shoe business and ran it quickly into the ground. The disaster had one happy effect at least; it brought our mother's parents to New York to live with us.

Of the experiences of my childhood only one influence was to have a clear effect on the course of my future; even so, it long lay dormant.

In a line of direct descent from my maternal grandmother and through my mother to me had come a passionate Jewish consciousness. With one exception, my grandmother's sister, we were the only ones to possess it. So intrinsic in nature was it, so indivisible, that, in spite of being negated and suppressed in me, taking many, many years to rediscover, it remained alive.

My grandmother's Jewishness was more active than my mother's; it was my mother's quiet way to live her convictions without, however, obtruding them on those around her.

I used to sit every day on a footstool at my grandmother's feet, listening in rapt attention to stories she told me from the Bible. She sat very tall and straight in a high-backed Victorian chair but in some wonderful way her hazel eyes, with bronze specks in them, brought her down close to me. Mine, and my mother's, eyes were like hers, only hers had more crinkles around them because she was old.

She would rest her hand tenderly on my head as she told the stories. I loved everything about her; the soft, billowy folds of her black silk dress, the way her white lace cap with the black ribbon bows set on her wavy brown-gray hair, her face shining with love for me as she stroked my hair.

More than anything I remember the day—though I was only five when she died—when, taking my face in her hands, and looking deep, deep into my eyes, she said, "Never, never, my darling, forget you are a Jew."

Always, after they were gone, my grandmother and my mother were identified in my mind as one.

My confirmation was the tremendous event of my youth. For a while I felt an acute regret that I was not a man, and therefore could not become a rabbi. I felt almost suffocated with wonder and joy at the moment when, before the open ark, my rabbi placed his hands on my head and blessed me. To myself I vowed that my life would forever be dedicated to my people.

What happened between that moment of exaltation, set to the deep, majestic tones of Handel's "Largo," and the time, only a few short years later, when there seemed nothing left of the burning faith that had been mine but the ashes that appeared to be without ember or spark?

Somehow the longing questions of a seriously inquiring child had been answered without affirmations she could accept. Could I, I wondered persistently to myself, be a Jew merely because of having been born a Jew?

Before doubts and questions assailed me, I loved going to temple with my mother on Saturdays, the only one of the children who really wanted to go. My father attended service only on the high holidays, and then merely to please my mother. He could make me laugh with funny things he would say, but I did not really like his saying them because everything in temple was to me too solemn and beautiful. When the organ poured forth its wonderful sound, and the choir sang, I felt myself lifted right up to heaven.

Because she was so devoted to us, mother was a worrier. It made for almost too cushioned a kind of life for us, overprotected. No matter how many servants there were—in time nurses, governesses, cooks, waitresses, chambermaids, finally a lady's maid, our darling, fat, French Marie—all picking up after us and tending to our slightest needs—our mother was always ready at any time to hurry to the kitchen and cook our favorite dishes as she knew that *we* knew only she could cook them; to sew for us, to knit beautiful stockings and sweaters for us, as later she would do for our children; to help us with our homework; from morning to night to add in whatever way she could to our happiness and wellbeing.

She taught us varied skills; though I could never seem to do very well at the drudgery of household cleaning jobs which in her wisdom she believed that we should master, in later years I could never be grateful enough that she had insisted that we learn them. Only long after she was gone, when I had allowed myself to grow rusty at such tasks, did I feel fortunate that I was able to call back some of the things she had taught me. However, I never learned the art of scrubbing a floor, and it took many grueling tries and much kindly direction before I could clean the floor of my tiny one-room shack in the kibbutz [collective settlement] and know that there was not more mud on it after I had worked than there had been before I started.

In view of our well-tended household life, it may seem paradoxical to say that before my sisters and I were grown there was never any extravagance in our home. Certain standards and amenities obtained, but they were based on fitness, not show. My mother knew instinctively how to husband material resources, utilizing them for necessary purposes; she was thoroughly in sympathy with my father's passion for saving to provide for our future, in healthy fear of a family being left unprotected, to face want.

This passion for saving to protect the future was altogether characteristic of German Jews of that period; indeed to this day it is considered something of a crime to spend more than one receives as interest on money. Capital is to be used only for investing.

The business was the big thing in life; the more money ploughed into it, the more profit would be stored up to take out later.

But when it came to our education, nothing was saved.

Contrary to everything which seemed so conducive to happiness and security, I was a lonely little girl, for a reason as painful and baffling to me as it was to my parents and the doctors.

I had been blessed in being born with the gift of a happy nature. My mother said I awakened to each new day with a smile. Regularly I was told that I was pretty. It was mentioned also that I was lucky, because of being "born in the caul," which I was happy to believe must be something exceptional. People said this brought luck to even those around me, and my father made me feel proud and important by telling me that it was when I was born that his real success in business began.

70

A MOTHER TO A SON LEAVING FOR AMERICA
1880

With tears in her eyes, Getty Bechmann wrote a letter saying good-bye to her son Heinrich, who was leaving for distant America. This was in September 1880. He set off for the Land of Unlimited Opportunity with two trunks and high hopes. The trunks contained his clothes, winter- and summer-weight, including red flannel underwear. Here in America, in Cincinnati, his hopes were realized, for as Nathan Henry Beckman (d. 1940), he became a wealthy clothing manufacturer. When he retired in 1910, he devoted himself to good deeds in the communal and religious fields. He was president of a Reform synagogue, treasurer of the Union of American Hebrew Congregations, and a member of the board of the United Jewish Social Agencies. In 1909, he endowed a clinic at the Jewish Hospital in memory of his parents. Getty's letter to Heinrich, translated and reprinted here, reflects the ethics, the piety, the idealism that characterized many a mother who sent a child out into the world. Be assured that N. Henry Beckman attempted to rear his children in the spirit that moved his beloved mother. His daughter, Mrs. Martha Ransohoff, was a highly respected Cincinnati educationist.

---

11 P.M., Sept. 30,
Night, eleven o'clock, 1880.

My dear good Heinrich, *may you live to be a hundred* [Hebrew]:

The long expected has come to pass, your trip to America. You realize, my dear son, the pangs I suffer at the thought of your going. But it is your wish and so shall it be. May the Almighty guide and protect you from all evil and be with you always. Put your trust in Him and everything will work out. Be good, as you always have been, good and kind, and you will get along everywhere. Dear Heinrich, do not forget our beloved religion. It will bring you comfort and consolation, patience and endurance in trials, whether it be your fate to be rich or poor. Always keep God before you and in your heart.

You are going out into the wide world far from parents and family. Don't be discouraged, for you are endowed with so many good qualities, and my heart tells me that God's blessing will accompany you in all that you propose to do. Commit your way unto the Lord and you will be successful. Be careful in all that you undertake, and particularly in your associations. Guard your health, know that it is the greatest gift on earth.

I would like to and I could say much more to you, dear Heinrich, but it is very hard and distressing for me. Therefore I can only say, finally: Go with God and may it be well with you. Be ever cheerful and put to good use all that you have been taught. Always consider very carefully what ever you do. Though a great distance separates us, my parental worry, my motherly thoughts of you, will never cease as long as my loyal heart beats. The thought that our separation will be of short duration is my only consolation in my great pain.

And so, my dear Heinrich, I bid you adieu. Write me and let me know everything that you experience and that happens to you. Do not play with the idea of settling so far away from us, and let me live in the expectation of not being without you too long. Tears come to my eyes; you will therefore have to excuse my poor writing although you know I have such good intentions.

Your ever faithful mama,
Getty

Amen, good luck, and blessing [Hebrew]
P.S. Tomorrow marks the advent of your twentieth birthday and the start of your big journey. May everything be for the best. Good luck, blessing, and prosperity!

71

THE EDUCATION OF A YOUNG LADY OF FAMILY
ca. 1881

Florentine Scholle Sutro (1864–1939) was the child of a wealthy German Jewish family which lived first in San Francisco and later in New York City. When but a child of four, her parents sailed for Germany, where they spent several years giving little Florentine ample opportunity to forget her English. On her return, she went to a private academy, studied with tutors, and was at home in French, German, and English literature. As a member of the first class of the Ethical Society's "Sunday School," she came under the influence of Felix Adler, who had by then begun preaching his gospel of social welfare. By the time she was seventeen, her formal education was finished, and she became a kindergartner and a volunteer social-welfare worker. The autobiographical selection that follows offers the reader some insight into the life, culture, and ideals of a well-to-do postbellum Jewish family.

One year before my class graduated, I left school to take a kindergarten training course. A year after my classmates graduated, a post-graduate course was formed for the purpose of studying English literature with Mrs. Froelich [at the private school for Jewish children]. It seemed quite natural that I should join this class, so after all I did not feel that I had not gone on to the end with my schoolmates. I got a good part of my education after I had left school. The influence that Mrs. Froelich left on my awakened intelligence through the study of literature, meant intellectually solid food for me.

Previous to this I had read the Elsie books [children's novels in which Elsie Dinsmore was the chief character. The author was Martha F. Finley.] and Grace Aguilar, Oliver Optic and later Thackeray, Dickens, Scott and Cooper. When I was thirteen I got hold of a copy of the Decameron and read it surreptitiously and enjoyed it with the keenness of forbidden fruit. After we started studying literature in school, I acquired a taste for better reading and we read Shakespeare, Milton, and other classics, in class. My home reading was never supervised and I was allowed to read anything. I do not feel today that it did me any harm. When my daughter Florence was growing up I offered her the Grace Aguilar [Jewish] books to read and she threw them aside saying they were too long-winded and too "goody-goody." I was not so critical and anything was grist that came to my mill. I had reached an age of maturity and appreciation of literature when I was about eighteen and read what might be called current classics with avidity and interest. It is easy for me to recall the pleasure I had in reading Oliver Wendell Holmes' "The Autocrat at the Breakfast Table." I felt impelled to write to the author because he had expressed my thoughts, for which I had no words and was naturally very grateful to him. His answer was as follows:

Beverly Farms, Mass. July 14th, 1885.

My Dear Miss Scholle,—I am much obliged to you for taking the trouble to tell me that my writings have given you pleasure or afforded you instruction. I did not think so pleasant a letter an intrusion, but a compliment for which I ought to be grateful.

Very truly yours,

(signed)   Oliver Wendell Holmes.

In 1878, a year after the Ethical Society was organized, Dr. Felix Adler formed a Sunday School Class for the sons and daughters of the members. I was a member of the first class, and we ranged in age between thirteen and sixteen. I was thirteen. This "Sunday" School Class met on Tuesday afternoons. Dr. Adler had been teaching at Cornell, having but recently returned from Heidelberg, where he received his Ph.D. He was filled with the idea of what we would now term social welfare work, and brought it forcefully before us in connection with his teaching of practical ethics.

At the age of seventeen I left school without much regret and took up a course in theoretical and practical kindergarten. Dr. Felix Adler had imbued us with the idea of doing practical work and he believed that girls as well as boys should be prepared for life, with a career, which was a new thought at that time. I grew exceedingly absorbed in the work and felt extremely flattered when the other teachers turned over their recalcitrant children to me, as I had so little trouble with those in my class. For some reason these new children fell into line and we were a very happy family. In the kindergarten course, I was happier in the practical than in the theoretical work,—teaching came natural to me.

The Ethical Society established the first free kindergarten in New York. It filled such a need that it was soon adopted by the Board of Education and introduced into the public school system of the country. I mention this fact because the origin of so many welfare movements originated in the Ethical Society through the stimulus of Felix Adler.

It was one of the purposes of the Society to send the teachers into the homes of the children and we were so successful in gaining the confidence of our pupils that the parents looked forward to our visits and, in many instances, we were able to be of real service in what is now called Americanization work. . . .

It was Dr. Adler's idea that there should be no race, creed or color discrimination, and a certain quota of colored pupils were admitted in the kindergarten from the beginning. At dismissal time each day the teachers took turns in standing at the head of the stairs to say "good-bye" and as the children filed out they all insisted on kissing us. With our present knowledge of hygiene, I feel sure that these fervent osculations would have been omitted.

It was in our kindergarten that the practice of medical examination of the pupils was first initiated. This received such widespread notice that before long it became incorporated in the public school system. A young doctor whom I knew socially was the medical examiner and because of my acquaintance with him the other pupil teachers turned over the children to be examined, to me, to prepare them. I remember one little boy who had a clubfoot. I took off his shoe and stocking, and I had never seen such encrusted filth so of course I had to bathe the foot before the doctor could see it. Another experience I had was with one of my own pupils, whose dress was stiff with dirt, and hair equally stiff with bear's grease, which had been used to keep the unwashed hair under control. I asked permission, of the principal, to bathe this child and it was granted. I had bought a new outfit of underwear, shoes, stockings, and a pretty pink dress for her. When the child saw the tub full of water she screamed with fear, never having seen such a quantity of water before. I petted her and finally induced her to get into the tub. When she felt the warmth, she relaxed and a wondrous change came over her. I gave her a good scrubbing, which she did not mind and also washed her hair. She came out of the bath like a new born child, and put on her pretty clothes. I placed her before the kitchen fire, so that she would not catch cold, and then took her back to the classroom. Nobody recognized her. When I told the class who she was, they could scarcely believe it was the same child. I had had considerable trouble with her before, because she apparently had been cowed, being one of eleven children, and I could not get her to speak or even take part in the exercises. After the bath episode, she became my devoted slave and followed me about like a pet puppy. Some years later, I told this story to a settlement worker in California, and she told me that that was always her method of bringing recalcitrant children into line. . . .

The method of our kindergarten training, although the course was only one year, was very efficient. We did such intensive work during our course that it compares favorably with the much longer term now required. Almost from the first day we entered school, pupils were assigned to us, and we began to teach, so that we got practical experience with the theoretical studies. We had the children from 9:00 to 1:00, then our lunch, and from 2:00 to 5:00, our lessons in theory. At 5:00 we went home and prepared our lessons and material for the next day. I worked until 10:00 or 11:00 o'clock every night during the entire year. . . .

My first awakening experience was during that time of strenu-ous study. Mother had gone to California after Aunt Rosa Scholle's death to bring Uncle William and his family back to New York. A well-known physician of our acquaintance had decided that he wanted to get married and made up his mind that I was eligible, probably considering my father's bank account as a big asset. He called on me one evening when I was very busy with my kindergarten studies. Presently he asked father to show him the paintings in the parlor. I was happy to get rid of him, but poor father little suspected what was coming his way. He had never had to tackle any problems pertaining to his children; mother always took care of them. Dr. H. asked my father for my hand, right there and then, which was, to say the least, a disquieting situation, as the man had never paid me any especial attentions. Father said he did not know anything about such matters and told my suitor that he would have to wait until mother's return from California. I was in no way consulted and felt thoroughly disgusted as I had never thought of him in the light of an eligible suitor. He seemed so much older and was most unattractive to me. After mother came home I told her about the incident. She promptly, with her habitual directness, went to the doctor's office, and told him that I was entirely too young and that matrimony was quite out of the question, and I considered the affair closed.

Several years later I was escorted to the wedding of an acquaintance by a young man who was a childhood friend. It was almost my first social function. As it happened, my would-be-suitor was the preceptor of my escort, who was studying medicine. In the course of the evening Dr. H. asked me to dance with him, after which he led me aside into one of the anterooms and formally proposed. I was startled to hear him say: "You may have been informed by your father and mother that I had asked for your hand? I wish to assure you once again of my admiration for you and I hope you will reciprocate the feeling." I promptly told him I had no intention of marrying, although I was already then in love with my future husband. Dr. H. later married a girl with whom I had gone to school who was reputed to be very stupid, but who had inherited a great deal of money. When someone asked him how he could have married this girl he replied: "It is sufficient that one of the family has brains." After my refusal he took me back into the ballroom and in his desire to get rid of me, introduced me to at least six men, who all seemed pleased to meet me but not one of whom asked me to dance so I went back to my escort and startled him by saying: "Alfred this is our dance, don't you remember?" He looked surprised, and then—remembered. After that a cousin of the bride came and talked with me for about an hour. I took it for granted he was going to escort me to supper, but was disappointed for he walked away just before supper was announced. Again I threw myself upon the mercy of Alfred who had in the meantime asked another girl, thinking I had been taken care of. Fortunately the girl was a close friend of mine and we were glad to be together. Before we sat down at table, four other men asked to sit with us, and the fateful evening ended in a burst of glory.

As I matured I somehow felt that any young man who evinced an interest in me did so from an ulterior motive. I had a peculiar under-estimation of myself and the feeling that no man could really care for me for myself alone. It made me very suspicious of any male attention, because I felt I was not good looking and thought that I was stupid. This lack of faith in myself was undoubtedly due to the fact that my parents constantly reminded me of my stupidity, which I am afraid was very much the parental attitude towards the children of that day. Consequently, as my father was a rich man I felt that the admiration of men was due to his purse and not to me. . . .

The annual charity ball took place at the time of my visit [to Chicago] and the young man responsible for my social career in Chicago, escorted me. As I had never been to a large evening affair, I had no idea what the proper dress was, nor had my friend, and so I came to the ball in a street dress, with hat to match. My escort was Master of Ceremonies and asked me to lead the march with him. I must admit I felt out of place. The invitations read "white neckties required." Although this was naturally meant for the men, they thought it would be a good joke that I should wear a white tie, and, Sir Walter Raleigh fashion, one of the men doffed his tie and placed it around my neck to give me the semblance of being in evening dress. I was game. I had a delightful time and am sure I had more partners than any other girl in the room. For the first time I felt myself a real person. My ego was considerably stimulated and as my social success continued I eventually lost my inferiority complex.

WHAT IS TO BE DONE: THE MEN WON'T CALL
1882–1883

It is a serious matter when eligible young men cease to call on the girls.
"Sophie"–whoever she was–uttered a protest and appeal for a solution to
this problem (A).

A number of people answered her. Among them was Lee C. Harby
(1849–1918). Lee was Leah Cohen Harby, a granddaughter of Isaac
Harby, the Charleston essayist, teacher, editor, and religious reformer.
Lee, like other members of the family, was a litterateur; she wrote poems
and short stories, a Texas flag song, and some articles on the history of the
Lone Star State. She had lived in Galveston, Houston, and New York,
though she was a native Charlestonian. Like many other Southerners, she
was an ardent patriot, a proud member of the Daughters of the Revolution
and the Daughters of the Confederacy. An early feminist, she vigorously
denied that women were inferior to men. Like other thoughtful club-
women of her generation, she was very much interested in the Jewish home,
in religion, and in the education of the younger generation of her sex. Her
answer to Sophie's query: "What Is to Be Done?" is in a way a blueprint
for the modern woman (B).

A

WHAT IS TO BE DONE?
1882

To the Editor:

You will pardon me, I am sure, for intruding on your valuable space with a subject which can hardly interest a journal so dignified as the *Messenger*. But while the matter may appear a trivial one, it is of some moment to the Jewish young ladies of the metropolis. I need hardly say that I refer to the absolute cessation of visiting by the young gentlemen. Last winter, it was bad enough, as all the girls know, but from present indications there is every reason to believe that the custom has, I am sorry to say, absolutely died out. Young men think of every way of passing away an idle hour, but the idea of spending it in a young lady's society never seems to enter their heads. I ask you, in all seriousness, what is the remedy for this abnormal state of affairs? Must we young ladies waste our time endeavoring to entertain those empty-headed youths of slender years, with their sickly moustaches and tight-fitting clothes, who imagine they are doing us a honor, by Jove, by calling on us, ye know? No, indeed! Some means must be devised, some plan effected to induce marriageable young men to once more indulge in the pleasure of social visiting. I hope some of my fellow-sufferers will come forward and ventilate their ideas on this subject.

Sophie

New York, October 8th, 1882

B

OUR WOMEN AND THEIR POSSIBILITIES
BY LEE C. HARBY
1883

"Woman is a creature between Man and the Angels," say the French; they well might have added, when she does not willingly descend to a lower plane, for the generality of the sex seem to take a certain delight in relegating themselves to a sphere of principle, thought and action, below that commonly assumed by men. The old, barbaric, Eastern idea of woman's inferiority and *irresponsibility* seems to have imbued the minds of generation after generation. Why it has not before this been totally eradicated, must be charged to an erroneous system of education, which fails to make them reliant and independent in their opinions, or brave enough to advocate and act up to them. Particularly is this the case with Jewish women, and, as one of their faith, it is to them that I address myself. In all kindness do I point out their errors; in all earnestness do I suggest the remedies. If I seem to prone to find fault, too exacting in my requirements, it is prompted by my desire to see my coreligionists as celebrated for their refinement and culture, as they have ever been for their beauty and domestic worth.

Society As It Is

It is a fact, sorrowfully conceded, that Jewish society is not what it should be. It is simply a mixture of handsomely dressed, fashionably attired persons of both sexes. Something more than this is needed to make our gatherings creditable to a race that is as noted for its intellect as for its antiquity. Our men of brains keep away from all such meetings; the few brilliant women we have are seldom found there, because certain elements are wanting that should be inherent in elegant circles. Repose of manner, polish, refinement, conversation in lieu of gossip, ideas instead of scandal, dress made subservient to the woman, not the wearer eclipsed by her attire—all these are component parts of polite society. Do we find them among the general run of Israelites? Unfortunately, we do not. . . . In this very essential of "good manners" our Jewess is often deficient, and under that head may be classed most of her errors in society. She is too much given to dress and fashion—valuing her attire by its *cost* rather than by its appropriateness to her style, or the occasion. She desires thus to outshine her neighbors with this evidence of greater means; and as she ranks herself according to the costliness of her garments, her respect for them is based upon the depth of their purse. A kind of self-consciousness is about her, which robs her of all repose of manner, causing her to attract attention by voice or exaggerated gesture. She is affected in her deportment at table while in company, but eats too much and too often when alone; hence the obesity of so many of our women when middle life is reached. The love of good living—a racial characteristic—may be carried to excess; it is the fostering of this taste, by both sexes, that makes so many mothers and wives in Israel fill the position of good cooks and housekeepers and—*nothing more.*

Our girls seldom engage in intellectual employments. They sew, embroider, crochet—keeping time to their needles with many a tale of gossip and many an unkind scandal. This arises from lack of reading and unstored minds. Having no inward resources, they soon exhaust the usual, every day topics of conversation—then they busy themselves with the affairs of others and repeat things to which they should never have listened. . . .

HOME LIFE

There is nothing more beautiful than Jewish home life, and no one appreciates it more than the average young man—but it must be a social home, not a fashionable one. I knew an old lady who was said to have married off her nine daughters, by having young men to drop in to her Friday night suppers. Her girls were so charming in their home, that their fascination was not to be resisted—and each one soon had the chance of forming just such a home for herself. If you would win a man away from the dangerous allurements of club and bar room, let him cast aside ceremony and enter your family circle; let him see your little home ways—how sweet and bright you can be, surrounded by the old folks and the children. If the gentleman is not one you can receive in that way, you had best not receive him at all—he can not be a desirable acquaintance. . . .

In this social visiting all your little accomplishments will come into play; a gay song, a merry air on the piano, the steps of the last new dance, your latest drawing, the subject of your next water color. This is your opportunity of showing your appreciation of good taste, or of impressing it upon your friend that taste, tact, and a certain sympathy with refined employments, are essential to polite circles and are tokens of education and culture. A mutual interest in each other's occupations is a necessary concomitant of pleasant social intercourse. . . .

EDUCATION—THE REMEDY

It is seldom that we hear complaints on this visiting question from women of culture, for they attract all those with whom they desire to associate. Their power lies in their scope of intellect and in the grace of manner that culture is sure to give—which brings us back to the remedy that we believe can be found for all social shortcomings—namely, Education. Here it is that woman's influence reaches its highest plane, moving children through their mothers, husbands through their wives, and men generally through that beautiful power wielded over their sex by all true womanhood. . . .

A girl's scholastic term is but the promise of what she can do. It depends upon herself whether she will develop into the intellectual, or the merely fashionable woman, with a thousand foolish caprices of dress and manner. It is not what a girl studies while at school or college—it is her course of reading, observation and self-culture, afterwards, that improves, exalts, and strengthens her mind and judgment. . . .

Good literature is a boon to mankind. The more we know of the works and thoughts of the scientists, philosophers and poets, the more do we approach their standard. A mind, strengthened and stored by a collegiate education, should be kept fresh and bright by a careful course of reading after scholastic exercises are done with. A couple of hours devoted to the best works of the best authors should be a part of each day's duties, and is time well expended. Then do not keep the knowledge so gained to yourself, but talk about it. Thus new ideas will spring from what you have read. Suppose your father or mother have not been blessed with advantages as great as yours, do you not see that they may learn from your lips, through your conversation, the information which has been denied to their early life?

The Art of Conversation

Physicians tell us that conversation at table is a great aid to digestion. Be sure that it is as healthful for the mind as the body. It is an art, made perfect by practice. Be you ever so wise, unless you have the power of imparting to others that which you have learnt, you will prove but an uninteresting and unprofitable member of society. Brilliant conversationalists are rare, but interesting conversers are happily often met with, and are generally self-made. Any intelligent, well-read woman, who determines to impart her information pleasantly, will, by trying, succeed in doing so. The first essential is to have something to say; the next is, to say it well. By "well" let it be understood that I mean in the most acceptable manner, to the person with whom you are speaking. Suit yourself to your company. Use good ideas, sound sense, broad views, no matter who may be your hearers; but your language, whether simple or ornate, must depend upon the culture of those whom you address. It is the extreme of bad taste—indeed of ill-breeding—so to construct your sentences and frame your thoughts, as to leave your listeners in doubt whether or not you desired to be understood, or to turn them into ridicule.

The best field for the practice of the conversational art is the home circle, whether suiting yourself to the babies' requirements in the nursery, telling a wonderful fairy story, boasting a moral, plain enough to strike their undeveloped minds, or merrily chatting at table, giving the *on dits* of the day—whether social or literary; or yet again, around the fire at night, where a recitation of a favorite poem, an anecdote, just learned of some great man, a discussion, a criticism, are all in order and give exercise to a faculty or an accomplishment, which adds a charm to its possessor. The girls, who the morning after a dance or theatre or opera, will sit around the breakfast board and relate a dozen amusing incidents, or tell the plot of the play and criticise acting and singing, not only perform their duty of making home pleasant, but teach themselves to clothe their thoughts in language and entertain those with whom they are brought in contact. Pleasant talkers are always sought after. They are really treasures at a dinner party, an acquisition at a country house, and a delight at a sociable tea gathering. At a ball they are never wall flowers, even if they do not dance; there is always a little group of *the best men* about them, for the male dancer of society seldom represents its intellect. Plain in face or figure these pleasant women may be, but, for all that, gentlemen pick them out to visit, to escort, to admire for a permanency. Remember, girls, a pretty fool may do very well for an evening's amusement, but it is the sensible women, who know how to demonstrate that they have sense, that a man will choose for his life time friend and companion, if he is a man of brain as well as form, and not simply an inane specimen of the masculine gender.

How many reading and debating clubs, literary circles or art societies, have we heard of among the Jewish ladies? Yet could anything be pleasant or more improving? I have been told that it was an impossibility to form such associations, that the material did not exist. That is a fallacy; the supply will grow to the demand. Improvement will come with the use of their gifts or faculties. The woman who discusses a question this week brokenly, hesitatingly, next week will do better, and in a month's time will be surprised at her own ease and fluency. So it is with writing, indeed with every power of man, for "Practise makes perfect" is the truest of all sayings. A girl should study quickness of thought, ease of speech, as a part of her education. She should train tongue and eye and ear, as she does her hands and feet. She learns to sew, and that is for utility. She learns to dance, and that is for beauty—a necessary accomplishment, the science of motion and grace. But do not let her stop there; why should she not learn to think, and to clothe her thought in words, to speak out or write down her ideas? Let her train her ear to catch the thousand voices of nature and her heart to answer their teachings, her eye to appreciate a beautiful scene, her soul to admire a noble action— then, as the brush or pencil imitates the one, let her deeds emulate the other.

A TIME FOR ACTION

It is time that something were done towards raising our social status, our intellectual average. I say educate, cultivate, read, listen, and discuss. Try and understand *yourself* physically, mentally, and morally. Study human nature, learn to look for motives, and judge of deeds by the thoughts and desires that prompted them. Do not be content with surface reasoning, but go to the depths of things. Take broad views, look on both sides of a question and appreciate the good they present, while eschewing the bad. A woman's idea of honor should be higher than a man's, as her purity is greater; yet her charity should be all-embracing, as she knows her own weakness and appreciates her own strength.

Cultivate self-reliance. A woman with resources within herself stands independent of fortune and imparts that quality to her children. Her resources are those of the minds that furnish refined pleasures, entertainment, and culture to the home whose ornament she forms. Such a home asks nothing from society, but gives much to it. A child raised in such an atmosphere will never value wealth above principle, or appearance more than worth. From such family circles will come those who will place Jewish social life upon its proper plane. Theirs will be an arduous task but a noble one, one of exaltation and redemption, to be extended to both sexes of those who share their faith.

Houston, Texas.

14. Emma Goldman

73

EMMA GOLDMAN, ANARCHIST
1885–1940

Lithuanian-born Emma Goldman (1869–1940) came to the United States in 1885 and over the years was recognized as one of the country's leading anarchists. A woman of high intelligence, she was a devotee of the arts and a person fully capable of expressing herself in excellent literary English. True freedom, she contended, was impossible under any form of modern society or polity, yet she insisted with equal vigor and conviction that the individual must be completely free. Thus, of necessity she was a "feminist," and by the same token a "masculinist." Though she condemned all extant forms of the State, it was her belief that an ideal form of group survival could be achieved through a cooperative ethical society.

The 1940 obituary printed below, as selection A, summarizes objectively the life and fortunes of a brilliant woman whose ultimate social goals are essential and moral by present-day standards. When she was sixty-five years of age, after years of exile from the America she loved, she was asked whether her life had been worth living. Selection B is her answer.

A

Emma Goldman, Anarchist, Dead
Internationally Known Figure, Deported from the U.S., is Stricken in Toronto

Disillusioned by Soviets

Opposed Lenin and Trotsky as Betrayers of Socialism Through Despotism

Toronto (Tuesday), May 14 (AP)—Emma Goldman, internationally known anarchist, died early today at her home here after an illness of several months. She was 70 years old.

Miss Goldman suffered a stroke in February and spent several months in a hospital. Until recently she had appeared to be improving in health, however.

Present when she died were a brother, Dr. Maurice Goldman, and a niece, Mrs. Stella Ballantine, both of New York. A sister, Mrs. Lena Cummings of Rochester, N.Y., also survives.

DEPORTED FOR OPPOSING DRAFT

Emma Goldman, apostle of philosophic anar_ism and of "voluntary communism," was born in Russia, s_ _t thirty-three years of her life in the United States fighting f_ /her ideals, for which she suffered imprisonment, and was an i_corrigible revolutionist to the end.

She was deported from the United States in 1919 for obstructing conscription, fled in 1921 from Soviet Russia, where she had hoped to find the realization of her social dreams but found only disillusionment, and saw her ideals defeated again in the civil war in Spain, in which she took an active part. In the social history of the United States she wrote a chapter all her own, and in the history of the worldwide revolutionary movement of her time she made a place for herself beside that of her teacher, Peter Kropotkin.

Miss Goldman was a writer of distinction and an able critic of the drama. Her autobiography, "Living My Life," published in 1931, is regarded as one of the important books of its kind.

THOUGHT IDEAL BETRAYED

After fighting for a generation against what she considered the ills of the social system in the United States, she opposed Lenin and Trotsky because she believed them guilty of betraying the Socialist ideal by establishing what she denounced as a new despotism. Her experience in Russia confirmed her in the belief that all government was wrong, and that the new society for which she stood could be established only on the basis of anarchism, through the free cooperation of the masses. She never ceased to search for that new society even after the defeat in 1939 of the social experiment in Catalonia, where she thought she had finally found it.

Miss Goldman always had a warm feeling in her heart for America, despite the long years of conflict with the authorities and public opinion in this country. In 1934 she was permitted to visit the United States for ninety days, and she lectured on political and literary topics.

It was not only because she had found an America that had undergone a profound transformation from the days when she had first come to know this country, but also because of the striking contrast presented by the United States in comparison with nations in the grip of totalitarian regimes that Miss Goldman hailed America as a land of hope. She said she had never ceased to regard this country as her real home.

Found U. S. Still Free

"You are still free in America," she said. "You are free to come here and listen to me, with no army of police descending upon you. No spies enter your homes for incriminating documents. No legalized assassins shoot you down in the streets."

Emma Goldman was born in Kovno, June 27, 1869. She spent her childhood in the Russo-German province of Kurland, where her father had charge of the government-subsidized theatre and where she received her early education. [Actually her father was a shopkeeper.] Later she was sent to her grandmother in Koenigsberg, the city of Immanuel Kant, in East Prussia, where she continued her education in schools and through private instruction.

In 1882, when she was 13 years old, her parents moved to St. Petersburg. It was a stormy period in the life of the Russian people. Alexander II had been assassinated the year before and Russian society was in violent fermentation, marked by the execution of the assassins and the imprisonment of their accomplices. It was the period of the celebrated revolutionary party of the Narodnaya Volia ["The Will of the People"], of activist "Nihilism." Young Emma was deeply impressed by figures like Sophia Perovskaya, who was among those executed for the assassination of the Emperor, and Vera Figner. [A Russian revolutionary, imprisoned for twenty years for her part in the assassination of Alexander II.] She determined to seek independence and an active career of her own. At the age of 17, with her sister Helene, she emigrated to America. They settled in Rochester, where she obtained employment in a clothing factory at $2.50 a week. There she gained her first knowledge and impressions of the labor problem.

Entered Anarchist Movement

In 1887 she was married to Jacob Kersner but the marriage soon broke up because of differences of opinion and ideas. Miss Goldman moved to New Haven, Conn., where she obtained employment in a corset factory. In New Haven she came into contact for the first time with anarchist circles. She read the *Freiheit*, the paper published by Johann Most.

These contacts, together with the impression made upon her by the execution of the Chicago anarchists in the Haymarket bombing tragedy of 1886, brought her actively into the anarchist movement. Made ill by her factory work, she returned to Rochester, where she remained until August, 1889, when she came to New York. Here she met Alexander Berkman. They became close friends and collaborators in anarchist work and propaganda.

This association was interrupted for fourteen years during which Berkman served a term of imprisonment in Atlanta for his attempt to assassinate Henry C. Frick during the Homestead steel strike in 1892. After his release from prison, Berkman rejoined his companion in her work of going up and down the country preaching the abolition of government through education of the people to the point where they could govern themselves.

Miss Goldman's first imprisonment was in 1893, when she was

arrested for inciting to riot at a Union Square demonstration in New York held in support of the Debs railway strike. She served seven months on Blackwell's Island. While in prison she acted as nurse in the hospital and devoted her leisure time to intensive study of American literature, with special attention to Bret Harte, Mark Twain, Walt Whitman, Thoreau, and Emerson. She also studied particularly Fourier, the French Socialist. These and other studies fortified her for the literary aspect of her career.

Miss Goldman was 25 years old when she left Blackwell's Island in 1894. In addition to her work as a propagandist of anarchism she published for many years *The Blast* and later, until her deportation, *Mother Earth*, a literary and philosophic journal which came to be recognized as the authoritative spokesman of philosophic anarchism in this country.

On September 6, 1901, Leon Czolgosz shot President McKinley at Buffalo. In his confession the assassin said he had been influenced by the writings of Emma Goldman and by some speeches which he had heard her make in Cleveland. She was arrested in Chicago and questioned for two weeks, the authorities being compelled to release her because of lack of evidence linking her in any way with the assassination. Eighteen years later, however, when the deportation proceedings were brought against her and Berkman, A. Mitchell Palmer, Attorney General, revived the subject, contending that there was some evidence that she knew Czolgosz at least by sight.

While she was often in trouble with the authorities because of her work on the lecture platform and in labor struggles, it was not until the war [World War I] that Miss Goldman came into serious conflict with the government.

SERVED TWO YEARS IN JAIL

Because of their agitation against the war draft and their opposition to the war, Berkman was sent to [the jail at] Atlanta and Miss Goldman fined $10,000 and sentenced to two years in jail in Jefferson City, Mo. The deportation proceedings were brought by the government upon their release. The case was fought through the Supreme Court and, finally, on December 1, 1919, together with 247 other aliens, they were deported on the transport "Buford."

"We expect to be called back to Soviet America," she said as the "Buford" drew away from the pier.

Because of the absence of diplomatic relations with Russia at that time, the deportees were landed in Finland, whence they traveled by rail to Petrograd. They received a gala reception from the Bolsheviki, but it was not long before Miss Goldman and Berkman discovered that the regime set up by Lenin and Trotsky did not correspond to their conception of the new society. Within six months she wrote to a niece in Rochester that the Soviet regime was a new despotism under which the Russian people were deprived of all liberty.

The suppression of the Kronstadt rebellion of the Spring of 1921 [when a mutiny was brutally suppressed] moved them to open opposition against the Bolsheviki. They fled to the Ukraine and in December of the same year arrived in Riga, enemies of the Bolshevik system. Early in 1922 Miss Goldman was in Stockholm, going in April to Prague and thence to Berlin. Berkman wrote a book called "The Bolshevik Myth," while Miss Goldman traveled about Germany lecturing against Bolshevism.

Wrote Two Books on Russia

In 1924 she published her book "My Disillusionment in Russia," followed next year with "My Further Disillusionment in Russia." This disillusionment was again emphasized in her autobiography. Incensed by her criticism, Communists in Germany tried to break up her meetings, just as the American police had frequently done in the earlier part of her career.

By 1924, Miss Goldman arrived in England, and two years later she turned up in Montreal as Mrs. E. G. Colton, wife of James Colton, a Welsh miner whom she had married in order to obtain British citizenship, having in the meanwhile lost her status as a Soviet citizen and become a woman without a country. From

Canada she returned to the South of France, where she lived quietly and wrote "Living My Life."

Three years later came her American visit. She did not conceal her happiness at having been permitted to return to this country, if only for a brief span. She was warmly received here by old friends and left with deep regret and some hope that she might yet be permitted to return to the United States permanently.

Her antipathy to Bolshevism was based upon a conclusion that the system had given "unhappy Russia a far worse tyranny than under the Czar."

Her impression of Russia was confirmed through the years in the establishment, finally, of the dictatorship of Stalin after the execution or exile of most of the old Bolshevik leaders. Lenin died in January, 1924. Ultimately, as Miss Goldman believed, Leninism, too, was dead, while nearly all the leading Leninists had been exterminated.

In July, 1936, while living at Nice, France, Miss Goldman suffered a shock in the death of her friend Berkman, who had committed suicide in a place near by.

B

WAS MY LIFE WORTH LIVING?*
By Emma Goldman

I have often been asked why I maintained such a non-compromising antagonism to government and in what way I have found myself oppressed by it. In my opinion every individual is hampered by it. It exacts taxes from production. It creates tariffs, which prevent free exchange. It stands ever for the *status quo* and traditional conduct and belief. It comes into private lives and into most intimate personal relations, enabling the superstitious, puritanical, and distorted ones to impose their ignorant prejudice and moral servitudes upon the sensitive, the imaginative, and the free spirits. Government does this by its divorce laws, its moral censorships, and by a thousand petty persecutions of those who are too honest to wear the moral mask of respectability. In addition, government protects the strong at the expense of the weak, provides courts and laws which the rich may scorn and the poor must obey. It enables the predatory rich to make wars to provide foreign markets for the favored ones, with prosperity for the rulers and wholesale death for the ruled. However, it is not only government in the sense of the state which is destructive of every individual value and quality. It is the whole complex of authority and institutional domination which strangles life. It is the superstition, myth, pretense, evasions, and subservience which support authority and institutional domination. It is the reverence for these institutions instilled in the school, the church, and the home in order that man may believe and obey without protest. Such a process of devitalizing and distorting personalities of the individual and of whole communities may have been a part of historical evolution; but it should be strenuously combated by every honest and independent mind in an age which has any pretense to enlightenment. . . .

I consider Anarchism the most beautiful and practical philosophy that has yet been thought of in its application to individual expression and the relation it establishes between the individual and society. Moreover, I am certain that Anarchism is too vital and too close to human nature ever to die. It is my conviction that dictatorship, whether to the right or to the left, can never work—that it never has worked, and that time will prove this again, as it has been proved before. When the failure of modern dictatorship and authoritarian philosophies becomes more apparent and the realization of failure more general, Anarchism will be vindicated. Considered from this point, a recrudescence of Anarchist ideas in the near future is very probable. . . .

Anarchism alone stresses the importance of the individual, his possibilities and needs in a free society. Instead of telling him that he must fall down and worship before institutions, live and die for abstractions, break his heart and stunt his life for taboos,

Anarchism insists that the center of gravity in society is the individual—that he must think for himself, act freely, and live fully. The aim of Anarchism is that every individual in the world shall be able to do so. If he is to develop freely and fully, he must be relieved from the interference and oppression of others. Freedom is, therefore, the cornerstone of the Anarchist philosophy. Of course, this has nothing in common with a much boasted "rugged individualism." Such predatory individualism is really flabby, not rugged. At the least danger to its safety it runs to cover of the state and wails for protection of armies, navies, or whatever devices for strangulation it has at its command. Their "rugged individualism" is simply one of the many pretenses the ruling class makes to unbridled business and political extortion. . . .

The fact that the Anarchist movement for which I have striven so long is to a certain extent in abeyance and overshadowed by philosophies of authority and coercion affects me with concern, but not with despair. It seems to me a point of special significance that many countries decline to admit Anarchists. All governments hold the view that while parties of the right and left may advocate social changes, still they cling to the idea of government and authority. Anarchism alone breaks with both and propagates uncompromising rebellion. In the long run, therefore, it is Anarchism which is considered deadlier to the present regime than all other social theories that are now clamoring for power.

Considered from this angle, I think my life and my work have been successful. What is generally regarded as success—acquisition of wealth, the capture of power or social prestige—I consider the most dismal failures. I hold when it is said of a man that he has arrived, it means that he is finished—his development has stopped at that point. I have always striven to remain in a state of flux and continued growth, and not to petrify in a niche of self-satisfaction. If I had my life to live over again, like anyone else, I should wish to alter minor details. But in any of my more important actions and attitudes I would repeat my life as I have lived it. Certainly I should work for Anarchism with the same devotion and confidence in its ultimate triumph.

74

SAN FRANCISCO'S JEWISH WOMEN: ASSORTED MODELS
1890's

Amy Steinhart (Mrs. Robert) Braden was born in San Francisco in 1879. Her father, William Steinhart, a businessman, was a committed Jew, highly respected as the first president of a Pacific Coast B'nai B'rith lodge and as one of the founders of the local Jewish orphan asylum. His girls were given a good education; Amy was a graduate of the University of California at Berkeley, class of 1900. Her brother Jesse (1881–1966) became one of the city's outstanding Jewish leaders and served as a regent of the University.

Selection A, part of an oral interview conducted by Edna Tartaul Daniel in 1960, reflects the early home life and background of a woman who later became a professional social worker. From 1925 to 1930, Amy Braden was Executive Secretary of the Department of Public Welfare for the State of California; her primary interest was in child care. Selection B is a summary chronicle of the activities of San Francisco Jewesses at the turn of the century. Item C is a charming account of a matron—and her husband—preparing to leave for the synagogue on the morning of the Jewish New Year.

A

BACKGROUND FOR A SOCIAL WORKER
1890's

I remember particularly—I have a very vivid recollection—we didn't have any Christmas celebration in our house; we didn't observe Christmas; we were brought up to be not altogether orthodox but to be aware of our Jewish background. We kept a mild form of Kosher [Amy ate oysters out]. My father had been brought up in a very strictly orthodox family. On the other hand

ny mother was brought up in a family that was not in the least bit
rthodox. After she married my father she conformed to all the
ustoms which he had learned in his youth in Germany. For
nstance we had a regular Seder service [Passover supper] in our
ome. I remember very well on the Day of Atonement that he
walked to the synagogue and never carried any money. On that
day we waited in the evening—I remember so clearly walking up
nd down Post Street until the first star came out—because he
wouldn't break his fast until the star had come out. We children
asted.

Daniel: Did you go to synagogue each Saturday?

Braden: We went to Sabbath school on Saturday where we
learned to read Hebrew and on Sunday we went to
learn Bible history.

Daniel: Did you go long enough to learn Hebrew really?

Braden: We learned to be able to read the prayers. Later I
studied Hebrew in college.

Daniel: To what extent had you any feeling of being in a group
that was different?

Braden: The only time I really felt it was at Christmas time
when my closest friend told me about all her Christmas
presents. Then I would magnify the fact that we had
hung up our stockings and had had an orange and an
apple and an anise seed cake.

Daniel: Cultures and religions and every aspect of human
behaviour have melted together in San Francisco.

Braden: But we had a pretty well separated social life. We went
to parties given by Jewish people with very few exceptions.

Daniel: You chose to circulate socially in the Jewish culture or
did it just happen?

Braden: It just happened that my closest friend in school was not
Jewish. She and I went all through school and all
through college and I was very happy because she
wasn't allowed to do anything that I was not allowed to
do. Her mother would always confer with my mother
about problems. But, by and large, I would say that
most of the parties that I went to were parties given by

the friends or children of my mother's and father's friends.

Daniel: Did you have any special awareness about this?

Braden: We just took it for granted. And I think there was a little bit of a feeling about people who broke away from Jewish friendships.

Daniel: This is what I am trying to get at. Actually there was rather a disciplinary effect of the Jewish group within itself.

Braden: Yes, very much so. It was very true. There was one friend in particular who was very beautiful and very attractive and was invited to the very select Greenway [dancing] assemblies. This is some years later. And one of the Saturday newspapers that picked up gossip wrote a column about this and they had to keep it away from her father so he wouldn't find out about it.

Daniel: I gather you were diligent about your studies.

Braden: Oh, very. There was no question of it. We were expected to do well in school. We were expected to get medals. In those days they gave medals. . . .

Daniel: Getting back to school—

Braden: My two older sisters graduated from Madame Ziska's. There was an article in the *Argonaut* newspaper which in describing this school said that there was better training in the social graces than in the three R's. The *Argonaut* wrote that many alumni learned to count on their fingers, and I remember going to visit my sister in Chicago and here she was counting out on her fingers!

Daniel: Then the *Argonaut* interpretation was accurate.

Braden: Yes. Many of the girls who went to that school became social leaders and married very brilliantly. That seemed to be their main purpose.

Daniel: What was a mother's number one choice of a husband for her daughter?

Braden: A man who could take care of her. A good man.

Daniel: How was the young lady launched?

Braden: In our home at the parties for my grandmother's

birthday, and frequent Friday evening parties. There were two big social clubs which had dances. These were Concordia and Verein.

Daniel: Did men and women belong to these clubs?

Braden: Men only were members. But they had parties for their wives and daughters.

Daniel: The Concordia Club was in existence already?

Braden: Oh yes. That's a very old and exclusively Jewish club. I think there were a few non-Jews in the Verein. It was a very German group. In recent years the two have combined.

Daniel: Was there an aristocracy within the Jewish group?

Braden: Yes.

Daniel: Probably the German group was more prosperous and had most cultivated tastes.

Braden: That's right.

Daniel: Were there any English Jews here?

Braden: Yes, there were just a few and they were considered very aristocratic. They had quite a standing in the community.

Daniel: Were they business people or visitors?

Braden: One family in particular came as business people and were very successful and had a very fine standing in the community. But I don't remember a great many of them. . . .

Daniel: Was it important at that time [1896] to belong to a fraternity or a sorority?

Braden: To me it was important because it was the first time that I came face to face with anti-Semitism.

Daniel: Weren't there Jewish houses [at the University of California]?

Braden: No. There were just three sororities on the campus at that time. And this very great friend of mine, with whom I had gone all through school, was rushed for all three and I was left out. Maybe that had something to do with my unhappiness.

Daniel: Did she join one of them?

Braden: Yes. Out of a private school she was considered ver desirable. She felt very sorry about it; it was unfortu nate.

Daniel: When did the Jewish houses start?

Braden: They are comparatively recent. Now they've broke down the lines, haven't they, over at the University?

Daniel: I don't know. I've never belonged to a social sorority What did your family friends and relatives think of you adventures in Berkeley?

Braden: They thought I was very enterprising, very, to go t college. . . .

Daniel: What sort of future did you envision for yourself?

Braden: I always felt that some day I was going to devote mysel to so-called "charities."

Daniel: Why?

Braden: I don't know. I was interested in helping my fellov man, I suppose.

Daniel: When did you get this idea?

Braden: I think I began to feel that in college more than I ha before. It was a natural thing, just as my mother ha certain activities; she went to a sewing society once month to sew for orphans. There's this, too, that m father was a very generous, charitable person. H brought over any number of relatives from Germany They did not live in our home but they came to dinne every night for many years.

Daniel: Did they seem pleased to be here?

Braden: No, I can't say that they were, without exception.

Daniel: Were you aware of the reasons for their coming here?

Braden: He had come himself; he was comfortable; he felt hi responsibility to his relatives. My mother brought he mother and her sister, and when the time came that m cousins were orphans she took three girls into our home It was just taken for granted that that was the natura thing to do.

Daniel: Being your brother's keeper was built into your con sciousness at an early age.

Braden: Also it was the natural thing for the people in our grouj to devote some time to some form of charity in those days. My father was one of the founders of the Eureka Benevolent Association which later became the Jewish Family Welfare Agency. [Actually the Eureka was founded in 1850; William Steinhart came to America in 1851].

Daniel: And you did call it "charity?"

Braden: Oh, yes, we didn't hesitate to call it "charity." I volunteered my services for a number of years. Gradually I realized that I wanted to carry on on a full-time basis.

B

1896
THE JEWESS IN SAN FRANCISCO.

The stranger in San Francisco seeing the Jewish maid or matron strolling along the principal streets bent on pleasure, business, or shopping excursions, forms an entirely erroneous opinion of her. As thus seen, she appears always well-dressed, sometimes a little dashing in her apparel; with dusky, flashing eyes, brilliant cheeks, and a figure that moves along with that swinging motion that indicates perfect health. With this hearty, well-groomed look, she seems a splendid creature physically, and one whose chief occupation in life does not extend beyond attention to her individual comforts or luxuries.

It is necessary to have lived for years in this city, to know that there is another side to this brilliant picture—one that perfects it and shows the Jewess developed not alone physically but mentally and spiritually—in fact that she keeps pace with the world's advancement equally with her sisters of other creeds. Of course in the charities of their own people, they are here, as elsewhere, deeply interested, and it is not necessary to mention the various organizations they conduct. But it is not for their own people alone they labor, but with broad-minded liberality, they are active in the most important societies that bring relief to the needy of all classes. The Fruit and Flower Mission has in its executive board several of this faith, and many others among its most zealous workers. [Hilda Steinhart, Amy Steinhart Braden's sister, turned this housebound patients mission into a free clinic.] In the Occidental Kindergarten the officers are all young ladies of this persuasion. Many a Jewish maiden leaves her luxurious home, puts aside some pleasure, and, threading the dark byways of the city, brings comfort to some poor woman by the assurance that her child shall be taught and cared for in this institution. In all the other large kindergartens the Jewish matron takes an active interest, devoting to them both leisure and money. The Woman's Exchange [to help genteel women in reduced circumstances] has on its board several Jewish names, and many are included among its members. These are but a few of the non-sectarian charities in which the Jewess is interested, but they prove that she has cultivated the noble qualities of generosity and thoughtfulness beyond her own narrow circle.

A further view shows her talented as well as generous. In musical circles there are a number whose accomplishments are of a high order. Miss Meta Asher, a girl of only fifteen years, is considered a musical prodigy. Her favorite instrument is the violin and those who have heard her playing predict for her a brilliant future. She is at present pursuing her studies in Europe. A pianist of more than ordinary skill is Mrs. Noah Brandt. She is a teacher of music and appears frequently in concerts at which her name is a guarantee of good music. Mme. Solomon is distinguished for her fine voice and her superior qualities as a teacher of singing. Miss Rose Adler is another well-known singer. Her voice of rare power and sweetness has won for her deserved recognition. The name Mme. [Julie] Rosewald is synonymous with music. As the mention of a flower recalls its perfume, so her name suggests a world of melody. For years she was the principal singer in the choir of the Temple Emanuel and is at present a teacher of voice culture at Mills Seminary. In every musical venture she is interested, and her influence has done much toward sustaining a high ideal in matters musical.

The mental aspect of the Jewess is equally favorable. There are three Jewish doctresses in the city. Dr. Adele Solomons Jaffa raduated from the Hahnemann Medical College about three ears ago; then spent some time in an Eastern college and upon er return began to practice her profession. She has found time, oo, to give weekly lectures to a class of young girls upon topics elating to the physical well-being of women. These have been ntirely free of charge, and with the one desire to assist young vomen in gaining a practical knowledge of the laws of health.)ne year ago, she was married to Mr. M. Jaffa, professor of griculture at the State University. Miss Natalie Selling, for-nerly a school teacher, is also a disciple of Æsculapius. Her uccess even during her brief career proves she has not mistaken er vocation and argues well for her future. Miss Amelia Levison 1as been a student all her life and no one marveled when her tastes ed her to the study of medicine. She is a thorough German and 1ossesses that determined, plodding nature that led her to overcome all obstacles in her path. She has been practicing for ome time with marked success.

The city may boast of a goodly number of Jewish women of nore than average literary and intellectual ability. Miss Emma Volf is the author of two popular books—*Other Things Being Equal* nd a *Prodigal in Love*. The former discusses the question of the ight of intermarriage between people of different creeds; the atter is a pretty love story pleasantly told. Her third book will be published at an early date. Her sister, Miss Alice Wolfe, has vritten a number of excellent short stories, and has lately published a book entitled *A House of Cards*. Its moral tone is a high one, and none who have read it can doubt the author's talent. Miss Selina Solomons pursues her way very quietly and unassum-ngly, and only those who know her best appreciate her scholarly attainments and are aware that she is constantly engaged in iterary work. She contributes to a number of magazines and has also written a play. Mrs. M. Prag occupies a high place in educational circles. She is a teacher in the senior class of the Girl's High School. She took an active part in the last session of the Woman's Congress, and her paper read before it was among the best. [Mary Goldsmith Prag was the mother of Congresswoman Florence Prag Kahn. Mary did not give a paper at the 1893 Chicago Jewish Women's Congress.] Miss Martha Shainwald is a contributor to the "Wave" and other city journals. Miss Miriam Michelson [sister of Albert A. Michelson, the future Nobel Prize laureate in physics] has written short stories of undoubted merit, and has been dramatic critic for the "Examiner," Miss Harriet Levy, a graduate of the State University, possesses brilliant intellectual qualities. She was at one time dramatic critic for the "Wave," and has lately written for the "Call." Mrs. I. Lowenberg is well-known in intellectual circles. She is president of the Philomath Club—the only Jewish literary club in the city. Mrs. Lowenberg is also at the head of the Laurel Hall Association—a literary circle that is non-sectarian and includes among its members some of the most talented women in the city.

Miss Ray Frank, the woman rabbi, may stand as an exponent of the spiritual elevation of the Jewess. Her mental qualities alone have given her rank among women of intellectual ability, but her efforts for the moral elevation of her race, her interest in all that concerns their welfare, have given her a prominence that extends beyond her own State. She is a graduate of the Oakland High School and has taken the regular rabbinical course in the Eastern college. [Miss Frank took no regular course at the Hebrew Union College.] She has preached in the synagogues here and in the North, and has been offered a permanent position, but she has refused.

Although broad-minded and advocating high aims for women, and the opening to them of all avocations, she does not believe in equal suffrage. Like her ancestress, whom she so closely resembles, the inspired prophetess Deborah, she would have woman rule beneath her "own vine and fig tree."

This sketch might be lengthened, and there could be added many names distinguished in school and college. But this cursory glance at the "Jewess in San Francisco" is sufficient to prove that, although there may be many instances among them where life has no higher motive than the pleasure of the moment, yet lofty self-denial, exalted ideals, and earnest progressive efforts are not exceptional cases.

San Francisco.   REBECCA J. GRADWOHL

C

GOING TO SYNAGOGUE ON ROSH HASHANAH, THE JEWISH NEW YEAR*

1890's(?)

The excitement began at eight in the morning, although my parents did not leave for the synagogue until nine-thirty. The preparations were the same year after year. One event followed upon another as if after careful rehearsal.

"Where are my cuff buttons, Yetta?" Every year the same question. [Yetta was the aunt of Albert A. Michelson, the Nobel Prize laureate.]

"They are in the buttonholes." Every year the same answer.

"There is only one."

"There are two."

"I can find only one."

"I put them both in myself."

"Where is it, then?"

Father clumsily lowered himself to his knees, but Mother ran to him, pushed him aside, stretched an arm under the bed, and arose with the white button between her fingers. "*Lahme Hände* [Lame hands]," she said, presenting it to him.

The white piqué vest with the small blue and yellow flowers had returned after a year of retirement. Like the *primavera*, it reappeared over the threshold of the bedroom, sprinkled with forget-me-nots and daisies. As long back as I could remember there had been no predecessor; it had always been the piqué vest. The starch of annual laundering had stiffened and shrunk it, the buttonholes had become slits, so that inserting the flat pearl buttons made a demand on Father beyond his dexterity. He had grown stout with the years; each New Year's Day found him heavier than the year before, while the area of the vest contracted; each year called for increased ingenuity. As he labored, his eye roamed the ceiling, leaving the operation wholly to his thumbs

*From *920 O'Farrell Street* by Harriet Lane Levy. Copyright © 1937, 1947 by Harriet Lane Levy. Reprinted by permission of Doubleday & Company, Inc.

and fingers. His face grew a pink that was pallor beside th
magenta that spread to the top of his head when he tried to butto
the vest across the arch of his abdomen. That he might hav
bought a new vest suggested itself to no one. New Year's, Fathe
the piqué vest, composed a normal trinity.

Watching Father, as he sought by deep breathing to induce
retreat of his abdomen into the constricted enclosure, awok
sensations piquant and varied. As I followed his struggle, I, too
inhaled heavily, held my breath to the point of dizziness, fumble
with clumsy fingers over moist button surfaces, suffered th
dismay of threatened failure until, suddenly, the button pene
trated the slit. Then I rejoiced with Father in the triumph of h
praiseworthy accomplishment. The result justified the labo
The waistcoat gave to Father a stamp of worldly smartness. But
was not always on a note of triumph that the struggle ende
There were other times when the slash of linen rooted Father t
the rug on which he stood; moments when he turned his head t
Mother helplessly, his fingers blindly fumbling with the faste
ings.

Without a word, her eyes shooting reproaches, Mother seize
the vest and hurried to the kitchen so that Maggie Doyle mig
make repairs. Here was double catastrophe. Had not the La
decreed that upon the sacred days neither manservant n
maidservant might labor, and did not Father know the Law? H
did, but though his eyes betrayed concern, fear of offense t
Mother must have triumphed over guilt in the sight of the Lor
for he raised no staying hand.

Mother returned, the bandaged vest was buttoned a secon
time, and Father, fortified by its snug support, entered into th
armor of his black broadcloth Sabbath coat (so heavily padde
that it looked as if it could stand by itself), and peacefull
continued his dressing. Taking from the commode drawer th
narrow, red-backed brush which had been there as far back a
memory carried, he caressed the perfect polish of his stovepi
hat and stood before the mirror to adjust it upon his hea
accurately. He was ready.

"Ready, Yetta?" he asked.

"Don't bother me." Mother had hardly begun.

The morning was not without importance to her, for Rosh Hashona was as Easter Sunday to the Gentiles in its opportunity for handsome raiment, and to Mother raiment meant a new winter bonnet. Wearing it she exercised, with one gesture, her full aesthetic impulse. Her bonnets were extravagant in price and elegantly spectacular. There would not be a more beautiful or higher-priced one in the synagogue. They were always of the same pattern, crushed folds of black velvet, framing the head tightly and broadly, with a "fantasie" on one side of finely threaded feather and jet, high and trembling, which to an ear sufficiently sensitive might have been heard to tinkle. Broad ribbons of satin-backed velvet met in a loose bow under the chin, the ends spreading to expose a rose-point collar and round diamond brooch. Mother looked in the glass with smileless approval.

"Ready?" Father asked again.

"Mind your own business," Mother remarked tranquilly, without removing her eyes from the mirror.

Directed by the heavy odor of gasoline, her hand reached toward the pair of white kid gloves upon the bureau.

"Why can't you put on your gloves on the way?" Father protested, his impatience mounting to anger. Mother's lips pursed and her eyes assumed a detached vagueness as she seated herself and slowly drew them on, finger by finger. Like the piqué vest they had suffered shrinkage under repeated purifications. We stood about fearful of a split; if it came, a neighboring finger would close swiftly over the break, denying its verity.

"Button it," Mother commanded; a cramped, reddened palm in its smelly casing reached out to us, and after delicate smoothings and pullings the glove was buttoned.

Father was already in the hall when Mother arose to receive the black all-over beaded cape, long tabs in the front, short in the back, which we dropped upon her shoulders.

"The books. Have you got the books?" Father called back sharply.

"Why should I have the books? I never keep them."

Father hurried to his closet and possessed himself of the two black gilt-tooled leather books of the service. At last they started,

Father leading until he turned and discovered that Mother was not following him.

"Where are you? Are you ever coming?" he demanded. Mother reappeared from her closet, two spots of red upon her cheeks. She carried a long-handled parasol of heavy black lace. Silently she stepped into the hall.

"Good-by, good-by," we called after them, encouraging them down the steps. "We'll be coming later."

"My stylish daughters," Mother said from the base of the stairs before she disappeared again, this time into the kitchen to warn Maggie Doyle not to forget to baste the chicken. Then she started toward the street door, but stopped to enter the parlor and pull down the shade that was letting in a beam of sunshine.

"For God's sake, come!" Father shouted from the street.

"Devil," observed Mother, slowly descending the steps to join him.

We crowded at the window to see whether they had really gone and to watch them down the street: Father, tall, short-necked, broad-backed, his feet shoving a path before him; Mother, short, erect, her bonnet firmly set upon her small head, above the double roll of pompadour, her back narrow and straight, the black grosgrain silk skirt flaring stiffly from a tiny waist. Each carried a book of the service under an arm. When they reached the corner, the large parasol opened and Mother disappeared under a canopy of lace.

15. Edna Ferber

75

EDNA FERBER, DISTINGUISHED AMERICAN WRITER*
1890's

Edna Ferber (1887–1968) was a novelist who described everyday people and made them interesting. In a way she was exceptional among successful Jewish writers, for she liked Jews and the Jewish way of life. She sang in the synagogue choir when she was a child, and when she grew up she admired Rabbi Emil G. Hirsch, the distinguished liberal. "All my life I have been proud of being a Jew," she wrote. One is almost tempted to say that there are two kinds of Jewish literary craftsmen: those who are careful to say nothing of their ethnic origins, and those who take pride in their ancestry, who are deeply interested in the fate of their people, who resent anti-Semitism bitterly. Edna Ferber might well serve as a model for the latter group. When bigots turned on her she never ran away; she fought prejudice valiantly; this is indeed unusual. The prejudice she encountered as a Jewess predisposed her to identify with the Jews who were being destroyed by the Germans.

Edna Ferber was a very successful writer of short stories, novels, and plays. In 1924 she won a Pulitzer Prize for her book So Big.

The following selections from her first autobiographical work describe her reaction to anti-Jewish prejudice.

Through the seven years during which we lived in Ottumwa [Iowa] I know that I never went out on the street without being subjected to some form of devilment. It was a fine school for a certain sort of fortitude, but it gave me a strong dash of bitterness at an early age, together with a bewildered puzzlement at what was known as the Christian world. Certainly I wasn't wise enough or old enough at five, six, seven, eight, nine, ten, to philosophize about this. But these people seemed to me to be barbarians.

On Saturdays, and on unusually busy days when my father could not take the time to come home to the noon dinner, it became my duty to take his midday meal down to him, very carefully packed in a large basket; soup, meat, vegetables, dessert. This must be carried with the utmost care so as not to spill or slop. No one thought of having a sandwich and a cup of coffee in the middle of the day, with a hot dinner to be eaten at leisure in the peace of the evening.

This little trip from the house on Wapello Street to the store on Main Street amounted to running the gantlet. I didn't so much mind the Morey girl. She sat in front of her house perched on the white gatepost, waiting, a child about my age, with long red curls, a freckled face, very light green eyes. She swung her long legs, idly. At sight of me her listlessness fled.

"Hello, sheeny!" Then variations of this. This, one learned to receive equably. Besides, the natural retort to her baiting was to shout, airily, "Red Head! Wets the bed!"

But as I approached the Main Street corner there sat a row of vultures perched on the iron railing at the side of Sargent's drugstore. These were not children, they were men. Perhaps to me, a small child, they seemed older than they were, but their ages must have ranged from eighteen to thirty. There they sat, perched on the black iron rail, their heels hooked behind the lower rung. They talked almost not at all. The semicircle of spit rings grew richer and richer on the sidewalk in front of them. Vacant-eyed, they stared and spat and sat humped and round-shouldered, doing nothing, thinking nothing, being nothing. Suddenly their lackluster eyes brightened, they shifted, they licked their lips a little and spat with more relish. From afar they had glimpsed their victim, a plump little girl in a clean starched gingham frock, her black curls confined by a ribbon bow.

Every fiber of me shrieked to run the other way. My eyes felt hot and wide. My face became scarlet. I must walk carefully so as not to spill the good hot dinner. Now then. Now.

"Sheeny! Has du gesak de Isaac! De Moses! De Levi! Heh, sheeny, what you got!" Good Old Testament names. They doubtless heard them in their Sunday worship, but did not make the connection, quite. They then brought their hands, palms up, above the level of their shoulders and wagged them back and forth, "Oy-yoy, sheeny! Run! Go on, run!"

I didn't run. I glared. I walked by with as much elegance and aloofness as was compatible with a necessity to balance a basket of noodle soup, pot roast, potatoes, vegetable and pudding.

Of course it was nothing more than a couple of thousand years of bigotry raising its hideous head again to spit on a defenseless and shrinking morsel of humanity. Yet it all must have left a deep scar on a sensitive child. It was unreasoning and widespread in the town. My parents were subject to it. The four or five respectable Jewish families of the town knew it well. They were intelligent men and women, American born and bred, for the most part. It probably gave me a ghastly inferiority, and out of that inferiority doubtless was born inside me a fierce resolution, absurd and childish, such as, "You wait! I'll show you! I'll be rich and famous and you'll wish you could speak to me."

Well, I did become rich and famous, and have lived to see entire nations behaving precisely like the idle frustrated bums perched on the drugstore railing. Of course Ottumwa wasn't a benighted town because it was cruel to its Jewish citizens. It was cruel to its Jewish citizens because it was a benighted town. Business was bad, the town was poor, its people were frightened, resentful and stupid. There was, for a place of its size and locality, an unusually large rough element. As naturally as could be these searched for a minority on whom to vent their dissatisfaction with the world. And there we were, and there I was, the scapegoat of the ages. Yet, though I had a tough time of it in Ottumwa and a fine time of it in New York, I am certain that those Ottumwa years were more enriching, more valuable than all the fun and luxury of the New York years.

There was no Jewish place of worship in Ottumwa. The five or six Jewish families certainly could not afford the upkeep of a temple. I knew practically nothing of the Jewish people, their history, religion. On the two important holy days of the year— Rosh Hashana, the Jewish New Year, and Yom Kippur, the Day of Atonement—they hired a public hall for services. Sometimes they were able to bring to town a student rabbi who had, as yet, no regular congregation. Usually one of the substantial older men who knew something of the Hebrew language of the Bible, having been taught it in his youth, conducted the service. On Yom Kippur, a long day of fasting and prayer, it was an exhausting thing to stand from morning to sunset in the improvised pulpit. The amateur rabbi would be relieved for an hour by another member of the little improvised congregation. Mr. Emanuel Adler, a familiar figure to me as he sat in his comfortable home talking with my parents, a quaint long-stemmed pipe between his lips, a little black skullcap atop his baldish head as protection against drafts, now would don the rabbinical skullcap, a good deal like that of a Catholic priest. He would open on the high reading stand the Bible and the Book of Prayers containing the service for the Day of Yom Kippur; and suddenly he was transformed from a plump middle-aged German-born Jew with sad kindly eyes and a snuffy gray-brown mustache to a holy man from whose lips came words of wisdom and of comfort and of hope.

The store always was closed on Rosh Hashana and Yom Kippur. Mother put on her best dress. If there were any Jewish visitors in the town at that time they were invited to the services and to dinner at some hospitable house afterward. In our household the guests were likely to be a couple of traveling salesmen caught in the town on that holy day. Jewish families came from smaller near-by towns—Marshalltown, Albia, Keokuk.

I can't account for the fact that I didn't resent being a Jew. Perhaps it was because I liked the way my own family lived, talked, conducted its household and its business better than I did the lives of my friends. I admired immensely my grandparents, my parents, my uncles and aunt. Perhaps it was a vague something handed down to me from no one knows where. Perhaps it was something not very admirable—the actress in me. I think, truthfully, that I rather liked dramatizing myself, feeling myself different and set apart. I probably liked to think of myself as persecuted by enemies who were (in my opinion) my inferiors. This is a protective philosophy often employed. Mine never had been a religious family. The Chicago Neumann family [mother's folks] sometimes went to the temple at Thirty-third Street and Indiana Avenue, but I don't remember that my parents ever went there while in Chicago. In our own household there was no celebration of the informal home ceremonies so often observed in Jewish families. The Passover, with its Sedar service, was marked in our house only by the appearance of the matzos or unleavened bread, symbolic of the hardships of the Jews in the wilderness. I devoured pounds of the crisp crumbling matzos with hunks of fresh butter and streams of honey, leaving a trail of crumbs all over the house, and thought very little, I am afraid, of the tragic significance of the food I was eating or of that weary heartsick band led by Moses out of Egypt to escape the Hitler of that day, one Pharaoh; or of how they baked and ate their unsalted unleavened bread because it was all they had, there in the wilderness. I still have matzoth (matzos, we always called them) in my house during the Passover, and just as thoughtlessly. Now they come as delicate crisp circlets, but they seem to me much less delicious than the harder, tougher squares of my childhood munching. . . .

My father and mother and sister Fan and I exchanged many friendly little calls with the pleasant Jewish families of the town—the Almeyers, the Adlers, Feists, Silvers, Lyons, living in comfortable well-furnished houses, conducting their affairs with intelligence and decorum, educating their children. They saw a little too much of one another. There was a good deal of visiting back and forth, evenings. At nine there would be served wine or lemonade and cake, a moment which I eagerly awaited. The Ferber specialty was a hickory-nut cake, very rich, baked in a loaf, for which I was permitted to crack the nuts and extract the meats. This was accomplished with a flat-iron between my knees and a hammer in my hand. The nuts went into the cake and into me fifty-fifty. Once baked, it was prudently kept under lock and key in the cupboard of the sitting-room desk, rather than in the free territory of the pantry.

My mother, more modern than most in thought and conduct, had numbers of staunch friends among the non-Jewish townspeople, and these enormously enjoyed her high spirits, her vitality, her shrewd and often caustic comment. She, too, was an omnivorous reader, so that when life proved too much for her she was able to escape into the reader's Nirvana. Certainly she was the real head of the family, its born leader; unconsciously she was undergoing a preliminary training which was to stand her in good stead when she needed it. . . .

There lived in New York a formidable old lady named Mrs. Wolcott. Her life's business was lion hunting. She was an inveterate and almost invincible dinner-giver. *So Big, Show Boat* and *The Royal Family* had made me fair game for her. Thus far I had escaped her careful aim.

Then, one day, when I was off guard, she said that she was giving a dinner for eight. Winthrop Ames [the theatrical producer] had said he would come if I would. I welcomed the thought of sitting next to him at a small dinner and having an hour of his stimulating talk and his gay glancing wit.

There was good talk and good food. Winthrop sat between the hostess and me. The conversation turned to books, someone mentioned G. B. Stern's novel, *The Matriarch*, which had been well received.

"That book!" shouted the hostess. "When I found it was about spawning Jews I threw it across the room."

A little silence fell. It was, I suppose, just about the nastiest little silence I have ever felt. I said, with laborious dignity, "It was a rich chronicle of a dramatic and cultured family. I loved it."

In leaped the gallant Winthrop. "Dramatic! That's it! I've often thought that if it hadn't been for the Jew in me I'd never have amounted to anything in the theater."

"*You*, Winthrop!" screeched Mrs. Wolcott.

"Certainly," he went on, equably. "Old Ameus, from whom we get our name of Ames. It's all in the book of the family tree in the library up North Easton. Old Ameus, the Jew, who was thrown out of England and into Spain, and out of Spain back into England, centuries ago. Where do you suppose I get this profile, if not from him!"

"That," I put in, lamely, "is exactly the way I feel about it. We Jews, because we've been suppressed for centuries express ourselves in the creative arts and sciences."

"Oh, are you Jewish—too?" faltered our charming hostess. "I didn't know—"

"Only," I replied cheerfully, "on my mother's and father's side, my grandmothers' and grandfathers', my great-grandmothers' and great-grandfathers', my great-great-grand—"

"There are Jews and Jews," interrupted Mrs. W., graciously.

"Yes, indeed. And Christians and Christians." With which I took my departure.

Now that's the sort of thing that interests me, psychologically. This beldame probably never had talked to three Jews in her life, knowing they were Jews. Her resentment of them was as pathological and unsound as the fear of, say, high places. If you multiply this one woman's ignorance and prejudice by one or two millions you have a very nice little anti-semitic group snugly seated in your own lap.

76

RAY FRANK, FEMALE "RABBI"
1890

"Oh, young Lochinvar (female) is come out of the West." Ray Frank (1864/65–1948) is the nearest approach to a female rabbi in the late nineteenth century. She was a San Francisco—Oakland, California, girl who, after receiving a good education, became a schoolteacher, writer, and popular lecturer. Actually she was a "missionary" who traveled about talking to Jews, urging them to document their devotion to their ancestral faith. Ray Frank was completely and utterly devoted to the religion of her fathers. By 1890, she had already become a celebrity on the Pacific Coast; by 1893, she was something of a figure in American Jewry: when the National Council of Jewish Women was organized that year, the "founding mothers" invited her to make one of the principal addresses. Some called her "The Prophetess"; others called her the "Female Messiah."

There can be no question that this brilliant, eloquent woman wanted to be a rabbi, but there is no evidence that she was willing at twenty-eight to go back to school and study Hebrew with teenage youngsters. Isaac M. Wise discouraged her; he preached a modest form of feminism, but made no real effort to bring women into the rabbinate. Indeed, the times were not ripe for a female rabbi. Her views of the rabbinate, moreover, were highly unorthodox, untraditional, and unrealistic (?), as the following letter of hers makes abundantly clear.

A JEWESS ON THE RABBI QUESTION

To the Editor:

Living in the "far West," your paper asking for replies to—"What would you do if you were a rabbi?" did not reach me in time to answer that interesting question, had I chosen to do so.

But I trust you will not think it too late to answer the question in a slightly different form, and one which is, I think, familiar to most minds. What I would not do if I were a rabbi.

RAY FRANK LITMAN
(Photograph taken in San Francisco,
California, *circa* 1897)

16. Ray Frank (Litman)

First, if I were one of the elect, one who deemed myself worthy to expound the law to men created like myself with an understanding, and a small but mighty organ termed by physiologists the heart, why, then I would not, if I were a rabbi, endeavor to impress the nature of my calling by loud and shallow words, nor by a pompous bearing unbecoming the man of God. I would not say to my fancied inferiors, "*I am the rabbi*," and you must therefore do this or that; but I would reach their actions through their hearts.

I would try and remember that example is better than precept. I would not imagine myself a fixed star around which lesser lights must move.

I would try the effect of a gentle demeanor, a quiet voice, an earnest will, and a helping hand. I would learn if an unfailing courtesy and a positive sincerity were not sufficient to announce and impress my high vocation to the stranger and to the sinner.

I would not, if I were a rabbi, consider a stylish residence, fine garments, including a silk hat, not any of the jewels representing the original twelve tribes, as absolutely essential to keeping up my position as a "priest of the temple." I would not make a business matter of my calling otherwise than for the good of my congregation or for humanity in general.

I would not say my services are worthy a salary of so much per annum because I do this or that, or because I preach oftener or more learnedly than Mr. A. or Rev. B.; but, after satisfying my own wants in a modest way, I would use amounts expended on "high living," on cigars, cards, and other pleasantries toward enlightening the ignorant of my people—if not in my own town, where perhaps they are blessed with both intelligence and wealth, then I would use it for the poor and oppressed abroad. I would be more like Judah Asheri; less like one type of Hebrew satirically mentioned as "Solomon Isaacs." [Judah Asheri was a very philanthropic medieval scholar; "Solomon Isaacs" was a late nineteenth-century contemptuous stereotype of the Jew.] It is, indeed, difficult nowadays to note the difference between the rabbi and his friend the clothier, or the broker; his dress, his diamonds, his language, his very walk is not bookish but business; is not piety but pence.

I would not, if I were a rabbi, attempt to be a politician, for religion and politics do not and cannot under existing circumstances walk hand-in-hand. I would not degrade my holy office by assuring any ward political "boss" that for a consideration I could capture the votes of my co-religionists, "because being the rabbi, they will do as I tell them," as one rabbi of my acquaintance is said to have remarked.

If I were a rabbi and the holidays were at hand, I would not make "stock" of my seats in *schule* [synagogue]; or in other words, I would not sell religion in the form of pews and benches to the highest bidder.

I would not treat disdainfully the moneyless fellow who comes on Rosh Hashanah, Yom Kippur, or Pesach to drink at the fountain of our faith, but alas! finds that unless he can pay for his drink of religion he must either go thirsty or beg it.

During the last holiday season a poor but faithful son of Israel travelled many miles afoot (he was a peddler) that he might reach a certain city before the morning services for Rosh Hashanah began. Weary and dusty he hastened to the synagogue, drawn thither by the teachings of childhood and an undoubted sincerity to be in God's holy temple.

When our shabby countryman entered, the *schule* was crowded almost to the doors by those who had *bought* religion at so much a seat; with difficulty the fellow found a resting place; but no sooner was he in it than the rabbi's aid-de-camp, the shamus, requested him to pay two dollars and a half for the privilege of saying his prayers in the place dedicated to God. Now it so happened this poor peddler had not the amount; so after having the attention of scores of more fortunate brethren called to his case, he was finally refused a *seat*—no, not in Heaven, but in a fashionable *schule*. I'm glad, very glad, that *schules* are but depots in one of the big way stations on the road to Paradise. Yet one cannot but regret that the ticket agents are not more thoughtful.

If I were a rabbi, I would not refuse any man a ticket for Heaven.

If I were a rabbi, I would not frequent such public places as street corners, cigar stands, nor business houses, until I was conspicuous only when absent.

I would not, were I a rabbi, canvass the town with tickets for a party if the funds went toward my own high salary. I would prefer less salary and have no soliciting to do.

If I were a rabbi of what is termed the reform type, I would not be funny or sarcastic at the expense of my orthodox brother. If I were orthodox in my ideas, I would not apply harsh names nor deny a state of future bliss to my brother of modern opinions.

If I were a rabbi, I would not direct my sermon to the costliest sealskin, handsomest bonnet, and smallest brain, but I'd divide my attention, as well as my remarks, among my audience.

If I had a Sabbath-school, I would so conduct it that each boy and girl should see in my conduct that which I preached in my sermon.

I would not correct evil-doers among children by physical pain, inflicted because "they do so in the old country." I would not, while an incumbent of one position, be on the "lookout" for another with a bigger salary, unless I felt I could do more good in the one than in the other.

I would not, at a wedding, be the first at the feast and the last to leave the wine; it looks too carnal for a rabbi.

There are many other things, too numerous to mention, which I would not do.

One thing more, and I have done. Were I a rabbi, none should insult my manhood by offering to pay me for praying at a funeral; nor would I dare accept money, unless for charity's cause, for any service I might do the living in memory of the dead.

Were I worthy to offer up a prayer for the departed, that worthiness and the honor of petitioning the King of kings, the consciousness that I was an ambassador to the Court of courts, the thought of pleasing the afflicted, would all be ample pay.

Would that the spiritual mantle of Elijah was more often donned, or at least thrown over the very material broadcloth of our modern rabbis.

Women are precluded from entering the Holy of Holies; but it is a great satisfaction to contemplate *what we would not do* were the high office not denied us.

Ray Frank

Oakland, Cal., May, 1890.

77

ANNIE NATHAN MEYER, AN EARLY ACTIVIST
1891

Annie Nathan Meyer (1867–1951) was a New Yorker who was very proud of her colonial Jewish background, her Revolutionary War ancestors, and the family traditions. She studied privately and took examinations at Columbia, because as late as the 1880's, women were not permitted to attend the lectures given there. In her later years, this gifted woman wrote plays and novels and lectured on education and art. She was a fine English stylist. About the year 1888, when only twenty-one, Mrs. Meyer succeeded in convincing Columbia's trustees of the need to establish a women's college as part of the university. She was successful despite bitter opposition, and Barnard College opened in 1889. There were men, and probably some women too in that generation, who were of the opinion that the ladies had neither the training nor the physical stamina to cope with the grueling challenge of four years of higher education.

That same year, 1888, she set out to co-opt a group of contributors to write on Woman's Work in America. *She was the editor of this volume, which made its appearance in 1891. The preface is reprinted below.*

Though she was very much interested in the advancement of women, Mrs. Meyer—unlike her sister, Maud Nathan—was vigorously opposed to equal suffrage. Voting women would not further democracy. Feminism and women's suffrage merely reflected a cult of discontent.

Editor's Preface. . .

It occurred to me that a volume on the work of women in America could be made equally valuable and interesting.

In the spring of 1888, therefore, I began to collect the necessary material. . . .

But before the task of selecting the contributors came that of dividing the whole great field of woman's work. Here I can only bow my head before the flood of criticism that is bound to bear

17. Annie Nathan Meyer

down upon me. I suppose it is inevitable that to many it will seem that undue importance has been accorded to one subject, and too little to another. I can but plead that in no case have I allowed myself to be influenced by prejudice, but only by the best judgment I was capable of bringing to bear. On mentioning this book to a well-known editor and poet (a man), I was gravely asked why I had omitted a chapter on "Woman in Marriage," as it would make a very readable and certainly a very prolific subject. My answer was that so far as I knew women had never been denied that privilege, and so it could have no legitimate place in my book. In that reply, although uttered lightly, lies the principle upon which I have worked; the fields of labor described here contain evidences of woman's progress; they are those in which women, if entrance were not absolutely denied them, were at least not welcomed, nor valued. Furthermore, they are phases of woman's work that have some direct bearing on the status of woman in this country.

And now a word on the object of the book, for many will shrug their shoulders and say: "Why separate *work* into *man's* work and *woman's* work? What is gained by this division? Why not be content with the simple word *work?* Is it not sufficient to be a factor in the world's growth, or must the ages keep a constant reckoning of *meum* and *tuum?*"

If the time has come when the word work is a neuter noun, I admit that the value of this book would be reduced; but even then I think it might justly claim a historical value, a value as a history of the struggle on woman's part to have her work accepted just as a "factor in the world's growth," judged on its own merits, not

> Mere woman's work,
> Expressing the comparative respect
> Which means the absolute scorn.

But aside from the value of the book as a record, it claims a value as an inspiration to greater effort; for in our eyes the time has not yet come when all effort should cease. The arguments against the development of woman have been many, and although centuries have passed, the changing years merely ring different tones upon the same theme. We may acknowledge that the day is past when it is necessary seriously to plead the capacity of woman to accomplish certain things; that victory has been won with tears of blood; but the fight still centers about the propriety of it. The large band of ignorant and prejudiced objectors is fast giving place to another of a more kindly, but more dangerous type. More dangerous because instead of employing the weapons of disdain, they use those of homage; instead of goading with scorn, they disarm with the incense of a false and hollow sentimentality. This new wave of feeling divides Life into Intellect and Emotion, the Mind and the Heart, Matter and Soul, etc., the one man, woman the other. These sentimentalists, who certainly include as many women as men, argue that every woman is the natural companion of man, and so is upheld by some strong shoulder. When faced by the awful statistics of unmarried females in the United States, they fall back on some hypothetical father, brother, or cousin. Therefore it is considered highly supererogatory that a woman should be taught to stand upon her own feet, when the adjacent shoulder answers the purpose as well. This belief holds its own with a peculiar tenacity, because there is a certain heroic satisfaction in retaining your sentiment notwithstanding all the arguments that can be brought forward by the low materialists.

This book is nothing else than a history of woman's slow, but sure, training to stand balanced upon her own feet. She has looked upon the thousands of falling sisters, and has very reasonably reached the conclusion that the only way to make sure of standing is to make use of her own feet.

Women have many so-called champions of their "purity," and "innocence;" champions that are shocked at opening so many new fields of "man's work" to women; but they are strangely ignorant of the very real contamination to which they expose their *protegés* by crowding them into the few already overcrowded channels, and refusing to let in fresh air and sunshine. Men and women both are born into the world helpless and unprotected; it may seem an ugly and bitter truth, but it is so, that in this struggle for existence daily going on about us, men and women do indeed stand "side by side,"—not, as with the poet,

Full summed in all their powers,
but each individually carrying on a struggle against suffering, starvation, crime, and death,—forces that remorselessly attack women, barren of the chivalrous regard of sex with which these sentimentalists seem to grace them.

And if it is true that both sexes fight the same battle for existence, who can honestly deny to women (at present physically the weaker) the best possible equipment that education of all kinds can furnish? I shall not even touch upon the other, and more poetic, argument of the divine rights of genius, which is of no sex; but I am content to employ only the prosaic one of the practical needs of life, an argument which here in America is by far the most potent one.

My own labors on this book have been purely editorial; and after selecting the chapters, and the authors, and laying down certain general principles and suggestions, my responsibility ceased. The principles laid down by me have been:

Facts and history rather than eloquence.

Truth before picturesqueness.

A total absence of railing against the opposite sex. (I do not mean for an instant to imply that these principles required emphasizing.)

The greatest care has been taken to assure accuracy; if mistakes do creep in, notwithstanding this, I must beg the reader not to judge too harshly, as the capacity for making mistakes in a book like this is illimitable. However, I trust the leniency of the reader will not be too severely taxed.

While being an ardent believer in the future progress of woman, it would be impossible to subscribe myself to every theory that may be found in these pages. To say one agrees in every detail with the opinions of eighteen women, all of whom are well known to be "women with opinions," is to boast of a breadth of mind, a roundness of judgment to which I am too modest to lay claim. But I can surely say that every one of the writers has cordially joined hands in the making of the book; the long hours spent in the writing of it, the many annoyances encountered in collecting historical data, all is forgotten in the hope that this book may serve:

1. To set certain plain facts, shorn of all sentiment, before the world in accessible form;

2. To preserve the record of a great, brave, and essentially American struggle;

3. To serve as a stimulus to many women who are working along a very weary road;

4. To hold up before the entire sex in every sphere of life only the highest standard of excellence.

In closing, I want to thank heartily, not only my collaborators, but also those whose names do not appear, but who have, nevertheless, added greatly to the interest and value of the book.

Annie Nathan Meyer.

New York, *January*, 1891.

78

REFORM RABBIS ON WOMEN'S SUFFRAGE
1892–1917

In 1892, two hardy souls among the Reform rabbis of the country offered a resolution that a paper be prepared for presentation to the Central Conference of American Rabbis—a paper recommending that women be permitted to hold office in congregations. The resolution was adopted and then ignored (A). Twice in later years, in 1913 and 1915, the liberals, now more numerous, returned to the fray to plead that women be allowed to vote at the civic polls. The Conference refused to take affirmative action (B and C). Finally, in 1917, the Reform rabbis did agree to recommend the enfranchisement of women; this was only three years before the adoption of the nineteenth amendment, which enfranchised America's females (D). Why had the rabbis been so dilatory, so cautious? They were well aware that many of their colleagues were adamantly opposed to political equality for women; the Jewish clergy wanted no conflict in the synagogue; the question was a hotly contested one, and most of them were afraid to take sides until they saw that the country as a whole was not unsympathetic to the pleas and demands of the suffragists. That same year, 1917, Rabbi Joseph Krauskopf published an address on The Ascendency of Womanhood. *It summarizes the arguments which induced the pro-feminist rabbis to support the cause of woman suffrage (E).*

The four resolutions of the rabbis and excerpts of the Krauskopf speech are reprinted below.

A

1892

Rabbi Clifton Levy offered a resolution, signed by himself and Dr. Berkowitz, in respect to the status of woman in Jewish congregations.

On motion of Rabbi Eisenberg, the resolution was adopted. The following is the resolution as adopted.

WHEREAS, We have progressed beyond the idea of the secondary position of women in Jewish congregations, we recognize the importance of their hearty co-operation and active participation in congregational affairs; therefore be it

Resolved, That the Executive Committee have prepared for the next Annual Conference a paper tracing the development of the recognition of women in Jewish congregations, and expounding a conclusion that women be eligible to full membership, with all privileges of voting and holding office in our congregations.

B

RESOLUTION ON WOMAN SUFFRAGE
1913

Whereas, Israel's demand for liberty at the Exodus was according to traditional accreditation the first historical assertion of liberty as a sacred right, and

Whereas, In every age since Israel's birth representative Judaism has ranged itself side by side with the foremost champions of the ever-widening and advancing cause of liberty, be it

Resolved, That this Central Conference of American Rabbis, by common recognition the largest and most representative organization of progressive Judaism to-day in the entire world, places itself on record as a body in sympathy with and in support of the latest appeal for the extension of liberty in civilization and recommends that its members individually in their pulpits, and through their ministry, advocate and advance the cause of woman's equal political suffrage with man's.

Moses P. Jacobson. . . .

VII. As regards the resolution relating to woman suffrage, the Committee feels that this is a matter for the individual Rabbi and deems it inadvisable for the Conference as a body to take action. Resolution No. VII was adopted.

C

1915

Resolution G:—Concerning the Enfranchisement of Women.

Whereas, the question of Woman Suffrage will be presented to the voters of a number of States in the course of the year,

Be it Resolved, that the Conference place itself on record as favoring the enfranchisement of women.

Horace J. Wolf. . . .

Your Committee recommends that we reaffirm the statement of the Conference made at the 1912 [1913] convention, to the effect that this is a matter for the individual rabbi, and we deem it inadvisable for the Conference, as a body, to take action thereon.

D

1917

WHEREAS, the Central Conference of American Rabbis recognizes the justice of thorough-going democracy, and,

WHEREAS, the Central Conference of American Rabbis recognizes that in a country which upholds democratic ideals and principles, it is unethical and unjust to exclude woman from active participation in choosing the leaders, and,

WHEREAS, the Jewish people have reason to know the hardship and bitterness of unjust and proscriptive political discrimination; and,

WHEREAS, in Peace and War, women have always shown their loyalty, patriotism, and eagerness to serve their country in every way possible,

Be it RESOLVED, that we, the Central Conference of American Rabbis, hereby feel it to be our solemn duty as ethical leaders in our various communities, as preachers of a religion which has stood throughout the centuries for justice and righteousness, to assert our belief in the justice and righteousness of the enfranchisement of the women of our country.

Horace J. Wolf. . . .

On this resolution the Committee is divided, the majority reporting that it be adopted, the minority reporting that this is a matter of individual decision for the rabbis in their respective communities.

Respectfully submitted,
Chas. S. Levi, Chairman

Resolution IV was taken up for consideration. A motion to adopt the minority report was lost. A motion to lay the whole matter on the table was lost. The majority report was adopted. The report was then adopted as a whole.

E

THE ASCENDENCY OF WOMANHOOD
1917

The largest number of women suffragists themselves, and by far the best part of them, do not want the franchise for the sake of mere voting, but for the sake of righting with it certain disabilities from which women suffer. They are no more desirous of doing the dirty work of politics than is the respectable element of the opposite sex. They are no more anxious to hang around the polls than the average male voter. They ask for nothing but their human rights. They believe that the franchise shall concern itself with responsible mind and moral character, and not whether the person dresses in trousers or in skirts. Possessing minds which, now-a-days, are as trained as those of men; souls which certainly are not inferior to those of men; bodies, which are capable of doing an adequate part of the world's work, they ask for themselves all the rights and privileges that are accorded to men,—that are accorded even to the most ignorant and brutish of the masculine sex.

Woman wants to see the sex element eliminated from the law. Its presence there is a relic of the long ages of barbarism. Having the same responsibilities as men, she wants the same rights. She wants efficiency not sex to be the determining force in legislation, and in the scale of wages. For the same labor she wants the same pay. She wants freedom to be and do, within the range of the law, what her ability and inclination prompt her to. She does not want man to deprive her of her rights, under the belief that he is thereby safe-guarding her sex. If he will but give her what is her due, he will find that she is amply able to look after her sex. Conscious of her powers to earn her own livelihood, she wants every obstacle removed that has been placed in her way because of her sex. She no longer wants to be a dependent creature, with no other purpose in life than to be made an object of sale or barter to the highest bidder in the matrimonial market. If marriage is to come to her, as she hopes it may, she wants it to come as a matter of choice and not of necessity. If single life is to be her lot, she wants to be able to maintain it without being a burden on others.

Being required to pay the same amount of taxes that man is obliged to pay, if she possesses property or other means, she demands the same right he has to determine how these taxes shall be expended and by whom they shall be administered. Like our revolutionary fathers, she believes that taxation without representation is tyranny. Responsible before God and before man for the health and happiness of her home, and for the education and usefulness of her children, she wants to have a voice as to who shall legislate and how, as to who shall manage the schools, and how the children shall be educated.

These are her demands, and this the cause of her uprising. Any one, therefore, who maintains that the "suffragette" movement has its origin in vanity, in a desire on the part of woman to play the role of man, either displays a woeful ignorance or he willfully perverts the truth. . . .

It is in the field of education, however, where she has made the largest progress. From having at one time been adjudged to possess but little mind, from women in general having at one time been taught but a few of the elementary branches, and the chosen few given but a smattering of the higher studies, her sex is fast becoming the better educated of the two, for the reason that she has longer time for study and greater enthusiasm for it. In 1833 only one small college admitted women; to-day, co-education is provided for, and made use of, in 75% of our colleges. Nearly one-half of the B.A. degrees are now-a-days conferred upon women. A number of our best colleges furnish higher education exclusively to women. While the male students have increased during the past decade 61%, the female have increased 149%. There are three times as many female teachers as male, in round numbers: 300,000 women teachers and 100,000 men, and each year the proportion is increasing. More than 100,000 of our women are trained nurses, and in that noble calling they render a service to our country which is second only to that of teaching our children. We find women in the medical profession, at the bar, among the clergy, among journalists and authors. We find them in the arts and trades, in the counting room and in the office, in the factory and in the shop. In fact, there is scarcely a pursuit in which woman is not represented. We find her even in callings which we had hitherto believed to be the special fields of labor of the opposite sex, such as locomotive engineers, elevator attendants, masons, pilots, blacksmiths, auctioneers, coal miners and the like. Of our wage-earning people, one-fourth are women. . . .

And all that woman's self-emancipation has thus far enabled her to do is but the prologue of the much larger work she is to do. The present is big with promise. A thousand ills that distract us to-day she will help to cure. A thousand wrongs she will help to right. Where the physical strength of man has failed, there woman's moral force will succeed. Woman's rights will yet obliterate man's wrongs. It was not her fault that she has been late in coming; but, coming now in mighty numbers, a new beauty will be discerned in Tennyson's lines

> "The woman's cause is man's; they rise or sink
> Together, dwarfed or godlike, bond or free."

79

THE JEWESS IN AUTHORSHIP
1893

By 1893, or somewhat earlier, Professor Abram Samuel Isaacs had written an article in the Ladies' Home Journal *on American and English Jewesses as writers. Rabbi Isaacs was, at various times, a professor of Hebrew, German, and Semitic languages at New York University. On the death of his father, he also served as editor of the* Jewish Messenger. *Of the names he reviewed in the article below, very few were notables; most of them had received recognition in their local communities alone. But, as the rabbi pointed out, American Jewry was small in numbers. Of the approximately 65,000,000 souls in this country, only about 450,000 were Jews; a very substantial minority of these were Central and East European immigrants; English was not their native tongue. All in all, the English-writing Jewish women in this country had made a relatively good start.*

THE JEWESS IN AUTHORSHIP
by Abram S. Isaacs

The literary and learned woman who used to be an object of profound curiosity has ceased to be a rarity. With the new education, and woman's rapid advance in all fields of activity she turns naturally to literature, and the world is the gainer. It is true France, Germany, Italy and England numbered their women writer[s] a century and more before Sorosis was organized, and America had women poets and novelists long before Vassar was founded, or Harvard dreamed of an annex. [Sorosis, the woman's club, was founded 1868; Vassar, 1861, Radcliffe, 1879.] But the recent awakening has been on a scale peculiar to our own age, and bids fair to assume still more imposing proportions in the near future.

What is the relation of the Jewess to this literary revival? What part does she take in authorship? Is she silent or responsive? What is her record?

Restricting ourselves to English and American literature, it is not to be expected that Jewesses as yet are closely identified with authorship to any large degree. In our own country, for instance, it is obviously unfair to compare the Jewess with the non-Jewess in the realm of literature. The former must have a little more time for development. As late as 1850 the number of American Israelites was limited to some thousands; today the Jewish population is still comparatively small—a few hundred thousand. Bearing in mind the vast proportion of emigrants who have to be fused into an American type, it would certainly be premature to demand any marked literary development. The great majority have to work for their daily bread in less fascinating fields than literature. . . .

Of Emma Lazarus it is unnecessary to say aught. "Her works praise her in the gates." [Prov. 31:31]. Like Grace Aguilar, she was inspired by high ideals, but she was more fortunate in her surroundings and enjoyed the friendship of prominent American authors, while Emerson was her guide, and she was a guest at his Concord home. She loved art and music, Heine and the Greeks. Her "Admetus" is a singularly polished and graceful poem; her translations from Heine show strength and beauty. Her "Alide"—a prose romance of Goethe's youth—is attractive in its luxuriance of phrase. But not all the claims of general culture made her silent when her voice was to be heard on a different theme, and her poems in behalf of the Russian Jews disclosed her spiritual fire. With no less enthusiasm she advocated manual training and agricultural pursuits for the Russian immigrants. Like Grace Aguilar she died too early to accomplish her ideals. In literary breadth and insight she was superior to her English sister, but not in intensity of religious conviction.

No literary Jewesses of the past or present compare with those two Esthers of the pen. Penina Moïse, whose hymns were the subject of an appreciative article in the "Critic" a year or two ago, Rebekah Hyneman, whose "The Leper and Other Poems," was published in Philadelphia in 1853, Mrs. Celia Hartog, the author of graceful tales and poems—the list is not a long one that survives. The encouragement given to young writers in the pages of Mr. Leeser's "Occident," a Philadelphia pioneer in Jewish journalism, and the favorable opportunity offered women writers in the Jewish press of today, have not been without their results in fitting them for a wider literary field, which some are already occupying with every indication of success. Lee C. Harby's earliest efforts thus won recognition. Helen K. Weil has done more than apprentice work. Mrs. Rosalie Kaufman, Josephine Lazarus, Mary M. Cohen, Mrs. Anna Nathan Meyer, Mrs. M. D. Louis, Ella Jacobs, Henrietta Szold (who translated an elaborate biography of Fleischer, the Orientalist, for the Smithsonian Report, 1889), Debbie H. Silver, Jennie W. Netter, Frances Hellman, Ruth Ward Kahn, Nina Morais Cohen, Mrs. S. A. Dinkins, are not unfamiliar names, and the list could be increased by Mrs. Rosa Sonneschein, Caroline Cohen, Myrtilla Mitchell, Annetta Kohn, Belle Moses, Isabella R. Hess, Elizabeth F. Aaron. . . .

The success of Martha Morton, of New York, as a dramatist, has been proven by her "The Merchant," and "Geoffrey Middleton, Gent." This list, which does not claim to be exhaustive, throws light on the versatility of the Jewess, at least. She can write graceful poetry, translate learned historical works, become historian and essayist, contribute stories and sketches to the magazines, publish tales for the young, edit special departments in the press, issue a Hebrew grammar—as did Ada S. Ballin— and enter into the spirit of Browning, like Mary M. Cohen. She can be critic, satirist, idealist, philosopher. She need not confine her efforts to Judaea. She can claim a hearing from the public at large on all themes dear to humanity, and if she does her work well recognition will follow. She is not likely to forget the claims of her own special race, their elevation and their enlightenment, but she will be qualified to advance on a line with cultured womanhood of every nation and creed.

It is not difficult to forecast the future of the Jewess in authorship. She is a partaker in the new education; she enters all the professions; she shares the ripest culture of the time; she responds to every movement that leads to honest, helpful living. The educated Jewess who graduates from Vassar or Bryn Mawr, from Cornell or Barnard, who pursues higher collegiate training at

Harvard or Yale, is on the same intellectual level as her non-Jewish chum. Her work in literature will follow the bent of her tastes and capacities, and will not be so much a question of her ancestral religion. Her womanhood and womanliness will guide her right, and as the religious instincts of the Jewess are innate, and her domestic qualities strong, one may expect her to champion all that is pure, and sweet, and wholesome.

She will be enthusiastic and resolute, but however positive her convictions she will not be less feminine in their utterance. Her ideals will be those of her age, and her inspiration the never-ending, ever-varying drama of humanity.

The work of the Jewess in authorship will hardly vary in quality and tone from that of her non-Jewish sister, and the charm and potency of her message will depend upon her spiritual insight and intellectual range. But there is every probability that for some years to come her attention will be largely devoted to education. The problems which are due to the Russian exodus, the spectacle of poverty, ignorance, over-crowding in our large cities must influence the sympathetic women of Israel. The American Jewish Publication and Historical Societies furnish a congenial field for her efforts, and in the department of Jewish Sabbath schools and devotional literature many can find ample opportunity for their talent. She has become a leading factor in charitable movements, and her experience in the class room and kindergarten, in personal service among the poor and agencies for sanitary relief, will prove fruitful in due time. One Jewess, prominent in her day in education, furnished the model of "Rebecca" to Sir Walter Scott, and the line of Rebecca Gratzes will never die.

We find, then, that despite obvious limitations due to small numbers and very recent disfranchisement of her race, the Jewess in English-speaking lands is in touch with the literary movement of her time and is utilizing her opportunities. She will become more and more closely identified with literature as she shares the intellectual tendencies of her environment and strives to influence mankind. With every barrier razed that once checked her progress, with the universities, the arts, the sciences all open to her, she feels keenly the double triumph of the century—as woman as well as Jewess. Whatever record may be hers in the future, whatever achievements she may claim as her own, she will write no unworthy line, utter no false note, if she be true to the ideals of Judaism and womanhood. She has everything to spur her on—in the broad republic of letters there are no distinctions of sex or creed, class or condition, race or nationality.—*Ladies Home Journal.*

80

LILLIAN WALD AND THE HOUSE ON HENRY STREET
1893

Lillian D. Wald (1867–1940) may well be remembered as American Jewry's most notable female social worker, but she was much more than that. She was a distinguished social reformer. In the course of her eventful life, she supported many worthy causes: child welfare, vocational guidance, classes for retarded children, scholarships for talented youngsters, the experimental theatre, women's suffrage. She fought to eradicate tuberculosis, child labor, militarism, and violations of civil liberties. In truth, Lillian Wald was one of the most highly respected liberals of the Progressive Age.

Her greatest achievement was in the field of public health nursing; it would seem that she was the ultimate pioneer in this type of social welfare, which, through the exemplary service performed by her and her associates, was adopted by municipal governments, public schools, the Red Cross, and industry too. It was largely through her initiative that a Department of Nursing and Health was established at Teacher's College, Columbia University.

This Cincinnati-born Jewess, daughter of a prosperous middle-class family, was a well-educated woman who turned to social service, especially to nursing, because she wanted to help others. In New York City, it was the day of the Sisterhoods for Personal Service. The first selection, A, describes how she began her career on the Lower East Side. That was in 1893. About two years later, she and a friend established the Nurses' Settlement, which was soon to become the Henry Street Settlement. By 1913, the Henry Street nursing service had grown to include over ninety women, who were making about 200,000 visits a year.

The second selection, B, in which Miss Wald recounts how a Jewish family reared a Christian child, has parallels in American Jewish history but is scarcely to be seen as typical.

400

18. Lillian Wald

A

1893

From the schoolroom where I had been giving a lesson in bed-making, a little girl led me one drizzling March morning. She had told me of her sick mother, and gathering from her incoherent account that a child had been born, I caught up the paraphernalia of the bed-making lesson and carried it with me.

The child led me over broken roadways—there was no asphalt, although its use was well established in other parts of the city, over dirty mattresses and heaps of refuse—it was before Colonel Waring had shown the possibility of clean streets even in that quarter—between tall, reeking houses whose laden fire-escapes, useless for their appointed purpose, bulged with household goods of every description. The rain added to the dismal appearance of the streets and to the discomfort of the crowds which thronged them, intensifying the odors which assailed me from every side. Through Hester and Division streets we went to the end of Ludlow; past odorous fish-stands, for the streets were a market-place, unregulated, unsupervised, unclean; past evil-smelling, uncovered garbage-cans; and—perhaps worst of all, where so many little children played—past the trucks brought down from more fastidious quarters and stalled on these already over-crowded streets, lending themselves inevitably to many forms of indecency.

The child led me on through a tenement hallway, across a court where open and unscreened closets were promiscuously used by men and women, up into a rear tenement, by slimy steps whose accumulated dirt was augmented that day by the mud of the streets, and finally into the sickroom.

All the maladjustments of our social and economic relations seemed epitomized in this brief journey and what was found at the end of it. The family to which the child led me was neither criminal nor vicious. Although the husband was a cripple, one of those who stand on street corners exhibiting deformities to enlist compassion, and masking the begging of alms by a pretense at selling; although the family of seven shared their two rooms with boarders—who were literally boarders since a piece of timber was placed over the floor for them to sleep on—and although the sick woman lay on a wretched, unclean bed, soiled with a hemorrhage two days old, they were not degraded human beings, judged by any measure of moral values.

In fact, it was very plain that they were sensitive to their condition, and when at the end of my ministrations they kissed my hands (those who have undergone similar experiences will, I am sure, understand), it would have been some solace if by any conviction of the moral unworthiness of the family I could have defended myself as a part of a society which permitted such conditions to exist. Indeed, my subsequent acquaintance with them revealed the fact that, miserable as their state was, they were not without ideals for the family life and for society of which they were so unloved and unlovely a part.

That morning's experience was a baptism of fire. Deserted were the laboratory and the academic work of the college. I never returned to them. On my way from the sickroom to my comfortable student quarters my mind was intent on my own responsibility. To my inexperience it seemed certain that conditions such as these were allowed because people did not *know*, and for me there was a challenge to know and to tell. When early morning found me still awake, my naïve conviction remained that, if people knew things—and "things" meant everything implied in the condition of this family—such horrors would cease to exist, and I rejoiced that I had had a training in the care of the sick that in itself would give me an organic relationship to the neighborhood in which this awakening had come. . . .

B

1913

There was the story of Mary, eldest daughter, as we supposed, of an orthodox family. When we went to her engagement party we were surprised to see that the young man was not of the family faith. The mother told us that Mary, "such a pretty baby," had

)een left on their doorstep in earlier and more prosperous days in Austria. "The Burgomeister [Buergermeister, mayor] had made)roclamation," but no one came to claim her, and the husband ınd wife, who as yet had no children of their own, decided to keep ıer. "God rewarded us and answered our prayers," said Mrs. L—, for many children came afterward; but Mary, blonde and)lue-eyed, was always the most cherished, the first-comer who ıad brought the others. When she was quite a young girl she was .aken ill—a cold following exposure after her first "grown-up")arty, for which her foster-mother had dressed her with pride. It ;eemed that nothing could save her, and the foster-mother in her distress thought with pity of the woman who had borne this sweet :hild. Surely she must be dead. No living mother could have ıbandoned so lovely a baby. And if she were dead and in the Christian heaven, she would look in vain there for her daughter. 'So, I called the priest and told him," said Mrs. L—, "and he made a prayer over Mary and said, 'Now she is a *Krist*.' The doctor, we called him too, and he said to get a goat, for the milk would be good for Mary; and she get well, but no so strong, as you ;ee, and that is why she don't go out to work like her brothers and ;isters. We lose our money, that's why we come to America, and Mary now she marry a *Krist*."

81

BEFORE WOMEN WERE HUMAN BEINGS
IDA H. HYDE AT HEIDELBERG
1893–1896

Ida Henrietta Hyde (Heidenheimer, 1857–1945), a native of Iowa, was the first woman to receive a Ph.D. from a German university. This was at Heidelberg in 1896. Thus she prepared the way for other women who wished to pursue graduate studies in that country. She was determined to make a career for herself in physiology and succeeded after heroically overcoming numerous obstacles. Ida Hyde was truly a remarkable person. After securing her degree, she returned to the United States and for a period did research at the Harvard Medical School. Here, too, she was a pioneer, for she was the first woman admitted to the school's research laboratories. In 1898, Dr. Hyde was given a teaching position at the University of Kansas; in 1905, she became professor of physiology. Three years earlier, she had been elected a member of the American Physiological Society, again the first woman to be accorded this recognition. In view of her fight for equality for women, it is obvious that she would be in favor of women's suffrage. In matters of religion, her affiliations were with the Society for Ethical Culture.

In the selection below, Miss Hyde describes her tribulations and her success in securing the coveted doctoral degree that would open a new world to her.

———————

BEFORE WOMEN WERE HUMAN BEINGS:
Adventures of an American [Female] Fellow in German Universities of the '90s
by IDA H. HYDE

Early in the last decade of the nineteenth century, a polemic between two European professors pertaining to the development of an organism they were investigating, led to bitter personal criticisms that finally appeared in print. The controversy aroused

19. Ida H. Hyde

Courtesy, University of Kansas Medical Center, Kansas City, Kansas

the interest of embryologists in this country, particularly a student in Bryn Mawr College, who without knowing of these professors was conducting experiments on the very problem about which the dispute centered.

The results obtained by the student in her investigation corroborated those published by one of the disputants, Professor Goette of the University of Strassburg. When Goette was informed of this fact he was very much elated. Eager to have his interpretation of the results strengthened and the investigation of the problem variously extended, he invited the student to come to the University of Strassburg and continue study of the subject in his department.

This invitation came to me as a complete surprise. Unfortunately it seemed impossible at the time to accept the tempting suggestion. But suddenly a way was unexpectedly opened through the splendid offer of the European Fellowship awarded in 1893 by the Association of Collegiate Alumnae for study in foreign universities. Thus in a short space of time and in a most extraordinary manner the realization of the dream to work in the promised halls of Strassburg University became a reality.

At the time the European Fellowship was awarded, it was not known to my professors nor to me that universities in Germany were not coeducational institutions, and that women had never studied in the University of Strassburg; in fact, that they had not been permitted to matriculate in any German university. Therefore we on this side did not appreciate the full significance and importance of the departure when Professor Goette, director of the Zoology Department in the University of Strassburg, graciously invited a woman student of Bryn Mawr College to work in his department.

It was not until I had worked many days in the splendid laboratory assigned to my private use that it dawned upon me that I was occupying a unique position, and that I was regarded by the students, faculty members, and their wives as a curiosity. In the university circle the news quickly spread that an American "woman's rights" freak, a blue stocking and what not, had had the boldness and audacity to force entrance into the college halls. At *Kaffee Klatchen* she was served for gossip and dissection. It was not unusual for a professor, student, or *diener* ["attendant"], seemingly by mistake, to open the laboratory door, look frightened, and quickly retreat. Or students would congregate at the windows of the botanical building opposite the laboratory, and from sheer curiosity stare across at my windows, greatly to the annoyance of the professors in both buildings.

My hostess, the wife of a professor of mathematics, occasionally invited me to accompany her to social affairs. At a dinner that we attended I met the charming wife of Professor Goltz, one of the most distinguished physiologists in Europe. Frau Professor Goltz was deeply interested in learning of the great independence enjoyed by women and women students in America. In the course of the conversation I remarked that I had specialized in physiology and had been assistant to and conducted investigations under Dr. Jacques Loeb, one of Professor Goltz's former assistants, from whom I had a letter of introduction to her husband. I ventured to inquire whether she thought Professor Goltz would allow me to work in his department. My heart sank when she replied that her husband was bitterly opposed to the admission of women to the Physiological Institute, the more so because it belonged to the Medical School, where women were taboo. However, she arranged for a meeting in her home, when the letter of introduction might be presented.

At the appointed time I found myself in the library of Professor Goltz's home, waiting for the eminent professor with little hope of success. Soon he appeared, followed by a fierce looking bulldog that greeted me with growls and terrifying barks. The stern, dignified professor attempted to calm the beast, and with strained gestures of welcome motioned me to a chair. He read the letter, apologized for the animal's behavior by informing me that the dog disliked women, and regretted that in spite of his high esteem for Dr. Loeb and the recommendations he could not admit me to the Physiology Department because the medical students would resent the presence of women there. However, he would be pleased on Sunday afternoon, following the dinner to which his wife had invited me, to show me the results of some experiments that his associate and he had recently conducted.

I reported the discouraging interview to Goette and to my host and hostess, who promised to speak in my behalf to Professor Goltz and to his associate, Professor Richard Ewald. The latter and his wife were also guests at the Sunday dinner, and accompanied us to the Physiological Institute.

When I saw the well equipped laboratories, museums, demonstration and preparation rooms, and remarkable experiments that had gained international renown, my interest and enthusiasm were deeply aroused. As we were leaving the building, I told Professor Ewald it was unfortunate that I was not a man with the privilege of working in his department. He assured me that there would be no objection to my watching experiments conducted in his private laboratory.

The following day, to my great delight, he invited me to witness the delicate technique required in experiments on the inner ear. Several times thereafter one or two of his research students and I were visitors at his demonstrations. I took pains to make a thorough study of the anatomy and technique involved, and to my surprise was rewarded by an invitation from Professor Ewald to cooperate in an investigation of the brain's relation to the peripheral center of sound—a study which was later published over our joint signatures.

Needless to say, I was overjoyed at the prospect of working in a physiological research laboratory where opportunity was offered to acquire valuable technique and experience in unusual operations. Now my time was divided between work in the zoological and physiological laboratories. Professor Goette was satisfied with the results obtained on the problem in which he was interested, and to my great surprise offered to accept my investigation for a doctor's thesis. Furthermore, he advised me to petition the Ministerium of Education in the Reichstag to permit the faculty of the University of Strassburg to allow me to work for the doctorate. It was necessary to obtain the consent of that august body and the approval of the faculty, because the constitution of the university did not contain a clause permitting women to take the examination for the advanced degree.

Before petitioning the Reichstag, however, it was deemed advisable to ascertain the attitude of the Strassburg faculty regarding the question of giving women the privilege of taking the examination. My petition, accompanied by many influential credentials, was presented for faculty action at the November meeting. It aroused heated discussion, and Professor Graf Solms, the director of the Botanical Department, announced that as chairman of the examining commission he refused to allow a woman to take the examination.

Believing that the disagreement aroused in the faculty by Graf Solms's attitude might prejudice the cause of woman students in Germany, I hastened to beg that my petition be withdrawn. This step, it proved, gained friends and no enemies for the cause.

When an American friend, engaged in publishing her late husband's manuscripts with the help of Professor Rosenbusch, the noted geologist in the University of Heidelberg, heard of Graf Solms's action, she urged me to try to obtain the degree in Heidelberg. But first I wished assurance that the university would actually grant me the degree. Accordingly a formal request was dispatched in November 1893 to the Reichstag's Ministerium of Education, "that universities in Germany permit women students, prepared in collegiate required subjects as thoroughly as were men, to matriculate, take the examination, and if successful in passing it, to receive the doctor's degree." It is noteworthy that this petition to the Reichstag pertained not only to my cause but to that of women in general. With this carefully prepared document were enclosed many credentials from noted educators and scientists.

After several weeks of waiting, a formidable-looking document from the Reichstag Ministerium arrived. It informed me that the petition had been presented to the High Commissioner of Education, and its object duly incorporated in the minutes of the day's proceedings. Furthermore, it advised that, inasmuch as I was hoping to enter the Heidelberg University, my petition should be sent to the Ministerium of Education and Justice in the Duchy of Baden, under whose jurisdiction the University of Heidelberg was governed. Also, my petition must receive the approval of the Grand Duke of Baden, who was rector of the university.

In considering the situation, it seemed best to finish the zoological and physiological investigations, and prepare them for publication before leaving Strassburg. In the meantime I addressed a letter to Professor Geheimrath Stengel, Dean of the Faculty of Natural Sciences and Mathematics of the University of Heidelberg, asking if the university would give me the degree of Ph.D. provided I presented a satisfactory thesis, pursued the required subjects in the university for the length of time deemed necessary, and passed the examination for the degree. This letter marked the beginning of correspondence that extended over a period of two years. The story may be briefly told here.

A most interesting letter, dated December 9, 1893, was received from Dean Stengel. He informed me that up to date no woman had petitioned the Natural Sciences and Mathematics Faculty for permission to matriculate and to take the examination for the doctorate. Furthermore, that there was in existence no record or constitutional clause stating that women shall or shall not be allowed to prepare for and take the examination. However, to obtain an official decision, a special printed blank, petitioning for the privilege of taking the test, must be executed and presented for faculty action.

It was so very important that this petition should receive a favorable vote from the faculty that I decided to go to Heidelberg to obtain an audience with the professors under whom I wished to study, and if possible secure their support. Therefore I wrote Professor Butschli (Hofrath Geheimrath Professor Doctor Otto Butschli), the renowned scientist and director of the Zoological Institute of the university, and begged for an interview during the Christmas vacation. This favor he kindly granted.

Arriving at the appointed hour, armed with my thesis, drawings, preparation-slides, and letters, I was shown by the *diener* to the professor's private laboratory. We found him bending over a microscope, absorbed in studying an object under it. With many apologies the *diener* announced a woman wished to speak to him, and inquired if she should be admitted. Turning his heavily bewhiskered face, and scanning me with searching eyes, he ejaculated "*Ja wohl*. What can I do for you?" Apologizing for the interruption and thanking him for the granted interview, I gave him Professor Goette's letter of introduction. Then I inquired if he would kindly examine the manuscript and illustrations, and let me know if I might work in his department toward a Ph.D. He asked me to leave my papers, saying that I might expect word from him in a few days.

Upon Professor Butschli's decision now depended my hope of entering the university. When on December 27 the *diener* brought my manuscript and letter, I opened the message with trembling fingers. Imagine my surprise and delight! Not only would he recommend the thesis for the degree, but he was also willing to enroll me with student's privileges in his department.

With such a delightful prospect, I dispatched the official petition blank to the Dean on January 11, 1894, to be presented to the faculty. Accompanying the petition were all of my letters and credentials and a personal letter in which I begged to be informed whether there existed any faculty ruling against admitting women to the examination for the doctor's degree.

A special meeting of the faculty was called to consider the petition. All members were present and took active part in the prolonged discussion. It was recognized that the questions asked in Miss Hyde's petition were for the first time in the history of the university presented for definite official action. After much discussion, two motions were voted:

(1) Women are admitted to the examination for the degree, under the same conditions outlined in the official regulations for men candidates, with the proviso that women are required to study in the University of Heidelberg in preparation for the examination. (2) A faculty rule does not exist against admitting women candidates to the examination for the doctor's degree.

Professor Quincke, professor of physics, cast the only vote against this motion. Further discussion finally influenced him to join the majority, making the vote unanimous.

The meeting also voted to petition the Senate to present the voted resolutions to the legislative and executive bodies for approval. On February 26 the Dean was notified that the resolutions adopted by the faculty were approved both by the Legislative Ministry and the Senate, with the proviso that in granting this petition it was understood that a precedent was not established justifying women in demanding admission to the university, since it had not as yet in any wise been decreed or announced by the superior Ducal Commission that women should be admitted to Baden's university on equal terms with men.

Shortly thereafter a letter bearing the seal of royalty reached me. From it I learned that my petition and letters, through the general adjutant to his Highness, the Grand Duke of Baden, had received due consideration and favorable judgment.

It may be imagined with what profound gratitude and appreciation I received these tidings. They established for the first time in the history of this institution the significant and victorious outcome of the struggle to gain recognition for women candidates for the Ph.D. degree. As a consequence, women thereafter met few obstacles in entering any—except the medical—department in the University of Heidelberg.

Although equal opportunities with men students were not obtained, nevertheless a beginning was made toward that end. With the passage of the decree any woman prepared to fulfill the university's requirements was permitted to study for the finals and if successful obtain the doctor's degree.

In Strassburg, in the meantime, my physiological and zoological investigations were completed. On my arrival at Heidelberg much time was consumed in fulfilling the customary registration regulations and in obeying the rules of etiquette. In accordance with the latter, I made a formal call on the Dean and asked for an opportunity to consult him on the subjects chosen for the finals. During the interview, granted late in March, he advised me to see the professors under whom I wished to study, obtain their consent to admit me to their departments and, when the time arrived, to conduct the examination. Furthermore, when all that had been attended to, I was to petition the faculty to approve the choice of subjects chosen, and beg it to invite the professors to be present at the examination.

The first steps taken in following the Dean's advice were to call on Professor Butschli, Director of the Comparative Anatomy and Zoology Departments, and Professor Victor Meyer, Director of the Chemistry Department. Both courteously welcomed me to their departments. However, they suggested taking some subject other than physiology, which I had chosen for the third subject required, since physiology was given in the Medical School, where women would not be admitted. Indeed, Geheimrath [Wilhelm] Kühne, professor of physiology, had recently announced in a public lecture that women's place was in the home and not in the university. They advised securing an interview with him at once, since the pre-semester faculty meeting, to which my petition must be submitted for approval, was scheduled for the following day.

Without further delay I called on Professor Kühne and presented a letter of introduction from his friend and colleague, Professor Goltz of Strassburg. He seemed a giant, seated in a huge armchair at a table in a spacious library. Without rising he expressed pleasure in receiving the letter and meeting me. When I told him that I was greatly interested in physiology, he kindly offered the use of his library, and asked what books he might send to my address. He expressed approval in the choice of books.

I then told him that I expected to work in the departments of Professor Butschli and Meyer, and wished to know if, after physiology had been sufficiently mastered, he would examine me in that subject for the degree. He appeared to regard the question as a joke, and laughingly said, "Certainly, if that time should ever come!" As he rose to show me out, he casually remarked that his conference hours were Saturday morning in his laboratory, where the books might be returned and where he would be pleased to discuss them with me.

I hastened to tell Professor Meyer the result of the interview. He expressed great surprise, and assured me that since Professor Kühne had given his promise, he was obliged to fulfill it. He also aided me in preparing the petition that was to be presented the following day for faculty action.

It was uncertain what attitude the members of the council would assume to the proposal to allow a subject belonging to the Medical School to be credited by the natural sciences and mathematics section as one of the three required subjects for the Ph.D. However, Professor Meyer reported after the meeting that finally a favorable decision had been reached.

But at the council meeting Professor Kühne had announced that he must be excused from giving the examination, and furthermore that he refused to let "skirts" enter his lecture room or laboratory. When questioned whether he had not promised to conduct the examination, if I should ever be prepared for it, he had admitted making that statement, in reply to what he considered a joke. He had had no idea that he was being made the victim of an American scheme in order to secure his favorable answer. To the statement that there was no proof that unfair methods had been employed or that the question had been put as a joke, he had replied that since it appeared that he ought to adhere to his promise, "as a gentleman he would keep his word." But without admission to the lecture room or laboratory, how could one master the subject sufficiently to pass the finals?

Even with this disappointment, the decision of the faculty meeting was more than I had expected. Was there not sufficient cause for rejoicing in the knowledge that a long stretch of the difficult pioneer route on the higher education of women had been traversed? The taboo chasm of tradition and prejudice that defied the aspirations and attempts of earnest women to reach the mecca of intellectual freedom had been bridged and actually crossed to the sacred road beyond leading to the open door of the seat of learning.

At an early hour of a spring morning in 1894, I entered the new Zoological Institute of the University of Heidelberg, selected a back seat in the lecture room, and was assigned to a well equipped laboratory. Over the table I hung a picture of the Grand Duke of Baden, writing below it *"Dankbarkeit erzeugt Ehrfurcht und Gehorsamkeit"* [Gratitude evokes veneration and obedience."],—an answer to the fear expressed by the Duke, that "if women became better educated, they would no longer respect, honor, and obey men, as they should." (The picture still hung there when I visited the laboratory thirty years later.)

In the Chemistry Department I was greeted by Professor Meyer, who placed my name on one of the most desirable places, where the experiments and demonstrations could most readily be observed.

Seemingly all was going well. But how to approach Kühne

without making an irretrievable mistake was a question that constantly haunted me. What if he should refuse to admit me to the lectures and laboratory courses in physiology? How would it be possible without attending them to prepare for the finals?

It is true, botany could be chosen as a third subject, and much heartache avoided. But I preferred physiology above every other subject, and had determined to specialize in it. To abandon that decision forever seemed to me a calamity. There was but one thing to do: study the books that Kühne had loaned me, and take them to the laboratory where on Saturday morning he held his seminar.

When the *diener* heard my request, he grinned most politely and led the way to the conference room. That gave me courage. Professor Kühne greeted me with extreme politeness. That greatly disturbed. He questioned me on subjects of investigations that had recently appeared in foreign publications, and on every subject except those dealt with in the books. Being unprepared for the attacks he successfully made to dishearten me, I ventured to ask the loan of literature about which he had quizzed me, and told him I regretted that the topics treated in the books had not been discussed. Thereupon he politely assured me that the examination might also deal with questions with which I was unprepared, and that as a matter of fact only a small per cent of the men students successfully passed the examination in physiology. Finally he advised registering in botany.

I replied that physiology interested me more than any other subject and if necessary I would devote a year or more in further study to master it, and asked if it were not possible to accomplish this with the aid of his assistants. He laughingly replied that his assistants had never attended his lectures; therefore it was doubtful they would be able to help me. He offered me a treatise on the physiology of blood, with the remark he would be interested in discussing the subject matter with me any Saturday morning.

During the ensuing weeks most of my thoughts were stained in blood. But when I came to the conference and begged to report on the topics dealt with in the books, Kühne, seemingly annoyed, inquired if I had heard that the professor of botany would admit me to his department. I replied that I had come to Heidelberg to study physiology and had just received word that the Phoebe Hearst fellowship for study abroad had been awarded me. I therefore felt in duty bound to make a success of my work in the university, and hoped he would assist me to that end.

I was dumbfounded when he rose, opened the door to the general laboratory, and beckoned to his assistants. He introduced me with the remark that I was determined to study physiology, and since he refused to let me attend his lectures, perhaps they would undertake to help me attain my object. They said that with his consent they were willing to try.

On the following morning, the medical students who crowded the physiology lecture room wondered why the two chief assistants were occupying the front seats. This was the first time in the history of his instruction that Kühne was honored by the presence of his associates in the lecture room. To his amazement and satisfaction they were actually taking notes.

The notes were taken for me, to be copied for study in preparation for the finals. Six hours daily were devoted to the subject. In the opinion of the instructors, this schedule followed for at most six semesters should prepare me for the most rigid examination.

During these months of arduous work, the thought haunted me that Kühne would do all in his power to frustrate my purpose. He bitterly resented the gossip aroused among his colleagues by the stand his assistants had taken, and he resented being an unwilling agent in permitting "skirts" to enter the Medical School.

Finally the morning of the first lecture in chemistry arrived. On reaching the building, I was dismayed to hear an uproar within, and awakened to the realization that I was late. The door of the lecture room was closed. As I stood before it, the chills ran up and down me, and my courage failed. It was impossible for me to face the excited crowd of noisy students. Turning to leave as quickly as possible, I saw students rushing upstairs. I realized that if I failed then it would require more courage to enter the classroom the next day. The students jostled each other and hastened by, leaving me standing in the open doorway.

A silence followed, so profound you could hear a pin drop. The men stood seemingly transfixed in their various attitudes. I never knew how I got to my seat. The blood was rushing to my head, and in the hush I distinctly heard an American voice say, "We shall next have them in the jury box."

To hear those taunting words in my profound embarrassment from an American would have proved too disheartening if the remark had not been instantly censured with hisses and scraping of feet by the German students who heard it. And to the credit of the Heidelberg students it must be said that in all the time of my attendance at the university, they always treated me with the greatest courtesy.

For three semesters I attended the lectures and demonstrations in chemistry conscientiously. At the beginning of the second semester I no longer was the only woman student in chemistry. Encouraged by my report of the opportunities offered in chemistry and geology for advanced work, two of my Bryn Mawr College friends had come to Heidelberg for special studies.

The time spent in the Zoological Institute was most happily employed in research, attending lectures, demonstrations, and seminars. I shall forever cherish the memories of my sojourn there, as among the most delightful of my college days.

As a matriculated student at the University of Heidelberg I devoted two years in preparation for the doctorate toward which my researches and thesis had already been accepted and credited in the Natural Sciences and Mathematics Faculty. While working here it was gratifying to meet women graduates from Russia and America, who were now admitted under the finally established resolutions not only to the lectures but also to the laboratories.

Finally the last lecture and laboratory experiment came to an end. I began a review of the subjects, especially of physiology, the one that caused most worry, in preparation for the finals.

In accordance with university traditions, a visit to the Dean was in order for the purpose of asking him to present my request to the faculty to be permitted to take the examination, if possible in November. The faculty's favorable decision was sent to Kühne for concurrence. In reply he announced that owing to ill health he was leaving for Italy for an indefinite period.

This information was disheartening, not only because prepaation for the tests was under way but also on account of the ncertainty of his return. Early in December Kühne appeared in Ieidelberg. Again a formal visit to the Dean was necessary, and nother petition was sent to the examining board asking at what late permission would be given to appear for the finals. The date vas set for January 8, and Kühne was invited to conduct the test n physiology. He replied that the date was noted, and that he vould be present.

While the process of cramming was going on, the weather ecame severely cold and damp. The change in temperature and ck of proper food and exercise no doubt contributed to a severe ttack of neuralgia, and it was necessary to petition the Board to ostpone the examination. This time it was set for 6 P.M. ebruary 12, 1896.

At last the day arrived when in formal attire, according to ustom, it behoved me to call upon and invite the professors to the xamination. The invitation was graciously accepted, but Kühne aid only that he hoped to be present. This implied uncertainty vas very trying.

The morning of the momentous day found me in a wretched ondition, unable to think or act. My loyal friend was deeply listressed. She feared that at the last moment my cherished hope vas doomed to disappointment. It was late in the afternoon efore I found it possible to take nourishment. By five o'clock we ealized that I must either be in the university hall or dispatch vord to the examining board that I was too ill to appear.

Suddenly an unaccountable consciousness of awakened power ossessed me. Telling my friend that my indisposition had niraculously vanished, with her assistance I dressed and set out n foot to the university. The invigorating evening air and nowledge of recovered well-being imbued me with a spirit of onfidence that stood me in good stead.

The *pedell* [beadle] in his elaborate uniform stood at the door. In condescending tone he requested me to wait in the ante-room ntil he should be notified to conduct me into the hall. He stood rect holding his mace, it seemed to me an eternity, guarding the oor, when he ventured to say, "Geheimrath Kühne has not yet rrived." Suddenly the room was pervaded by an overwhelming chilliness. But presently the door was opened, and I was escorted to a chair at a long table surrounded by what appeared to me to be countless professors.

As I entered the room, wine glasses were being passed, and Kühne rose and handed one to me saying, "We shall celebrate this event with a toast in champagne." In thanking him I humbly asked permission to drink water before and champagne to the toast after the examination. Laughingly they rose, and as the *diener* handed me the water, all drank to my success.

Professor Butschli placed his watch on the table, and Kühne, as Dean of the Medical Faculty, had the honor of opening the quiz. He was keen in his questioning, and made no comments upon my answers. Suddenly Butschli pointed to the watch and inquired if he was aware that the allotted time had elapsed? Jocularly Kühne replied that in the enjoyment of the test he had entirely forgotten the time.

The examination lasted until ten o'clock, when the *pedell* entered, showed me to the anteroom, and asked me to wait until the professors had left the hall. While adjusting my wraps, I heard discordant voices issuing from the hall, and feared the worst. When the *pedell* opened the door, some of the members, among them Butschli and lastly Kühne, came toward me, extending their congratulations. The ordeal was over!

My friend was awaiting me in a cab at the entrance to the building. She kindly inquired if she might have my professors taken to their homes. Butschli accepted the offer, saying his wife was anxious to hear the result of the game, and to see me in the gown which she had heard I had made for the occasion.

The Frau Professor seemed so very pleased that I had come. Excitedly she asked her husband how Kühne had behaved. He answered that I had deserved *Summa Cum Laude*, but that the "brute" had objected to giving a woman that honor. Finally a compromise had been agreed upon, and a new term, *Multa Cum Laude Superavit* [praiseworthily excellent in many things], with the title, Doctor of Philosophy and the Natural Sciences, was conferred upon me. Before I left, Frau Professor Butschli invited me to a dinner in my honor.

On the following day a great honor, an invitation to a dinner

om Frau and Professor Kühne, was received. Most unfortu-
ately, this was for the day set for the dinner of Frau and
rofessor Butschli, and could not be accepted. An invitation from
ie students, asking me to participate in a parade, was also
eclined. However, an enormous chocolate cake in the shape of a
octor's chapeau sent with congratulations was accepted most
eartily.

I was the first woman to obtain the Ph.D. of Heidelberg not as a
ourtesy but as a *bona fide* university student in the Natural
ciences and Mathematics Faculty who had met in every detail
ie requirements of that institution's decree of March 7, 1894.
he university, be it said to her honor, had established a
recedent of far-reaching importance.

82

THE NATIONAL COUNCIL OF JEWISH WOMEN
1893–1902

At the Chicago World's Columbian Exposition in 1893, women's denominational religious congresses met to listen to papers. Among the essays read at the Jewish Women's Congress in September was one by Julia Richman, the well-known New York City educator. The subject assigned her was: "Women as Wage-Workers, with Special Reference to Directing Immigrants." This essay of hers is a good introduction to the economic life of the New York Jewess. Selections from it are reprinted below (A).

One of the purposes of the Jewish Women's Congress was the hope of creating a national organization for Jewish women. The appeal to establish such an association was made by Sadie American, one of the country's leading Jewish clubwomen. In her rather lengthy address, she reviewed the work then being carried on by Jewish women in various communities. Brief selections from her appeal are reprinted below as item B. After she had finished her call to organize, a resolution was introduced and adopted, which brought to birth the National Council of Jewish Women. These resolutions constitute item C. Throughout the 1890's, the individual sections submitted reports on their programs and achievements. A number of them are reprinted below as selections D, E, F, and G. They enable the reader and student to gauge the nature of the work carried on by the branches of the Council in different parts of the country. In 1902, Hannah G. Solomon, the first president and a prime founder of this association of Jewish women's societies, made an address in Washington before a Council group. The excerpts printed here serve very well to summarize the accomplishments of the Council over the preceding decade.

Mrs. Hannah G. Solomon (1858–1942), a member of one of Chicago's most prestigious Jewish families, was a highly respected welfare worker in both Jewish and non-Jewish philanthropic organizations. In the late 1870's, when only nineteen years of age, she was invited to become a member of the Chicago Woman's Club. Prior to this time no Jewess had been asked to join that exclusive group. While still president of the National Council of Jewish Women (1893–1905), she helped organize the Federation of Women's Clubs and played an important role, too, in the

rger nondenominational National Council of Women and in the
iternational Council of Women, which met abroad.

She was an outstanding civic reformer, a devoted suffragist, and an
idefatigable worker on behalf of the incoming East European immi-
rants. The National Council of Jewish Women was launched by her with
ie help of her able associate Sadie American.

A

WOMEN WAGE-WORKERS: WITH REFERENCE TO DIRECTING IMMIGRANTS.
by Julia Richman, New York.
1893

This is an age of progress; and, surrounded as we are to-day by
very evidence of the astounding advance that the nineteenth
:ntury has carried in its train, I feel that I am flinging down a
iallenge that will, perhaps, bring me face to face with a volley of
ietorical bullets, when I assert that in no other country and in no
ther direction is this progress more noticeable than in the relative
osition to man and the affairs of the world that woman occupies
›-day. This advance has been made in almost every grade in
)ciety, in almost every walk in life; but so far as my own personal
bservations have permitted me to go, so far as my own experi-
nces have enabled me to judge, it is my belief that this change,
iis revolution, yes, this progress is more noticeable in the
osition held by the Jewish women of America (notably the
escendants of European emigrants driven from their homes
irty or fifty years ago), than in that of any other class in our
osmopolitan community.

Many conditions have conspired to bring about this change: the
eneral advance in the education of women; the desire to give
hildren greater educational advantages than the parents enjoyed;
ie financial value of woman's work; the frequent necessity for

women to contribute to the support of families; the growing conviction that there is not a sufficient number of marrying men to supply all the marriageable girls with good husbands—these are but a few, with only one of which it is my privilege to deal, viz., the financial value of woman's work.

Perhaps it was due to custom and tradition, perhaps due to our oriental origin, but notwithstanding the fact that there may have always been among us a certain number of Deborahs, Ruths and Esthers, in general, the wives and daughters of Jews were, and in many parts of the world unfortunately still are, regarded as man's inferiors, their chief mission in life being to marry, or rather to be given in marriage, to rear children, to perform household duties, and to serve their lords and masters.

This is an age of progress; and thousands of women, many of them good, true, pure, womanly women, have discovered for themselves, or have been led to discover, that there is, at best, only an uncertain chance of real happiness facing the woman who calmly settles down in her parents' home, to perform, in an inane, desultory way, certain little household or social duties, who lives on from day to day, from year to year, without any special object in life, and who sees no prospect of change, unless a husband should appear to rescue her from so aimless an existence. Having made this discovery they try to join, and frequently, in the face of opposition, succeed in joining the ever-increasing army of women wage-workers, striving to lead useful, if sometimes lonely lives with the hope of making the world, or that little corner thereof into which their lines have fallen, a little better and a little brighter than they found it. . . .

Who are our women wage-workers? . . . Perhaps the simplest classification on practical lines would be in general terms:

Women engaged in professional work.

Women engaged in domestic service.

Women engaged in store or factory work.

The professional workers, excluding writers, artists and all other classes requiring special talent in addition to long training, let us, for convenience, divide again into two classes; the one class including teachers, governesses, companions, kindergartners typewriters, stenographers, bookkeepers, trained nurses, etc emands, first, a general education, in a greater or less degree, ith a thorough knowledge of the English language; and, second, ome special course of instruction, to which, in most cases, ronths, sometimes years must be devoted. The other class, a ype best represented by dressmakers, milliners, manicures, rasseuses and hair-dressers, demands little general education— r which a thorough knowledge of the English language is not an ssential—a marketable value of which can usually be acquired y a special course of instruction which can be completed in a few veeks. . . .

The workers, whom, in general terms, I have placed under the ead, "Women engaged in domestic service," are the cooks, rundresses, waitresses and chambermaids, children's nurses, eamstresses, ladies' maids, and general houseworkers. And vhen we have found a sound, practical, reasonable plan for irecting the tide of immigration into this channel, we shall have olved the most perplexing woman's problem of the day. . . .

And now we come to the third class, "Women engaged in store r factory work." Perhaps this class comprises more grades of vork than could be classed under any other general head.

The manager of one large dry-goods house reports to me that e employs women as buyers, forewomen, dressmakers, milliers, saleswomen, cashiers, stock-girls, office-assistants, bundlers, perators, addressers, and scrub-women; while a manufacturer f tin toys uses female help exclusively for painting on tin, cutting in, packing toys, making paper boxes, and working foot presses. 'here are almost as many grades of woman's work as there are ranches in every style of factory work. A word, now and again, i all that I can say in reference to these.

Saleswomen in large establishments are, on the whole, fairly vell paid; but this avenue is closed to the immigrant, until she hall have mastered the English language to such an extent that here is no room for misunderstanding between herself and her ustomer.

"Figures" [models] in wholesale cloak and suit houses are well aid; their hours are short, their work never onerous, and between seasons" they have little or no work to do. But, perhaps, o other class of working women in large cities is so directly placed in the way of temptation, and the mother who lets her daughter, particularly if she be attractive and vain, take a position as a "figure," has need of all our prayers added to her own to protect her girl. You, who are doing such zealous work among working girls, try to reach this class. God help them! They have need of you.

Until I commenced to systematically collect data for this paper, which data have been furnished me by the owners of large manufacturing industries in New York City, and by working girls with whom I am intimately acquainted, I am afraid I shared the only too general opinion, that factory girls are an overworked, underpaid, much persecuted class of wage-earners. Now, I am hardly prepared to say that girls are never overworked or never underpaid, but I am prepared to assert and to prove that in New York City, at least, there are hundreds of shops and factories, well lighted, well ventilated, controlled by humane forewomen, where girls can be contented if not happy; and where the pay for satisfactory work is good, in many cases excellent. I do not, for one moment, claim that there are no factories, life in which must be torture to the poor girls therein employed; but these are in the minority; I think vastly in the minority in those industries largely controlled by Jews. . . .

Probably, the manufacture of clothing and cloaks gives employment to a larger number of immigrant Jewish girls and women than does any other single industry in New York City, and, unfortunately, many, perhaps even most, of these women are compelled to run heavy machines, in badly lighted, worse ventilated dens. The manufacturer is only indirectly to blame for this, owing to the pernicious "middleman" system; and let me say right here that if *"the kindest proprietor in the world is a Jew of the better class,"* there is no employer of our Jewish working girls who shows less kind-heartedness to his employees than these Jews of the other class, call them middlemen, or sweaters, or what you please. They are, with few exceptions, so hard, so harsh, so grasping, so unreasoning, and so unreasonable, that on several occasions, in my capacity as president of a Working Girls' Club, tried to find better paying positions for some of these girls in order to take them away from shops owned or controlled by their own athers. I recall one case distinctly—a girl, not over fifteen, whose father runs a shop for the manufacture of ladies' wrappers—over twenty machines in two small rooms lighted by kerosene lamps, the air vile, the language not less so, the employees paid by piece-work, laboring from seven in the morning until after ten at night, and for this, the girl I refer to received three dollars a week, of which she paid her father two dollars and a half for board. I saw her growing hollow-eyed, round-shouldered, narrow-chested, with a never-ceasing pain in the back. It was not until I found a place for her in which she earned six dollars a week, working daily from 8 to 6, that her father would let her leave his shop, and then only upon her promise to pay him four dollars a week for board. . . .

The Jews of America, particularly the Jews of New York City, are, perhaps, the most charitable class of people in the whole world. Time, labor, and money are given freely in some directions. But charity is not always philanthropy; and we have reached a point in the development of various sociological problems which makes it imperative that philanthropy be placed above charity. The need of charity must disappear as we teach the rising generation how to improve its condition.

Almost all the female immigrants who come to this shore, through lack of knowledge as to the means by which they can swing themselves above the discouraging conditions which face them, sink down into the moral and intellectual maelstrom of the American ghettos, becoming first household or factory drudges, and then drifting into one of three channels: that of the careless slattern, of the giddy and all-too-frequently sinful gadabout, or of the weary, discontented wife.

We must disentangle the individual from the mass. We must find a way or several ways of leading these girls, one by one, away from the shadows which envelop them, if not into the sunshine of happiness and prosperity, at least, into the softening light of content, born of pleasant surroundings, congenial occupations, and the inward satisfaction of a life well spent.

Working girls' clubs are doing a grand work, but these clubs never reach the lower strata. There must be something before and beyond the working girls' clubs, something that shall lay hold of the immigrant before she has been sucked down into the stratum of physical misery or moral oblivion, from which depths it becomes almost impossible to raise her.

In this age of materialism, in these days of close inquiry as to the "Why?" of every condition, it has been claimed that the ever-increasing proportion of unmarried women among the Jews of America is largely due to the independent position women make for themselves, first, by becoming wage-earners, and second, through the development of self-reliance brought about by societies, working girls' clubs, and kindred movements. If marriage always meant happiness, and if celibacy always meant unhappiness, to make women independent and self-reliant would be a calamity. But, in the face of so much married unhappiness and so much unmarried contentment, it is hardly pessimistic to wish that there might be fewer marriages consummated until the contracting parties show more discrimination in their selection of mates.

The saddest of many sad conditions that face our poor Jewish girls is the class of husbands that is being selected for them by relatives. It is the rule, not the exception, for the father, elder brother, or some other near relative of a Jewish working girl, to save a few hundred dollars, by which means he purchases some gross, repulsive Pole or Russian as a husband for the girl. That her whole soul revolts against such a marriage, that the man betrays, even before marriage, the brutality of his nature, that he may, perhaps, have left a wife and family in Russia, all this counts for nothing. Marry him she must, and another generation of worthless Jews is the lamentable result.

I wish it distinctly understood that there is no desire on my part to disparage matrimony; indeed, happy wifehood and motherhood are to my mind the highest missions any woman can fulfill; but in leading these girls to see the horror of ill-assorted marriages, I intend to teach them to recognize the fact that many of them may never find suitable husbands; and recognizing this fact, they must fill up their lives with useful, perhaps even noble work. Should the possible husband fail to appear, their lives will not have been barren; should he come, will a girl make a less

20. Sadie American

faithful wife and mother because she has been taught to be faithful in other things?

And so I could go on showing how, in every direction, the harm and the evil grow, until the day will come when charity, even with millions at her disposal, will not be able to do good. It is easier to save from drowning than to resuscitate the drowned. Disentangle the individual from the mass; create a new mass of disentangled individuals, who shall become the leading spirits in helping their benighted sisters, and with God's help, the future will redeem the present and the past.

B

ORGANIZATION
by Sadie American, Chicago.
1893

The foregoing days of this Congress have shown what some Jewish women have been, have done, have thought, and what a few are thinking and planning. This Congress would not be complete without some record of what many Jewish women have done, and are doing. Therefore, an attempt has been made to bring into a short, presentable form, the present work of Jewish women. . . .

There are in existence several working girls' clubs [in New York City] for evening instruction and one—the Working Girls' Alliance—for mutual improvement and culture. This is a self-supporting institution, and is a pioneer in a field that should be actively and energetically worked.

In New York and in other cities during the past few years have been formed in the various congregations what are known as Sisterhoods. They teach the value of personal service, and practically show it in visiting the sick and poor, in providing and teaching crèches and kindergartens.

Their work is divided into four sections:

(1) Visiting the poor;

(2) Work in Kindergartens, etc.;

(3) Work in Sabbath Schools and sewing classes, combining religious and practical work; and

(4) Work among working girls.

Prevention is their watchword, as it must come to be that of us all. The first three of these sections are in most active operation. Work among working girls is being pushed but has assumed no such proportions as it should and will.

In addition to these sisterhoods, there exists in Baltimore a society doing much the same work but on a different plan. The organization, known as the Daughters in Israel, is an organization composed of small bands of ten, each doing the special work itself decides upon; its small size insures all workers and no drones. Among the good things brought into existence through its instrumentality are visiting among the needy, dressmaking classes, the establishing of a fresh air fund for the care of sick children, the instituting of a temporary home where Russian immigrants are cared for during a few days till they can find employment; mothers' meetings, at which kindly advice on home matters is given to poor mothers and at which they are also taught to sew; a small kitchen-garden or household school, and a working girls' club for social approach. This club holds meetings every Saturday evening; often there are informal talks by some outsider on popular subjects, such as physiology, etc. Here, too, their sympathies have been quickened for those *most* unfortunate in this world—the sick and absolutely poor—and they find that out of their small means they still have enough to give something of money, of time, and of friendliness, to help those poorer than themselves. The Daughters seek to procure employment for specially talented girls. They have extended their influence even to children. There is one band that gives such things as children prize—fruit, and flowers, and candies, and good food for the mind in entertaining books. The Daughters in Israel may feel they have indeed deserved to be told, "Well done, thou good and faithful servant" [Matt. 25:21].

There are, too, in Baltimore, congregational societies "for promoting the interests of the congregations," furnishing prizes and entertainments for their Sabbath School children and decorations for the synagogue on Holy Days. There is the night school of the Hebrew Literary Society, arranged primarily to meet the needs of adult immigrants, to teach them English and act as an Americanizing influence. For the more advanced pupils here, the history of the United States is taken as a textbook, and some have this year been reading Lamb's Tales from Shakespeare, with frequent passages from the great bard himself. Sunday evening lectures in winter are a feature of this school; but the best feature is the fact that it is partially supported by the small tuition fee of thirty cents a month, paid by the pupils, and giving them that feeling which is only theirs who know that they are not a burden nor a drag on others.

In Philadelphia, the institutions deserving special mention are, a Wayfarers' Lodge, established by Russian women for the temporary housing and feeding of their persecuted brethren driven to seek new homes; the Household School, providing as an adjunct to itself weekly inspiriting entertainments; and the Personal Interest Society, composed of women, each of whom looks after some one family, inculcating principles of thrift, and cleanliness and culture, and seeing that the children get all the benefits of education open to them.

In Rochester, beside the general run of societies, there is one for encouraging and distributing good reading among children, a club giving monthly entertainments, a musical society, and a Shakespeare class.

In St. Louis, the Mothers' Club, and the Pioneer Society, a society established for mutual culture and improvement, must be mentioned.

In Detroit stands forth pre-eminent the Woman's Club, established on the fine principle of bringing rich and poor, women of all social conditions together in frequent meetings, that they may learn to know and to help one another. Sewing classes, readings, lectures and general social intercourse are its work; and it has proved its practicability and elevating tendency through the several years of its existence. . . .

There are among the Jewish women various benefit and secret societies, such as the Treue Schwestern [United Order of True Sisters], whose purpose is mutual aid in cases of sickness and death, and noble friendship and endeavor, together with some charitable work among the very poor.

There is in existence, too, a society called Sons of Zion with branches called Daughters of Zion, whose aim is (I read from the report), "To propagate the national idea among the women of Israel by meetings, lectures on history and literature, and a circulating library.

"Secondly, to assist Jewish colonization in Palestine, with the special aim of colonizing the Russian Jews. These societies, comprising in all about 30,000, exist in Russia, France, Germany, England, and a small number in America, as the Americans think not at all on this subject."

The existence of this society will be a surprise to many of us; yet, while we do not in the least share in the national idea, in fact, scarcely comprehend it and strongly oppose it, we can all see here in the colonization of Palestine another chance of bringing happiness to the persecuted of our religion. . . .

To the sewing of garments for the poor, by the poor, I also desire to call attention. In New York there exists a Young Ladies' Society which gives work to the very poor, to be sewed for distribution by the Hebrew Relief Society. But the like society in London is on a higher round of the ladder, since it arranges that the poor work directly for the poor, and be paid by them. This work should be copied.

There are three institutions in my own city [Chicago] which I must, however, mention. Though not entirely woman's work, women have done more than their one-half share in starting, managing and providing for them, and working in them—and therefore I include them.

In addition to the general run of philanthropic societies in which women are interested, we have the Jewish Manual Training School—the model of its kind in the United States, and an institution of which we are justly proud. We have the Elise Frank Fund, of which we are equally proud, for its application of funds to the support and bringing up of orphans in private families has proved so successful that it has demonstrated this manner of caring for the parentless to be no longer an experiment, but a finer, a better and, to the practical, a more economical way of solving this great question. In this country, this fine woman, following the plan laid out by the late lamented Dr. [Samuel] Hirsch, of Philadelphia, is the first woman to apply money to this purpose.

In addition to this there is about to be formed a Social Settlement of Jewish Young People. While it will be non-sectarian, welcoming all co-workers, and doing its work among whom it may find, yet its main purpose is the elevation of the Jews in whose midst the settlement will be situated. Its work will not be charitable, but philanthropic. The distinction between these terms should always be carefully noted. The raising of the people from their outward and inward degradation, the helping of working men and women, girls and boys, to learn, to cultivate themselves—to play and relaxation and recreation—that is their mission—to inculcate the principles of independence, of self-dependence, of self-reliance; by living and working directly among them to become their friends, not their benefactors nor patrons, and thus to teach and to influence them as only personal contact can teach and influence. . . .

C

1893

The committee appointed to draft resolutions setting forth the objects of the National Council of Jewish Women then reported through its chairman, Mrs. [Minnie D.] Louis.

The following resolution was presented and adopted:

RESOLVED, That the National Council of Jewish Women shall (1) seek to unite in closer relation women interested in the work of Religion, Philanthropy and Education and shall consider practical means of solving problems in those fields; shall (2) organize and encourage the study of the underlying principles of Judaism; the history, literature, and customs of the Jews, and their bearing on their own and the world's history; shall (3) apply knowledge gained in this study to the improvement of the

Sabbath Schools and in the work of social reform; shall (4) secure the interest and aid of influential persons in arousing the general sentiment against religious persecutions, wherever, whenever, and against whomever shown, and in finding means to prevent such persecutions.

D

Chicago Section of the National Council of Jewish Women 1895

The Chicago section, of which Mrs. Conrad Witkowsky is president, has two hundred and fifty members, one honorary life member, Mrs. Ellen M. Henrotin, the president of the Federation of Women's Clubs, for whose encouragement and assistance in our Congress work we are deeply thankful. [Mrs. Henrotin, a Gentile, helped establish the Parliament of Religions in 1893.] There are ten study circles with from ten to twenty members in each. One of these circles pursues its work in German. The general meetings are very successful. It has decided upon two lines of philanthropic work, the first that of charity organization. To this end it called a conference of Jewish Women's Charity Organizations in Chicago, of which there are twenty-six, and after considerable work a conference committee has been created made up of two members of each organization. This committee has agreed upon one plan of records [of the charity clients] and is now considering the plan of visitation. It is hoped that in time we will have a complete charity organization. For its special philanthropic work the Chicago section has established a summer sewing school. Girls from ten to fourteen years of age are taught sewing and employed to sew garments for the poor. They are paid twenty-five cents a day for five days of each week during the summer months. Fifty children were employed last summer and each was given an outing of two weeks in the country. A teacher was paid to teach them and one accompanied them to the country. The amount of money which this cost was less than $1,000 and was raised by voluntary subscription. It is hoped that enough money will be provided this year to extend the work, and that a class of boys as well as girls, may be benefited.

The study work of the Council is by no means narrow. Such programs as the following are the work of the circles: "Myths of Creation," the "Myths of the Greeks," "Norsemen," "Germans," Character Study, "Eve," Milton's Creation, "Lilith." The following are some of the subjects for papers at general meetings: "From Fetichism to Monotheism," "Saul," Browning's poem, the "Biblical Saul," the "Attitude of Women of Leisure to her Wage-earning Sister." "Institutional *vs.* Home Influence." "I am a man, nothing in human life can fail to have its interest for me."

E

REPORT OF THE NEW YORK SECTION.
1896

The New York Section has 590 members, with 7 circles for religious study and 3 circles for philanthropy. These circles have been organized in various parts of the city, and have been exceptionally well attended.

The circles on Religion are led by the different Rabbis, who have taken the greatest interest in our work, the members of the Section not feeling themselves capable of imparting Bible instruction.

The Section was organized through the efforts of Mrs. M. D. Louis in May, 1894, but a permanent organization was not effected until the following November; and yet in this remarkably short time it has grown from a membership of 70 to the present number.

The monthly meetings have been well attended, and we trust the past is an earnest of the future.

The Committee on Religion have had special lectures each winter, the lectures this year being on "The Philosophy of Jewish History," by Mr. Joseph Jacobs of London. Sabbath observance also received special attention, and the interest in Bible study has very materially increased.

Through the generosity of Mrs. S. Berg, the Committee on Philanthropy had a special course of lectures by Mr. Reynolds of the University Settlement and Mr. Jacob Riis, well-known for his experience in philanthropic work, and more particularly as author of "How the Other Half Lives." A Boys' Club, a Cooking School, two Home Libraries, a Home for Convalescents, a Directory of the Jewish Charities and some reform work have been the results of the efforts of this committee.

The Sabbath School Committee has established two Mission Schools whose average attendance is 200, reaching a class of children who have never received religious instruction. This Committee has also been instrumental in forming a Union of the Teachers of the Religious Schools of this city.

The Council, it seems to me, is part of the prophecy fulfilled! It can succeed because it deserves to succeed, if religion, Judaism, be the groundwork upon which we build. The work of our section can be considered a perfect success, and the mission of the Council will not have ended until every Jewess shall have learned to read her Bible and to know the history of her people. With that knowledge must come a love for Judaism, interest in the Temple, more spirituality in all our doings.

Rebekah Kohut, President.

F

REPORT OF THE QUINCY, ILL., SECTION.
1896

Date of organization of the Council—April 25, 1894.

Number of members who signed the Constitution, 22. Number of members at present time, 28. . . .

Two Saturday afternoons per month our time is devoted to the study of Jewish History; papers are written and discussed by the members of the study circle.

On the third Friday of each month our regular business meeting is held, and the program that follows includes the study of "Daniel Deronda." [This 1876 novel by George Eliot emphasizes Jewish nationalism.]

Up to the present time our Philanthropic Section has had no work to perform, but the past week this section joined the "Woman's Exchange" in serving a dinner for the benefit of the "Associated Charities."

The Philanthropic Section has been made a section of personal service—visiting the Russian families and attempting to educate them to the ways of the American citizens, and seeing that their children are sent to the public as well as the Sunday School.

Our entire Sunday School Board is composed of women, six of the members of the Jewish Council.

Considering the size of our small Jewish community, we feel that the Council is doing some good, and we have succeeded in interesting a few of our women who have thought their study days were a thing of the past.

Wishing the Council success, I remain,

Mrs. Emil S. Nelke, President.

G

REPORT OF THE ST. PAUL, MINN., SECTION.

St. Paul, January 10, 1897.

The formation of the St. Paul Section took place October 21, 1894, under much difficulty, having to contend with the fewness of workers. Through the persistence of the president, the society struggled slowly along until the following summer, when an Industrial School for girls was opened.

The work of the St. Paul Section is divided by the seasons, winter and summer. During the winter months we study the Bible, and during the summer months the members are interested in work among the children.

The St. Paul Section has a membership of forty-five (45) ladies. General meetings take place the second Tuesday of every month; an Executive meeting is held once a month. There is a also a study circle.

Much credit is due to Mrs. Nina [Morais] Cohen, the state Vice-President, who arranges the literary program and generally is present to lead the work, and with the efforts of the President, Mrs. Haas, there has been much study accomplished. The works that have been read are the Five Books of Moses, Joshua, Judges, Ruth, Samuel, Kings, Chronicles, and Psalms; also historical, literary, and poetical works, alluding to each book under study. The following are a few of the noted authors used in giving interest to these Bible studies:

Byron, Browning, Milton, Racine, and Grace Aguilar.

The members are now making an effort to purchase Biblical books not obtainable in the city library.

The Industrial School for girls is the summer work of this section. A donation of one hundred dollars ($100) from the fund of the Hebrew Ladies Benevolent Society did much to aid in this work, and with numerous contributions and gifts this work is proving very successful. The number of children generally in attendance is about seventy-five (75), ranging from six to fourteen years, meeting Wednesday of each week. Under the supervision of Mrs. J. Wirth the children are taught the value of cleanliness and the use of the needle. Instructive readings are given and patriotic songs; visits are repeatedly made to the homes of the children.

In making comparison with the work in the various sections, we feel assured that the St. Paul Section has given excellent results, and promises great possibilities for the future.

Mrs. H. Haas, President.

H

WASHINGTON, D. C.
1902

It is with much pleasure that I accepted the invitation to be with you this evening and to speak to you of the work of the Council of Jewish Women, whose president I have had the honor to be since its organization. Almost ten years ago, 1893, in the year that "swords had been turned into plow-shares and spears into pruninghooks," when the nations of the world had formed an alliance to worthily represent the arts of peace in honor of the discovery of America, the belief in the brotherhood of man had as its expression the Parliament of Religions. Under this the committee planned the Congress of Jewish Women, and our council is the outgrowth and perpetuation of the spirit of the time. The congress was the first national gathering of Jewish women ever held in the world. It was most successful, but after all it is easy to achieve success for an occasional happening, but difficult to win a place for that which shall be enduring and lasting, and which shall call for constant effort and support.

Our council would build for all time and therefore has carefully laid the foundation for its growth. It has as its aim the popularizing of the study of our religion and history, the development of the best philanthropic methods of increasing the value and extent of the Sabbath-school, of interesting the young men and women in religion as well as to establish co-operation between cities and non-sectarian organizations in all lines pertaining to the civic and national good and to the advancement of the human family. I take it that here there is no woman question, that what is still agitating the mind of some sections of the country has here ceased, that woman's sphere, like man's, is the whole earth, and that her rights to use the powers she has are unquestioned; that, not like man, yet his equal, she may do those things for which she is fitted. I also take it for granted that you are not worried by what is known as the feminizing of the synagogue, that you realize that women predominate because they are the leisure class, that not our opinion of what Judaism is prevails, but as ever the leaders and teachers are those whom we consider the specialists in Jewish laws and lore. Nor would I grant that our presence necessarily indicates a preponderating amount of sentimentality or that we alter the tone of the religious life, but that for all alike, men or women, Judaism is the blending of thought and feeling, the product of the clear mind, the pure heart and the reverent spirit, and like every religion requires enthusiasm as the motive power which must stir it to action.

It was natural that, organizing in Chicago, we would have a free platform, with no thought of establishing unity of opinion, but rather to develop better understanding of our religion, greater knowledge of our history, to create a more generous response to Jewish religious and philanthropic endeavor. It is needless to say that we have settled none of the problems that confronted our forefathers, that we still have them all and a few added, but we are trying to study and comprehend them. Our work is planned by five national committees on religion, philanthropy, Sabbath-schools, reciprocity and junior sections. In eighty cities, with a membership of nearly eight thousand, we are aiming to establish the importance of religious study. In sixty study circles, with two thousand members, we are considering Jewish questions. Some are studying the Bible. It is much to be regretted that more of our sisters do not take advantage of these excellent opportunities, but our time, as a rule, is not systematically planned and we allow all sorts of one-night performances or one-day affairs to crowd out the uniform employment of certain hours for each week, yet the interest is growing. There are, of course, many whose lives are full of serious work, who are regretfully leaving the good which life offers because duty demands it. Yet we all require the stimulus of great minds, and no organization can better furnish these than the council to whom all teachers so willingly respond, and we need the training that comes with writing and speaking upon a definite subject.

Our circles should be the best allies of the temple, spreading the teachings of our pulpits. We owe a debt of gratitude to the rabbis who give their time and service so willingly, asking nothing in return but our interest and enthusiasm. For our Sabbath-schools we are endeavoring to enlist the earnest support of the parents. The boy of thirteen in the reformed temple does not count as he did in the orthodox. The time of confirmation, instead of being the day which witnesses his going into temple, generally marks his departure. We have endeavored and to some extent succeeded in raising the age of confirmation to fifteen years. The necessity no longer exists among a large number of our coreligionists to force the boys at an early age to seek their own livelihood, so that a longer term at school is possible. Women have been placed on Sabbath-school boards at the request of the council, seventy-nine are now serving. Our own religious school and its welfare require our attention quite as much as do those organized in the poor districts, and the mothers of Israel ought to have the will to make them perfect in their equipment. We have established about fifteen mission schools in which nearly two thousand children are studying the principles of our faith. All the conditions for healthful development are lacking in the lives of these children and it is necessary that we give them every assistance that we can in order to prevent that waste of human life, since every child is God's creature.

It is with the hope of interesting our young Jews and Jewesses that junior sections have been organized. They now number thirteen. We cannot have too many forces at work to retain as religious men and women those who belong to us in faith by an accident of birth. It is impossible to separate our duty to God and our duty to man. Our philanthropies are the necessarily active expressions of our work, and all of these are organized upon the newest and the best methods. Our sections have given their assistance to the work of federating the charities, a necessity for all large cities, as well as to the National Federation of Jewish Charities, although one hundred active philanthropies have been established by the Council. Most of all we must give ourselves to some service. Individuals are more important than funds. Our teachers of the orthodox school or of the radical alike tell us that it is not a creed to die by but one to live by. In olden times every act of the day was brought under the law. Today these traditional laws have largely fallen into disuse, yet their ethical and moral basis is with us.

Our reciprocity bureau attempts to form a union between the sections, furnishing papers and speakers when desired. We are also united with the women of England, who, through the influence of Miss American, our representative in England at the International Council in London, organized a society similar to our own. We exchange study programs and syllabi and are united in our work. The council by organized effort supplied nearly $10,000 in cash and supplies during our recent war with Spain, more than $600 for the India and Bessarabia funds, and during the past year nearly $1,000 for the Denver Hospital for Consumptives. Our sections are members of the state and city federation of clubs, of the needlework guilds, and the other non-sectarian organizations, and have members on all committees on civic work planned by women. We are members of the National Council of Women of the United States, representing an aggregate of over a million women, through them with the International, thereby coming in touch with the leaders of women throughout the world and bringing what influence we can to better mutual relations.

· *83* ·
MEMORIES OF A HOOSIER GIRL
1893–1906

Ruth Sapinsky was born in 1888 in a southern Indiana village where her father, an East European immigrant, had achieved success as a merchant. Her memoirs—reprinted in part below—are in a way typical of the careers of those Russian, Polish, and Rumanian Jews who settled in the hinterland, Americanized themselves, and educated their children. Many of these second-generation youngsters were in later decades to become men and women of some distinction. Miss Sapinsky, after graduating from Wellesley, became a social worker and writer. Her husband, Henry Hurwitz, founded the Menorah Movement.

Since my older brothers and sisters were now all at school, my favorite make-believe was that I too was learning the "three R's." I would sit out front on the stone steps pretending to do sums on my slate or read from my books—a discarded almanac, [Sir Walter Scott's] *Ivanhoe* with pages missing, and [E.G.E.L. Bulwer-Lytton's] *The Last Days of Pompeii* minus binding. As soon as I was five Mother yielded to my pestering, took me to the near-by school, and bade the teacher examine me. The older children at home had taught me the alphabet, to spell a few simple words, and count by fives and tens. So to my delight the teacher put me, not in the first term "first," but in the second term "high first." This premature start meant that I was to be in high school by the time I was twelve. . . .

By nine or ten I became somewhat more conscious of differences between my playmates and myself. None of them were Jewish. There were at the time only four or five Jewish families in the town. Only one had children about my age—the meek little rag and iron man and his booming-voiced wife, a ménage decidedly out of social bounds. My cronies were flaxen-haired and blue-eyed, with names like Goodbub, Zimmerman and Beck. Their parents or grandparents had settled in New Albany several decades before to work at the skilled trades of boat building and glass making. The children attended mostly the German Lutheran and German Catholic churches. Their talk contained quite a few German expressions, since both at home and ʲⁿ their Sunday Schools German was spoken. I didn't understand German; my olive complexion and brown eyes and thick dark hair, I decided, bespoke a "Russian" origin; my "church" was in Louisville, and I explained to my best friends that it wasn't really called a church but a synagogue.

Anyway, it was due to my "church," I made clear to the inquisitive, that our meat was never bought at the local butcher's, that Father killed our chickens with strict regard to certain religious regulations, and our meat, "cow not pig," was delivered to us twice a week from Louisville. We never had butter and milk when meat was served at our meals, and for one whole week in the spring, I explained, to commemorate the delivery of our people from bondage in Egypt, all bread even to the tiniest crumb must disappear from our homes and we must eat of the crackly unleavened squares my schoolmates called "matches."

However, there was no explaining why we didn't celebrate Christmas, since our store in December was gay with tinsel and red bells and the show-windows crammed with Christmas gifts of all descriptions. I early learned to use considerable guile in order to show off Christmas gifts to my playmates. Luckily my December birthday (which always brought gifts from my brothers and sisters), and Hanukkah (when Mother gave each child a present), and a gaily boxed scarf or belt I regularly purloined from the store, built up for me a fairly satisfactory stockpile of "Christmas gifts."

My eagerness to celebrate Christmas came simply from a longing to be like everybody else, certainly not from any dearth of holidays in the Jewish calendar. It is tempting to dwell on them all—Purim, Pesach, Shabuoth, Sukkoth, Hanukkah—every one with its rich emotional associations, its special food delicacies, the parties and best dresses of china silk and flounced challis.

Through the years Mother's weekly euchre club in Louisville was her chief social outlet. The club consisted of her relatives and friends who had also come to America as young girls and had shared the early poverty and struggles of their hard-working men. Now, their husbands well established in trade and most of their children grown up, they could begin to take life easy. The card games being not at all such dressy affairs as balls and weddings, the women wore their second-bests of wool or silk, beaded or lace-trimmed. Their coats in winter were of black seal (real or imitation); their earrings were diamond drops, some quite huge; and they wore breast-pins of gold, set with large or chip diamonds, each according to her husband's economic status.

On one occasion, an early May afternoon when "The Races" at Churchill Downs in Louisville were as pervasive and inescapable as the weather, the euchre club adjourned to the tracks. It was before the day of the pari-mutuels. A tout prevailed on the ladies to make up a pool of ten dollars for a bet on a horse. The horse won and Mother received two dollars as her share of the windfall. "Think of it—to make two dollars so easy!" she exclaimed to the family that evening. "If I had known that horse would surely win I would have put up another dollar.". . .

A very industrious man, it was Father's habit to rise at six in the morning and be at the store by seven. With his eldest clerk Mr. Streepey, he served the railroad men, the rolling mill workers, and the farmers whose shopping hours were decidedly matutinal. By mid-morning there would be a lull. Then Father, an ardent admirer of Henry Watterson and his Louisville *Courier-Journal*, would repair to a quiet corner of the store and read the newspaper methodically from first page to last. Home for dinner (our heartiest meal served at mid-day was a leisurely affair), Father would discuss the news and "Marse Henry's" editorial with my brothers. Being precociously eager to keep up with these serious discussions, I began to read for myself not only Watterson's editorials but the *Literary Digest* which came regularly to the house—when most of my schoolmates were just about able to stumble through McGuffey's *Fifth Reader*. . . .

Mother didn't read the *Courier-Journal* nor trouble her head with politics. Her favorite paper (and what a favorite!) was the *Yiddishe Gazetten*, a news and literary weekly from New York. It arrived, as a rule, on Friday morning, and I would stop any game to run indoors with the precious *Gazetten*, so eager, I knew, was

Mom to see her paper, her link with the great outside world. On Fridays she was always up at six and busy with the *Shabbas* cooking and baking: three fat loaves of bread with the glazing of egg-yolk atop them, huge cinnamon coffee cakes, the Friday night *gefuellte* fish, the Saturday chickens. By eleven o'clock (when the mail arrived) she could leave the steamy kitchen to the hired girl, repair to the screened side-porch and lose herself in her paper. . . .

Aunt Dvorie, a widow with five small children, was "poor relations." Her chief respite from her cares was to come from Louisville once a fortnight to spend the afternoon, have tea with home-made hartshorn cookies in winter and lemonade and vanilla wafers in summer, and remain for supper. Between her and Mother there would be transactions involving gifts of money (about which Father was not supposed to know too much), gifts of clothes (both used garments and "seconds" from the store), and saved-up copies of the *Yiddishe Gazetten*. It was when (as often) the ignorant hired girl had used one of the serial's precious chapters to start the fire that Mother, speaking in English but with many vivid Yiddish expressions for immorality and sin, would supply the missing episode. Playing not far away from the two utterly absorbed women, I would drink in great gulps of sexy romance. . . .

When my youngest brother Lee was ten, a teacher was engaged to come over from Louisville twice a week to give both of us instruction in Hebrew. Compared with present-day methods of teaching Hebrew as a living language—a progressive course with attractive books and art materials carefully designed for various age levels—our instruction was indeed medieval. We began with the *aleph-beth*, learned to recite by rote a few prayers and blessings, and then were plunged cold into portions of the Pentateuch and Prophets!

Always able to take considerable educational punishment, I might have stuck to my Hebrew for several years had our teacher been in the least tolerable. But he was a huge, shapeless, smelly man who knew not a single word of English and was equally innocent of child psychology. Very near-sighted, he had a comical habit of first pushing his spectacles atop his head and then, when he wished to use them, dropping them down to his nose by a mighty wrinkling of his brows. There was a cup of hot tea always before him which he sipped with a noisy gurgling. Behind his back I would mimic his gestures and mannerisms for the amusement of my brother. Under these circumstances our lessons lasted only a few months. . . .

Father was most ambitious for his children to be well-educated. Self-taught, he honored American educational institutions often beyond their worth. When I entered high school at twelve, it was taken for granted I would go on to college, just as two brothers had already done and a brother and sister were preparing to do. But high school, oddly enough, meant a sudden drop in my zeal for learning. There were various reasons. The building was superannuated, and most of the teachers were equally so. Some subjects, like "literature" and "history," I found too easy. New Albany had a good public library, and even before high school days, guided by my brother Joe who was eight years older and an omnivorous reader, I had been devouring Scott, Dickens, Dumas and Kipling, Mark Twain, Jack London, and O. Henry. Other high school subjects were bores. I detested mathematics and physics, both required subjects. (Later, my elder son, in revenge, was to become a mathematical physicist.) I disliked Latin but scorned to use a pony like many of my classmates.

A final reason for my abrupt loss of interest in school, which had once been a passion, was that my cronies—three lush girls several years older than I—were not only boy-crazy, they were seriously talking of marriage. Though precocious in some respects and aware of the facts of life (I had learned what I thought were all of them around the livery stable several years before, and not many years later D. H. Lawrence and Marcel Proust were to supplement aplenty) matrimony seemed a remote, far-off state. Moreover, my parents, while voicing no objections to their daughter mingling with *shkotzim* (Gentile youths) in casual groups, frowned upon anything that smacked of a serious interest. Thus cut off from the usual boy-and-girl relationships, I went in strongly *pour le sport.* . . .

As my four years at high school were drawing to a close I

debated "What College?" Credits from our school would admit me to the State University or other mid-Western universities. But I was bent on going East to college, though women's colleges of standing had more language and science requirements than I could offer. Just then *The Ladies Home Journal* began to run a series on Eastern women's colleges. For no reason except that I liked the pictures of Wellesley better than those of other colleges, and preferred to be near Boston rather than New York or Philadelphia (having seen none of these cities), I decided on Wellesley.

My sister Bertha, who had graduated from high school several years before, now decided she too was going to college. We sought out Professor Abraham Flexner, of Louisville, owner and principal of one of the first progressive schools in the country. Here my sister prepared for Wellesley during part of a year, and I followed her in 1905. . . .

One spring day I invited three of the school's lions and a girl classmate nearer to my own social level for an afternoon of tennis at New Albany. Before their arrival I was as much in a dither as though my guests were to be the Prince of Wales and his entourage. What if it suddenly began to teem? The weather was perfect. What if Rick, our young blood of a Negro houseboy who rolled and lined the court, should be in jail (from which brother Julius had periodically to rescue him)? Rick showed up cheerful, free of any snarled *affaires d'amour*. But perhaps the pineapple frappé and the angel food cake that I made myself would suddenly turn out a fizzle. The cake was of a heavenly lightness and whiteness, and the ice-cream, turned by Rick to just the right solidity, was golden and velvety. But in the tub those last minutes, before putting on my starched ankle-length tennis clothes, I suddenly remembered to my horror that this was the afternoon for Aunt Dvorie's fortnightly visit, and Mother had gone to her dressmaker's. Whenever Mother wasn't home, Aunt Dvorie, fortified with jelly bread and tea, would invariably seek me out to ply me with questions about my parents, my seven brothers and sisters, and our *Shapinsky* aunts, uncles and cousins in Louisville (there were over fifty of them, all told.)

Heaven be praised, Aunt Dvorie was not on the trolley with the tennis party, so I had a half hour's respite. But two of my young gentlemen were openly critical of the court. It was too short by at least a foot; moreover, a rise of ground just beyond one end should have been graded to give a better runback. "But that would mean cutting down the silver maples," I protested. Two fine tall trees stood on the hillock and the Kentucky cardinals, handsome crested birds of olive green and red, made the spot their home all summer long. "The maples make no difference," snapped the youth. "Either you have a good tennis court or you don't." Another complained, "Your crazy calliope gets me off my game." (This calliope, on an old river boat, "The Queen City," which had been recently acquired from Cincinnati, was one of our town's prides; the calliope operator, a friend of brother Julius, gave us a tune every twenty minutes or so when he passed our neighborhood plying to and from a Louisville amusement park.) Only one of my guests politely refrained from criticism, but she so far outclassed me that mixed doubles were out of the question.

My spirits were at their lowest ebb when I suddenly heard Aunt Dvorie's voice. No Southern lady's gentle drawl was hers. My aunt lived in a crowded, ghetto-like neighborhood in Louisville, and her English was not only broken, it was shattered.

But just as I was about to pass out, I heard Mother's voice. The seamstress had disappointed her, so she returned home early. Meanwhile my Southern gentlemen were so busy wolfing ice-cream and cake they paid not the slightest attention to my little aunt hovering at the edge of the court.

When at supper that evening Julius asked me how the big party went I answered ruefully, "Catch me ever again inviting those snobs to play here!" But in my heart I knew it wasn't only the criticisms of the court that had riled me. I realized that the lives of the young Kentuckians were utterly different from mine. Aunt Dvorie, a part of big-hearted Mother, belonged, whether I liked it or not, to the pattern of my life.

There is a humorous and touching Jewish folksong about an *arme Tante* [a poor aunt] who comes unbidden to the wedding feast. Why shouldn't she be there, she asks. Didn't she give the bride some feathers for the bridal featherbed? Isn't she part of the family? Why shouldn't she be present at the wedding? Well, I owed my aunt no feather-bed. But I admitted her right to visit her sister on a lovely spring afternoon. I suddenly respected the bright-eyed, courageous little widow. She was giving her five children a decent bringing-up, despite all obstacles. To be ashamed of my relatives before my supercilious guests was to lose my own self-esteem.

The following month, clad in a simple white dress (no flounces and furbelows for me at that serious period of my life) I sat on the stage of a pretty club auditorium in Louisville ready to graduate from the University-Flexner School. The audience was wealthy and fashionable. With an air of affected boredom and indifference I rose to read my essay on "The Child Characters in Dickens."

In September, when the hot midwestern summer was nearly spent, I donned a wine-colored tweed suit and a stiff black sailor hat, and carrying several popular novels, a new suitcase and a long-handled silk umbrella (patterned after the parasols in the famous musical comedy of the day, *Floradora*), I took the Louisville and Nashville for Cincinnati. There I boarded the Pullman that would take me East for the first time in my life—East to college.

84

BACKGROUND FOR A FUTURE TRADE-UNION LEADER, ROSE SCHNEIDERMAN
1895

Two Jewesses carved out distinguished public careers as officeholders in the early twentieth century. Both were immigrants. It is worthy of note that neither was of German or colonial stock; obviously the race is not to the swift. The one was Anna M. Rosenberg, the other was Rose Schneiderman (1882–1972).

The latter, a native of Poland, went to work in a department store at the age of thirteen; she was paid about $2 a week. In order to make more money, Rose went into a factory as a cap maker, helped organize a women's union, and in a relatively short time became the secretary of her local and a member of the executive board of the overall organization, the United Cloth Hat and Cap Makers Union—all this by the time she was twenty-two. It was the first time that a woman occupied so high a post in the labor hierarchy. By 1905, she had joined the Women's Trade Union League, an association of working women and their bourgeois sympathizers dedicated to the furtherance of unions and women in industry. In later years, Rose became the president of the New York section of the League and finally head of the national organization.

Rose ran a strike, served for a number of years as an organizer for the International Ladies' Garment Workers' Union, fought to secure the ballot for women, ran for the United States Senate on the Farmer-Labor Party ticket, and, in 1933, sat on the Labor Advisory Board set up by the National Recovery Administration. Miss Schneiderman was the only woman thus honored. In 1937, the governor of New York appointed her Secretary of the State Department of Labor.

She never married; the furtherance of working women was her whole life. The progress of women in this country, said the New York Times, *was her monument. The following autobiographical account relates her beginnings.*

How does one go about getting a job? I knew nothing about it. Again the United Hebrew Charities helped. In those days poor Jews looked to them for everything. Someone from the organization took me to Hearn's Department Store on Fourteenth Street, one of the best shops in the city and an extremely busy place.

I got a job as an errand girl and was stationed on the first floor where tables were laden with sales merchandise. After each individual sale, the clerk would call out "Cash!" and it was my job to rush up and take the customer's money and the sales check, both tucked in the sales book, to the cashier. If change was due, it was placed in the book, which I then took back to the clerk.

My weekly salary was $2.16 for a sixty-four-hour week. The sixteen cents was supposed to cover the weekly cost of laundering the over-all apron I was required to wear on the job. It was navy blue muslin with white polka-dots and it was most unattractive, but I saved the sixteen cents by laundering it myself.

One day during a particularly busy sale, I rushed the book to the cashier and was to bring back fifty cents in change. When I got back to the sales clerk, there was no change in the book. To this day I don't know whether the cashier forgot the change or it simply dropped out. Whatever the case, I was fired at the end of the week.

Once more I turned to the Hebrew Charities. This time they placed me at Ridley's on Grand Street, then the fashionable shopping center of New York City. Besides Ridley's, Lord & Taylor's, Kurzman's, and Stern's were located there.

I was check girl in a department selling women's muslin underwear, babies' dresses, coats and caps, and white shirtwaists. My wages were $2.25 a week and here, too, I had to wear an apron.

I worked with a group of kind women who treated me as if I were their child. In fact "child" is what they called me but I didn't feel like one. I was the wage-earner for a family. Even today I remember them all. There was Sarah Bennett, the head of the department, not good-looking but with such wit and charm. Martha Apple, who headed the shirtwaist section, astonished me by confiding that after working there for fourteen years, she was getting only $7.00 a week. Fanny Fuerst in babies' dresses was another agreeable girl. During the slow time right after the Christmas rush, she and I took to singing duets back of the counter. We harmonized quite well and had a good time learning all the popular new songs from the inexpensive song sheets on which the lyrics only were printed. Among our favorites were "After the Ball," "The Little Lost Child," and "She May Have Seen Better Days" [These three songs were written between 1894–1899. The first two were written by Jews.]. . . .

All the stores on Grand Street were open on Saturday nights all year around. Before Christmas, however, they stayed open until ten o'clock every night. From eight in the morning to ten at night made a mighty long working day for an entire month. By the time Christmas Eve came along, all of us were completely exhausted. I still remember that I was so tired I could barely walk home. There was no such thing as overtime pay or supper money.

In spite of the long hours and small pay, I was a happy girl, thrilled by the lovely presents the women had given me. There was a piece of blue material for a dress, and a felt hat with three little plumes to match. Our time-keeper, Mrs. Havemeyer, gave me a doll and doll carriage and a cornucopia, filled with candy and an orange, all to take home to my little sister. I was so happy that Jane would have her doll. . . .

When I went to work, I was determined to continue my studies at night school. That fall I enrolled and went faithfully every evening for about four weeks. But I found that it was not the same as day school. The instructor seemed more interested in getting one-hundred-percent attendance than in giving one-hundred-percent instruction. He would joke and tell silly stories until he thought all the students had arrived. Only then would he start the lessons. I soon realized I was wasting my time, and so my attempt to continue my formal education came to an abrupt end.

To my great joy I found there were other ways of acquiring knowledge. Mother, who had always loved books (although she could read only the Hebrew prayer book), asked me to read the Bible stories in Yiddish to her. We started with the story of Joseph and his brothers which Father had dramatized years before, and we had a wonderful time as I tearfully read about the inhumanity of Joseph's brothers. Then we went on with other

Bible stories. After a while we turned to more current books. At that time the Dreyfus case was uppermost in everybody's mind and heart, and Mother and I anxiously read Emile Zola's now famous, "J'accuse," which ran serially in the *Abendblatt* [the Socialist Labor Party Yiddish daily].

We discovered, in the same newspaper, serial stories about Henry VIII and Anne Boleyn, and Thomas à Becket. Later on I began reading English novels in the ten-cent paperback editions of the day that I somehow managed to buy. The only money I ever had was six cents Mother gave me every day for my lunch—a sandwich and a piece of fruit. But the saleswomen would send me out to buy their lunches, paying me a penny each. I saved those pennies until I had enough for a book. I knew nothing about going to a public library and taking out any book my heart desired.

I devoured everything I could lay hands on. Miss Healy, who was the cashier on our floor at Ridley's, read a great deal, too, and she would occasionally lend me some of her books. I was especially thrilled when she let me read [Corneille's tragedy] *Camille*. It was considered quite risqué but Miss Healy knew she could trust my sense of propriety.

Now I realize that my reading would have been much more worthwhile if I had been guided by a competent person. The people we lived among were mostly illiterate and I had no one to direct me. I did not even know about the College Settlement House which was only a block away. There I could have found companionship and guidance. In later years I discovered those marvels, the great English classics, and only then did I realize how much I might have profited had I read them earlier in life.

My adolescence was a far from happy one. All the romantic novels I consumed made me a most romantic young woman, and when I looked at myself in a full-length mirror I was very unhappy. Then I would despair. I wanted to be tall and I thought I had several other counts against me. First of all, I was a redhead with curly hair, and neither the color nor the texture was stylish at that time. Then, you were supposed to have a bosom, the larger the better, and good-sized hips. I possessed neither of these but the hips I could do something about. I discovered that if you wore a short corset and laced it tight, your hips stuck out. The bosom was more difficult, even though I wore corset covers. I weighed only a little over ninety pounds but I was small-boned and not skinny, and with my eighteen-inch waistline I would be right in style today.

From the books I read I had also developed a special taste in men. Among other traits, I wanted them well-read and cultured. I never dreamed of marrying a rich man. That was entirely out of my ken. My idea of what a man should be didn't quite match up with the boys Ann Cypress [a fellow-worker at Ridley's] and I were meeting at the Saturday-night dances in the neighborhood. Most of them were loud and dull and suffered when compared with the heroes in my books. I didn't enjoy their company, but I did love to dance and was pretty good at it, so I put up with them. Ann, on the other hand, enjoyed the idle chatter very much. She took all the banter in her stride and always managed to have a good time. As for me, small talk was never in my line.

In time, when my trade-union interests started me on what proved to be a long career in the labor movement, though always concentrating my efforts on working women, I met many interesting men and discovered that I could fall in love very easily, though unsuccessfully.

But being poor was the worst part of growing up. I was ashamed to have anyone come to my house. Even Ann never visited me until years later when we were living in better quarters. To give a party was unthinkable. In those early days we had only two rooms, one of them a bedroom; you couldn't ask anyone up to sit around in a kitchen, furnished only with a couple of hard wooden chairs and cluttered with dishes and cooking equipment. Besides, there was no money for refreshments. . . .

After working at Ridley's for three years, my salary was all of $2.75 a week! Ann, who worked in a factory making artificial flowers and feathers, was earning much more than I, and more than Martha Apple, who still made only $7.00 a week. I decided I couldn't possibly wait fourteen years, as Martha had, and so must find another job. Mother and I talked it over and I went to see Cornelia Jastrowitz, a former neighbor, who was working as a lining-maker in the cap industry. She promised to take me in at Fox and Lederer, where she worked, and teach me her trade.

The men's cap industry was a very stable one because most men could not afford to wear hats, especially derbies, which were very fashionable. They wore caps to work and after work. The men did the cutting of the caps as well as the sewing, while women employees made the cap linings.

Like all lining-makers, I had to furnish my own sewing machine. One could be bought from Singer on the installment plan for one hundred dollars. But since Mother had been able to save a little money, how I'll never know, we bought a Wilcox and Gibbs one-thread machine for thirty dollars cash. I also had to furnish the thread I used. And not just one color either. You had to have several colors handy to match the colors of the lining. The cost ran up to at least fifty cents a month.

I learned to use the machine in three or four weeks and after a trial period with Cornelia, I was on my own. The first week on the job I earned six dollars, more than twice as much as I had earned at Ridley's. However, Mother was far from happy. She thought working in a store much more genteel than working in a factory. But we needed that extra money. When I gave her five dollars out of my first pay, she wanted to know where the envelope was. I told her that I had it and that I had taken out a dollar for my own expenses. She didn't like this, either. She thought that as a dutiful daughter I ought to hand over all I earned and let her give me what she thought I needed for the week. I didn't agree, so we continued my way. That was my first revolt toward independence.

The dollar I kept had to cover the cost of lunches and expenses in connection with my job, such as paying for thread and needles. Later, when I was earning more, I kept a little more for myself. I certainly needed it for clothes. There were no ready-made clothes in those days, and one of the trials of my life had been that I could not afford a dressmaker and had to rely on Mother to run up a dress in her spare time. She meant well but she was hardly a professional seamstress. Something always went wrong. More often than not the seams were crooked and I would end up in a burst of tears.

Though the workmanship was not of the best, people did not look too closely and I gave the impression of being fairly well-dressed. Later, I learned to make shirtwaists and skirts which were the working-girls' uniform. One of the first results of my new affluence was a dress I had made for the wedding of a girl I worked with. It was a lovely wedding and I enjoyed every minute of it, especially all the dancing and my dress, which was pearly gray with a deep bertha of ecru lace lined in pink.

My friend Cornelia became a sample-maker and, a year later when she left to get married, I was given her job. A sample-maker was not paid more than the others, even though her work was much more exacting, but during the slow season she was given preference when work was available.

Meanwhile, Cousin Koppel was prospering. But his life was not an enviable one. He had married a shrew who was insanely jealous. As a result, he had become careless about his clothes, almost slovenly, a far cry from the dandy he had once been.

About this time, he bought a tenement on Suffolk Street and asked Mother if she would be the janitor in exchange for free rent. Not knowing what she was undertaking, Mother accepted. We had three rooms on the first floor, so we took a lodger in the living room.

Koppel had assured Mother that there would be very little for her to do. During the summer it wasn't too bad. Of course, the garbage cans had to be carried out to the sidewalk and brought back after they were emptied, and the toilets in the backyard cleaned. For some reason the tenants in this building were not required to scrub their own halls and stairways, so Mother had to do that too. But in winter the job was hard because it meant shoveling snow off the roof and the sidewalk. Before the cold months were over we came to regret her decision, even though it meant that the money I earned and the rent from our tenant could be spent on food and clothing.

But we had some fun during this time, too. For the first time in our lives, Mother and I went to the theater. We became regular attendants, thanks to a friend of Mother's who worked as a cook in a restaurant frequented by theatrical people. They often gave her tickets and since she cared nothing about the theater, she passed the tickets on to Mother.

Meanwhile, there was a big fire at the factory. Fox and Lederer were amply insured but we workers all lost our machines. They were not covered by insurance and we had to replace them. This time I bought one on the installment plan instead of paying cash, for if there was a fire, it would be covered until the last payment was made by the company from which I bought it.

85

THE MODERN JEWESS
1895

Quite correctly, Emil G. Hirsch maintained that the emancipation of women began in the last decade of the nineteenth century. The rabbi, in his generation America's most scholarly and distinguished ultra-liberal, declared in the rather rhapsodic statement printed in part below, that a new era had dawned for the Jewesses of this land. He even promised the women in 1895 that the ballot would be theirs. Certainly, he was a true prophet—but it would take a good twenty-five years for Reform rabbis to endorse equal suffrage. In 1895, Hirsch's thinking reflected the views of a mere handful of his colleagues.

THE MODERN JEWESS
by Emil G. Hirsch

The last decades of the nineteenth century will probably live in history as the age of woman's emancipation. Mighty as are the changes, both social and political, which have marked the flying years of the latter half of this wonderful century, there is none which in its far-reaching consequences may be held to surpass the movement, the impelling motive of which was to admit woman to a plane of equality with man. What the American and French revolutions accomplished for the male half of human-kind, this quieter, but all the more persistent struggle, wrought for their sisters. Every war has its heroes. The generals in this fight will also live in song and memory.

Ridicule was the first battery to be silenced. But its shots once proven to be harmless against the cuirass of a stout resolution, the battle for recognition was more than half won. All that was needed was for woman by her own capabilities to demonstrate her eminent fitness for the position coveted by her. Medical science in league with deep rooted prejudices had long countenanced grave doubts as to woman's strength to endure the excitement and withstand the wear and tear of the fierce race. Her staying qualities riddled the most strongly fortified demonstrations to the contrary of her sceptical opponents. Nor did the other doleful predictions come true. Woman by entering the lists for public honors and responsibilities did not sacrifice her womanliness. Perhaps she gained in all the essentials that make up the true woman. Her self-reliance and self-consciousness heightened, she herself learned to put a new and better value on herself. As an equal, she could meet father, husband and brother. And where the responsibilities of motherhood had fallen to her lot, her broadened horizon conferred on her a rational understanding of the sanctity and importance of her opportunity. Business and the professions, no less than literature and the arts and sciences have welcomed her to full citizenship in their respective realms. Soon, also, the last citadel will capitulate before her victorious siege; the political ballot will also be hers. . . .

The history of the Jew will be repeated in the record which the Jewess is about making for herself. If her father and brother for long spells of circling time were doomed to be in the world but not of the world, the Jewess was barred from the outer throng and its interests by a double restriction. She shared the fate of every adherent of Judaism, but in addition she was under the despotism of home Orientalism, sanctioned by unyielding religious rigorism. It is true, Jewish history names many of the sex that shine with the light of beauty and heroism. The prophetic spirit even fell to the lot of some of the sisters, while others live on in the fame of wisdom and learning. But on the whole, the Jewish woman's universe was her home. Her position was not without ideal compensation. The Biblical description of a true woman reveals a busy and useful, and what is more, an honored and trusted station. To-day, the Synagogue has ceased looking Eastward. Orientalism in thought, views and symbols gleans but a romantic tribute in the reconstituted and broadened Temple of Israel's God. Into Western life the Jew has thrown himself. From it he draws his inspiration, and to it would he contribute his historic idealism. And the Jewess without hesitation follows her brother's lead. She has turned her eyes Westward.

Often is the Jewish woman held by prejudice to be under the spell of Eastern fancies. Upon this mistaken judgment rests the ascription to her of a love for fineries, gems and loud colors. But a more serious purpose runs through the modern woman's life, and the Jewess has sacrificed with no greater zest than her non-Jewish sister at the shrine of frivolity. In fact it is the ambition of the Jewess to be a woman so womanly as to exclude all qualifying adjectives. Her Judaism inculcates and emphasizes this ambition. She would take her place at the side of her sister in all that makes for the nobler freedom. Her culture is no narrower than that after which the non-Jewess aspires. In the struggle for fame and position, the Jewish woman, when predisposition or necessity have pointed her path in this thorny field, bears bravely the brunt of the battle, and is no less anxious and competent than is woman generally to equip herself for the fray. She has had to conquer twofold difficulties, those arising from home prejudices and those due to opposition to her sex generally. Her Judaism was no passport to willing reception, as it was no godspeed to her at the threshold of her own parental residence. But she has won the day, in spite of bias and obsolete misgivings and capricious interference.

The opportunities for the Jewish woman to-day to reform her own religious home are many. What the Synagogue now needs foremost is intelligent enthusiasm. It is woman who owns this gift. Let her place her new culture into the service of her old faith and the winters of indifference will yield to springtides of young and hopeful life. At home let her be the priestess of the Ideal, abroad the prophetess of Purity and Refinement and through her will Judaism and the Jewish name be exalted to heights never before attained.

86

SUCCESSFUL BUSINESSWOMEN
1895

By the 1890's, women from middle-class families were entering the job market in increasing numbers. The industrial revolution was making an impact on the Jewish community and its mores. East European immigrant girls were not the only Jewish female wage earners. The following article describes the business success of three enterprising New York women. The poem at the end of the selection is Emerson's, misquoted.

SUCCESSFUL BUSINESSWOMEN.
1895

Since innumerable avenues of work have opened up to women, and legions of them have everywhere eagerly availed themselves of the long desired opportunities, it is surely futile to still discuss the advisability or non-advisability of woman entering the active fields of labor. It would be just as well to realize that we stand before an accomplished fact and deal with it accordingly.

To those depressing pessimists, who with doleful shakes of the head predict as a consequence dire disaster for the nation and the entire human race, I would say: "Good gentlemen, your quarrel is not with woman, but with society. It is the conditions of society in all monogamous countries, with their large feminine surpluses, that have forced women into active competition with men."

In the scheme of nature, woman has assigned to her a distinct task—the reproduction of the race. But this throng of surplus femininity, which is of necessity debarred from fulfilling its natural destiny—what is to be done with it?

Medical authorities assert that the grayish matter in an average woman's cranium falls four ounces short of that in the average man's, still, none will dispute that some women possess a much greater cerebral development than the majority of men. Can any just or logical reason be adduced why such women should not be encouraged to follow the God-given bent of their natures? Surely every fair-minded being must consider it a subject for congratulation and a clear gain for humanity at large, that the greater and lesser lights, the radiant arc light and the modest tallow dip, are no longer huddled, perforce, in one indiscriminate mass beneath the stifling bushel measures of millinery, mantua-making, and household servitude. And even in these feminine occupations *par excellence*, it is passing strange that the great prizes have been won by men, thus proving again that occupation is of the neuter gender.

Another argument, advanced by those who see darkly, is the baneful effect that contact with the every-day working world will produce upon the essentially feminine attributes of the fair sex. These fears have little or no foundation in fact. Most of my readers, undoubtedly, number among their acquaintances gracious and charming women whose creed has passed beyond the "There is but one God and the kitchen stove is his prophet" boundary. On the other hand, the most heartless, envious, uncharitable and all-around disagreeable woman it has ever been my fate to meet was an excellent cook and model housekeeper. Heaven be praised, true femininity lies deeper than such externals.

Any mode of life that would destroy or even tend to lessen the womanly attributes of beauty, grace, and self-abnegation, I would sincerely deprecate. But because my girl prefers driving a nail to threading a needle and my boy would rather run the machine or make the coffee than play marbles, must I cry alarm? Surely such predilections do not seriously imperil either her feminine charm and beauty or his masculine strength and independence. Women have claimed business rights and privileges. Their claims have been allowed and all barriers practically removed. The time for argument has passed; the time for action is come.

Of women who have made good their claim to compete in the fields of business activity with men, I know of no better example than the subjects of this sketch, the Rosenfield sisters of New York city, proprietors of the largest stenographic and typewriting establishment in the United States.

The father of these young women, Joseph Rosenfield, a Bavarian by birth, came to this country at the age of eighteen and settled in New Orleans. His polished manners and winning personality gained for him a host of friends and at twenty-two he obtained a position of trust with the New Orleans branch of the house of Rothschild. . . .

Zerlina Rosenfield, elder member of the firm, graduated from the St. Louis High School with special distinction. Business interests finally necessitated the removal of the family to New York, where a few uneventful years elapsed. Then sickness and misfortune invaded the happy home. With stern necessity staring her in the face, Zerlina, the eldest daughter, took an inventory of her marketable accomplishments. She found that she was a good penman and mathematician and possessed a fair knowledge of bookkeeping. She finally secured a temporary position as assistant bookkeeper after which she entered a publishing house where she remained seven years. She then decided to identify herself with the stenographic and typewriting business, and, familiarizing herself with all classes of work, she soon ranked among the ablest women law stenographers in New York city.

Laura Rosenfield, junior member of the firm, also attended the St. Louis public schools but was graduated from a New York seminary. After the death of the parents, Laura decided to adopt her sister's profession. She succeeded in securing desk room in a prominent theatrical exchange. Naturally bright and quick, she was not slow in grasping the favorable situation. Her one machine soon gave place to two, then four and so on until desk room would no longer suffice and large offices were taken. About this time, the largest contract ever awarded for typewriting was given to the two sisters, a contract competed for by all the copying offices in Washington and New York city. This work was the compilation of a legal index covering 375,000 pages or about 11,000,000 words. Work of such magnitude required co-operation, and a partnership was formed in 1889 between Zerlina and Laura Rosenfield. To-day these enterprising women have six thoroughly equipped typewriting offices with from forty to fifty typewriting machines. In addition to their facilities for typewriting and stenographic work, they associated with them several compilers and translators of both modern and classic languages which makes the execution of dramatic, literary, legal or commercial work in the English or other languages possible.

To a query of mine regarding the secret of their success, Miss Zerlina Rosenfield responds as follows:

"Perhaps the true secret of our success lies in our unity. Three striving for the same goal can obtain infinitely more than if each pursued a separate avocation.

"I manage the down town offices and my sister Laura the uptown, the character of the business being quite distinct. My sister Laura is, according to the general verdict, the most popular woman in the profession. Her firmness and keenness in deciding business problems would do credit to an old and able financier.

"Our younger sister Alice, an expert stenographer, has an interest in both the finances and glory of the firm and strives, as far as possible, to keep all the work in the family. Hence it rarely becomes necessary to call in outside assistance.

"We are never too busy nor too tired to take an order. We are always ready for an emergency. We never have to send a customer elsewhere for assistance of any kind.

"We have a staff of thoroughly competent, reliable, and ladylike assistants who attend to their work not alone as a matter of duty, but because they like it. These are some of the reasons why the firm Z. & L. Rosenfield, although one of the last in the field is not the least."

We have here a brief sketch of the remarkable business career of three young and inexperienced girls, who carved out their fortunes simply by energy and unremitting hard work, tools within easy access of everyone, irrespective of sex or condition. Asking no favors, devoid of any extraneous influence, endowed with but the usual quantum of brains, they have by sheer pluck, persistency, and faithful work rapidly risen to the heights of their profession. Nor has this eminence been obtained at the sacrifice of any truly good or womanly quality.

Contact with the business world seems but to have enlarged their sympathies and brought them into closer touch with the great pulsing heart of humanity. Although the busiest of women, they stand ever ready with word and deed to aid those who seek their advice.

Most dutiful and devoted of daughters, when death deprived them of their natural protectors, they turned all their loving care and kindness to the five helpless orphans left in their charge and have since striven faithfully to be to them both father and mother. Bravely and cheerfully, casting aside all thought of self, they have taken up life's burdens and fulfilled life's duties. In contemplating such lives, we feel the full force and significance of the poet's uplifting words:

> "So nigh to Heaven is our dust,
> So nigh to God is man,
> When duty whispers low, 'I must,'
> The soul replies: 'I can.' "

PAULINE S. WISE.

Chicago.

87

CHICAGO'S LADIES' AID AND LADIES' SEWING SOCIETIES
1895

Few communities lacked a Ladies' Aid Society in one form or another. The women wanted to help others and—what was equally important for most of them—were eager to meet socially with kindred souls. In the larger cities, where Jewry was socially stratified, it was inevitable that there would be numerous women's organizations catering to different social groups and cultivating diverse philanthropic and cultural areas. Chicago's Young Ladies' Aid, founded in 1882 with Mrs. Henry Gerstley as its first president, was originally a hospital-visiting society. Later, as the Chicago Woman's Aid, it was noted for its innovative approach. Though its members were Jewish, its work embraced the entire community; it was patriotic and civic-minded, not at all parochial in its eleemosynary outreach. The Chicago Woman's Aid helped introduce penny lunches in schools, hired a dietician for a dispensary, and provided a visiting nurse for the Associated Jewish Charities. One of the sewing societies described below employed impoverished women, who were paid to sew garments for distribution to the needy. Let it be noted, too, that there was a North Side and a South Side Ladies' Sewing Society. Distances in metropolises made travel difficult; women were impelled to set up societies in their own part of town. Centrifugality, not centripetality, is frequently the norm in the Jewish community.

The selections below reflect the diversified philanthropic activities of Chicago Jewesses.

CHICAGO YOUNG LADIES' AID SOCIETY.

The Young Ladies' Aid Society is an organization numbering nearly four hundred members. The officers are: Mrs. Henry Adler, president; Mrs. Leo Fox, vice president; Mrs. Henry

Gerstley, secretary, and Mrs. Jos. Beifield, treasurer. The object of the society is general philanthropic and literary work. For the better execution of its object the society is composed of committees representing its different lines of work, namely: Education, Art, Literature, and Philanthropy. The special work of the Philanthropic section is to further the interest, by active work and financial support of the new Sheltering Home and Crèche for poor Jewish children, which was opened the 1st of February on West Twelfth street. To this most necessary institution the Young Ladies' Aid Society has donated $500 toward the furnishing, besides subscribing $1,000 annually toward its support. Advanced methods of philanthropy are studied, and one of the hopes of this section is to establish a loan fund for the assistance and relief of the respectable and self-respecting poor. The Art and Literature departments consist of regular meetings of the club. A course of lectures by Mrs. Sara Hubbard has been completed, as well as a course on Shakespeare, by Mrs. Mary H. Ford. The meetings held at Sinai Temple vestry room are always largely attended. The lectures are followed by discussions, in which all are invited to participate.

The Young Ladies' Aid Society desires to promote literary and philanthropic work, and a closer fellowship among our women. Its members are women of advanced thought and action, foremost in all affairs tending to the advancement and improvement of humanity in general, and self-culture in particular. While composed of Jewish women only, non-Jews will be heartily welcomed who feel the need of belonging to an organization of this kind. . . .

South Side Ladies' Sewing Society, Chicago.

Officers: president, Mrs. J. Schmaltz; recording secretary, Mrs. Fannie H. Regensberg; financial secretary, Mrs. Florence F. Leopold.

The society numbers 404 members and a good idea of its work may be gathered from the following:

We had in our midst such ardent and indefatigable workers that the success of the society was assured, philanthropically, financially and socially. The plan of making many of our poor Jewish women self-supporting is steadily increasing. Our disbursements have amounted to $5,187.49, out of which we have supplied 400 families, numbering more than 1,850 persons, with bedding and clothing as well as boy's underwear and complete children's outfits.

North Side Ladies' Sewing Society, Chicago.

The society has a membership of 226 ladies and at the last report showed a balance of $162.53 in the treasury. The receipts for the year were $2,175.20 and the expenditures, $2,093.90, but there were thousands of pieces of wearing apparel made and distributed which do not appear as cash. The following fragment of the report speaks for itself:

"Every mother here among us knows how her heart beats with gratitude when at night she tucks her little ones up snug, and remembers that they have been warm, well-fed, and consequently happy during the day. I think of those other mothers who also love their children tenderly, who would willingly sacrifice their lives to keep them from want, and who can only say at night, 'I thank God that my little ones sleep, that they may forget that they are hungry and cold.' One afternoon a week spent in sewing will not put any one out much, and may be the means of making many comfortable, and is far more charitable than the giving of dollars and cents."

88

MARRIAGE ON NEW YORK'S LOWER EAST SIDE
1898

*The following description of the marriage ceremony at the turn of the
nineteenth century is not too different from the arrangements that still
prevail in some metropolitan catering establishments in the late twentieth
century. Some of the wedding customs and rituals go back to ancient times.*

GOING UNDER THE CHUPAH

Curious Ceremonies at East Side Jewish Weddings.
Elaboration and Display on Even the Humblest Occasions.
Dancing in the Hall—The Luncheon and the Supper.

Uniting people in wedlock according to the old Jewish customs
and with the pomp and display which indicates their Oriental
Origin is one of the industries which always flourishes in the
New-York Ghetto, and is affected by none of the mercantile or
political disturbances which frequently influence ordinary business. The East Side weddings come under the head of business,
because they give employment to many people, and these and the
many public halls, where most of the weddings took place, could
not exist if the business fell off.

Such a thing as a strictly quiet wedding, with no witnesses
except the immediate members of the family, is almost unknown
in the Jewish quarter. When the wedding contract has been
signed and the schatchen's [marriage broker's] work completed,
there is usually an "engagement party," at which the parents of
the bride-elect make public announcement of the engagement of
their daughter, and break a glass in the presence of their guests to
indicate that the contract is not fragile, like the works of man, and
cannot be broken like them.

All those who come to the engagement party are usually asked to the wedding ceremony, and receive invitations which are printed on fancy embossed cards in English and "Yiddish," and sometimes in German also. These invitations are worded nearly like the ordinary wedding invitation, but in every instance a line follows the address where the ceremony will take place, which tells the "bride's residence."

DIFFERENT DEGREES OF MAGNIFICENCE

The people who are the least blessed with worldly goods have the ceremony performed at the home of the bride; those who have more hire the synagogue for the occasion, and those who are of the highest circle in the Ghetto have the ceremony performed in the synagogue and hire a hall for the wedding dance and dinner. But the largest number of weddings takes place in the halls which are arranged for the purpose. These halls usually contain a women's reception-room, a dining-room and a ballroom, and are rented for evening weddings and balls for from $5 to $10. This does not include what is known as the "hatbox," where the wardrobe of the guests is left. The proprietor of the hall usually charges from 10 to 30 cents a couple for taking care of hats and wraps. "When people are very swell," said the proprietor of one of these halls, "they hire the hatbox, and their guests don't have to pay for hatchecks."

The invitations usually give 5 or 6 o'clock as the hour for the ceremony, and at the time named the bride and bridegroom arrive, with their respective kinspeople. The bride is attired in white satin and long veil and has many flowers, and the man in evening clothes. They take stations in different rooms, and as the guests arrive the ceremony of Kabolath-ponim, or presenting, takes place. This lasts until the guests have all arrived—generally an hour or two later than the time named on the invitation cards—and then, if it is a large company, the young people have a dance or two. This over, the bridegroom takes his place under the chupah, or canopy, in the large hall, and there awaits the coming of the bride, who is brought to him by her father. The chupah, or canopy, has been an important feature in the Jewish wedding ceremonial ever since there has been any record, and one of the East Side rabbis said that a verse of the Bible refers plainly to the "joyous voice of the bridegroom from under the chupah" [Ps. 19:6].

The Canopy and Its Significance

The canopy is made of velvet and may be of any color, although it is usually purple or deep red, and is trimmed with gold lace and has the star of David embroidered in gold on one end. Under this canopy, which symbolizes the future home of the family, the bride is taken by her parents, and the rabbi performs the marriage ceremony. When the couple have taken wine from the same glass to show that they will be partners in joy, and the ring has been placed on the bride's finger, a glass is again broken, which ceremony the rabbi explained thus:

> At no joyous occasion should the Jew forget that the glory of the Jewish nation is broken, and the broken glass reminds him of that. It also reminds the young people that sooner or later all must return to dust, and even like the beautiful glass, be shattered and destroyed.

The ceremony over, everybody congratulates his neighbor as well as the bridal couple, and then, under the leadership of the chief actors, the whole party goes to the dining-room, where luncheon is served. Since early in the morning the kitchen has been in charge of a Kochfrau [female cook], under whose direction a luncheon as well as a supper, which is served later in the evening, has been prepared. The luncheon lasts only a short time, and then the dancing begins and lasts until supper is served at about 11 o'clock.

The synagogue wedding, when the chupah is reared in the sanctuary, is more expensive than the hall wedding, because, aside from the fee paid to the rabbi and the hall rent, there is an expense of $5 for the use of the synagogue. There are several ewish houses of worship on the East Side which are particularly popular, and the one at No. 38 Henry St. rarely has less than two, and frequently as many as four, weddings on a Sunday.

DANCING SCHOOL AND SANCTUARY

There is a hall in East Broadway where many of these weddings and wedding balls take place which is used on two nights every week as a dancing school, and the sanctuary at one end, containing the sacred scroll behind embroidered curtains, and the little sign on the wall, with the words, "No refusals," seem to clash, until one is told that "No refusals" is posted for the benefit of fastidious East Side maidens, who are warned in that way not to bring about any unpleasantness in the dancing class by refusing to dance with any "gent." At two points in the hall there are automatic machines, where a cent in the slot brings forth a dash of perfume, and a dumb-waiter communicates with the bar, which is in the basement.

89

MAIMIE PINZER: A COURAGEOUS WOMAN
1898–1899

In 1898, a thirteen-year-old girl was thrown into jail as an "incorrigible." The following account is the story of her imprisonment as she described it years later.

The child was Maimie Pinzer, born in America to East European immigrant parents. After the death of her father, a moderately successful businessman, this teenager left school and before long found it necessary to go to work. She became a saleslady, but soon started consorting with men. Salesladies were underpaid. Her unsympathetic mother reported her to the police, who threw her into jail and then sent her to a home for "fallen" women. After her release from the Magdalen Home at fourteen years of age, she became a discreet occasional prostitute in order to supplement her income from odd jobs. Instinctively a "lady," she never consorted with "trash." This went on for about ten years; she preferred a life of lazy vice to one of domestic drudgery.

In 1909, aided by a social worker, Herbert Welsh, and the Bostonian notable Fanny Quincy Howe, an understanding friend, Maimie found herself. She gave up the "sporting life," cured herself of morphine addiction, and set out to help other unfortunates as far as it lay in her power. She was kind, intelligent, a gifted writer, a linguist. Above all, she was an honest, courageous woman who made a desperate and apparently successful effort to build a new existence for herself, one in which she at least maintained her self-respect.

She identified whole-heartedly with her fellow-Jews when she deemed them honorable; she avoided those who were uncouth.

The significance of her story? It reflects the seamy side of the life of a girl in precarious economic circumstances in this golden land of opportunity. It suggests also that hundreds if not thousands of girls—and boys too—were helped by devoted men and women who had dedicated themselves to aid others less fortunate.

Most of Maimie's letters were addressed to Mrs. Howe. The name "Maimie Pinzer" is a pseudonym, as are the names given many of her intimates.

"This picture of me and Poke
was taken in San Antonio, Texas,
in the summer of 1909."

21. Maimie Pinzer

November 27, 1913

It is a bit cold in my room, and my fingers are stiff, but I will write in spite of all this, for I feel in the mood. And perhaps at such times when the room is warm, I will be drowsy—and that accounts for some of the long waits between letters.

I received the booklets. Thank you again. The cookbooks had the first attention, for I am beginning to really like "domestic labor"; and hints as to cooking, etc., seem quite interesting—where, before, I used to look on one who found interest in such things as an "old hen," and one who would be likely to have all sorts of time for reading rot of the sort the Sunday papers print on their magazine pages. Possibly, my predilection is due to the fact that I am sometime going to have a home of my own. (I think I will have to consult one of the clairvoyants of which Montreal boasts many. If so, I may at least have what pleasure I can derive from anticipation.)

The Ballad of Reading Gaol is certainly gruesome. I had a copy—of part of it—that was printed as a prospectus by some publisher who sold Oscar Wilde's complete works, I think. At the time I read it, I felt it was a wonderful poem of its kind, but I couldn't grasp the meaning of but snatches of it. At the time, I excused myself, and (though I did think it a bit over my head) because the poem was incomplete. I felt reasonably sure, had I had it *all* to read, I would have understood it better. Since reading the copy you sent, I find I am still very much at sea. Much of it is Greek to me. Some of it is brutally plain; but when he writes: "Yet each man kills the thing he loves, / Etc., etc., etc., / The coward does it with a kiss, / The brave man with a sword!"—then, speaking of the man who was hanged, he says: "He had but killed a thing that lived, / Whilst they had killed the dead"—I would like to understand both of these more than the occasional thing or two in the poem that is beyond my powers of comprehension. If you know, and it is not too much of an explanation, I'd like it immensely if you'd explain it to me, when you write again. I read the entire ballad to Miss Brown [a Montreal friend, a teacher] and she seems to understand it even less than I—for I had much to explain to her. . . .

I do not recall whether I wrote you that I had, among my many experiences, spent some time in the Phila. prison. Perhaps I told you, but I know I've told no one else but Mr. Welsh. And of course my immediate family know it—for it was they who were the cause of my being sent there. I don't think I did tell you; and since I feel in the mood tonight, I will tell you what I remember of it. It was such a terrible experience, and I was only past thirteen years old! It was the regular prison, and not the place of detention that they use now to send juvenile offenders to. I think of it but seldom. Tonight I thought of it due to re-reading *The Ballad of Reading Gaol* and talking about prisons to Miss Brown.

I had left school directly after my father's death, and was put to work in the house, doing the sort of work I despised, because I had never been taught how—and, too, because I loved school and books and the things that school meant. I was thirteen in July, and in September—my second term at the Phila. high school—I was not permitted to go back to school. Prior to my father's death, we had a general servant in the house, and a laundress and scrub-woman who came, each two days in the week. After his death, I was given it all to do but the laundress's work—and I did it very poorly, and always only after receiving severe whippings. In October, or perhaps November, I told a young girl who was librarian in a city library close to my home, of the reason that I did not come for books any more—which was, that my mother wouldn't permit me to read them, and a book for which the librarian wanted to collect 80 cents had been thrown into the fire when I had been found reading it. Of course, I had no 80 cents to pay her, and I was very much ashamed of it. I think this was my original reason for getting work in a neighborhood store, to work at night for a small weekly sum, as a "saleslady." After this—and after a violent scene with my mother, who told me if I didn't like my life at home, that I should get out—I went to the city, and there got a regular job in a department store, at $5.00 a week, though I was only past thirteen years old. I was a "saleslady"— and this store, to this day, is quite the place for men to come during the afternoon hours to make "dates" for the eve. I found I could stay away from dinner, and go along with some boys, and come home and tell some sort of story—and that it was accepted, lue to the $5.00 I was bringing home! Once, there was some kind of a fuss again—and when I threatened to leave home, my mother said she hoped it was soon.

Of course, the inevitable thing happened. Some young chap took me to his room; and I stayed three or four days before I put in an appearance in the neighborhood of my home. As I neared our house, a man spoke to me by name, and told me he was a "special officer" and that he had a warrant for my arrest. He took me to the Central Station, which is in the City Hall—the large building which is in the center of the city of Phila. Of course I was terribly frightened—but imagine my horror when I was placed in a cell! It was a horribly filthy, vile-smelling hole. I cried and begged they should send for my mother—and though they did, after awhile, she refused to come. It was nighttime, and there was no light; and I could hear the rats, which I feared more than death. I was terrified, and pleaded to be taken out of there. It was only after I permitted one of the men, who seemed to be in charge at the time, to take all sorts of liberties with me, that I was permitted to come out of the cell; and I sat up for the rest of the night in the room where he, too, sat all night. The man was perhaps fifty, or even older.

In the morning, there was a hearing. My mother was present; and I recall my uncle was with her—and he was acting with her to persuade the "Commonwealth" that I should be sent to some house of refuge as being incorrigible. This uncle is the same one who did me the first wrong, when I was a tiny girl, and any number of times since then. It seemed that in order to prove me immoral, so that I should become a public charge (without excuse to my mother), it would have to be proven that I had committed a crime, and the man produced. A further hearing was demanded for this—as, in my terror, I had told the name and address of the chap, and of course they were going to arrest him. I was led away to the same cell, pleading to my mother, in shrieks, to take me home. It was morning, and not so bad as at night; but as I had nothing to read, and the terrible fear of spending another night there seemed imminent, the hours seemed years. There was only a bench and an exposed toilet in the cell, and it was, as I thought, terrible.

At noon, there were footsteps and the jangling of keys, and the cell was opened. I thought for sure my mother had relented, and was so grateful. I put on my hat and coat, and came out to the large room—and though I did not see anyone I knew, I was laboring under the delusion that I was being taken home. I saw some men in line, and I was told to get behind the last one. Still, had no suspicion of what was coming. The line moved, as did I. And oh! what a lot they were! There were perhaps eight men (three Negroes), and they were the dregs and scum of the earth. I looked on them with alarm, and was dismayed that I had to walk with them, though I did not even guess at my destination. We filed down the stairs, and the line in front got outside; and as I was last, I saw them filing into a prison van—the kind called "Black Maria." They are usually painted quite dark, and resemble a closed box with air- or peep-holes on top. It was just at noon; and there were thousands going thru the courtyard, enroute to their lunches. Quite a crowd had gathered to watch the prisoners; and as I saw that, I became so mortified that I could not move—though, due to the imprecations of the guard behind me, I really wanted to. Of course, little ceremony was wasted on me. I was fairly dragged to the van, and thrown in. When I recovered my senses, I found the wagon was moving. The men were each in a compartment. Though there was no door between there were sheets of iron that made semi-walls, permitting only one person between each wall. Yet they all seemed to disregard this, and sat out on their seats, talking and laughing. The ride lasted perhaps an hour. Time can never efface my impressions thru that ride. Their humor was shocking—such obscenity and scurrility! One of them told me to cheer up, and said he would look out for me after he got out—for he would only get thirty days, whereas no doubt I'd be sent away for a number of years, until I was of age. I then knew for sure I was going to prison—and oh! how I feared it! The ride was probably the worst of the whole harrowing experience.

In the prison, which was the Moyamensing Prison, I was led away by a woman to a room where a man sat before a large book—no doubt to enter the names, etc., of the prisoners. It was to this same prison that my father had given a library of

wo-hundred books, printed in the Yiddish language, for the
enefit of the few Jewish prisoners who were kept there and who
ould not read English. I recalled, as I stood there, hearing my
ather speak of the place, and the pity of sending Hebrews
here—who generally committed an offense only because they
vere not familiar with the laws. I was overcome with the thought
f what my father would think of my being there; and I don't
emember what happened, exactly, only that later, I found
nyself in a little bed, in what seemed to be another cell. As there
vas a woman sitting beside me, I did not seem to mind it so much,
or I only cried quietly. Presently, the man who had sat by the
ooks came in with a notebook in hand, and asked me many
uestions, which I recall I answered freely. I know now, that he
new from my name—which was not a common one—that it was
ny father who had given books and money to help Jewish
awbreakers, and that he communicated with my uncle; but no
tep was taken by him to have me released from there. I recall
earing him and the woman who sat by me, comment on the fact
hat I was sent there; and they both didn't seem to understand it.
After the man left, the woman brought me some very coarse,
ough-looking clothes and took away my own, though I cried
readfully to not have to put them on. Then they took me to
nother room, and before I knew what they were going to do,
hey had combed my hair out—it was cut off to the ears.

I was taken back to the cell, which was similar to the one I had
ccupied in the Central Station, only larger, and had a pallet of
traw on a black iron frame bed. Besides, there was a chair and a
amp and a stone floor, and one tiny window, with bars, that
aced a courtyard; and on the other side—perhaps three or four
ards away—was another wall with the same window, at which I
ould see faces that were pressed against the bars and fingers
lutching them. The woman left me after awhile, and brought me
a Bible—for which I was grateful enough. She said the books
vere all taken that day, but tomorrow she might get me a real
ook. I entreated her to remain with me—for she was indeed
ind, and had much commiseration for me. She assured me she
vould return as soon as she could. When she left, I went to the
vindow. And immediately I was seen, the persons began to call

to me, asking what I was put there for. They were women and, take it, saturated with the spirit of prison life. I don't think they could see me any plainer than I could them, so they took it I was a little girl. There was food brought me. All I can recall of it was that it was given to me in a metal dish that closely resembled a pie plate. I believe I tried to eat it, but couldn't. I had gotten quiet by night, and then the lady returned. And though I had to put the light out, she sat by me until I fell asleep.

I awakened in the night, and then it was that I became panic stricken. I beat on the bars of the cell and cried until someone came. This time, it was a woman and a man. The woman was of the grim-visaged sort, entirely, without compassion, and threatened me with all sorts of dire things unless I was quiet. cannot remember how I passed the remainder of the night though I know I did not get back into bed.

The next day, the kind lady came, and I recall she gave me two chocolates that were very stale, and a book which I think was *Robinson Crusoe* or *Pilgrim's Progress*. I found when reading, it did not seem so terrible to be there. I recall I was ashamed of the fact that I didn't seem to mind it so much, and that I rather enjoyed the privilege of reading undisturbed. I was all right until night (or, rather, evening) came, when I became unnerved again. And must have gotten some privilege thru this lady, for at eight o'clock at night, she took me to another place, where I slept in a bed, with other women in the room. I think it might have been the prison infirmary. Before daybreak she took me back to the cell; and I was given a book, closely printed, of Shakespeare. Some time around twelve, they brought me my clothes, and I was taken back to the Central Police Station. This time, I am glad to say, it was in [a car], accompanied by a maid who belonged to the court.

It seems there was some sort of talk, of which I remember little but my mother and uncle were there—and then this man took me to the Magdalen Home, where I stayed a year. It is a mild sort of reform school for girls who have gone astray. Though I was the youngest girl there by four years, still, I taught the ones who had little or no schooling, during our school hours. I received absolutely no school training there whatever—except what derived from teaching girls of seventeen and eighteen their alphabets and the simple sums.

22. Rebekah Kohut

90

REBEKAH KOHUT, AN EXEMPLAR OF THE NEW INDEPENDENT WOMAN
1899

n 1887, Rebekah Bettelheim (d. 1951) married the famous scholar Alexander Kohut; when he died at New York in 1894, he left his widow vith eight children by a previous marriage, a number of them still young. Five years later she had to go to work; much of the family fortune had been wept away. The following account describes her successful effort to provide for her numerous dependents. Clearly, she was a competent person. Employing her skills as an educator—she had graduated from a California normal school with a teacher's certificate—Rebekah became a volunteer social worker in New York City shortly after her marriage and was appointed director of a ghetto kindergarten. In later years she achieved recognition as one of the city's better-known workers in civic and Jewish communal enterprises and institutions. The women elected her president of New York's first section of the National Council of Jewish Women; the city and state exploited her expertise in the field of unemployment; Rabbi Stephen S. Wise appointed her a trustee on the board of his Jewish Institute of Religion. Women selected for positions of importance in Jewish national enterprises were few and far between.

The following autobiographical account describes Mrs. Kohut's achievement in establishing the Kohut College Preparatory School for Girls, a boarding and day institution, one of many such private Jewish academies which had made their first appearance in 1840.

And now the crisis came.

My mother and sisters, who had been living in Richmond, returned at this time to Baltimore. I visited them and learned that a tremendous problem faced us. A bad investment had swept away their meager capital and also a considerable part of the small Kohut estate.

Somehow I felt I must not only make good to my children the money lost through no fault of my own, but determined that I

must also take up the responsibilities of my mother and sisters. My
father and brother were gone, and I saw myself taking their place
as the breadwinner.

When I returned to New York, I spent the hours in anxious
thought. The wakeful nights were dedicated to a number of
schemes whereby I might earn enough to replace at least the
interest lost to the Kohut estate and to assist in the maintenance of
the family in Baltimore.

Why had God put it upon me to assume so much responsibil
ity? I stood at Alexander Kohut's grave and said the burden was
greater than I could bear.

There were, besides, difficulties other than economic, such as
always arise in the managing of a large family. I had long since
learned that without my husband I had not the same confidence in
the management of the children that I had enjoyed while he was
alive.

Volunteer service was now precluded. The joy of feeling I was
rich enough to give myself was to be denied me.

I went to Jacob H. Schiff [the New York banker and philan
thropist] and in my inexperience, shall I say youthfulness, I asked
him if he could not invest our meager capital so that we could have
larger returns. He assured me that he never did a thing of that sort
for anyone. He told me I could sleep soundly in the knowledge
that Alexander Kohut's money was invested in four per cent gold
bonds.

Now that we were once more face to face with poverty, I
wanted it not to gnaw too much or even at all. Egotistically
sensitive, I was ashamed to tell the children that part of our
money had been lost; money which had been left to me as a sacred
trust. There was not even the comfort of discussing it with my
oldest son, with whom I might have established another secret.
He was in Europe.

But no bewailing what could not be helped. Something had got
to be done. The whole question was—what? I cast about and cast
about in my mind for some good plan. I rehearsed my capacities.
Not writing for newspapers, not lecturing. Teaching, perhaps.
Yes, teaching. My life, in a sense, had been a preparation for it.

since acquiring a teacher's diploma, I had never quite left the schoolroom atmosphere. I understood children, had studied pedagogy, and there was my experience with Dr. Kohut's Sunday-school and the confirmation class of Temple Emanu-El.

Teaching in itself, however, was not highly remunerative. The thing to do was to start a school!

Once more I went to Mr. Schiff and told him of my plan. I told him that though the need for money was the mainspring of my ambition, the school was not to be conducted for that end alone. I pledged myself to give girls the best education New York offered and all the moral and spiritual training of which I was capable. He asked for time to consider the matter before advising me. Walking through the park, after I left his home, the notion came to me, somehow, that he intended to give me the benefit of a good investment.

A few days later he called upon me, and gave the plan his unbounded approval. He had inquired into all its features, saw that there was need for such a school, and advised me to go ahead.

I was a little resentful at the time that he did not offer to aid me financially. I felt burdened with responsibilities, and somehow entertained the fantastic notion that Mr. Schiff would throw a bag of gold at my feet and encourage me to lead a life of luxury.

Under all circumstances, however, his approval of a plan meant that I must carry it out, whatever the difficulties. Almost immediately I commenced visiting schools, studying curricula and text-books, and drawing up a prospectus. Through my class at Temple Emanu-El I made efforts to obtain a few private pupils. The Council sections, too, were informed of my project.

Soon the last series of lectures under Mrs. Schiff's auspices were under way. The subject was "Dreamers of the Ghetto," inspired by Israel Zangwill's book. This helped me to increase the income and contribute in a small way to the support of my mother and sisters. . . .

The Kohut School for Girls, in its formative stages, had the advantage of excellent counsel. Dr. Henry Leipziger and Julia Richman [high officials in the New York City educational system], both educators of great experience, gave an enthusiastic

novice the benefit of their seasoned knowledge; and through thei
aid teachers with desirable qualifications were secured and man
pitfalls avoided.

Upon my return to New York, I again applied myself t
organization, perfecting all the groundwork of management. A
building was secured in West Fifty-eighth Street with our own
apartment a few doors away. In addition to providing mainte
nance for our family and a vocation for me, the school was t
provide a partial outlet for George's abilities [Rabbi George
Alexander Kohut, her stepson]. With physical resources in
adequate for the strenuous duties of a large congregation, he
could give classes the benefit of his training without ill effect and
thereby provide a competence for himself.

The time approached for the opening of the school, and I wa
busied with a thousand details. It was a very tired but happy
woman who sat in her office that afternoon, her dream translated
into action, her school functioning at last. In the various class
rooms throughout the building, one hundred pupils who had
been entrusted to her care were becoming acquainted with their
teachers.

As I sat there, happy for my task in the immediate present bu
also wondering what the future held in store, a card was brough
in. Jacob H. Schiff.

He came to congratulate me upon my venture.

"I have watched your progress," he said, "and I am delighted
that you have done what you wanted to do." Then he laid a chec
upon my desk. "I hope you will not feel offended. Until now
would not have dared to offer you money, because I knew you
wouldn't accept it. But now you are in a business venture, and
that is different. Please take this as a loan for an indefinite period
to tide you over financial worries."

He walked quickly out, before I could answer. I picked th
check up. It was for $10,000. A few months before I had been
resentful at his apparent unwillingness to ease my financia
struggles. Now I felt how untrue that resentment was to the bes
that was in me. Was it not finer that I had consummated my wish
through my own efforts, and was not Mr. Schiff's loan doubl
sweet in its compliment to my ability to help myself? What

wonderful first day for my school! That evening I walked up Fifth Avenue with the check and a note expressing my deepest gratitude and left them at the Schiff house.

Busy days followed. The pedagogic machinery functioned well. My teachers took complete charge of the general education. I assumed as my special responsibility the girls' religious instruction. To communicate my own religious enthusiasm to my pupils was my aim, and I did not count my work well done, unless, in addition to knowledge of the Bible and ceremonial observance, I instilled into them certain moral and ethical standards which would strengthen them for the future. And so I tried to make religion so significant and beautiful and stimulating to the imagination that the young girls whose lives had been entrusted to me might be stirred to the soul. In my efforts I reached new outposts of my own soul. While expounding certain subjects, new vistas were suddenly flung open to me, too. The view was thrilling.

As there were both boarding and day pupils, I had not only class-room work to manage but also a household on a large scale with high standards. On Friday evenings we had religious services for resident pupils. My son [George A. Kohut] presided at the services, and I blessed the Sabbath lights in the fashion of the true mothers of Israel. Friday evenings we often succeeded in recapturing the spirit of joy that had prevailed in our home in the San Francisco days; we sang and told stories and filled the hours to the brim with merriment and healthy laughter. Saturday mornings I attended services with the girls at one of the temples, and the morning of the following day I held classes in Jewish history. Happy those Sunday mornings, as I recall them.

Because of his years at the University of Berlin, George was qualified to teach German; he also taught history which had been one of his major subjects at Columbia. I conducted a class in current events, taught English literature, and now and then substituted in mathematics which had always been my favorite subject in school.

Once the assistant principal asked me to take a class in geometry in place of the teacher who was ill. Fortunately I had an hour in which to prepare. The problem happened to be one that had been a stumbling block to my classmates in San Francisco days. It came to me in a moment. My success with the geometry class in that one period led me to undertake teaching mathematics regularly the next season.

As time went by and I grew more experienced in school management, I was in a state of perpetual dissatisfaction with results. Perfection was what I strove for and, as there is no point in education where one can say that the summit has been reached, it was a continuous effort. Meanwhile, the standards of the institution rose and rose. I visited the best schools of the country to observe their methods and attended classes in pedagogy at New York University. "Keeping school" was by no means easy. There were exacting parents who would have been dissatisfied under any circumstances because it was their nature to be dissatisfied. There were unappreciative pupils. What institution is without them? I spent sleepless nights.

There were other troubles. From the moment the school was started and commanded my entire attention, my family felt neglected. Their apartment was only a few doors away, but they saw little of me and their feeling of neglect grew into resentment. There arose a conflict of interests which troubled not only my children but myself. . . .

Five years had gone by and the Kohut School for Girls was firmly established, but perhaps I should have taken a longer road to prosperity. Perhaps the time had not yet come when I could relinquish my hold upon the Kohut family. I felt pressure from without and from within and my conscience troubled me not a little. It was pleasant enough for me to know I had rescued my mother and sisters from poverty. It was a triumph to know that I had replaced the money lost to the Kohut estate. It was satisfying to know I was a success. But then, feeling I would rather lose my school than my children, I gave up the school.

91

INTERMARRIAGE
1899–1903

At the turn of the century, according to available statistics, the percentage of intermarriage among East European newcomers was minuscule. Actually, the number of those marrying out was probably larger than the figures reported. At any rate, Jews were concerned about the threat of assimilation. Fear of intermarriage and of defection from Jewry is mirrored in a ballad entitled "A Rabbi's Daughter" (1899), by Charles K. Harris (1865–1930), a Milwaukee Jew, one of the country's most popular songwriters. Harris' "After the Ball," written in 1892, brought him a fortune; it was still selling at the rate of 5,000 copies a year in the early 1920's. There is no evidence, however, that "A Rabbi's Daughter" ever became popular (item A).

That intermarriage was not uncommon in the ghettos of the Lower East Side is reflected in the advice-to-young-women column of Rose Harriet Pastor (1879–1933). Born in Russian Poland, Rose came to America in 1890 from London. All told, she had had about two years of formal schooling in a London free school for the poor. In Cleveland, she became a cigarmaker, but somehow or other managed to educate herself; she was a very ambitious young woman. At an early age she began writing poetry and in 1903, after the family moved to the Bronx in New York, was invited to join the staff of a Yiddish paper, the Jewish Daily News *(Yiddishes Tageblatt). Her column was part of the English Department page. It was called "Just Between Ourselves Girls" and was signed Zelda. Selection B, reprinted below, exemplifies the nature of her assignment.*

A

1899

A Rabbi sat one ev'ning with Bible on his knee,
His daughter knelt beside him for she loved him tenderly.
Come tell me child, the Rabbi said, Why do you weep and sigh,

Don't be afraid to trust me dear, tell me the reason why.
She gazed into his dear kind face and said: will you forgive,
I love a man with all my heart, without him I can't live.
The Rabbi looked down at his child, one question answer me,
Is he of Jewish faith or not—her head sank on his knee.

Chorus

You are a Rabbi's daughter, and as such you must obey,
Your father you must honor unto his dying day.
If you a Christian marry, your old father's heart you'll break.
You are a Rabbi's daughter and must leave him for my sake.

Second Verse

The hour of midnight sounded, the world seemed all at rest,
The maiden kissed a picture and she held it to her breast.
I'm told I must not love you, dear; I ne'er must see your face,
And that you cannot marry me, for you're not of my faith.
But I shall have no other love and though my heart should
    break,
To you my love I'll faithful be, though I may never wake.
Her words came true that very morn, for on her bed so white,
The Rabbi found his only child, had died for love that night.

Chorus

B
1903

Just Between Ourselves Girls
"Twixt Passion and Conscience"

One of my girls unburdened her heart to me and asks my advice in
the following letter:

My dear Zelda:
    Being a reader of your columns in the *Jewish Daily News*, I
would like to have your advice. I am eighteen years of age and I

am in love with a Christian young man who is two years older than myself. He loves me, too, and he wants to marry me, but my father objects. My father says that a Jewess should not marry a Christian. He tells me that a Jewess should marry a Jew. I call my father an old-fashioned man because he objects to a marriage between a Jewess and a Christian. I love my Christian friend very much. He tells me that when I will marry him I will be happy. I always quarrel with my father on account of my lover. My lover is a tall man. He has blue eyes, black hair, and a blonde mustache. My lover is a nice looking man. I told my father of the good qualities of this young man and still he objects. I think it very nice that a Jewess should marry a Christian. Don't you? People say that my father is a clever man, but I think that if a man objects to a mingling of Jew and Christian he can not be very clever. What would you advise me to do? Marry my Christian lover or listen to my father? I am,

Yours truly,
"B.C. (Broken hearted)"

My dear B.C.: I do not intend to advise you because I do not think you need my advice. If you had decided to marry a Christian, if you had thought it right and "nice" (as you express it) to marry a Christian, if you had thought your father was wrong to object, you would not have asked my advice. It is because you know it would be wrong to marry him; it is because you are not so absolutely sure that it is *nice* to marry a Christian; and it is because you know your father has lived years and years before you saw the light, and is a sensible man, far more sensible than you, perhaps, can ever hope to be; and because you know in your soul your father objects to such a marriage because he wants to save you from misery and shame, from social excommunication and from moral death—you know all this in the depths of your heart in spite of what you are trying to fool yourself into believing— and that is why you write and ask for advice.

My dear, my advice to you would be superfluous. *I know that you will not marry a Christian.* Your letter betrays it. I can read it between the lines. I know what the "wee voice" tells you in the night when your head has touched your pillow and you cannot sleep; when you lie awake thinking, thinking, thinking: "Is it right?" it questions you, "is it right for you to marry a Christian; nay, is it good that you should marry a Christian? A Jewess—think!—no one will speak to you; no one will come to your house. You will be shunned by all your friends and all his friends will despise you."

"You will break your father's heart," says the voice; "you will break your mother's heart. Think! They will not be able to look a friend in the face for the shame you will have brought upon them; they will lie awake nights thinking of the disobedient child they no longer see—for they will not come to see you—and your father will curse you and your mother will become near blind with weeping. Can you bear to do all this to the two beings whom God has commanded you to honor?"

And the voice nags at you and nags at you and you can not sleep; you are forced to listen. Then your passion answers blindly: "What do I care! I must be satisfied. Why should a father or a mother care whom their daughter wishes to marry, Jew or Gentile? Is it my fault if they are foolish and their hearts break?"

"Yes, it is your fault," says the voice, "and no matter what you say, you can't get away from it."

And you can't get away from it. That voice talks to you and you are compelled to listen in spite of yourself. You are not happy though you try to make yourself believe you are; and you know your father's judgment is right in spite of your being angry with him for opposing your marriage with a Christian. But I know that the true voice within you will get the better of you; you will respect your father's wishes and do the thing most worthy of a loyal daughter; you will give up your Christian lover and save yourself and your parents the life-long misery that is in store for you if you do the contrary. So, believe me, my dear, I am very much in earnest when I say you do not need my advice, for I have not a doubt but that if the test should actually come you will do what the "still voice" bids you; you will give him up.

Zelda

23. Belle Lindner Israels Moskowitz

· 92 ·

BELLE LINDNER ISRAELS MOSKOWITZ, SOCIAL WORKER AND POLITICAL ADVISOR
1900

In 1900, Belle Lindner Israels Moskowitz (1877–1933) became a full-time member of the staff of the Educational Alliance, a Jewish settlement house on New York's Lower East Side. It was the beginning of what would be a notable career.

Belle, the daughter of a Polish or East Prussian immigrant watchmaker, was born in Harlem, then an area of second settlement for immigrants leaving New York's ghetto. After a year's study at Teachers College of Columbia University, the energetic young woman turned to social work, then began raising a family, and finally, eager to prove herself, accepted the challenges that confronted her in the world of business, politics, and social reform. She took a job with the Dress and Waist Manufacturers Association, handling the grievances of the workers. Capable, shrewd, and wise, she did an excellent job. Never losing her interest in social reform, she busied herself with the supervision of dance halls, proper housing for young girls, pure milk for infants, workmen's compensation, and good government. She had an opportunity to implement her ideals from 1918 on when, as a public relations counsellor, she became a confidante and mentor of Governor Alfred E. Smith, whom she influenced profoundly. Unlike Rose Schneiderman or Anna M. Rosenberg, she never held a political office, but in her unofficial capacity as an advisor to the governor she was in no small measure responsible for shaping his sociopolitical policies. She strove doggedly to win the presidency for him. Had he been elected, she would have been one of the most influential persons in his administration. Because of her close identification with Smith's political career, Franklin D. Roosevelt chose not to exploit her talents. The following obituary from the New York Times sums up her life and activity.

Mrs. Moskowitz, Smith Aide, Dies

Adviser to Governors Wielded Wide Political Power Behind the Scenes.

Pioneer in Social Work

Never Held Public Office, but Molded Legislative Trends—Hurt in Fall Dec. 8. [1932]

Mrs. Henry Moskowitz, who during former Governor Alfred E. Smith's ascendency in the Democratic party wielded more political power than any other woman in the United States, died yesterday of heart disease in her home, 147 West Ninety-fourth Street.

Holding no public office, she occupied a unique position during Mr. Smith's four terms as Governor. She was his adviser on matters of statecraft as well as politics and many times she was the unseen advocate of progressive legislation which he sponsored.

Mr. Smith she always regarded and often spoke of publicly as "a great leader—a man of destiny," and in 1928 when, partly as a result of her efforts, he won his party's nomination for the Presidency, she came nearer than any woman had come before to being the maker of a President.

Heart Attack Followed Fall.

Mrs. Moskowitz was in her fifty-sixth year. She had enjoyed good health until Dec. 8, when she tripped and fell down the steps of her home, breaking her right arm and left wrist. Until last Thursday she showed steady improvement, but then she was stricken with a heart attack. She grew weaker and a recurrence of the attack yesterday at 2 P.M. proved fatal.

Mr. Smith was in Albany for the inauguration of Governor Lehman. He was told of the death of his friend and counsellor by telephone at the Albany home of his daughter, Mrs. John A.

Warner. There were tears in the former Governor's eyes as he replaced the telephone receiver on its hook and turned to a group of friends to say:

"Belle Moskowitz is dead. I'm going to New York."

Canceling social engagements connected with Governor Lehman's inauguration, Mr. Smith boarded the first train he could get for New York. Before leaving the capital, the former Governor, his voice a little huskier than usual, paid this tribute to the woman who for many years was his political alter ego:

"She had the greatest brain of anybody I ever knew."

SMITH OVERCOME WITH GRIEF.

Persons who traveled to New York with Mr. Smith said he was overcome with grief. When he emerged from the trainshed into the big waiting room at Grand Central, his head was bowed and he walked slowly. The crowd that had gathered there—many of them unaware of the death of Mrs. Moskowitz—seemed to sense that it was not an occasion for cheering and was still.

Reporters pressed around the former Governor. To them he said:

"When I was asked in Albany to comment on the death of my friend, I had to refuse, because it was simply impossible to collect my thoughts. The sad news put a damper on everything that had happened in Albany. It would not have been possible for any news to have come that would have distressed me more. I regard the passing of Mrs. Moskowitz as a disaster."

With Mrs. Moskowitz when she passed away were her husband, Dr. Henry Moskowitz, former Municipal Civil Service Commissioner, and two sons of a earlier marriage, Josef and Carlos Israels. Dr. Moskowitz, who shared his wife's admiration for Mr. Smith as a political leader, was one of the authors of "Up From the City Streets," a biography of the former Governor, whose father was an Oliver Street teamster!

Funeral services will be held in Temple Emanu-El, Fifth Avenue and Sixty-fifth Street at 11 A.M. tomorrow. Dr. Nathan Krass, rabbi of the congregation, and Dr. Stephen S. Wise, rabbi of the Free Synagogue, will preside. Many persons prominent in social and civic life are expected to attend the services. Burial will be in Sleepy Hollow Cemetery.

HAD WIDE, VARIED INTERESTS.

Mrs. Moskowitz's interests were wide and varied, and while she purposely avoided public office and public notice, she was active in many private welfare movements, including the Council of Jewish Women, the Travelers' Aid Society, the Committee of Fourteen and the Association to Promote Better Housing for Girls.

She also held the following positions during her career: Manager of the labor department of the Dress and Waist Manufacturers' Association, secretary of the Mayor's Committee on National Defense, secretary of Governor Smith's Reconstruction Committee, secretary of Governor Smith's Labor Board, secretary of the Educational Council of the Port of New York Authority, special advisor to the State Department of Labor, director of the Women's City Club and director of publicity for the Democratic State Committee.

Mrs. Moskowitz was born on Oct. 5, 1877, in Harlem, the daughter of Isidor and Esther Lindner. Her father, a watchmaker, gave her the name of Belle. She received her formal education at Horace Mann High School and Teachers College, which she left at the age of 18 to become actively engaged in social service work.

She obtained her first position as director of entertainments and exhibits for the Educational Alliance on East Broadway. It was while living at the Educational Alliance that she met Henry Moskowitz. There also she met Charles H. Israels, a successful architect, who was leader of a boys' club at the Educational Alliance. She was married to Mr. Israels in 1903.

In his lifetime, Mr. Israels designed the Hudson Theatre and the Warrington and Devon Hotels. He also designed the exterior of the Hall of Records, which is regarded as one of the most beautiful public buildings in the State. Mr. Israels died in 1911. Their three children are still living. Carlos is an attorney, Josef a writer and publicity man and the daughter, Miriam, is married to Cyril Franklin of London.

NOTED FOR HER AID TO GIRLS.

After her first marriage, Mrs. Israels maintained an active interest in social service work, with special emphasis upon preventive work among delinquent girls. In the era of the "lounge lizard" and "tango teas," she organized her Committee of Amusement Resources for Working Girls and was instrumental in bringing about the passage of the dance hall license act. This gave her her first legislative experience.

In her leisure hours, Mrs. Moskowitz began to take an interest in politics. At about the time that Mr. Smith was obtaining an important part of his social education as a member of the factory investigating committee after the disastrous Triangle factory fire, Mrs. Moskowitz, then Mrs. Israels, joined the Progressive party and seconded the nomination of Oscar Straus for Governor.

Forced to seek gainful employment after her first husband's death, Mrs. Moskowitz, through her friendship with Dr. Moskowitz, became manager of the labor department of the Dress and Waist Manufacturers' Association. In the four years she held that position, from 1912 to 1916, she adjusted more than 10,000 disputes between employers and workers and devoted herself to a close study of labor laws.

With the advent of Mayor Mitchel's administration, she became secretary of his Council of Women and in 1914 married Dr. Moskowitz, who then was president of the Municipal Civil Service Commission. In the fusion campaign which placed John Purroy Mitchel in the City Hall, both Dr. and Mrs. Moskowitz were in the forefront of the anti-Tammany drive.

FIRST MET SMITH IN 1918.

The first association of Mrs. Moskowitz with Mr. Smith came in 1918 when, at the request of Judge Abram I. Elkus, a partner of former Supreme Court Justice Joseph M. Proskauer, Mrs.

Moskowitz became chairman of the women's division of the citizens' committee working for Mr. Smith's election as Governor.

Mrs. Moskowitz arranged for the use of a theatre, then closed because of an influenza epidemic, for an afternoon women's campaign rally. Mr. Smith was the speaker and afterward Mrs. Moskowitz prevailed upon him to accompany her to another gathering at the Women's University Club. Mr. Smith, it was told later, went along with but little grace, protesting on the way that he did not enjoy the prospect of speaking before a "highbrow" women's club. He would just go in, shake hands and leave, he said.

At the club, however, Mr. Smith, after meeting several of the leading women, agreed to make a speech. Some who heard it declared it was the best he ever made. Many in his audience were women who were active in the women's suffrage movement and, choosing that for his topic, he revealed a more thorough knowledge of his subject than that possessed by some of those who heard him. He spoke also about his experiences in public life and concluded:

"You see, I know what it is to run a great State. You can check up on me, for if I do wrong it will not be a case of ignorance but of willful intent."

PLANNED SOCIAL LEGISLATION.

It was not until after the campaign that the association between Mr. Smith and Mrs. Moskowitz began to develop into the close relationship which existed in later years. Soon after assuming office the Governor telephoned to Mrs. Moskowitz and suggested that she bring to his office such social workers as she should select to plan the social legislation which was called for by the party's platform.

As a result of this conference the Reconstruction Commission was appointed. It was not an official body, but it became one of Mr. Smith's favorite creatures. Mrs. Moskowitz was its secretary. She developed a comprehensive program for relieving the housing shortage that existed after the war. Great stress was laid also on public health, food and markets.

Since that time, Mrs. Moskowitz has been a definite factor in Mr. Smith's career. Although she often said that no one ever did Mr. Smith's thinking for him, it was known that he often consulted her in matters of policy and that she frequently assisted him in the preparation of his speeches and public papers.

For years she was the tireless tender of the Smith political beacon, always with the hope of one day seeing him in the White House. Prior to his nomination in 1928, Mrs. Moskowitz kept a steady stream of political literature flowing from her tiny office in the Prudence Building on Madison Avenue to meet the overt and insidious attacks and propaganda of the Ku Klux Klan against the New York Governor.

Long before the nominating convention met, she began keeping a card-index file containing the name and address of every person who wrote Mr. Smith a commendatory letter or telegram, together with such other data about the sender as she could gather. Sometimes, when new help was needed in a doubtful State, this index proved extremely valuable.

RELIED ON INTUITIVE SENSE.

Mrs. Moskowitz had an experienced and infallible intuitive sense for choosing issues, for popular feeling. She had another quality, a genius for organizing and generalship. She was a realist, fully awake to the shortcomings of herself and her sex. She said once:

"Because I am a woman, I have certain intuitions, certain powers of sensing reactions on the part of others that men lack."

Another time, she made a public speech in which she said:

"Women have qualities of mind peculiarly feminine, but they are not the intellectual equals of men. Their intuitive sense is the biggest thing they bring to politics. Combined with the thinking ability of men, this makes a splendid working team."

Throughout the 1928 campaign Mrs. Moskowitz had the title of director of publicity of the Democratic National Committee.

When that campaign ended, almost if not quite as bitterly for her as it did for Mr. Smith, she became president of Publicity Associates, a company with offices in the Empire State Building, continuing to serve Mr. Smith in private life as she had during much of his public career.

EVEN SOLOMON IN ALL HIS GLORY WAS NOT ARRAYED LIKE ONE OF THESE
1900

Jewish girls who came here from Eastern Europe acculturated speedily; they did not want to be damned as greenhorns. They were very eager to become real Americans; that meant they had to dress like natives and faithfully observe the dictates of fashion. The following article describes how the young ladies of New York's Lower East Side triumphantly met the challenges of Dame Protean Fashion.

EAST SIDE FASHIONS.

They Keep Pace with Those of Fifth Avenue, and Perhaps Outrun Them a Little

As Broadway [is] to upper New-York, so is Grand-st. to the lower East Side. Here and in the streets immediately adjoining one sees what lower Manhattan considers "the glass of fashion and the mould of form." Of "form" there may be something lacking, but fashion is there in full force. Grand-st. out-Broadways Broadway. Here one sees all the styles ever devised by the brain of man—sees them in all their glory, having their fullest scope, allowed to expand at their own sweet will. Does Broadway wear a feather? Grand-st. dons two, without loss of time. Are trailing skirts seen in Fifth-ave.? Grand-st. trails its yards with a dignity all its own. Are daring color effects sent over from Paris? The rainbow hides its diminished head before Grand-st. on a Sunday afternoon. Grand-st. is Broadway plus Fifth-ave., only very much "more so." Its wide sidewalks show more fashion to the square foot on a Sunday than any other part of the city.

"Millinery Lane."

In Grand-st. the East Side buys its dresses, coats, and a thousand and one other things. For its hats it goes to Division-st. Division-st. begins its picturesque career at Chatham Square, and runs along to Clinton-st. From Chatham Square, for the length of a couple of blocks or so, the neighborhood christens the street "Millinery Lane," for good and obvious reasons. Let no unwary traveller, unversed in the ways of the East Side shop-keeper, set foot in this spot, under pain of being forced to buy the most marvellous creations of the modiste's brain that were ever designed to assist Cupid in subjugating the heart of man (East Side man). There are fully twenty millinery stores in the "lane," and each store has one or more "sidewalk ladies" to "pull in." The term "puller in" is not wrongly applied. They smile seductively as they ask, "Anything in a stylish hat, ma'am?" But if the fascination does not work properly the "puller in" gently but firmly takes hold of the arm of the passer by and proceeds to argue the question. These enterprising ladies devise the hat fashions for the lower East Side. The system is simple. Whatever a hat may lack in quality, there is never anything to be desired in the matter of quantity. The East Side, though poor enough in all truth, is ever generous. So far as the people can afford there is no stint in hospitality or charity, and the same rule is applied to hats.

It is not easy for an unpractised eye to judge of the quantity of chiffon or silk used on an ordinary summer hat, but on one recently seen in Millinery Lane there was a bulwark certainly no less than ten inches high all around the huge brim of the "creation." And it cost only $4—all that chiffon for $4, not to mention the handful of flowers and fruit which grew in the centre! Purple and yellow is a favorite combination, and may truthfully be said to give more show for the money than any other "effect." Black, except in large black velvet hats with feathers, is not popular, and when a black straw is used a microscope is needed to distinguish it at the bottom of a pyramid of peacock colors. The average East Side girl, who earns a few dollars every week and is not in destitute circumstances, buys every winter a hat with feathers. It is always a large one, and sometimes it groans beneath the weight of nearly or quite a dozen plumes which may once have called an ostrich their parent, although it is certain that the bird would disown her offspring at sight could she again see them.

Nothing if Not Up to Date.

It is to hats that the young girl's fancy lightly turns not only in spring, but in autumn also. She cares for dress, but it would be impossible to maintain throughout the high standard of elegance set by the headgear. Nevertheless, she does very well in this respect. The "habit back" flourished on the East Side from the first moment of its arrival from Paris. If skirts are long, no self-respecting girl would be seen in any costume that did not sweep a yard or two behind. If sleeves are tight, she would consider it a disgrace to be able to raise her arms above her head. She ties her neck scarf as low on the waist of her dress as it is shown in Paris fashions, and just a little lower, at the same minute that Fifth-ave. adopts the same style. If overskirts are worn, there is nothing else to be seen in Grand-st. But in the matter of dresses it is natural that the East Side should be strictly up to date, for does it not furnish clothes for the rest of the town? If my lady wears a velvet gown, put together for her in an East Side sweat shop, may not the girl whose tired fingers fashioned it rejoice her soul by astonishing Grand-st. with a copy of it on the next Sunday? My lady's is in velvet, and the East Side girl's is in the cheapest of cloth, but it's the style that counts!

The artistic taste of the East Side men is also highly developed, but the cruel hand of fashion has shut to them the door to its full enjoyment. Only in the matter of collars, neckties and socks can their fancy display itself. But if the field is restricted it is worked with energy. There are "sports" and "hot sports" and "stiffs." The "sport" is known by his necktie or his socks. The point is to combine on the small space allowed as many colors as possible. Purple and lavender, green and red, dark and light blue make contrasts which, as the wearers say, are "not to be beat." A "hot sport" is the common or garden "sport" in the superlative. A "stiff" is known by his collar. There are many gilded youths on the East Side who would never be guilty of wearing a "standup" collar when "high turndowns" were in fashion.

Is it funny, or is it pathetic? One is at loss to decide, and compromises by a smile and sigh. The girls enjoy it, and they are so pretty, many of them, that two dozen feathers, instead of merely a paltry ten or twelve, could not make them anything but attractive. As to the men, they are hardly attractive at the best, and, after all, a manly heart beats as truly under a green and red striped shirt as under one of purest white. It is only an expression of love of beauty. It does not happen to be the right idea of beauty, but it fills a place in the human soul which is better filled with even an idol of clay than left empty. Is it better for a girl to neglect her personal appearance or to deck herself with rubbish? If the latter is vulgar, the first is unwomanly, and the East Side may safely be said to have chosen the lesser evil.

Girls With Good Taste.

There need not be any evil to choose, however, as many East Side girls realize. Not all overdress, by any means. The uptown world is always underestimating the amount of refinement and ends from which she had fashioned the pretty thing. The skirt her brother-in-law, who "works at skirts," had made for her at odd times, and it cost, getting the material at wholesale, $2.50. Her hat her "chum" made at an expense of 60 cents. To the uninitiated the costume represented an outlay of $20, at least, although she had achieved it at an expense of $3.30, and was able to go abroad without proclaiming to the world the dire poverty at home. Her cleverness and the kindness of others had saved the proud old mother a severe humiliation. There are many such on the East Side.

But, although such girls are not rare, the other kind forms the great majority. It is apparently a part of the process of becoming Americanized. The girl whose Russian mother knew but the wig of the religious Jewess and a soft shawl; the girl who, had she remained in bright Italy, would have kept but one kerchief for week days and another for Sunday—these girls feel vastly fine in a "three story hat" which might well vie with the historic coat of Joseph. In the land of equality shall not one wear what another wears? Shall not Fifth Avenue and Grand Street walk hand in hand—the lion and the lamb lie down together? It would be rank heresy to insinuate that there is anything faulty in the process of "Americanizing" as it goes on on the East Side.

· 94 ·
LOVE AND MARRIAGE ON NEW YORK'S LOWER
EAST SIDE
1900–1901

When the East European Jews first started coming in large numbers to America in the late 1800's, they made every effort to follow the pattern of life of their Slavonic homelands. Psychic security was imperative. The marriage broker—the shadchan—was something of a tradition in the Russian and Polish ghettos. Over here some Jews continued to turn to him, although by 1900 he was on the way out. Sensible though they might be, arranged marriages were deemed un-American; love had taken over. The first article below, A, recounts the plaint of a former marriage broker who sniffed at love marriages and praised those where common sense prevailed. The implication was clear: papa, mama, and the broker know best.

The second selection that follows, B, describes the efforts of parents and girls to improve their social station by marrying a professional, especially a physician. Jewish women were ambitious, eager, anxious to make their way in life socially, culturally, and financially. Often they had little choice. But in no sense were they resigned to remain proletarians or petit bourgeois; they were always reaching out. To attain their goals they were prepared to struggle, to sacrifice. An inner daemon possessed many of them.

502

A

Love And All That Rot
1900

Jews Wed Without Brokers

Schatchens Find Business Bad and Deplore the Unhappiness Sure to Follow.

This has been a hard year for the Cupids of the Ghetto, as the matrimonial agents of the Jewish quarter might be called. To the Jews he is known as the schatchen, but unless the marriage business picks up the broker is going to drop out of sight. Already he is branching out into other ways of making a living. He writes letters for the illiterate, acts as interpreter in business transactions or does odd jobs around the synagogues. Marriage brokerage used to be one of the best-paying businesses on the East Side, but that day has passed, and the schatchens think it will never return.

When the Jews began to come to this city in large numbers and to crowd the Germans out of the East Side district they brought the marriage broker with them. They had always been accustomed to having a professional matchmaker arrange their marriages, and at that time they did not know how to get along without it. The young men were bashful and were more than willing to give up 10 per cent of the girl's dowry if some one else would put the question. Besides, they made sure of getting a wife in this way. They would go to the broker, or schatchen, and outline their ideal of a wife, not forgetting to mention the amount of dowry they expected. The schatchen would take note of all of the young man's advantages—personal appearance, education and money making ability. Then he would go among the young women of his extended acquaintance, and speedily find some one who was willing to wed on the terms which the broker had to offer.

The schatchen's fee was paid as soon as the engagement was announced. It usually amounted to 10 per cent of the dowry, but in some cases a stipulated fee was charged where the girl was very pretty and her people unable to give a large marriage portion.

Sometimes the schatchen had trouble collecting his fee, and in these cases he evened things up by breaking off the match. There were many ways of doing this. If the man was at fault the schatchen would get the girl a more desirable match, and as love had not entered into the first engagement it was speedily broken, leaving the man sadder but wiser. If the schatchen discovered that the girl had objected to paying the fee he found a prettier girl for the man.

This was the way it used to be done. Let the oldest schatchen in the colony tell why it is that his services are no longer in great demand. He is to be found in Hester-st., and the sign outside his door asserts that he writes letters, makes translations and teaches Hebrew or English.

"I would starve to death in a month if I depended on matchmaking for a living," he said bitterly. "Once I lived on the fat of the land, and most of the marriageable young men and women in the quarter depended on me to make them happy for life. Now they believe in love and all that rot. They are making their own marriages, and many of them will be unhappy. Several things combined to bring about the change. In the first place there are too many girls in the Jewish quarter. There are six or seven girls after every man. This makes the young fellows hard to deal with. They can marry into almost any family in the block just for the asking. Some of the women still come to me, but it is hard to find mates for them.

"They learned how to start their own love affairs from the Americans, and it is one of the worst things they have picked up. How can a Jewish couple expect to be happy in a marriage of their own making when it has been the custom of their fathers and mothers for ages not to see each other until after marriage? The love which they have learned to put so much faith in dribbles out in trips to Coney and walks around the parks before marriage. In a month they are figuring out ways of getting rid of each other. In the old way every month of married life made the young people more attached to each other. They may come back to the old way of doing things, and for their own sakes I hope they do."

B

Her Father Bought a Doctor for Her

1901

East Side Weddings.

The Curious Etiquette That Prevails in That Quarter of the City

If any one thinks that, below Houston-st., Mrs. Grundy [Madame Social Arbiter] either does not exist or is a lady addicted to slumber, that person is mightily mistaken. The outward and visible signs of her power may be, to the casual observer, less noticeable than in Fifth-ave., but she is there, and her power is, in certain particulars, all supreme. The desire to outshine the neighbors arose doubtless on the very day when a cave dweller, killing an ostrich, tore out the tail feathers to brush away the flies, and found that his wife appropriated them for her hair. The more neighbors one has the more, one would think, should be the social rivalry; ergo, there being a score of times more neighbors on the East Side than in any other equal space in the city, this form of aspiration should be found there in a high degree. Perhaps the reasoning does not hold good; but the code of etiquette is none the less severe.

The field of activity is rather restricted on the East Side. Social entertainments are not many. Balls are affairs of tickets, and each man pays his own way and that of "his lady." The one occasion on which the ambition of the aristocratically inclined may manifest itself is that of a wedding. Mrs. Grundy has woven around this ceremony all the red tape she expends on "functions" in a different sphere. A wedding must be large. There must be abundance of food and drink and plenty of carriages, and to secure these advantages many families are willing to sacrifice the savings scraped together for years. But before the ceremony comes the question of the suitability of the bride and bridegroom, and this point, or at least the latter part of it, is of the greatest importance. The choice of the son of the family may be poor and of inferior connections, and there will be nothing worse than disappointment; but should the daughter look beneath her, there are storms and entreaties, and even curses.

So great is the desire for sons-in-law above the rank of the family that extraordinary measures are taken to secure a desirable specimen. The son-in-law for whom the soul of every East Sider pines is a professional man—a doctor preferably. Now, there are not so many physicians to be had, and there is only a slight chance that one of the number will look kindly on any given girl, so the affair cannot be left to chance. An ambitious youth is "caught young," his fancy fired with pictures of social and professional glory, financial help is promised him, and then like a pill in jelly is tucked the condition, "marry my daughter afterward." This practice is so common that there has arisen a saying, used when any girl marries a physician. "Her father bought a doctor for her." The young men do not seem to object. Indeed, at the age of seventeen the prospect of marriage is little worthy of consideration to a boy, and if repentance comes after, he manages to keep it to himself and to live up to the bargain.

The case of one young man, recently married, will serve to illustrate the practice. At the age of eighteen, the father of a girl a year or two his senior made a contract with him, the one side promising a medical education, and the other side, marriage and social elevation. The boy agreed, went through the medical school, and duly announced his engagement. The girl's father furnished his office and living rooms, paying the rent and promising support until the young man's practice should pay. Then, in order to call attention to the value of their purchase, the family invited about two hundred guests to a large hall, paying $2.50 each for supper. The cost of this outlay will take probably every dollar of their savings, but they do not consider it extravagance. They have pushed their daughter a rung higher up the social ladder; they shine with reflected glory. Henceforth their conversation will be peppered and salted with "my son-in-law, Dr. So-and-so," "my son-in-law—he's a doctor, you know," while, should he be present when the neighbors visit, his title will be hurled at their heads at least once a minute.

Still more extraordinary is the case of a girl doing the purchasing of a doctor quite without assistance. Some ambitious maidens have negotiated the whole affair alone, either having their parents lacking in social ambition or failing parents altogether. These cases are kept quiet, naturally, but the neighbors usually find out and spread the news that such a one "is buying a doctor."

When the son chooses a girl whose parents are not well-to-do, a large wedding is none the less necessary. On the East Side, as elsewhere, the bride's family pays the wedding expenses, but if they are not able the bridegroom will step into the breach and cover the fact that the parents of his bride are poor. The alternative of a quiet wedding does not appeal to anybody concerned. There must be music and dancing and wine unlimited, whoever pays. One family, paying the wedding expenses of the son's wife, spent more than half the savings which up to that time had been the comfort of their hard worked lives, their own assurance of a decent old age.

Certain minor conventions are also strictly observed. The custom of giving a ring and a gold watch to one's fiancée divides the social sheep from the goats. Should a young man fail in this the omission is remedied at social affairs which the newly wedded pair attend by borrowing the necessary articles from some intimate friend. Only in this borrowed finery does the bride feel able to face the inquisitive eyes of her friends and acquaintances.

These gorgeous marriage ceremonies do not have their rise in a base mercenary desire for presents. Guests do not offer tribute as universally as in higher circles, although the members of the family do their best. The desire to shine socially is at the bottom of it, pure and simple, if, indeed, social aspiration is ever pure and simple. It leads parents to educate their children so that they may rise higher and cast into the shade the children next door—thus mingling good and evil in odd fashion. But it amuses them, it excites them, and perhaps the game is worth the candle, after all.

95

THE GHETTO JEWESSES OF NEW YORK CITY
1902–1905

One of the best studies of the New York ghetto was written by a Gentile journalist, Hutchins Hapgood. With the help, no doubt, of Abraham Cahan, a fellow-reporter on the New York Commercial Advertiser, *Hapgood's* The Spirit of the Ghetto *(1902) succeeded in recapturing something of the essence that imbued the men and women of the Lower East Side. To be sure, his book contains passages testifying that even he did not fully fathom the psyche of the émigrés whom he attempted to view sympathetically. To understand Jews, especially recent arrivals, perhaps one had to be a Jew oneself—a most sensitive, most tolerant Jew.*

The passages reprinted below, selection A, portray ghetto Jewesses as Hapgood saw them; his descriptions are, in turn, supplemented by excerpts, item B, from Charles S. Bernheimer's The Russian Jew in the United States *(1905), a cooperative work. The author of the excerpted passages from this latter book was Abraham H. Fromenson, the editor of the English Department of the Yiddish-language* Jewish Daily News. *Objective yet sympathetic, he was thoroughly conversant with his subject.*

A

1902

The women present in many respects a marked contrast to their American sisters. Substance as opposed to form, simplicity of mood as opposed to capriciousness, seem to be in broad lines their relative qualities. They have comparatively few *états d'âme* [emotional facets]; but those few are revealed with directness and passion. They lack the subtle charm of the American woman, who is full of feminine devices, complicated flirtatiousness; who in her dress and personal appearance seeks the plastic epigram, and in her talk and relation to the world an indirect suggestive delicacy. They [the ghetto girls] are poor in physical estate; many work or have worked; even the comparatively educated among them, in the sweat-shops, are undernourished and lack the physical well-being and consequent temperamental buoyancy which are comforting qualities of the well-bred American women. Unhappy in circumstances, they are predominatingly serious in nature, and, if they lack alertness to the social nuance have yet a compelling appeal which consists of headlong devotion to a duty, a principle or a person. As their men do not treat them with the scrupulous deference given their American sisters, they do not so delightfully abound in their own sense, do not so complexedly work out their own natures, and lack variety and grace. On the other hand, they are more apt to abound in the sense of something outside of themselves, and carry to their love affairs the same devoted warmth that they put into principle.

THE ORTHODOX JEWESS

The first of the two well-marked classes of women in the Ghetto is that of the ignorant orthodox Russian Jewess. She has no language but Yiddish, no learning but the Talmudic law, no practical authority but that of her husband and her rabbi. She is even more of a Hausfrau than the German wife. She can own no property, and the precepts of the Talmud as applied to her conduct are largely limited to the relations with her husband. Her life is absorbed in observing the religious law and in taking care of her numerous children. She is drab and plain in appearance, with a thick waist, a wig, and as far as is possible for a woman a contempt for ornament. She is, however, with the noticeable assimilative sensitiveness of the Jew, beginning to pick up some of the ways of the American woman. If she is young when she comes to America, she soon lays aside her wig, and sometimes assumes the rakish American hat, prides herself on her bad English, and grows slack in the observance of Jewish holidays and the dietary regulations of the Talmud. Altho it is against the law of this religion to go to the theatre, large audiences, mainly drawn from the ignorant workers of the sweat-shops and the fishwives and pedlers of the push-cart markets, flock to the Bowery houses. It is this class which forms the large background of the community, the masses from which more cultivated types are developing.

Many a literary sketch in the newspapers of the quarter portrays these ignorant, simple, devout, housewifely creatures in comic or pathetic, more often, after the satiric manner of the Jewish writers, in serio-comic vein. The authors, altho they are much more educated, yet write of these women, even when they write in comic fashion, with fundamental sympathy. They picture them working devotedly in the shop or at home for their husbands and families, they represent the sorrow and simple jealousy of the wife whose husband's imagination, perhaps, is carried away by the piquant manner and dress of a Jewess who is beginning to ape American ways; they tell of the comic adventures in America of the newly-arrived Jewess: . . . More fundamentally, they relate how the poor woman is deeply shocked, at her arrival, by the change which a few years have made in the character of her husband, who had come to America before her in order to make a fortune. She finds his beard shaved off, and his manners in regard to religious holidays very slack. She is sometimes so deeply affected that she does not recover. More often she grows to feel the reason and eloquence of the change and becomes partly accustomed to the situation; but all through her life she continues to be dismayed by the precocity, irreligion and Americanism of her children. Many sketches and many scenes in the Ghetto plays present her as a pathetic "greenhorn" who, while she is loved by her children, is yet rather patronized and pitied by them.

In "Gott, Mensch und Teufel" [*God, Man and Satan* by Jacob Gordin], a Yiddish adaptation of the Faust idea, one of these simple religious souls is dramatically portrayed. The restless Jewish Faust, his soul corrupted by the love of money, puts aside his faithful wife in order to marry another woman who has pleased his eye. He uses as an excuse the fact that his marriage is childless, and as such rendered void in accordance with the precepts of the religious law. His poor old wife submits almost with reverence to the double authority of husband and Talmud and with humble demeanor and tears streaming from her eye.

begs the privilege of taking care of the children of her successor.

In "The Slaughter" there is a scene which picturesquely portrays the love of the poor Jew and the poor Jewess for their children. The wife is married to a brute, whom she hates, and between the members of the two families there is no relation but that of ugly sordidness. But when it is known that a child is to be born they are all filled with the greatest joy. The husband is ecstatic and they have a great feast, drink, sing and dance, and the young wife is lyrically happy for the first time since her marriage.

Many little newspaper sketches portray the simple sweat-shop Jewess of the ordinary affectionate type, who is exclusively minded so far as her husband's growing interest in the showy American Jewess is concerned. [Abraham] Cahan's novel, "Yekel," is the Ghetto masterpiece in the portrayal of these two types of women—the wronged "greenhorn" who has just come from Russia, and she who, with a rakish hat and bad English, is becoming an American girl with strange power to alienate the husband's affections.

THE MODERN TYPE

The other, the educated class of Ghetto women, is, of course, in a great minority; and this division includes the women even the most slightly affected by modern ideas as well as those who from an intellectual point of view are highly cultivated. Among the least educated are a large number of women who would be entirely ignorant were it not for the ideas which they have received through the Socialistic propaganda of the quarter. Like the men who are otherwise ignorant, they are trained to a certain familiarity with economic ideas, read and think a good deal about labor and capital, and take an active part in speaking, in "house to house" distribution of socialistic literature and in strike agitation. Many of these women, so long as they are unmarried, lead lives thoroughly devoted to "the cause," and afterwards become good wives and fruitful mothers, and urge on their husbands and sons to active work in the "movement."

They have in personal character many virtues called masculine, are simple and straightforward and intensely serious, and do not "bank" in any way on the fact that they are women! Such a woman would feel insulted if her escort were to pick up her handkerchief or in any way suggest a politeness growing out of the difference in sex. It is from this class of women, from those who are merely tinged, so to speak, with ideas, and who consequently are apt to throw the whole strength of their primitive natures into the narrow intellectual channels that are open to them, that a number of Ghetto heroines come who are willing to lay down their lives for an idea, or to live for one. . . .

As we ascend in the scale of education in the Ghetto we find women who derive their culture and ideas from a double source—from Socialism and from advanced Russian ideals of literature and life. They have lost faith completely in the orthodox religion, have substituted no other, know Russian better than Yiddish, read Tolstoi, Turgenef and Chekhov, and often put into practice the most radical theories of the "new woman," particularly those which say that woman should be economically independent of man. There are successful female dentists, physicians, writers, and even lawyers by the score in East Broadway who have attained financial independence through industry and intelligence. They are ambitious to a degree and often direct the careers of their husbands or force their lovers to become doctors or lawyers—the great social desiderata in the matchmaking of the Ghetto. There is more than one case on record where a girl has compelled her recalcitrant lover to learn law, medicine or dentistry, or submit to being jilted by her. An actor devoted to the stage is now on the point of leaving it to become a dentist at the command of his ambitious wife. "I always do what she tells me," he said pathetically. . . .

PLACE OF WOMAN IN GHETTO LITERATURE

Ibsen's "Doll's House" has been translated and produced at a Yiddish theatre; and an original play called "Minna" registers a protest by the Jewish woman against that law of marriage which binds her to an inferior man. Married to an ignorant laborer,

Minna falls in love (for his advanced ideas) with the boarder—every poor family, to pay the rent, must saddle themselves with a boarder, often at the expense of domestic happiness—and finally kills herself, when the laws of society press her too hard. Another drama called "East Broadway" presents the case of a Russian Jewess devoted to Russia, to idealism and Nihilism, and to a man who shared her faith until they came to New York, when he became a business man pure and simple, and lost his ideals and his love for her. In a popular play called "The Beggar of Odessa," lines openly advocating the freest love between the sexes accompany other extreme anarchistic views put into the loosest and most popular form. "Broken Chains" is a drama which criticises the relative freedom of action given to the man in matters of love. The heroine reads Ibsen at night while her husband amuses himself in the quarter. A young bookkeeper is there who serves to make concrete her growing theories. But her sense of duty to her child restrains her from the final step, and she dies in despair. Suicides in sketches and plays abound, and as often as not result simply from intellectual despondency. "Vain Sacrifice" is the fierce outcry of a woman against the poverty which makes her marry a man she loathes for the sake of her father. In the newspaper sketches there are many pictures of sordid homes and conditions from the midst of which fierce protests by wives and mothers are implicitly given.

An appealing characteristic of the "new woman" of the Ghetto is the consideration which she manifests towards the orthodox "greenhorn" who may be her aunt, her mother, her mother-in-law or her grandmother. The sense of infinite form prescribed by the Talmud is dead to her, but extraordinary love for the family bond is not, and, moved by that, she observes the complicated formulae on all the holidays in order to please the dear old "greenhorn" who lives with her; eats unleavened bread, weeps on Atonement Day in the synagogue, and goes through the whole long list. Her conduct in this respect is in striking contrast to the off-hand treatment of parents by their American daughters, and to that of the Orthodox Jewish woman in relation to the theatre. The law forbids the theatre, but even the slightly disillusioned ladies of the quarter will go on the Sabbath; and it is said that they sometimes hypocritically relieve their consciences by hissing the actor who, even in his rôle, dares to smoke on that day. This is on a par with the hypocrisy which leads many Orthodox Jewish families to have a Gentile as their servant, so that they can drink the tea, and warm themselves by the fire, made by him, without technically violating "the law."

Love in the Ghetto is, no doubt, very much the same as it is elsewhere; and this in spite of the fact that among the Orthodox marriage is arranged by the parents, a custom which is condemned in "The Slaughter," for instance, where the terrible results of a loveless union are portrayed. The system of matrimonial agents in the quarter does not seem to have any important bearing on the question of love. In this respect the free thinking of the people grows apace, and love-marriages in the quarter are on the increase. In matters of taste and inclination between the sexes, however, there are some qualities quite startling to the American. The most popular actor with the girls of the Ghetto is a very fat, heavy, pompous hero who would provoke only a smile from the trim American girl; and the more popular actresses are also very stout ladies. From an American point of view the prettiest actresses of the Ghetto are admired by the minority of Jews who have been taken by the rakish hat, the slim form, and the indefinite charm to which the Ghetto is being educated. It is alleged that at an up-town theatre, where a large proportion of the audience is Jewish, the leading lady must always be of very generous build; and this in spite of the fact that the well-to-do Jews up-town have been in America a long time, and have had ample opportunity to become smitten with the charms of the slender American girl.

B
1905

And where the cigarette smoke is thickest and denunciation of the present forms of government loudest, there you find women! One wishes he could write these women down gently. But to none would gentle words sound more strange than to the women of the radical coffee "parlor," who listen to strongest language, and loudest voices, nor fail to make themselves heard in the heat of the discussion. Yet it is hard to criticise them. The hall-bedroom is such a dingy, dreary place; the walls so close they seem to crush the unfortunate whose "home" is within its oppressive limits. The "coffee saloon" is light and cheerful; the noise is only the swelling chorus of spirits with whom they are in harmonious accord. If they are not the objects of fine courtesies and considerateness, they do not miss them; perhaps they never knew them. The stern realities of life, the terrible disappointment of thwarted ambition, the bruising friction of tradition and "emancipation," the struggle for existence—all these have conspired to rob them of the finer attributes of womanhood. These are the stalwarts of the radical movements, the Amazons, or, as they have been dubbed, "die kaempferinen" [the battlers], whose zealotry rallies the flagging courage of their "genossen" [comrades]. Unromantic, perhaps, and yet we hear of them toiling, slaving, denying themselves until some man has won a degree and an entry into one of the professions. But, as they sit there in an atmosphere of tea-steam and cigarette smoke, one who does not know sees them only as unwomanly women; pallid, tired, thin-lipped, flat-chested and angular, wearing men's hats and shoes, without a hint of color or finery. And to them, as to the men, the time of night means nothing until way into the small hours. When one must sleep in a hall-bedroom there is no hurry about bedtime. . . .

The ladies of the Ghetto are never "at home," but the welcome visitor is always sure of his glass of tea, his dish of preserves, and some fruit. There are no "Kaffee Klatches" here; nor progressive euchres, or bridge-whists. Hospitality is simple, homely, genuine. There are no social circles, "social life" as that term is understood does not exist. "Parties" are given; not "coming out" parties, but "engagement parties," "graduation parties," "bar-mitzvah parties." The wedding, of course, is the big function. Hundreds of societies give dances and "receptions" (the latter being a more pretentious name for the former) during the winter, to which anyone may come if he can pay the price of a ticket and "hat check." Some societies couple entertainments with these receptions. The great social events are the "entertainment and ball" of the Beth Israel Hospital, the Hebrew Sheltering House and Home for the Aged, the Daughters of Jacob [a home for the elderly], the Young Men's Benevolent League, and the New Era Club [a settlement house with Jewish educational goals]. It is at these functions that the East Side makes its most gorgeous sartorial display, and it is by no means either a crude or cheap display. The women for the most part are as exquisitely clad as their sisters who visit the Horse-Show, and the diamonds worn at these affairs can be outblinked only by the collection on the grand tier at the Metropolitan Opera House. Strange as it may sound to many, the East Side is not all poverty and suffering.

The Harlem contingent has acquired some "society" manners, but like newly acquired things, these manners do not fit very snugly, and their wearing is very amusing. Perhaps, with much effort some of the social aspirants will become accustomed to the new burden. The "climbing" is confined, for the most part, to the wives of physicians and lawyers and manufacturers. The great mass regards it all with quiet derision, and will have nothing to do with "visiting lists" and the rest of what they call "blowing from themselves." With the mass, relatives and friends are to be visited when time allows, or when occasion demands.

Owing to home-conditions on the East Side there is only such social life for the young folks as is made possible by organization membership, and as may express itself in the dances mentioned above, or in "open-meetings," indulged in by the "literary" societies, the Zionist societies, and the clubs in the settlements. In the summer time there are the picnics, which are dances in an open pavilion, with a few patches of grass surrounding it, all enclosed with a high fence. Much has been said against these "picnics" and it must be admitted that many of them are not very desirable. There is great need for healthy, wholesome recreation, for expression of the buoyancy of youth; and it is greatly to be regretted that the facilities for the things that help to make boys and girls better, purer men and women are so very few.

96

THE SETTLEMENT COOK BOOK
1903

In 1900, during the days of the Sisterhoods for Personal Service, a group of Milwaukee Jewesses established a neighborhood house which they called "The Settlement," the first institution of its type in the city. As in similar charitable enterprises, a cooking school was established. In order to expedite their work, the instructors published a cooking and housekeeping textbook or manual. It appeared in 1901 under the auspices of The Settlement; its title was The Way to a Man's Heart: Under the Auspices of "The Settlement." *The compilers were Mrs. Simon Kander and Mrs. Henry Schoenfeld.*

The original cookbook sold for fifty cents; as sales increased, new revised editions appeared. The proceeds were used to fund the local "Settlement House," to provide scholarships for students, and to finance a nursery school. Ultimately, the Settlement Cook Book *was to run to some forty editions and to sell over a million copies. It is no great exaggeration to maintain that this book rivals beer as Milwaukee's most notable product. The royalties that came pouring in still accrue to the Settlement Cook Book Company, a charitable trust. After a few printings, Mrs. Kander became the sole editor. She had been an indefatigable social worker since the middle 1890's; Milwaukee saluted her as The Settlement's "Lady Bountiful." By 1906, she was also a member of Milwaukee's Board of School Directors, filling an office in which her husband had served over a decade earlier.*

Because the first editions of the work were for immigrants, it was necessary to be most explicit. The newcomers, hailing from tiny Slavonic villages, had cooked under the most primitive of conditions. The new cookbook was indeed an important medium of acculturation, as becomes quite clear in the excerpts from the second edition published below. Though the cooking instructions were intended for these newcomers, most of whom kept kosher, nonkosher foods and recipes were included because many of the purchasers were acculturated Jews who loved forbidden delicacies. Pork, however, was taboo in the early editions.

To Clear the Table After a Meal.

Brush the crumbs from the floor. Arrange the chairs in their places. Collect and remove the knives, forks and spoons. Empty the cups and remove them. Scrape off the dishes—never set any food away on the dishes used for serving—pile them up neatly and remove to the place where they are to be washed. Brush the crumbs from the cloth and fold it carefully in the old crease, as it lays on the table. If the napkins are used again, place them neatly folded in their individual rings.

Washing Dishes.

Have a pan half filled with hot water. If dishes are very dirty or greasy, add a little washing soda or ammonia.

Wash glasses first. Slip them in sideways, one at a time, and wipe instantly.

Wash the silver and wipe at once, and it will keep bright.

Then wash the china, beginning with the cups, saucers, pitchers, and least greasy dishes, and changing the water as soon as cool or greasy.

Rinse the dishes in a pan of scalding water, take out and drain quickly.

Wipe immediately.

Then wash the kitchen dishes, pots, kettles, pans, etc.

A Dover egg-beater should not be left to soak in water, or it will be hard to run. Keep the handles clean, wipe the wire with a damp cloth immediately after using.

Kitchen knives and forks should never be placed in dish water. Scour them with brick dust, wash with dish cloth, and wipe them dry.

Tinware, granite ironware should be washed in hot soda water, and if browned, rub with sapolio, salt or baking soda. Use wire dish cloth if food sticks to dishes.

Keep strainer in sink and pour all dish water, etc., in it, and remove contents of strainer in garbage pail.

Wash towels with plenty of soap, and rinse thoroughly every time they are used.

Hang towels up evenly to dry. Wash dish cloths.

Scrub dishboards with brush and sapolio, working with the grain of the wood, rinse and dry.

When scrubbing, wet brush and apply sapolio or soap with upward strokes.

Wash dish pans, wipe and dry.

Wash your hands with white (castile or ivory) soap, if you wish to keep smooth hands, and wipe them dry.

Wash teakettle.

Polish faucets.

Scrub sink with clean hot suds.

To Build a Fire.

It is necessary to have:

1st, Fuel.—Something to burn.

2nd, Heat.—To make fuel hot enough to burn.

3rd, Air.—To keep the fire burning.

To Dust a Room

Begin at one corner and take each article in turn as you come to it. Dust it from the highest things to the lowest, taking up the dust in the cloth. Shake the duster occasionally in a suitable place, and when through, wash and hang it up to dry.

In sweeping a room, sweep from you, holding the broom close to the floor.

97

FANNY BRICE, COMEDIENNE
1905

*Fanny Brice (Borach, 1891/92–1951), a New York East Side young-
ster, made her debut on the stage at the tender age of thirteen. It was the
beginning of a great career as a singer, mimic, and comedienne. When still
a young woman, she had become one of the country's best-known stars of
stage and radio. By the 1930's, she had made a name for herself on the
screen as well. Her career is important because it highlights the
opportunities open to the children of the East European newcomers who
aspired to make a name for themselves in the theatre. Most of the Jews who
achieved national recognition as singers and comedians were men; Fanny
Brice was the exceptional female. Few women in the world of comedy were
more admired than this incomparable actress whose mimicry made her the
darling of millions. The obituary below tells the story of her career.*

FANNY BRICE DIES AT THE AGE OF 59

Comedienne, Famed in Role of Baby Snooks, First
Scored with Song, "My Man"

"DISCOVERED" BY ZIEGFELD

She Got $75 a Week to Play in "Follies"—Also Starred on Radio
and in Movies

Special to *The New York Times*

Hollywood, Calif., May 29—Fanny Brice, stage and screen
comedienne and the Baby Snooks of radio, died at 11:15 A.M.
today at the Cedars of Lebanon Hospital. Her age was 59.

Miss Brice suffered a massive cerebral hemorrhage last
Thursday morning and was rushed to the hospital from her home

24. Fanny Brice

in Beverly Hills. She never again regained consciousness, although she was placed in an oxygen tent.

With Miss Brice when she died were her son, William Brice and her daughter, Mrs. Frances Stark, the children of her marriage to Jules W. Arnstein, and her son-in-law, Ray Stark, and daughter-in-law, Mrs. Shirley Brice.

Also surviving are a brother, Lew Brice of Hollywood, a sister, Mrs. Caroline Russak of New York, and three grandchildren, John Brice and Peter and Wendy Stark.

TORCH SONG BROUGHT FAME

Although known chiefly as a comedienne, Fanny Brice first became internationally famous for singing a torch song, "My Man." Channing Pollock wrote English words to the French tune, "Mon Homme," which Miss Brice introduced in "The Ziegfeld Follies." It proved a "natural," since it appealed to every woman who had ever been in love.

Her classic burlesque and pointed satire formed a hardy perennial of the "Follies" almost every year starting in 1916, when she first did a comic version of a dying swan ballet. Her lampoon of sultry Theda Bara, her take-off of "Camille," with W. C. Fields as the maid, and her travesty on fan dancers and the modern dance, were part of the repertoire of the actress whom Brooks Atkinson of *The New York Times* described as "a burlesque comic of the rarest vintage."

She was billed with Eddie Cantor, Will Rogers, W. C. Fields, Willie Howard and other top Broadway performers through the years in which she appeared in such shows as the "Follies," "Music Box Review of 1924," "Sweet and Low," and Billy Rose's "Crazy Quilt." She also put across the song, "Rose of Washington Square."

She created the character Baby Snooks, originally acting the part of the annoying little girl at parties for the entertainment of friends. Later Snooks was regularly featured in sketches in the "Follies" and was introduced to radio in 1938.

After an eleven-year run, Baby Snooks went off the air when

its sponsorship on the Columbia Broadcasting System network was withdrawn by General Foods. In November, 1949, however, Miss Brice resumed the role under a long-term contract with the National Broadcasting Company. The company announced yesterday that the program would be off the air for the remainder of the season, the spot being filled by an orchestra.

Born on East Side

She was really Fannie Borach, daughter of a saloon-keeper on Forsythe Street in the crowded Lower East Side, where she was born in 1892. Her first appearance on any stage took place when she was 13 at Keeney's Theatre in Brooklyn, where she won an amateur night contest singing, "When You Know You're Not Forgotten by the Girl You Can't Forget." The prize was $5 and numerous coins hurled by the audience, and from that night on Miss Brice gave up school for the stage.

Then followed a job as jack-of-all-trades in a movie house, playing the piano, singing and helping out in the projection room. When she was 16 she applied for the chorus of the George M. Cohan–Sam Harris review, "Talk of New York." She remained in the chorus until Mr. Cohan found out she could not dance and fired her.

She then sang in various burlesque houses in New York. One night Florenz Ziegfeld "caught" her act and offered her a job at $75 a week. When she left the stage after introducing "My Man," Ziegfeld gave her a check for $2,500 and said, "You've earned it." Her weekly salary soon reached $3,000.

Only once did she try straight drama. In 1925 she was starred in the Belasco production, "Fanny." It was unsuccessful. The critics called for Fanny the comedienne, not the dramatic actress.

She first went to Hollywood to appear in the silent film, "My Man." She returned to Broadway only to find herself in Hollywood again when talkies came in, playing herself in "The Great Ziegfeld" and appearing in "Everybody Sing" and "Be Yourself."

She was married three times. Her first husband was Frank White, a barber, whom she met in 1911 in Springfield, Mass., when she was touring in "College Girl." The marriage lasted only a few days and she brought suit for divorce. In 1918 she was married to Jules W. (Nicky) Arnstein, only to divorce him in Chicago in 1927, after she had stood by him during his two years' imprisonment, starting in 1924, in Leavenworth, in connection with the mysterious disappearance of $5,000,000 worth of securities.

Two years after her divorce she was married to Billy Rose, the showman, by Mayor James Walker in New York. In 1937 she sued Mr. Rose for divorce, and shortly after it was granted he married Mrs. Eleanor Holm Jarrett, swimming champion.

98

THE IMPACT OF A SETTLEMENT HOUSE ON IMPRESSIONABLE JEWISH GIRLS
ca. 1905–ca. 1920'

Quite a number of settlement houses in the Jewish ghettos were supported and staffed by Gentiles. The following memoir recounts the influence of a pious Christian social worker on a group of Boston girls, children of recent immigrants. The supervisor and leader, Julia Frothingham (d. 1925), introduced her charges to the world of art, poetry, politics, and also to her exemplary Protestant Christian concept of morality. There can be no question that the influences which impinged upon these Jewish girls helped make them finer Americans, nobler human beings.

Girlhood in the Old North End
By Celia Stanetsky (Mrs. Moe) Cohen

About a half century ago, I was fortunate to meet one of the most splendid and wonderful personalities that ever lived. Her influence on my life as well as upon a great many others was beautiful and everlasting. Her name was Julia Frothingham and she will always be remembered by anyone who ever met her.

My parents were immigrants, and we lived in the North End. There was a settlement house called "The North End Union" on Parmenter street. In those days we had no Jewish Centers. The result was that most young Jewish children affiliated themselves with clubs and met people in the local settlement houses. A group of sixteen girls about ten years old started a club called the "Jerusalem Stars." We thought of Jerusalem because we were all Jewish girls and "stars" because we were bright and wideawake.

Our supervisor and leader was Julia Frothingham and she took us under her loving and protective wing. We sewed while she read to us and soon we were listening to the beautiful poetry of Alfred Tennyson and Robert Browning and others. We loved to hear the sweet gentle voice of Miss Frothingham while we worked diligently and made hundreds of bandages for the Red Cross. Those more skillful made pajamas and layettes. As we were very young we used to come to the Settlement House from 4 to 6 p.m. The older girls, a larger group, went in the evening. Since their work was sedentary during the day, Miss Frothingham provided a gymnasium class once a week in the evening.

We became the Frothingham Girls Club and another group of older girls was organized under Miss Frothingham's leadership as the "Progress Club."

Miss Frothingham wanted us to learn as much as possible and all the advantages she had she shared with us. She told us about her travels abroad and we took an imaginary trip to Europe and studied Art and made beautiful Art Books with illustrations by Perry pictures. We learned about Rome, Florence and Venice with its great history and magnificent Art treasures. We visited the Uffizi and Pitti Palaces and became familiar with the works of Fra Filippo Lippi, Michelangelo, Masario, Giotto, Botticelli, Donatello and Leonardo da Vinci. . . .

We all went to hear Burton Holmes' lectures on his travels and we sat in the gallery and enjoyed it immensely. Later one of the girls gave a stereopticon lecture of our imaginary travels and with the money we raised the entire club went to Washington, D.C.

We were all interested in Women's Suffrage and we had a debate on Suffrage with the young men of the Settlement House. Of course, the girls won the debate! Therefore we were thrilled to be with the Women's Suffrage group in Washington and shake the hand of the great American, Theodore Roosevelt, President of the United States. We roamed about the White House, wide-eyed with excitement and joy from our wonderful experience. This was a great opportunity for us girls of immigrant parents, and many of us foreign-born. We sang "My Country 'Tis of Thee," "The Star Spangled Banner" and "America the Beautiful" with extreme fervor and devotion, proclaiming our love for our country with all our hearts and souls.

We associated ourselves with all civic movements which would benefit society. We debated Prohibition and the Eighteenth Amendment. We studied current events and were interested in the League of Nations and the World Court. The peace of the world was very dear to Miss Frothingham's heart and we attended the lectures at Ford Hall. We all became vitally interested in making the world safe for ourselves and posterity.

We joined the Massachusetts Federation of Women's Clubs, a most worthy organization. Once we attended meetings in Montreal and quaint Old Quebec. We sailed up the St. Lawrence River and saw the beautiful Chateau Frontenac and the scenic grandeur of Canada. We visited the shrine of St. Anne de Beaupre, where thousands of cripples leave their crutches yearly because of their tremendous faith in God. As I write, I am wondering where the money came from for this wonderful trip. There must have been a fairy God-mother and one can easily guess. This noble and gracious lady gave her time, her money and all her love and devotion to people less fortunate. It wasn't the fun we had or the things we learned or the joy of travel that I remember, but Miss Frothingham's love and consideration for all kinds of people. She admired Booker T. Washington, the great educator of the Negroes, and at an early age we realized that we should help them. Miss Frothingham stressed tolerance and taught us to have respect for others and their opinions. We all worship God, but not in the same manner.

An old English professor of Boston University once said that by the conduct of the students, their zeal for study and learning, their ability to make friends, they set a splendid example for all the others.

A young lawyer once said that Miss Frothingham left her stamp on each and every one of us. You can always recognize a Frothingham girl. Her ideals are high and she will not swerve one iota from those ideals. We learned that we were created in the image of God and that our aim is perfection. Our thoughts are like a magnet and like attracts like. If we think good thoughts, more good thoughts will come to us. "To him who hath more will be given." I could never understand that statement until Miss Frothingham explained it.

We were warned to count ten before we lost our tempers, as self control is important. We must also have the right attitude towards life and count our blessings instead of envying others. Jealousy is the green-eyed monster which can devour you and make you most unhappy. Happiness is within our own hearts and is in the reach of every one of us. Material things may buy comforts but real true happiness is within. Nothing anyone can say to hurt you will affect you if you have the right feeling within you, and your enemies' remarks will roll off like water from a duck's back. If you listen to that small faint voice within you and heed it carefully you have nothing to fear from anybody. Pray to God for all your needs in the quiet and seclusion of your own room and he will answer your prayers, for God is interested in your every desire great or small.

We know there is a God because of the perfect order in Nature. Even scientists admit to a Supreme Power because of this orderliness. The human body testifies to God's handiwork because of its perfection. . . . God can perform miracles and the lowly can be raised while the mighty can be made low. Therefore we must never think we are better than other people. Fear and worry are the scourge of mankind. Since worry never helps us but can bring only harm, we must do the best we can and leave the rest to God. Many of the fears we have never materialize anyway.

Miss Frothingham always emphasized gratitude and she wanted us always to express that feeling promptly whenever the occasion arose. Ingratitude is horrible! If we see something beautiful, a fine picture or any work of art, and it inspires us, don't waste that inspiration, but act at once and do something worthwhile. I am forever grateful to God for my meeting Miss Frothingham, for she has been and still is my guiding light, showing me the beauty of life and how to live it.

The influence of Miss Frothingham will be felt by many generations to come. Our beloved leader gave each girl a memento, a beautiful picture from the walls of her Beacon street home. We went to her home frequently and partook of hot chocolate and Bailey's cocoanut cakes. We will always remember her loving kindness to us.

On her demise, every Frothingham girl was left a personal bequest, a small token. In my particular case, it is a lovely silver dish which I have treasured these many years.

I have tried in my humble way to give you a picture of Julia Frothingham, the friend of my childhood days in the old North

End of Boston—my friend and the friend of other little Jewish girls who came under the influence of this Christian lady. To do justice to this noble character is an Herculean task and one which I am unable to do. But if I have given you a glimpse of her beauty, sweetness, kindness and love for humanity, I am deeply grateful. For the lessons she taught us of gracious living in Peace and Brotherhood abide with us always.

99

THE EAST EUROPEAN IMMIGRANT JEWESS:
TROUBLE, TROUBLE, TROUBLE
February–March 1906

Abraham Cahan, the editor of the revamped Forward, *a Yiddish socialist newspaper, began publishing a personal column in 1906. It was called "A Bintel Brief," a Bundle of Letters. Most of the letters which reached the editor's desk were sent by recent arrivals, troubled young immigrants in need of advice. What were the chief concerns of the women among them? Family tensions, love, marriage, desertion, divorce, broken homes, sexual freedom, Jewish-Christian relations, religion, education, working conditions. Are these letters authentic? Yes, though undoubtedly many, if not most, of them were modified as they were prepared for publication. A few, indeed, were actually fabricated in the editorial offices.*

Do the plaints fully reflect the life of the typical East European female immigrant? No. From 1906 into the 1930's, well over 10,000 letters poured in; only a few were published; those printed were the result of a highly selective winnowing process. The Forward, *it must be kept in mind, was a socialist newspaper, while only a minuscule number of the new arrivals were Marxists. Its readers—some of whom were indeed not socialists—did not represent the rank and file of Yiddish-speaking American Jewry. What is equally true is that this column mirrored only the social pathology of the proletarian and petty bourgeois newcomers as they moved from a despotic Slavic agrarian village economy to a Western-type democracy in an Anglo-Saxon metropolitan industrial economy. The transatlantic crossing confronted these newcomers with traumatic challenges. One is tempted to venture the opinion that these letters overaccentuated the anguish of the new settlers as they were driven to surrender treasured prepossessions. Nevertheless, they did accurately reflect the problems of tens of thousands of ghetto Jews here in this land of "unlimited opportunity."*

People read this column. They wept and found solace in common sufferings. Through the editorial answers, a whole generation of devotees found advice, comfort, and Americanization.

Letter A reflects the heartache of a lonely widow; her beloved only

daughter has married and established a home of her own; item B embodies
the doctrinaire convictions of a young lady who balks at religion and the
formality of a marriage ceremony; item C tells the story of the slave of the
alarm clock, a servant girl. Judging by her pseudonymous signature
"Trilby," she identifies with Du Maurier's tragic heroine. Selection D
emphasizes the problems of juvenile delinquency, a social dysfunction
which is almost inevitable where there is a large body of impoverished
immigrants. Two years later, in 1908, New York Police Commissioner
Theodore A. Bingham accused the Jews of being the major contributors to
the city's crime rate. Furious because he had bared their shame, the Jews set
out in the Kehillah Movement to clean house. The last letter, E, illustrates
the difficulty of observing the traditional Sabbath.

A

THE LONELY MOTHER

February 7th, 1906

Most Worthy Editor of the "Forward"!

I doubt whether my writing is worthy of publication. I suppose
I am writing for your waste basket. Anyhow, I will write. Let the
heart become a little lighter. I have been a widow for more than 12
years; until a month ago however I considered myself happy
because I was not alone. My only daughter was with me. And we
lived together not like mother and daughter, but like two friends.
I was going to write: "two sisters," but are then sisters always
friends? In short my daughter did not do the least thing without
me and I without her. [We] always consulted one another, always
talked everything over, took walks together, ate, always drank
together, and of late even wore the same clothes. When I observed
that a fine young man was paying attention to her, I naturally
considered myself happy being a mother, but I must confess that
my heart severed. Will I remain lonely? I ask myself. I saw how a
stranger suddenly steps into my intimate life and tears my
treasure, my friend, out of my arms. My heart bled; I observed

my daughter; I saw how the flower of love grows in her young heart, but to me it was not a flower, but weeds. Still I rejoiced in her happiness and did my duty as a mother, and the wedding was not delayed by me for a single day. At last it happened.

My daughter is married; she belongs to a different world, and I am lonely, alone with my wounded heart. She always receives me with love, but I am of course not more than a mother, an appendage. The great world, naturally, is the husband, and I do not begrudge him his happiness and wish them eternal happiness from the bottom of my heart. But why deny? When they sit and talk softly and show manifestations of their love in a corner and I sit at a distance, like a stranger from whom secrets are kept, I am jealous to tears. Yes, more than once I went to the kitchen for water, but in truth, to shed tears, not to get water. When I cry out my heavy heart, I feel better. I know that it cannot be otherwise, I too acted in the same manner once with my mother, but that helps me little with my heart's wound. I am so lonely, so unhappy, the world is empty and desolate for me. I wish my daughter at least understood me and sympathized more with me, but no! She is too occupied with her hubby and her happiness. May they spend their years happily. I have at least made my heart lighter.

A Mother Left Lonely

B

A Freethinker Balks at Formal Marriage

February 20th, 1906.

Dear Mr. Editor of the "Forward"!

Before I tell you of what my trouble consists, I would like to give a short introduction about myself. I have not been long in this country, a year and a half altogether. I am only 18 years old. At home, in Russia, I participated in the revolutionary movement, and I also had a very good opportunity to develop. A famous revolutionist gave me lessons in the native tongue and in French and she especially exerted her utmost strength to make an atheist out of me. That was her passion; if one mentioned the

word God, she would close her ears. Her teachings made a strong
impression upon me and I became her devoted disciple to the last
dot. At the same time a letter came to me from a rich uncle of mine
in Chicago, and he asked me if I had any desire to come to
America. He promised me golden mountains and, knowing that
study, he promised to send me to high school. I seized upon this
and after an intense struggle with my parents, who in no wise
wanted to let me go (I am their only child), I left.

The uncle received me very kindly and he assured me that
would be happy here. He engaged a teacher for me, and in the
course of half a year I made good progress in English. My uncle's
house too is English [speaking] and that is why I learned so
quickly to speak like a Yankee girl. When my uncle realized that
was no longer green, he decided that nothing in particular will
result from my studying at a college or high school, and he
proposed that I become a saleslady in his department store. It is
true that the proposal mortified me very much, but it would have
been very foolish for me to start bickering, when my uncle was so
kind and friendly to me. Having no way out, I became a
saleslady. It is perhaps not necessary to mention in this letter that
my uncle changed completely, that he began to exhibit too much
affection for me . . . and that a few ugly scenes of jealousy took
place between him and my aunt and between my aunt and
myself, but this has no relation to my trouble.

My troubles really began in the same store but my uncle is not
the guilty one. At my uncle's store there also worked a clerk, a
very handsome and highly intelligent young man, but he was a
Gentile. To me it was not a great blemish; I was already too much
of a freethinker to stop at such a trifle, and I became acquainted
with him. But our friendship became in time greater and more
intimate; he already began spending on me. He took me to the
theatre almost 2 times a week and, in short, he fell seriously in
love with me. I, to tell the truth, was not in love with him, but I
respected and esteemed him very much. But when his relations
with me at last became so friendly, that they could not be
friendlier in the case of a couple in love, I willy-nilly was caught in
his net and I gave myself to him. I did not believe in a wedding
and ceremonies, as I did not think of later consequences. But the

consequences soon came of themselves. Firstly, my uncle and aunt soon became aware of my love-relationships with the clerk, and they hinted that I would not be able to remain any longer in their house. But this was a minor trouble. My lover really wanted that I should leave my uncle, and the day when I moved into his two rooms was a great holiday for him . . . but for me the day was the beginning of my future suffering. . . .

A few days after I moved into my "free" husband's, he began bothering me that I marry him legally. He has a big family, he said, in New York, and he would not be able to show himself to them if I lived with him illegally.

I did not like this proposal at all. If I was going to live with a Christian then I wanted it to be a free relationship. But if legally and to go to church yet, which I condemn so strongly, I did not want it and I told him plainly that he will never carry it out. His attitude to me immediately became different; I realized at once that his education was not worth a pinch of snuff if he is only religious in this respect. And a miserable time began for me. "Scenes" with us were already a daily occurrence. In a word, my life became unbearable. In the meantime he was discharged and he got employment with a New York store. He took me, naturally, with him to New York. And coming here and realizing that he was firm in his decision, I left him. I went to a *landmaidel* [woman compatriot] of mine, also a comrade, and seeing your paper at her house and reading through several articles in your *Bintel Brief* it occurred to me to ask for your advice: What shall I do now?

I am to become a mother soon, and I do not want to give a new *goy* [Gentile] to the Christian church. I want my child to be a man. But I do not want a Christian. My "husband" would take me back even today, if I only wanted to be united to him legally.

Chajah Ritz
42 Broadway
Brooklyn

C

SERVANT GIRLS: SLAVES OF THE ALARM CLOCK

[Denver,] February 26th, 1906

Dear Mr. Editor of the "Forward"!

Permit me, please, to relate several sad experiences of my unhappy life and, if it is possible to give me too some advice, then, please, do it. I will write the truth: It would have never occurred to me in all my life to go and bother anyone about my troubles. But when I realized that in our "Forward" many readers tell of even worse troubles than those which I have to bear, a great desire to write down on paper all I feel took hold of me. But the greatest impetus to write about myself was given me by one of your articles on servant girls. It seemed to me as if the writer of that article was a good friend of mine and knew my whole biography.

I have been a servant girl these 2 years. I came to America six years ago. For 4 years I worked in a shop and I lost all my strength which I had gathered while at home, but I was still strong enough to be employed as a servant girl and to work with more strength than I had. But I am not worrying about my hard work. A poor man must work nowadays in order to make a living, but my moral troubles, which I had to endure being a maid, made me thin and emaciated. When I worked in the shop, so when I came home, I would sit quite contentedly at the table and enjoy myself along with the entire household, but I contracted consumption and had to go to Denver, Colorado. I feel quite well here, I get better, but as there are no [work] shops here, I am compelled to be a servant girl. My first job was with Gentiles and with an upstart real estate operator to boot. And here is what happened: Not an evening passed when the house was not full of guests. The tables were set with all good things, and I, tired out, broken, sat in the kitchen at the table with the dog and the cat. And in case the son or the mistress wanted to spit, they found no other place to spit in than the kitchen and exactly at the time when I ate.

I believe every human heart can feel how depressed I felt sitting in the kitchen alone, separated from human beings. Besides no guest left without poking his nose into the kitchen to see who the maid was and to abuse her in obscene language. And when I made myself a dress, I noticed how it aggravated my mistress. In short, it is impossible to imagine the pain I suffered there. Well, now I am with rich German Jews, so I tell you, that I feel even more depressed and unhappy than when I was with the Gentiles. I am writing you this letter, in order that servant girls the world over might understand their plight, as I do, and might understand as I do as to who it was that humiliated them and brought them to such a horrible position. And then if they only knew it, they would have united [in socialistic unions] and our position would then have been greatly bettered.

> With socialist greetings
> "Trilby"

D

JUVENILE DELINQUENCY

> February 27th 1906.

Dear Mr. Editor of the "Forward"!

I read the troubles of family life in your *Bintel Brief* each day very attentively. But my own troubles are so great, so enormous, that I will not even ask for your permission to print my few words in your paper, as others do, but simply: I ask you right on the spot: Help! Save me and save also thousands of other unhappy fathers.

The story I want to tell you is this. I have two little girls, one is 10 years old and the other, 13. Both girls go to school. The school is on the East Side. A few months ago a friend of mine told me that he saw one of my girls walking about arm-in-arm with a little boy, who probably goes to the same school with her. I happen to be a busy man; I have a stationery store and am always occupied; I cannot even get away for a minute. Then my wife is busy with a little tot, and she too cannot leave the house. So with tears in my eyes I begged my friend to stop working for a few days at my

expense and watch my 2 girls. My friend did not refuse me thi
favor, and he watched my 2 girls on the other side walk, as soon a
the children left school. And he saw something horrible. As soo
as my daughter walked out of school, they walked up to th
corner of the street and stood waiting . . . About 15 minutes late
two boys of the same school, really, walked up and the 4 of ther
went away. My friend followed them and he saw the boys too
candy, chocolates and peanuts from their pockets and treated m
daughters. The girls would take the presents and for this woul
drag around for many hours through tens of streets.

It would not have grieved me because they walked around, bu
my friend saw such wicked behavior on the part of the boys, wh
are very much like the "gang" of the great bandits. At each stree
corner they would go into a hall[way]. My daughters would laug
out loud and my friend heard both times how they agreed to mee
in the evening at a certain spot in Hester Street Park. My frien
watched them in the park, too, and his face burned for shame a
what he saw the little bandits do, and at the indifference of the
girls. Walking home from the park they several times walked int
other hall[ways]. What they did there, this my friend did not see
because I told him not to show himself to my daughters (the
know him).

I myself am afraid to ask them about it. In dear Americ
thousands of cases happen where children run away from hom
altogether for shame and may even do harm to themselves.

But just imagine my position and my wife's position when my
daughters are already so corrupted in their childhood days; wha
will become of them as grown-ups?

I cannot keep them in the house: they claim, that they have t
go to their friends and have to study together. And so I am dyin
of my troubles and can find no way out. I am afraid to turn to th
police, lest they be given over to the "Gerry Society" and eve
there, I think, they do not turn into nuns. [The New Yor
Society for the Prevention of Cruelty to Children was a favorit
philanthropy of Elbridge Thomas Gerry (1837–1927).]

What is to be done, dear Editor? How can one save young
children from eternal shame? Cry it aloud to all parents; the
should take council and see what can be done. I am sure I am no

he only one; there are thousands of such unhappy fathers besides me who do not know yet of their misfortune.

But I beg you to give me some advice personally, if I ought to tell them in strong terms to stop carrying on with the boys. I really cannot do it; I love them too much and I fear unfortunate results, but I decided to do as you will advise me.

Not hoping, but being sure that my words will be printed in your worthy paper, I remain with greetings,

The Unhappy Father

E
THE PROBLEMS OF SABBATH OBSERVANCE

March 13th, 1906.

Dear Editor!

I see that you satisfy everyone in your *Bintel Brief* with your answer. So I decided to ask you a question. I am very interested to know whether or not I am acting correctly. My question consists of the following: My brother-in-law, who is not long in this country, does not like the education I give my children. He says that when I do not tell my children that one must not write on the Sabbath, it is very bad. I tell him however that I cannot help myself. I have a store, to which I must attend on the Sabbath, and naturally there is writing to do. I cannot teach my children that I may and they may not. But my brother-in-law says that I act very badly. This grieves me very much. I want them to hear your opinion, dear Editor!

With respect,

Philadelphia
Chaver [Comrade] Rosenberg

100

ROSE HARRIET PHELPS STOKES AND THE WORKING WOMAN
1906

Rose Harriet Pastor Phelps Stokes (1879–1933) might well be referred to as a proletarian Cinderella. Born in Poland, she was helping her mother make a living when only four, and went to work in a cigar factory in Cleveland, Ohio, when little more than a child. After the family moved to the Bronx, New York, this gifted young lady, then twenty-four, became a writer on the staff of the Yiddish-language Jewish Daily News. *Two years later, in 1905, she married James Graham Phelps Stokes, a wealthy aristocrat who advocated Socialism.*

In 1906, an article by Rose on the condition of American working women appeared in the Annals of the American Academy of Political and Social Science. *Excerpts of it are printed below. Her approach was that of a Socialist. After the Bolsheviks seized power in Russia, she became a Communist and barely escaped going to jail for ten years when indicted under the Espionage Act of 1917 for a letter she had written attacking the government. Her conviction was later reversed on appeal.*

Despite the fact that she had but two or three years of schooling, she became a cultured woman, a poet, and a painter. In 1925, Mr. Stokes divorced her; in 1933, she died in a hospital in Frankfort on the Main, Germany, where she had undergone an operation for cancer.

THE CONDITION OF WORKING WOMEN, FROM THE WORKING
WOMAN'S VIEWPOINT
by Rose H. Phelps Stokes,
New York City

The topic, "The Condition of the Working Woman," itself suggests forcibly the chief evil which working women have to face. The selection of this particular topic by those who have arranged the program of the annual meeting of the Academy calls attention to the assumption prevailing throughout our country, particularly among men and women of the employing class, that a rather natural distinction exists between women who work and women who do not. It is not uncommon to find the view held by people of culture that it is entirely proper for women to be thus divided: for some to produce far more than they require to supply the needs of themselves and their families, and for others to consume far more than their own efforts produce.

Obviously it would be improper to regard the products of manual toil as the only products necessary to human welfare. It is evident that grace and culture and refinement are in themselves human products of much usefulness, and that a world devoid of these would be a cold and dreary place in which to pass our days. Grace and culture and refinement, where these are expressions of real feeling and of depth of human desire to be just and courteous and true, are evidently of large human value; so much so, that where economic and industrial conditions prevail such as to hinder or prevent their development, it becomes desirable to ask whether the conditions are necessary which thus thwart progress, and whether they could not be so modified and changed by human effort that none need be deprived of opportunity to make constant progress toward all that is admirable in manhood or womanhood.

It must be perceived by even the casual observer that working women, as a rule, are permitted to retain but a portion of the value of what they produce; that they add more value to the material upon which they work than they receive in payment for their labor; that the average working woman produces, on the whole, more than she consumes, and that the excess is consumed by those who produce insufficient for their own maintenance, and who would probably resent being called working women; yet who are thus as dependent as any pauper is upon the labor of others. In other words, much of the hardship of the working classes is consequent upon the fact that they are obliged not merely to support their own families, but to contribute, whether they will or not, to the support of other families which live in idle luxury upon the products of working people's toil. It is the nearly universal recognition of this fact among the working people of our country that leads more than all else to strikes and industrial disturbances, to ill-will, to class hatred, and to that craving for larger justice which underlies the socialistic program. . . .

Every working man and working woman feels the need of recreation and social enjoyment, and particularly so after hours of arduous toil. . . .

It is true that many employers of women's labor seek to supply the need to which I have alluded by the introduction into their industrial communities of what has become known as welfare work. . . .

Far be it from the working girl to object to improvement of industrial conditions, however inadequate such improvement may be. But, while appreciating the improvement, she knows that even with it she must necessarily get less than the fair reward for her labor if she receive for her day's work barely enough to hold body and soul together, while those who exploit her labor live in luxury and wastefulness, and spend in extravagant living what she has earned. She often realizes that the idle classes harm not only the working classes by their extravagances, but themselves as well. She sees in a vague sort of way that they make themselves unjust, and she can see neither rhyme nor reason in an economic system that checks tendencies toward spiritual perfection—the goal and reason of all human life.

An enormous majority of working women live and labor under conditions inimical to health and happiness. Nearly one-third of the deaths among working women between the ages of twenty and forty-five occur from tuberculosis alone, and these deaths are due almost always to needlessly bad conditions of tenements and shops. The bad conditions are maintained, usually, by people of the employing and propertied classes, who prefer to continue them rather than suffer such slight curtailment of revenue as improvement might cause. . . .

Throughout the length and breadth of our land the terrible question faces our people: Shall the health and lives of our workers continue to be jeopardized and sacrificed to swell the incomes of the few?

The working girl does not object to the accumulation of wealth when accumulation harms no one; but her soul cries out in revolt

gainst the callousness and heedlessness of those who in their mad
reed for gain ignore the conditions under which the gain is
roduced. She sees herself and her sisters struggling ten or twelve
r fourteen hours a day under conditions destructive to health and
) progress, in order that the incomes of employers and their
imilies may be large enough to sustain them in luxurious living.
he and her working sisters see the daughters of their employers
ad idle and self-indulgent lives upon profits wrung from the
ealth and strength, and often from the virtue of those who must
gnore industrial injustice or starve. "By what right," she cries,
whether divine or human, am I and my sisters compelled to
xhaust body and soul that other human beings may be idle and
vasteful, and even destroy their own souls in vicious and
noughtless living?"

The working woman sees the women of the employing class
nock the teachings of their great religious leader by manifesting
verywhere, contrary to His injunctions, pride, vain glory, and
ypocrisy. Instead of "remembering the Sabbath day to keep it
oly" they choose that day of all others to "make broad their
hylacteries and enlarge the borders of their garments," and to
gnore His injunctions to humility and consideration of one's
ellows. [It is interesting, ironic, to note that in order to make a
oint, she does not hesitate to cite a New Testament passage
·hich criticizes severely Jewish religious leaders (Matt. 23:5).

"Love thy neighbor as thyself" sounds hollow and derisive to
ne working girl, who on the Sabbath day, and many other days,
ees wealth and fashion "pass by on the other side" in all their
now and glitter, while the victims of greed and oppression lie
.ck and poverty stricken in tenements close by.

As to the subject of religion, it is difficult for the working girl to
ely upon its teachings, when on every hand she see the wicked,
ne dishonorable and the covetous in high places, and the
najority of honest workers abased, and compelled by cir-
umstances beyond their control to toil and suffer excessively;
articularly is it difficult for her to respect those churches in
·hich "uppermost seats" are bought and paid for, like so much
nerchandise, with money unjustly earned. The working girl who
eceived her first Christian precepts from a hard-working mother

may have a deep and abiding respect and love for Jesus and His teachings, and faith in the ultimate triumph of right, but she cannot respect that false religion miscalled Christianity, and those false teachings of its preachers, which confine themselves to blasphemously singing praises of God while repudiating the great commandment to "Love thy neighbor as thyself." For there is no loving one's neighbor as one's self, says the working woman, where one's self lives in wealth and luxury and affluence while one's neighbor, like the victim in the parable, lies robbed wounded, starved and dying on the Jericho road, priests churchmen and pharisees seeing his affliction, but "passing by on the other side". . . .

A word must be said in regard to the working girl's attitude toward that patronizing, condescending type of interest shown so often by rich women toward working girls' clubs. It is far too common in our settlement houses and elsewhere, even in tenement homes themselves, to find wealthy women very expensively dressed attempting to encourage the so-called unfortunates by visiting them and telling them what they should do. Not long ago in one of the principal settlement houses of New York, a very fashionably dressed woman, a lorgnette dangling from her finger tips, opened the door of a working girls' club, uninvited, and raising her lorgnette to her eyes, surveyed the group before her and, as though desiring to compliment the girls, remarked in the hearing of all, "What a very attractive looking lot of working girl these are!" This sort of thing is by no means rare. Wealthy women visiting settlement houses, as they do in large numbers feel offended if their desire to visit intrusively every club in the building is discouraged by those in charge. In some of the large settlement houses an evening rarely passes without from two to one-half dozen groups of such visitors showing their lack of regard for the feelings of others by intruding upon the privacy of one club after another, inspecting them successively as they inspect animals in their cages at the zoo. As a rule the poorer girls members of these clubs, have sufficient good breeding to refrain from manifesting resentment at the intrusion, but too often such intrusions on the part of merely curious persons, slumming parties, and so forth, are carried to the degree of extreme discourtesy and become intolerable. But good-will and pleasure are always manifested by the members when they are visited out of pure friendliness, without condescension and without patronage.

And now a word as to the attitude of the working girl toward organized charity. She knows that there is no true charity except where there is true sympathy, and that true sympathy can exist only in proportion as there is true understanding of personal needs and feelings. To be sure, there are many working women who will readily accept donations of money or food or clothing, whether the gifts be given by ward politicians seeking the votes of the husbands, or by such of the rich as seek through "charity" to "cover a multitude of sins," or by societies which advertise conspicuously the donors to their funds; but most self-respecting women would rather go without asking for aid of any kind until they are half starved and half frozen than accept the doles of hard-hearted men in high places, or the doles of ostentation, hypocrisy, or sham, wherever or however offered. . . .

This prevailing distinction that is so commonly made between "worthy" and "unworthy" applicants for relief is, in the opinion of the writer, most mistaken and unfortunate. Not that every drunkard and loafer should be maintained in vice and idleness by the gifts of well-meaning people, or that any one should be given anything inimical to his or her highest welfare, but no man or woman is so degraded as to be unworthy of aid to a better and worthier life. The more degraded men and women are, the more worthy they are of aid to nobler living, and of relief from the thralldom of evil ways and evil environments. We cannot have too much of the kind of relief that does truly relieve, or too much aid of the kind that does enable men and women to become more self-respecting, self-sustaining, self-denying members of a community. There is no relief in throwing an anchor to a drowning man or in throwing money to one who is being morally and spiritually drowned in vice and profligacy. What the struggler needs in either instance is an opportunity to live and labor under conditions less destructive of physical or moral welfare. The relief must be suited to the sufferer, but relief of the right kind need never be withheld.

More fellow-feeling is what the world most needs, more true sympathy, more determination to promote justice and right living, by being just and living right one's self; more readiness to subordinate one's personal desires in consideration of the needs of one's fellows, and of the underlying causes which occasion those needs; more of the sort of charity which leads the individual not merely to offer aid to those who suffer, but to search out and remove from human environments the needlessly harmful conditions and the far-reaching manifestations of human greed and injustice that usually underlie the conditions to which, in last analysis, most of the suffering is due.

101

A NEAR MASSACRE
1906.

The American ethos was not easily understood by many of the mothers who hailed from the relatively primitive lands of Eastern Europe. Most of the Jewish immigrants who lived on New York's Lower East Side had received little secular education; they were not a sophisticated lot. No less than 27 percent of the newcomers landing at New York's Ellis Island in 1906 were illiterate. The women among them, though illiterate, were not a submissive lot, nor were they easily cowed. Mass demonstrations by them were not an unusual form of protest. In 1902, they rioted in New York, Newark, Boston, and other cities because of the high cost of kosher meat. At that time, large numbers stormed butcher shops, with dozens being arrested and fined.

When, in June 1906, these women heard that their children attending New York's public schools were being killed, they came to the rescue. Thousands rioted in the city, moving against the schoolhouses until the police reserves were called in to disperse them. It should not be forgotten that most of these women had come from Russia and Poland, where pogroms were common; during this very month of June 1906, seventy Jews were murdered in Bialystok with the connivance of the government.

What actually happened to arouse these apprehensive mothers in New York City is described below.

East Side Women Riot.

Stone Schoolhouses

Minor Operations on Children Spread Rumors of Murder

Rioting women and children by the thousand swept into a senseless panic by an absurd story that children's throats were being cut by physicians in various East Side schools, swarmed down on those buildings all over the lower East Side in great mobs yesterday, intent on rescuing their children and companions. Excitable, ignorant Jews, fearing Russian massacres here, knowing nothing of American sanitary ideas and the supervision exercised over school children by the Health Board, outdid all previous resistance to vaccination. They stoned the schoolhouses, smashing windows and door panels, and except for the timely intervention of police reserves from several precincts, would without doubt have done serious injury to the frightened women teachers.

As it was, the affair was a tempest in a teapot. One or two minor arrests were made, and the police had their hands full for a couple of hours. The serious rioting, which would have become dangerous if the men had had time to join in it, occurred just before noon. Teachers, learning what the trouble was, dismissed their pupils, and the sight of the multitudes of uninjured children stifled the mothers' wrath.

The excitement lasted all the afternoon, however. Three or four patrolmen were kept on duty at each schoolhouse in the East Side, and the doors and windows of each building were closed. These guards adopted summary methods for quelling what excitement was left. Almost every one armed himself with a long, supple slat from one of the numerous new buildings all through that section, and when voluble Yiddish women of luxuriant flesh or chattering young Hebrews formed a group before the schoolhouses, they were persuaded to depart by vigorous application of the slats to the most convenient section of the nearest "Yiddisher."

"There's goin' to be no spoilin' of these childer," explained a patrolman, who was engaged in this unusual occupation, to a passerby. "We're not sparin' the rod any. They want riot over here all the time—bread riots, meat riots, coal riots, and now the wimmin and childer is havin' one for thimsilves. They'll git it," he declared grimly as he set about hastening the departure of some half grown boys who had become obstreperous. They got it, soundly.

The panic grew out of minor operations by Health Board

physicians on several of the children, and a great deal of vaccination among the children in preparation for the usual summer disease epidemic. Such vaccination is always accomplished only by force in the lower East Side.

Last week Miss A. E. Simpson, principal of Public School 100, at Broome and Cannon streets, found that many of the children were suffering from adenoids, a fungus growth at the back of the mouth and nasal passages, which can be removed by a simple operation. The consent of parents is necessary before physicians may perform such an operation. Miss Simpson weeded out the cases and explained the situation, telling them that, if possible, their children should go to private physicians or hospitals; but if not, the Board of Health physicians would do the work. Most of the parents probably misunderstood, but last Thursday public physicians operated on many of the children.

Since then a rumor has been afloat that a slaughter of the innocents surpassing Herod's was in prospect [Matt. 2:16]. This story, several of the teachers suspect, has been augmented by the reports of ignorant mischief makers, and possibly by some of the cheap "fake" physicians, of whom the East Side has at least its share.

The trouble came to a head in half an hour yesterday. The mobs of women descended on the schools, crying out that their children were being murdered and buried in the school yards. The riot belt extended from Rivington street to Grand, and from the Bowery to the East River. In the more easterly section the violence was greatest. In almost every case the windows of the schoolhouses were riddled with stones. . . .

Captain Byrne of the Delancey street station, as soon as he learned of the rioting, sent out all his reserves, but the trouble by that time had spread to so many schools that he was forced to call for help from several West Side precincts. The Essex Market police court, in the heart of the district, was closed for half an hour, that the court officers might help in quelling the riot at School 37, Grand and Essex streets.

A physician connected with the Board of Education, while attempting to leave Public School 36, at 9th street and Avenue C, was set upon by the mob gathered in front of the school and his hat was knocked off. He ran from the crowd, which followed him, aiming blows at him from all sides.

He ran into a drug store at Avenue C and 8th street, hatless, and asked for protection against the crowd, part of which followed him into the store and repeated their threats and blows. Patrolman Burke, of the Union Market station, forced his way through the crowd and entered the shop, where he found Max Scott, seventeen years old, of No. 643 East 13th street, holding a loaded revolver at the physician's head, while the latter stood with his hands above his head.

Burke drew his revolver and disarmed and arrested Scott. In the confusion the physician got away without his name being taken.

Captain Cooney, of the Union Market station, who single handed tried to disperse the angry crowd in front of Public School 188, at Houston and Manhattan streets, received a bad beating from a couple of irate mothers. The captain at last managed to telephone for the reserves of the Union Market station to come and help him. All the reserves and detectives, however, were out at other schools. Doorman John Falway went to the captain's aid, and the two managed to keep the crowd in fair order until more assistance could reach them.

Much excitement was caused at the school at Attorney and Stanton streets, when Leon King, brushing aside women, children and policemen, made a dive for the iron doors shouting in Yiddish that his children were being murdered and he must save them. He had battered himself half insensible before the patrolmen could check him. He was arrested for disorderly conduct. Women in the various mobs got to fighting among themselves to get nearest to the doors. They tore out handfuls of hair, and their dresses after the fray were a little more open than is customary even in East Side social circles.

And then, as suddenly as it had risen, the trouble lost its serious aspect. The teachers had learned its reason, and line after line of children began marching out of the buildings. The screaming, fighting mothers caught their own progeny and hurried home, helped along by indignant police reserves whose sleep had been spoiled. Commencement exercises in many schools were postponed. No fatalities were reported, but the East Side lost all interest in the discussion of Kosher "wurst" to gossip over this "near massacre."

102

JENNIE FRANKLIN PURVIN: CHICAGO CLUBWOMAN
1907–1958

Jennie Franklin Purvin (1873–1958) was anything but a typical Chicago Jewess. She was a most unusual and exceptionally able woman. While still young, she left the university, during the panic of the 1890's, to run her father's cigar business after he had suffered a physical collapse. In a relatively short time, she became one of Chicago's best-known clubwomen. She was active and creative in both the Jewish and larger civic communities. Two men influenced her, both clergymen—Emil G. Hirsch, a Reform rabbi, and Jenkin Lloyd Jones, a Unitarian minister. Her biography documents the accomplishments of one woman in many fields of civic, cultural, and even commercial endeavor. Jennie Purvin's achievements were many, but what is even more significant, some of them were very important. It is difficult to believe that one person—even in a long lifetime—could be so effective. She was no joiner; she was nearly always an important executive in the institutions with which she was associated, often the initiator of productive, original programs.

The list of organizations enumerated in the following biographical sketch does not exhaust her interests. In addition to those recorded here, she worked with Hadassah and other local Zionists; she sponsored public open-air concerts, labored for international peace, and also found time to publish numerous articles and short stories.

JENNIE FRANKLIN PURVIN: A STUDY IN WOMANPOWER

by Neil Kominsky

When one finds a woman credited with almost single-handed responsibility for so major an institution as public bathing beaches in the city of Chicago, there is a certain tendency to sit up and take note. When one finds the same woman called "the Jewish Jane Addams" in Miss Addams' own home territory and during

25. Jennie Franklin Purvin

her lifetime, one is likewise inclined to pay attention. This is as it should be, however, for Jennie Franklin Purvin, who enjoyed this reputation, made a career—in fact, several careers—of making people sit up and take notice. In more than half a century of activity, Jennie Purvin left her mark in the fields of art, politics, business, philanthropy, education, recreation, and literature, among others, and her efforts influenced the lives of millions of Chicagoans. She had, in fact, two distinct careers, each of them of a quarter century duration, each of them full, varied, and highly successful. The first of these careers began when Mrs. Purvin, already in her middle thirties, married, and the mother of two girls, became a leader in the P.T.A., Chicago Women's Aid, Chicago Women's City Club and numerous other organizations concerned with civic and humanitarian interests. Her accomplishments in this field between 1907 and 1933 constitute, in themselves, the first of a long and useful career in voluntary public service. Yet, in 1933, at sixty years of age, Jennie Purvin undertook a second career as library trustee and, shortly thereafter, as director of a complex of service functions in a large department store, a career fully as long and as fruitful as her previous activities as a clubwoman. The sum of the accomplishments of these two careers represents a monument to the effectiveness and determination of one very thorough, efficient, and remarkably tenacious woman.

Jennie Franklin Purvin was born in Chicago in 1873, the daughter of Henry B. and Hannah Mayer Franklin. Her life seems, from the very beginning, to have been woven into the fabric of Chicago. Her maternal grandfather, Louis Mayer, came to Chicago in the 1840's and was one of the founders of Sinai Congregation. She was also proud to point out that her granduncle, Leopold Mayer, was the first Hebrew teacher in Chicago. Her mother was born and educated in Chicago, and in 1872 married Henry B. Franklin, who had emigrated from Germany five years before and established himself as a cigar manufacturer. The Franklins were the first couple to be married in Chicago by Kaufmann Kohler. Jennie graduated from the North Division High School in Chicago and planned to attend the University of Michigan. When her father fell ill, however, she went to work full-time assisting him in his business. She attended a business school briefly, continuing her education over many years as a night and extension student at the University of Chicago.

Jennie was apparently independent-minded even as a child. As a footnote to her campaign for bathing beaches, she told the story of her battle for permission to be given swimming lessons, permission which was withheld by her father because swimming was not considered to be a suitable activity for young ladies at that time. Only after her brother almost drowned was permission grudgingly granted, and surreptitiously, with great care not to scandalize the neighbors, Jennie was taught to swim.

In 1899, Jennie Franklin married Moses L. Purvin and settled down to the business of being a housewife and raising a family, and in her spare time joined Chicago Women's Aid. This marked the beginning of her first career, clubwoman extraordinaire and outspoken advocate of the public interest. . . .

Jennie Purvin's Jewish interests, as may be gathered from what we have already said, were extensive. Her diary regularly recorded the subject and quality of the Sunday morning services at Sinai Congregation. She was an organizer and secretary of the Chicago branch of the Jewish Welfare Board, president of the Chicago chapter of the National Council of Jewish Women, president of the Sinai Congregation Sisterhood, and a very active member of the Board of Jewish Education of Chicago. She also established and administered a loan fund to assist Hebrew Union College students who wanted to spend a summer studying at the University of Chicago. Her correspondence with these students indicates that she not only assisted them financially, but also befriended them and, in many cases, maintained contact with them for years afterward. . . .

The bathing beaches were perhaps Jennie Purvin's most notable accomplishment. In 1911, swimming in Chicago meant trespassing on debris and garbage-covered beaches for an unprotected, unsupervised dip in the lake. Jennie Purvin's articles and speeches portrayed this situation in graphic detail to anyone who would lend her an ear. Her reports to the Women's City Club on the activities of the Bathing Beaches Committee document a remarkable series of one-woman forays into the darkest depths of the Chicago municipal bureaucracy. No detail was beneath Jennie Purvin's attention when she went to work on a problem. From mayor's office to alderman's office, to city engineer, city architect, city legal counsel, wherever the problem of the bathing beaches led, she followed. With incredible tenacity, she followed every lead, investigated every excuse, extorted promises from harried city officials and was back the next week to see that the promises had been fulfilled. One cannot help suspecting that more than one municipal official was less than overjoyed to find Jennie Purvin in his office. Gradually, the dream in Mrs. Purvin's mind became a reality, as land was set aside and cleared, lifeguards hired, rights of way obtained, all obstacles overcome, so that every year Chicagoans found themselves with expanded and improved public bathing facilities.

As a woman who was closely identified with the beaches in Chicago, Jennie Purvin became involved in many interesting situations. One in particular illustrates well the wry sense of humor and open-mindedness which seem to have contributed much to her success. A letter from a Baptist minister to a local public decency organization concerning bathing suits was referred to Mrs. Purvin. The good clergyman, much perturbed by "indecent" women's bathing suits that actually climbed above the knee, demanded action to correct the problem. Mrs. Purvin, who seems to have shared the minister's basic dislike for immodest dress, took to heart the swimmers' protest that it was healthful to expose greater areas of the body to the sun and consulted several physicians on the subject. To her distress, the doctors informed her that the maximum benefit from the sun was to be derived from total exposure of the body. This being impossible, she concluded, it was best to "evade the situation by letting bathing suits take care of themselves."

Jennie Purvin's activities concerning comfort stations and recreation facilities followed the pattern of her bathing beaches campaign. Relentlessly running down necessary facts and arguing persuasively both with civic organizations and public officials, she convinced the city to build public comfort stations in busy areas, forced the institution of a merit system for the appointment of municipal playground and recreation supervisors, and brought about the expansion and improvement of public recreation facilities for both children and adults. . . .

The library and her club work, however, were apparently not adequate to occupy Mrs. Purvin's time. In 1934, she approached Col. Leon Mandel, president of Mandel Brothers Department Store, with the idea of delivering book reviews—a frequent club activity of hers—under the store's auspices. Col. Mandel, impressed by the value of her activities, suggested instead that Mrs. Purvin move all her club work into the store. Jennie Purvin went even a little further than that and established three entirely new areas of activity in the store, the Club Women's Bureau, the Camp Advisory Bureau, and the Art Gallery, all of which were under her personal direction until her retirement in 1957. The Club Women's Bureau, a rather elaborate name for an operation that generally consisted of Jennie Purvin and two secretaries, provided meeting facilities, programs, and service for the city's women's organizations. The packed monthly schedules which fill Mrs. Purvin's reports to Col. Mandel attest to the utility of this service. Immediately before and during World War II, Jennie Purvin entertained troops in Chicago with tours, programs and refreshments under the auspices of the Club Women's Bureau. . . .

The Mandel Brothers Art Gallery which Jennie Purvin established fulfilled a special role in the cultural life of the city. For twenty-three years—it outlasted Mrs. Purvin's retirement by only three months—the gallery provided a showing spot for native Chicagoan art talent. No attempt was made to compete with major museums and galleries for classics and big names. Rather, the emphasis was constantly on local, unsung talent. Although claiming no special artistic training or taste herself, Jennie Purvin ran a gallery which won the applause of the artists of Chicago for its non-commercial nature. The citation of honor which she received from the Chicago chapter of the Artists Equity Association after her retirement from Mandel Brothers attests to the esteem in which she was held.

At eighty-four, Jennie Franklin Purvin commented in an interview: "I didn't have many diversions . . . I never knew how to dress, never used power until I was fifty or lipstick until a month ago. I never had a group of my own, or a social circle. I just worked. But life owes me nothing. I've had such a good time!"

In the course of having a good time, Jennie Purvin spent more than fifty years serving the interests of the people of Chicago. She left in her wake bathing beaches, public comfort stations, well-tended and supervised public recreation facilities, and, through her activities on the Library Board and at Mandel Brothers, helped to provide cultural and educational experiences for millions of people. Few people, at the end of their lives, can look back on one significant accomplishment which has affected the lives of others. Jennie Purvin could look back on many such accomplishments. The secret behind her success was the energy, determination, and intelligence of a one-woman-power dynamo. In a way that very few private citizens can match, Jennie Franklin Purvin left her mark on the society in which she lived.

103

THE BIRTH OF A SINGER, ALMA GLUCK
1909

Alma Gluck (Reba Fiersohn, 1884–1938) was born in Rumania, but brought to America while still a child. After studying in the public school of the Lower East Side, she became a stenographer until her marriage in 1902. In 1909, this charming, attractive women, a lyric soprano, made her debut in opera. Her forte, however, was not opera but classical European lieder and heartwarming American ballads and folk songs. She was one of this country's most notable musical recitalists. It is reported that almost 2,000,000 copies of her recording of "Carry Me Back to Old Virginny" were sold. Among the several bequests in her will was one to St. Thomas' Church in New York City. She had become a convert to Christianity.

The following obituary outlines her life and career.

ALMA GLUCK DEAD, OPERATIC SOPRANO

Former Star of Metropolitan Was Among Most Popular Recitalists of Her Day

HELPED MUSICAL CAUSES

Aided in Launching of Many Music Organizations—Wife of Efrem Zimbalist

Alma Gluck, wife of Efrem Zimbalist, the violinist, and an internationally famous soprano in her own right until her retirement in 1925, died yesterday at 9:30 A.M. at Rockefeller Institute Hospital at the age of 54. She had been ill for a long time and had been taken to the hospital several days ago.

The funeral will be of the utmost simplicity, according to Mme. Gluck's own wishes. Only the immediate family will be present.

26. Alma Gluck

Surviving besides Mr. Zimbalist, are three children: Mrs. Marcia Davenport, a daughter by a previous marriage and a prominent writer, Mrs. Ogden Goelet, who is the former Maria Zimbalist, and Efrem Zimbalist, Jr.

Mme. Gluck made her mark as a singer thirty years ago. For a short time she was a member of the Metropolitan Opera. Thereafter she became one of the most popular concert singers in the period before the World War. She was also one of the most successful makers of records.

When her career as an active artist diminished and ceased Mme. Gluck did not disappear from the musical scene. She became one of the most important figures in American musical life by virtue of her activities in behalf of music.

Gave Famous Musical Parties

Until she became ill she was one of New York's celebrated hostesses. Her musical parties became famous. Musicians of every land and persuasion gathered at her home to exchange ideas and to make music.

Alma Gluck was born in Bucharest, Rumania, on May 11, 1884. Her name was Reba Fiersohn, and she took Alma Gluck as her stage name. She was brought to this country by her parents at the age of 3. She attended the public schools and the Normal College here and then went to Union College in Schenectady. After her college course she went to work in a New York law office. [Alma Gluck's formal education stopped when she left high school.] She was married to Bernard Gluck, an insurance salesman, before she began to cultivate her voice in earnest. They parted after her success as a singer.

She studied with Arturo Buzzi-Peccia who was a friend of Giulio Gatti-Casazza and Arturo Toscanini. It was Signor Buzzi-Peccia who arranged one day to have Signor Toscanini visit him at his studio. By prearrangement Alma Gluck called during the maestro's visit. Toscanini was attracted by her beauty and poise. When Signor Buzzi-Peccia observed that Alma had a fine voice, Signor Toscanini asked to hear her. She sang for the maestro and he immediately recommended her engagement at the Metropolitan.

Alma Gluck made her debut in New York as an opera singer on Nov. 6, 1909. She had sung several days before as a member of the Metropolitan in a Philadelphia visit as Gilda in "Rigoletto," a performance in which Titta Ruffo made his American debut in the title role. Her New York debut occurred at the New Theatre (later known as the Century) which was operated as an adjunct of the Metropolitan. Her first local role was Charlotte in "Werther."

Sang Eleven Roles First Season

Her success was immediate. In that first season she sang eleven roles which was something of a record for a freshman in the company. She remained at the Metropolitan until 1913, but found time to appear in recital and as soloist with orchestras. She did not hestitate to continue her studies, coaching with Jean De Reszke and Marcella Sembrich after establishing the foundations of her career.

It was during this period that she established her reputation as a recitalist. In the period before the war there were perhaps only two other women—Ernestine Schumann-Heink and Johanna Gadski—whose names had such magical effect on the box-office receipts. Her fame rested not only on the refinement of her singing, the delicacy of her style, and the intelligence and musicianship that informed everything she did, but also on her attractive appearance and personality.

Alma Gluck, a handsome woman, knew how to dress beautifully. She was one of the first singers to realize that her appeal as an artist would inevitably be enhanced by charm and personality.

Made Popular Records

Alma Gluck's voice and art were among the most successful in recording for the phonograph. One of her records, "Carry Me Back to Ol' [Old] Virginny," sold more than 1,000,000 disks. Her royalties from records in the years between 1914 and 1918 amounted to $600,000. Only such names as Enrico Caruso and John McCormack earned comparable or larger sums.

In 1914 she was married to Mr. Zimbalist. For three years after meeting her in 1911, he admits, he pursued her. He used to wait at the Metropolitan like any ordinary stage-door John.

Their marriage was one of the happiest in the annals of alliances between artists. As musicians, each went his or her own way. Occasionally they appeared in joint programs. Several times Mr. Zimbalist played accompaniments for his wife. In 1925 she retired from active singing and thenceforth devoted herself to her family and to the artistic world.

Mme. Gluck was one of the founders of the American Guild of Musical Artists and a vice president at her death. She helped to start the Musical Art Quartet on its way; the young musicians met and played at her home before they appeared in public. She was one of the chief supports of the Musicians Emergency Fund. She sang for the Red Cross and for the Actors Fund. She appealed for help for the Society of the Friends of Music.

Always her voice was raised for causes and persons she believed in. She was one of the signers of a statement supporting the work of the Musicians Committee to Aid Spanish Democracy.

104

FANNIE HURST FALLS IN LOVE WITH A KIKE AND GOES TO NEW YORK TO BECOME A WRITER
1909

In 1909, Fannie Hurst (b. 1889), daughter of a St. Louis shoe manufacturer, fell in love with Jacques S. Danielson, a Russian-born Jewish musician. Mama was very unhappy: she was "German"; Danielson was a "kike," an offensive epithet describing an East European Jew. Many, probably most Jews of German origin despised Jews from the "East." Mrs. Hurst should have consoled herself with the thought that a kike ceased to be a kike when he became a son-in-law. Fannie married "Jack" some five years after she first met him, though even after marriage they maintained separate households. The following document describes her love for her husband-to-be.

While sweating out her love affair with Danielson, Miss Hurst left home for New York, where she took a variety of jobs in order to understand "life" and prepare herself for a literary career. By 1914, she had achieved a degree of success and soon became one of the country's best-known short-story writers and novelists. It was then, a century after the appearance of the first literate American Jewesses, that women of Jewish origin were for the first time recognized as writers who had "made it" by American standards. In the 1890's, Martha Morton was one of the country's most successful playwrights; Edna Ferber pushed her way to the top in 1912; Fannie Hurst, in 1914. Hurst belonged to the new generation of Jews who did not lower their voices when they uttered the word "Jew" in public. As a woman interested in social reform, she did not hesitate to respond to appeals for help when Jewish organizations turned to her. Like Ferber, she identified with her people. By the early twentieth century, Jewish women had not only become celebrities, they had become mature.

Who has not, at one time or another, indulged in the conjectural game of what-if!

What if I had done this instead of that! What if I had not turned that particular corner, or taken that particular plane! What if I

27. Fannie Hurst

had not decided to study pharmaceutics? What if someone besides John had collided with me that Easter afternoon?

What if, on my See-America-First trip with Papa, I had not suddenly inquired, while thumbing through a timetable en route from Buffalo to Detroit: What is this next stop, Mount Clemens?

Mount Clemens, replied my father, is a famous watering place about twenty miles this side of Detroit. Americans don't have to run to Europe for mineral baths. Mighty fine ones right here.

It was a clear autumn day, the countryside flashing past the train windows.

Let's get off here, Papa. I've never seen a watering place.

It was my first use of my prerogative to change the itinerary and, true to his word, Papa did not demur. He called the porter for the Redbook of hotels and, bag and baggage, off we got at the Mount Clemens station. . . .

I first saw Jack in what might have been the stage setting for a romantic drama by one of those lady writers with three names.

Wandering about the hotel that first day of our arrival, exploring writing rooms, lounges, and solaria, I came upon a small, darkened parlor dominated by a grand piano, my future husband seated before it, his head highlighted by a floor lamp.

I stood unnoticed in the doorway. Had I known him then, I would have realized that he had stolen quietly into the remote room, while most of the guests were at the baths or taking siesta, in order not to be heard.

Something of his sensitivity must have been telegraphed to me. He played the Chopin Etude with that special lacelike quality of his, and I stole away just before he concluded.

It was not love at first sight. It was love before first full sight, because I caught only his silhouette, the nobility of his lowered head, the mobility of his hands.

I did not see him again for two days. Papa expressed surprise at my desire to remain on at the Park Hotel, where there were chiefly older people taking the "cure" and few recreations outside of tennis or boating on the St. Clair River, which flowed past the hotel and on out into Lake St. Clair.

Don't remain here on my account. I enjoy the baths, they are toning me up, but I don't believe there is much here for you.

I lied magnanimously. That's all right. The baths are what you need.

Meanwhile, what had become of *him?* Had he been a mirage? I returned again and again to the dim room with the grand piano, the floor lamp, and the potted palms. I ran my fingers over the keys. In later years he was to tell me that he could always tell when I had touched the keyboard of his piano, and, curiously, he could. I imagine what he meant was that my impact had made them shudder.

Perhaps he had been a one-day guest from Detroit, after the manner of Philadelphians on flying visits to Atlantic City. I scanned the hotel register for a possible clue.

An acquaintance of Mama's had seen our name on the register and sought us out.

Afflicted with a hip ailment, she had been taking the baths for several weeks and appeared to know most of the guests. Several times I stationed myself beside her wheel chair, not quite daring to ask her directly, but waiting.

Mr. Hurst, she said to Papa, I must commend your daughter. How many young girls would take the time to help an old woman while away the hours?

Papa said to me later: It goes to show that modest and considerate behavior is admired. Just you let the flighty girls go their way.

The second day brought its reward. The hotel, remarked Mama's friend, has been unusually quiet since you arrived. Mr. and Mrs. Thal from New Orleans, such lovely people, immensely rich, and their five children left yesterday. The eldest girl, about eighteen, was beautiful and the mother as young looking as the daughter. Did you ever hear a name like Renalda?

No, I had not. Well, it seemed Mrs. Thal had named her eldest after a girl in a novel, and she certainly acted like one. She is engaged to a man down in New Orleans, but her mother had to lock her in her room to keep her from making a complete fool of herself. She went just crazy about a guest in this hotel, who did not seem to know she was on earth.

My ears pointed.

A lovely young man, so handsome, and a splendid musician,

here from New York with the pianist, Rafael Joseffy. If I were twenty-five years younger I would be crazy about him myself. They will be back tonight from a couple of days in Detroit, where Joseffy had a concert. Now, don't you be the next one, she concluded playfully, to have to be locked in your room.

I haunted the poor lady all that afternoon and evening, remaining at her side when she played bridge, joined her after dinner while Papa talked politics with a group of men.

Late in the evening, he walked into the lobby accompanied by a stubby elderly man with a shock of gray hair.

Tall, slim, and straight, the same soft elegance about him that had characterized his Chopin, he had none of the shaggy qualities of his companion, the great Maestro Joseffy. His dress was impeccable, his heavy black hair groomed, his head beautiful in the way that Greek runners and discus throwers were beautiful.

I was smitten to the extent of pain. Pain that he existed outside of my experience. For the first time an overwhelmingly disturbing thought assailed me. He might be married! Why else lock a girl in her room?

Mama's friend sang out: Well, it is about time you two returned from your gallivanting in Detroit. They stopped to exchange pleasantries and I was introduced. I had looked into eyes that for all the lovely years were to light my way, until they closed to this world. And still they light it.

The following morning I sat on the veranda trying to think it through. Papa had remarked at breakfast that it was time for us to be moving along. At best we would have only three or four days left for New York if we were to be back in St. Louis on schedule.

He would probably be in Mount Clemens all the while I would be in New York. It became all important to be in Mount Clemens.

I rocked furiously, I racked my brain furiously, I suffered furiously.

Mama's friend rode by in her wheel chair on her way to the baths and remarked that I had on such a pretty dress, too bad there were not more young men in the hotel to see it. I could not have been less interested in more young men.

Then he came along with Joseffy, so renowned and so hitherto unknown to me. We exchanged good mornings, and after they had passed me three or four times Mr. Joseffy stopped, mopped his brow, and dropped into a chair, his companion beside him.

Mr. Joseffy had a foreign accent. He was jolly and asked me where I came from. When I told him, he wanted to know if I had any Anheuser Busch beer with me and said he had played in the St. Louis Odeon.

Then Mr. Joseffy's attendant came to escort him to his sulphur bath. *He* stayed on.

I do not recall much of that first conversation. Jack has always teased that I did most of the talking. But the probability is I was struck dumb, even though the figure in the lamplight playing Chopin became a rather humorous young man in a checked sports coat, saying teasing things.

And how is your rheumatism this morning? he asked.

I haven't rheumatism.

Then what are you doing at Mount Clemens?

Have you rheumatism?

No.

I wanted to add: Have you a wife?

Gradually, I, with a burning inner intensity, and he, with apparent casualness, drew each other out. He was there as a teaching assistant, friend, and disciple of the great Joseffy. They were returning to New York the following week.

And my father and I will be leaving New York just before you return there.

Do you canoe? was his retort. I do, every afternoon. Would you like to come along today?

I was deathly afraid of canoes. But would I come along! . . .

It is true that by the time we drew up once more at the hotel dock I had learned that he shrank from public appearances necessitated by concertizing; that besides assisting Maestro Joseffy he had his own teaching studios; that he loved the theater and was a *first-nighter*, a phrase new to me; that he had never until now been more than two hundred miles out of New York; that he had been born within the shadow of the Czar's Palace in Moscow, where his father had been royal sculptor; and that he had come to the United States as a lad of sixteen.

He left me at the elevator with a light impersonal handshake.
Will I see you before we leave tomorrow?

In case we don't, he said, be a good country girl when you get to
the big city. That was all there was to it. . . .

In all the months, there had been at most a half dozen postcards
from Mr. Danielson, simple, informal, half humorous, wholly
unamorous. . . .

Mama, of course, had inquired about these cards.

Oh, just a man I met in Mount Clemens.

It's like pulling teeth to get a word out of that child. What man?

You wouldn't know. A musician staying at the hotel with
Rafael Joseffy.

Who?

You wouldn't know. A famous musician.

Is Joseffy the man who writes to you?

No, he was with him.

I asked who is the man who writes to you?

A musician too, Mama. A wonderful musician.

That's all we need. A musician. They don't earn salt. Leave it
to you to find the men who don't. Did your father meet him?

No.

Funny.

We just met once or twice.

Mama softened. Who are his people?

How should I know?

Well, if I met a young man and corresponded with him I would
know. Is he a New Yorker by birth?

Here it came!

No.

Where do they come from originally?

What difference does that make?

Kikes? The word that usually went through me like a knife
drew blood this time.

I don't know and I don't care. All I know is his little finger is
worth more than all the smug ones in this town put together.

Where was he born?

I don't know, I lied a little wildly.

I can see now why you didn't want your father to meet him.

Mama, I only met this man a couple of times. He was with a great celebrity. Isn't that enough?

I don't see why I worry myself. If you don't want to take your parents into your confidence, all I can say is when you go to New York keep away from such. New York, they say, is filled with them—Russians and Galicians. . . .

Tumultuous indecisions continued to sweep over me. The fleeting glimpse of New York, so dazzling, had nevertheless given me an idea of its immensity. Papa had felt that sense of aloneness in the crowds. This town certainly makes one feel insignificant, he had remarked as we stood on a street corner, looking upward at the buildings reaching for the sky.

What assurance had I that Jacques Danielson would have time for me in all that vastness? Or that editors would be any more receptive to my writings than they were a thousand miles away? Simultaneously, I wanted to go with the same old overwhelming urgency, and yet I wanted to stay with Mama and Papa, safe and sound on Cates Avenue. . . .

Likewise, Mama, during these weeks of preparation, sobbed as she packed my clothing. Once, in the act of cramming into my trunk more pairs of stockings than I would use in a year, she cried out suddenly, reaching her arms toward me: Baby, don't leave me. You're my life. Don't leave me and Papa. . . .

I won't, Mama, I cried. I love you so much. Take my things out. I'll stay with you and Papa always and ever.

Such unprecedented fireworks of emotion reduced us both to limpness. When Papa came home, we met him with assurances that things had resolved themselves; and then Papa, also on the verge of tears, used the strongest term of endearment I had ever heard from him.

Sweetheart, he said, this is the most sensible decision you have ever made. It will add years to your mother's life.

What had I done!

Compromise with me, Papa, I cried. Let me get it out of my system for a little while, and then I'll be satisfied, I feel sure, to do as you say. Just let me try it!

This time Mama, poor dear, flared into one of her most frightening states.

Sam, before you leave this house tomorrow, I want you to see that she has her ticket to New York. She goes, or I'll go to the lunatic asylum.

Looking back, I marvel at the ruthlessness which drove me on. For us on our tight little island of three, this tempest was not in a teapot. It was a holocaust. For two more weeks, while all about us Cates Avenue stood embalmed in its static quiet, that holocaust raged in the little house with the stone facade and the brick sides.

The day I departed for New York, with brand-new luggage and my cousin Lester Hurst in his Ford waiting at the door to take me to Union Station, Mama was crying so that Papa feared to risk the strain of train farewells and remained behind with her.

My baby, come home to me soon, screamed Mama after me, and the lace curtains of neighbors parted discreetly.

I rode beside Leslie through rain-streaked streets, admonishing and admonishing my cousin, and Papa's favorite nephew.

Leslie, be good to them—take care of them—go and see them often. . . .

Yeth, said kindly Leslie, who lisped, I'll come often to thee Aunt Rose and Uncle Tham. . . .

105

CLARA LEMLICH SPARKS THE UPRISING OF THE TWENTY THOUSAND
1909

On the evening of November 22, 1909, over 2,000 New York shirtwaist makers assembled at Cooper Union to discuss the possibility of calling a general strike in the industry. Working conditions were almost unbearable. The union leaders, including Samuel Gompers of the American Federation of Labor, hesitated to ask the toilers, mostly young girls, to go out on strike. They knew the sacrifices the young women would have to undergo and the violence they would encounter at the hands of police and thugs. In the midst of the debate, Clara Lemlich made her way to the front and sparked the great assembly with an impassioned plea to go out on strike at once. This was the beginning of the Uprising of the Twenty Thousand, the first successful large-scale protest in the garment industry. It began with a twenty-year-old girl who had come from the Ukraine in 1903; it was a successful job action in which the overwhelming majority of the rebels were young female immigrants.

Remaining loyal to her early social ideals, Clara Lemlich fought throughout her long life for the betterment of her fellow unionists and for world peace. When the Marxist workers split into Socialist and Communist factions in the 1920's, she moved over to the left. Clara was one of the charter members of the Communist Party, United States of America. The following article gives the highlights of her career.

CLARA LEMLICH SHAVELSON: 50 YEARS IN LABOR'S FRONT LINE
by Paula Scheier

1909

It was not a usual union crowd that met at Cooper Union in New York the evening of November 22, 1909. It was large, but that the speakers on the stage had expected. It was tense, but they had seen tenseness before—eyes strained from watching stitches peering up at them, backs bent from years at cutting boards bending toward them. What was strange about this crowd boards bending toward them. What was strange about this crowd was the women. Not even women, most of them . . . girls. How fresh their faces were, fresh from the small towns of the old country. How innocent they looked in those high starched shirt-waists and big picture hats. Did they realize what they were getting into?

One by one, they rose to speak, in English and in Yiddish— Goldstein of the Bakers Union, Weinstein of the United Hebrew Trades, Mary Dreier of the Women's Trade Union League, Meyer London of the Socialist Party. . . . The word "strike" was always greeted with applause. But, each one hastened to warn, a general strike in the industry was a serious affair. It might run into months . . . the manufacturers would not give in easily.

The crowd was growing restless. This was not what they had come to hear. They knew it would be hard. But what about the six-dollar salaries, the cheating on the piece-work? What about the foremen that yelled at you and the stinking toilets that overran into the workrooms? They had heard all about scabs and thugs and police. But would they ever have a union if they didn't strike now?

When Samuel Gompers, president of the AFL, got up, a new eddy of excitement ran through the hall. The waistmakers should not act too hastily, he said, but "if you can't get the manufacturers to give you what you want, then strike . . . and let the manufacturers know that you are on strike."

If they couldn't get the manufacturers . . . ? Suddenly, in the front of the hall, one of the girls jumped up. "I want to say a few words," she said.

The crowd buzzed. That was Clara Lemlich from Leiserson's —they were on strike already—for 11 weeks! "Get up on the platform," somebody shouted. "Yes, get up on the platform," other voices joined in.

They lifted her up: she was barely five feet tall; she was no more than 20. But they could also see the proud set of that head, the passion in those great, dark eyes. "I have listened to all the speakers," she cried in Yiddish, "and I have no further patience for talk. I am one who feels and suffers for the things pictured. I move that we go on a general strike!"

Instantly they were on their feet, men, women and girls, cheering, stamping, crying approval. With one motion, Chairman Feigenbaum sprang to Clara Lemlich's side and thrust her right arm into the air. "Do you mean faith?" he cried. "Will you take the old Hebrew oath?"

For answer, two and a half thousand right arms shot up at him. Two and a half thousand voices repeated the Yiddish words: "If I turn traitor to the cause I now pledge, may this hand wither from the arm I now raise." By the morning, one of the garment industry's first great strikes was under way—and a new labor heroine had been born.

The newspapers called it the "Revolt of the Girls." Clara Lemlich, they said, was its Joan of Arc. She was "the soul of this young woman's revolution," wrote Mary Brown Sumner in *The Survey*, "a spirit of fire and tears, devoid of egotism, unable to tolerate the thought of human suffering." Clara Lemlich explained "Why the Waistmakers Strike" in her article in the New York *Evening Journal* on November 26, 1909.

At nine, on the morning of November 23rd, thousands of shirtwaist makers left their shops in Manhattan, Brooklyn's Brownsville and the Bronx to march to Clinton Hall, the union's headquarters at 151 Clinton Street. Four-fifths of them were women.

But the strike was as well organized as it was dramatic. Each shop formed a strike committee, which set up headquarters in some East Side hall. Every midnight, the committees reported to the general executive at Clinton Hall. There each day's campaign was mapped; pickets and speakers were assigned. Even a special Italian headquarters with Italian literature was set.

That winter, the strike was Clara's life. She was up at six for the picket line, out during the day to raise money and speak at meetings, working far into the morning as a member of the executive committee.

The manufacturers answered the workers' militancy with violence. A year before, the Triangle shop, destined for its place in labor infamy, had hit upon a novel method for dealing with women strikers. Since the usual male thugs seemed inappropriate, they hired their female counterparts—prostitutes—to taunt and start fights with pickets. In 1909, a number of their colleagues copied the fashion.

The police, too, could be called upon to break up picket lines. On one pretext or another, they would arrest whole bunches of girls and haul them off to stand trial in the lower East Side's Jefferson and Essex Market courts. On December 3rd, the union protested the continuing arrests with a march of 10,000 strikers on City Hall. The mayor offered no help but public sympathy was aroused. The Women's Trade Union League, an organization of middle class, suffragette sympathizers, with the aid of such society suffragettes as Mrs. O. H. P. Belmont and Ann Morgan, held a meeting at Carnegie Hall to protest police brutality. Across the wide stage sat a row of "convicts," the youngest 15 years old, wearing streamers over their shoulders reading, "I am a criminal."

A number of the manufacturers had signed with the union at the beginning of the strike. As the winter went on, the holdouts were faced with the gloomy prospect of losing a whole season's profits. In January, 1910, when Leiserson's fell, it was the beginning of the end. By March, 354 of the 400 struck shops had signed contracts with the Ladies Waistmakers Union of New York. A closed shop, a 52-hour week, a substantial pay raise and abolition of many abuses had been won. And, not least, the union had grown from 800 to 20,000 members, its treasury from next to nothing to $2400 a week. Only a few months later, the giant cloakmaker's strike was to settle on its feet once and for all the International Ladies Garment Workers Union.

But perhaps the most important thing established by that strike was a fact. Not only the journalists, but sober Samuel Gompers himself had called it a "revolution." Until then, women had always been considered labor's weakest link, its most negligible and expendable part. The liberal weekly *Outlook* was echoing all the press when it said (July 2, 1910), "These young, inexperienced girls have proved that women can strike, and strike successfully."

"That is what you must write about!" The small woman with

the vivid eyes would still rather talk about the strike's meaning than her part in it. "They used to say that you couldn't even organize women. They wouldn't come to union meetings. They were 'temporary' workers; they would always undercut men. Well, we showed them!"

It takes a while before you get Clara Lemlich Shavelson to talk about herself. When I visited her one evening last March, the news from the Caracas conference was just coming over the radio. "Look—" her tongue still has fury, "who tries to talk for Latin America!" On her end table was a ticket for a meeting to protest intervention in Guatemala. The phone rang with a query from a friend in her shop. While she talked, you noticed that the room is filled with books. No matter how many newspapers she reads each day, she must have a book "for dessert."

Music has been vital to Clara Lemlich from the time she was a young girl in Gorodok, on the Austrian border of the Ukraine. The rebellious daughter of an orthodox Jewish scholar and grocery-storekeeper learned her songs from the children, frowned upon by the family, of non-Jewish shoemakers and peasants who lived, as the Lemlichs did, on the outskirts of the town. She then promptly compounded the heresy by using her singing to make friends with the daughters of wealthier Jewish families who subscribed to the city libraries and gave her Russian books. The two-grade village school did not admit Jews, and Clara's parents, protesting in the only way they knew, would have no Russian—either in speech or in print—in their home.

Not only learning, but the money for it had to be gotten by stealth. Though the family was poor, ownership of the little grocery store made them too proud to let her work. She used to steal time from the housework to go and make buttonholes in the tailor shops—the only places of employment open to Jews—for money to pay the students who taught her to read. A few more kopeks for books were made by writing letters from parents to children in America. The books had to be hidden. Once, when her father found their hiding place—under the pan where meat was made kosher—he threw the whole painfully accumulated lot into the fire.

She would read late at night, creeping out of bed after the

family was asleep, or on the Sabbath, when she would climb up into the attic and perch herself on a bare beam to pore over Turgeniev, Gorky and Tolstoy. One Saturday afternoon, when she was about ten, the neighbor who shared their semi-detached house stumbled upon her up there. He was so impressed by her passion for reading that he not only heeded her tearful pleas not to tell her parents, but brought her more books, among them her first revolutionary tracts.

By the time of the great Kishinev pogrom of 1903, when the Lemlichs, along with thousands of Jewish families, fled the Ukraine, Clara was singing revolutionary songs. In England, where they stayed for a few months, she was taken to Anarchist meetings. But her rebellion was still only personal.

In America, she was determined to become a doctor. But in America, as many an immigrant family was discovering, employers preferred to hire children rather than their parents. Within a week of her arrival, 15-year-old Clara was at work in a shop.

Almost immediately she started to study at night. One of her first great discoveries in America was the East Broadway branch of the New York Public Library, which had a great collection of literary classics in Russian. Oddly enough, she says, she learned more Russian from that library than she did in her years in the Ukraine. "I should have spent more time learning English correctly," she says, "but I was so eager to learn *things.*" History and literature were her passions. After an 11-hour day in the shop, she would walk through half the East Side to the Gordon free school on Madison Street, stopping only for a penny or two's worth of milk. She ate her mother's dinner at 10 or 11 when she arrived home.

"All week long I wouldn't see the daylight. I remember once, when things were slow, they let us out in the middle of the day. 'What!' I said, 'are all the people on strike!' I had never realized that there were so many out during the daytime."

It was not at all strange that the first thing to come to her mind then was a strike. For not only at school was she learning new things. The older workers in the shops talked constantly about trade unions; in some shops there were even lunch-time discussion groups on trade union theory; small knots of workers, escaping the bosses' watchful eyes, would walk the streets, talking and arguing.

In the workers' constant struggles with the manufacturers, there were many individual shop stoppages, but none had the backing to succeed. The International Ladies Garment Workers Union was a weak six-year-old, consisting mostly of male cloakmakers, when, in 1906, Clara joined a delegation of waistmakers that went to the *Jewish Daily Forward* to ask how to go about forming a union. That spring, only two years after her arrival in America, she was one of the seven young girls and six men who founded the waistmakers' Local 25, I.L.G.W.U.

The organizing, at first, was slow, monotonous and discouraging. There were scores of shops and thousands of waistmakers. Clara, by then a skilled and relatively well-paid draper, was still hoarding money for medical school, but she could not work in a shop without trying to organize it. She began to gravitate toward the smaller places where an individual organizer might exert more influence.

Her first strike came in 1907, at Weisen and Goldstein's, an "uptown" shop in West 17th Street. It was new and considered a very desirable place to work, until the workers realized that the modern conveniences were being paid for out of a still greater speed-up. They held out for ten weeks, against every kind of attack.

One night during a meeting Clara heard a fierce argument break out over the general objectives of the union. When it was over, she went up to one of the cutters. What did he mean by attacking Samuel Gompers as a "pure and simple trade unionist?" she asked. The older man started to explain, then took another look at her eager face and asked if she would like to go for a walk.

"We walked 40 blocks," she says, "and he gave me my first lesson in Marxism. He started with a bottle of milk—how it was made, who made the money from it through every stage of its production. Not only did the boss take the profits, he said, but not a drop of that milk did you drink unless he allowed you to. It was funny, you know, because I'd been saying things like that to the girls before. But now I understood it better and I began to use it more often—only with shirtwaists." She also started to take classes in labor theory at the Rand School.

The great 1907 depression broke the Weisen and Goldstein strike, but others were still to come. In 1908, trade union consciousness among the waistmakers had reached such heights that the girls at the Gotham shop, where Clara was working, struck in protest against their boss firing men to make room for cheaper women workers. And in the fall of 1909 the strike at Leiserson's broke out.

The union was then divided into crafts and the operators, who were men, went ahead with their plans without consulting the workers of other crafts, many of them women. They were more than a little surprised when, suddenly, at their strike meeting, there was Clara, asking for the floor. Didn't they know, the teen-age girl scolded them, that if they went out alone they would lose! The only thing to do was to take the whole shop with them. She managed to convince the operators and, with their help, the rest of the workers. Even Leiserson seemed impressed by her: in 11 weeks of picket line scuffles she was arrested 17 times and six of her ribs were broken.

"Ah—then I had fire in my mouth!"

Her hands fly to her head when she remembers the famous speeches. "I read about them now—all those important people and Clara Lemlich here, Clara Lemlich there! What did I know about trade unionism? Audacity—that was all I had—audacity!"

The union and the public at large, however, seemed to think otherwise. The Socialists, whose meetings she constantly attended, never asked her to join their party because they took it for granted that she was already a member. Professor Charles Beard, whose wife was an active strike sympathizer, was so struck by her that he offered to get her into Barnard and help her through college. The great dark eyes grow a bit wistful when she thinks of the lost education. "But it was too late. I was swallowed up by the trade union movement."

The strike over, the sleepness nights and months of inadequate food at last made themselves felt. Clara broke down completely and had to be taken to the country to recover. When she returned a few months later, it was to the blacklist. She was only one of the rank-and-file strike leaders, who for several years thereafter, could find work in the industry only under assumed names, constantly being fired when their identity was discovered.

However, her loyalty to the union remained undiminished. She kept up with all its activities, attended every convention. Late in 1910, it finally rewarded her with a job as factory inspector—to see that the reforms she had played such a large part in winning were being carried out. The union appointed its own inspectors, with official city sanction, because of the city inspectors' apparently strange lapses in observation when it came to factory working conditions.

At the same time she returned to her activities in the Women's Trade Union League, which she had joined during the strike, and to whose executive board she was soon elected. The League had close ties with the Woman's Suffrage Party. Even though most of its middle class ladies did not agree with Clara's outspoken socialist views, Mary Beard could not resist asking her to speak for them.

In the years before World War I, Clara spoke for woman's suffrage on Riverside Drive and, more frequently, outside the gates of factories that employed women. She remembers particularly the Butterick Pattern and Uneeda Biscuit plants in downtown Manhattan, where the men workers would come out and call: "Go home and wash your pants!"—often driving home their point with rotten tomatoes. The women would usually stay inside, peering out the windows, somewhat frightened and not too sure what was in it for them.

Their attitude soon changed, however, when Clara's ideas of what should go into a suffrage speech prevailed. Shortly after she became an active suffragette, Jessie Ashley, a prominent socialist, died and left the Suffrage Party a fund for the express purpose of bringing the fight for the vote to working women. Clara then became a paid organizer of labor groups within the party and special material was printed to show the relation of suffrage to child labor, sanitary conditions and other workers' problems. On the soap boxes and ladders outside plant gates now, she talked about women in the labor movement and women as the wives of workers. When she told her audiences about the families burned out of their tents after being evicted from company houses during the Colorado mine strike of 1914, she had no trouble getting rid of her leaflets. The men took them, as well as the women.

In 1913, Clara married Joseph Shavelson, a printer and an old comrade from the strike days. "He was a fighter," she says. It is her highest praise. Her husband's family had taken part in the Russian revolution of 1905; Joe, then a gangling teen-ager, had been a member of the Social Democratic Underground, traveling from town to town with illegal leaflets hidden underneath his coat. "He was so thin that no one could tell." Clara would listen by the hour to the Shavelsons' stories, sometimes feeling that she almost wanted to go back to this revolutionary country of her birth.

But, even if it had been a serious thought, there were to be no wedding trips for the young Shavelsons. Joe, unable to get into the printers' union, was earning $17 a week. They went to live on DeKalb Avenue in Brooklyn with one of his sisters and her two children. "I still hoped," says Clara, "that I could finish school." By then, without any grade schooling, she had managed, in ten years' time, to accumulate 48 out of 60 high school points, and she still had not given up her dreams about medical school. But in a year she had had her first baby and the family's finances were still lower.

When her son, Irving, was two-and-a-half, she went to work in a tie shop on the ground floor of the building where her sister lived. Her second child, a daughter, Martha, was just old enough to walk when Clara began taking the youngsters with her to Socialist meetings. Soon she was speaking for a Socialist women's group to protest profiteering on food prices. When the landlord who owned the two-family houses on the East New York block where they then lived tried to raise the rent, she organized a rent strike—which ended with the Shavelsons being evicted. They moved then to Grafton Street, in Brownsville, where Clara's second daughter, Rita, was born.

Clara reacted to these personal burdens characteristically: she became an organizer for the United Council of Working Class Women, a housewives' community organization that allied itself closely with the growing labor movement. Besides fighting on prices and rents, it set up kitchens and joined picket lines during many a strike of the late twenties, including the famous Passaic strike.

The onslaught of the depression in the thirties found Clara in Brighton Beach organizing that working class community's first Unemployed Council. She went on both the 1930 and 1932 hunger marches.

Hardly a single one of the dramatic struggles of the thirties was not to become a part of her. In 1935, when the United Council had become the Progressive Women's Council, it followed up a successful 1932 bread strike with a great battle against the high cost of meat. Clara was among the leaders of both fights in Brighton Beach, organizing picket lines and mass meetings and making her fiery speeches as of old. The meat strike became so successful that it spread throughout the country.

Among the earliest active anti-fascists, in 1934 she attended the first International Women's Congress Against War and Fascism in Paris. She remembers that trip well not only for the conference but for her travels after it, which took her, for the first time since her childhood, to the country of her birth. "We went by train to Moscow," she says, "and there was a bus there to meet us. But I wouldn't get on it. I told the others to go ahead without me. This was the country where they wouldn't even let me go to school— where if I walked into a city they would have made me wear a prostitute's badge. And now—I wanted to stand there for a long time with my feet on the soil of a workers' country."

She returned to the United States to lecture and show slides of the USSR to some 30 clubs of the Progressive Women's Council. As educational director of the Council, she gave courses on fascism, war and peace. And soon she was a familiar figure at Brighton Beach street corner meetings, rallying the Jewish workers with her own passionate clarity against the Hitlerism that threatened them.

When the United States entered World War II, Mrs. Shavelson was back at it again with the old energy. The Progressive Women's Council had merged with the women's clubs of the International Workers Order. By then PWC president, Clara became New York City secretary of the IWO's Women's Division, working day and night to organize first aid classes, knitting circles, aluminum campaigns, bond rallies. And in 1944, when she realized that her husband's strength was failing, she went back to the shop and was in the union again.

For nine years, until her retirement this past spring [1954], she remained in the shop, a hand-finisher on cloaks and a rank-and-file union member. She still went to union meetings, fought with both boss and foreman, and found time for her many outside activities.

During the Stockholm Peace Petition campaign she got 500 signatures—93 of them the day after the Korean War started. She also collected 1200 signatures to the 1951 petition for a five-power peace pact.

In 1951 she made her second trip abroad, this time as a member of a trade union delegation. In France, Italy, Czechoslovakia and the Soviet Union, she heard about wages and working conditions, housing and health problems, and always and foremost, about peace. "Peace was the most important issue to all those European workers," she says. "We heard that everywhere we went. It was on all the walls and all the banners. If any of us had thought that there was a danger of war from the Soviet Union or anywhere in Europe, we were convinced now we had been wrong. We were convinced that our job was to go back and tell American workers that if they too would struggle for peace, there could be no war."

When she returned home, Mrs. Shavelson gave the message of peace in countless speeches to countless meetings. She brought it back into the shop with her and to the women of the Emma Lazarus clubs with whom she now works.

It is not only the children and the six grandchildren (Joseph Shavelson died in 1951) that make Clara Shavelson say now, "I'm not a poor woman; I have dividends." First among them, she counts the union. (When the ILGWU broke a rule, requiring 15 consecutive years of work in the industry, to give her a pension last spring, she wrote to David Dubinsky—in a letter which was reprinted, in part, with a story about her in the union paper, *Justice*—"I feel that this is in some measure a tribute to the early band that struggled and fought to eliminate the sweatshop system and bring the benefits of unionism to thousands of workers.") Then, there is the growing respect for women as unionists, which she helped establish. There was that election day in 1921, when she cast the first precious vote she had helped win. There is the unemployment insurance that she helped fight for, the defeat of fascism that she helped bring about, the socialism she has always worked for triumphant in half the world. And she still may count.

If there is any further dividend still owing to Mrs. Shavelson, it is the recognition of Clara Shavelson, and not only of Clara Lemlich. Clara Lemlich was a brilliant youngster of whom she can rightfully be proud. But Clara Shavelson, she feels, has accomplished much more. Clara Shavelson is no Grand Old Lady of progressivism, no symbol of the past. She is as young as Mother Bloor was in her eighties, or Elizabeth Gurley Flynn is at 64, because she, too, will never stop fighting.

106

WOMEN LABOR ORGANIZERS IN THE INTERNATIONAL LADIES' GARMENT WORKERS UNION
1909–1944

It took time before the male-dominated unions began according female workers a degree of equality. The following document deals with the difficulties experienced by three women organizers who worked selflessly for the International Ladies' Garment Workers Union (ILG): Pauline Newman, the ILG's first organizer, Fannia Cohn, and Rose Pesotta. They ran into one formidable barrier—and this was one which the male unionists also faced—a great deal of virulent anti-union sentiment in this country. The problems of these organizers were compounded because they had to work closely with the middle-class humanitarians in the Women's Trade Union League (WTUL), people whose social background was altogether different. What was even more exasperating and disheartening was the fact that the women unionists frequently met with rebuffs from the males who ran the union and who shared the common prejudice that females must at all times play a subordinate role.

Organizing the Unorganizable:
Three Jewish Women and Their Union
by Alice Kessler-Harris

Women who were actively engaged in the labor struggles of the first part of this century faced a continual dilemma. They were caught between a trade union movement hostile to women in the work force and a women's movement whose participants did not work for wages. To improve working conditions for the increasing numbers of women entering the paid labor force, organizers painstakingly solicited support from labor unions that should have been their natural allies. At the same time, they got sympathetic aid from well-intentioned women with whom they otherwise had little in common. The wage-earning women who undertook the difficult task of organizing their co-workers also faced yet another problem: they had to reconcile active involvement in labor unionism with community traditions that often discouraged worldly roles.

Understanding how women who were union organizers experienced these tensions tells us much about the relationships of men and women within unions and throws into relief some of the central problems unionization posed for many working women. It also reveals something of what feminism meant for immigrant women. Evidence of conscious experience, frequently hard to come by, exists in the papers of three women who organized for the International Ladies Garment Workers Union [ILG]: Pauline Newman, Fannia Cohn, and Rose Pesotta. All were Jews working for a predominately Jewish organization. Their careers span the first half of the twentieth century. Taken together, their lives reveal a persistent conflict between their experiences as women and their tasks as union officers. Their shared Jewish heritage offers insight into the ways women tried to adapt familiar cultural tradition to the needs of a new world.

Like most of the women they represented, Newman, Cohn and Pesotta were born in Eastern Europe. Cohn and Newman emigrated as children before the turn of the century, Pesotta as a teenager in 1913. In the United States, poverty drove them to the East Side's garment shops. There they worked in the dress and waist industry, a rapidly expanding trade in which Jewish workers predominated until the 1930s, and in which women made up the bulk of the work force. . . .

To choose a militant and active future among a people who valued marriage and the family as much as most Eastern European Jews did must have been extraordinarily difficult. Women who chose to be continuously active in the labor movement knew consciously or unconsciously that they were rejecting traditional marriage. In her autobiography, Rose Schneiderman, just beginning a career in the Women's Trade Union League, recalls her mother warning her she'd never get married because she was so busy. One woman organizer, who did marry, made the following verbatim comment to an interviewer who asked her about children: "I wouldn't know what to do with them. First of all I never . . . we were very active, both of us, and then the unions. I don't think I . . . there were always meetings . . . so we had no time to have children. I am sorry now. . . ." Even after so many years, her discomfort at talking about her unusual choice was apparent. Despite difficulties, many in the first generation of immigrants, Newman and Cohn among them, did not marry and there are numerous examples of women whose marriages did not survive the urge to independence. Rose Pesotta divorced two husbands, and anarchist Emma Goldman and novelist Anzia Yezierska one each before they sought satisfying lives outside marriage. . . .

Faced with the exploitative working conditions characteristic of the early twentieth century United States, many women turned naturally to unionism. The ILG, founded and nurtured by socialist Jews from New York's Lower East Side, offered an appropriate organizing agency, and early expressions of enthusiasm indicate something of its romantic appeal. "I think the union is like a mother and father to its children. I'd give my whole life for the union," said one young woman in 1913. Half a century after she joined the union in 1908 an eighty-year-old woman wrote to David Dubinsky, the ILG's president, "And I still have my membership book of that year. And I will keep it with reverence until the end of my days." Another recalled her experience on the picket line: "I felt as if I were in a holy fight when I ran after a scab." . . .

Women who had had to struggle to create and enter trade unions, who were baited, beaten, and arrested on picket lines, and who had already rejected traditional roles sought help from other women, identifying their problems as different from those of male workers. Large numbers indicated their need for organization by participating in spontaneous strikes. Workers on women's clothing (largely female) tended to strike without union support more than half again as many times as workers on men's clothing (largely male). In the early years of organizing, attacks against other women often elicited support from co-workers. Clara Lemlich, whose proposal to strike sparked the 1909 uprising of 20,000 in the dress and waist trade, had been badly beaten by thugs. A woman who had participated in the Chicago garment strike of 1911 recalled that violent attacks against other female strikers had persuaded her not to return to work until the strike was won. As she and her fellow workers were negotiating with their employer to call a halt to the strike, they heard a terrific noise. "We all rushed to the windows, and there we [saw] the police beating the strikers—clubbing them on our account and when we saw that we went out." A sense of female solidarity joined the oppressed together. A 1913 striker who said she was "in good" at her job refused to work without a union "for the sake of those that didn't have it good." In jail women strikers passively resisted when their captors tried to separate them. . . .

"American" women, as the organizers persistently called them, were hardest of all for Jewish women to unionize. It was a necessary assignment in order to prevent some shops from undercutting the wages of others, enabling them to charge lower prices for finished goods. But it was dreaded by Jewish organizers who saw "shickses" as at best indifferent to unionism, and more often as strike breakers and scabs. Success at organizing "Americans" evoked unconcealed glee. Pauline Newman wrote to Rose Schneiderman from Massachusetts that they had "at last succeeded in organizing an English-speaking branch of the waist makers union. And my dear not with ten or eleven members— but with a good sturdy membership of forty. Now what will you say to that!" Long after most Jewish women were comfortable within unions, Rose Pesotta complained that she was having a "hell of a job" with the Seattle workers she had been sent to organize. They were, she said, the "100% American white daughters of the sturdy pioneers. They are all members of bridge clubs, card clubs, lodges, etc. Class consciousness is as remote from their thoughts as any idea that smacks with radicalism." Women from such an ethnic background could severely inhibit the success of an organization drive. Pesotta complained that she could not call a strike as women would not picket. "No one will stand in front of the shop . . . as they will be ashamed. Not even the promise of getting regular strike benefits moved them."

Isolated from the mainstream of the labor movement and divided from other working women who came from less class conscious backgrounds, Jewish women gratefully accepted help from middle class groups like the Women's Trade Union League. But the financial and moral support of the WTUL came at a price. Jewish women had been nurtured in the cradle of socialism, and for them, alliances with other women were largely ways of achieving a more just society. Many middle class members of the WTUL, in contrast, held that political, social, and biological oppression of women was the major problem. They saw labor organization among women as a way of transcending class lines in the service of feminist interests. Contemporary testimony and filtered memory agree that the WTUL provided enormously valuable organizing help. . . .

Pauline Newman became the ILG's first female organizer in the aftermath of the "Great Uprising" of 1909. She had a stormy relationship with the union until she settled down in 1913 to work for the Joint Board of Sanitary Control—a combined trade union and manufacturers unit designed to establish standards for maintaining sanitary conditions in the shops. Fannia Cohn worked for the union from 1919 to the end of her life. For most of that time she was educational director though she also served as an executive secretary and briefly as a vice president. Rose Pesotta (some 10 years younger than the other two) became a full time organizer in 1933 and a vice president of the union in 1934. She remained active until 1944 when she returned to work in the shops.

Their lifestyles varied. Pauline Newman, warm, open and impulsive, had a successful long-term relationship with a woman with whom she adopted a baby in 1923. Fannia Cohn lived alone—a sensitive, slightly irritable woman, concerned with her ability to make and retain friends. Rose Pesotta married twice and afterwards fell in love with first one married man and then another. Cohn and Newman called themselves socialists. Pesotta was an anarchist. No easy generalization captures their positions on women, or their relationships to the union. But all felt some conflict surrounding the two issues.

From 1909 to 1912 just before she went to work for the Joint Board, Newman vacillated between the union and the middle class women of the WTUL. Frequently unhappy with a union that often treated her shabbily she nevertheless continued to work for them throughout her life. . . .

Her disagreements were not simply matters of style. She was more than willing to give way when she thought a well-spoken woman could influence a stubborn manufacturer. But she thought it bad strategy to raise issues of morality when they threatened to interfere with negotiations over wages and hours. It may have been true, she argued, that a factory owner's son and his superintendent had taken liberties with female employees: "There is not a factory today where the same immoral conditions [do] not exist. . . . This to my mind can be done away with by educating the girls instead of attacking the company."

Caught between the union and middle class allies, Newman called for help—a pattern repeated by other women involved in the labor movement. Her letters to Schneiderman are filled with longing: "all evening I kept saying if only Rose were here. . .;" and with loneliness: "No matter how good the people are to me, they do not know me as yet." At times one can only guess at the toll her job took. She wrote repeatedly of trying to "get away from the blues" and complained, "I am just thrown like a wave from one city to another. When will it end?" Respite came at last in the form of the Joint Board of Sanitary Control. With the struggles to organize behind her she could spend her energies improving working conditions for women in the factories. . . .

It was just in this period that Fannia Cohn climbed to a position of authority in the ILGWU. In many ways she was fully aware of women's issues. In 1919, in the aftermath of a successful shirtwaist strike, she pleaded for tolerance from male union members. Recalling the militancy of the young female strikers she wrote: "Our brother workers in the past regarded with suspicion the masses of women who were entering the trades. They did everything to halt the 'hostile army' whose competition they feared.". . . She wrote, "The labor movement is guilty of not realizing the importance of placing the interest of women on the same basis as of men and until they will accept this, I am afraid the movement will be much hampered in its progress.". . .

Rose Pesotta took no shelter and asked no quarter. By 1933

when she began full-time organizing for the ILG, it had become clear to many that women, married and unmarried, were in the work force to stay and the ILG willingly committed both money and resources to organizing them. Membership campaigns no longer focused on the East Coast cities. In the garment centers of the Far West and in places like Buffalo and Montreal, Jews took second place to Mexican, Italian, and "American" women. But Pesotta was a Russian Jew who worked for a still Jewish union and, like her predecessors, she suffered the turmoil of being a woman in ambivalent territory. Sent by the ILG to Los Angeles in 1933, she moved from there to organize women in San Francisco, Seattle, Portland, Puerto Rico, Buffalo, and Montreal before she became involved with war mobilization.

None could question her awareness of women's particular problems. Persuaded by the argument that there were no women on the union's General Executive Board, she accepted a much-dreaded nomination for Vice President. "I feel as if I lost my independence," she confided to her diary. She often berated the union leadership for its neglect of women: "our union, due to the fact that it has a WOMAN leader is supposed to do everything, organizing, speechmaking, etc., etc." She was not shy about asking for courtesies that men might have had trouble obtaining. Women who earned meager wages could not be expected to pay even modest union initiation fees, she urged at one point. At another, she demanded that ILG pay not only the expenses but make up the lost income of a Spanish woman elected to attend the biennial ILG convention. And she knew the advantages of solidarity among women, making personal sacrifices to "win the support of the ladies who might some day be of great help to the girls.". . .

Pesotta carried the scars of the woman organizer. "A flitting happy little whirlwind," her friends called her. It was an image that did not fit. "Nobody knows how many cheerless, sleepless nights I have spent crying in my loneliness. . .," she confided to her diary. Unlike Newman and Cohn, she sought solace in men and depriving herself of close women friends exacerbated her isolation. Tormented by the gossip of her female colleagues she struggled with her self-image. Occasionally she confessed "I feel so futile . . .," or sorrowed "everybody has a private life. I have none." In an effort to avoid entangling herself with a married man she exiled herself to Montreal in 1936. It was no use. She wrote from there to her lover: "Why must I find happiness always slipping out of my hand . . . I'm sinking now and who knows where I will land." For ten years, Rose Pesotta battled against police alongside her union colleagues. Then she returned to the comparative peace of the garment shop from which she had come.

By the middle 1930s, with unionism apparently secure and the ILG's membership expanding rapidly, it looked as though women might at last begin to raise issues peculiar to them within the confines of the union. Fannia Cohn wrote a play in 1935 which raised critical issues. Intended for presentation at union meetings, it described a husband and his "intellectually superior" wife. Both worked, but, because the wife had to devote her evenings to caring for the home, the husband rapidly developed more interests and became increasingly discontented with his spouse. The wife, wrote Cohn, brought with her the resentment and "the protest of a woman worker, wife and mother against an economic condition that compels her to work days in the shop and evenings at home." Chivalry, Rose Schneiderman had said, "is thrown away" when a girl enters the factory or store: "Women have to work and then are thrown on the dust heap the same as working men." Working men were by no means chivalrous in 1935, but enough women had been organized in the ILG so that the union, no longer afraid of imminent disintegration and collapse, could lend an ear to the women's issues. Perhaps in consequence the solidarity of women within the unions diminished.

Those who came before walked an uneasy tightrope—slipping first to one side and then to the other. Tempted sometimes by the money and support of middle class women, at others by the militance of a changing labor union leadership; alternately repelled by "ladies" and repeatedly hurt by their union's male leadership, women who tried to organize their sisters were in a precarious position. They were not feminist—they did not put the social and political rights of women before all else. They did draw strength and support from the solidarity of women inside unions and outside them. Their lives illustrate the critical importance of "female bonding" and of female friendship networks. Newman and Cohn, who had particularly strong relationships with women and who managed to find relatively passive roles within the union, maintained their relationship with the ILG far longer than Pesotta who relied on men for support and who stayed in the front lines of battle. All were class conscious, insisting that the class struggle was preeminent. When their class consciousness and their identification as women conflicted, they bowed to tradition and threw in their lot with the working class.

107

THE TRIANGLE FIRE
1911

At 4:35 on a Saturday afternoon, March 25, 1911, a fire broke out in the Triangle Waist Company factory in New York City. About 145 people died, most of them girls and women, Jews and Italians. They perished in the fire or when they jumped to the pavement 100 feet below. The fire escapes were inadequate. It was the greatest tragedy in the history of the city since 1904, when the General Slocum, *an excursion boat, burned in New York Harbor with a loss of 950 lives. After the Triangle fire, a new industrial code was enacted by the United States—a social advance of consequence.*

In a memorial meeting held at the Metropolitan Opera House, Rose Schneiderman, the labor leader, said: "The life of men and women is so cheap and property is so sacred." The following is the New York Times' *account of that tragic conflagration.*

-----

141 Men and Girls Die in Waist Factory Fire Trapped High Up in Washington Place Building; Street Strewn with Bodies; Piles of Dead Inside

The Flames Spread with Deadly Rapidity Through Flimsy Material Used in the Factory.

600 Girls Are Hemmed In

When Elevators Stop Many Jump to Certain Death and Others Perish in Fire-Filled Lofts.

Students Rescue Some

Help Them to Roof of New York University Building, Keeping the Panic-Stricken in Check.

One Man Taken Out Alive

Plunged to Bottom of Elevator Shaft and Lived There Amid
Flames for Four Hours.

Only One Fire Escape

Coroner Declares Building Laws Were Not Enforced—Building
Modern—Classed Fireproof.

Just Ready to Go Home

Victims Would Have Ended Day's Work in a Few Minutes—Pay
Envelopes Identify Many.

Mob Storms the Morgue

Seeking to Learn Fate of Relatives Employed by the Triangle
Waist Company.

Three stories of a ten-floor building at the corner of Greene
Street and Washington Place were burned yesterday, and while
the fire was going on 141 young men and women—at least 125 of
them mere girls—were burned to death or killed by jumping to
the pavement below.

The building was fireproof. It shows now hardly any signs of
the disaster that overtook it. The walls are as good as ever; so are
the floors; nothing is the worse for the fire except the furniture
and 141 of the 600 men and girls that were employed in its upper
three stories.

Most of the victims were suffocated or burned to death within
the building, but some who fought their way to the windows and
leaped met death as surely, but perhaps more quickly, on the
pavements below.

All Over in Half an Hour.

Nothing like it has been seen in New York since the burning of the "General Slocum." The fire was practically all over in half an hour. It was confined to three floors—the eighth, ninth, and tenth of the building. But it was the most murderous fire that New York has seen in many years.

The victims, who are now lying at the Morgue waiting for some one to identify them by a tooth or the remains of a burned shoe, were mostly girls of from 16 to 23 years of age. They were employed at making shirtwaists by the Triangle Waist Company, the principal owners of which are Isaac Harris and Max Blanck. Most of them could barely speak English. Many of them came from Brooklyn. Almost all were the main support of their hard-working families.

There is just one fire escape in the building. That one is an interior fire escape. In Greene Street, where the terrified unfortunates crowded before they began to make their mad leaps to death, the whole big front of the building is guiltless of one. Nor is there a fire escape in the back.

The building was fireproof and the owners had put their trust in that. In fact, after the flames had done their worst last night the building hardly showed a sign. Only the stock within it and the girl employes were burned.

A heap of corpses lay on the sidewalk for more than an hour. The firemen were too busy dealing with the fires to pay any attention to people whom they supposed beyond their aid. When the excitement had subsided to such an extent that some of the firemen and policemen could pay attention to the mass of the supposedly dead they found, about half way down in the pack, a girl who was still breathing. She died two minutes after she was found.

The Triangle Waist Company was the only sufferer by the disaster. There are other concerns in the building, but it was Saturday and the other companies had let their people go home. Messrs. Harris and Blanck, however, were busy and their girls—and some men—stayed.

LEAPED OUT OF THE FLAMES.

At 4:40 o'clock, nearly five hours after the employes in the rest of the building had gone home, the fire broke out. The one little fire escape in the interior was never resorted to by any of the doomed victims. Some of them escaped by running down the stairs, but in a moment or two this avenue was cut off by flame. The girls rushed to the windows and looked down at Greene Street, 100 feet below them. Then one poor little creature jumped. There was a plate glass protection over part of the sidewalk, but she crashed through it, wrecking it and breaking her body into a thousand pieces.

Then they all began to drop. The crowd yelled "Don't jump!" but it was jump or be burned—the proof of which is found in the fact that fifty burned bodies were taken from the ninth floor alone.

They jumped, they crashed through broken glass, they crushed themselves to death on the sidewalk. Of those who stayed behind it is better to say nothing—except what a veteran policeman said as he gazed at a headless and charred trunk on the Greene Street sidewalk hours after the worse cases had been taken out.

"I saw the Slocum disaster, but it was nothing to this."

"Is it a man or a woman?" asked the reporter.

"It's human, that's all you can tell," answered the policeman.

It was just a mass of ashes, with blood congealed on what had probably been the neck.

Messrs. Harris and Blanck were in the building but they escaped. They carried with them Mr. Blanck's children and a governess, and they fled over the roofs. Their employes did not know the way because they had been in the habit of using the two freight elevators, and one of these elevators was not in service when the fire broke out.

Found Alive After the Fire.

The first living victim, Hyman Meshel of 332 East Fifteent
Street, was taken from the ruins four hours after the fire wa
discovered. He was found paralyzed with fear and whimperin,
like a wounded animal in the basement, immersed in water to hi
neck, crouched on the top of a cable drum, and with his head jus
below the floor of the elevator.

Meantime the remains of the dead—it is hardly possible to cal
them bodies, because that word suggests something human, an
there was nothing human about most of these—were taken in
steady stream to the Morgue for identification. First Avenue wa
lined with the usual curious east side crowd. Twenty-sixth Stree
was impassable. But in the Morgue they received the charre
remnants with no more emotion than they ever display ove
anything.

Back in Greene Street there was another crowd. At midnight i
had not decreased in the least. The police were holding it back t
the fire lines, and discussing the tragedy in a tone which thos
seasoned witnesses of death seldom use.

"It's the worse thing I ever saw," said one old policeman.

Chief Croker said it was an outrage. He spoke bitterly of th
way in which the Manufacturers' Association had called
meeting in Wall Street to take measures against his proposal fo
enforcing better methods of protection for employes in cases o
fire.

No Chance to Save Victims.

Four alarms were rung in fifteen minutes. The first five girl
who jumped did so before the first engine could respond. Tha
fact may not convey much of a picture to the mind of a
unimaginative man, but anybody who has ever seen a fire can ge
from it some idea of the terrific rapidity with which the flame
spread.

It may convey some idea, too, to say that thirty bodies clogge
the elevator shafts. These dead were all girls. They had mad

heir rush there blindly when they discovered that there was no
hance to get out by the fire escape. Then they found that the
levator was as hopeless as anything else, and they fell there in
heir tracks and died.

The Triangle Waist Company employed about 600 women
nd less than 100 men. One of the saddest features of the thing is
he fact that they had almost finished for the day. In five minutes
nore, if the fire had started then, probably not a life would have
een lost.

Last night District Attorney Whitman started an investiga-
ion—not of this disaster alone, but of the whole condition which
nakes it possible for a firetrap of such a kind to exist. Mr. Whit-
nan's intention is to find out if the present laws cover such cases,
nd if they do not to frame laws that will.

108

THE YIDDISH PRESS AS AN AMERICANIZING AGENCY
1912

One might be tempted to think that the Yiddish press, a foreign-language medium, was a deterrent to speedy Americanization. The opposite is true. The foreign-language newspaper which the immigrant woman read taught her how to survive in this country, so different in culture and economy from her East European homeland.

The following account in the January 2, 1912 edition of the New York Warheit ("The Truth") offered mothers instruction in the feeding of babies. The newspaper imparted the latest findings of pediatrics to mothers anxiously concerned about the health of their children.

THE MOTHER AND HER BABY.

One of the greatest experts on the question of the bringing up of babies says the following, in his book called *The Nursery* (p. 171).

"Formerly a mother had to bring twelve children into the world in order that three might live. Now she brings three and all three live. There is no reason why a child born healthy should not grow up to be healthy. Merely ignorance on the part of the mother or the governess can result in the fact that a healthy child should not remain alive."

These words are true from beginning to end.

Every intelligent woman who can read a book in English, German, French, or Russian can learn all the rules and requirements regarding the rearing of the child. By the word "bringing up" we mean here not spiritual or material but simply the nursery attention

Englishmen and Americans have written a number of books on this question. Almost all of them were written by experts. A certain doctor has devoted years of study to this question, and his

596

book is the result of careful observations, which are usually very accurate. Every woman ought to have a book which explains the questions of wifehood and motherhood, and then regarding the duties of bringing up a child. . . .

In such a large city as New York there die annually thousands of children from summer complaint. Every mother in any tenement can prevent that.

We will tell you, for instance, regarding several false notions of old-fashioned and ignorant mothers. They nurse a child and allow it to nurse at any time when it cries. That is wrong. The child ought to nurse for several minutes (from about ten to fifteen minutes) every two hours, before it becomes four months old, and after that every three hours.

Many mothers begin to feed their children when they become three or four months old. No babies should be given anything but their mothers' milk before they become a year old; then they should be weaned and given a little milk and stale white bread, occasionally a baked potato, etc.

How many mothers know that when a baby is a day or two old it should be given water to drink?

How many mothers are there who do not know that a child must cry in order to develop its lungs and certain organs of its body, and that when a child cries it does not necessarily mean that it is sick?

Take the children who are being reared according to modern rules. You would be surprised to see how clean their bodies are, how bright their eyes are, and how splendid their general condition of health is.

The mother who has the opportunity to know all this and does not know it is actually guilty of criminal negligence.

Any woman that does not know where to obtain such books or who does not have any money to spend, may obtain these books in all public libraries. Any librarian will give her the necessary information.

It is really high time that women in modern times should take life a little more seriously and should know that they are responsible for the lives of their children.

109

GOLDIE STONE, LIAISON COMMUNAL WORKER FOR THE NEW IMMIGRANTS
1912

Goldie Tuvin (Mrs. Julius) Stone was a Lithuanian who came to the United States in 1880 and settled in Chicago. The family came later, and in 1892, at the age of eighteen, Goldie was married. Unlike most Slavic Jewesses who emigrated here, Goldie had a background of culture and learning. Drawn at a very early age into social work on behalf of her fellow Russian immigrants, she became identified in the course of years with some of Chicago's outstanding philanthropic institutions: the Chicago Hebrew Institute—a settlement house—the Marks Nathan Orphan Home, the Federated Orthodox Jewish Charities, the Josephine Club—a home for immigrant girls and young ladies from the hinterland—the Orthodox Home for the Aged, and the Jewish Committee for Palestine Welfare.

Mrs. Stone is important because she represents an immigrant segment not hitherto given its just due. These were educated, bourgeois-minded immigrant women from Eastern Europe who were eager to cooperate with the native Jewish elite, to adapt the pattern of American Jewish institutions to the needs of the newcomers, and, finally, in a later decade to amalgamate their recently created philanthropies with those of the older settlers into a common unified federation. In Chicago, Goldie served as a prime instrument of liaison with the older established Jewish community. Today, in the late twentieth century, the children of these new settlers—some women, too—have been admitted into the inner circle of the communal elite.

Excerpts from her autobiography which illuminate her activities are reprinted below.

———————

Community service is at one and the same time difficult and satisfying. No sooner is the desired goal reached than its importance diminishes and newer distant goals beckon. Inherent in human nature is the desire to reach out, to seek to grow, to branch out into new fields. The will to advance reveals the magic of untried, and sometimes almost unsuspected, power.

Each successful project brought to our attention other needs. The Orthodox Home for the Aged inspired the Marks Nathan Home for Jewish Orphans, and that in turn was followed by the Maimonides Hospital, more recently known as the Mount Sinai Hospital.

Unfortunately it was necessary for each organization to follow its own method of fund raising. Mr. Julius Rosenwald had often discussed these unstable methods at our numerous conferences.

"We can learn much by studying the methods of other similar organizations," he urged. "You must understand that I am interested in the needs of any people regardless of race, color or creed. It happens that there are some ethnic groups who are not able to help themselves because they have been downtrodden and because as a people they are impoverished. Often in their desperate anxiety for themselves they forget the needs of their fellows. Other peoples lack a tradition of giving. Fortunately, the Jewish people have a tradition of charity. They don't have to be taught to give—even the poorest of them give, but that giving must be organized so that it can do the most good."

Mr. Rosenwald then turned to me with this question.

"Do you believe, Mrs. Stone, that we can federate all of the West Side Jewish Charities [of the East European immigrant Jews]?"

I did not hesitate to reply.

"Mr. Rosenwald, that is exactly where we have been heading. All these projects that we have been undertaking have proven to the people of the West Side that we want to share their problems. I think that is a firm enough basis upon which to build right now."

He smiled at my answer and after a moment's hesitation said,

"Very well, then, I will contribute five thousand dollars a year to this federation if you can make it a fact."

My heart pounded with excitement at the suddenness of this proposal.

"Will you act as president of the meeting when the representatives of the different organizations will be summoned?" I asked eagerly.

"Yes, Mrs. Stone, if you will act as secretary of the meeting."

The Assembly Hall of the Jewish People's Institute was crowded to capacity [1912]. Naturally everyone was eager to hear the message of the great philanthropist and the meeting was indeed an historic event. The Federated Orthodox Jewish Charities came into being at that assembly, and when the discussions were over I had been made financial secretary of the Federation. This caused a buzz of conversation in certain corners of the hall where numerous representatives had expected a man to be appointed to that office. Mr. Bernard Horwich, an acknowledged leader and philanthropist on the West Side of the city, was elected president of the [Orthodox] Federated Charities of Chicago.

Mr. Rosenwald was in the center of an eager group of orthodox rabbis who were fairly bursting with questions. One old man seemed particularly perturbed. "Why a woman for financial secretary? A man should have that position. Such responsibilities are too heavy for a woman to assume."

Before Mr. Rosenwald could answer, a rabbi in the group said witheringly: "Why, what are you talking about? Was not Miriam a Prophetess and Deborah a Judge in Israel?" And thus the skeptic was squelched.

At the first meeting of the newly formed Federation pledges of fifty thousand dollars were signed. Flushed with success I asked Mr. Rosenwald a question that had been propounded to me by my friends.

"Why is it that you always pledge an amount *on condition* that an equal or proportionate amount be subscribed by others? Why don't you make your gift an outright donation?"

He made a wry grimace. "Mrs. Stone, surely you know the answer to that; why ask it? Some people have to be prodded into bearing their fair share of the responsibility, and that is my method of prodding.". . .

One evening when we were conversing, after the rest of the guests had gone, Mrs. Rosenwald said softly to her husband,

"Do you know, Julius, what I should like to do now above all else?"

"What organization is it this time, Augusta?"

"No, this wish concerns just you and me. I should like to escap nd take you with me. We would run away from all the ties and responsibilities of our daily life. We would go to a little log cabin somewhere in the north woods where I could do again some of those little things that meant so much to us in the early days of our marriage when you were struggling to get started. Most of all, I would like to cook your favorite dishes. I would be gloriously selfish and have you to myself alone."

Mr. Rosenwald leaned toward her and patted her hand. "I wonder, my dear, whether that could ever become a reality again even if we went to your little dream cabin in the woods. We are attuned to a life that is far more complex. There are too many hands holding on to the dream chariot that would take us there, and you cannot rap their knuckles, my dear, to make them let go. They are our responsibilities and we cannot run away."

"Well," she sighed, "it relaxes me just to think about it."

Although I had enjoyed the privilege of her friendship for many years, it was when the two of us organized the Chicago Jewish Committee for Palestinian Welfare [1913] that I got to understand and appreciate more fully the honesty and sincerity of her spirit. She was so splendidly comfortable about being a Jewess. She moved in and about the problems of her people as a great lady moves about her stately halls, familiar with every furnishing, with every tiny piece.

"You know," she said to me with a twinkle in her eyes, "Dr. Rabbi Emil G.] Hirsch is not, and has never been, an adherent to the Zionist cause, so I must confess that I am looking forward to the visit of Miss Henrietta Szold with the greatest of interest."

Then I met Miss Henrietta Szold. Her every gesture was a magic brush painting a truly fascinating picture of the miracle that was happening in Palestine.

"You must understand that Palestine is a blackboard upon which the Jewish people can once for all demonstrate to the whole world their creative and vital spirit."

I ventured to interrupt. "But, Miss Szold, are not the Jews creating and enriching the culture of the lands of which they are citizens?" I felt that I was the echo of Dr. Hirsch's sermons.

She was patient with me.

"But among the nations of the world their contributions

become lost; that is to say, no one recognizes or bothers to point out what our people have contributed. It goes into the general heap. The fault or sin of an individual Jew, however, is chalked up against the entire people so that in the eyes of many of our neighbors, the red side of the ledger is very vivid and the black not even known. There can be no mistake about Palestine where it is clearly a case of *creatio ex nihilo;* the demonstration is entirely convincing."

"I called Palestine a blackboard," she continued. "It is one that doesn't readily take the chalk. Trachoma, malaria, diseases of every sort arising out of swamps filled with poison—hills where the rocks have to be blasted with dynamite and the stones have to be torn out with the fingers to expose a barren earth which in turn must be watered by irrigation and by sweat—this is a real challenge, isn't it?"

I was watching Mrs. Rosenwald as Miss Szold was speaking. Her face was alight with interest. I at once suggested that Miss Szold come to my home the following day when a group of my friends would be there to discuss her message more informally and more intimately.

Some of these women were at first apprehensive. "After all, you know what Dr. Hirsch thinks of Zionism," said one. Another one timidly ventured, "But isn't that sort of a disloyalty? Won't people think that we are un-American if we interest ourselves in the Zionist movement?"

Miss Szold bowed her head for a moment.

"That is our tragedy, my friends. We live in slavery even in a free land. We try to mold our lives to what we think our Gentile neighbors would like us to be. We are so afraid to show our love for our traditions that we lean in the other direction and become antagonistic to them. An Irishman may sing to his heart's content, 'Ireland Must Be Heaven.' Children in schools sing among their school songs, 'Die Wacht am Rhein,' but let a Jew sing of Zion and he trembles for fear that he might be thought disloyal."

Nevertheless, several of the women persisted in their resolution that they did not want to be affiliated with the Zionist movement as such, but that they were perfectly willing to help unfortunate people regardless of where they were, and thus the Jewish Committee for Palestinian Welfare came into existence. . . .

To our great surprise, Dr. Emil G. Hirsch gave us wholehearted cooperation, although he insisted that he would not and could not be interested in any national home for the Jewish people in Palestine.

Most of our members were so far removed from a knowledge of Jewish tradition and Jewish history that it was as though they were contemplating something entirely alien to their experience.

An elderly lady, whom I called Aunt Sarah, urged me to stay to lunch one day as she had prepared some baked ham which was always greeted with paeans of praise by those whose palate it had pleased. Her daughter reminded her that I didn't eat ham.

"Oh, yes," she said, "how stupid of me—I forgot—I didn't think." And then to her daughter, "Let's prepare a little bacon for her."

She was very much in earnest and when I demurred at the second suggestion, explaining briefly the reason for my refusal, she said in a tone of amused surprise, "Are you a stomach Jew, Goldie?"

I patted her upon the arm and answered,

"Once we didn't classify Jews as heart Jews, head Jews or stomach Jews. Once a Jew loved his traditions and felt quite comfortable under them."

Aunt Sarah nodded somewhat chastened but zealous to show me the error of my ways. "Now look here, Goldie, you are not a fanatic. Once upon a time the pig was a very filthy animal and carried no end of diseases, and no doubt that is why the Jews were prohibited from using it as food, but now—"

"Now," I interrupted gently, "the pig is milk-fed, bathed regularly, wallows in whipped-cream instead of mud, and rests upon the digestion lightly as an airy cloud."

She wanted to continue along the same vein, but I felt that the subject had been discussed far enough, and so I merely added, "Call my reasons merely sentimental, but all through the ages Jews were ready to die and many actually did die rather than touch the flesh of swine which seemed to them to be the symbol of everything unclean. It would seem as though I were jeering at their spirit and courage if I were to eat what was so abhorrent to them and what I can get along very well without."

I was not extremely religious. My faith could be summed up in a simple phrase—"Be kind." I could not expect myself to *love* every person that I met, but I could *be kind* to every one; that was not expecting too much and the world would be so much more pleasant for it.

28. Mary Antin

Courtesy, New York Public Library, Astor, Lenox and Tilden Foundations

110

MARY ANTIN, EUPHORIC AMERICAN
1912

Mary Antin's The Promised Land, *published in 1912, ecstatically praised the freedom its author enjoyed in this best of all possible lands. In her writings, Antin (1881–1949) attempted to emphasize the spiritual obligations which, in her view, constituted America's mission. As the pages reprinted below testify, her love of the new homeland knew no bounds. An immigrant herself, she respected the newcomers and, more than most, knew what they had achieved: "What we get in the steerage is not the refuse but the sinew and bone of all nations." Because the new Promised Land meant everything to her and had given everything to her, Judaism meant little. How could it have been otherwise? She came from the Russian Pale of Settlement, where Jews were degraded as Jews; she had never had an opportunity—because she was a Russian, a Jew, a woman—to learn much about the history, the ethics, the beauties of the religioethnic community into which she was born. It was virtually inevitable that, for her, acculturation would spell assimilation, though she never cut herself off from her people.*

Mary Antin came to these shores from White Russia at the age of thirteen; she wrote and published poetry and a book by the time she was eighteen. This eager, starry-eyed lass studied at Columbia and Barnard, but never earned a degree. The Promised Land *made her a national celebrity by the time she was thirty-one. Mary had married a Gentile while still at college. Since civil religion was the only altar at which she worshiped, it was probably no wrench for her to marry out. The marriage, apparently, was not a happy one. She was in some respects a very difficult person. This highly intelligent, sensitive woman never became a literary figure of enduring significance, though her books are beautiful. She ceased to write and made a living in her latter years as a social worker. For some reason, she lost faith in herself; psychically, it was no light thing to make the Atlantic crossing. Maybe she lost her soul when dread reality throttled her dream.*

In after years, when I passed as an American among Americans, if I was suddenly made aware of the past that lay forgotten—if a letter from Russia, or a paragraph in the newspaper, or a conversation overheard in the street-car, suddenly reminded me of what I might have been—I thought it miracle enough that I, Mashke, the granddaughter of Raphael the Russian, born to a humble destiny, should be at home in an American metropolis, be free to fashion my own life, and should dream my dreams in English phrases. But in the beginning my admiration was spent on more concrete embodiments of the splendors of America; such as fine houses, gay shops, electric engines and apparatus, public buildings, illuminations, and parades. My early letters to my Russian friends were filled with boastful descriptions of these glories of my new country. No native citizen of Chelsea took such pride and delight in its institutions as I did. It required no fife and drum corps, no Fourth of July procession, to set me tingling with patriotism. Even the common agents and instruments of municipal life, such as the letter carrier and the fire engine, I regarded with a measure of respect. I know what I thought of people who said that Chelsea was a very small, dull, unaspiring town, with no discernible excuse for a separate name or existence. . . .

The public school has done its best for us foreigners, and for the country, when it has made us into good Americans. I am glad it is mine to tell how the miracle was wrought in one case. You should be glad to hear of it, you born Americans; for it is the story of the growth of your country; of the flocking of your brothers and sisters from the far ends of the earth to the flag you love; of the recruiting of your armies of workers, thinkers, and leaders. And you will be glad to hear of it, my comrades in adoption; for it is a rehearsal of your own experience, the thrill and wonder of which your own hearts have felt.

How long would you say, wise reader, it takes to make an American? By the middle of my second year in school I had reached the sixth grade. When, after the Christmas holidays, we began to study the life of Washington, running through a summary of the Revolution, and the early days of the Republic, it seemed to me that all my reading and study had been idle until then. The reader, the arithmetic, the song book, that had so fascinated me until now, became suddenly sober exercise books, tools wherewith to hew a way to the source of inspiration. When the teacher read to us out of a big book with many bookmarks in it, I sat rigid with attention in my little chair, my hands tightly clasped on the edge of my desk; and I painfully held my breath, to prevent sighs of disappointment escaping, as I saw the teacher skip the parts between bookmarks. When the class read, and it came my turn, my voice shook and the book trembled in my hands. I could not pronounce the name of George Washington without a pause. Never had I prayed, never had I chanted the songs of David, never had I called upon the Most Holy, in such utter reverence and worship as I repeated the simple sentences of my child's story of the patriot. I gazed with adoration at the portraits of George and Martha Washington, till I could see them with my eyes shut. And whereas formerly my self-consciousness had bordered on conceit, and I thought myself an uncommon person, parading my schoolbooks through the streets, and swelling with pride when a teacher detained me in conversation, now I grew humble all at once, seeing how insignificant I was beside the Great. . . .

My father, in his ambition to make Americans of us, was rather headlong and strenuous in his methods. . . . My father gave my mother very little time to adjust herself. He was only three years from the Old World with its settled prejudices. Considering his education, he had thought out a good deal for himself, but his line of thinking had not as yet brought him to include woman in the intellectual emancipation for which he himself had been so eager even in Russia. This was still in the day when he was astonished to learn that women had written books—had used their minds, their imaginations, unaided. He still rated the mental capacity of the average woman as only a little above that of the cattle she tended. He held it to be a wife's duty to follow her husband in all things. He could do all the thinking for the family, he believed; and being convinced that to hold to the outward forms of orthodox Judaism was to be hampered in the race for Americanization, he did not hesitate to order our family life on unorthodox lines. There was no conscious despotism in this; it was only making manly haste to realize an ideal the nobility of which there was no one to dispute.

My mother, as we know, had not the initial impulse to depart from ancient usage that my father had in his habitual scepticism. He had always been a nonconformist in his heart; she bore lovingly the yoke of prescribed conduct. Individual freedom, to him, was the only tolerable condition of life; to her it was confusion. My mother, therefore, gradually divested herself, at my father's bidding, of the mantle of orthodox observance; but the process cost her many a pang, because the fabric of that venerable garment was interwoven with the fabric of her soul.

My father did not attempt to touch the fundamentals of her faith. He certainly did not forbid her to honor God by loving her neighbor, which is perhaps not far from being the whole of Judaism. If his loud denials of the existence of God influenced her to reconsider her creed, it was merely an incidental result of the freedom of expression he was so eager to practise, after his life of enforced hypocrisy. As the opinions of a mere woman on matters so abstract as religion did not interest him in the least, he counted it no particular triumph if he observed that my mother weakened in her faith as the years went by. He allowed her to keep a Jewish kitchen as long as she pleased, but he did not want us children to refuse invitations to the table of our Gentile neighbors. He would have no bar to our social intercourse with the world around us, for only by freely sharing the life of our neighbors could we come into our full inheritance of American freedom and opportunity. On the holy days he bought my mother a ticket for the synagogue, but the children he sent to school. On Sabbath eve my mother might light the consecrated candles, but he kept the store open until Sunday morning. My mother might believe and worship as she pleased, up to the point where her orthodoxy began to interfere with the American progress of the family.

The price that all of us paid for this disorganization of our family life has been levied on every immigrant Jewish household where the first generation clings to the traditions of the Old World, while the second generation leads the life of the New. Nothing more pitiful could be written in the annals of the Jews; nothing more inevitable; nothing more hopeful. Hopeful, yes; alike for the Jew and for the country that has given him shelter.

29. Ernestine Heller

111

ERNESTINE HELLER AND THE MAXWELL STREET SETTLEMENT HOUSE
ca. 1912

The Chicago Jewish native-born, so-called Germans, thought it necessary, if not imperative, to establish a settlement house in the congested West Side district. The example of Jane Addams' Hull House was constantly before them. The conscientious Jewish elite, determined to "Americanize" the immigrant and, if possible, do something to solve the problem of juvenile delinquency, established the Maxwell Street Settlement House in 1893. It was not successful at first; it was a resented philanthropy; the newcomers thought they were being patronized. Not until Ernestine Heller (1865– 1955) took charge in the early twentieth century was this neighborhood house accepted by its East European clientele.

Ernestine Heller is usually bracketed with her sister Louise (1866– 1958), a nurse. They were known as "The Girls." Both were born in Prague, as was their brother Max, who was to become one of the country's leading Reform rabbis and a pioneer Zionist. Ernestine, originally an office manager at the settlement, finally became the headworker. The following account was written in 1954 by their niece Ruth Heller (Mrs. Alfred) Steiner. The excerpts reprinted below deal primarily with Ernestine in her role as a very successful social worker and administrator.

Hull House had done pioneering work in its depressed Irish-Polish neighborhood, and Maxwell Street, with a distinguished Jewish board of directors, extended the deeply human technique of the settlement house to the poorest Jewish neighborhood. As at Hull House, its workers were residents—they not only worked within the doors which always stood open to their neighbors, they lived there and shared their daily lives.

How Ernestine moved up from office head to head worker, I don't really know. She seemed to think the considerable jump, over the heads of trained personnel, was unremarkable, and she merely said it was because the former head worker transferred to another job. That can't be the whole story. It couldn't have happened today, what with B.A. and M.A. degrees and job analyses and all the semi-scientific paraphernalia of social work. But when she took over, a quiet force behind the keen, brown eyes hit that neighborhood and made itself felt for many years.

Ernestine had the advantage of understanding Yiddish, through her knowledge of German; she gathered around herself a group of workers whom she helped train and many of whom she still has as close friends. I saw her at work at the Maxwell House at a formative period in my own life, and it helped me toward a decision on my own profession.

The following clipping was handed to me by my cousin in Chicago; I have no way of knowing the year, or the paper from which it was taken:

One Woman's Wisdom
by E. L. Valentine

Miss Heller is the amiable and greatly respected head of the Maxwell Street social settlement house. Her influence has permeated the region roundabout and it has come to be the common custom to refer to her as arbitrator of all the disputes that arise in the thickly settled community of which the house is the natural center.

The talent she has shown repeatedly in leaving both sides satisfied with her decision has gained her a reputation of the sort that Solomon of old enjoyed. But in nothing has her wisdom been manifested more strikingly than in an incident which happened a few days ago.

Mrs. Braunschwiger's little boy, Lester, had a penny—money is the root of all evil. Desiring to invest it in such food as would vary and supplement his rather limited culinary range at home, he approached the slot machine on the corner presided over by Mrs. Kohn, duly inserted the coin in the orifice provided and awaited the peanuts tacitly promised.

Just what took place in respect of Lester and the machine is still a matter of dispute. Lester averred that no peanuts were forthcoming whatever, and that the heartless machine retained the penny. Mrs. Kohn states solemnly that not only did a full penny's worth of peanuts discharge themselves into Lester's grimy hand, but he so shook the machine at a critical moment that he obtained another cent's worth on the spot.

The droves of children which pervade the neighborhood took up the side of their small fellow. Lester repeated his story to gathering crowds of urchins and future mothers of the republic and obtained their indorsement.

As a result the street was soon black with boys and girls who were pointing the finger of scorn at Mrs. Kohn and her slot machine and saying things that no small child should say about an elder person.

More than that, the mothers appeared also to take up the cause of their little ones and also pointed the finger of contumely at the peanut vendor and her apparatus.

The street was assuming the look of a riot when some cool-headed person bethought him of Miss Heller and rushed to the settlement house.

Miss Heller appeared, took in the situation at a glance, sniffed the air critically in full view of the gesticulating crowd, and remarked:

"I think I smell somebody's meat burning."

And the street cleared like magic, mothers taking their young.

Ernestine purposely kept the settlement house small and intimate and used the facilities of the nearby public schools and of her old hang-out, the Girls' Training School. She got the Marshall Field Company to lend their old busses for picnics in Lincoln Park. Many of the neighbors had thought, up to then, that trees and flowers grew only in the old country. One woman asked her wistfully, "When we move out of here some day, do you think we can arrange to get the right kind of fish for our gefillte fish?"

Across the street from the settlement was the Russishe Shul, the Russian synagogue, where a fight always developed at Passover time with the free distribution of matzos—the first to come grabbed too much, and the latecomers got no matzos.

Those in charge asked Miss Heller to take over and called her thereafter the Queen of the Matzos. Nearby was a shelter house for the destitute, whose workers were always in hot water with the State Board of Charities over their mixed-up records and expenditures; she took on their application and record work in addition to her own and linked it up with that of the settlement. She supervised another separate project a block away from the settlement, a day nursery for young children of working mothers, and raised the money to replace its cold, inadequate building with a fine, modern one.

One of Ernie's deep concerns was the fact that the neighbors, living in cold, unheated tenements, bought their coal in bushel baskets which bulged at the bottom and did not really hold a bushel. Angry at the short weights, she established a coal fund so that her people could save and buy coal by the ton. A board member underwrote the fund, and when eventually Maxwell House closed, that fund was entirely paid up. There was one bathtub to a block in the neighborhood; she convinced the city that a fine gymnasium and swimming-pool were needed.

Everyone knew that the firm, practical Miss Heller was a softy, too. A tramp could sleep in the basement of Maxwell House if the shelter house turned him away. And her courage was renowned; at the nearby Jefferson Market, the politicians had always extorted fees from the small proprietors of stalls and stands. Ernestine brought charges against them, haled them into court, and cleaned up the mess, at very real risk to her life. Probably no mere politician could have taken on the consequences of any harm to her. One or two of the neighbors across the street used to tell her, "Your light burned so late last night! I never go to sleep until your light is out!"

Ernie has fond memories of the time a mother stood up at a settlement party and yelled for her daughter, "Becky, come home. You're engaged!" And one story that we loved when we were children was of the little boy who fell silent when the worker who filled out his admissions card asked him his father's occupation. "You won't tell?" he begged anxiously. "Indeed I won't," she promised. Still he couldn't speak. "If I get Miss Heller and she promises too, will you tell us what your father does?" "Yes," he breathed in relief. And when Miss Heller came, he whispered in her ear, "My father's the bearded lady in the Dime Museum." . . .

This coming April [1955], Louise will be eighty-nine and Ernestine, who lives in fear of having a fuss made over it, will be ninety. "Really," said Louise recently about her sister, "isn't she remarkable for her age?"

112

HENRIETTA SZOLD, HADASSAH, AND PALESTINE
1912–1945

In 1912, Henrietta Szold (1860–1945), the daughter of a modernist Baltimore rabbi, joined the Daughters of Zion. This was the beginning of Hadassah, the Women's Zionist Organization of America, the largest Jewish association in the world. More than any other person, Henrietta Szold was the one who built this great American institution.

In 1920, she settled in Palestine and helped provide the medical services which have since done so much to eradicate malaria, trachoma, and other diseases in that territory, so woefully neglected for generations by the Turks before World War I. To a substantial degree, America's female Zionists are responsible for the growth of the Hadassah–Hebrew University Medical Center, which is said to practice the best medicine in the Middle East. After Germany began to persecute the Jews, Szold turned her attention to the rescue of Germany's Jewish children (1934). The Youth Aliyah ("Going Up" to Israel) program which Hadassah soon sponsored (1935) brought deliverance to thousands of young boys and girls. Many of their parents perished in the concentration camps.

Here in the United States, Henrietta Szold encouraged the Jewish cultural studies which were later to mark the Hadassah programs. Hers was a binationalist Zionism, for she envisaged a conjoint state of Jews and Arabs. Her Judaism, however, was traditionalist; she had little sympathy for Classical Reform. She was a feminist, that is to say, a woman who expected recognition for the work she was doing; yet this did not preclude her yearning for a husband and children. She was no "glamour girl." Of her it may be said that the race was definitely not to the swift. She was a hardworking, determined, self-sacrificing woman who labored for a cause to which she was utterly devoted. No Jewess in the first half of the twentieth century did more for American and Palestinian Jewry than Henrietta Szold.

In selection A, Miss Szold describes the problems facing Jewish Palestine during World War I; item B is an account of the medical work carried on by Hadassah; the third document, C, is a report on the arrival of Jewish girls and boys from anti-Semitic Germany. This was the beginning of Youth Aliyah, immigration to Palestine.

30. Henrietta Szold

A

1915

New York, January 17, 1915

[To Mrs. Julius Rosenwald]

Your night letter has come to hand, and you will receive a copy of all recent telegrams that have reached the Provisional Executive Committee for General Zionist Affairs concerning the situation both in Palestine and among the refugees in Jaffa. Most of our information at present concerning Palestine comes from a group of Palestinians who have taken up their abode in Alexandria, in order that they may serve as intermediaries between Palestine and ourselves. If it were not for them, we should lack information about many points, and we should not be able to get money to our people in Jaffa.

I asked them to do so in order to make up for the meagerness of the letters received from our own nurses. I am enclosing the most recent *Bulletin* issued by Hadassah, in which you will see that we received only postcards.

You will notice that though Mr. [Aaron] Aaronsohn [a Palestinian pioneer and agronomist] advises the nurses to return to the United States, they have made no move to do it as far as we know.

Let me congratulate you and Palestine upon having secured, as you tell me in your telegram, a "splendid response from local organization" [Chicago Jewish Committee for Palestinian Welfare]. I wish there were a way of Hadassah's being kept informed of all you do. I have requested Mrs. [Lee J.] Lesser to employ a stenographer at our expense and to dictate to her a full account of what has happened for our benefit. It would be so valuable to us from the point of view of propaganda.

However, the paramount consideration is that you are advancing the cause of Palestine. From my point of view, as I need not tell *you*, that is the cause of the Jew and, most important of all, of Judaism. In many respects the war catastrophe has left me bewildered and uncertain. In one respect I see more clearly than ever—that is in respect to Zionism. The anomalous situation of the Jew everywhere—the distress, misery, and in part degradation (witness Poland!) of seven millions, more than half, of our race; the bravery of the Jews who are serving in all the armies; the size of the contingent we are contributing to every front—means to me that the Jew and his Judaism must be perpetuated and can be perpetuated only by their repatriation in the land of the fathers.

It is a miracle that, though we Zionists were not hitherto able to bring many to our way of thinking, nevertheless many in these days of stress think with pity of our little sanctuary. They have come to us and said: "Even if we do not see eye to eye with you, we are going to help you save the sanctuary you have established." Perhaps they feel that it will yield sanctuary, refuge, and protection in the days of readjustment soon to dawn, we hope.

If you succeed, in your appeal to the Federation of Temple Sisterhoods, in conveying to the Jewish women of America the need of such a sanctuary for the Jew, the need of a center from which Jewish culture and inspiration will flow, and if you can persuade them to set aside one day of the year as a Palestine Day, on which thoughts and means are to be consecrated to a great Jewish world-organizing purpose, you will have accomplished a result that will bring immediate blessing to those now in distress and in terror of life, and a blessing for all future times redounding to the benefit not only of those who will make use of their sanctuary rights in Palestine, but also those who like ourselves, remaining in a happy, prosperous country, will be free to draw spiritual nourishment from a center dominated wholly by Jewish traditions and the Jewish ideals of universal peace and universal brotherhood.

If you and they do not follow us Zionists so far, at least they will respond to the appeal for material help—at least they will recognize that for the sake of Jewish dignity and self-respect, even the purely philanthropic work in Palestine, for which so large a part of Jewry has long felt a keen responsibility, may never again be allowed to relapse into a pauperizing chaos. They may refuse to accept the whole Zionist ideal. But the wonderful vitality shown by the Zionist settlement in the Holy Land—the resourcefulness of the colonists, who could supply the cities with grain and food for months, and the usefulness of the Zionist bank in averting panic and the direst distress—they make of me a more confirmed and conscious Zionist than ever. I need not analyze the elements I have enumerated for you. You, who have been in the Holy Land, even if you do not—may I say, not yet?—agree with me, your mind will instinctively understand the leap mine makes in these troublous days to the Zionist conclusion.

Troublous days? I have often wondered during these months how many of us Jews here in America realize that we are living through times comparable only to the destruction of the second Temple and of our commonwealth by the Romans, and exceeding by far the horrors of the exodus from Spain and Portugal, and the abject misery and suffering of the pogrom years 1881, and 1903, and 1905 in Russia.

The Jew speaks of the first *Hurban*—the utter destruction of Solomon's Temple. He speaks of the second *Hurban*, the ruin of the second Temple by Titus. I feel that a future Graetz will speak of this war as the Jews' third *Hurban*. [Heinrich Graetz was the great Jewish historian.]

There is only one hope in my heart—the effective aid being rendered to Palestine by all Jews without difference. In the first *Hurban* the Jews could not protect their sanctuary against the hordes of Nebuchadnezzar. In the second *Hurban* the Roman legions destroyed the Temple, leaving only the western wall, the last vestige of glory, now turned into a place of wailing. There is no third Temple on the hill of Zion to be destroyed in this third *Hurban*; but in Zion, nevertheless, there is a sanctuary, the refuge that has been established by Jewish pioneers, with the sweat, blood, and labor of those who believe. As American Jewesses they cannot possibly reject the centralized organization of Palestine, an endeavor for which Zionism stands first and last.

With cordial wishes for success, and, may I add this only once only, with Zion's greetings.

B

[Addressee not given]

I can give you no idea of the bigness of the [Medical] Unit work in the field and in the office—actually and administratively. For the administration of the work we have an inadequate personnel, inadequate in number and in efficiency. The result is that everyone in the head office must work at a constant high pressure. Please picture me sitting from morning until night inside of a mountain of letters and notes which I myself create. I cast them out faster than they can be picked up and executed and carried to their destination. For one removed, I vomit forth a dozen.

But I'd rather tell you of my days away from the office. There were nine of them, during a tour of inspection through Upper and Lower Galilee. I touched at thirty-one points in which the Unit has some interest, either a doctor, or a nurse, or a sanitary inspector. That gives you an idea of the extent of our undertaking. I hasten to admit that it is not so intensive as extensive. I have been oscillating between these two poles, without being able to decide which should have been sacrificed to which. We cannot have both without a budget out of all proportion to the financial powers of the Zionist world. What the extent of our work should indicate to you is that the criticism made against it very freely before the [12th Zionist] Congress at Carlsbad, that we are doing nothing for the halutzim and workingmen in general, the "productive" Jewish population, is false. Most of the thirty-one points are camps, workingmen's groups, colonies, etc.

Some of our critics went to the Congress with the intention of proposing that our hospitals be given up and all our available funds be devoted to the immigrants, the proper charge of the Zionist Organization. There is logic in this contention. Indeed, from my point of view, which is that everything of a public character ought to be thrown on the shoulders of the mandate government, the Medical Unit ought to cease to exist. Unless we make the government concern itself with us, it will never be our government in any sense of the word. The Zionist Organization pledged itself to take care of every immigrant for one year after his arrival. This, then, should be the extent of its medical task—logically.

But the course of Zionist development has not been any more logical than the rest of life has the habit of being. By force of circumstances, the Zionists have evolved a medical service which has served, and some time to come will continue to serve, as a standard to the government itself. The government establishments cannot compare with ours. And Jews being Jews, with a very proper regard for their bodies, must have a better service than the Palestinian government can now give them. Then it is folly to think of abridging the Unit work—or to think of caring for the immigrant at the front without good, modern hospitals behind the lines. I should urge the Zionist Organization to make one magnificent effort and secure a great sanitary fund. The malaria-sanitary problem in Palestine is so well defined that it can be solved without residue in a short time and with not too much money.

First I'd like to tell you more about my trip, especially about the malaria-sanitary work, which, in a way, is the best we are doing. Most interesting of all is the anti-malaria experiment carried on since last March, by means of a fund of $10,000, the special gift for the purpose made by Mr. [Louis D.] Brandeis. The settlements at the north and south end of the Sea of Tiberias were chosen as the scene of the experiment. They comprise some of the well-known pest-holes of malaria. At Migdal Farm, for instance, a paradise—oranges, lemons, palms, bananas, almonds, and what not—with the anopheles mosquito playing the part of serpent—there were seventy-eight victims of malaria last summer, out of a possible eighty employees and laborers. You must consider what that means—on the average two attacks a season for each victim. Can you calculate the economic loss? This summer, so far—the malaria season ends only in December—the record is reversed: only two cases of malaria! In the whole region, comprising a population of about 1000 to 1200, there have been only five cases of malaria.

The results are all the more interesting because part of the population is shifting. It includes two road-builders' camps to which new forces from malaria-ridden sections are constantly being brought, and also it includes a few Arab villages which have been treated along with the Jewish settlements. The whole paraphernalia developed in Panama and Arkansas, etc., has been applied: petrolization of swamps, canalization and regulation, treatment of carriers, quinine prophylaxis under strict supervision, mosquito-nets, clearing of grassy spots that serve as breeding-places, etc. There is a microscopist on the spot, the doctors are enlisted for the therapeutic treatment, and a small corps of sanitary inspectors watch the swamps, execute the works, administer the quinine, look out for dripping faucets, etc. Result: the men sleep in the open, without nets, and remain unstung! It is a miracle.

When the money arrived in the spring for the purpose, we called a little conference of the physicians who had been in the country for more years than our Unit and who consider themselves malaria experts. The conference was to work out a plan of prevention within the limits of the budget. The best known among the physicians was rather contemptuous when he heard that the conference was expected to plan on a $10,000 basis. The Palestinians are very magnificent in their notions. Six ciphers is the minimum they are willing to manipulate with, especially when malaria is to be handled.

The experiment has proved conclusively that for three-fourths of Palestine the malaria problem is not a million-dollar engineering enterprise at all. In all but a few remote spots, it is a "thou-art-the-man" problem. The individual or rather the community of individuals can grapple with it. To be sure, there must be supervision, propaganda, education. I wish I could find time to write to Mr. Brandeis and give him a description of what has been done with his $10,000—which, by the way, has not been used up by a long shot.

It is such a pity I haven't time to keep in touch by correspondence with people in America. I have much material stored up, some of which would stimulate the interest of certain groups, and some of other groups. Do you know that in addition to the snug sum I carried with me from friends in America when I came here—it amounted to about $1300—to be applied as I saw fit, I have received $4150 since I am here for all sorts of purposes, named and to be named by me? Most of the sums came in response to letters of mine containing a bit of description of something or other out here. I never asked for money, never even thought of it. Isn't it a pity that I always get entangled in a multitude of administrative details?

You asked whether I have made friends with any of the Arab neighbors. Alas! the language difficulty. Three or four months ago a huge family took possession of the home next to us, which the head of the household has been building who knows how long. Since we have been here he has been working assiduously, but practically single-handed, laying stone upon stone, patiently. the whole harem down to the third generation visited us time and again. We—that is, Sophia [Berger]—talked to them with the aid of the glossary in Baedeker. Sophia has some Arabic from her Red Cross days here. The trouble began when they talked back. Baedeker does not provide for the second half of the conversation. A week ago they invited us to a betrothal party. I am charitable to surmise that the men's part was interesting. In the women's apartment it was deadly dull. My only emotion was aroused by the sight of the sick babies nursing at their mothers' breasts— eternally. I wanted to pick them up—oh, but they were so dirty!—and carry them to my hospital.

C

GERMAN YOUTH IMMIGRATION INTO PALESTINE
by Henrietta Szold

1934

(This article consists of excerpts from a report prepared by Miss Szold for the Central Bureau for the Settlement of German Jews in Palestine.)

On Monday, February 19, on the Steamship "Martha Washington" of the Lloyd Triestino Line, the first group of boys and girls organized for settlement in Palestine by the Juedische Jugendhilfe, the Federation of German Jewish youth organizations, arrived at the recently opened port of Haifa. There were forty-three of them, eighteen girls and twenty-five boys. An older comrade, Hanoch Reinhold, their trainer and leader, accompanied them. The group was destined for settlement in Ain Harod [in the Jezreel Valley].

Everything from quarantine to customs and from customs to the first meal on Palestinian soil moved flawlessly—except the weather. The vessel came in under a heavily shrouded sky, driven by a gale with the rain pelting down steadily. Good humor prevailed nevertheless. The merciless wet could not damp the enthusiasm of the young travellers nor the joy of their grandparents, brothers, sisters, aunts, and friends who were on hand to greet them. All of them, travellers and relatives, apparently forgot their discomfort, and swiftly adopted the point of view of the Palestinian farmer, who was rejoicing in the blessed downpour, a welcome change from the devastating drought of the three years preceding this winter of 1933–34.

The luggage heaped up on the dock was a formidable pile. Amid the suitcases of every conceivable shape, size, and material, there stuck up flagpoles and cellos and mandolins and, first and foremost, bicycles. In addition, some of the boys and girls had chunky rucksacks strapped to their backs. In spite of the careful preparations made beforehand and the numerous willing and expert helpers and the courtesy of the officials, the formalities stretched out over hours, from the early afternoon until long after seven in the evening. Finally, in the dark and through the rain, stimulated by the hope of the first square meal of the day, the troop trotted gayly across the wide expanse of the new wharf to the Workingmen's Kitchen facing the shore.

Through the foresight of the Ain Harod hosts, a special car had been secured for the transportation of the group and a considerable part of its belongings. On the railway journey of about one hour and three-quarters, there was much craning of necks and darting from windows on the one side of the train to windows on the other side, to catch a glimpse of Yajur, Nahalal, Kfar Yehoshuah, Kfar Yecheskel, and, finally, the twin Kewuzot [cooperatives] of Tel-Joseph and Ain Harod. All these were names not unknown to the boys and girls, also a gift of their youth organization training. They greeted them as acquaintances, and when the cross-road sign of Ain Harod and Tel-Joseph hove into sight, they sang out merrily: "Main Station of Ain Harod." Again they broke out into song, responding to the greetings of the older pupils of the Ain Harod and Tel-Joseph school who had descended to the railroad tracks to welcome their new companions. In the crowd were two lads belonging to the German group who had preceded it to Palestine. Boisterous greetings!

All the way up to the settlement, the troop was met by members of the Kewuzah streaming down to catch a first glimpse of the new contingent added to the six hundred, among them ninety recently come from Germany, which constitute the cooperative community of Ain Harod. At the top, in front of the dining room, the veranda of which was crowded with the rest of the residents, the ubiquitous photographer snapped the scene.

The travellers were hurried into the dining room for lunch and again, to the delight of the long-established Ain Harodians, they sang out lustily one Hebrew song after the other, their hosts joining in with a will. After the meal came the inevitable Horah [a round folk dance], which at once integrated the new arrivals into the company of the old residents.

At the order of the leader Reinhold, calm fell upon the dancers. The lull had been called for in order to assign rooms to the members of the group. The business was well-planned and executed, another evidence of the preliminary camp and group discipline practiced by the organizations in Germany which are taking care of the Youth Aliyah. There was but little challenging of the order established by those in charge, and such as there was expressed quietly and with precision. Then the troop was marched off to the storerooms to disengage sheets and pillows and pillow-cases and other necessities for the night from suitcases and trunks. It is characteristic of the thoughtful attitude of the Ain Harod hosts that even the first routine act in the new surroundings was made a festive ceremonial. The boys and girls were guided to the storehouses, not by the most direct route, but via the incubators, the workshops, and the stables, thus becoming familiarized at once with the lay of the land, within the precincts that are to be home for them for at least two years. On all sides there were expressions of amazement at the completeness of the Meshek [settlement]. It was beyond the expectation of the newcomers, they agreed. For the rest of the afternoon there was carrying to and fro and scouring the houses of the older settlers for blankets and what-not to supply the needs of those whose baggage had had to be left behind at Haifa for the next morning's transport.

The boys and girls will be housed in wooden barracks until the permanent concrete houses under construction for them are completed, which will be in about two months. The temporary arrangement is fully adequate. The barracks are well-built, the flooring firm and closely laid, and the walls protected against wet and wind inside and outside. On the second day, the rest of the baggage having arrived, the rooms were stocked and beautified with the equipment provided by loving hands at home. Within they lost all semblance to barracks and assumed a homelike, cozy air.

Meantime the teachers and other leaders were holding sessions to discuss details of a plan long ago laid out for work and study. In general terms the idea underlying the plan is study half the time, work the other half. For the first six months the studies will center about the Hebrew language, the geography of Palestine, the history of Israel and the Bible, and the work to be done by the young labourers will be such as to introduce them by means of the lightest tasks gradually to all the details of the Kewuzah life in the houses, in the stables, in the workshops, and in the fields. There will be planned walks to the neighbouring settlements—applied geography lessons—and there will be lectures and supervised reading. On the basis of what is achieved during the first six months, further plans will grow up.

113

CHICAGO JEWESSES, BREADWINNERS AND MANHUNTERS
1912–1920

In the depths of the depression of the 1930's, the government established the Works Progress (Projects) Administration to provide jobs for the unemployed. Many men with advanced cultural backgrounds were absorbed into the Federal Writers Project. In Chicago, the workers in the FWP made translations from earlier Yiddish newspapers in a Foreign Language Press Survey. The results of some of their labors are reprinted below.

The data reproduced here deal with two social groups among the Yiddish-speaking immigrant Jewesses, older matrons and young acculturated girls. The matrons described here were breadwinners. It is interesting to note that all of them worked in the garment factories. The younger women, girls in their early twenties for the most part, were all immigrants who had come as children and succeeded in securing a college education. Their problem was not one of keeping body and soul together, but finding a mate of equal cultural caliber. Basically, their goal was not to advance their careers; it was to establish a home with the right man.

The Daily Jewish Courier, July 8, 1912

Jewish Women

It is a great error to think that women are capable only of raising children and taking care of a house. The best illustration of this error is the Jewish women of Chicago. Several and even hundreds of Jewish women carry on business alone, work in shops [factories], and canvass from door to door. They are the only breadwinners of the entire family. One must naturally possess a great deal of energy and courage to carry all this through, but the Jewish women show that they have more than is needed, and these types of Jewish women are, without a doubt, the most clever in Jewish life.

True that this is an unfortunate phenomenon of our life, because women are more than capable, suitable, and obligated to raise children, run a house, and so forth. And it is also true that when they neglect to take care of the home, it's very bad. But what shall the Jewish women, whose fate compels them to carry on such life, do? You may rest assured that they do not engage in other activities for the sake of pleasure or happiness. Want, privation, and hunger drives them to do other things than housekeeping. Many are employed in other work because their husbands are handicapped and earn too little.

Upon visiting Jefferson Street, Maxwell Street, and many other streets you will witness how women run stands of fruit, clothing, fish, and other products, and several manage complete stores. In other localities you can meet Jewish women running candy stores, groceries, butcher shops, cleaning and dyeing stores and so forth. At times, the strength of our Jewish women is to be marvelled at. They endure heat, cold, rain, snow, winds, from early morning until late at night on the street or in poorly ventilated stores. The tragedy of such families cannot be overestimated. The children are not brought up as properly as they should be. Food is never dished out in proper time or proper manner. Walking through the West Side, one can observe dressmaking signs in the windows. These are practically all family women who are compelled to make dresses in order to help along the family budget. . . . A great number of Jewish women can be found in the tailoring shops working together with the opposite sex. Most of the women are unskilled and, therefore, are employed in the sweatshops where they work long hours with little pay. Speaking in general, we should not feel ashamed of our Jewish women.

Sunday Jewish Courier, November 14, 1920

The Plight of the Educated Jewish Girl

Miss Newberger's letter on the subject of the educated Jews in Chicago makes interesting reading. She states her case intelligently and formulates a problem the solution of which is difficult.

The semi-educated Jewish girls, whose only business in life is clothes, cosmetics, and good times, have no right to complain about the peculiarities of the Jewish young man. Since they have no ideals, they deserve their lot. It is quite different, however, with the educated, serious-minded, and modest Jewish girl who has to spend her youth in loneliness because she cannot find decent Jewish male companionship. The fact is that there are more educated Jewish girls than there are cultured Jewish men. Jewish parents in Chicago are often more anxious to send their daughters to college than their sons, and are more interested in the intellectual careers of their daughters than their sons because the sons are supposed to embark upon a business career and to make money as soon as possible, while the daughters are allowed to continue their studies. What is more, the Jewish intellectual sets a value upon himself even before he leaves the University, and is anxious to be a success financially as well, while the cultured Jewish girl is more idealistic and her attitude toward men and life is more refined. She is not obsessed with the idea of making money, as the Jewish professional man is—and if she has not been blessed with rich parents, she is, as a rule, ignored by her male colleague.

This may seem to be an exaggerated statement, but it is true, nevertheless. The materialism of the young Jewish professional is too well known to require any further discussion. It may be that this is an unpleasant passing phenomenon, but the reality of the phenomenon cannot be denied, and the cultured Jewish girl suffers most from it. It is, of course, true that in many cases the parents of the girls are to blame for the tragic lot of their daughters because they frighten young men away from their homes by attempting to "brand" them at once as *Chosons* [bridegrooms]. They do not permit a friendship to grow, to develop, to mature. No Jewish boy wants to be "captured." However, this hastiness on the part of the Jewish parents is only partly responsible for the plight of the cultured and refined Jewish girl. The main causes are: one, she outnumbers the cultured Jewish male youth; two, the young Jewish man is overly conscious of his own worth and is eager to become well-to-do as soon as he graduates by marrying a girl of means; three, there is no refined intellectual Jewish center in Chicago where both can meet on equal terms and become friends.

Can the situation—a very unpleasant situation—be remedied? We think that it can be remedied to a certain extent only. It would be difficult, if not impossible, to break the materialism of the young Jewish professional who differs in no way from his Gentile colleague; it would also be difficult to break the bad habit of Jewish parents of greeting their daughter's boy friend as the future son-in-law. It should not be difficult, however, to give both the boy and the girl an opportunity to meet and to make friends by establishing a Jewish intellectual center. This is our opinion on the matter.

It may be that there are other ways and means of improving the condition of the cultured Jewish girl. We confess that we are not experts in the field. This is the second time that the problem has been brought to our attention. We are convinced that there are many more things to be said on the subject and that a more exhaustive discussion would be of benefit to all concerned. Let the educated Jewish girl come forward and not only explain her case more fully, but also make suggestions and proposals as to how to remedy the situation.

The Daily Jewish Courier, November 30, 1920

SEEK SYNCOPATORS, NOT EDUCATORS

Editor, *Daily Jewish Courier*

Sir: We have been much interested recently in some letters in the *Courier* from young Jewish college girls. As school teachers, we have associations with some of the most cultured young Jewish girls in the city; and although almost all of them are teachers, they are good-looking, fashionably dressed, interested in sports, athletics, etc., and all are under twenty-two years of age. Although we are far from being snobbish, we consider that it would be a waste of all our training and hard work at school to choose as our associates young men who have not had as good a training as ours; yet it is practically impossible for us to meet the kind of man with whom we should like to associate. The clubs that are formed in the temples seem to be frequented by dance-crazy boys and girls in whom we are not at all interested, although we too like to dance. Our attempts to organize a college people's club at our temple have been unsuccessful. The men do not attend. Tell us, dear editor, are our young Jewish doctors, lawyers, and other professionals too busy to enjoy the company of girls who are not only pretty but also intelligent or are they, too, too much interested in the flapper to notice us? We should like to know.

Very sincerely,
Some Young Schoolma'ms

114

BELLE FLIGELMAN, SUFFRAGIST
1913–1917

Belle Fligelman, whose father was the owner of Fligelman's New York Dry Goods Company in Helena, Montana, is a native of the Treasure State. Her husband is Norman Winestine, one of Montana's most prominent Jewish citizens. In her younger days, Belle was active in politics, campaigning to secure the vote for women; later years found her active in the League of Women Voters and in the struggle to eliminate child labor.

Like many other cultured Jewish women of her generation, she is a writer; one of her short stories appeared in Atlantic Monthly.

In the following autobiographical account, she records her initial forays as a suffragist and her work as an aide to Jeannette Rankin, the first woman to serve in the United States Congress.

MOTHER WAS SHOCKED
by Belle Fligelman

The first time I got involved in the suffrage movement was somewhat accidental. It was in 1913, when I was a senior at the University of Wisconsin in Madison, then one of the intellectual centers of the reform spirit known as Progressivism. One afternoon a woman called me on the telephone and said, in a brisk voice, "This is state headquarters for women's suffrage in Wisconsin. The woman suffrage bill is to come up for a public hearing tonight before a joint session of the House and the Assembly."

"Oh," I said blankly.

"We feel because you are president of the women students at the University, you must come down to the capitol tonight and tell the legislators why women should have the right to vote."

"You'll have to excuse me," I protested, "I couldn't possibly."

My sister, Frieda, was interested in the women's suffrage

movement, and I knew that it was right for women to vote, but I didn't know that you had to have a reason for being right.

"You will talk ten minutes," the voice continued. "Please be at the capitol at 8:00 o'clock. . . . Put on your prettiest dress and look as feminine as possible."

Then there was a click. She had hung up. I was terrified. I told my friend, Mabel Search, who was a great deal smarter than I, what had happened.

"All you have to do," she said, "is give them a reason for voting."

"But I have no reason," I said. "I just know it's right."

"Look," she said, "both senators and assemblymen will be there. Tell them they are investing thousands of dollars every year to educate men and women in the university. By letting only the men vote, they are cutting only half the coupons on their investment."

"That's wonderful," I said, "but that will take only half a minute. I have to talk ten minutes!"

"You'll think of something," she said reassuringly. "I'll stand in the back of the room, and if I see you hesitate, I'll start clapping. If one person claps, the whole audience claps. That will give you time to think of more reasons."

That night I put on my blue velvet dress, tied a ribbon in my hair, and went down to the capitol. The great chamber where the hearing was to be held was already packed. The people in charge of the hearing noticed that I was not quite five feet tall and sent for a box for me to stand on. All of a sudden I was aware of the most appalling silence. I began talking about investments and dividends. Then came what seemed like thunderous applause and the ten minutes had somehow passed. To this day I don't know whether they clapped for what I said or for what I didn't say.

After graduation, I worked for newspapers in Milwaukee and in New York City, and in 1914 returned to my home in Helena, Montana, as a reporter on the *Helena Independent*. As it turned out, I was just in time to get involved with the state's suffrage campaign. The suffragists had persuaded Governor Sam Stewart to proclaim May 2 as Woman's Day to launch their campaign with a flourish.

In order to attract attention, the Helena suffragists arranged for some mild sensation. On May 2, three carloads of women drove up and down Last Chance Gulch, Helena's famous main street, tooting horns, waving flags, and tossing literature. Then we all converged on a main street corner for speeches.

I recall that a man who passed by called out, "I ain't got no interest in this here women's suffrage stuff." Lucille Topping, who headed the Helena suffrage branch, called back, "But you will after November!"

In June the Montana Federation of Women's Clubs met in Lewistown, and the editor of the *Helena Independent* assigned me to cover a speech there by Jeannette Rankin. Although I had never met Miss Rankin, the chairman of the state women's suffrage organization, I had heard a great deal about her and was anxious to meet her.

I had never left Helena before to cover a news story, and I wasn't sure how it was done. I didn't even know how to telegraph news to a paper. All the telegrams I knew about were ten words long and ended with "love." The editor advised me that if I got stuck, the editor of the Lewistown paper would help me.

The meeting at Lewistown was packed with women from all over Montana. When Miss Rankin came forward to speak the air became electric. She immediately dispelled the notion that suffragists were all middle-aged and masculine. Young, attractive, energetic, and glowing with friendliness and reason, Jeannette Rankin commanded attention as soon as she spoke. She wore a gold-colored velvet suit, and the Lewistown editor said she looked like a young panther ready to spring.

In her speech, Miss Rankin attacked the defensive posture which some of the suffragists had assumed. Women should not have to give their reasons for voting, she said, for men were not called upon to explain theirs. She went on to point out that although people asked what women planned to do with the franchise if they won it, no one asked men to make any such defense.

Echoing many of the themes of Progressive thought about the role of women, Jeannette said there were many reasons why women must vote. Women had work to do with the vote, not because they wanted to be like men but because women *were different* and represented different interests. She pointed out to the club women that governmental actions directly affected their lives, but they had nothing to say about any of them. For instance, she noted, Montana's infant and maternity mortality rates were among the highest in the nation. She also emphasized the need to do something about the working conditions of women in factories and industry and the need for food and safety inspectors. Women needed the vote because all of these were things which needed attention. . . .

Up to that time, no one in Montana, or anywhere else for that matter, had heard of a respectable young woman making a public street corner speech. Yet we knew we would have to adopt all the normal political techniques if we were going to win the vote. I remember my first speech distinctly. I was terrified as I took my place on what was supposed to be a busy Helena street corner. Suddenly, it seemed, there was not a soul in sight. But I had something to say, so I just started talking to the world. Miraculously, someone stopped to listen, and then another came running, and soon I had a big audience, all listening attentively— partly, I suppose, because they had never heard a woman speaking on the street.

My mother was horrified. While it was all right for women to vote, she said, no respectable lady would speak on a street corner. She warned me that if I made one more speech on the street, I needn't come home. That night I slept at a hotel and charged it to my father. After that I was allowed to speak on street corners, although Mother was still horrified in spite of her feelings that what I was doing had a high purpose. As time went on, she had to accept even more "unladylike" techniques from me and other campaigners for the rights of women. We had a long ways to go.

On the Fourth of July, 1914, I attended a four-county picnic in Absarokee, a little town near Billings, where State Senator J. B. Annin, Miss Rankin, and I were to be the speakers. We gave our speeches while standing on the back seat of an open car. The audience seemed to enjoy our talks, and I was well on my way to becoming a seasoned speech maker.

Some weeks later Lucille Topping and I went to Marysville, a little gold-mining town up in the mountains twenty miles northwest of Helena. We had a buggy with two horses to pull us up the steep mountain road. Lucille did the driving. We arrived in the evening and gave our talk in the Miners Hall. All the miners came in their high rubber boots, listening attentively to what we had to say. When we were finished, someone got out a fiddle, and we danced. And while we pushed these men in their rubber boots around the dance floor, we thanked them earnestly for the votes they were going to give us in November.

On the way back to Helena, after midnight, Lucille drove the team down the mountain while I stretched forward and held a lighted kerosene lantern over the horses' tails so that she could see the road. I think Marysville voted for us.

One evening I gave a talk in front of a saloon in Augusta, a ranching community some seventy-five miles north of Helena. As far as my mother was concerned, this was far worse than speaking on street corners. No lady would ever even stop in front of a saloon in those days, much less talk to a man who came out of one. Nevertheless I started to talk, and a few men came out to listen. I don't think they thought much of it: on election day someone in Augusta wrote my name in as Lewis and Clark County sheriff.

After a summer of meetings and speeches throughout the state, we sponsored a booth at the Montana State Fair, where the *Suffrage Daily News* which I helped to publish, was handed out. Our campaign concluded with a triumphant parade in Helena, in which hundreds of men and women from all over the state marched. Dr. Anna Howard Shaw, president of NAWSA (National American Women's Suffrage Association), led the parade with Jeannette Rankin. . . .

On election day, November 3, 1914, Montana's suffrage amendment was approved, 41,302 to 37,588. At first it looked as if it would not pass. We heard that at some polling places anti-suffragists held their locked ballot boxes and refused to count the votes for several days. We figured that they were waiting so they could delete as many yes-votes as necessary to defeat us. Miss Rankin announced to the press that she was going to hire lawyers if necessary to get the ballot boxes opened, and with that threat, the boxes came out of hiding. From that day, women in Montana have voted on equal terms with men. Even now I never go to the polls without a silent thank you to those many energetic, earnest women in Montana and supporters from other states who made it possible.

Even with this victory, however, we knew it was not enough merely to have the vote. Women had to be persuaded to use it. It was suggested that Jeannette Rankin run for Congress. This was a staggering and somewhat amusing proposal for the men in our state to consider. But of course they thought she would never win. While we felt that most women would vote for her in gratitude for what she had done for them, the question was, would the men support her, and indeed, what about the vocal anti-suffragists among women? . . .

We set up headquarters in the Helena law office of her brother, Wellington D. Rankin. I left my position as manager and editor of the *Montana Progressive* and was in charge of remobilizing the organization which had been formed for suffrage. We sent out mountains of literature and hundreds of personal letters. Press releases went to the newspapers every day. As election day neared, we sent out a flood of postcards.

In those days we could still buy "penny postcards" that cost only one cent. We bought hundreds of them and dozens of women volunteered to address them to names on voting lists throughout the state. They bore the folksy handwritten greeting: "Dear Friend: We are enjoying it here. We're going to vote for Jeannette Rankin for Congress. Hope you will. Greetings." The card was signed with the initials of the writer. We hoped this would keep the voter sufficiently curious to remember the unknown friend's advice on election day. . . .

Although the election in November, 1916, proved a landslide for the Democrats, Jeannette, a Republican, was elected to Congress. Because she was the first woman in the world to be elected to a national parliament, she attracted a great deal of attention in the papers and in magazines. She was commissioned by the *Chicago Herald* to write a weekly syndicated column, and Jeannette asked me to go along to Washington as one of her secretaries to write that column and assist in the office.

In the meantime, the world situation was deteriorating rapidly, and it began to seem that the United States would inevitably enter the war in Europe. The war spirit became so strong that President Woodrow Wilson called a special session for April 2, 1917, to announce that he could no longer keep us out of the conflict. . . .

On April 2, 1917, the special session began at noon. . . . After some discussion, the voting began at 3:00 o'clock in the morning. When Miss Rankin's name was called she did not respond at first. After the second call, the first woman in Congress arose. "I love my country and I cannot vote for war," she said. "I vote no." Thus, the first vote ever cast in Congress by a woman was for peace.

The papers the next morning announced that the Congresswoman from Montana had voted against war, then swooned and wept, and had to be carried out of the chamber. It made a dramatic story, but it was without truth. Fiorello La Guardia, later New York's coloful mayor, but then a freshman Representative from his state, received a letter from one of his constituents, a woman, who asked whether it was true that Miss Rankin had "disgraced them" by weeping when she voted. "Dear Madam," La Guardia replied, "I am sorry, but my own eyes were so full of tears, I couldn't see how Miss Rankin voted." . . .

One of Miss Rankin's most significant achievements was cleaning up the Bureau of Engraving and Printing where Liberty Bonds were being produced. There was an eight-hour law on the books for all governmental departments, but because of wartime demands, personnel in that bureau worked ten to twelve hours a day with no overtime compensation. About 2,000 girls worked under those conditions and several of them had fainted at the printing presses; two had been institutionalized because of tension. An entire issue of Liberty Bonds had been thrown out because of printing errors brought on by overtime pressures and exhaustion.

This situation was brought to Jeannette's attention by the sister of one of the girls, who lived in Montana. Miss Rankin went down to the bureau to talk with the director and look over the situation. He was friendly and charming and assured her that everything in his department was working smoothly, that the girls were happy in their work. Miss Rankin was not convinced. She sent me down the next day to talk with the girls during their lunch hour. They were very upset not only by the long hours but by conditions in general and expressed the hope that Miss Rankin could help them. This was the only bureau in Washington where girls from the District of Columbia could work, they said. Although the pay was low (25¢ an hour), all the good jobs went to constituents of the Senators and Representatives from the various states. (My salary was $125.00 a month).

I suggested that they meet with Miss Rankin at her apartment on Sunday morning, and thirty of them showed up. Convinced by their pleas, at her own expense, Jeannette hired Elizabeth Watson, a professional social investigator from New York, to come to Washington to work on the case. Within a week Miss Watson brought to the office a pile of signed affidavits attesting to the abuses in the bureau.

The next day all the government offices were to close for the long Fourth of July holiday. Miss Rankin, however, put the affidavits in her briefcase, and we went down to the Treasury Department to talk with Secretary William McAdoo, who had jurisdiction over the Bureau of Engraving and Printing. We sat in the waiting room until McAdoo came in. He said he was sorry, but he was leaving for a boating party, and had only a few minutes to spare.

Miss Rankin got right down to business: "The Bureau of Engraving and Printing will have to be put on an eight hour schedule on July 5."

McAdoo smiled tolerantly. "The fifth of July! That's the day we get back from our vacations!"

"Yes," said Miss Rankin.

"Well, we don't work that way," he said, still smiling. "That isn't the way we do things in Washington. You're new here. I'll let you talk to my assistant. I'm sorry, but I have to leave now."

When his assistant came in, Miss Rankin told him why she had come. He leaned forward and shook his finger in her face.

"You can't do that in Washington," he said. "It's a government bureau. Things take time. You're new here. It takes months to reorganize things and change schedules. You'll learn when you're here for a while."

Miss Rankin opened her briefcase. "I have these affidavits," she said, "and if this bureau isn't put on an eight-hour schedule on the fifth of July, I'll have to turn them over for a Congressional investigation."

"You can't do that!" His face got very red and he shook his finger in her face again. "You'll have to learn how we do things here."

Miss Rankin arose. "Thank you," she said. "We won't take any more of your time."

We had been back in her office almost an hour when the phone rang. It was someone from the Treasury Department: "There will be a hearing at the Bureau of Engraving and Printing at 1:00 o'clock today. We would like you and your secretary to be there. The girls will be excused from their work to testify."

We put on our hats and went down to the bureau again. Jeannette thought the girls would not testify because they would be afraid of losing their jobs, but when we arrived, the long corridors were filled with girls waiting to testify. After several hours of testimony the chairman suggested we adjourn until the next day. Within the hour, however, the bureaucratic wheels began to turn, and by 8:00 o'clock that night, newspapers were on the stands announcing the institution of an eight-hour schedule at the bureau beginning July 5. It was the swiftest change ever made in a governmental department, they said. . . .

Although she knew her vote against the war had ended her chances for re-election, Jeannette Rankin never regretted it. She was returned to Congress in 1941 in time to vote against war a second time. When she was ninety years old, this courageous lady said she would like to go back to Congress again to cast one more vote against war. That, she thought, was the great job yet to be done by women. And so it is.

31. Sophie Irene Loeb

115

SOPHIE IRENE LOEB: SOCIAL AND CIVIC REFORMER
1913–1929

Russian-born Sophie Irene Loeb (1876–1929), who came to these shores at the age of six, was one of America's outstanding social and civic reformers. This woman, it has been said, was responsible for more beneficial welfare legislation than any other woman in the United States. Sophie Loeb employed her tremendous energy to implement the social ideals to which she had dedicated herself. She identified with Jewish causes, and among the several books she wrote were two which documented her sympathy for Zionism and her interest in the Palestine Jewish settlements.

Loeb made her living as a reporter for the New York Evening World. *Lest one think of this influential journalist as a sobersides, one has merely to turn to her* Epigrams of Eve *(1913). The excerpts below, in item A, are taken from the chapter on "Woman." In 1915, Sophie Loeb edited a symposium on woman suffrage in which disparate views were presented (B). The third selection, C, an obituary (1929), chronicles her achievements.*

A

1913

A brainless beauty is but a toy forever.

Men may come and men may go, but the nagging woman goes on for ever.

Many women think that they have poise when in reality it is avoirdupois.

If a woman is a rag, a bone and a hank of hair, at least there are many willing ragpickers.

A woman purrs at being termed a kitten but scratches when called a cat.

B

1915

SHALL WOMEN VOTE?

A SYMPOSIUM PREPARED BY SOPHIE IRENE LOEB

[THE VIEWS OF SOPHIE IRENE LOEB]

I am a suffragist.

Every woman does not want the vote.

Every woman does not need the vote.

Every woman will not use the vote.

Yet, if only one woman wanted, needed and would use the vote, every other woman should see to it that she gets it.

This woman is the woman of industry. Her needs form the fundamental foundation for the right to vote. Man brought it about himself.

There was not enough of him to carry on the work of the world. "Nothing is permanent but change," says Socrates.

Man made so many machines and developed so many industries, that he had to call woman out of the home to run them.

And the day that he mobilized women, in the battle of business, that day he took away her dependency of him; that day she marched side by side with him, sharing his economical and political burdens, but not always the blessings—blessings that are lacking because her voice through the vote is silent.

The sphere of woman is changed. She needs the vote to adequately meet that sphere.

Not many years ago we were shocked when woman claimed her first great right—the privilege of collecting her own wages. Not the right of working, bless you, she has always done that, but the right to demand a day's pay for a day's labor. . . .

Nor does the ugly duckling need the aid of a magic stick to make her beautiful so that she may marry the wondrous god-man and live happy ever after. But from the day she held her first pay envelope in her hand she has acquired the wand of wisdom that has been the open sesame in the magic lantern of life—activity.

No longer does my ringless sister of long ago need count her rosary of days, months and years with its everlasting Ave Maria of "When will he come! When will he come!" The term of "old maid" has lost its sting. She has a fighting chance to forge her own future should he fail her.

We now have, instead, the self-respecting, self-sustaining bachelor girl. Her face is toward the east. The east is all aglow! Today the woman who works chooses marriage not as an escape course but as an elective course. . . .

It is now a fact that thousands have refused the first man that came along, preferring their own bank accounts to "washing the windows, scrubbing the floor and polishing the handle of the big front door," of some lord of creation, who on a moonlight Wednesday in a moment of madness chronicled another epoch between a question mark and a period.

That we have left behind the good old days when this was the only honorable course for self-respecting female persons to pursue no one may gainsay.

For, while the cry of the race suicide faction rings with the woman that isn't married to some man and ought to be, the real tragedy of the hour is the woman who is married to him and oughtn't to be.

The direction of the compass has changed for woman; it does not point only to the home. The ideal marriage with its peace and security is welcome in any age.

Formerly when woman accepted friend husband as master he represented her vote. Today, being mistress of her own life, she wants to represent herself. At present she is numbered only in the tax books or census lists. . . .

When he [man] grants her the vote, he gives her the place she has earned beside him on the throne of government.

STRONG STATISTICS BY MRS. [MAUD] NATHAN. . . .

"I strongly urge every Jewish woman to use her influence in the home and wherever possible to secure the vote that will give her a voice in her government—the one government that gives to the Jew the equal chance. There are hundreds of Jewish women in positions of importance.

"There are thousands of Jewish women in the industrial world all of them should have something to say in the making of the law that govern them.

"When you think that laws are made appropriating moneys laws not nearly as vital as those of human life, the only answer is Votes for women to secure them.

"Congress during the last session appropriated $2,224,000,000

"Among the appropriations were $600,000 to prevent hog cholera.

"$400,000 to prevent tick among Southern cattle.

"$375,000 for cotton boll weevil.

"$293,000 for a Bureau of Standards.

"Yet there was great opposition to giving Miss Julia Lathrop the $165,000 which she asked for in order to reduce the infant mortality in the United States. (Death rate twice as large in United States as in New Zealand.) The appropriation was finally granted, but only after much opposition.

"However, when the women of the District of Columbia asked for $6,000 for an investigation of the conditions of work, low wages, etc., of women and the high cost of living for them—this was refused, although $250,000 was granted to the Agricultural Department for the free distribution of seeds! And these seeds are even sent to people living in cities who only have flag-stones in which to plant them!

"One hundred and forty-seven girls lost their lives in the Triangle factory fire. Out of 34,000 factories we are told that in 15,000 there exist today the same conditions as were found in the Triangle factory.

"Thirty-eight per cent of the New York City tenement houses we are told, do not come up to legal requirements in regard to light and ventilation.

"We need the vote to compel such needful reforms.

"In Chicago, Illinois, since women have become political factors, a bill has passed giving women who hold government positions the same pay as men, when they do the same work." . . .

"Now why do so many organizations urge equal suffrage? Can it be that they do so without having studied facts and results? Is it not rather because they know, for instance, that in New Zealand since women have voted, the infant death rate has been reduced until it is now fifty-one per thousand, less than half that of the United States; that in the State of Washington—an equal suffrage state where there are many women food inspectors and a woman on the State Board of Health—we have the lowest death rate of any state in our Union; that the only states that have an eight-hour law for working women are equal suffrage states, that the majority of the states that have passed widows' pension laws are equal suffrage states; that according to the National Vigilance Association, every equal suffrage state has a good law against the white slave traffic, that in all of the equal suffrage states except one, the age of consent is 18, and in this one—the newly enfranchised state, Nevada—it is 16; whereas, in several non-suffrage states, it falls as low as 10, 12 and 14. Is it not because they know that laws relating to the welfare of women and children, and therefore to the welfare of all humanity, are passed far more quickly when women are the constituents of the legislators—laws which women before enfranchisement have been unable to get passed?

"Is it not because these associations know that there are 3,000,000 women wage-earners in the United States and that these women should have a voice in the selection of the legislators who make the laws controlling and governing the conditions under which they work? . . .

MISS LAUTERBACH PREFERS MAN-MADE MANDATES

Miss Helen Lauterbach, daughter of the well-known attorney Edward] is an ardent anti-suffragist. . . .

"Men and women are not born equal. Women are the superior of men in certain attributes. To them was given the noblest function—that of producing the human species—and of guiding their offspring through the stage of infancy and of adolescence.

"While woman should reign supreme in her life function, man should be allowed to act untrammelled in his.

"He being the stronger, his work is adjusted in the field where strength is needed. Therefore my preference is for a virile, man-ruled government and not an effeminate one. An effeminate government would seem to me to be a calamity.

"In all these thousands of years woman has done noble work, but it differs from the masculine kind.

"In neither Philosophy, Art, Science has woman ever shone. She has produced the race (a noble work), but man has done the things that advanced it. That woman should remain the beautiful, still, small voice of life's conscience, rather than the ugly, noisy, voice of the political platform is my preference.

"Woman's power can be exercised, as it now is, quietly and serenely non-partisan. It would seem wiser not to disturb the great yet gentle influence she now sways. The machine politic will hardly be improved when guided by her more impulsive temperament. In ages to come should she have accomplished any of the great work that man has done it would seem then to be time enough to upset the machinery of government by giving her the power some few now crave. If man's last exclusive tool were given her now to wield how would she improve the world?

" 'These ages to come' may well be allowed to take care of themselves. At present it would hardly seem that woman is fitted for this added power. When woman has produced in her own sex a Moses, a Jesus, a Buddha or Confucius, a Plato, an Aristotle, a Shakespeare or a Dante, a Michael Angelo or a Rembrandt, a Newton or a Copernicus—a Franklin or a Fulton, aye, or even an Arkwright or a Howe—then it will be time to give her the privilege of men, and not before."

C

1929

SOPHIE IRENE LOEB IS DEAD AFTER BUSY LIFE DEVOTED TO MOTHERS AND CHILDREN

Noted Welfare Worker and *Evening World* Writer Won Many Reforms

"I'M SO GLAD THOSE CHILDREN WERE HAPPY."

These were the last words that passed from the lips of Sophie Irene Loeb, since 1919 a writer for *The Evening World*, and one of the leading welfare workers of her generation.

Miss Loeb died shortly before 6 o'clock last evening in the Memorial Hospital, 106th Street and Central Park West, with her last conscious thought on the happiness of the children to whose welfare she had devoted the best years of her life.

She had had in mind the fourteenth annual Christmas Party under the joint auspices of *The Evening World* and the Board of Child Welfare for youngsters benefiting from the Child Welfare Act. It was the first such function Miss Loeb had missed. In the Capitol Theatre the children and their mothers stood and bowed their heads while prayers were offered for her speedy recovery. . . .

DOMINATING STRENGTH

The story of Miss Loeb's life is one of intense activity and irresistible determination. Of less than average height, she was endowed with a courage and tenacity of purpose that were overwhelming. So pronounced were these characteristics that Mayor [William Jay] Gaynor used to say:

"I can always tell when Sophie Loeb is coming up City Hall steps. It's then the aldermen are jumping out the back windows. That's the only way they can keep from giving her what she wants."

History of the last twenty years furnishes ample proof that the astute old man was right.

When Miss Loeb reached New York from Pittsburgh in 1910 she joined the staff of *The Evening World*. Her assignments took her into the slums of the east side and there she became so impressed with the suffering of widows and children that she began the campaign which has resulted in a Nation-wide organization for the establishment and liberalization of child welfare laws, usually referred to as "widows' pensions" or "mothers' aid."

That work was closest to her heart. From her bed in the hospital, and as recently as the day before her death, Miss Loeb had mapped out a campaign for legislation this year in New Mexico, Texas, Oregon, and South Carolina. As president of the Child Welfare Committee of America, a national organization created as the result of her own determination, mothers' aid propaganda has been co-ordinated throughout the United States and a legislative program for every State has been laid down.

To Miss Loeb the most dramatic moment in her life was when the Assembly in Albany passed the first Child Welfare act in 1915. It marked the end of a fight that would have broken the spirit of almost any one else. At the same time it marked the beginning of her national campaign.

NOTED ACHIEVEMENTS

Before telling that story, and to give a truer picture of the accomplishments of Miss Loeb during the years from 1910 to 1929, her activities as a writer of *The Evening World* are related.

Campaign for inaugurating penny lunches in the public schools.

Passage of an ordinance making motion picture places in New York City free from fire hazard and setting up sanitary provisions.

Investigation of the Public Service Commission which resulted in the ousting of the then Chairman Edward E. McCall when Miss Loeb disclosed that he held public utility stock.

First for the 80-cent gas rate in Brooklyn, and later, when the Supreme Court held that rate confiscatory, establishment of the $1 rate for New York City.

Establishment of public baths in New York City.

Commutation of the death sentence by Governor Whitman imposed on Charles E. Stielow, up-state farmer, who five times had been reprieved as he was about to go to the electric chair.

Passage of a bill regulating taxicabs and their rates, and later a bill compelling all cabs to be bonded.

Acted as mediator in taxi strike, the first time a woman had officiated in settling a labor dispute.

Stimulated Congressional inquiry into the coal trust.

Opening public schools for community forums and community centers.

Enactment of the anti-scalping bill limiting theatre ticket agencies to a 50-cent premium over the box office prices.

Encouragement of better housing in the slums.

And the list could be extended still further.

During the years she campaigned for child welfare legislation, liss Loeb had been invited to address Legislatures in many ates. Missouri, Florida, and Mississippi passed special resotions inviting her to talk to them in joint session, and to be the rst woman ever to be so honored by the States.

To all these legislators she told of the earnest pleas which idowed mothers had made to her for a little help with which to cep the home together, so the children might be brought up in reir own homes until they could be self-supporting. From this re derived the slogan, "A Home for Every Child.". . .

Miss Loeb was an unusually forceful speaker. She had an itimate, conversational manner that readily responded to a burst f indignation or an emotional surge. In many of the places she irried her message there was deep antagonism. Nevertheless, re invariably succeeded, before her address was half through, in voking applause or tears, according to the mood. In more than ne instance her speech saved from almost certain defeat legislaon to keep dependent children in their homes.

Although she could have had any one of a number of public ffices Miss Loeb was satisfied to serve only on the Commission to ivestigate Child Welfare Laws, and later as the first President of re Board of Child Welfare in New York City. Mayor [James J.] Valker reappointed her a member to that board for a term of nine ears. The first appropriation for that board, in 1915, was 100,000. The budget for this year provides more than 7,000,000. More than 30,000 children live in homes which ceive the benefits of the Child Welfare Law.

In liberalizing the law through the years Miss Loeb succeeded i extending its provisions to include not only families where the ither has died, but where the father is imprisoned, in an istitution for the insane, in a sanitarium, or where the mother as been deserted. Amendments have also made it possible to rant aid not only to a mother but to any blood relative within re second degree who is responsible for rearing the child.

One of the recent pieces of legislation Miss Loeb sponsored, hich gave her satisfaction second only to the original enactment of the Child Welfare Law, was the act prohibiting the use of the word "illegitimate" in referring to a child born out of wedlock. This was the first such law ever passed in this country.

Miss Loeb was responsible for legislation creating the Anna Heckscher Memorial Fund which provided the playground in the southwest corner of Central Park. She also participated in the fight for the emergency rent laws, and more recently had been identified with August Heckscher in his plans for housing betterment. She was instrumental in forming groups of east side businessmen who pledged themselves to erect blocks of model homes for wage earners in connection with Mayor Walker's plan to use the city's right of excess condemnation.

Two years ago Miss Loeb addressed the First International Child Congress in Geneva, and her resolution "Home Life for Children as Against Institutions" was unanimously adopted. Later she prepared a report at the invitation of the League of Nations on conditions among the blind in the United States.

The walls of Miss Loeb's home at No. 145 Riverside Drive, and her office at the Child Welfare Committee of America, No. 730 Fifth Avenue, bear graphic witness to her achievements. Among those whose commendations and praise are found framed are Woodrow Wilson, Calvin Coolidge, Governor Smith, Mayor Hylan, Mayor Walker, Aldermanic President Mcee [Joseph V. McKee], Governor Flem D. Sampson of Kentucky, Governor Sam A. Baker of Missouri, Governor John W. Martin of Florida.

In addition to her news stories and special articles in *The Evening World* and magazines Miss Loeb has written plays, motion picture scenarios, and the following books: "Everyman's Child," "Palestine Awake," "Fables of Everyday Folks," "Epigrams of Eve," and "What Eve Said."

She was born in Russia, July 4, 1876, and when very young came with her mother to McKeesport, Pa. That city has erected a monument to her. Miss Loeb, in that monument, is shown holding an infant in one arm and laying a protecting other arm about an older child at her side. In 1896 she was married to Anselm Loeb but was divorced.

Miss Loeb was a member of the National Institute of Social

Sciences, the National Social Science Honor Society of Pi Gamma Mu, League of American Pen Women, Women's City Club, Society of Arts and Sciences, and Authors' League of America.

· 116 ·
TILLIE LEWIS, INDUSTRIALIST*
1913–1966

Very few women in twentieth-century America have headed corporations doing business in the millions of dollars. It is worthy of note, however, that in this minuscule group there is a disproportionate number of Jewesses. Among the companies they have owned or managed are a toy business, a fabric design enterprise, a garment manufactory, a chemical research laboratory, and a newspaper. One woman, Tillie Lewis (b. 1901), built a business from scratch. When she finally sold Tillie Lewis Foods, Inc., to the Ogden Corporation, she became the first and only woman director of one of the country's great corporations.

The selection reprinted below describes her rise; hers is a record of remarkable achievement, a success story in the classical American tradition.

Defense contracts [during World War II] enabled new small enterprises in many industries to survive their growing pains and grow big. One who made good use of this opportunity was one of the first women to get a cannery going in California. Manpower was short on the farms and in the canneries, but the armed forces were begging for more production, and the only way to deliver it was to find and train workers who had never seen the inside of a cannery.

During World War II, this woman stood along the assembly line of her plant personally showing new workers how to peel Italian tomatoes. When they couldn't do the delicate operation fast enough, she tried canning tomatoes in their skins. It worked, and other hard-pressed canners followed her lead.

Tillie Lewis (b. 1901) introduced the Italian tomato industry to California in the first place. One of a very small group of self-made enterprising women, she had long dreamed of growing.

*Selection is reprinted from *Enterprising Women* by Caroline Bird, with the permission of W. W Norton & Company, Inc. Copyright © 1976 by Caroline Bird.

canning, and selling the small, tangy, pear-shaped tomatoes called pomodoros that make Italian spaghetti sauce unique. She was born Myrtle Ehrlich in Brooklyn. Her father was a Jewish immigrant who ran a music store. Her mother died when she was a baby. She didn't like her stepmother, and nobody objected when Tillie quit school at 12, lied about her age, and went to work folding kimonos at $2.50 a week for a Brooklyn garment manufacturer. When Tillie was 15, she married a grocer twice her age just to get away from home.

The way she likes to tell the story, the idea of growing pomodoros popped into her head the only time she volunteered, on a Sunday, to help take inventory for her husband. Looking over his stock, she wondered why the high-priced tomatoes and tomato pastes were all from Italy. Why couldn't these special tomatoes be grown in the United States?

Nobody seemed to know. She asked experts at the Brooklyn Botanical Gardens. "Wrong soil and climate," they explained, but they didn't say what soil and climate were right. She did learn that people had said the same thing about French grapes but that wine makers had transplanted the vines successfully to California and made fortunes. She had never been to California but figured that what worked for grapes and wine might work for tomatoes.

She read about tomatoes in the public libraries and wrote to experts asking why pomodoros couldn't be grown in the United States. Those who replied were not encouraging and some suggested she forget the whole idea. She didn't forget it, but it was years before she could do anything about it.

After she divorced her husband, she worked as a "customer's woman" for a stockbroker for a time and went to business school at night. Soon she was selling securities on commission, and she was good at it. In 1932, one of the gloomiest years of the Depression on Wall Street, she earned $12,000.

One day in 1934 she read on the office news ticker that Congress had imposed a 40 percent tariff on pomodoro imports. If she was to do anything about her long-cherished dream, she realized this was the time. She bought a new hat and a Berlitz book of lessons in Italian, and invested her savings in a second-class passage to Naples aboard the S.S. *Vulcania*.

On the way over she had the luck to meet Florindo del Gaizo, a Naples canner who was the leading exporter of pomodoros. He was interested in the tariff too, and feared that it would cut down on the 700,000 cases a year he sold in America. He was also fascinated by the little red-haired woman in the big hat who had never been in a cannery but talked confidently of growing and canning pomodoros in the United States. The courtly Italian toured her through his cannery, showed her pomodoros growing around Naples, and entertained her in his home.

She left happily two weeks later with a cashier's check for $10,000 and four bags of pomodoro seedlings. Under the arrangement with Florindo del Gaizo, he would send her canning equipment and an expert to install it. She would undertake to grow, can, and market Italian-style tomatoes in the United States, and for this she was to be paid a salary of $50 a week.

Florindo was the closest thing to a male sponsor Tillie ever had. "I will never forget him," she says. "He was the first person to believe in me."

She named their enterprise Flotill Products, Inc., a combination of his first name and her nickname, and, in commemoration of its casual launching, designed a trademark picturing a champagne glass and a sprig of pomodoros. She had never been to California, but she had the names of business people who might be able to help, and they suggested various sites for her to visit. The San Joaquin Valley looked like the best place because it had soil and climate much like that of Naples. She found a canner who agreed to pack on a cost-plus basis.

The first real snag was the reluctance of farmers to plant the seedlings she farmed out to them. They were used to growing round tomatoes, onions, and potatoes, and they didn't think pomodoros would grow in the San Joaquin Valley.

Tillie induced them to promise to plant enough to can 100,000 cases of whole tomatoes and 100,000 cases of tomato paste. Then she set out on a one-woman tour of the East to get wholesalers to buy the crop she expected. Before the tomatoes were even grown, the whole crop had been sold.

The pomodoros grew beautifully, but there weren't enough of them. The farmers had been so doubtful that the pomodoros would grow that they had not been willing to risk all their acreage on the new crop. Tillie had to answer to the angry wholesalers. The second year she had her own cannery in Stockton, the crop was bigger and there was a profit, but there were always problems. Tillie had to learn all about commercial canning. In the beginning, she used secondhand equipment that was always breaking down. Once, just when tons of tomatoes were waiting to be processed, a steam boiler stopped working. At the very moment Tillie was wondering what to do, the wail of a railroad whistle reminded her that locomotives produced steam.

"I called up the Santa Fe and asked how much they would charge to lend me a locomotive," she recalls. "The man who answered was sympathetic and said they would charge only the switching fee of $7.50. 'Good,' I said 'I'll take two.' The tomatoes were saved."

Florindo del Gaizo died in 1937, and to keep control of the enterprise Tillie had to borrow $100,000 to buy his stock. A vice president of the Banco di Napoli in New York loaned her the money, and she gratefully said: "If I can ever do anything for you, please don't hesitate to call me." Pearl Harbor ended operations of the Banco di Napoli in New York, and in a letter the banker reminded Tillie of her promise. She sent him tickets to California for himself and his family and created the job of vice president and treasurer for him in the company. He held the post for 27 years.

In 1940, AFL [American Federation of Labor] cannery workers struck her plant, though she was paying more than the union asked and providing additional benefits. The strike was settled with the help of Meyer Lewis, western director of the AFL, and a year later he became her general manager. Seven years later, they were married.

As an independent canner, Tillie had to find some way to establish consumer recognition of her brand name. One of her assets was the attention she attracted as the only woman canner in the business. Her own attempts to reduce led, in 1952, to the first artificially sweetened canned fruit. The diet pack turned out to be popular and profitable. When she sold her controlling shares in Tillie Lewis Foods, Inc., to the Ogden Corporation in 1966 for $9

million, she became that billion-dollar company's first woman
director.

World War II made large-scale enterprises out of small firm.
producing something that was needed for the war, and a few o
these were headed by women like Tillie Lewis and [the aircraf
executive] Olive Beech who made the most of the opportunity
But most women went to work because extra hands were needed
and industry became accustomed to the convenience of being abl
to call on them.

Each major American war has permanently liberated womer
from some restriction on their freedom. The Civil War had mad
it respectable for them to leave their homes to work in public
Their contribution to World War I secured them the vote. Worl
War II offered married women the option of working for money
when they needed it, and at the same time gave to industry a
badly needed flexible labor reserve.

117

RUTH KATZ, GRANDMOTHER: THE CHALLENGE
TO SURVIVAL
1913–1976

Ruth Katz was sixteen when she came to this country from Eastern Europe in 1913. In the following account, she tells of her struggle to make a living; she describes her marriage; she explains her philosophy of life. Her relatively brief narrative would make an excellent outline for a massive Slavic immigrant chronicle, Jewish style. "I think that I contributed to this country quite a bit," said Ruth. "I felt that I'm just as good as any American." She was.

———————

Let me tell you something. I say we are the forgotten people. It isn't a blessing to live long. You know, I may look outwardly happy-go-lucky and in perfect health, but there's no such thing at the age of seventy-eight. And recently—I lose my balance; it's a little frightening. And I never write to my daughter my problems. Everyone has their own problems—why should I burden her? She's so far away [in California.] My granddaughter goes to work and writes her. My daughter got alarmed. "Mother, I'm so worried; I'm so worried." I called her and I say, "Honey, don't worry about Mother; Mother is perfectly all right. I am an old woman and I pay a price for reaching my age. Your mother has her own coffee pot hidden in my little place where I'm in nobody's way. I don't have to ask anybody to support me. I can still get up in the morning and make my own coffee and take care of myself during the day. So you have nothing to worry . . ." I said to my daughter, "Being old is not a blessing."

And I'm telling you the same thing. You go downstairs here [an apartment building for the elderly], and you see how much the old people suffer and how many children don't bother with the parents. And what good is old age for? . . .

You know, every night before I go to bed—I'm not religious—I say a prayer of thanks for the blessings of the day, that I could go through the day peacefully, and I say, "God dear, if my time is up, I should not wake up." But we don't die when we want to die, and we don't have the courage to finish it either. That takes an awful lot of courage.

Something else I'll tell you. I didn't know what old age meant. You see, I wasn't home with my parents when they got old, so I didn't know what old age meant till I moved in here. That opened my eyes. I go up to the laundry. And I see a woman there—new face—and I says, "You just moved in?" and she says, "Yes." I says, "What do you pay for your apartment?" She says, "Two hundred dollars. What do I care? I lived with my daughter. My daughter came here and rented the apartment. She pays the rent." Do you see? The daughter wanted to get rid of the mother; she came and rented an apartment. She paid way above [the going rate], just to not have her around. . . .

Now there is a story about how I came to America [when] I was a little over sixteen years. We had a neighbor in Russia and he paid the soldiers that let boys [draftees] cross the border. So he was caught and he was sent to jail. My father went to the state and vouched for him and told them that he'll never do that business again if they'll free him. So that neighbor had a brother in Baltimore, who brought the whole family to Baltimore. And they wanted to be grateful to my father. They got a synagogue and they sent a contract for the whole family to come to Baltimore. Who wouldn't want to go to America? It was the most fascinating word—America. We thought nothing but America is paved with gold. Everybody in Europe thought that in those days—that the streets were paved with gold and you dressed beautifully. You didn't have to work.

But my mother said that she will not leave unless she sells everything; and she was particular whom she wanted to sell, that [might] take a little time. So that neighbor wrote, "Send me the two younger girls first. And by the time you'll sell, they'll go to school and get a little English education." So an older sister and I came to Baltimore.

It was a terrible boat. [We went] lower class. And my parents ave us enough food to take along, we shouldn't have to eat *trayf* ood. It took us twenty-one days.

When the boat reached Baltimore, the girlfriends of the girl of he people that I came to, they all came to look at the greenhorns; nd one asked me to see my stockings. She wanted to know if greenhorns wear stockings with all different colors, and I wore lack stockings.

I was very lonely, very homesick, and I got sick. And the loctor advised that either I go back or else [go to] a sister here in America (she was also married to a rabbi, in Chicago). So she took is to Chicago. I wasn't in Baltimore very long—maybe about two nonths. That was in 1913, and in 1914 we had the war. After the var, my parents were too old and too broken up and too sick to ome. The rest of the family never came. There were three girls nd two brothers here.

I guess [my father] did [worry about sending us to America], ut he didn't show it if he did. He knew that he's sending up to eople that will really take care of us. It turned out different and 'm not sorry, because it made independent people out of my ister and me. I had to provide for myself for today and for omorrow. I had to find a way of being independent. It's onditions that pulls you into it. When you know that you have to ay rent, and you have to support yourself, that in itself makes an ndependent person out of you. If somebody shelters you, you lepend upon someone.

[In Chicago] we met a woman that came from the same town [as ve did in Russia]. She was the most wonderful person. On a 'riday night, she invited us to have dinner with her. So one 'riday, it was slippery. It was December, and my sister and I valked there to have dinner. My sister fell, and [her] appendix usted. She was very, very sick for about six to eight months. She vas in and out of the hospital, but I had to work and make enough o cover a little bit of the hospital and support myself. And do you now how much I was getting a week? Five dollars! *And that was ood.* Some people got three or four dollars.

In those days there were a lot of fancy bows and collars; I vorked on that. A very nice guy I worked for—he was a German

Jew, I think. Then I thought maybe if I'll change jobs, I'll make little bit more. I went in and applied to work by machines and tha was by the dozen [piecework]. Men wore garters and suspenders Seven cents a dozen. I worked and made ten dollars or twelv dollars or fifteen dollars a week. On work there was no limit. used to come in early in the morning and work to six, seve o'clock.

As soon as I got a job, I rented a room with a family. That wa practically a basement apartment; a Jewish family had fou rooms—a husband and wife, boy and girl. So one bedroom the used. The other bedroom they had for rent. I rented it for fou dollars a month. I told them I had a sick sister in the hospital, an when she comes out she had to share the room with me—"so it' cost you five dollars." I didn't cook. You could get for twent cents a good dinner in a restaurant. So about three times a week used to go out. The rest I used to buy smoked fish, cheese, cream lox.

I met my husband after I was a year here. To begin with, w used to go out, the four of us. My sister and I, and his brother an him. We bought a nickel ice cream cone; for twenty-five cents w went to Jackson Park and you took a boat for an hour. Ther wasn't such a thing as going out for dinner; they went home, w went home. On weekdays, we didn't even go. Sometimes, whe you were more serious with a girl, you took her out Wednesda for a movie—for ten cents you went to the movies; for ten cent you went into the ice cream parlor and you had an ice crean soda. *Who* was chaperoned? Not in this country. But no sex; I tel you I was five years going with my husband, and we neve mentioned that word sex.

I got married, I was in my twenties. Not for the money—h couldn't give me anything. The boys weren't prepared to suppor us; they also came from Europe, unprepared. You just go married at that time. In this country I think all my generation go married for love. You think it's love, but when you're married fo a while, life settles down more serious. It's not what you dreamt but we make the best of it. One good thing about it is you ge companionship. I know I went through a lot of surgery, and n one would do more for a wife than my husband did. When I wa in the hospital, he neglected the business and everything. He was right there with me, and that's what it means, companionship. If you look for something else, there is no excitement in marriage. You both got to work both ways. You've got to meet him halfway. You must, regardless how modern we are. I must tell you one thing; a man's ego gets hurt very easily, and to have a halfway happy marriage, you must feed your husband's ego. I can only tell you from my own experience. You take me, I worked with my husband. We worked together, we slept together, we ate together, and that is *not* the best recipe for a happy marriage.

I always stood up for my rights as a wife. You know, too much togetherness, the novelty is worn off, and there was a lot of friction to begin with. When we got into the ladies' and children's line, naturally it was me more than my husband. If a woman came in and she wanted a foundation garment, she wouldn't approach my husband, or even a dress, she preferred me. My husband's feelings got hurt very much. One incident really changed our life to the better. On a Saturday night I was almost busted from busyness; every customer that my husband approached [said], "We'll wait for Ruth." When we closed the door, my husband made a terrible remark, and he was so worked up. I didn't say a word. I walked out and I took the bus and I went home. In the morning (my husband all the years that we were married made breakfast), he came up to me and he says, "Won't you come to the table?" I says, "On one condition; that we sit down and we talk things over." I says, "I'm your wife, and your partner, and I'm also your business associate." (We had a girl, Celia was her name.) "You talk with respect to Celia. This is what I expect of you, and if you can't do it, we might as well break up right today, but I will not stand for another insult or outburst of temper. Now otherwise I don't go to the store with you." So he says, "How can we do it any other way?" And I said, "You cannot wait on customers, because it's women's work. But you want to be active. Fine, I need you. You take care of the books, the finance, and the stock buying, and selling will be mine." You know, that was the best thing. There was hardly friction between us; he didn't mix with mine, and I didn't mix with him. Otherwise I don't think I could go through forty-two years working together.

Whatever I have, we both worked for, both of us, and my husband always valued my opinion. He never done anything without consulting me. Every marriage has a lot of adjustments, and mine wasn't any different. My husband bathed my daughter till she was three months old, and he washed diapers (you know, in those days, you washed diapers by hand), and he washed the dinner dishes and the china. As a whole, it was a good partnership.

I'm grateful I was married. I don't know if you call it pleasure; I would call it satisfaction of life. [The kind] you get out of family life, nothing else satisfies you that much. There is something when you have a family—the hopes, the things that you want to do for them. Then when they get married and they leave you, it's a sad time in life but still you know that there is somebody in the world that cares for you. It's just a wonderful feeling to become a mother. And much more wonderful is when you become a grandmother.

I'll never forget. My husband and I were in the hospital when my granddaughter was delivered, and the doctor knew me. So the first thing, he said to the nurse, "Before you bathe the baby, take it out to the grandparents." And you know, with me, I still swear when the nurse brought Barbara, Barbara looked at us; they say a newborn baby doesn't see, but I swear that she looked at us. That was a wonderful feeling.

At the time I came [to America], the woman was home cooking and cleaning and raising the children. Women weren't supposed to go out and work. In fact, during the Depression when we lost everything, when my husband couldn't get a job, I went out and I got a job selling dresses. I came back and I told him that I'm going to work tomorrow and he says, "Not as long as I live." He wouldn't let me go. That was a disgrace. That I think we brought from Europe, that a Jewish wife should not go to work.

I would advise it to any woman: don't become a housewife only. It's good to be a good housewife. But you got to have outside interests to stimulate you. You'll become stale before the time. I don't think I'm stale yet. My husband considered me aggressive and so does my daughter. I don't know if it's typical, it's circumstances. You know, when you have a child, you want the child to get the best education, and if I would sit still, and must sit in the house, I could never reach it. Only through my aggressiveness, I am protected now.

You see there were good times in business and bad times, especially the years that you begin with. I had so many different businesses. To begin with, we had nothing to start with. My husband didn't have at that time a trade that he could go back to work. He used to pick up odd jobs, so I said to my husband, "I'll work and you work, and whatever we can, we'll arrange a life." I took care of a little candy store, lived back of one room. If I wouldn't be aggressive, you couldn't do that. That little candy store that I took care of paid my rent. The only thing that I didn't like working is, when I lived in the back of the store, my company were rats, that I was afraid of.

In the three months after I was married, I became already pregnant and the room was cold. I stayed there for seven months. I sold the store for $500. Then I thought that with $500 I was a rich woman. $500! I took a little apartment, and I had my daughter and raised her in the back of the business—selling bakery goods—and when my daughter was ten weeks old, my husband bought a little delicatessen, and I lived in the back. This is the honest truth; my husband used to go to the market, and buy a barrel of apples and I used to keep my daughter on one hand and dip the apples in taffy with the other—sold them a penny an apple. Ten cents a corned beef sandwich and they used to say, "Put a little bit more corned beef on." So my daughter was about three years old and I had a little cigar store and I also lived in the back and my husband used to go out and do *any* kind of a job. Then [one of my friends] had a department store. She thought that the neighborhood, it was Lithuanian and German, is not good for her children; especially no young man wanted to come out to that neighborhood to take the youngest daughter out and bring her back in the evening. So she said to me, "Look, this place will be good for you. You'll make friends and make a nice living." But it was hard to bring a little girl seven years to that neighborhood. I said. "Hannah, if I'll succeed as a mother, I'll succeed there. And if I'll fail, I'll fail anywheres." We wanted that store, and I had a friend whom I met at that factory where I was making the garters, and we remained friends. She came in one afternoon for a newspaper and I told her; the next day I found in the mail a check of $200 from her (and I felt some people are the most wonderful people and you don't know what a help it can be). When I told my husband about it, he said, "I have a brother in New York. I will ask him if he can help us," and he got $500. We started a department store and in one year we had merchandise of $18,000. We really did tremendous.

I had mostly my customers Gentiles. There was always respect. I was never insulted as a Jew and neither was my husband, because I would never cheat, I would never take advantage. I was brought up to be honest and considerate and helpful. To understand if there are less fortunate people, you've got to help them, if you are more fortunate. That's the values that my parents gave me, and if you take something that doesn't belong to you, I know I'm not going to be punished by God, but I'll be punished by my conscience.

So we were doing very well and the Depression came along. We got wiped out again. We had to start from scratch. We couldn't start that big so we opened a little children's shop on Twenty-sixth near Kedzie. Then gradually I took in ladies' apparel too. And that was going very well till I took sick; I couldn't work. Then I was at the hospital and my husband came to see me and he said he's liquidating the business. I said, "Who kills the goose that lays the golden egg?" and he said he'd rather be a poor man here than a rich man on the cemetery. He sold it. Then we bought a little real estate so I didn't have to work, and my husband took care of the apartment.

One thing, I am very happy that whatever I did, I made friends. I made friends with my customers. When I was in the hospital, my daughter says, "The door doesn't close. Everybody opens the door to find out how you are." Then the real estate that I sold, I also made many friends. They still come to visit me. That means something, because I didn't treat them like they're tenants or my customers. I treated them like a human being. If they asked me for something, I used to tell them, "It's your home and if I possibly can do it I will. But lose money I cannot afford." And they were not just tenants to me. When we had bought the building, there was an old Jewish family who had an invalid daughter. She must have been even in her forties and was in a wheelchair, and they had one daughter that had a nervous breakdown several times, and the old mother and father. So who could raise their rent? We never raised their rent. You have to be human. You know, a lot of people, if they wouldn't be human, I don't think I would survive.

I think that I contributed to this country quite a bit. I felt that I'm just as good as any American. Because when I came here, what was Chicago? What was this country? If you read history, you know what, I don't have to tell you, and I contributed a lot helping it develop. God knows what difficulty I had financially and I never went for any help.

118

THE NATIONAL FEDERATION OF TEMPLE SISTERHOODS (NFTS): ORIGINS AND ACHIEVEMENTS
1913–1931

Largely at the instigation of Mrs. Abram Simon, of Washington, D.C. and Rabbi George Zepin, the Director of Synagogue and School Extension of the Union of American Hebrew Congregations, the sisterhoods of the Reform synagogues of this country were federated in 1913. Undoubtedly the sisterhood confederation was established to counter and rival the National Council of Jewish Women, which, by the second decade of the century, was no longer primarily interested in furthering religion. It had begun to emphasize civic and cultural work. A leading American rabbi was unhappy that "a board member of one of the sections of the Council of Jewish Women, who in a city that prides itself upon possessing some of the foremost Jewish congregations in the land, belonged to none of them, had none of her children taught in a Jewish Sabbath School, and was, herself, an attendant upon the services of a Unitarian Church." Eased out of their charities by the new modern family services, the sisterhoods emphasized their religious role as auxiliaries and supporters of the synagogue. In selection A below, David Philipson (1862–1949), the dean of the American Reform rabbinate, described the beginnings of this national organization of Reform sisterhoods.

At the time of its establishment, the NFTS was already the largest Jewish women's religious organization in the United States; by the late 1970's, it had well over 600 affiliates. What do they do nowadays? The latter-day sisterhoods have raised their social sights. There is almost nothing in which they are not interested and in which they are not active. This eager band of more than 100,000 women serve Jewish and humanitarian causes all over the world. They are in the forefront of many important social causes, work for world peace, and further good will between Jews and Christians. It was the sisterhoods which built the Hebrew Union College dormitory in Cincinnati and even today finance scholarships for rabbinical students. They subsidize new congregations,

*help religious schools, work with youth, publish a beautiful art calendar,
and dispatch pilgrimages to Israel.*

*Typical of the philanthropic social welfare in which they are engaged is
their concern for the blind. As far back as the 1920's, they addressed
themselves to the needs of the sightless and, in 1931, became the chief
sponsor of the Jewish Braille Institute of America, an agency ministering
to the cultural and religious needs of the thousands of Jewish blind in this
country. The Institute publishes a magazine and has built up a circulating
library of thousands of braille volumes in English, Yiddish, and Hebrew.
It prepares blind boys and girls for bar and bat mitzvah. Through long
hours of fatiguing and exacting labor, members of the sisterhoods,
competent braillists, have succeeded in creating this library for the blind.
The Institute prepares tapes, long-playing records, and books with large
type not only for Jews, but for others too. They were happy to transcribe a
textbook for a Catholic parochial school in Maine. The sightless now have
access to prayer books and educational texts for college use. If a blind bride so
desires, she may send away for a transcribed or even a talking cookbook. As
they practice these deeds of loving-kindness, the sisterhoods have not failed
to turn for help to women in Orthodox and Conservative synagogues. In
1965, Mrs. Irving E. Hollobow, the president of the NFTS, related how
the Jewish Braille Institute of America came into being (B).*

A

Davɪᴅ Pʜɪʟɪᴘsᴏɴ Dᴇsᴄʀɪʙᴇs Hᴏᴡ Hᴇ Hᴇʟᴘᴇᴅ Oʀɢᴀɴɪᴢᴇ ᴛʜᴇ
Nᴀᴛɪᴏɴᴀʟ Fᴇᴅᴇʀᴀᴛɪᴏɴ ᴏғ Tᴇᴍᴘʟᴇ Sɪsᴛᴇʀʜᴏᴏᴅs

1913

In that same month of January, 1913, I assisted at the birth of
what was destined to be one of the great organizations in
American-Jewish religious life, namely, the Federation of Temple Sisterhoods. Some time previously, Mrs. Abram Simon, of
Washington, D.C., the wife of Dr. Abram Simon, had written
me on the subject which she had so closely at heart, namely, a
national organization of Jewish women along religious lines. I

encouraged her greatly in the contemplated project. She laid her plans and in January, 1913, at the time of the dedication of the new home of the Hebrew Union College, she saw her dream come true. For it was then that her brainchild, the Federation of Temple Sisterhoods, first saw the light of day. It was indeed a great achievement. The Council of Jewish Women, the other national organization, was more general in character. This new organization laid particular stress upon the synagogal and religious life of the American Jewess. It was to be the feminine counterpart to the Union of American Hebrew Congregations. In fact, it was largely because of the sympathy and encouragement of Mr. J. Walter Freiberg, the fine-spirited president of the Union, that Mrs. Simon was enabled to bring her plans to fruition. She had asked me to speak the opening words at the organizational meeting, January 21. I had taken as my subject for this keynote address, "Woman and the Congregation." In that opening address I said:

I have been asked to speak the opening words at this meeting, which will prove of momentous significance in the organized religious life of American Jewry, if the hopes of its projectors are realized. There is no one who would not consider it an honor to address the first gathering of delegates of Jewish women's congregational organizations in the history of the world, and of that honor I am deeply sensible; and so also it is a privilege to give utterance to a few thoughts on the subject of woman and the congregation in the presence of so representative an assemblage. The very title of this address, 'Woman and the Congregation,' indicates in what a progressive age we live. Before the coming of what is called 'the modern era' no one would have dreamed of speaking on such a subject, for woman as such had no share in congregational life as such. The Oriental origin of Judaism appeared in the inferior position that woman held in all public and official Jewish life. However, it must never be forgotten that, although this was true of woman's place in public congregational and other functions, her position in the home and in private life has always been on the highest plane among

Jews, as Israel Abrahams put it well and strikingly in his fine book, *Jewish Life in the Middle Ages*, when he wrote, 'The anomaly is presented of woman filling legally a low position indeed, but morally a most exalted one in Jewish esteem.' Woman's position among the Jews as wife and mother has always been a distinguished one. . . .

Let me refer briefly to some reforms which were introduced to accentuate the new point of view as to woman's position in the synagogue. The family pew has been mentioned above. This did away with the woman's gallery, whither woman was relegated and which was indicative of her religious inferiority, of her disbarment from active participation in the service, and of the Oriental idea of the separation of the sexes in the place of worship. The confirmation ceremony was introduced first in addition to the Bar Mitzwah ceremony, and later, notably in this country, as a substitute for the Bar Mitzwah. In the olden days, when woman had no participation in the synagogue service, there was naturally no provision for her giving any public expression to her assumption of religious responsibilities. The religious majority of the boy was expressed by the Bar Mitzwah ceremony. For the girl there was no institution of this kind. The Reform movement changed all this when the confirmation ceremony for boys and girls became one of the most prominent features of congregational life.

The changed view of the position of woman gave rise also to a number of changes in the prayer book, the most notable of which was the elimination of the benediction, spoken by men in the morning service, 'Praised be Thou, O Lord our God, who hast not made me a woman.' This reform, I am sure, requires no defense in this company.

But the most telling reform involving woman's position in the congregation was in the matter of counting her among the number necessary for the conducting of a religious service, or a *minyan*, to apply the usual term. . . . According to the traditional view, no religious service could be conducted unless ten men were present. If there were one hundred women present and only nine men, the service had to be delayed until a tenth lord of creation made his appearance. But we have changed all that. . . . In all Reform congregations, woman is accounted on a par with man in this matter. But we should go farther. The last word in woman's relation to the congregation will not be spoken until she is received into full membership if she so desires, on the same footing as man. This is the case in some congregations, but not in all. If a woman is willing and desires to bear the full burden of membership and to incur all the responsibilities involved, why shall she not be permitted to do so? There is no valid reason against this and all reasons for it.

Already in some congregations women are performing splendid service as members of working committees. . . . All this fine and necessary work and other work of a similar kind can be, and in all likelihood largely is, accomplished, through the women's congregational organizations, yclept in many instances sisterhoods. You are here as representatives of those organizations. Your work is primarily for the congregation and for the religious interests of our communities. In union there is strength. By federating all these women's organizations you will forge a mighty weapon in the service of Judaism. We have organizations galore for philanthropic, charitable, and humane purposes. We have not organizations enough for specifically religious work and for the strengthening of our congregational life. Here lies your great opportunity.

B
THE WOMEN HELP THE BLIND

1931

On the eve of the First World War in 1914, Sir Edward Grey, the British Foreign Minister, said: "The lights are going out all over the world. I shall not see them lit again in my lifetime." Sir Edward was a prophet. The thirty years war which followed from 1914–1944, from Hohenzollern to Hitler, not only created general havoc for the Jews in East European villages and cities, it snuffed out the lights of entire populations so that the world of Sholem Aleichem is no more, and its only self-contained Jewish communities are cemeteries.

For a young graduate of Hebrew Union College, Rabbi Michael Aaronsohn of Cincinnati, a soldier in the First World War, Lord Grey's prediction had personal meaning. He returned from the war totally blind and wrote of his experiences with evocative sensitivity in his book, *Broken Lights*, which became a braille "best-seller." Among his profoundly moved readers was an extraordinary blind man, Leopold Dubov, now of blessed memory, who immediately began an avid correspondence with Rabbi Aaronsohn. In the course of his writing, Mr. Dubov related to his correspondent both a frustration and a dream.

For the Jewish blind, Mr. Dubov lamented, the lights had been out since creation. While they could read in braille what Chaucer had thought of the Jews in the *Canterbury Tales*, what Shakespeare had said in the *Merchant of Venice*, and Dickens' character portrayal of Fagin in *Oliver Twist*—of Jewish literature, culture, religion, and scholarship, there was nothing [in braille].

Rabbi Aaronsohn was fired by Leopold Dubov's vision of a Jewish Braille Institute of America to end this blackout for the Jewish blind. He brought this vision to the delegates of the April, 1931, convention of the National Federation of Temple Sisterhoods. They responded as one and enlisted themselves and the entire Sisterhood membership of NFTS as shock troops ever after to the end of making the dream a reality. On that day, more than thirty-four years ago, the Jewish Braille Institute of America was conceived. The evidence of how well they succeeded is all about us. Throughout the United States, Sisterhood volunteers contributed countless hours of devoted braille transcription to the new Jewish Braille Institute library. Beginning ten years ago, volunteer groups and individuals—both men and women—began recording the more than eleven hundred complete titles in the Institute's Jewish Talking Books library.

Further, we have ardently welcomed as allies, throughout all the years, our sisters of the [Conservative] National Women's

League of the United Synagogue of America and the Women's Branch of the Union of Orthodox Jewish Congregations of America—as well as other men and women of the American community. Together we serve the sightless interested in Judaica regardless of nation, race, or creed.

This cooperation was established so that the Jewish Braille Institute of America might truly be Jewry's official ambassador for the Jewish blind of the world. Through the dedication of Jews and non-Jews alike, men as well as women, the Jewish Braille Institute of America has restored to the Jewish blind everywhere the once broken light of their cultural and religious heritage.

32. Jennie Grossinger

119

JENNIE GROSSINGER
1914–1972

In 1914, after suffering a nervous breakdown, Selig Grossinger, a New York East Side restaurateur, bought a rundown farm in the Catskills and soon began taking in summer boarders. Papa was aided by his wife and his Galician-born daughter Jennie, whose formal education did not include more than four years of public school. The farm was too barren to afford the family a livelihood, but out of this tiny summer boardinghouse came a hotel complex which grossed millions annually and in time became a national enterprise, "Grossinger's." Here indeed was a family of petty businessmen and pants pressers that lifted itself up, as it were, by its own suspenders. The huge resort was built primarily by the skills, the courage, the imagination of two people, Harry Grossinger and his wife-cousin, Jennie.

Jennie (1892–1972) was the hostess; Harry, the inside man. Together they made a team which expanded this "papa and mama store" into a gastronomic empire larger than the principality of Monaco. Though the kitchen was kosher—or because it was kosher—the thousands of Gentiles who have patronized Grossinger's over the years have become true believers worshiping at the shrine of lox, matzo balls, and gefilte fish. For Jewish food, it has been said, one needs the strength of a Gentile; the Grossingers' Gentile patrons have not only survived, they have thrived on this trans-Vistula diet.

In a larger sense, the story of Jennie and Harry is the familiar saga of an East European family in which the woman did her share—often more than her share—of carrying the load. She was indeed a woman of valor, stretching out her hand to the needy, and for years to come her own works shall praise her in the gates.

The following obituary (1972) chronicles in some detail the history of the Grossingers.

671

JENNIE GROSSINGER DIES AT RESORT HOME
by Richard F. Shepard

Jennie Grossinger, the gentle Jewish mother who transformed a modest Catskills family hotel into a luxurious resort, died early yesterday morning in a ranch cottage on the vast property the world calls Grossinger's but she called home. Her age was 80.

Mrs. Grossinger had been in ill health for several years. Her death, attributed to a cerebral vascular stroke, caused sadness among the countless scores of guests and employes, known and unknown, who had passed through Grossinger's over the years.

For more than half a century, Mrs. Grossinger and her family worked to bring the little farm her father bought in 1914 to the rank of flagship of the fleet of landlocked luxury liners anchored in the Catskills 100 miles northwest of New York City, and she ruled, with regal dignity, a 1,300-acre domain larger than Princess Grace's Monaco.

Many Grossingers have worked at Grossinger's, but it was Jennie who epitomized the tone of the place, an atmosphere that combined urgent family solicitude for guests with an elegance that gave to many an opulent feeling they never enjoyed at home. She was the sole owner of the Sullivan County resort.

For the guests, as many as 150,000 a year, Mrs. Grossinger was the voice of the recreational plantation. On Saturdays, after the lavish entertainment had bedazzled the viewers in the 1,700-seat auditorium, she would often take the stage and, in her quiet voice, thank the visitors for taking the trouble to come.

Whether she was greeting guests who had endured the long trip up with the "hackie" who had picked them up between Brooklyn and the Bronx, or such dignitaries as Governor Rockefeller or Senator Robert F. Kennedy, who came by chauffeured car, Mrs. Grossinger was the symbol that they were visiting a family, not merely an impersonal hostelry. Mr. Rockefeller said yesterday she would "be missed by the many thousands of persons in New York and throughout the nation who knew and loved her."

The gentle, slender, blond, blue-eyed, philanthropic and genuinely sociable Jennie often kissed people spontaneously, not in the ritual theater-district style, but with real affection. She was a poised woman who dressed with quiet elegance, not at all the flashy type of sleek Borscht Belt that is so often caricatured in depictions of life in the Catskills.

She achieved instant rapport with people, although she was not a brilliant, quotable wit. She was, in the words of an old associate, a real mother figure. She abhorred boxing, yet felt protective toward the prize-fighters who trained at Grossinger's. She had no great messages for guests such as Dr. Ralph J. Bunche, Cardinal Spellman, Senator Jacob K. Javits, Jonas Salk or Alfred Gwynne Vanderbilt. Yet she met them with no pretension and usually hit it off amiably and successfully.

SPOKE FLUENT ENGLISH

Although she spoke fluent English, occasionally tangled, Eisenhower fashion, she sprinkled Yiddishisms in her speech and professed a simplicity that encompassed all the homely virtues.

"I don't know from those hochmas," she might say, referring to sophisticated expositions that abounded in casuistry.

Quentin Reynolds, who was working on a biography of Mrs. Grossinger when he died, wrote of one incident that characterized lack of shyness in the proximity of the mighty.

One morning she received a call from her son Paul, now president of the corporation. Paul, then general manager of the hotel, said, "Rocky just phoned. He's speaking at Pines Hotel this afternoon and is landing at the airport in about an hour. He asked if he could stop in and see you. Remember how he liked those egg rolls last time he was here?"

"Egg rolls?" Mrs. Grossinger answered, in surprise. "Rocky has been to my house a dozen times, and he never asked for egg rolls. And what do you mean, he's landing at the airport in an hour? Where has he been? I saw him in the dining room last night. He was talking to Ingemar."

"I don't mean Rocky Marciano," her son explained. "I mean Governor Rockefeller."

For all that Mrs. Grossinger was the heart and soul of Grossinger's, she was not considered to be a great business operator. She had the sagacity to choose perceptive associates and she was naturally effective in human relations. If she was the "outside man," her husband, Harry, who died in 1964, was the "inside man" who made the place run.

An old employe recalled that she treated the workers as members of the family. In the early days, when the family was pinched for ready cash, some of the help would not take their salaries from her, but insisted on getting by on their tips. "Use it, Jennie," they would say.

3 Swimming Pools

Today, with three swimming pools, a ski slope, 600 rooms, a dining room that seats 1,700, an airport, a post office and a gross estimated at $7-million a year, not including two nearby independent motels that house the rush season overflow, Grossinger's is a long way from the $81 net profit it took in that first season in 1914.

But the diversity had, and still has, a Jewish flavor—no smoking in the public rooms Friday night and Saturday during the Sabbath, and a strictly kosher cuisine that is nonetheless Lucullan and universal even without mixing milk dishes with meat dishes.

The future lady of the house was born on June 16, 1892, in Galicia, then a part of Austria. Her father, Asher Selig Grossinger, who had once owned property, had become an estate overseer. Because of the poverty, Asher emigrated to New York, got a job as a presser and, three years later, sent tickets to bring the rest of the family: his wife, Malke, and their two daughters, Jennie, 8, and Lottie, 5. A brother, Harry, was born in America.

Jennie entered Hebrew school and later Public School 174 in their new home on the Lower East Side. When she was 13, she went to work, sewing buttonholes during a 10½-hour day that added up to $1.50 for the first week's wage. On May 25, 1912, she was married to a cousin with the same surname, Harry Grossinger, who worked in a garment factory.

"We started as a Jewish hotel, and still are, in a resort area," Mrs. Grossinger wrote several years ago. "But today, about 25 per cent of our guests are non-Jewish. The first time Gentiles came, of course, they were celebrities and big names. Now they come routinely." A more recent estimate puts the non-Jewish trade at one-third of the total.

Mrs. Grossinger was proud of the diversification in clientele that made the resort a meeting place of all races, classes and castes, including kings (Baudouin of Belgium), baseball stars (Jackie Robinson), Arabs (with visiting United Nations groups), and Rothschilds, several varieties.

"Quietly and without fanfare, Grossinger's has become a social laboratory," Mrs. Grossinger once observed upon receiving an Interfaith Movement award.

A grabbag sampling of celebrities who made the Grossinger's scene comes up with Bobby Fischer, Robert Merrill, Red Buttons, Mrs. Franklin D. Roosevelt, Vice President Alben W. Barkley, Chaim Weizmann, Dore Schary and two Nobel Prize winners, Dr. Selman A. Waksman and Dr. Arthur Kornberg.

Eddie Fisher was an unknown singer at the hotel when he caught the ear of Eddie Cantor, a guest, and started on the road to glory from the hotel.

What was to become one of the larger facilities in the world dedicated to man's rest and recreation was once a rundown seven-room house with an old barn and chicken coop on 100 acres of rock-strewn land that would intimidate any farmer. It soon became clear that agriculture was not going to sustain the family, and Jennie suggested that they take in boarders.

In that first season, 1914, Grossinger's had nine boarders a week at $9 apiece. Everyone in the family worked, even Jennie's husband, Harry, who recruited guests in New York.

By the spring of 1915, the Grossinger destiny was clear. Six rooms were added to the spruced-up house, suitable for 20 guests. Everyone worked an 18-hour day. That summer Grossinger's took on its first hired hand, a chambermaid.

In 1919 Jennie negotiated the purchase of a neighboring hotel, a lake and 63 wooded acres. Ten years later, Grossinger's was entertaining 500 guests and Milton Blackstone was hired as press agent. He came up with the idea that couples who first met at the resort should get a free honeymoon there. Grossinger's has never wanted for publicity.

HOME AWAY FROM HOME

It was another idea of Jennie's, in 1934, that made Grossinger's a home-away-from-home for the famous names of the era, and succeeding eras. She had read about a Jewish boxer, said to observe the rules of his religion, who was going to try for the welterweight title against Jimmy MacLarnin. The fighter was Barney Ross and, accepting an invitation, he set up training at Grossinger's.

The project was a success for both Ross, who won, and for Grossinger's. Training for pugilists became a resort staple.

Mrs. Grossinger was more than routinely involved in philanthropy and community responsibilities. She helped charities for all causes and denominations and was solicitous of Grossinger alumni who served in the armed forces. During World War II $1-million worth of bonds were sold at the hotel, leading to an Army plane's being named "Grossinger."

A clinic and a convalescent home in Israel bear her name, and her activities led to several honorary recognitions by academic institutions.

Mrs. Grossinger lived in a ranch house on the property, called the Joy Cottage. As a friend put it, "Jennie was always on the phone and the door was never closed."

Besides her son, Mrs. Grossinger leaves a daughter, Mrs. A. David Estess; six grandchildren, and a great-grandchild.

A funeral service will take place at 1 P.M. Tuesday at Ahavath Israel, the Orthodox synagogue in nearby Liberty of which she had been a member for many years. She will be buried beside her husband on a hill in Ahavath Israel Cemetery, overlooking the hotel that was her life's work.

120

MARGARET SANGER, BIRTH CONTROL, AND THE JEWS
1914

Margaret Sanger (1883–1966), the founder of the birth control and Planned Parenthood movement in the United States, was a Gentile, a nurse, and a social reformer; some of her staunchest supporters were Jewish men and women who rallied around her in the early days when dissemination of contraceptive information was against the law.

In 1927, the Hebrew Union College talmudist, Dr. Jacob Z. Lauterbach, wrote a responsum *demonstrating that the Jewish codes were not adverse to some forms of birth control. Following his lead, his students at the College and in the Reform rabbinate were most sympathetic to Mrs. Sanger's crusade. Although initially cautious, the Reform rabbis were soon in the vanguard of the country's religious leaders in insistence on the right of women to secure information on contraception.*

The following selection from Margaret Sanger's autobiography describes how the death of an unfortunate ghetto Jewess, about the year 1914, moved the notable social reformer to make data on birth control available to the women of this country.

Pregnancy was a chronic condition among the women of this class. Suggestions as to what to do for a girl who was "in trouble" or a married woman who was "caught" passed from mouth to mouth—herb teas, turpentine, steaming, rolling downstairs, inserting slippery elm, knitting needles, shoe-hooks. When they had word of a new remedy they hurried to the drugstore, and if the clerk were inclined to be friendly he might say, "Oh, that won't help you, but here's something that may." The younger druggists usually refused to give advice because, if it were to be known, they would come under the law; midwives were even more fearful. The doomed women implored me to reveal the "secret" rich people had, offering to pay me extra to tell them; many really believed I was holding back information for money.

They asked everybody and tried anything, but nothing did them any good. On Saturday nights I have seen groups of from fifty to one hundred with their shawls over their heads waiting outside the office of a five-dollar abortionist.

Each time I returned to this [ghetto] district, which was becoming a recurrent nightmare, I used to hear that Mrs. Cohen "had been carried to a hospital, but had never come back," or that Mrs. Kelly "had sent the children to a neighbor and had put her head into the gas oven." Day after day such tales were poured into my ears—a baby born dead, great relief—the death of an older child, sorrow but again relief of a sort—the story told a thousand times of death from abortion and children going into institutions. I shuddered with horror as I listened to the details and studied the reasons back of them—destitution linked with excessive childbearing. The waste of life seemed utterly senseless. One by one worried, sad, pensive, and aging faces marshaled themselves before me in my dreams, sometimes appealingly, sometimes accusingly.

These were not merely "unfortunate conditions among the poor" such as we read about. I knew the women personally. They were living, breathing, human beings, with hopes, fears, and aspirations like my own, yet their weary, misshapen bodies, "always ailing, never failing," were destined to be thrown on the scrap heap before they were thirty-five. I could not escape from the facts of their wretchedness; neither was I able to see any way out. My own cozy and comfortable family existence was becoming a reproach to me.

Then one stifling mid-July day of 1912 I was summoned to a Grand Street tenement. My patient was a small, slight Russian Jewess, about twenty-eight years old, of the special cast of feature to which suffering lends a madonna-like expression. The cramped three-room apartment was in a sorry state of turmoil. Jake Sachs, a truck driver scarcely older than his wife, had come home to find the three children crying and her unconscious from the effects of a self-induced abortion. He had called the nearest doctor, who in turn had sent for me. Jake's earnings were trifling, and most of them had gone to keep the none-too-strong children clean and properly fed. But his wife's ingenuity had helped them to save a little, and this he was glad to spend on a nurse rather than have her go to a hospital.

The doctor and I settled ourselves to the task of fighting the septicemia. Never had I worked so fast, never so concentratedly. The sultry days and nights were melted into a torpid inferno. It did not seem possible there could be such heat, and every bit of food, ice, and drugs had to be carried up three flights of stairs.

Jake was more kind and thoughtful than many of the husbands I had encountered. He loved his children, and had always helped his wife wash and dress them. He had brought water up and carried garbage down before he left in the morning, and did as much as he could for me while he anxiously watched her progress.

After a fortnight Mrs. Sachs' recovery was in sight. Neighbors, ordinarily fatalistic as to the results of abortion, were genuinely pleased that she had survived. She smiled wanly at all who came to see her and thanked them gently, but could not respond to their hearty congratulations. She appeared to be more despondent and anxious than she should have been, and spent too much time in meditation.

At the end of three weeks, as I was preparing to leave the fragile patient to take up her difficult life once more, she finally voiced her fears, "Another baby will finish me, I suppose?"

"It's too early to talk about that," I temporized.

But when the doctor came to make his last call, I drew him aside. "Mrs. Sachs is terribly worried about having another baby."

"She well may be," replied the doctor, and then he stood before her and said, "Any more such capers, young woman, and there'll be no need to send for me."

"I know, doctor," she replied timidly, "but," and she hesitated as though it took all her courage to say it, "what can I do to prevent it?"

The doctor was a kindly man, and he had worked hard to save her, but such incidents had become so familiar to him that he had long since lost whatever delicacy he might once have had. He laughed good-naturedly. "You want to have your cake and eat it too, do you? Well, it can't be done."

Then picking up his hat and bag to depart he said, "Tell Jake to sleep on the roof."

I glanced quickly at Mrs. Sachs. Even through my sudden tears I could see stamped on her face an expression of absolute despair. We simply looked at each other, saying no word until the door had closed behind the doctor. Then she lifted her thin, blue-veined hands and clasped them beseechingly. "He can't understand. He's only a man. But you do, don't you? Please tell me the secret, and I'll never breathe it to a soul. *Please!*"

What was I to do? I could not speak the conventionally comforting phrases which would be of no comfort. Instead, I made her as physically easy as I could and promised to come back in a few days to talk with her again. A little later, when she slept, I tiptoed away.

Night after night the wistful image of Mrs. Sachs appeared before me. I made all sorts of excuses to myself for not going back. I was busy on other cases; I really did not know what to say to her or how to convince her of my own ignorance; I was helpless to avert such monstrous atrocities. Time rolled by and I did nothing.

The telephone rang one evening three months later, and Jake Sachs' agitated voice begged me to come at once; his wife was sick again and from the same cause. For a wild moment I thought of sending someone else, but actually, of course, I hurried into my uniform, caught up my bag, and started out. All the way I longed for a subway wreck, an explosion, anything to keep me from having to enter that home again. But nothing happened, even to delay me. I turned into the dingy doorway and climbed the familiar stairs once more. The children were there, young little things.

Mrs. Sachs was in a coma and died within ten minutes. I folded her still hands across her breast, remembering how they had pleaded with me, begging so humbly for the knowledge which was her right. I drew a sheet over her pallid face. Jake was sobbing, running his hands through his hair and pulling it out like an insane person. Over and over again he wailed, "My God! My God! My God!"

I left him pacing desperately back and forth, and for hours I myself walked and walked and walked through the hushed streets. When I finally arrived home and let myself quietly in, all the household was sleeping. I looked out my window and down upon the dimly lighted city. Its pains and griefs crowded in upon me, a moving picture rolled before my eyes with photographic clearness: women writhing in travail to bring forth little babies; the babies themselves naked and hungry, wrapped in newspapers to keep them from the cold; six-year-old children with pinched, pale, wrinkled faces, old in concentrated wretchedness, pushed into gray and fetid cellars, crouching on stone floors, their small scrawny hands scuttling through rags, making lamp shades, artificial flowers; white coffins, black coffins, coffins, coffins interminably passing in never-ending succession. The scenes piled one upon another on another. I could bear it no longer.

As I stood there the darkness faded. The sun came up and threw its reflection over the house tops. It was the dawn of a new day in my life also. The doubt and questioning, the experimenting and trying, were now to be put behind me. I knew I could not go back merely to keeping people alive.

I went to bed, knowing that no matter what it might cost, I was finished with palliatives and superficial cures; I was resolved to seek out the root of evil, to do something to change the destiny of mothers whose miseries were vast as the sky.

121

MAY WEISSER HARTMAN: SELF-TAUGHT SOCIAL WORKER AND SUPERB FANATIC
1914–1932

May Weisser was born to Russian immigrant parents in the New York ghetto in 1900. At the age of fourteen, she went to work for an orphanage later known as the Hebrew National Orphan Asylum. Several years later, she took a job at the Israel Orphan Asylum established by Gustave Hartman, a judge in the City Court. By 1923, she had been appointed superintendent, and in 1928 she married the judge, though she continued serving as the institution's chief administrator. After her husband's death, she continued to direct the asylum, which was renamed the Gustave Hartman Home for Children.

In 1960, Mrs. Hartman wrote her autobiography, I Gave My Heart. *In the first of the two selections reprinted below, she describes her entry into the field of orphan care. In the second, she tells the reader how she and her husband induced Fannie Hurst to broadcast a radio appeal for the Israel Orphan Asylum. Such orphanages set up by immigrants with little or no means are an evidence of their determination to provide for their own social needs in accordance with their own way of life.*

1914–1915

My First Job

Into the lower East Side, swarmed not only Jewish immigrants but Italian immigrants, who lived in the tenements on First Avenue and along Thirteenth and Fourteenth Streets from Second Avenue to Avenue B. They had their markets and pushcarts all along these streets.

Many families of German Christian origin lived along Avenue A. On the extreme East near the river were Irish immigrants. The lower West Side of Manhattan was Italian and Irish.

The immigrants, who had come to these shores to find the

freedom and opportunity denied them in the lands of their birth, had these things in common—an intense love for the land of their adoption and a deep sense of responsibility towards their coreligionists. Churches, synagogues, hospitals and welfare agencies sprang up everywhere, supported by men and women of very modest means. They had understanding and compassion in their hearts and sought to help each other out. When one of them contributed fifty cents or a dollar to a charity, it was a real sacrifice, and in some instances the denial of a meal.

After a long, hard day's work in a factory, or a store, or at home raising a large family, these men and women would go out to raise funds for charity. They would climb steep flights of stairs to upper-floor assembly halls, to make appeals at lodge and society meetings. When such an evening's effort resulted in a collection of a few dollars, there was elation.

The Orthodox Jews collected funds for hospitals and homes for the aged and for orphanages, where kosher food could be served and other religious customs of their forefathers observed. The Hebrew Immigrant Aid Society, Beth Israel Hospital, and the ["old folks"] Home of the Daughters of Jacob were among many East Side institutions that were to become famous.

Bessarabia, a Rumanian-speaking province of Russia, was the birthplace of my parents. The Bessarabian Verband Association was composed of many lodges and societies, organized by immigrants from the little towns of Bessarabia.

There was a crying need for a home where orphan boys, between the ages of six and fourteen, could be raised in the orthodox tenets of the Faith, and the Bessarabian Verband started the organization which was to become the Hebrew National Orphan Home.

My parents were among the founders and much of their activity took place in our home. My mother helped organize the first Ladies Auxiliary and my sisters Sally and Minnie started the Young Folks Auxiliary.

The Verband purchased and renovated a fine brownstone house for the orphans at 37 East 7th Street, between First and

Second Avenues, on the lower East Side. It had been the home of Rabbi Philip Klein, who was famous on the East Side. A charter was obtained from the State Board of Charities.

The official opening was scheduled for June 7, 1914, with a celebration to last an entire week. This would be a fund-raising event.

For several months, the Board and Auxiliaries had been selling raffle tickets and collecting thousands of prizes from merchants and manufacturers. Tickets of admission to the celebration were fifty cents each and entitled the owner to a prize, according to his luck when he pulled a number.

I volunteered my services and at the age of fourteen I started, at the beginning of June, to work in the Home.

My plan for the handling of the prizes had proved so successful that the Board and Auxiliary members turned over all sorts of jobs to me.

This certainly was not going to be any permanent job for me, I thought, but there was so much to do that I stayed on way beyond the summer. Then I found the work so fascinating and stimulating, especially when the children began arriving, that I continued to stay on.

The first to be admitted were four pitiful little brothers, parentless and neglected, who were brought in by a very sick grandmother. Since no house staff had yet been hired, the women of the Auxiliary took turns looking after the children.

Each day one would bring in the meals prepared in her own kitchen. Another stayed with the children during the day, until another relieved her in the evening. They rendered this service with love and earnestness.

When I could slip out of the office, I would play with the little boys in the backyard; and I always came around on Saturday to be with them.

On Sundays our office was like a beehive, with directors and members all over the place.

With the arrival of more children a superintendent was engaged. Soon a medical staff was set up and we had a complete organization to look after the children.

The Superintendent distrusted me at first because of my

closeness to the directors and their wives, but he overcame his prejudice, when he realized that I never carried tales or sought information or favors, but was only interested in doing a good job. I became his right hand.

The Superintendent was a very able man. He knew how to make people cry when he made a speech, because he was sincere in his own feelings. This made him a good fund-raiser, which, of course, is necessary for running a charitable institution. He also was able to recruit volunteer workers.

From him, I learned my first lessons in public relations.

There were now three of us on the office staff and my salary, which I had just started receiving, was raised from five to six dollars a week.

Though only fifteen, I was in charge of the office and handled all the funds. Besides, I was secretary to the Board of Directors and to all committees. I worked every evening, except Friday.

At meetings, I not only took notes but participated in the discussions.

During a House Committee meeting on which my mother served, the chairman suddenly turned to her and said, "You'll see, someday your daughter May will be the president of a great institution." All the members nodded their heads in agreement.

My mother was pleased and proud, but to me it sounded very farfetched.

So accustomed was I to being sent on errands that I wasn't surprised when the Chairman of Finance said to me, "May, I want you to go over to Rabbi Philip Klein. Tell him we are short of funds and unable right now to meet the interest on the mortgage. Ask him for an extension of time."

I had never met Rabbi Klein, from whom the orphanage building had been purchased. I had heard that he was a great spiritual leader and a learned scholar and that he was of Hungarian origin.

He received me very kindly. I was impressed with his distinguished appearance and courtly manner.

He listened to me earnestly, and then said, "How come that they send a child to ask me this?"

In all innocence, I answered, "I suppose they were too

embarrassed to come themselves." A smile flitted across his handsome face and he answered, "All right, my child, you can go back and tell them that you accomplished your mission. I'll wait until they have the funds."

He then asked me about our work and was pleased that the children were being well cared for, and especially that we were adhering to the rules of Orthodoxy.

I was sent on a similar errand to the Bank of the United States at the Delancey Street Branch, when a note, that we were unable to meet, fell due. I walked in and asked for Mr. Joseph Marcus, the President.

A stocky, gray-haired, little gentleman, wearing a frock coat and striped pants, came forth. He received me courteously and, after listening to me, inquired just as Rabbi Klein had done, why the directors had sent me on this important errand.

I gave him the same answer I had given the Rabbi.

He threw his head back and chuckled, "You know, you are a very smart and nice little girl. I wish I had someone like you in my bank. Tell the committee that I will extend the note for three months."

A secretary of one of the lodges gave me a check to be used as a deposit on a purchase. After a few moments' reflection, he said, "I think it would be a good idea if you went over to the bank and asked them to 'satisfy this check.' "

I looked at him in bewilderment and said, "What shall I ask?"

He repeated, "To satisfy this check." When I asked a third time he showed his annoyance and made me feel stupid.

I approached the teller in the bank and in a faint hesitant voice said, "I would like to have this check satisfied."

"What?"

I repeated my request.

He walked over to an officer of the bank, then came back with a grin on his homely face and said, "Here is your satisfied, I mean *certified*, check."

I blushed to the roots of my hair.

When I returned to the office, I said to the secretary, "Here is your certified check," and unable to control my indignation, I hissed, "Not satisfied."

He shrugged his shoulders and calmly replied, "When that stamp is on a check, everyone is satisfied."

FANNIE HURST

One hot July evening in 1932, I was having dinner with Gus [my husband] who had just returned from the Republican National Convention in Chicago. At an adjacent table, a most attractive woman was seated with a gray-haired, distinguished-looking man. I said to Gus, "That's Fannie Hurst."

He shook his head sideways and said, "No, it isn't."

I repeated, "Yes, it is. I wouldn't have recognized her either, because she has taken off so much weight, but last week I saw her at a tea where she was the guest speaker. Isn't she stunning?"

Now convinced by me, Gus stopped on our way out to speak to the couple. As he introduced himself, Miss Hurst replied, "I know you, Judge Hartman and your lovely wife, and this is my husband Jacques Danielson. I attended your show at Madison Square Garden right after you were married and again the following year. My friend, Daniel Frohman, never missed your annual parties, and he took me to two of them. Your Madison Square Garden events are phenomenal and your work for orphan children is an inspiration. If I can ever be of service to you, please call on me."

We were thrilled by Miss Hurst's graciousness. This gave me an opportunity to tell her about arrangements we had just made with our friend, Donald Flamm, President of Station WMCA, for a series of seven weekly half-hour broadcasts. Each broadcast would have an orchestra and soloist, to be followed by an address by a person of distinction regarding the work of our Home, and concluded with a five-minute appeal by the Judge. I asked Miss Hurst if she would be our first guest speaker.

Gus quickly and earnestly added his invitation to mine, and Miss Hurst accepted. Then she and her husband were invited by us to visit our children at our Far Rockaway Summer Home, so that they would form their own impressions firsthand. This they readily agreed to do.

A few days later, Gus and I called for Miss Hurst at her fascinating apartment. We then picked up her husband in his music studio in Carnegie Hall and drove to Far Rockaway. During our drive, Gus and I spoke of the wonderful books she had written and said we were looking forward to seeing the movie of *Back Street* which was to have its first showing in a theatre in Far Rockaway the following week.

Gus asked Miss Hurst if her writing depended solely on inspiration. With a laugh and a sigh, she said, "Writing is only one percent inspiration and ninety-nine percent perspiration."

The visit to Far Rockaway lasted all day. Miss Hurst and her husband couldn't tear themselves away from the children.

In her broadcast that evening, Miss Hurst said:

"What I have seen today deserves to be passed on to the somewhat heavy-hearted world which is wallowing in the strange and temporary interlude of depression. Because what I have seen helps make one realize that certain cardinal qualities in the human race simply will not be submerged under man-made ills, and, that amazing muscle, the human heart, is capable of swinging high over any temporary depression in worldly affairs.

"I have just returned from the summer home of the Israel Orphan Asylum at Far Rockaway where I was taken by Judge and Mrs. Hartman. There, in a pleasant countryside retreat, is one of the finest examples of a happy handling of a problem of the orphaned and dependent child I have ever seen, and my observations include a recent firsthand study of similar institutions in Russia where intensive experimental study of this particular problem is now under way. . . . Surely no problem of a troubled era is worthier of loving concern than that of the mental, spiritual, and physical well-being of the children we are rearing to meet the ideal of tomorrow's happier universe. Not only does today's world owe every child a living but a decent, happy, healthy, and idealistic one.

"Apparently something like that is the underlying principle of the Israel Orphan Asylum. It isn't an institution in the asylum sense of the word. It isn't a private home in what may, in many cases, be the cramped and sordid sense of that word. It is a cross between. It is a home for youngsters; a home small enough to reckon with the personal equation; a darling home of sand piles, bright playrooms, dining rooms with lilliputian tables, and cribs in pinks and blues. It is a small community presided over by those rare qualities of the human spirit, a loving and intelligent comprehension of its mission. And its mission is to tide youngsters over the formative periods of their minds and bodies to adolescence unscarred by orphan memories.

"I would advise theorists and those interested in the experimental aspect of child welfare, in fact, all those who have been children themselves, have children, or expect or hope to have them, to look at this unpretentious and going concern known as the Israel Orphan Asylum. Its moving spirits are Judge Hartman, its founder and his wife—a pair of superb fanatics. In a world harried by economic, industrial, and spiritual crisis of one sort or another, these two people, under the simple banner—life must go on—are preparing, with a quality of mercy and rare understanding, denied youngsters of today for tomorrow's better world. As I pronounce these words, two hundred children between one and seven, lie sleeping in the immaculate Far Rockaway beds, safe and sound, and cared for in the most constructive sense. A student in St. John's College wrote recently to Albert Einstein asking him the necessary qualifications for success in the world today. 'Only a life lived for others,' replied Einstein, 'is worth while.' This reply, in its purest and noblest sense, applies to the moving spirits behind the Israel Orphan Asylum."

This eloquent address brought wonderful results.

We were also fortunate in the six guests who followed Miss Hurst on the remaining broadcasts, Judge Frederick E. Crane, Chief Judge of the Court of Appeals; General James C. Harbord, Chairman of the Board of the Radio Corporation of America; former Ambassador to Germany, James W. Gerard; Surrogate John F. O'Brien who later became Mayor of New York City; Dr. William J. O'Shea, Superintendent of Schools; and the Honorable George Gordon Battle.

· 122 ·
POLLY ALDER: BORDEL MADAM*
1914–1917

In the second quarter of the twentieth century, Polly Adler (b. 1900, achieved notoriety as the madam of one of New York's best-known brothels. The following selections from her autobiography, A House Is Not a Home, describe her fall as a girl of seventeen. For the social historian, Polly's account is illuminating, for it reflects some of the hazards to which young immigrant girls were exposed: the temptations that faced these impoverished youngsters, the unsupervised dance halls, the sexual harassments by foremen in the shops. The unions were very active in fighting for collective bargaining, for a clean shop, for fewer hours and better pay, but they waged no moral crusade against the men who annoyed women in the factories. Jewish female social workers stepped into the breach; they were eager to protect working women molested by their bosses.

"Goldine Madina" Means "Golden Land"

I was born in Yanow, a White Russian village near the Polish border, on the second Sunday before Passover, April 16, 1900 [actually April 1, 1900]. Isidore, my father, was a tailor, a talkative, temperamental man with big ideas and a correspondingly large sense of his own importance. In his eyes, as in the eyes of the village, a wife's place was either in the kitchen or in childbed, and Sarah, my subdued self-effacing little mother, alternated uncomplainingly between them. I was the eldest of their nine children. After me were to be born one girl and seven boys. . . .

My father, who was always toying with the idea of transplanting the family to America, finally had hit upon the plan of sending us over in installments, and when he heard that a cousin of ours

---

was about to set sail for the Golden Land, I, as the eldest, was elected to accompany her. A husband's word, of course, was law, and my mother's tears, her protests that I was only a baby, cut no ice with father. At first I was upset at the thought of leaving home, but once I grew used to the idea, I was excited and eager to be on my way. After all, it wouldn't be long before we were all together again—at least so father said—and I tried to comfort my mother by reminding her of this while she packed my belongings in a potato sack (the Yanow substitute for a Vuitton trunk). . . .

I sailed . . . on the ship *Naftar*. Being the youngest passenger, I rated penthouse accommodations—the top bunk—which served both as bedroom and dining quarters. The food served in steerage was not as good as we gave our animals back in Yanow, and I thought how lucky it was that my mother had tucked four loaves of black bread, four salamis, garlic and apples into my potato sack.

My fellow passengers—all going to seek their fortunes in the Golden Land—were a mixture of nationalities: Russian, Polish, Danish, Swedish and Italian. Since the voyage was very rough, nearly everyone was seasick, but not me. It was my first taste of freedom, and my spirits were high. I would stay up most of the night snacking on salami and singing Russian folk songs—to the annoyance of my ailing shipmates who quite often rewarded my vocalizing with a cussing-out. But when the epidemic of seasickness subsided they made a pet of me, and for the rest of the voyage I had it—as the saying goes—good.

The climax of the trip came one morning when everyone rushed to the rail and began screaming and waving. I was certain that we were sinking and stayed where I was, too frightened to move. Then one of the men grabbed me and set me up on his shoulder.

"Look!" he shouted in Yiddish. "The American Lady! The Statue of Liberty!" . . .

When I arrived in Brooklyn, I was startled by the signs of poverty in the neighborhood where my cousins lived. . . . Nonetheless, I was glad I had come, for after I'd explained who I was, my cousin Lena really made me feel that I was being welcomed from the heart. Pulling me over the threshold, she gave me a big bear hug, the children kissed me and patted me and fussed over me, and Lena kept exclaiming she couldn't wait until Yossell, her husband, came home and found the wonderful surprise. The Rosens were poor; they lived in what amounted to a tenement, but they lived like human beings with warm blood in their veins, not like cold fish.

Almost immediately, I found a job in a corset factory. I made five dollars a week, out of which I paid three dollars for room and board and a dollar twenty for carfare and lunches. That left eighty cents for clothes and shoes and all the things a growing girl needs. I learned to shop for remnants from the bearded pushcart men on Dumont Avenue, and sewed blouses and skirts and underwear for myself by hand. I had to get up at six to be at the factory on time, and I came home just in time for supper. . . .

In April, 1917, when the United States entered the war, the corset factory closed down, and I found a new job in a Blake Avenue factory which manufactured soldiers' shirts. At first I was doing all hand work, but as soon as I had learned to operate a machine, the foreman put me on piece work, saying I could work overtime if I wanted to make more money. I worked overtime.

Along with my hunger for an education, I had developed a new craving—I wanted finery. There was a Japanese mink (dyed cat) cape in a store window on Pitkin Avenue, and every day I walked an extra two blocks just to see it. I used to go over and over my budget, trying to figure out a way of getting that cape. But of course it was a pipe dream—I was doing well to own more than one pair of drawers.

Now, at seventeen, I had matured physically. I had reached my full height of four feet eleven, and my chest had taken on a new look. In those days life would have held little for the columnist Earl Wilson since bosoms were out of style and the boyish figure all the rage. In order to make myself as flat in front as possible, I used to bind myself with strips of white cloth—so tightly that sometimes when I was bending over my machine I'd nearly pass out. It was only after the girls at the factory found out about my "mummy wrappings," and as a result of much kidding, that I finally unpent myself.

Sidonia did most of the kidding. She was a heavy-set redhead, full of bounce and wisecracks, and rumor had it that she was a bit of a rounder. One day after work she announced that she had a date lined up with a couple of sports, and how about me coming along? When I hesitated, she laid her hand on my arm. "Listen, kiddo," she said, "I know you're a good girl, and no guy's gonna get fresh with you or give you drinks while I'm around. You tell your folks not to worry—Big Sidonia's lookin' after you."

So that night after supper I joined Sidonia and her friends and we went to the Nonpareil Dance Hall. Technically, I guess, this was my début as a "painted woman," for I had daringly dusted my nose with cornstarch and rouged my lips with coloring obtained by soaking red tissue paper in a bowl of water. It was also my début on the dance floor, and after five minutes I was convinced that was where I wanted to spend the rest of my life. Before the evening was over, I had mastered the waltz and one-step, the two-step and the cakewalk, and had been informed by my partner that I was a "real cute little trick" and had "the makin's of a nifty stepper.". . .

At that time—the fall of '17—dance halls all over America were crowded as never before, and reformers and blue noses viewed the scene with alarm. From their sanctified soapboxes, they expressed their horror at fashions in dancing which brought male and female bodies into such uncompromisingly intimate contact. They denounced the aphrodisiac quality of a new kind of music called "jazz"—music born (low be it spoken) in a New Orleans barrel house. They warned the parents of the nation to keep their daughters away from "the gilded hell of the *palais de danse*" in terms which strongly suggested that a sort of mass defloration was a nightly event in such places. Well, if so, I never got in on any such doings. Far from being a "gilded hell," the Nonpareil was more like a gymnasium, and, as in a gymnasium, the goings on though strenuous were disciplined.

Since no escorts were necessary, I began going there Sunday afternoons with a girl from the factory, and before long we made friends with the "regulars"—the kids who, like us, were dance mad. By dint of spending every spare moment practicing, I got to be very good (in fact, almost as good as I thought I was) and entered all the dance contests, competing for candy, kewpie dolls, cups and sometimes even cash. It was considered very hot stuff to jump into a split in the middle or end of a number, and my favorite partner was known as Jack Split because of his skill in this department. I danced with other boys, of course, but it was understood that the contest dances belonged to Jack. Like other teams, we had a small but devoted "fan club," an unofficial claque, who did their best to applaud us into the prize money when we appeared at the Halsey Theatre on amateur nights. Mostly we finished second, but on a few banner occasions copped first. . . .

I got a raise at the factory and was promoted to a more difficult machine. For a few days I was proud of myself and felt like quite a career girl. Then it dawned on me that I was still sleeping on the leather couch, still grindingly poor, still minus an education, still without a place in the sun. I was restless and discontented. I kept thinking that surely life must offer me other alternatives than a factory job and a Willie Bernstein [an unattractive swain who suffered from acne].

One day a new foreman came to work. His name was Frank, and whenever he walked past my machine I got weak in the knees. If he so much as looked at me, even though his glances were impersonal and cold, my heart thumped like a tom-tom. He affected the other girls the same way. They all raved about Frank—how handsome he was, how sexy, what a spiffy dresser. When I saw him swagger down the aisle between the machines, every girl giving him the eye, when I saw the lordly way he acknowledged their homage and disdained it—well, let's face it, I was a dead pigeon.

Up to that time I had never even thought of making a play for anyone, but this was different, this was love, and I bragged to Sidonia that Frank was as good as in the bag. Sidonia looked me over appraisingly. "Well, if you can't be good, be careful," she said. "You sure got mischief in your eyes."

That day I really gave out every time Frank was in the vicinity, and finally he sauntered over by me and bent down as if he were inspecting my work.

"Come to my office right after lunch," he said.

I almost strangled. From then until noon hour I was on tenterhooks. He had been so businesslike I didn't know whether he was going to fire me or ask for a date. But when I went into his office there was no longer anything cold or impersonal about the way he looked at me. What he wanted to see me about, he said, was would I care to go out to Coney Island with him that night?

Would I? My voice has always been low and husky, but it dropped a full two registers on that "Yes."

Frank asked me if I'd mind coming along while he picked up some clothes he'd left in a cottage out there. It was the end of the season and the place was being closed for the winter. We arranged to meet.

As I went back to my machine, walking on air, I gave Sidonia the high sign, and she passed the word around to the other girls. All afternoon my conquest was the only topic of conversation, and when one girl—trying, I guess, to figure out what I had—said, "Well, you know, Pearl does look kinda like Theda Bara [the popular cinema actress of the day]," my cup was full. I felt like the *femme fatale* of all time.

It was a long walk from the station to the cottage where Frank was to pick up his things. The boardwalk was deserted, and there were shutters on the concessions. An icy wind flattened against us as we walked along, and by the time we reached the cottage, I was shivering with cold and glad to get inside where it was warm.

We kidded about mutual acquaintances at the factory while Frank packed. When he closed the grip, I stood up, ready to leave.

"What's your hurry?" he said. "The evening is young."

He put a record on the talking machine—a comedy song, Scotch brogue (I think now it must have been Harry Lauder). Then he sat down on the couch and patted the place beside him, beckoning for me to come and sit there. I complied, and after a moment he leaned over and began pulling the pins out of my hat. All of a sudden I got scared. I jumped up from the couch and said it was time to go. Instead of answering, he went over to the door and locked it.

When I resisted him, he knocked me cold.

The next morning I told Lena I was too sick to go to work. Since my jaw was badly bruised and my eyes swollen nearly shut from crying, I kept my face hidden from her in the pillow. Later I made up a story about falling down, and she seemed to believe it.

I stayed away from work the next three days. It seemed to me I could never face the girls at the factory again, and even worse was the thought of seeing Frank. On the evening of the third day, Sidonia came to inquire about me, and I poured out the whole story. She called it rape, and though I winced on hearing this ugly word, still it did reduce what had happened to a size where I could handle it. I had heard the girls talking about it, I had seen the word in the headlines, and the knowledge that I was not the only one who had been through such an experience helped to restore my sense of proportion. I accepted that such things happened and still the world did not come to an end.

After I had been back at work a month, I discovered I was pregnant. Though my feelings about Frank were the same I would have for a dangerous reptile, only more so, the child inside me was his, and I asked him to marry me. His answer was to kick me out of his office.

So what was there left to do? Sidonia and I talked it over, and she took me to a doctor for an abortion. But his fee was a hundred and fifty dollars and all I had was the thirty-five dollars I had been accumulating toward the Japanese mink cape. Again Frank refused to help out, and at last Sidonia found a Dr. Glick who would do the operation for what I had saved. But when he heard my story, he would only accept twenty-five and told me to take the rest and buy some shoes and stockings. . . .

When I got back to Brooklyn, Lena did not mince words. I had stayed out all night, my dress was in rags, she was not interested in hearing my story. All she wanted was for me to get out—and to get out as of that minute. I did not argue with her. I wrapped my clothing in a newspaper and went.

In the subway station, my bundle came undone and all my belongings spilled out on the floor. As I scooped up the blouses and stockings, I could not help thinking that at least when I left

Yanow I'd had a good stout potato sack in which to carry my possessions. I began to laugh—I couldn't help it. So far, I had certainly racked up a row of goose eggs in the Golden Land. I had failed in my quest for the education I might have gotten in Pinsk, I had lost my virginity, my reputation and my job. All I had gotten was older.

So far, the joke was on me.

123

PAULINE STEINEM OPTS FOR WOMAN SUFFRAGE AND THEOSOPHY
1914

One of the leaders of the women's movement in the United States in the late twentieth century was Gloria Steinem (b. 1934), the editor of Ms *magazine. She came by her interests honestly. Her grandmother, the suffragist Pauline Perlmutter (Mrs. Joseph) Steinem, was born in Poland but accompanied her family to Bavaria, where she received an excellent education in a teachers' seminary. Most of her life, however, was spent in Toledo, Ohio, where she was one of the town's leading citizens, playing an important part in general and Jewish organizations. She was the first woman in the city to be elected to public office. This was in 1904, when her admirers elected her a trustee of the Board of Education. The ladies of Toledo also chose her to preside over their Federation of Women's Societies; in the state she graced the Ohio Woman's Suffrage Association as president. As a Jew she was called upon to lead the Reform temple's women's auxiliary, the Jewish free loan association, and the city's section of the Council of Jewish Women. At national headquarters the Council asked her to chair the Sabbath School Committee for the entire country. Her election as president of Toledo's Hebrew Associated Charities merits more than passing notice. To be chosen to guide the most important Jewish social welfare institution in town, in a day when very few women were accorded such recognition, is high tribute to her.*

The mainspring of all her activity was ethics, a social conscience. The desire to help others motivated her to join the Christian-tinged Golden Rule Mothers' Club, to fight for political rights for women; to attend the 1908 convention of the International Council of Women. She approved heartily of the reform mayor, Samuel Milton ("Golden Rule") Jones, and supported him in his social and economic reforms. She was very much a devotee of theosophy, convinced that it furthered the brotherhood of all human beings.

In the following public statement she affirmed vigorously her faith in theosophy and the right of women to equality.

33. Pauline Steinem

WHY I AM A SUFFRAGIST
by Pauline Steinem

I believe in woman suffrage because I believe that the perfect equality of men and women is founded on Divine Wisdom. Divine Wisdom, or, in the Greek term, Theosophy, teaches first of all the brotherhood of man without distinction of race, creed, color or sex. The foundation for such brotherhood lies in the fact that there is but One Life, whatever we may call it, permeating and sustaining the universe. In human beings this life exists in a more highly evolved form; it has become individualized, self-conscious, and we know it as the Ego, the Thinker, the real man. The body which the man wears is merely a garment, put on today and laid aside tomorrow, the real man is external, like the Source from which he sprang, taking on new bodies life after life, for the purpose of gathering that experience which eventually shall make him "more than man."

Since all human beings partake of this One Life, and since women must be considered human beings, it follows that men and women are the same in essence, differentiated only by the outer garments, the bodies they temporarily wear, and that therefore they have certain duties and certain responsibilities shared by all human beings alike.

Theosophy or Divine Wisdom teaches—as does science—that the purpose of life is growth, evolution, and that all growth is the result of use, exercise, expression; that, in fact, without expression there can be no growth, for muscles long unused become atrophied, and faculties or powers long neglected, or tendencies receiving no encouragement, are in course of time lost altogether.

In the light of this knowledge, have women been fairly treated? Has not woman's lot been largely one of repression, while man had every opportunity for expression?

Women were constantly reminded that they were ruled by their feelings, that they lacked logic and reasoning power; they were born and bred in an atmosphere of prejudice and suppression, which could not but have its influence upon them, with the result that they did not use the talents they possessed.

People say: "Women cannot succeed in certain fields." How do we know what women can do, when we have never yet allowed them to try? No man knows what woman would do, if she were free to develop the powers latent within her, nor does she herself know as yet.

Theosophy further teaches that service is the duty and at the same time the privilege of every human being, for service to humanity is considered a short cut to perfection. Woman's right to service has never been questioned; rather has she always been expected to serve, but the sphere of service was carefully marked out for her, and never by any chance was she allowed to step out of it.

But times have changed. New conditions have arisen. Women do not do their own milking and churning, their own spinning and weaving any more. Factories and machinery have taken much of woman's work out of the home, and a large army of women are following their work by going out into the world. However, another army still remains, constituting today the leisure class. Shall we allow these women to become parents? Are we going to take away from them the right to labor and to serve in whatever may be best suited to their individuality? To do so would be fatal to the race, as Olive Schreiner so forcefully points out in her book on "Woman and Labor."

Women need today the larger vision and the wider experience which the world's work would give them. They need that all-around development so essential in the building of character, in order that they may become better wives, better mothers and better home-makers. And the world needs them; it needs its mothers, if we are to enter upon the new era, promised by the teachers of the Divine Wisdom, and earnestly hoped for by every lover of humanity, an era of co-operation, of brotherhood, and of universal peace.

124

THE JEWISH COLLEGE GIRL
1916

Ruth Sapinsky (1888–1961), who married Henry Hurwitz, the founder of the Menorah Movement, was one of the few Jewesses of the early 1900's who had gone to college; she graduated from Wellesley in 1910. The following article is a study of American Jewish college women and at the same time an appeal to the young Jewesses of that generation to seek a higher education. Mrs. Hurwitz ignored the fact that the majority of Jewish women were at the time either recent East European immigrants or their native-born daughters. Most of the newcomers were poor. Even if they had the desire to send their daughters to universities—and most did not—they lacked the means.

THE JEWISH GIRL AT COLLEGE
by Ruth Sapinsky

At this advanced stage of higher education for women, when the once distrusted sex is admitted freely to all branches of learning and our women's colleges are announcing with a pride not at all feminine that they are nearing their half-century mark, public interest has shifted entirely away from women college-goers. Women soldiers, women aviators, even women voters have all come in for their fair share of popular attention recently, but the college girl, just in proportion as she has become less and less of a novelty, has become less and less interesting to the fickle public. It is the purpose of this article to turn the spotlight on the college girl once more—not upon college girls in general, it is true, but upon one group in particular, the Jewish college woman.

Is the Jewish girl, daughter of a race that takes to books as naturally as the Dutch take to bulbs or Germans to music or Renaissance Italians took to paint pots, conspicuous for her presence at America's universities? And if she is not attending college, why is she not? Does the trouble lie with the college? Or with the professional world which the graduate enters upon receiving her degree? Or does the blame lie nearer home—with the Jewish parent, perhaps, who realizes the need for giving his son an education, but maintains towards his daughter's intellectual yearnings the *laissez-faire* attitude typical of all parents a few generations ago?

In order that these divers questions might be answered as accurately as possible a questionnaire was sent out at the close of the academic year last June [1916] by the Intercollegiate Menorah Association to women's colleges throughout the country, personal letters were written to and personal talks had with Jewish college women, graduate and undergraduate, and the following bird's-eye view of the whole matter is the result.

Men go to college in about twice the numbers of women. The inhabitants of the United States (exclusive of the Jews) send their sons to the universities at the rate of 2.2 boys for every 1,000 persons and their daughters at the rate of approximately 1.1 girls for every 1,000 persons. The Jews, however, make a much better showing. Although there are little over 2,500,000 Jews in the United States out of a total of 100,000,000 inhabitants, the attendance of Jewish young men at the institutions of higher learning runs up to 9,000, or 3.6 boys for every 1,000 Jews.

How Many Jewish Girls Go to College?

One's pride at this laudable figure receives a decided jolt when the Jewish girl is considered. The figures obtained last summer revealed the fact that all over this broad land there are little more than 1,000 Jewesses prolonging their education beyond the narrow reaches of high school. In other words, the Jewish girl is going to college in only one-ninth the number of her brothers and in less than one-half the number of her Gentile sisters. To put the matter briefly, it takes 1,000 Jews to send to college .4 of a daughter.

It must be admitted in all fairness to the Jewish girl that when the figures of her attendance at representative Eastern colleges are studied, she does not make so slender a showing. At Barnard, Radcliffe, Smith, Wellesley, Vassar and Bryn Mawr there were last year enrolled 335 Jewesses, 5 per cent. of the entire student body. At six colleges and universities for men near these institutions—Columbia, Harvard, Yale, Dartmouth, Princeton, and the University of Pennsylvania, there were enrolled 2,179 Jewish men, 8 per cent. of the entire student body. The discrepancy then at these Eastern colleges between the number of Jewish girls and Jewish men or between the number of Jewesses and non-Jewesses is not large enough to cause any concern.

But these are the figures viewed in their most favorable light. No mention has been made of a New England college of eight hundred girls where there is not one Jewess in attendance, nor of a Southern woman's college of about the same size which has graduated only five Jewish girls in twenty-four years of its existence. In Russia where the ban against higher education for the Jews has recently been lifted, thanks to the exigencies of war, 55 Jewish women have this year eagerly entered the Woman's Institute in Petrogad, forming 12 per cent of the total of 450 students there.

In America the Jewish girl not only knows no such education privation as her Russian sister has suffered heretofore, but even the prejudice sometimes encountered by the Jewish boy at college has been spared her. This is due, if you will, to the fact that the Jewish girl has not been present at America's institutions for higher learning in large enough numbers to bring the question of anti-Semitism to an issue. But even were the caitiff prejudice lurking behind the cloisters of America's women's colleges, it seems that the normal, healthy part that Jewish girls are taking in the lives of their college communities should quickly put the bugaboo to rout.

The Social Position of the Jewish Girl at College

Answers to the questionnaire sent to the women's colleges show that the Jewish student is participating in all branches of college activities with the same variety of interest as her Gentile sister. Perhaps she "goes in" for dramatics and journalism to a greater extent than for other pursuits, but her name is found on debating teams or basket-ball, hockey and rowing squads, in the Deutscher Verein, in the Alliance Française, in the socialist club and on suffrage and settlement and college relief committees. Public offices come her way in a very fair proportion cosidering the paucity of her numbers. At Lake Erie College near Cleveland, Ohio, a Jewess was the first president of the Student Government Association, at Wellesley during the past year a Jewess was the House President (the student government head) of one of the dormitories, at Barnard the Jewish girls receive a goodly share of class and association offices.

In colleges where there are fraternities and sororities, Jewish girls have been discriminated against in "bids" to join these secret societies; just as many Gentile girls have been discriminated against, but nowhere is there a policy of absolute exclusion. A young college girl recently phrased the situation in this wise: "No, we're not exactly kept out, but whenever a Jewish girl of extra charm or ability happens to make a frat, you can bet her name goes down in history!"

The attitude of the sorority toward the Jewish girl, however, is not one to occasion much alarm, as the policy of most women's colleges toward the secret society is fast becoming one of radical reconstruction or of complete abolition. Smith College has only two sororities and they are more like large democratic clubs than like exclusive sisterhoods; Wellesley has reorganized its six fraternities so that membership is by application; Vassar, Barnard and Bryn Mawr report no secret societies of any kind.

Her Academic Standing

The social position of the Jewish girl at college, then, is practically no better and no worse than that of her Gentile sister. Her academic standing needs only a word in passing. At Smith during the past college year, where the Jewish girls comprised only 3 per cent of the student body, they comprised 9 per cent of the number receiving Phi Beta Kappa keys; at Bryn Mawr in

June, 1916, where only 4 per cent of the Senior class were Jewish girls, they formed 9 per cent of the number receiving "cum laude." The registrar of a woman's college of 276 students in the state of New York who writes that her college has only three Jewish students but that they are all doing work above the average, and the President of a college in Colorado who says of the Jewish girls he has had that they were good students, very loyal and painstaking, are but voicing the esteem in which the Jewish girl student is held generally by college officials.

So much for the part played by the Jewish girl once she gets to college. But most girls do not go to college without the consent of their parents. And most parents do not give their consent until they have carefully considered the all-important question, "After college—what?" The young Jewish girl pleading to be allowed to prepare for college along with her Gentile friends Alice and Jane and Sue meets this question lightly. "After college, why I'll go to work at something interesting and then some day, I hope, I'll get married."

The average Jewish parent views this rather general program a bit skeptically—he hasn't much faith in his daughter's ability to earn her own livelihood, he has less faith in the power of a college education to enhance her matrimonial chances. Accordingly, the Jewish girl is kept safely at home by her well-meaning father and mother against the day of her marriage or else she is sent off to boarding school where in one year's time, two at the most, she is supposed to imbibe that learning and culture which will suffice for all of the emergencies she is likely to meet in life.

The Preference for Boarding Schools

That Jewish girls go to boarding school in much larger numbers proportionately than they do to college was first brought home to me when as a freshman at a New England college I spent the Thanksgiving vacation with a friend in a boarding school not many miles away. At the boarding school, where tuition and board cost almost twice as much as they did at my college and where "a little prejudice" was supposed to exist among the students, there were 25 Jewesses out of a total enrollment of 140; at my Alma Mater there were only 20 out of a total enrollment of 1,400.

A questionnaire sent to boarding schools simultaneously with the questionnaire sent to the colleges revealed the fact that the Jewish girls comprise 9 per cent of the total attendance at five of the most representative boarding schools in different parts of the country. This does not take into account finishing schools in New York and in other large cities of the South and West that are almost exclusively for Jewesses.

Of course, it must be said in all justice to the Jewish parent that whenever colleges are conveniently located in the city of his residence, he sends his daughters to these colleges in a fairly commendable number—the attendance of Jewish girls at Barnard and Hunter Colleges in New York, at Goucher in Baltimore, at the University of Chicago in the city of Chicago serve to illustrate this. But the majority of Jewish fathers and mothers are loath to permit their daughters to attend colleges at a distance when for approximately four years these daughters are divorced from family and friends and where, the parent fears, they learn habits of liberty and independence not at all compatible with a future of wifehood, motherhood and domesticity. . . .

THE OCCUPATION OF THE JEWISH COLLEGE GRADUATE

It must be admitted, however, that upon first graduating from college the question of a choice of a husband is not a matter of such immediate concern with the new B.A. as the question of a definite occupation. . . .

The Jewish graduate is showing quite the same eagerness as her Gentile sister to put her college training to practical use. During the year 1914–15, 5½ per cent of the women registered at the Intercollegiate Bureau of Occupations were Jewesses, a very favorable number in view of the fact that the Jewish graduates comprised much less than 5½ per cent of the total number of women college graduates.

It is true that in seeking employment, the Jewish college girl sometimes meets with prejudice, a handicap that she often experiences for the first time in her life. (This fact has been stated by Miss Frances Cummings, manager of the Intercollegiate Bureau of Occupations.) Yet one need not look much farther than his own circle of acquaintances to discover Jewish college women well toward the front in every line of endeavor that is open to women at all, be the affiliation with Jews or with Gentiles.

Not only as professional women but also as volunteer workers in various civic and philanthropic undertakings, Jewish college graduates are proving themselves invaluable members of their communities. One finds them either individually, or through the medium of clubs, committees and various organizations and institutions, devoting a goodly part of their leisure to work along correctional, health, religious, industrial and recreational lines.

Her Affiliation with Jewish Undertakings

Concerning the question whether the Jewish college woman is tending to Jewish or non-Jewish interests, a Southern club woman conspicuous for her work along both Jewish and non-sectarian lines recently wrote me, "Whenever Jewish work is of broad and dignified character, it draws the majority of well educated Jewish women." This same friend stressed the value of Jewish women of education as representatives of Jewish organizations in state and national Federations of clubs of all sects.

The head of a large Jewish institution in New York City, herself a college woman, answering the same question concerning the affiliation of Jewish college women with Jewish undertakings, said, "The Jewish women who are doing things in New York are often not college women. But I do not mean to imply by that that the Jewish college graduate is lacking in initiative or energy. Every college woman I know is doing something. But up until now there have been so few Jewish college women in the community, they have not as a class been able to make their presence felt." . . .

THE OPPORTUNITIES OF THE TWENTIETH CENTURY

Looking back through the centuries one finds the Jewish woman everywhere a potent influence in the life of her people. In ancient days, when, as Olive Schreiner [the non-Jewish South African author, 1855–1920] points out, the ideal was one of physical labor, the Jewish woman bore the major weight of agricultural and domestic toil, "from Rachel whom Jacob met and loved as she watered her father's flocks, to Ruth the ancestress of a line of kings and heroes whom her Boaz noted laboring in the harvest fields; from Sarah, kneading and baking cakes for Abraham's prophetic visitors, to Miriam, prophetess and singer, and Deborah, who judged Israel from beneath her palm tree."

Miriam and Deborah, however, seem to foreshadow the Jewish woman of the twentieth century, the Jewess who serves her race and her age not through physical labor perhaps but through that "mental industry" which is taking its place. Yet for this mental industry the modern Jewess must be thoroughly equipped.

That equipment is at hand in the form of the most wonderful educational opportunities ever held forth to her—either in the history of her sex or in the history of her race. If she seizes and makes the most of these opportunities, despite the minor obstacles that are in her way, some twentieth century psalmist should arise like the famous feminist psalmist of old to sing her everlasting praises; if she neglects her opportunities she deserves to be left in ignominy by the wayside, while the voices of her Jewish ancestresses of the past who "ate not of the bread of idleness," and the voices of her Gentile sisters of today who are pressing forward into constantly broadening fields of art and labor, unite to proclaim her guilt to the ages.

125

HELLO MINNIE: MUSIC FOR MILLIONS*
1918

In 1918, Mrs. Charles S. Guggenheimer (Minna, Minnie, 1882–1966), a youngish matron, began her career as chief fund-raiser for Stadium Concerts, Inc. These open-air summer programs at the Lewisohn Stadium on the campus of the City College of New York brought good music to literally millions of people. From about 1918 into the early 1960's, music lovers could listen to symphonic music and notable virtuosi for as little as twenty-five cents a ticket. The expenses for a six-week summer season were huge; Minnie herself gave liberally, but the deficits were still substantial. It was her job to raise the needed funds, and for decades she did, beloved by her mass audiences for her devotion—and her malapropisms. In the following account, Minnie's daughter, Sophie Guggenheimer Untermeyer, details some of her mother's more memorable verbal distortions.

<hr/>

It has been estimated that almost as many people trek up to New York's Lewisohn Stadium on clear summer nights to chuckle over the intermission antics of Minnie Guggenheimer as to hear any of the world-famous singers, instrumental virtuosi and conductors she lines up for appearances with the Stadium Symphony Orchestra in her full-time, unsalaried job as impresaria of the world's largest-scale musical project.

Minnie's perennial tussles with such tongue twisters as Khatchaturian and Slenczynska over the Stadium loudspeakers; her persistent public confusion as to whether Moiseiwitsch is a ballet dancer, Szigeti plays the piano, or Beethoven wrote the Verdi *Requiem*; the unabashed bloopers and blithe malapropisms she perpetrates while rattling off advance programs and introducing celebrity guests; and the utter lack of inhibition with which she shares intimate household secrets and problems of

*Excerpted from *Mother Is Minnie*, by Sophie Guggenheimer Untermeyer and Alix Williamson. Copyright © 1960 by Doubleday & Company, Inc. Reprinted by permission of the publishers.

dress and digestion with crowds running into the tens of
thousands have become as immortal a part of the New York
legend as the remembrance of an unknown Negro girl named
Marian Anderson, whom she presented to the public as winner of
a city-wide talent search in 1925; a shy young composer [George
Gershwin] she persuaded to play his own *Rhapsody in Blue* for the
first time at the Stadium in 1927; or a tall, curly-headed Texan
[Van Cliburn] who tied up traffic for half a mile in each direction
when he came to Claremont Heights in 1958 to repeat the two
piano concerti in which he had just carried off first prize in
Moscow's International Tchaikovsky Competition.

A short, busty, gray-haired dowager who might have stepped
right out of a Helen Hokinson cartoon, Minnie will float from the
wings of the vast outdoor stage at around 9:30 of a June or July
night—in all likelihood wearing the same heavy, rubber-soled
sport shoes and dowdy, five-year-old cotton dress she put on to
walk the dog before breakfast, with a frumpy inverted flowerpot
of a hat borrowed at the last minute from the cook—and, waving
her right hand giddily in mid-air, chirp a cheery "Hello,
everybody" to a motley mass that choruses its reciprocal "Hello,
Minnie" in ecstatic unison. Then, planting herself behind a
standing microphone and sliding her framed spectacles down the
not inconsiderable length of her nose, she'll proceed to forecast
the musical highlights of the week, identifying *Richard* Strauss as
the composer of "The Beautiful Blue Danube" and *Pinafore* as
everybody's favorite by Gilbert and *Solomon;* promising that
Anton Rubinstein will play the Tchai-COW-sky *Violin* Con-
SERT-o, Jan Peerce will sing the role of *Aïda,* and *Rodger
Hammerstein* "personally" will conduct a number from *South
Pacific;* and interrupting herself from time to time to implore the
echo of her own voice to "shut up" or exhort her listeners to "Tell
everybody you know to come to the Stadium. And tell everybody
you don't know too, because unless we have people in the empty
seats I'll simply go bust!"

Habitual Stadiumgoers recall with particular delight the night
in 1947 when she came out to herald the upcoming appearance of
"one of the best-known names in the musical world," then,
hesitating for an anguished moment, reached into her overstuffed

pocketbook for the crumpled bank check on which she had written her notes and identified him as "Ezio Pinza, *baass.*" "Oh dear, that can't be right," she corrected aloud. "A bass is a kind of fish!"

They'll recollect the time she was tendering official thanks of the Stadium Concerts Corporation to the President of City College, on whose campus Lewisohn Stadium is situated, and sighed, "I don't know what I'd do without him"; then, removing her glasses, scrutinized the eminent educator from head to toe and admitted, "I don't know what I'd do *with* him either." Or how, anticipating a wartime performance of *La Bohème* by the late Grace Moore, she explained, "Miss Moore has just been abroad for the boys, you know," unflusteredly inquiring, "What's wrong with that?" when the crowd broke into loud guffaws.

They'll never forget her asking an audience of 10,000 whether they preferred jazz to Beethoven and requesting them to answer "one by one." How, announcing a last-minute program change, she once said, "We won't be able to have that thing by Smetana tonight, but I don't think it matters very much. Smetana is some kind of mustard or sour cream, isn't it?" How, attempting to drum up box office for a future Ballet Russe appearance, she asked the legion out front not to "tell a soul" that she had always cherished a secret ambition to be a ballet dancer herself and forthwith demonstrated by raising her skirt well above one knee and kicking high enough to reveal a pair of long cotton knit underpants such as haven't been sold across a counter in thirty years.

Or they'll remind you of how, faced with imminent eviction from her Park Avenue apartment because the building was being torn down, she once told a capacity Stadium throng, "Now somebody out there must know a place where I can live when they kick me out on the streets!" How, making one of her innumerable appeals for contributions to underwrite the concerts' deficit, she suggested to the shirt-sleeved subway strap-hangers in the twenty-five-cent seats along the stone tiers that "you people should stop eating those fancy lunches at the Plaza and the Pavillon and send me the money instead!" Or how, while three of the Metropolitan Opera's highest-paid stars waited to resume their part in the evening's musical program, she punctuated another plea for funds with the promise, "If I get enough money, I'll be able to give you *better* artists in the future."

They still remember the time she summoned Sweden's Crown Prince onstage with a snap of her fingers and a "Here, Prince, Prince!" And the night she confessed, "I have a beau in the wings. He's the minister from Junkoslavia" and called upon Laurence Steinhardt, then U. S. Ambassador to Czechoslovakia, to take a bow. Or how, by way of expressing gratitude for the sponsorship of one concert by the brewers of Rheingold beer, she raved on before several hundred of their employees and distributors about how much she had always enjoyed *Budweiser*, especially to set her hair!

They love to tell about the occasion on which, staggering under a mass of orchids large enough to blanket a midget's coffin, she coyly gushed, "I suppose you're wondering where I got these gardenias. Well, I'm not going to tell you. The Mayor sent them to me and nobody's supposed to know about it!" Or the time she apologized publicly for her own late arrival at a concern, explaining that she'd eaten some sweetbreads that didn't agree with her and had been obliged to take "a big dose of citrate of Carbona!"

Then there's the time Fiorello La Guardia came up to the Stadium to confer New York City's Certificate of Merit on a star of the evening. "The Mayor's going to decorate our soloist," Minnie Guggenheimer began, "that is, if he can find a place where she isn't already decorated!" Or the 1948 season-opening concert when, following Bill O'Dwyer's announcement that a new stage would be erected by the city for the following season, she invited Stadium subscribers to participate in the ground-breaking ceremonies. "We'll all go down there and lie . . . lay," she started, then abruptly halted and amended, "I mean we'll do something with spades!"

Or the night she sauntered out in the face of lowering thunder clouds and petulantly exclaimed, "What in hell am I going to do about this weather?" And the time when a sudden torrential downpour interruped the 1950 Stadium season's sold-out Rodgers and Hammerstein Night and sent thousands scurrying for shelter. "Now come back every single one of you," Minnie remonstrated. "It'll be over in a few minutes, I promise." When, contrary to all weather bureau predictions, the rainfall stopped as suddenly as it had begun and the moon and a hundred stars came out an instant later, she rushed back to the microphone, pleading, "Good heavens, I hope you won't all think I'm a witch!" Or when, after being shown the lengthy background material on a prominent political figure in a reputable directory of facts, she carefully prepared a written introduction for him, then decided at the last minute to scrap it and made short shrift by announcing: "I can only tell you that his Who's Who is six inches long!"

As a matter of fact, I am quite probably the only one of the millions of New Yorkers and their summer visitors attending summer concerts at the Stadium with any degree of regularity who doesn't recall a single one of these incidents or cherish some favorite story of her own concerning Minnie Guggenheimer's weird and wondrous platform behavior. That's because Minnie is my mother and, like my father before me and my brother Randy to this day, I run for cover whenever the sound engineer comes onstage to connect the microphone indicating that Mother is bent on making one of her famous intermission speeches. I hide out in the nearest telephone booth or subterranean locker room until I hear the orchestra strike up the second half of the program and can be sure that the worst is over. Then I retrieve Mother from the backstage men's washroom into which, still blissfully unaware of the legend on the door, she regularly ducks for emergency relief, and escort her to our seats at table 5E out front without comment.

126

IRMA L. LINDHEIM: ZEALOUS CONVERT TO ZIONISM
1918

In 1918, Irma Levy Lindheim (1886–1978) became a convert to Zionism. This was rather unusual, since Irma came from a Central European family of some means and most middle-class turn-of-the-century American Jews were anti-Zionists. An apprehensive generation eager to acculturate, they dreaded the thought that they might be accused of dual loyalties. Irma's mother-in-law was a Virginia Guggenheimer; they, too, were unsympathetic to a Jewish philosophy which they associated with ghettoism.

In the following account, Mrs. Lindheim, a highly intelligent, educated child-care worker, describes how she became a Zionist. William James, author of The Varieties of Religious Experience, *would have enjoyed reading how this young matron turned to a Jewish way of life condemned by most of her social peers. Once a Zionist, Mrs. Lindheim rose rapidly in the hierarchy. The Zionists were delighted to have her; she was an elite convert, who helped give the movement status and respectability. She succeeded Henrietta Szold as president of Hadassah and, after the death of her husband, emigrated to Palestine, where she made her home in a collective settlement. Her commitment to the movement left her no alternative.*

I was one of the few Jewish women then in the Motor Corps [during World War I], the only one later to become one of its high officers. I felt it a debt of honor to balance time, given away from home and family to Motor Corps service, with creative attention to my children. I was appalled at the way some women used war work as a welcome relief from family responsibilities; it gave me the consciousness that, whatever I could contribute of time and work to the war effort, I must make doubly sure not to neglect the rights and needs of my family.

Our eldest son had begun lessons at home when he was six, to learn something of his people's history. My husband and I agreed that he was not to be a spiritual parvenu. Therefore he received instruction in the history, the legends, and the customs of the Jews from a well-qualified teacher, able to impart knowledge according to the boy's capacity, not his age. A child should at the very least become acquainted with the line of his inheritance, historical and individual. Well remembering that questions of my childhood and teen years had received answers which did not satisfy me at all, unlike my parents with their children, I decided that I too must study, to fit myself to answer questions as they would inevitably arise.

Available at the time was a course of lectures by a leader of the Ethical Culture Movement. The subject was "The Bible as Literature," the group composed mostly of Jewish women.

Discussing the Book of Job, the lecturer said one day, "The Book of Job is to be ranked with the world's greatest literature, including the writings of Shakespeare and Goethe." He startled us then by changing abruptly from the coolly intellectual to intellectual indignation, throwing out a question shocking in its pertinence.

"Should I, a non-Jew, have to reveal to you, who are Jews, the greatness of your own literature?"

No whipped dog could have felt worse as, humiliated and inwardly disgraced, I left the lecture hall. I thought I had been studying conscientiously for some years: philosophy, history, sociology, politics. But now I realized how I had neglected—perhaps subconsciously avoided—subjects which were intrinsically Jewish. I had read the Upanishads—yet not the Bible! Early marriage having cut short formal education, and feeling the urgency of catching up with a brilliant, highly educated husband and fitting myself to raise our children, for me Jewish history might as well have stopped at the fall of the Second Temple. Even though I could recall having won a medal at Sunday School graduation for knowing all the "answers" at the back of the lesson book, a non-Jew had—very properly—made me feel the disgrace of my basic ignorance as a Jew.

I then knew that I must do something positive to close the gaps in my knowledge and understanding. But what? How?

A short time after that shattering episode in the lecture course, I was given a weekend leave from my Motor Corps duties and went to Baltimore to pay a brief visit to my husband's cousin, my friend Hortense Guggenheimer Moses. A Jewish life had developed in Baltimore which had in it nothing of the negative, formless, creedal limitations which had impelled me to look for new, positive answers to life. Hortense was a leader among the younger women of the Jewish community; of exceptional intelligence, she was active too, in the life of the city. To her it was incomprehensible that I was not a Zionist. In the few days of my visit, conversation revolved frequently around that subject. To me it was equally incomprehensible that she was a Zionist, no doubt mainly because of my antagonism to it, for I knew little if anything about the movement.

The final evening of my visit started out, as I thought, uneventfully. I took merely polite interest in my hostess' decision to expose me to strong Zionist influence, by means of our going to call at the home of Dr. Harry Friedenwald, an eminent Baltimore physician, and an ardent and prominent Zionist.

Another guest was Dr. Ben-Zion Mossensohn.

Introduced to me as the principal of the *Gymnasium* in Tel Aviv, first institution of its kind in Palestine, he was the first Palestinian I had ever actually met.

I was jolted out of my passive frame of mind by the first impression made upon me by this thoroughly exotic-looking man. One felt astonished by a man who seemingly might have stepped forth from the pages of a tale from *The Thousand and One Nights*. The combination of his appearance—luxuriant, meticulously square-cut, black beard; glistening black-brown, magnetic —almost mesmeric—eyes; expressive long-fingered hands; a body suggesting boundless vitality—and the manner of his talk—a remarkable vocabulary, conveyed in a soft voice of great resonance—was saved from melodramatics only by a tremendous sincerity and conviction. All this was bound to be fascinating to any woman, a fact pointedly noted sometime later by my mother-in-law, who seemed well informed as to his romantic reputation and feared its effect on a daughter-in-law whom she considered woefully impressionable.

Oddly enough, his conversation that evening with Dr. Friedenwald about Zionism—to which it was intended I should listen and learn from—was boring to me at first, and I heard it with only surface attention.

However, I could certainly not deny to myself that I felt emotionally stirred by this apparition among men. Subtly, however, it became as though my mind were being exposed to a slowly unrolling scroll, silken, marvelously illuminated. I was presented with a series of images, the best of Zionist literature and thought, taken like rubbings of ancient tablets. With consummate skill Dr. Mossensohn gave to forces and events the status of oracle. The combined impact of personality, intellect, and dedication was enormous. Perhaps the effect on me was secondarily intellectual, due to some unreckoned vulnerability within me.

As I knew myself, one side of my nature was wonderfully and completely satisfied in my marriage. Another side, engrossed in a drive for self-fulfillment, was acutely receptive to external impression, like copper plate under the engraver's burin. My thinking still leaned to the abstract and the philosophical. Though little recognized as such by myself, deep within my being ran a revivalist's rushing fervor. Restrained, kept within bounds by the calm rationalistic atmosphere of our home, and a strong streak of inherent common sense, I was protected against the dangers of ever going off at "religious" tangents.

Later, looking back with objectivity on that evening at Dr. Friedenwald's home, it was possible to realize that my host as well as Dr. Mossensohn had deliberately plowed up a spirit and mind they divined to be ready to be sown with the right seed; they divined also, in a person showing few outward points of contact with the Jewish heritage, that some spark lay deep, still, which in time might be fanned into flame.

I left for New York the following morning. Boarding the train I can recall my state of mind as only one of *waiting*. I had a misty sense of something coming toward me, but no premonition as to what it might be.

I opened a book, let my eyes follow lines of print, looked out the window, absently took my tickets from my purse. The train rushed along; it passed a red barn, a white wooden church, a shallow pond, cattle standing placidly in lush meadowland.

A Morse Code of facts, ideas, questions, answers, arguments, hummed along my mind. *National being of a people, captive for centuries. . . . Isn't it enough to be an American? Untrue that Jews are not a people, only a religion. . . . Jews are victims of their homelessness. . . . If I am an American, am I at the same time a Jew? Where does my allegiance, my responsibility lie?*

Without being able to identify what was happening to me, I had the feeling of growing bigger than I knew how to be—

Must not I, so wanting to be free and to find fulfillment, be part of the drive of a people to be free, to reassert their creativity in a homeland of their own? *I am an American. . . . I am a Jew. . . . Instead of an enigma to myself, am I not thereby doubly blessed, doubly responsible? What better fulfillment than to take my place with those who have suffered for centuries for their beliefs? To share in rebuilding a national life in the land where our forefathers held that very concept of freedom, equality, brotherhood on which the greatness of America—my America?—is built?*

So went the stream of my consciousness as I looked out at the countryside and saw it only vaguely, looked at lines of print in a book without taking in their meaning. Looked—and waited—

If, as the Zionists such as Dr. Friedenwald and this Dr. Mossensohn held, Jews retained the courage, the vision, and energy to rebuild a home in the land of their beginnings, how could I look for greater fulfillment than to be part of the great adventure?

Bits and pieces of old prejudices and antagonisms swam past the lens of my mind like motes in a shaft of sunlight—and passed into a sudden nothingness. *Zionism is not an abstract term, framed in space,* I thought. *Zionism is a saving way of life to a people, Zionism is alive—*

To what moment can one point, saying, *There in that moment my life was mystically changed?* That then one experienced the awakening, as from the unconsciousness of long sleep, to the spiritual revelation of a purpose which could become a lodestar for the rest of one's life? How express the experience in terms of a chemical composition of emotional and intellectual parts?

What had been coming toward me happened, while the train rushed onward. Zionism reached out to me and took my hand. A new way opened in front of me and there was no fear. Mystically, yet it seemed tangibly as sunlight, a great purpose and its glory touched me. Reason murmured in my mind, *There will be conditions.* Of course. Great purpose is never without conditions.

For example, how convey to my husband, at the end of this train ride within an hour or so, even a fraction of the vision I had caught, with its accompanying marvelous evaporation of inhibitions, doubts? How make real to those I loved, and who loved me, what was now so real to me? I so wanted my family to travel with me, side by side. How present this way to them, so that of their own accord they would want to travel it with me?

Unbidden, my mind moved back to my confirmation. How I had been exalted by it! And how far I had strayed from the font of my exaltation!

Now I was returning home. This was my conversion.

As love released me years earlier from the confines of my stammering, now the signs and symptoms of love were again all around me. I had a matchless feeling of weightlessness, of freshness of spirit, an essence of spring. Life was falling into a mosaic. There were depth, breadth, harmony, beauty in prismatic color. Puissance flowed through me.

The train crossed the Jersey marshes. My husband would be at the station to meet me. I could face him in the security of discovery that my life had reached a threshold of true purpose. No atheist ever had farther to come, or arrived with greater certitude.

When I told my husband that I had experienced a conversion and become a Zionist, would he understand?

A more phlegmatic—or less uplifted—person doubtless would have waited to get home, or at least into the privacy of the family automobile, before conveying to a quite unprepared husband so vital a piece of news; besides its inherent importance as deep human experience, it inevitably must affect the life of our family.

As it was, stepping from the train, I said, "Darling, I'm a Zionist."

His answer was equally direct. "You mean you want to live in a ghetto?" A few short days earlier, if he had been the one to make an announcement like mine, my reaction would probably have been no different than was his.

I was not disturbed. In our ten years of marriage I had learned to rely on osmosis as a method to overcome certain essential differences between us in approaches to things. In his question I had caught an edge of irony. But it would take more than irony to swerve me from the course on which—so inexplicably—I had been set. I was convinced that he could and would be won over. In terms of his own personality, the way his mind worked, it would not come about in a hurry. Time, reason, circumstances, and great caring must be given opportunity to work changes.

127

FRANCES STERN: DEAN OF FOOD CLINIC DIETICIANS
1918–1941

The Bostonian Frances Stern (1873–1947) was a woman of many careers. She was a kindergarten teacher, a visiting housekeeper and homemaker, an industrial health inspector, a director of an American Red Cross clinic for children in Paris during World War I, a pioneer in the science of home economics, the founder of the food clinic movement, and the author of many books and pamphlets in her professional field. Her approach in her writings was popular-scientific. In later years, after she had received recognition, Mrs. Stern became chief of the food clinic in the Boston Dispensary and Assistant in Medicine at Tufts College Medical School.

She has been included in this documentary on Jewish women because of what she accomplished. In 1918, she founded at the Boston Dispensary one of the first food clinics in this country; by the 1940's, there were at least fifty such clinics in the United States and other lands. Mrs. Stern succeeded in meshing together science, social work, income, and nutrition, a synthesis particularly important for low-income workers. In the following article Mrs. Stern recounts the highlights of her distinguished career.

DIETETICS AND THE FOOD CLINIC DEVELOPMENT. . . .
by Frances Stern

1941

The privilege to reminisce can be allowed, I suppose, to one who has almost reached the age of three score years and ten. Can this be used as an excuse for one's indulgence in recalling the interesting people and events that have influenced her life?

One often hears reference, in these days, to "a concentrate." In the vitamin field the term "a concentrate" is significant of research and victory, with contribution to the health and welfare of countless people. For my part I think of the Food Clinic as "a concentrate." It came into being as the result of varied and rich experiences, the direct impact of which is seen today in many phases of its activities. When, in 1939, the Food Clinic of The Boston Dispensary celebrated its twenty-first birthday, an article was written entitled "The Food Clinic Comes of Age." In a sense, a certain phase of my life was born in the year 1918.

It was many years before, in 1895, while I was taking a graduate course in kindergarten training, that I first became interested in teaching nutrition to children at the Louisa May Alcott Club in the South End of Boston, as co-director with Miss Isabel F. Hyams. It was our belief that if children were properly trained in home-making, they could help to lead the world to the "art of right living." We took the first floor and basement of a tenement house in a crowded district. The group of seventy children were of many nationalities and ranged from pre-kindergarten age through adolescence.

At the Louisa May Alcott Club the equipment for teaching housekeeping to little children was unique. It was adapted to the various age levels.

Besides the preparation of food, we used, in teaching food values, the analyses of several foods carried out at Pratt Institute under the direction of Mrs. Ellen H. Richards [1842–1911]. I wish I still had in my possession the rows of bottles showing the amounts of the constituents in various foods, and the blocks that represented a 70 kg. (154 pound) man, nearly six feet tall, with the bodily composition of essential nutrients printed on them, as well as smaller blocks descriptive of the food intake and outgo.

I was becoming aware that the desire for social betterment was not sufficient; I was beginning to recognize the need of relating science and education to life. It was a happy chance, with unforeseen developments, that led to my meeting Mrs. Ellen H. Richards at the Massachusetts Institute of Technology. It was in reality a milestone in my life, for Mrs. Richards, although devoted to pure science, was also feeling the need of applied science. "Research has to step aside," she said, "when I feel the pressure of sociological problems."

Mrs. Richards' belief in the application of science to daily life took her directly into the community. She was especially pleased to be asked to help secure efficiency and happiness for the industrial worker. How well I remember preparing the petri dishes for a talk to a group of waitresses. By this means of visual education they could see if microbes would grow upon "the garden" of sterile gelatin—an indication of unclean hands.

Even as early as the 80's, Mrs. Richards believed that children were ready for health education and that the community was on the threshold of this work. The use of "penny booklets" that were published at this time by the Health Education League, in the interest of teaching health, is little known. In an early edition of the Journal of Home Economics, I found an article of mine describing Mrs. Richards' interest in the school lunch—a question still before the public. The days when I helped her arrange equipment for these penny lunches, sometimes perforce in the janitor's quarters in the basement of the school, are still vivid in my mind.

These years in the employ of Mrs. Richards were rich indeed. My activities included organizing her files, reading her papers, gathering material for lectures on food and related problems, talking to various groups and assisting in the preparation of Mrs. Richards' book, "Euthenics." How interesting and delightful it was to accompany her to the conferences at Lake Placid, where the beginnings of the home economics movement, the forerunner of the American Home Economics Association, were discussed!

All these activities stimulated my desire for further scientific knowledge and I became a special student at the Massachusetts Institute of Technology. The curriculum did not include courses in what is today termed nutrition but centered on the chemistry and sanitation of foods. An outstanding affiliated course was on Industrial Hygiene with Professor Sedgwick, whose interest in public health also helped prepare me for my later work. Perhaps the remark of one of my instructors will illustrate the difference between our past and present attitude toward nutrition. "I am interested in the methods of water analysis," he said, "while you care more for the welfare of human beings and whether they are poisoned or not." Only within recent years has the Massachusetts Institute of Technology included nutrition in its course in Public

Health asking me to present a series of lectures on applied dietetics.

Mrs. Richards' death in 1911 was a tragedy for me as well as for countless people in the field of public health and nutrition. What path would I follow now? One of Mrs. Richards' interests had been Instructive Visiting Housekeeping, a phase of work which had also intrigued me. The following year I became Instructive Visiting Housekeeper for the Boston Tuberculosis Association and later for the Boston Provident Association. This work brought me in close contact, both in the home and in clinics, with many underfed patients on low incomes. The usual instruction given them in the clinics was the vague direction, "nutritious diet." Out of this work grew the book "Food for the Worker," written with the assistance of Miss Gertrude T. Spitz to show the need for the unification of science, social work, income and nutrition. These were the days, too, when the need for a center in the community for teaching nutrition to the worker began to develop in my subconscious thoughts. I had known the woman in the home as well as the child in the school. Now I looked forward to knowing more about labor—the man in the factory. When the Massachusetts Board of Labor and Industries was established, I became an Industrial Health Inspector. The influence of nutrition upon efficiency had been given little thought by either the industrialist or the worker. In my visits to industrial organizations I investigated lunch rooms and other facilities for food, and again realized that abundant health, which meant the ability to work, required the right food in kind and amount.

With the first World War came the call to go to Washington and work in the Food Conservation Division of the United States Food Administration. During a visit to Professor William Hurd of Amherst State College, then assistant to Secretary of Agriculture David G. Houston, we discussed the problems embodied in my book "Food for the Worker." Upon my return to Massachusetts, Professor Hurd wrote me a letter stating that he had long been considering a project of nutrition in relation to the industrial worker but that he had never known how to carry it out. He said, "Now I know how it can be done. Will you do it?" I answered, "Yes."

My work kept me in close contact during the war period with

the Home Economics Committee of the Massachusetts Committee on Public Safety, of whose executive committee I was a member, as "Specialist on Food for the Industrial Worker." I tried to reach out to many types of groups and talked at patriotic meetings, trade-union meetings, and to wives of the workers. My activities took me into the factory, where I sometimes assisted the nutritionist and industrial physician. At one time I helped a librarian, who was translating recipes into Polish. In other words I tried to contact the workers and their families as well as industrial executives, to help them to become aware of the value of food to the body as a means of conservation of health and income.

At last my wishful thinking concerning a center for teaching nutrition to workers was to become a reality. Dr. Michael Davis, Director of The Boston Dispensary, with whom my work had brought me in close contact, believed that unfortunate changes in the dietary had been brought about by the war. He asked me to plan a study for evaluating the food intake of families under the care of the agencies of the League of Preventive Work, of which The Boston Dispensary was a member. The results were published in a pamphlet, "Food Supply of Families of Limited Means." In this report Dr. Davis pointed out with great vision that social and health agencies could not deal adequately with the serious problem of inadequate food supply and that there must be a nutritionist in a community organization.

Still working on the project of food for the worker, I approached Dr. Davis with a plan for establishing a Food Clinic in The Boston Dispensary. A one-page administrative report *is the authentic beginning of the Food Clinic movement.* At last the dream of many years came true and the Food Clinic opened its doors to about four patients one day a week. As chief of the Food Clinic, I have watched it grow so that now I have a staff of four workers to assist me in caring for 1500 patients, of thirty nationalities, who yearly average a total of 7000 visits. How grateful I am today to Tufts College Medical School for its recognition of our work, including my honorary degree and appointment as Assistant in Medicine; for in 1918 few physicians recognized the value of a Food Clinic.

A department of Health Education became affiliated with the

Food Clinic. It was the first to be established in any medical institution. The result has been the publication of a book for teachers, "Food and Your Body; Talks with Children," written with Miss Mary Pfaffmann; as well as the preparation and distribution of leaflets, the creation of exhibits, the production of a film entitled "Fun in Food," and talks and lectures given both within and without The Boston Dispensary.

Today the Food Clinic is no longer an experiment but a successful and important reality for the food treatment of the ambulatory patient. A graduate course for Students Training in Food Clinics is given in The Boston Dispensary and is approved by the American Dietetic Association. Other courses are given for students of home economics, social work, medical students, graduate physicians, graduate nurses and students in allied fields of health and education. Methods and material for the education of students and patients have been developed, including the book "Applied Dietetics," which I wrote especially for purposes of teaching.

The Food Clinic believes that the "Nutritional History," which it has developed and uses with every patient, is essential for complete understanding of the patient's life. The information called for in this history is a reflection of my many experiences in educational adventure, study of housing here and abroad, practical interest in labor and study of the labor movement in the London School of Economics, work with many nationalities including the organization of the first settlement house in Paris during the first World War—in other words, my experience with Food and Life. As far back as 1929 we published an article "The Nutritionist Looks at Mental Hygiene." Truly we may relate the Food Clinic to almost every phase of life and many fields of knowledge. Rightly nutrition can be called the first line of defense and the dietitian is necessary wherever there is concern for the health and happiness of human beings.

Would that the pioneers who were interested in the art of cooking and the science of food, so meagerly understood in those days, could realize the great contribution made by pure science to nutrition, and to its application through education, reaching into every home, including those of wealth and of poverty, and in innumerable ways making a finer, stronger nation! A great accomplishment of the last half century lies in the integration of the thinking and doing of various groups, in relation to nutrition, and in the belief that the dietitian or nutritionist is necessary to the science and art of living.

128

JESSIE ETHEL SAMPTER: ARDENT JEWISH NATIONALIST
1920

Zionism, Jewish Palestine, the State of Israel—these have appealed to a number of Jewish women who had found little comfort in Judaism, but finally made their way back to their people through a love for Zion. Influenced by Henrietta Szold, the left-wing traditionalist Mordecai M. Kaplan, and Emma Lazarus' brilliant sister Josephine, Jessie Ethel Sampter (1883–1938) became a devoted member of the people who gave her birth.

Her family on both sides were of antebellum stock, well-to-do, cultured, on the road to assimilation. Her father was an early follower of Felix Adler, the founder of the Ethical Culture movement. Jessie, a semi-invalid all her life—unhappy, lonely, unattractive—was a "seeker," constantly searching for spiritual peace and a rewarding purpose in life. She found it first in Unitarianism and then, at long last, in Zionism, in poetry, and in a dedication to the challenge of the new Palestine, where she settled in 1919. There the special object of her attention was under-privileged Yemenite newcomers.

She wrote on Zionism and published several modest volumes of poetry. The following rhymes are for children. Her purpose in these poems was essentially didactic; she was eager to make Jews, their customs, their history, their beliefs, attractive to the children who, she hoped, would be the stalwart Jews of tomorrow.

BLESSING

Blessed art thou, O God our King,
The Lord of life and everything,
Who kept and brought us all the way
Alive and strong until to-day.

PETACH TIKVAH
The Gate of Hope

I know a little village
That's called the Gate of Hope.
It lies in blessed Palestine
Upon a gentle slope.

Its orange-trees are golden,
As golden as the day,
And singing Hebrew melodies,
Its happy children play.

But silent in the graveyard,
The bones of heroes sleep,
Who died to build this Gate of Hope
That others live to keep.

When all the singing children
Have grown to man's estate,
Will then, at last, the Hope come true
Where they have built the Gate?

HADASSAH
Esther

I love to think of Esther,
A simple Jewish maid,
When in her uncle's house she lived
And happily obeyed.

Before she thought of Shushan,
Its splendor and its gloom,
Or dreamed her deed of faith might save
Her people from its doom.

Her mind had then the sweetness,
Her heart the courage high,
That later bade her say, "I go,
And if I die, I die."

129

ROSE HAAS ALSCHULER, CHICAGO ARISTOCRAT
1920's

Rose Haas Alschuler (1887–1979) was descended from a pioneer Chicago Jewish family, the Greenebaums. Her grandfather, Michael Greenebaum, who had come to Chicago in 1846, was a Jewish communal leader in antebellum days and not without influence in the city itself. In 1853, he led a group of outraged citizens in a successful effort to liberate a fugitive slave from the clutches of a United States marshal.

Over the years, Mrs. Alschuler achieved recognition for her social work. Chicago knew her as a pioneer in providing nurseries for preschool children of the needy and unemployed. Not only was she the founder of the first private nursery school in the city, but she also organized many similar schools for the Board of Education. During World War II she served as chairperson of the National Commission for Young Children. As a Jew she helped found Glencoe's prestigious North Shore Congregation Israel, led the North Shore Bonds for Israel Committee, and accepted election to the board of the American Technion Society.

During the decade of the 1920's, it was relatively common for people of distinction and culture to write a confessio fidei, *a statement of their philosophy of life. This was the day of "I Believe" pronouncements. It is probable that, though undated, the following statement was written by Rose Haas Alschuler during that decade.*

"I BELIEVE—TODAY"

Life is a mirage and life is an effort—and the fullness of life for every individual depends on the strength and beauty of his effort.

And I would have my child know that one lives by truth—but that truth is only relative. That in this great world so full of positive impressions, sensations and experiences, there is only one unchanging truth, and that is the spirituality of the world. This spirituality is evidenced in power—human and superhuman, in the re-creative powers of nature, and the creative powers of man.

I would tell my child and live for him an inner freedom—a freedom from fear, a freedom from the out-lived traditions of the past, and from the futile allegiances of the present—a freedom which should enable him to think thru every experience, to act and to react freely, and to realize daily living with all the capacity of a free spirit.

I would tell him that life must be lived constructively, that love should be the motive power of action—I would have him know that hatred, envy, malice, evil in any form is a boomerang and consumes its begetter.

I would have him think that every human being has unrealized and almost unlimited possibilities which it is his joyous responsibility to fulfill. But I would have him keep his sense of personal accomplishment balanced by realizing that any individual accomplishment is infinitely small, if one thinks in terms of the cosmos—of what is being done, what has been done and what remains to be done.

And in time I hope he shall come to know that a talent for living consists in a capacity for adjustment, that happiness and fulfillment consist in realizing life to the fullest at every moment and in losing one's self thru giving one's love and one's power to the sum of human welfare.

Can we teach those things—appreciations of truth and beauty—understanding of inner freedom—the joys of world love and service? Probably not! One can only sense them and perhaps impart them thru the quality of one's own being.

Rose H. Alschuler

· *130* ·
LEFT-WING SOCIOPOLITICAL DEVOTEES
1920's–1950's

After 1920, a number of able, self-sacrificing, dedicated Jewesses worked to further the underprivileged of American society. They felt that they could best reach their goals by affiliating with left-wing political groups, primarily the Communist Party, United States of America.

Rose Wortis (1894–1958), an active member of the leftist faction in the International Ladies' Garment Workers Union (ILGWU), was one such woman. To her, the right-wingers were reactionaries. Selection A, below, briefly recounts her career as a militant Marxist. She was an outstanding trade unionist, and an ardent Communist. Her friends looked upon her as a working-class hero.

Alice Citron, another left-winger, worked in an entirely different sphere. She was a cherished public-school teacher in the Harlem of the 1930's and 1940's. Her particular concern was helping the impoverished black children in her classes. In 1950, Alice was suspended because she refused to disclose her political affiliations. The late 1940's and early 1950's were a time of political reaction. Anti-Communist laws were passed and enforced; Jews who were members of the Communist Party, or even thought to be members, were dismissed, even though they could in many instances point to notable records as teachers, civil servants, and citizens. Neither Alice Citron's devotion to her pupils nor her capacity to teach were ever questioned. A generation later a New York court ruled that the dismissal in 1950 was unconstitutional.

In article B, she describes her goals as a teacher and a humanitarian.

A

1920's–1950's

WOMEN WHO MADE AMERICA

ROSE WORTIS, GARMENT LEADER
by Lena Gold

The history of our country is rich with accounts of men and women who have courageously fought for the rights of the working people. Among them is Rose Wortis, devoted champion of her class. Born in Kiasilov in 1894, she left her family there and joined the tens of thousands of Jewish and other immigrants who fled from oppressive Czarism to seek freedom and work in the new world.

She came with dreams and hopes for a life that would put her childhood's memories of poverty into a forgotten past. Life's reality found her scrubbing dirty floors in a chocolate factory in Williamsburg. For $3 a week she slaved from 7 in the morning until 6 at night. A harsh and cruel foreman drove her and abused her. Though exhausted, she would still snatch a few hours of reading and studying in order to make the grades at a part-time school she attended eagerly.

From the chocolate factory to the operating machine, she found herself among the thousands emerging from hard fought battles to improve working conditions and to strengthen the Union. She was not yet in the maelstrom of the turbulent life of the East Side's organizations and political activities. Of necessity, she clung to the closely knit family circle, although lonely and missing people of her own age.

The turning point in her life came when she attended a meeting at which [a left-wing rebel] Elizabeth Gurley Flynn spoke. The impression and impact was immediate and lasting. Eloquent and persuasive, the young Miss Flynn pointed the way out of exploitation, out of the enslavement and poverty of the working people; that unions are the essential for a better, freer life.

From then on, never wavering, following and searching for

every bit of information about unions, she was dedicated to the ideals of freedom and happiness of the working people in this, her beloved land. "Bent over my machine in the daytime," she writes in her yet unpublished autobiography," my mind was busy with a multitude of ideas and activities for the evening. The shop and the union, my political work and work in the women's suffrage movement, all those bits fitted into one picture—a better life for all people."

The years of World War I found her speaking out at this unnecessary tragedy, while organizing against the high cost of living.

The war was the beginning of a war against the working people here. The cost of living soared, and the demands, the strikes for higher pay to meet it were beaten down. The Gompers and Greens did nothing on behalf of the workers. [Samuel Gompers and William Green were presidents of the American Federation of Labor.] The reactionary leaders of the ILGWU took their cut from above, and retreated in face of the employer attempts to destroy the hard-won rights of unions.

To Rose Wortis, this was a great challenge, for not only living standards, the return to sweat-shop conditions, but every democratic right was involved.

The workers in the ILGWU were aroused to stop this betrayal. One of the leaders of this movement was Rose Wortis.

Organizing, speaking, and writing she gained recognition and responsibilities.

"The struggles in the twenties were much more complicated and required much more understanding and class consciousness than the earlier battles," she says. For the enemy was not only the bosses, but the union officials.

No group deserves more recognition than the dressmakers who fought with determination, courage and self-sacrifice. When the whole sordid story of the subterfuge, trickery, expulsions and blacklisting on the part of the Dubinskys, Kahans against the unions is unfolded, the bright spirit of Rose Wortis stands out. [David Dubinsky and Abraham Cahan were anti-Communist Jewish leaders.]

As a leader in the Joint Action Committee, she participated in negotiations, striving to bring about peace and harmony. [This Joint Action Committee was an instrumentality of three Communist locals which had been suspended by the more conservative International Ladies' Garment Workers Union.] Confident and steadfast, she was nevertheless at times hesitant about her own powers as an effective speaker. At a rank and file meeting at the packed Yankee Stadium she became nervous before her appearance on the platform. But like lightning the whole background of decades of working people's struggles and sufferings flashed before her, the issues became real in terms of human beings struggling for air to breathe and she enchanted the audience. She was in demand as a speaker, as an educator and traveled to many cities and towns in the country.

Active in the Trade Union Educational League, as a writer in the Labor Herald, also writing articles in the Freiheit, the Daily Worker and in women's magazines, she brought the issues to the public. The new socialist Soviet State found in her a staunch supporter, for she rejoiced with the Russian workers over their new-found freedom.

In the Needle Trades Industrial League, she was a leading board member. The special training of women for leadership was its concern, as was the unity of the Negro and white workers.

Serious illness keeps Rose Wortis away from direct participation in labor affairs. Her interest and concern, however, are as alive as ever. We hope she will soon be back and continue in her leadership.

B
1930's–1950's

AN ANSWER TO JOHN F. HATCHETT
by Alice Citron

[Comment of the Editor of *Jewish Currents:*
Alice Citron taught in Harlem schools for 19 years until she was suspended May 3, 1950 in a witch hunt that fired scores of teachers dedicated to democracy in the schools. . . . Delegations of Negro mothers came to witness the hearings of Miss Citron. There it was reported that she had introduced the study of Negro

history in the schools, had freely given after-school coaching to slow learners, had bought eye-glasses, books, shoes and food out of her own salary to help needy pupils, had gotten toilets repaired, walls painted, badly soiled textbooks replaced, and had led movements of teachers and parents. . . .]

The July–August issue of *Jewish Currents* contains a story (p. 33) about John F. Hatchett, a Negro substitute teacher dismissed because he took his class to a Malcolm X Memorial. While supporting his defense, *Jewish Currents* also points out that he made the following remark in a signed article: "We are witnessing today in NYC a phenomenon that spells death for the minds and souls of our Black children. It is the systematic coming of age of the Jews who dominate and control the educational bureaucracy of the N.Y. Public School system . . ."

It is time to recall some glorious history made by Jewish teachers in the fight for Negro children and other oppressed youngsters. This history has long been buried and lives perhaps only in the minds of the participants.

In the very early '30s a small but valiant group of young Jewish teachers in Harlem started the battle that was to continue until 1950. During the struggle they won the support of Negro teachers and the entire community. What did we do? These are only highlights, for we worked unceasingly.

1) No parent associations existed at the time but from the beginning we fought for and won the right of parent participation in the conduct of the schools.

2) We fought to eradicate the filthy conditions in the schools, the overcrowding. We demanded new schools. As the years went on, these demands were partly won.

3) During the horrible depression of the '30s, when hunger stalked the land and was unbearable in Harlem, we won free lunches served in the public schools for all poor children.

4) In 1935 Harlem rose up in all its anger against the poverty of the day. The press, as it still does, called these actions "riots." The then Mayor Fiorello H. La Guardia ordered an investigation into the conditions of the area. Together with the parents, we

forced the appointment of a Subcommittee on Education. This Subcommittee among its conclusions reported: "We have already established that the unhappy school conditions in Harlem have been one of the most potent factors in creating the unrest and unhappiness which set the scene for the disorders of March 19." Further on the report said, "It is a fact that in no section of the city is overcrowding greater; and this is immediately reflected in the school system. Practically unanimous testimony shows that most of the Harlem schools are compelled to hold two or even three sessions, beginning in some cases as early as eight a.m. and running through until five o'clock. . . . There are between 40 and 50 pupils per class in fully half of the elementary schools."

This report was made possible because we were able to get 100 Jewish and Negro teachers to testify in secret before the Commission. Mayor La Guardia permitted this secrecy to protect the teachers against Board of Education reprisals.

5) In order to educate Harlem teachers, we organized forums at the Harlem YMCA on "The Contributions of the Negro to Civilization." Not a single prominent community leader failed to respond to our invitations to participate. Some of the names and organizations that come to mind are: A. Philip Randolph of the Brotherhood of Sleeping Car Porters, Dr. Max Yergan, then at C.C.N.Y. [City College of New York], the N.A.A.C.P. [National Association for the Advancement of Colored People], The Urban League, Frank Crosswaithe of The Negro Committee, Roy Wilkins of *The Crisis*, Alaine Locke, Countee Cullen and many more.

6) We initiated the fight against biased texts. We issued a pamphlet, "Bias and Prejudice in Textbooks in Use in the New York City Schools." In addition to the vile insults against Negroes, we indicated slanders against Puerto Ricans, the foreign born, Mexicans and others. The pamphlet also stated: "It is noteworthy that little or no attention is paid in most texts to the contributions of the Jews to American democracy, despite the fact that including such material would be an important step in overcoming misunderstanding and prejudice. . . . nor are even passing references ever made to the outstanding record of Jewish abolitionists in the fight against slavery." This pamphlet, issued

by The Teachers Union under the leadership of its Harlem Committee, received wide distribution.

7) We prepared materials for the use of teachers such as "The Negro in Africa," which was widely disseminated.

8) The celebration of Negro History Week became a practice in many of the schools.

9) Some of the schools rang out with achievements of the Negro people. Even the most reluctant teachers had to become involved. In my school, this was done through invitation to prominent Negroes to come to our assemblies. One of my most cherished mementoes, dated Feb. 11, 1949, was written to me by my Jewish principal: "You carried the ball beautifully. I am sure our visitors, Jackie Robinson and Roy Campanella, were just as impressed with the work of our children as our children were awed by these 'greats'—thanks to you."

I do not wish to imply that there were no Jewish teachers who disliked black children. But the collaboration of the militant Jewish and Negro teachers changed the atmosphere and none in our presence dared utter derogatory remarks.

All this came to a halt when, during the McCarthy witch-hunt days, the cowardly Board of Education dismissed or caused to resign hundreds of the finest teachers in any school system. [In 1950–1954, Senator Joseph R. McCarthy, a conservative, made irresponsible attacks on many loyal Americans.] My personal estimate is that 99 per cent of the fired teachers were Jewish. Eighteen years after our dismissal the Board of Education is beginning to do under community pressure but a trickle of the things we started 37 years ago.

Edgemere, N.Y., July 12 [1968]

34. Martha Neumark (Montor)

131

SHALL WOMEN BE ORDAINED AS RABBIS?
1922

The problem of ordaining women became actuel *in 1922, inasmuch as the nineteenth amendment, granting the vote to women, had been adopted in 1920. Could Jews be more conservative than the United States government and deny equality to women? Jews were well aware that the Congregationalists had ordained a woman, Antoinette L. B. Blackwell, as early as 1853. The issue was exacerbated by virtue of the fact that Martha Neumark (later Mrs. Henry Montor) was studying at the Hebrew Union College and, God willing, would soon be ready for ordination. Confronting this problem in 1921–22, the College faculty and the Central Conference of American Rabbis reluctantly decided that women "cannot justly be denied the privilege of ordination." The final ruling, however, rested with the Board of the College, which in 1923 limited ordination to males. Martha Montor stayed on until 1925, when she left the school; her class was to graduate in 1926. In 1972, fifty years after the faculty and the Conference agreed to accept women in the rabbinate, Sally Priesand was ordained and received her degree as rabbi.*

The selections below limit themselves to the discussion and pronouncements of the rabbis of the Central Conference in 1922.

RESPONSUM ON QUESTION, "SHALL WOMEN BE ORDAINED
RABBIS?"
by Jacob Z. Lauterbach.

The very raising of this question is due, no doubt, to the great changes in the general position of women, brought about during the last half century or so. Women have been admitted to other professions, formerly practiced by men only, and have proven themselves successful both as regards personal achievement as well as in raising the standards or furthering the interests of the professions. Hence the question suggested itself, why not admit women also to the rabbinical profession?

The question resolves itself into the following two parts: first, what is the attitude of traditional Judaism on this point, and second, whether Reform Judaism should follow tradition in this regard. At the outset it should be stated that from the point of view of traditional Judaism there is the following important distinction to be made between the rabbinate and the other professions in regard to the admission of women. In the case of the other professions there is nothing inherent in their teachings or principles which might limit their practice to men exclusively. In the case of the rabbinate on the other hand, there are, as will soon be shown, definite teachings and principles in traditional Judaism, of which the rabbinate is the exponent, which demand that its official representatives and functionaries be men only. To admit women to the rabbinate is, therefore, not merely a question of liberalism, it would be acting contrary to the very spirit of traditional Judaism which the rabbinate seeks to uphold and preserve. . . .

Now we come to the second part of our question, that is, shall we adhere to this tradition or shall we separate ourselves from Catholic Israel and introduce a radical innovation which would necessarily create a distinction between the title rabbi as held by a reform-rabbi and the title rabbi in general. I believe that hitherto no distinction could rightly be drawn between the ordination of our modern rabbis and the ordination of all the rabbis of preceding generations. We are still carrying on the activity of the rabbis of old who traced their authority through a chain of tradition to Moses and the elders associated with him, even though in many points we interpret our Judaism in a manner quite different from theirs. We are justified in considering ourselves the latest link in that long chain of authoritative teachers who carried on their activity of teaching, preserving and developing Judaism, and for our time we have the same standing as they had (Comp. R. H. 25a). The ordination which we give to our disciples carries with it, for our time and generation, the same authority which marked the ordination given by Judah Hannasi [a third-century rabbinical leader] to Abba Areka or the ordination given by any teacher in Israel to his disciples throughout all the history of Judaism.

We should, therefore, not jeopardize the hitherto indisputable authoritative character of our ordination. We should not make our ordination entirely different in character from the traditional ordination, and thereby give the larger group of Jewry, following traditional Judaism, good reason to question our authority and to doubt whether we are rabbis in the sense in which this honored title was always understood.

Nor is there, to my mind, any actual need for making such a radical departure from this established Jewish law and time honored practice. The supposed lack of a sufficient number of rabbis will not be made up by this radical innovation. There are other and better means of meeting this emergency and that is, by the rabbis following the advice of the Men of the Great Synagog [a rabbinical council centuries before Christianity] to raise many disciples and thus encourage more men to enter the ministry. And the standard of the rabbinate in America, while no doubt it could be improved in many directions, is certainly not so low as to need a new and refining influence such as women presumably would bring to any profession they enter. Neither could women, with all due respect to their talents and abilities, raise the standard of the rabbinate. Nay, all things being equal, women could not even rise to the high standard reached by men in this particular calling. If there is any calling which requires a whole-hearted devotion to the exclusion of all other things and the determination to make it one's whole life work, it is the rabbinate. It is not to be considered merely as a profession by which one earns a livelihood. Nor is it to be entered upon as a temporary occupation. One must choose it for his lifework and be prepared to give to it all his energies and to devote to it all the years of his life, constantly learning and improving and thus growing in it.

It has been rightly said that the woman who enters a profession must make her choice between following her chosen profession or the calling of mother and home-maker. She cannot do both well at the same time. This certainly would hold true in the case of the rabbinical profession. The woman who naturally and rightly looks forward to the opportunity of meeting the right kind of man, of marrying him and of having children and a home of her own, cannot give to the rabbinate that whole-hearted devotion which comes from the determination to make it one's lifework. For in all likelihood she could not continue it as a married woman. For, one holding the rabbinical office must teach by precept and example, and must give an example of Jewish family and home life where all the traditional Jewish virtues are cultivated. The rabbi can do so all the better when he is married and has a home and a family of his own. The wife whom God has made as a helpmate to him can be, and in most cases is, of great assistance to him in making his home a Jewish home, a model for the congregation to follow.

In this important activity of the rabbi, exercising a wholesome influence upon the congregation, the woman rabbi would be deficient. The woman in the rabbinical office could not expect the man to whom she be married to be merely a helpmate to her, assisting her in her rabbinical activities. And even if she could find such a man, willing to take a subordinate position in the family, the influence upon the families in the congregation of such an arrangement in the home and in the family life of the rabbi would not be very wholesome. Not to mention the fact that if she is to be a mother she could not go on with her regular activities in the congregation.

And there is, to my mind, no injustice done to woman by excluding her from this office. There are many avenues open to her if she choose to do religious or educational work. I can see no reason why we should make this radical departure from traditional practice except the specious argument that we are modern men and, as such, we recognize the full equality of women to men, hence we should be thoroughly consistent. But I would not class the rabbis with those people whose main characteristic is consistency. . . .

DISCUSSION

Rabbi [Louis] Witt: I was present at the meeting of the Board of Governors [of the Hebrew Union College] when the matter came up, and it was decided to refer it to the Conference. After reading the responsa [responsum] that was prepared by Rabbi Lauterbach

I feared that there would be much opposition. I trust that our action in this matter will be unanimous. It is not a matter of tradition at all. I must confess I was not in the least interested in Rabbi Lauterbach's presentation. It seemed reactionary to me. I did not feel that it was the proper presentation of the subject. I need not say that I honor Dr. Lauterbach for the learning contained therein but the point he presents is not the point at issue. We have witnessed the revolution in the status of woman. Five years ago I had to argue in favor of women's rights when that question came up in the Arkansas legislature, but I did not feel that there would be need to argue that way in a liberal body of men like this.

There is a principle involved, and I hope that the stand we take will be one in line with all the progressive tendencies of our day: That we will have the vision to see what is before us and from the standpoint of to-day shall we say to women that they shall not have the right to function as we are functioning?

The question is, Have they the qualifications to function as spiritual leaders? What does it require to be a spiritual guide? It requires a great spirit and the quality of leadership. Some women have it and some women have not. Some men have it and some men have not. If we had a great leadership we would not have the questions which were so ably presented yesterday among the practical questions of the ministry. The one thing that was stressed was that if we had devoted leaders who could inspire following all the problems would vanish.

I believe that this body of men should do nothing that would stand in the way of any forward movement in behalf of the womanhood of America. I cannot believe that a religion that is so splendidly spiritual and forward-looking as our religion will stand in the way of such a movement. I feel that this Conference can only act in one way, and that is to fall in line with what is the destiny of the women of the future. . . .

The following statement was submitted, and was adopted by a vote of 56 to 11:

The ordination of woman as rabbi is a modern issue due to the evolution in her status in our day. The Central Conference of

American Rabbis has repeatedly made pronouncement urging the fullest measure of self expression for woman as well as the fullest utilization of her gifts in the service of the Most High and gratefully acknowledges the enrichment and enlargement of congregational life which has resulted therefrom.

Whatever may have been the specific legal status of the Jewish woman regarding certain religious functions, her general position in Jewish religious life has ever been an exalted one. She has been the priestess in the home, and our sages have always recognized her as the preserver of Israel. In view of these Jewish teachings and in keeping with the spirit of our age, and the traditions of our Conference, we declare that woman cannot justly be denied the privilege of ordination.

HENRY COHEN, *Chairman.*

35. Estelle Miller Sternberger

132

SUMMARIZING THE ACHIEVEMENTS OF THE AMERICAN JEWESS
1923

In 1923, the Executive Secretary of the National Council of Jewish Women gathered information on the careers of American Jewish women and published her findings. Her report is important; it is an excellent summary of what the Jewess in this country had accomplished in the three decades since she determined to carve out a career for herself. Had Rebecca Gratz been given the opportunity to read the survey, she would certainly have been astounded—but, in all probability, gratified. The Jewess of 1923 was no longer the retiring gentlewoman of 1823.

The author of the study was Estelle Miller Sternberger (b. 1886). Mrs. Sternberger was an outstanding example of what a person could do to raise herself up, as it were, by her own bootstraps. Starting with at best a high school education, she became a communal worker and radio commentator of national stature. She served as editor of the Jewish Woman, *as Executive Secretary of the National Council of Jewish Women, as the Executive Director of World Peaceways, Inc., and as a Vice-President of the nondenominational National Council of Women of the United States.*

CAREERS OF JEWISH WOMEN
by Estelle M. Sternberger
National Executive Secretary, Council of Jewish Women

All doubts concerning the talents of women have experienced a rapid revision within a single generation. As soon as popular prejudices and legal barriers were somewhat mitigated, woman seized upon her opportunity and showed powers that were unsuspected even by those who had championed her cause. The sceptic was effectively silenced by the careers and successes of those women who dared to be pioneers.

The Jewish woman in America has displayed talents and

abilities that reflect the general abilities of womankind. Laboring under the double handicap imposed, generally, by the world and, particularly, by some ancient but outgrown traditions of her faith, she has risen to a position of influence in a varied field of interests. There is hardly a phase of American life that remains untouched and unexperienced by her. She has assumed her role in the economic spheres of society, in the realm of the professions, in education, in the arts and in the sciences.

To ascertain with a measure of definiteness just what careers our women in America have chosen, "The Jewish Woman" made a study of a group of 87 cities, in which Council Sections are found, excluding New York City and Chicago, where the inquiry would require a more extended pursuit because of their large Jewish populations. The information that has been gleaned reveals a very interesting variety and preference.

The career of teacher claims the largest number, totalling far beyond the thousand mark. The world of social service follows next in rank, with a host of able executives and professional workers. Here are to be found several superintendents of local federated Jewish charities, heads of detention homes, of community centers, of Young Women's Hebrew Associations, and of homes for girls.

In the professions of law and medicine, the former has attracted the greater number. Twenty-three cities reported 69 lawyers, and two cities boasted of 15 and 14 respectively. Nineteen cities enumerated 40 physicians, the largest number in any single community, namely five, being found in Baltimore and San Francisco. It is to be presumed that these figures would be greatly exceeded in New York City and Chicago. The city of Philadelphia reports only four Jewish women physicians, one of whom is on the faculty of a local medical college. In the last of the three traditional professions, namely the ministry, not a single woman is to be found. In view of the favorable action of the Central Conference of American Rabbis, on the question of admitting women into the Jewish ministry, it may be anticipated that the liberal and progressive Jewish seminaries of the United States will, before long, remove the obstacles that now stand in the way of woman's ordination.

It is in the field of commercial activity that we find the next largest group of women. A very great proportion of them own very successful enterprises, including an extensive chain of business establishments. Some function with remarkable acumen as general managers, and others as credit managers. One of the most gratifying bits of information revealed by this inquiry is the increasing number of women who are assuming academic careers. Twenty-four teachers appear on the staffs of seventeen different colleges and universities in the United States. The departments they represent include English, French, Spanish, chemistry, economics, sociology, history, biology, medicine, philosophy, mathematics, art, and secretarial work. They are also teachers on the faculties of our conservatories and colleges of music.

"The Jewish Woman as Author" has already been discussed in this periodical in an article contributed by Elma Ehrlich Levinger. No less than twenty-nine authors are claimed by fourteen cities, including poets, novelists, short story writers, authors of memoirs, of books on Jewish history and Jewish life, on public health, citizenship and dietetics. The arts are well represented by an abundance of vocalists, several teachers of voice culture, dramatic readers, professional accompanists, organists, sculptors, panel painters, portrait painters, illustrators, composers, opera singers and photographers.

Relatively prominent is the field of public health. In addition to the many young women who become nurses, there are those who have risen to the responsible posts of hospital superintendents. Dietetics has been selected by a comparatively significant group.

Though of lesser proportions, the following careers have also been reported: dentists, journalists, advertisers, librarians, architects, designers, psychologists, interior decorator and civic director. They are significant in that they suggest avenues and opportunities that have not yet been fully appreciated by our women.

The participation of the Jewish woman in political and civic life is indicated by the various offices they fill. Some of them are elective and some appointive and cover city, county, state and federal offices. Five are members of local Boards of Education;

three, members of Boards of Charities and Corrections; and there is one each in the following civic positions: Member of Labor Arbitration Board; Commissioner of Charities; Director of Public Health; Director of Charities; Assistant City Attorney; member of Minimum Wage Board; member of Playground Commission; Justice of the Peace; and Probation Officer. In County offices are to be found an Assistant County Prosecuting Attorney and an Assistant District Superintendent of Schools.

Pennsylvania has two Jewish women in the State Legislature and Arizona has one. In a western state, a woman heads the Widows' Pension Bureau, and in another there is a representative on the state's Board of the Hall of Fame. Other states report a Regent of the University and a Secretary of the State Public Welfare Board. Finally, in the National Department of Labor, there is a divisional chief.

As one reviews the scope of talent in these many careers, there is born in our hearts an inspiring appreciation of woman's ability. The vital fact that cannot be forgotten or brushed aside is that this record of achievements has been built up by a generation of women, faced constantly by a hostile public and heavily weighted with the chains of restrictive legislation, masculine prejudice and feminine timidity. The careers of today are only the gateways to a larger world that shall lie open to the women of tomorrow.

36. Florence Prag Kahn

133

FLORENCE PRAG KAHN, CONGRESSWOMAN
1925–1937

Florence Prag Kahn (1868–1948), the wife of Congressman Julius Kahn, was chosen to fill the vacancy caused by his death in the mid-1920's. Mrs. Kahn, a Republican, was the first Jewess to sit in the United States Congress. She served her San Francisco constituents from 1925 to 1937, when she was swept out during the Roosevelt landslide. Congresswoman Kahn was a third-generation Californian; her grandmother, the wife of a Polish shohet, had arrived in San Francisco in 1852. Her mother, Mary, a high school teacher, had helped organize one of the first San Francisco Sabbath schools. For lack of something better, Mary had not hesitated to adapt a Christian religious tract for her purposes.

Florence went to college and taught school. When she married Congressman Kahn, she became his secretary. In taking over his job in Washington, she was no novice; she already had twenty-five years experience as his aide and mentor. Her election to Congress is mute testimony that women were making their way politically and that a Jewess could be elevated to a position of responsibility in the national legislature of the most powerful country in the world.

The following article describes in some detail her career in Washington.

FLORENCE PRAG KAHN: THE FIRST JEWISH CONGRESSWOMAN
by Irena Penzik Narell

In 1925 Florence Prag Kahn entered the United States Congress, the first Jewish woman to do so. No novice to politics or Washington, she had been the wife of a congressman, his advisor-secretary-critic and hostess since 1899. Gray-haired, high-spirited with flashing brown eyes, she was the mother of two grown sons when elected to the vacancy created by her husband's death. Florence Kahn had accompanied the California congressman Julius Kahn on over 30 transcontinental journeys from their native San Francisco to the nation's capital before making her trek alone to face new responsibilities.

California had enfranchised women in 1911, but it was only five years before Florence Kahn's election that universal suffrage had been enacted. Only one other woman would serve with her in the 68th Congress. Mrs. Mary [Mae] Nolan, widow of congressional veteran John Nolan of San Francisco, was also elected to her husband's seat.

MADE HER MARK IN CONGRESS

Given Florence Kahn's character and personality it would be hard to picture her as unequal to the challenge. Present in the gallery for countless debates, she was an astute politician. Her ancestors had made the arduous journey to the west during the gold rush period, surviving with family values and Jewish tradition fully intact. The inheritor of their pioneer spirit, she would make her own mark in Congress.

Her mother, Mary Goldsmith Prag, at the age of seven and feverish with malaria, crossed the Isthmus of Panama propped up on the saddle before her bearded, pious father, Isaac Goldsmith. The Goldsmith family had taken a steamer to Nicaragua, the most popular route to gold-crazed San Francisco, in July 1852. Mary's father, a *shochet* (ritual slaughterer) born in 1816, had emigrated from Poland to New York. The discovery of gold in California proved irresistible to the Goldsmiths.

In Panama City the family discovered that the paddle-wheeled Pacific steamer that was to take them to their destination had been wrecked on the downward trip. They were forced to wait two weary weeks until a steamship came around Cape Horn. Designed to hold 400 passengers, the steamer was already bursting with a thousand. Somehow they managed to scramble aboard.

San Francisco, an obscure western outpost of 300 inhabitants in 1848, within a scant three years had grown into a mushrooming tent and shack city of 50,000. Hundreds of Jewish merchants traded in the busy auction houses and stores of the makeshift city, built haphazardly atop sand dunes. Brothels and saloons outnumbered other establishments two to one and all transactions were conducted in gold tender. Soon Mr. Goldsmith was advertising his skills as a *shochet* in the local Jewish press.

By the time the Goldsmiths arrived, the Jews of the "City" had already organized into several benevolent societies and religious groups. They had even managed a good-sized ritual quarrel and had split into two major congregations—Sherith Israel and Emanu-El.

On the first Rosh Hashanah after their arrival, Mary's father took her and her sister to services at the orthodox Temple Sherith Israel, where the girls were seated in the gallery, separated from the men. Only two other females were present at the services. In 1856, Mary, whose family would become close to the grandparents of most of the prominent Jewish families of today's San Francisco, was taken along with her schoolmates to view the sight of a Vigilante double hanging.

In the honky-tonk atmosphere of the gold rush capital, Mary's family retained all the old world qualities of Jewish traditionalism and pride of achievement. Mary became the first Jewish schoolteacher in San Francisco, then a principal of Girls' High. In 1865 she married Conrad Prag, a forty-niner, present at a historic first Yom Kippur service that took place in a San Francisco tent in September, 1849.

Prag had tried his hand at prospecting in San Andreas [Calaveras?] County, then turned to the minding of a general store. He took his family to Utah for several years where Florence was born in 1869, and he became a friend of Brigham Young. Mary, surrounded by Mormon neighbors, wrote reminiscences entitled, "My Life Among the Mormons." She taught for over fifty years, and upon her retirement at 82, was elected to the San Francisco Board of Education. She served until her death seven years later, and acquired the nickname "Little Gibraltar" for her fervor in fighting for teachers' pensions and women's rights.

Florence, who had lost her father at ten, was highly influenced by her remarkable mother. She graduated from U.C. Berkeley, and following her mother's example, also became a teacher of English until she married the newly elected Congressman Julius Kahn.

Kahn was a character in his own right. His parents came from Prussia in 1866 in search of economic opportunity in the mining settlements of the West. After a time in the mining town of Mokelumne Hill, the elder Kahns opted for San Francisco where the father opened a bakery and the son was his delivery boy. But Julius dreamed of another career entirely. By the time he was eighteen he was making an auspicious debut as "Shylock" at the Baldwin Theatre. He was handsome in those days, full-faced with thick, curly hair, prior to developing the famous pot-belly of his congressional years. In his heyday as a thespian, he hobnobbed and played with such theatrical greats as Edwin Booth. After eleven years as an actor, Kahn turned to politics and law, in both of which professions he profited from his acting experience. By 1892 he was already a member of the state legislature, and in 1898 he became Congressman Kahn.

Two Party Candidate

The Kahns were Republicans, as was the overwhelming majority of their constituency. Patriotically devoted to the United States, Julius was so popular with his electorate that no one could be found to run against him. In primaries he often captured both the Republican and Democratic nominations.

The power structure in San Francisco "loved him." Though never wealthy, the Kahns were members of the exclusive Temple Emanu-El, where their sons were bar-mitzvahed. They counted most of the influential San Francisco Jews among their friends and fans.

An advocate of a large navy and a standing army, Kahn [ultimately] became Chairman of the Military Affairs Committee, supported President Wilson's conscription bill of 1917 and [helped sponsor] the National Defense Act, adopted in 1916.

But he made a serious error in judgment. Because of political considerations and loyalty to his largely anti-Chinese constituents, he co-sponsored the Kahn-Mitchell Chinese Exclusion Act in 1902, a notorious anti-Oriental piece of legislation. Yet he had great redeeming features. He refused to condone Congressional hypocrisy and was scrupulously honest. When he died he left an estate of only $4,430.

Florence shared her husband's loyalty to San Francisco, and to military preparedness, but was strongly individualistic in both her convictions and style. An independent, highly opinionated California woman, she was elected to six successive terms. During her tenure she accomplished more for San Francisco than her husband had done in all the years of his service. Through uncanny legislative ability she obtained funds for a new Federal office building, a marine hospital, the construction of a new mint, as well as several important military installations, and piloted legislation for the construction of the now indispensable San Francisco–Oakland Bay Bridge. The San Francisco Chronicle in August 1926 called her "a Republican who knows how to get things done."

In April 1929, while the military budget was under discussion, Speaker of the House Nicholas Longworth paid Mrs. Kahn the ultimate compliment of asking her to take the chair for a day.

A witty, brilliant woman, she would often meet the press with her hat slightly askew on top of her carelessly done up hair. She wore a black velvet band around her neck, refused to "slick" herself up, get a permanent or go on a diet. When asked in 1928 to what she attributed her immense plurality over her husband's votes, she replied without batting an eyelash: "Sex appeal."

"Would she favor a birth control law?" "I will if you make it retroactive," came the flashing reply. Her lack of vanity extended to the discarding of all her clippings and personal letters. Thus a great store of Kahn witticisms has been lost forever.

UNCONVENTIONAL BEHAVIOR

For example, a congressman of mighty self-importance was known to walk up and down the corridor between the House and Senate, his head bowed in meditation.

"He's walking again," a seat neighbor whispered to Florence Kahn, "all wrapped in his own thoughts." "My God," exclaimed the lady from California, "he must be almost naked!" Unhappy with Attorney General Cummings' selection of Alcatraz Island in mid–San Francisco Bay for a "Devil's Island" type of prison for the nation's worst criminals, she read that Democratic chieftains planned to buy an island for a weekend retreat. Florence dispatched a note to the Attorney General:

> I see by the papers that the Democrats are looking for an island for their rest and relaxation. Permit me to suggest Alcatraz. . . .

Her reputation for unusual pronouncements as well as for unconventional behavior prompted one of her more exasperated contemporary Washingtonians to write: "You always know how she is going to vote but only God has the slightest inkling of what she is going to say."

When she first appeared on the Washington scene as a congresswoman, Calvin Coolidge was in the White House and conservatism was king. Florence Kahn subscribed to the conservative viewpoint of "minimum government on the federal level." Yet she maintained that she voted on the basis of the merit of each question, "not on mere party loyalty."

She proved it after the election of Franklin Delano Roosevelt, when she joined a congressional majority in voting to give the President the power to act decisively, "not as a Republican but as an American." Florence had met young Franklin in San Francisco at a 1915 reception when he was assistant secretary of the navy, and was the first Republican dinner guest at the Roosevelt White House.

While a member of the House Education Committee Florence stood firmly against motion picture censorship. A fellow member of the Committee claimed that anyone objecting to censorship was unclean. The *American Mercury* reported her reply in Oct. 1929. Mrs. Kahn flounced up and yelled: "Don't you dare call me unclean!" She had already publicly expressed the view that "one cannot legislate morality into people." Censorship of art, education or religion was "un-American, unconstitutional and ineffective."

In an era when the women's vote was generally considered to be on the "dry" side, Mrs. Kahn became a vociferous spokesperson against Prohibition. She was supported in this by her California wine-producing constituency, and a firm belief that the law (The Volstead Act) was hypocritical and unenforceable, needing drastic reform. At a mass meeting in Carnegie Hall in April 1930 Congresswoman, mother and grandmother Kahn said:

. . . had our worst enemy designed a scheme to vitiate our youth, undermine our morale, inculcate a disrespect for the law, increase crime and warp our ideas of right and wrong, he could have conceived of no plan that would have accomplished it as has the prohibition law.

In 1936 Mrs. Kahn was defeated in a Roosevelt landslide, and returned permanently to her San Francisco family and a host of friends. In praising her Eleanor Roosevelt wrote: "Mrs. Kahn would be welcomed to the House with open arms."

Florence Kahn died of a heart attack in 1948, eight days after her 80th birthday, and nearly 100 years after her mother's danger-fraught journey to the West. As the bride of Julius Kahn she had walked with him to the Executive Mansion to have dinner with President McKinley because it cost $1 to hire a carriage. "In what country," asked Julius, "could two poor Jews be on their way to dine with the head of state?"

Her district had been a melting pot of middle and upper class Germans, French, Chinese, Irish and Jews. She had been at home with them all, friendly as an old hat. She had dined at the White House with eight presidents, heard secret confessions and given advice to presidents' wives. Rabbi Alvin I. Fine and Cantor Reuben R. Rinder officiated at her funeral from San Francisco's Temple Emanu-El, attended by hundreds.

The Kahns' two sons, Julius II, a retired attorney, and Conrad Prag, a former Los Angeles motion picture executive, fondly recall their indomitable mother. Julius II has had the unique experience of voting in public elections for his father, his mother, and his grandmother.

American Jewry can indeed reflect with pride on the life and career of a unique woman—Florence Prag Kahn.

134

DAVID A. BROWN'S BIRTHDAY POEM FOR HIS MOTHER
1928

On March 18, 1928, David Abraham Brown (1875–1958) read a poem at a dinner given in honor of his mother on her seventy-fifth birthday. From the aspect of literary structure and artistry, his effusion may well leave much to be desired; emotionally, it is the outpouring of a devoted son who loved and cherished the woman who bore him. It is cast in the best Jewish tradition, even if almost matriolatrous in its fervor.

Obviously Mama had influenced David, in his heyday one of the country's most influential Jews. Brown, a native of Scotland, came to this country at about the age of four and grew up in Detroit, where he stood out as a successful businessman and communal worker. Because of his skill as a fund-raiser, he was co-opted by the country's Jewish elite to organize drives for the impoverished Jews of Eastern Europe. Under his dynamic and imaginative leadership, millions of dollars were collected for philanthropic purposes.

Brown's poem, "To My Mother," which follows, was apparently issued as a private print.

When God from his heaven
Looked down upon earth,
   And saw that all was not right.
He called to his angels,
Come gather around,
   So all might behold the sight.

Then from all corners,
The angels appeared,
   All clad in garments pure white.
They look down upon earth
And are greatly disturbed
   And counsel with God through the night.

With God in the center,
The angels around him,
   The heavens ablaze with their glory,
With silence about them,
They listen all quietly,
   As he interprets for them the story.

Listen, my loved ones,
There is need upon earth,
   For a soul of the purest gold.
A mother in Israel,
Must be born at once,
   Born from an angel's mould.

We'll send upon earth,
A mother so noble,
   So beautiful, so good, so fine,
Bettered the world,
By her example,
   Proud, I, to call her mine.

So God looked about him
At his angels superb,
   More beautiful one than the other.
And tried to decide
The angel who would
   Make for the most perfect Mother.

The angels were waiting
The verdict of God.
   Which of them would he elect?
So many to choose from
Made the choice hard,
   The purest of all to select.

Then God's face lit up,
As it does, when
   A blessing he wants to bestow,

As His judgment he rendered,
To the angels assembled,
  To be sent to earth below.

Instead of one angel,
A dozen I'll send.
  Who stands ready to sacrifice all?
To give up their heaven
For life upon earth?
  Who'll volunteer at my call?

Then hundreds of angels
Cried out as one,
  Take me, I'm ready to go.
The spirit of angels,
To give of themselves
  In heaven, has always been so.

Out of the hundreds
A dozen or more
  God's most beautiful angels made glad.
While those not chosen
Went quietly away,
  Not unhappy, but yet quite sad.

Into God's mighty hand
So powerful, so strong,
  The angels were placed one by one.
When all were there
God gently said,
  Come back when your work is done.

As slowly his hand
Crushed them all into one,
  Their songs of joy could be heard.
We'll soon be on earth
Our task to begin,
  Oh, hearers, our hearts should be stirred.

As God opened his hand
Came a flood of light,
  A light of rare dazzling beauty.
Angel's souls most precious,
Had become as a jewel,
  To enlighten the world to its duty.

In the stillness of night
God sent on to earth
  This jewel which he dropped from above.
To be born as a child
And give to the world,
  An example of pure mother love.

O Mother, dear Mother,
It's you were the jewel
  That God did send from above.
The angels in heaven
Are dancing with joy,
  As they see how you've poured out your
    love.

O Mother, dear Mother,
Your love has been ours,
  And our love has been yours through the
    years.
God's blessing upon you,
May he spare you and keep you,
  I cannot say more for the tears.

· 135 ·

DOROTHY FIELDS: "I'M IN THE MOOD FOR LOVE"*
1928–1974

In a man's world of lyricists and librettists, one woman stood out, Dorothy Fields (1905–1974). She began life with the advantage—or handicap—of having a great comedian for a father, Lew Fields. After teaching art in a high school, she turned to the writing of lyrics in 1928. From then on, for over forty years, she was recognized as one of America's leading writers of lyrics and "books," scripts of plays. Many of her notable successes were produced in collaboration with male composers whose names are household words.

The following autobiographical interview turned out to be a summary of her life and its achievements, for she died a year after its publication.

I'M IN THE MOOD FOR LOVE

You never ask a lady her age. But if your parents grew up singing such songs of the '20s as "I Can't Give You Anything But Love" or "On the Sunny Side of the Street" and *your* kids are wriggling to "Hey, Big Spender!" and if you know that Dorothy Fields is responsible for the lyrics to those songs (as well as a truckload of other hits in between), then the subject of her age can be dropped and we can concentrate on her amazing career.

"When I was born," she says, "my family were spending the summer down at the Jersey shore. I must have arrived ahead of time, because I've always heard how Lee Shubert and Willie Collier, the actor, who were both good friends of my father, Lew Fields, ran through the streets looking for a doctor or a midwife."

Perhaps that last word dates Miss Fields' entrance into the world, but nothing else about her is passé. She's an attractive woman, so soft-spoken and essentially female (her maid

*Reprinted by permission of Atheneum Publishers from *They're Playing Our Song* by Max Wilk. Copyright © 1973 by Max Wilk.

apologized on the phone that Miss Fields couldn't answer—she was having a pedicure) that it's almost impossible to realize that this charming lady has been a successful survivor in an essentially masculine jungle, the music business, for more than forty years. And it's not only as a top-flight lyricist that she's left her indelible imprint on our popular culture of the past forty-odd years. Dorothy Fields and her late brother Herbert fashioned the books of *Something for the Boys, Let's Face It, Up in Central Park, Mexican Hayride*, and wrote another one called *Annie Get Your Gun* which still stands as the textbook of musical comedy—that is, what to do right in two acts if you're planning to have yourself a smash-hit show.

Her roster of songwriting collaborators sparkles with talents: Messrs. Jerome Kern, Sigmund Romberg, Harold Arlen, Arthur Schwartz, Burton Lane, Jimmy McHugh, Morton Gould, Harry Warren. ("Wait a second," she cautioned, "I'm sure you left some others out. Albert Hague, J. Fred Coots, and what about Cy Coleman? He and I are writing a show right *now*.")

How did she manage to write successfuly with so many complex and disparate men? ("I just remembered, I also wrote lyrics to a melody by Fritz Kreisler, 'Stars in My Eyes.' ") One lady lyricist, a dozen gentlemen composers. Is there some magic formula she might divulge?

"I don't know, she says. "In my case, I guess it just evolved."

In a milieu where every fourth word is "greatest" and every second word is some grammatical form of "I/me," the lady's laconic understatement is refreshing.

We sit in her large and beautiful apartment on Central Park West in that old building, the Beresford, which houses such a large population of successful songwriters that it should perhaps be renamed the Brill Building North.

Had she always wished to be a lyricist?

"I didn't really know what I wanted to do," she said. "Pop, of course, was a famous producer, and he didn't want any of us in the theatre. (Lew Fields, partner to Joe Weber in one of the great dialect-comedy acts of American show business, later turned to successful production.) So out of four, three of us ended up here—Joe, Herbert, and myself! I was married very early; my first husband was a doctor who's now dead. I taught school, and I was a lab technician. But I'd written a few poems that had been published in Frank Adams' famous column, 'The Conning Tower,' in the old *World*. I was introduced to a songwriter named J. Fred Coots, and the two of us began writing songs. (J. Fred Coots has written such hits, with others, as "Love Letters in the Sand," "Why?," "You Go to My Head," and "Santa Claus Is Coming to Town.") We wrote a few bad ones, and, boy, if you've ever heard bad lyrics, they were the ones. We went around to all the publishers, and the response I got was, 'Well, if you're so great, why doesn't your father do something for you?' Which of course militates against you, if you know what I mean.

"Coots introduced me to Jimmy McHugh. . . . Then McHugh said, 'Would you like to do some songs for the Cotton Club in Harlem?' And I said, 'I would write for the Westchester Kennel Club. I don't care what it is!' So we did a few shows there. Three, I think, before Harold Arlen and Ted Koehler came in. We didn't have any hits. And the curious thing about the Cotton Club was that they had their openings on Sunday nights so that all the stars could come. Big celebrity nights. The night that our show, our first, was to open, they also had Duke Ellington and his orchestra—first time he appeared in New York. We'd rehearsed with a woman—let's not mention her name. We'd rehearsed her in some nice songs. Opening night, Walter Winchell was there because he was a good friend of my father's. Huge family table—my mother, my father, my first husband, Joe and his wife, and Herbert. And she came out after intermission and she sang three of the dirtiest songs you ever heard in your life. 'Easy Rider' was mild compared to these songs. ("Easy Rider" is a blues song made famous by Bessie Smith.) My father looked at me and asked, 'Did you write these lyrics?' And I was green. I said, 'Of course I didn't. So Winchell said, 'You'd better do something about it, Lew.' So Pop went to the owner, a man named Block—he was partners with a gangster named Owney Madden. He said, 'If you don't make an announcement that my daughter Dorothy didn't write those lyrics, I'm going to punch you right on the floor.' So they made an announcement: 'These lyrics of Miss Blank were *not* written by Dorothy Fields. The music was

ot written by Jimmy McHugh.' That was my first experience in
ɪeatre.

"And the second was with a man named Harry Delmar, who
ɪad a show called *Delmar's Revels*. He asked us to do a song about a
ɪoor little Brooklyn boy, who was Bert Lahr, and a poor little girl
ɪamed Patsy Kelly. They're sitting practically in rags on a cellar
ɪtep. The song we wrote was 'I Can't Give You Anything But
ɪove.' Well, they did one verse and one quick chorus, and the
ɪurtains parted and there were the girls of the chorus, practically
ɪude, dressed as rubies, diamonds, opals, amethysts, sapphires,
ɪverything! Next day Delmar said, 'This is a lousy song. Take it
nd get out of my theatre.' "

She smiles. "Rude beginnings. R-u-e-d . . .

"Then Lew Leslie hired us to do a show called *Blackbirds of
928*. First, we'd written songs for a show of his in a club called
ɪes Ambassadeurs, on 57th Street, where we had Roger Wolfe
ɪahn—he was Otto Kahn's son—and his orchestra, and a lovely
ɪady named Adelaide Hall, who sang. We tried again with that
ɪong. Horrible reviews for *Blackbirds*. Panned. Everybody
ɪoathed it. Gilbert Gabriel, who later became a close friend of
ɪnine, wrote, 'And then there was a sickly, puerile song called "I
ɪan't Give You Anything But Love." ' So we waived royalties
ɪnd the show limped along until Leslie got the idea to do midnight
ɪhows on Thursdays. And that became the rage of New York.
ɪverybody went to *Blackbirds* on Thursday midnights. Woollcott
ɪe-reviewed it, Gabriel, everybody re-reviewed it, and it ran for
ɪwo years! Ran in Paris, ran in Chicago, everywhere. And that
ɪsickly, puerile song' became an enormous hit. Sold over three
ɪnillion copies.". . .

Then came her collaboration with Jerome Kern.

"It's a curious thing how I started to work with Kern. Of
ɪourse, he knew my father and he knew my brothers, everybody
ɪn the family. He was a little older than I. And I was with RKO
Radio Keith Orpheum]. Pandro Berman was producing *Roberta*,
ɪnd he asked me if I'd take a couple of days off and work on it. He
ɪaid, 'We have a curiously uneven melody of Jerome Kern's that
ɪhe's given us to add to the score; it needs a lyric. It has to be sung
ɪby Irene Dunne, who comes down the steps all in ermine for a

fashion show, and it can be a love song.' So I wrote 'Lovely t
Look At,' which absolutely astounded Mr. Berman. And he ha
the nerve to shoot this whole sequence without Jerry okaying th
lyric! But Jerry loved it. And when he signed with RKO to do
picture with Lily Pons, *I Dream Too Much*, he said, 'I'd like t
work with Dorothy Fields.' That's how we got to be such goo
friends.

"I always found Jerry easy to work with. We'd sit down at th
piano together—first at the Beverly-Wilshire Hotel, before h
built the house on Whittier Drive. He always had next to him o
the piano a basket of pencils and a little bust of Wagner. He didn
play the piano very well—not a great pianist like Arthu
Schwartz, or Harold Arlen, or Cy Coleman, who play beauti
fully. He'd play something he'd written, and if there was a
expression on your face that showed you didn't care for it—he'
react very quickly to what you thought—he'd turn this littl
statuette around facing away and say, 'Wagner doesn't lik
it.' " . . .

"Oh, it was a lovely collaboration. Don't let anybody tell yo
Jerry was unhappy in Hollywood; he loved it out there. He mad
an excellent living and he did a lot of good work. And he wa
never difficult . . . except perhaps once," she muses. "This is th
only time he ever let *me* have it. When George Gershwin bought
Cord. Remember the Cord car? It was beautiful.

"We went down to Palm Springs. George started to teach m
how to play golf down there. I fell in love with his car, and h
said, 'Well, why don't you get one too?' So I went out and bough
a Cord. I always used very blue pencils to write with, and I ha
the car painted that bright blue color. I used to drive Jerry to th
studio every day, because he didn't drive. And I drove up in my
brand-new bright blue Cord, very proud, to pick Jerry up. Ther
he was, waiting for me. But he became very incensed, the only
time he ever lit into me. He said, 'I won't drive with you in tha
vulgar, repulsive car!' Do you believe I had to take it back and
have it painted black?" . . .

"Jerry was wonderful, just wonderful," she murmurs. "He wa
always obsessed by hats. Had all sorts of them—jockey caps,
captains' caps, all sorts of funny hats, just like Ed Wynn. One day

we were all going to the races at Santa Anita, Jerry and his wife, Eva, me, and Sigmund Romberg—Rommie, the oom-pah-pah boy. He'd been here almost forty years, but he always garbled the language so. Ockie [Oscar] Hammerstein called them Rommie-isms. We drove up to the Kerns', and on this day Jerry came out wearing a checkered cap. Rommie took a look at him and said, 'Jerry, you look like a race-horse trout!' " . . .

Miss Fields departed Beverly Hills in 1939 to write the score, with Arthur Schwartz, of a Broadway musical that satirized Hollywood film-making, *Stars in Your Eyes*. The stars of this joyfully mad venture were Ethel Merman and Jimmy Durante, and anyone who was a witness to the sights and sounds of Merman and Durante dueting the Schwartz-Fields ditty "It's All Yours," with Miss Merman aping Jimmy's inimitable strutaway —complete with hilarious jokes, head-wagging, and hot-cha-cha ("he actually *taught* her how to do him")—was party to a titanic display of talent, a perfect meld of material and per-formers. . . .

That talent for pleasant yet professional working relationships also extended into the more complex and demanding field of musical-comedy librettos. Dorothy and Herbert Fields wrote a string of smash-hit books for Cole Porter: *Let's Face It*, *Something for the Boys*, and *Mexican Hayride*. . . .

What about Cole Porter? What was it like working with him?

"Wonderful," she says promptly. "Herbert and I never had any set pattern with Cole. He didn't care too much about the book. He came to some rehearsals. But generally he just wrote songs and he'd rewrite them, and then Herbert and I would have to fit them.". . .

Did she ever find it difficult to retire as a lyricist and bequeath that spot to Mr. Porter?

"Oh, honey, let me tell you, it's great," she says fervently. "The book is always the toughest thing to do; one doesn't need the added responsibility of doing the lyrics, I can assure you."

She managed the same shift most successfully in 1946 when Irving Berlin wrote both music and lyrics to the Fieldses' book for *Annie Get Your Gun*. On the American musical-comedy scene *Annie Get Your Gun* almost instantly assumed classic status. It's been filmed, done as a TV special, played all over the world. ("When it opened in London, the producer made records of the opening night and sent them to us. It's remarkable. Four sides of nothing but applause and cheers. And on closing night, that British audience wouldn't let the cast go, they loved them so.") And just a couple of seasons back *Annie* was revived in Lincoln Center, with Ethel Merman in her original part. . . .

Hadn't there ever been one of those creative "dry spells"?

"Oh, honey," she says, "of course. They can happen to anybody. I just seem to manage to write my way out of them. I remember working with Fritz Kreisler, back in the '30s, when we were doing a picture at Columbia for Grace Moore, called *The King Steps Out*. Fritz says to me, 'You know, Dorothy, darling, for months, months, *months*, nothing comes out. Nothing. Break my heart, and break my head, and break the piano . . .' And that was Fritz Kreisler! I don't care who you are, you hit those patches. Ockie Hammerstein, Irving [Berlin], we've all gone through them."

The word "through" is the key word. Hammerstein also observed that the professional writer does not wait for inspiration to strike. To that, Miss Fields would add her own footnote; she keeps a book, one in which she records ideas, titles, lines for future reference, random thoughts. And she has a further piece of pragmatic advice: songwriters must not become married to one particular song. "You keep on writing. If the one you've written doesn't work, you write another."

She has a schedule worked out for audience acceptance as well. "You do a song in a show. Give it four performances. Monday, Tuesday, Wednesday—matinee and evening. If it hasn't clicked with the audience by then, take it out."

A rather ruthless timetable, isn't it?

"Sure it is," she concedes. "But remember, when I'm working on songs, I'm still a book-writer. I'm not out to write popular song hits, though I've written songs that have *become* popular; I'm writing a song to fit a spot in the show. To fit a character, to express something about him or her . . . to move that story line forward. You can't fool that audience out there. They'll always ell you whether a song is right or not." She shakes her head eminiscently. "And they're not polite about it, either."...

Sweet Charity was also remarkable for having in its score "Hey, 3ig Spender," which proved to be a show-stopper and went on to)ecome a popular song hit, with attendant record sales and TV .nd radio plugs. And, as anyone around Broadway will be very ad to tell you, these days you don't hardly get those any more. A 3roadway musical show may run to capacity houses for one or wo seasons, but song hits from its score are harder to come by oday than a parking space along 45th Street. So if Miss Fields vas able to make contact with the record buyers of the '60s, omething she started doing back in 1926, she has to be doing omething right.

Perhaps the underlying element of Dorothy Fields' remarkable pan of activity is embodied in the title of one of her own lumbers, a song she wrote with Arthur Schwartz for Ethel Merman to chant in *Stars in Your Eyes* back in 1939. She called it 'A Lady Needs a Change." Here, in her fifth decade of creativity, he's abiding by her own words, living a life compounded of various parts: loving parenthood, domesticity, auditions, confer- nces, Long Island summer retreats, rewrite sessions, theatre- oing, socializing, public service (she's long been involved in vork for the Girl Scouts and for the Federation of Jewish Philanthropies), more rewrites . . . and pedicures.

And she's already off on a new tack. She and Cy Coleman have nade a musical version of William Gibson's hit play *Two for the eesaw*. "Which is very much in the contemporary idiom of the 70s—not at all hard rock," she says, "because that period's lready over. Now there's a whole new sound. We're very lucky, Cy and I. Work fast when the ideas flow. We wrote the title song for *Seesaw* in three hours."

And if, because of some as yet unforeseen set of circumstances, *eesaw* flounders—Broadway being the chanciest, costliest crea- tive crap game ever devised—what then?

"I'll start another one, what else?" she quips instantly.

Which is something you learned early, and never forgot, if you were Lew Fields' daughter.

136

THE OLD MORALITY AND THE STRUGGLE FOR PEACE
1930's

The 1960's and 1970's have witnessed the rise of a new morality in the lives of young men and women. Complete sexual freedom is not only exercised by them, but condoned by parents and benignly tolerated even by many theological seminaries. Serial monogamy is the order of the day. It is, therefore, instructive to read Leah Parnes' story of the premarital conventions governing the conduct of a young Jewess in the 1930's (selection A).

In selection B, Lillian Cantor Dawson recounts the efforts of the socialistically-oriented order, the Workmen's Circle, to aid America's Jewish garment workers. In a most realistic fashion, she brings to life the suffering of millions during the decade of the Great Depression. This fourth decade of the twentieth century also marked the height of the postwar peace movement on the campuses of the country. Most Americans were beginning to think that World War I had been a terrible mistake; American casualties had run to well over 300,000, but what good had resulted? Lillian's narrative also reflects her fervent devotion to the cause of peace, her presentiment of coming evils after the rise of Hitler to power in Germany, and her fear of what might happen to the world and to the Jews.

A
LEAH PARNES'S STORY*

By 1930 I was eighteen and that was a marriageable age. A girl thought primarily of where she was going to attach herself and find an eligible husband who would make a living. It was a time when I went out and got socially oriented.

Women who were working at that time were confined to

*Reprinted by permission of Follett Publishing Company, Chicago, Ill.

factories or shops, or if they were really intelligent, they went to college. Most of us were looking for husbands, and it was a big city. New York City was *the* city of the whole world. There was no better place to live and grow up.

I was born on 127th Street and St. Nicholas Avenue . . . it wasn't Harlem nor was it the East Side as it is today. The cream of Manhattan lived there. My mother had a tailor shop there and worked from morning 'till night, seven days a week. As a child, I helped by delivering suits to the hoi polloi, but I always had the feeling that whatever I was taking was costing my mother her health. Young people had a conscience in those days toward their parents; we pitched in and did our bit. My mother never said to me, "Leah, you have to go out and work." I automatically helped; there was never any question.

So I had been working at this and that for years when I realized that I had to get married; otherwise there was a terrible stigma on a girl. If you reached the age of twenty in the 1930s and you weren't married, well then, you were an outcast.

After I got out of high school, I went to Woods Business School on 125th Street—it was a commercial business college—and on my way to school I met a young man in the subway. In those days you weren't afraid to say "hello" to somebody. Since I had met him three times in one day, I thought it was fate, so I said, "hello."

He was attending business school just across the street from my college. So we began to travel together, and we became very much acquainted.

He was Russian-born and had enrolled in the business school to improve his English. Well, as time went on we became very much enamored of each other—and he gave me a beautiful lavaliere. But he took ill and died the following week . . . a terrible experience for me.

By that time I was almost nineteen years old, and that's when I met Morris, my husband. I met him at a club; it was called the Matrimonial Club. Several people started it as a way to make money. You paid your dues, and these people eventually made off with them. But I didn't know that at first. I went for the social functions and dances. I would sing for the club members and put on a show for them. Attractiveness was vital, but if your personality was such you didn't have to be beautiful. A little extra talent, that made you stand out . . . then you became popular. That's how I met my husband. He walked in with my girl friend's boyfriend, and I looked up and said to myself: "That's the man I'm going to marry." When we talked, I found out his mother's name was Esther and my mother's name was Esther; his father's name was Morris and my father's name was Morris; and we were both the babies of our families. I thought this must be fate.

To get back to the Matrimonial Club: If a couple met at the club and married, they were given $500. Now that was a great sum, so naturally people were interested. But during the time my husband and I were keeping company, the organization went bankrupt and was investigated by the police. They said the organization had set up phony marriages and had been milking the funds. It was just one of many frauds in those days. People were poor and everybody was scheming to make money, so they'd dupe the public.

Those clubs were not really unusual—we didn't have places where we could go to meet. A young lady couldn't go anywhere unescorted, and when I was growing up I was instilled with a sense of respectability. We had to do the right thing. If you wanted to be a good girl, you could be one. A fella that took a girl out in the thirties would try things, but if a girl came from a respectable home she was expected to reject his advances . . . and of course no girl made advances to men.

Morality was well-defined. Women didn't sit by themselves at restaurant tables. They never, never went into bars. And they never went all the way.

The result of any of these indiscretions was ostracism by her immediate family, her friends, and her temple group. Every girl knew right from wrong. Our behavior was governed by the Ten Commandments and all the unwritten laws as well.

The only thing my mother worried about with my three brothers was that they might get a girl from a good home "involved"—pregnant she meant. That would have meant marriage—an arranged wedding—and immediately, too.

So there was always this fear—boys and girls went together

ometimes for four or five years and sexually didn't go beyond a
ertain point until marriage . . . and I think that was the way it
vas for millions of us. We all accepted this. I knew that boys were wary of girls who
vere loose in their morals. I knew of cases where a girl would "get
oose" out of love for the boy—and she was dropped, like that . . .
ike a hot potato!

B

Lillian Cantor Dawson's Story*

I had just finished my first year teaching when the Depression
iit hard in Pittsburgh. Women were laid off so that men could be
out in their place. There I was . . . after a very short career. I was
out, and I had spent my life preparing to teach. Even though my
salary was helping my family, it didn't matter. This was one of
he things that women had to accept at that time.

However, during my school years I had taken about twelve
credits with Dr. Marian Hathaway who was one of the first
people to give social work a professional standing. Anyway, we
had met socially once and she'd said to me, "If ever you change
your goals, will you come into social work? I think you're a
natural." So, when I lost my teaching job I went right to her:
'Well, here I am without a job." She asked me if I would consider
a position with the temporary emergency relief group of Al-
legheny County; of course, everybody thought it was going to be
temporary then.

The first thing I knew I was made supervisor of aid to the aged,
blind, and children. I went into the neighborhoods—remember it
was when John L. Lewis was trying to organize the coal miners. I
found the children didn't have enough to eat, and many out-of-
work mining families were coming in from outlying areas,
resulting in terrible overcrowding.

Personally, I don't think John L. Lewis used the best methods,
but they were certainly effective. During the middle of winter in
'30, the miners decided to march . . . yes, and the women and

children marched with them, and they all sat down in silence on the steps of city hall.

The police couldn't get rid of them because they were hungry and they desperately wanted some kind of help. The mayor—I can't remember his name because I've tried for years to block the whole thing from my mind—was not a thinking or feeling man. He ordered the firemen to turn hoses on those people to get them moving. I saw mothers throw their bodies around their children when the water hit, and it was so cold—nine degrees above zero that day—that those women froze in a few minutes. It was one of the blackest days in the history of Pittsburgh.

No, the women didn't die that day; they got pneumonia and died later. Their orphaned children were taken into Catholic homes. But it did get headlines in the newspaper, and Lewis won that battle.

I saw it all. I was downtown, like many social workers, trying to pull strings, trying to get somebody to take these people in out of the terrible cold. We couldn't budge the bureaucrats. You know, when a man has a political job he isn't going to buck a Carnegie or a Sloan. [Alfred P. Sloan, Jr., was president of General Motors Corporation from 1937 on.]

I saw many families around that city living in hovels with no coal, no heat. Young children went along the train tracks picking up bits of coal that had dropped from trains. If they were caught they were arrested or smacked very thoroughly. Those women, the mothers, tried in every way to keep their children alive. We tried to help them, but relief in those days was not organized to take care of all of them.

The number of professional women and blue-collar women who had been ousted out of jobs impressed me. Some of them were family breadwinners. It didn't matter as long as a man was available for a job. Remember, we're talking about a male-oriented society. When I was a young high school girl and marched for women's suffrage, we had eggs and tomatoes and stuff thrown at us. The underlying attitude really hadn't changed much by 1930. Teachers were let out right and left. Nurses were getting thirty dollars a month. Women in labs with degrees in pathology got fifteen dollars a month. Working women paid a heavy price during the Depression, and many of them actually stood between the coming generations and death.

I worked for nine months in those conditions, and then I needed a vacation. I was very young and dedicated. I stopped sleeping, and I wouldn't allow myself a day of sickness. I told myself, "All right, so if you give in and get sick, who's going to take your caseload?" But after awhile, this took its toll, and I needed to get away for a few weeks.

I went to New York City and visited relatives, but about the tenth day of my vacation somebody told me Workman's Circle needed a director. I went to see the executive secretary and he hired me on the spot. It meant leaving my family in Pittsburgh which I didn't care to do, but at that time I was very ambitious. So with fifteen assistants, I started the social service bureau of the Workman's Circle.

The Circle had been organized since 1920 [1900] for the needle trade—for garment workers in New York City who were chiefly Jewish and from Poland. They had literally been in a slave situation so they banded together into the kind of union they called Workman's Circle. They probably had the best social medicine that there ever was in this country—for nine dollars a month a whole family was covered from birth to death. They were known worldwide for their treatment of TB and had a famous sanitarium. TB is what happens when ten or twelve people sleep in one room. This was a way of life then: one greenhorn moved in with another until there were thirty people in three rooms, and when one had TB it went to the others.

Included in this medical coverage was a psychiatric clinic which must have been one of the first in the country. Day after day, I saw droves of women coming in with problems. Most of these women were working in the needle trades with their husbands . . . many were doing piece work in their homes when they could get it. One of the first benefits these women received at the Circle was that they began to space their children better, except for the very orthodox who felt about contraceptives the way Catholics did. At any rate, the women would come, walking from the Bronx to Brooklyn, walking six to ten miles to be able to talk about their problems.

Many of these women carried double loads. Their husbands weren't working steady, and their children were crying because they weren't fed well enough. It was just a massive problem. We tried to feed them and we tried to have fairs in order to get clothes for them. These beautiful women would take clothing twenty sizes too big and somehow make it fit their children so they could go to school.

One time the women came to me and said: "We have an insurance policy. Can you get it cashed for us?" And I said: "But you've had it so many years. You don't want to lose it." But they convinced me their children needed clothing and food more than they needed the policy.

I went to the Metropolitan Insurance Company—these were policies you paid ten cents a week for—and the policy was not supposed to have any turn-in value. At first I talked with assistants, but I couldn't get anywhere until I insisted on seeing the top man. I told him about the women; I painted as true a picture as I could. He finally agreed, and I got a cash surrender value for those policies. Now for these women, that was their nest egg; they had saved for it a penny at a time.

When WPA [Works Progress Administration] came in, they had a project in which they said taxi companies could hire men three afternoons a week at fifteen dollars if those men were certified by a social agency. That meant I had to fight for recognition as a social agency. And I did, and we *were* recognized. I placed 300 doctors as taxi cab drivers . . . 300 *medical* doctors. Nobody realizes what the Depression meant in large urban centers. These men pleaded for a chance to earn that pittance. It meant that they at least could bring some milk or bread into the house.

There are a hundred stories like that; but I don't think men could have done what they did if they hadn't been backed by their women. The women carried such a load. I came to believe in those years that the female of the species is entrusted with the perpetuation of life at her own expense. Perhaps nature compensates for this burden in a way: women develop the strength to survive anything. . . .

In 1934 there was a convention of the Women's International

League for Peace and Freedom at The Hague—I was so happy to get to go. I had already met my future husband, but I left him and went off, and I was gone for almost eight months.

There were women representing some thirty nations, some of the finest women you ever would want to meet. Austria, England, and Germany were represented. Of course, Madame Doty from France was there . . . to this day I can see that flaming young woman—a wow of a woman.

Of course, our goal was disarmament—always disarmament. But we were never to see that. The most positive outcome of the conference was that women realized they were a power. Women, at that time, were finding that their natural female role of helping the culture survive might lead to peace. We were finding that we weren't prisoners—as Freud was saying then—of our biological selves.

After the conference, I went on to Palestine. I went for six weeks and stayed seven months. And there I met that superb pacifist, Henrietta Szold, and I told her of my friendship with Jane Addams and the others; this was what she wanted to hear about.

Let me tell you about Miss Addams, while I'm on the subject. She was a little, nondescript, almost mousy woman. Not the fiery type at all—very subdued. You listened because of her sincerity. It was obvious to everyone that she was genuinely devoted to the idea of peace. It was such a strong thing that you felt its power, even when she spoke so softly that you had to strain forward in your seat to catch all her words. Even when she spoke to a large group she didn't raise her voice. She was a Quaker, and Quakers believe the message speaks for itself.

When I came back from Palestine in 1935, Miss Addams took me to tea at the White House. She introduced me to Eleanor Roosevelt: "This is our baby pacifist and, just like all babies, she creates quite a stir."

I thought Mrs. Roosevelt was one of the great women of the day. In her heart she was a pacifist but, of course, she couldn't openly take a position. Here was a woman whose personal troubles never defeated her but helped her develop into a magnificent human being.

She had a despotic mother-in-law, and she had many more children than was usual in those days for a woman in her position. And then with her husband's polio—well, out of painful experience the great strength of the woman appeared.

I met her again two years later and she said, "Oh, here's the baby pacifist." She was a remarkable woman.

About that time—at the WILPF's 1935 convention—some of us in the peace movement began to be very concerned about the Nazis who were gaining at such a rate in Europe. We were hearing of the persecution of Jews and Christians, too. So we tried to introduce a resolution from the floor condemning the senseless, immoral things that man Hitler was doing. But Jane Addams, who was chairing the convention that day would not entertain the motion, and so about a hundred of us walked out—both Jews and non-Jews.

There was no effort to bring us back, and so that was the end of my contribution—although that was not the end of my pacifism.

I just could not believe that the world should stand by and let Hitler happen. But at the same time I thought war was the greatest scourge of mankind. It was, of course, a difficult personal decision for me.

The peace movement was one of the great experiences of my life; it also caused some of the greatest emotional disappointments.

137

THE AMERICAN JEWESS: INFINITE VARIETY
1930's–1950's

Esther Bengis is married to a blind rabbi, Harry Bengis (b. 1898[?]). The rabbi served for years as the spiritual leader of a congregation in Batavia, New York, and as chaplain at Veterans' Hospital and Attica State Prison. He is the man who prepared the Hebrew braille code in common use. In the 1930's his wife Esther wrote an autobiography. With sympathy and objectivity, she described her experiences in the traditional congregation which she and her husband had served. Selection A is an excellent introduction to the accomplishments of American Jewesses during the 1930's. Her chapter focuses primarily on those associated with the synagogue. It cannot be overemphasized: the synagogue—the Jewish community, too—was, and still is, dependent upon women. With all due deference to Saint Peter, it can be said of the Jewish woman: "Upon this rock I will build my church" (Matt. 16:18)!

A poetic reply to a rabbi's wife who bemoaned her lot was published in the January 1954 issue of American Judaism, *the official publication of the* Union of American Hebrew Congregations. *In this journal, which circulated among the 160,000 families affiliated with* Reform Jewish *congregations, an anonymous rabbinical spouse had written about "the juicy pinpricks and the wounds which often make the rabbi's wife long for a divorce, if not from her husband, at least from his current congregation." Complaining that it was hardly possible for the wife of a rabbi to satisfy her flock, the writer, who called herself A. Rebbitzen ("A Rabbi's Wife"), declared that the "congregational grapevine" often spread the news of her pregnancy before she herself was aware of it, and frequently contained exaggerated reports of her household management. "The congregational censors know," she wrote, "that the daily contents of the rabbinical garbage pail would feed a family of four; the living room drapes were as good as new, but* she said she was tired of them; *and did you notice the hat she wore in temple on Yom Kippur!" A reply to the article in the form of a poem, selection B, written in the Ogden Nash manner, informed the magazine's readers that "This Rabbi's Wife Can Help Herself!" The poet was Helen A. Wilner, whose husband, Dr. Herbert J. Wilner, at that time served as rabbi of Congregation Ahavath Sholom, Bluefield, West Virginia.*

A

1930's

WOMEN

The work of women is of great importance in the community. In many communities the labors and achievements of "women of valor" surpass the efforts of the men. Often, this becomes so apparent that the masculine leaders will hesitate to undertake any community or congregational project of any magnitude, unless they feel certain of the moral backing and support of the women.

My husband would ask the congregational Board of Directors to appoint two women of the Ladies' Auxiliary as members of the Board. Usually the Auxiliary president and another of her officers would serve. This proved most helpful. By attending Board meetings, these ladies would keep in close touch with congregational needs, and be prepared to present these needs at their own Board or general meetings.

To the congregation, the Ladies' Auxiliary is all that the name implies. Often it is even more. I have known Auxiliaries to cover Hebrew School deficits, raise funds to pay the mortgage interest, contribute a good portion of the general congregational budget, maintain the synagogue office and secretary and render a host of similar valuable services.

During the depression period, especially, the women proved most heroic. They often succeeded where the men failed. Jobs that the men despaired of they gladly undertook, and as a rule they succeeded. Whether it was a bazaar, the raffling of an automobile, the publishing of a congregational year book, or running a kitchen for a week in one of the leading stores downtown—they undertook these tasks courageously, worked faithfully, and secured results.

One Auxiliary president stands out preeminently in my mind. She had served most faithfully and capably for nearly a score of years. Hers was a long record of usefulness and of achievement.

I have often wondered why it is that women who have servants and do no hard work at home will, on the eve of an Auxiliary affair, come to the synagogue and cheerfully cook, wash dishes, scrub and do other such tasks they would not dream of doing at home. I can ascribe it to one thing only, an earnest and spirited desire to be of service. This readiness to serve is a tribute to their loyalty. As a rule, the work of the women is earnest and sincere. Feuds and squabbles among the leaders of women's organizations are inevitable, but less frequent than among the men.

In the furtherance of congregational and community projects Rabbi Bengis realized and appreciated the value of the women. He was always prepared to give them full credit and recognition for their labors, as well as encouragement in all their undertakings. His relations with the Auxiliary, its officers and workers were most cordial and pleasant. He attended their meetings, helped them in their plans and cheered them in their endeavors.

It is a most happy memory that the Ladies' Auxiliary in one of my husband's early positions was responsible for the gift of an automobile to us. Many other gifts which adorned our home, including floor lamps, articles of silver and even our radio came from the Auxiliary.

Besides the congregational Auxiliary there is the Hadassah which is really the Zionist Auxiliary, doing splendid work in sanitation, hospitalization and child welfare in Palestine. The leaders of these organizations, unless they were tactful and clever, would sometimes come into conflict, since one stressed local synagogue work and the other emphasized the national, or Palestine need. The rabbi, who urged the support of both, would now and then be called in as mediator and arbitrator of these disputes. Of late, a better understanding of both needs is being cultivated and developed with beneficial results. Thus in our last position it was nothing new for both organizations to enter into a partnership on a rummage sale proposition or jointly sponsor a picnic. Of course, there will always be the rabid and fanatic extremists who will not listen to reason but fortunately they are few in number and their influence is not felt.

There is still another organization worthy of note: namely, the Council of Jewish Women. While giving itself mainly to civic and philanthropic work, it has other worthwhile achievements to its credit. I have known small communities in which the Council of Jewish Women maintained a synagogue or a Hebrew School. The Council does one other commendable work, and that is, the aiding of Jewish college students. Its Student Loan Fund and scholarships have proved a blessing to many a Jewish student. I knew a number of young men and women who owed their college education to the Council.

The Council also fosters and aids Jewish boys and girls who have talent for drama and art.

There are other women's organizations, such as Auxiliaries to the Hebrew School, Relief Societies, etc., each doing a definite and specific piece of work. There is scarcely a Jewish woman in the community who is not affiliated with one or more of these organizations. Many women are members of all.

The wise and successful leader of any of these organizations, while belonging to all or most of the others, and contributing to their support, concentrates her energies on the one which is nearest to her heart.

I have known quite a few able and talented women who made the mistake of attempting to simultaneously lead two organizations. Usually the results are disastrous.

Of course, there are also shirkers among the women as among the men. These women, who are spoiled by ease and luxury, will accept no responsibility and will do no work, but will be the first to criticize those who try. Their energies are usually expended in the two pastimes in which they excel, bridge and gossip.

At these bridge parties many women in public life, the rabbi's wife especially, afford a convenient topic for gossip. Little did I know that while making a sick visit, I was at the time being picked to pieces by these ladies who are past masters at this operation.

Most of my heartaches came from such sources. I might meet one of these women on the street or in a store. I nod to her or civilly greet her, but for her it is not enough. Ever looking for trouble, she broadcasts that I have ignored her. She will never forget or forgive this, which she considers an insult. This type is most difficult to get along with. She would never meet me half way. I must come to her, or suffer the unpleasant consequences. She will also criticize whatever I do or wear.

There are, too, the women who are social climbers. Their mad chasing after social prestige and keen desire to be in the company of the elite becomes an obsession with them. No sacrifice is too great to achieve this double purpose. Their husbands usually follow them—even if reluctantly. These men have already exhausted every reasonable argument, and have despaired of swerving their determined Amazons, who are bent on conquest. It might even happen that these women are made to feel unwelcome in high places, but this, instead of being a deterrent, only spurs them on.

In the early days in one of our positions, a woman of influence solicited my friendship, letting me plainly see that she considered her wealth of paramount importance. I replied to her, "I don't measure friendship by the size of the pocketbook."

I was introduced to another lady, similarly swelled with the importance of her wealth. As there were a number of other families by the same name in town, and fearing that she might be confused with these more humble ones, she hastened to volunteer the information: "I am the rich Mrs. ———."

Our women have the reputation of being most charitable, and appropriately so. I recall one striking exception, the wife of a very wealthy man. She was habitually grouchy. Being an officer of the charity organization, she would attend all meetings. Her pet complaint became a mania. There was a poor and almost physically disabled man, who was receiving a meagre weekly allowance. He had a wife and children in Europe, whom he couldn't bring here because of immigration difficulties and because he lacked the means. He would stint himself and send them a portion of his allowance. The lady in question was incensed at this. At every meeting she would give voice to her complaint: "I don't see why our money should be sent to

Europe!" Had this lady ever experienced the pinch of hunger, the misery of want and the sting of poverty, she might have been more tolerant and considerate.

On New Year's eve the socially-mad women will choose the fashionable hotel party in preference to their own Auxiliary homelike celebration. There they will receive and swallow a goodly portion of abuse and insult, but they are willing to pay even this price.

What is worse is that these women often infect their children with this harmful and distorted notion of superiority. Other children naturally resent this and trouble ensues. If the afflicted child is bright and intelligent he later discards his mother's teaching. When they reach this stage, these children are as a rule most sociable and democratic.

When these mothers think that the children of their congregation are not good enough company for their children, or below their own social standard, they hit upon the plan of sending them to the Sunday School of the reform temple. But here they are often disappointed—for these children whose company they wish their own children to avoid, have mothers who reason and plan similarly—with the result that instead of meeting these children at their own synagogue they meet them at the reform temple!

On the whole, the worth and service of energetic and conscientious women in the community cannot be overestimated. They frequently set the pace for the men workers, inspiring them to greater efforts and achievements by their own heroic example. Their beneficial influence lends color to and shapes the character of many a community.

I have visited in small communities where there are only a handful of Jews, far removed from any Jewish center. In these remote places I have seen a Jewish organization or school for Jewish children, a spark of Jewish life tenderly fostered and bravely kept alive by a few devoted daughters of Israel!

It is women of this type who brought much joy to our hearts. Our association and comradeship with them in a common cause constituted, in the midst of our ministerial trials and labors, a source of solace for which we shall always be grateful.

B

1954

THIS RABBI'S WIFE CAN HELP HERSELF!

There is always a great deal of comment in our worship houses
Concerning the activities of the rabbis' spouses.
For the most part 'tis the opinion consensus that ours is a sorry lot,
And that our chances of pleasing our husbands, our congrega-
tions, and still retaining our sanity are not so hot.
For example, if the rebbitzen's dresses are smart instead of so-so,
Then the whole congregation begins to think the rabbi is getting
too much dough;
But if, God forbid, she should go to the A&P on a Friday morning
shabbily,
Then everyone immediately starts treating her crabbily.
And if you stay at home and tend to your business and your
babies, and Sisterhood responsibilities should shirk,
The hue and cry goes up: "She doesn't do a bit of work!"
It goes without saying that everyone knows how much you pay
your maid, what's in your garbage pail; but most of all you
despair of it
When everyone in town knows you're pregnant before you are
even aware of it!
On the other hand, rabbis are pretty swell guys, and put this in
your bonnets:
I'll bet none of you have ever received from your husbands on
your anniversaries written-to-order sonnets!

They say we have no privacy, we live in a glare of publicity;
But let me tell you, any gal who denies she loves it is guilty of
flagrant duplicity.
In conclusion, had my husband chosen garbage collection as the
work of his life,
Then I should be proud and happy to be the garbage collector's
wife!

138

ANZIA YEZIERSKA: A HUNGRY HEART
1935

*When Anzia Yezierska's family immigrated here in 1901, she was
sixteen. In the attempt to keep body and soul together, she worked in a
sweat shop and in a laundry; she cooked in a private home; she worked in a
factory. Hers was a "hungry heart" yearning to be free, to create.
Somehow or other she secured an education and began to write. Her first
success came in 1919, when a short story of hers was acclaimed as one of the
"best" of the year. This quondam cook was even called to Hollywood, but
failed there; once more she was reduced to the edge of poverty.*

*Although by 1935 Yezierska had already published six volumes of
fiction, that depression year found this fifty-year-old woman desperately
in need of a job. The following account, taken from her autobiographical*
Red Ribbon on a White Horse *(1950), tells how she was finally put on
the payroll of the Works Progress Administration (WPA). To be sure, her
vivid description of those sad days is her recall of what happened fifteen
years earlier; nevertheless, even though her autobiography is not untouched by fantasy, it may be assumed that her narrative is essentially
authentic.*

*Today, a generation after this ghetto novelist stopped writing, her
naturalistic works may, to a degree, be looked upon as historical
documents. She held up the mirror to reality, for she wrote of the
heartaches, the labors, the despair of a generation long gone. Her stories
are a healthy antidote to the latter-day literary veneer that threatens to
conceal the miseries and the hardships of a ghetto existence.*

RELIEF

A new life opened to me with my new-found young friends,
the jobless writers and painters. Night after night, I joined their
meetings at Stewart's Cafeteria. For a five-cent cup of coffee we

37. Anzia Yezierska

could sit for hours, discussing the one topic of conversation among hungry people everywhere—jobs.

They were in the midst of planning another hunger march to Washington when Harold Gordon, the organizer of the Unemployed Artists' Union, came in waving the evening edition of the morning tabloid.

"We did it! It's come! It's here!"

He spread the newspaper out on the table and every one followed the words as he read the headlines:

PRESIDENT SECURES FOUR BILLION DOLLARS TO CREATE EMPLOYMENT

Special Projects for Actors, Painters, Musicians, Writers

These were the people who had worked for it. The old-timers had been planning this for months, years. Petitions, demonstrations, picket lines, mass delegations, leaflets to unemployed to join the fight for jobs. At last it had come. We read it over and over again.

FOUR BILLION DOLLARS FOR JOBS . . .

One after another picked up the newspaper, disbelieving. Perhaps because they had fought so hard for it they were stunned. It was too good to be true. And when they were finally convinced that their dream was about to be realized, the discussion became a joyous shouting celebration.

A new world was being born. A world where artists were no longer outcasts, hangers-on of the rich, but backed by the government, encouraged to produce their best work.

The President said so.

People who no longer hoped or believed in anything but the end of the world began to hope and believe again.

In the weeks that followed, radios boomed with it. Everywhere—at grocers, cigar stores, lunch counters, in the streets—people were discussing the President's plan to end unemployment. Every day we read announcements in the newspapers of the prominent men and women appointed by the President to direct the various departments of W.P.A.

One morning as I was in the kitchen of my rooming house fixing breakfast, the radio broadcast a special news item about W.P.A.: a headquarters had just been set up for the new Writers' Project. I hurried to the address, eager to work. Ever since I had marched with the unemployed I was full of ideas for stories. All I needed to begin writing again was the security of a W.P.A. wage to get my typewriter out of the pawnshop.

A drab office building of narrow windows and faded stone housed the Writers' Project. Newly painted government signs stood out against the scarred, dirty walls.

In the lobby I joined the crowd heading toward the elevator. A uniformed guard stopped us.

"Freight elevator!" he barked.

"What's wrong with the passenger elevator in the front?" some one asked.

"That's for officials only."

As we scrambled through the long dark hall to the back of the building, I recalled the Free Vacation House of immigrant days. We for whom the house had been donated were consigned to the back part. The front of the house was reserved for the board of directors meetings. We charity vacationists sat on long wooden benches in the back yard, furtively spying on the committee ladies in the front parlor, planning our food and directing our destinies.

The freight elevator was in use moving office equipment. We lined up behind a rope, waiting to get on. In the noisy confusion of loading and unloading, more people kept coming, joining the crowd behind the rope. Some shabby, well-pressed gentility held aloof, edging closer to their own kind. The rest of us were intent only on getting into the elevator.

At last the guard raised the rope. With the crowd, I was pushed into the elevator and dumped on the twelfth floor. White placards above rows of desks indicated the various departments.

I walked up to the guard at the first desk.

"I've come to work on the Writers' Project—"

"What's your relief number?"

"I don't want relief. I want work as a writer."

"You have to be on relief to get on W.P.A.," he stated.

"Isn't there a ten per cent quota who do not have to go through relief?"

"Those are the big names. They have already been chosen," he said and turned to the next applicant.

I walked away, remembering stories I had heard of what people had to go through at the relief mill. Then I thought of Harold Gordon. He had been among the first to get on W.P.A.

I went to his loft on West Third Street under the shadow of the El. Seated about his cluttered studio, young people were drinking and laughing.

"Hi, Yezierska!" Gordon hailed me. "Have a beer and catch up with us. We're celebrating payday."

"Did all of you have to go through relief?" I asked.

"What in hell did you expect? Utopia?" Gordon demanded. "They have to handle crowds of people. And so they resort to charity methods of administration."

"I still don't see why we have to become paupers to get work."

A dark, solemn-faced young girl turned on me. "Why do you make such a fuss? We all had to go through it. Look at me. I'm supposed to be an art teacher. I have a diploma from Hunter. But the schools aren't appointing any new teachers, and on the Art Project a diploma is nothing. You've got to be a goddamn charity case."

She had had to swear to the relief authorities that her mother was dead, that she had no home, no means of support.

"Sure I got a mother." The girl gave a bitter imitation of a laugh. "Mother keeps roomers, but most of them are out of work. My mother's close to the bread line, but that would make no difference to them."

As long as she had a home, she explained, it made her ineligible for work on the Art Project. She was forced to build up a careful structure of lies to prove that she was living with another girl: letters from friends to that address, testimony from others that she was destitute.

"At least you're *working* for your money—not rotting away," an oldish woman consoled.

"Listen! Going on relief is just like passing an examination," a red-lipped girl advised. "There's nothing to it. Just remember the rules: Two years' residence in the city. No relatives. No friends. No insurance. No money. No nothing—you've got to be starving to death."

A tall, gaunt man with an enormous black mustache added helpfully, "You've got to be careful about the two years' residence. Now, I've been in the city only a month, but I proved the required two years' residence okay. I had a friend say that I lived in her house. She gave me some of her mail and I rubbed out her name with ink eradicator and put my own name on it."

"I couldn't do that," I protested.

"It's being done by the best people," Gordon assured me.

I was so horrified that they stopped their laughter.

"What's the good of a job if you have to sell your soul for it?"

"For Christ's sake! Don't be so tragic! You need a job, don't you? To hell with pride. The relief mill has to put the stamp of a legalized pauper on your forehead. Shut your eyes and go through with it. It's like having a tooth pulled."

Next morning I stood in line again, waiting for the doors of Home Relief to open. Endless hours we stood on the sidewalk where passers-by could stare at us creeping one step at a time—only to meet at the door the uniform with the brass badge: "That's all for this morning. Come back this afternoon."

Afternoon. More waiting in line. When we got inside, the waiting began once again. Misery huddled on benches; bent heads, furtive eyes watched the investigators at their desks. The air was a hot, greasy fog. If they would only open the windows— But so drained from waiting were we all, no one had the courage to approach the guard.

"How long? God! How long?" some one whispered.

A bearded youth with bloodshot eyes took up the whisper. "Christ! I'm hungry! My head is splitting!"

"Why don't you try Christian Science?" another mocked.

"Thanks! I'd rather have ham and eggs."

Next to them sat an old woman locked in silence. All at once the air was torn by her hysterical shriek. "How much longer you make me wait? You bastards!"

I jumped up to aid the woman.

"Number thirty-nine!" My relief number was called. At the voice of authority, instead of going to the woman, I automatically walked to the desk.

The investigator looked me over as I sat down.

Then the questioning began. "Name? . . . Address? . . . Name of your father? . . . Have you any brothers? Sisters? Husband? Children? . . . Where were you born? Have you any money saved? How much rent do you pay? Can any member of your family, relative, or friend support you? Have you a piano, a radio, automobile . . . anything you could turn into money? Do you have any insurance that could be cashed?"

He scribbled my answers on a printed form. "How did you live until now? You had a hundred dollars three months ago? What did you do with it? How long have you lived in New York? Before that? And before that? Have you proof of these statements?"

"You'll have to take my word for it."

"Where would we be if we took every one's word? All right, that's all. Go home and wait till your case is investigated."

So the waiting began again. Each knock, each ring of the bell put me in a cold sweat of excitement. I could not read. I could not see friends. I could only wait.

At last the investigator brought me a food check with a number on a ticket. I had successfully passed the relief test. Hooray! I was a pauper!

I rushed to the Writers' Project. I thrust my ticket into the hands of the application clerk. "I have it! I have it! I have my number. Now I'm eligible for work!"

The man smiled at my elation. "Very well. I'll take this up with our personnel man."

"When do I start to work?"

"I'll get in touch with you."

"I'm ready. I have my ticket. Oh, God, how long I've waited!"

"Every one has to wait."

A day passed. Another, and another. And still I waited. At

every delivery I hurried to the mailbox. I questioned the janitor. No use. There was nothing for me.

At last I got the relief clerk on the telephone. "You said you would get in touch with me."

"You'll have to wait your turn. You're on our list."

Wait again? Weeks had already passed, waiting. Nothing but waiting. Waiting, tortured by the hope of work . . .

I picked up the food check and stared at the printed name—my name—and over it the words "HOME RELIEF BUREAU." And then a number. A number for a dole. The hope of work ended in a food check.

I tore the card to pieces, tossed them into the wastebasket.

I stormed out of the house. I did not know where I was going or what I would do. But I would starve rather than submit to the demoralization of relief any longer.

The air of the street cooled the turmoil within me. Suddenly, everything I had been through became clear. I had to write it. Write it to President Roosevelt himself. Is this "upholding the hands of the forgotten man"? Grinding him through a relief mill more deadly than the old-time charities? Holding out hope of work to the unemployed—only to madden them with hopeless waiting?

It was evening when I returned. Automatically, I stopped at the little table in the hall where the mail was spread. There was a letter from the Works Progress Administration. I tore open the envelope and read:

> You have been appointed to the Writers' Project. $23.86 per week.

The ticket! I ran upstairs. I looked into the wastebasket. Thank God! I sat down on the floor and fitted the torn pieces carefully together again.

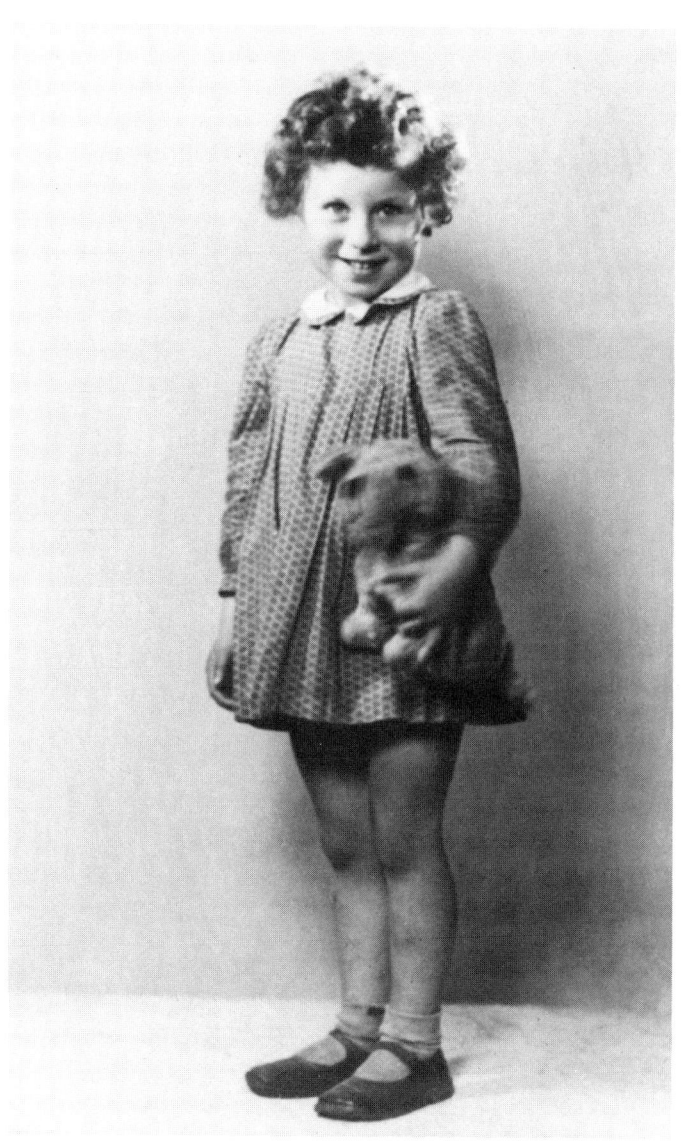

38. Susie Weinberg (September, 1945)

· 139 ·
SUSIE WEINBERG: A BRAND PLUCKED FROM THE BURNING
1940

In 1978, one Frank A. Harris sponsored a reunion here in the United States of certain Jews who had survived the Holocaust. They had all been members of the same Jewish school in Fuerth, Bavaria, in the late 1930's. Among those present was Lisl Weinberg, wife of Professor Werner Weinberg of the Hebrew Union College in Cincinnati. Mrs. Weinberg read a paper describing how their daughter Susie was saved by a Dutch Gentile family, the Van Heeckerens. Mrs. Weinberg's paper, the following narrative, recounts in some detail how the child was restored to her parents after their release from Bergen-Belsen Concentration Camp. It is a story with a happy ending.

When Frank Harris, organizer of this historic meeting, gave me a choice of subjects to talk on, I combined a few of his suggestions by deciding to tell you the story of our daughter. It is as unique a story as it is typical, and, luckily—a "story with a happy ending."

Susie was born on July 6, 1941—the second year of the German occupation—in a little town in Holland. At that time, Werner, my husband, was connected as a teacher with the Hachsharah ["training"], which prepared young people for Aliyah [immigration to Palestine]. The Hachsharah was considered by the Germans as important for the war effort, seeing that most of its members worked on farms, and therefore Werner was given several privileges—like permission to travel inside Holland, ride a bike, stay out after curfew-time, etc. But the nightly German raids on Jewish men got more and more frequent and Werner's privileges ceased, one after the other. Many nights I was alone with the baby—waiting for the worst. Then, in the spring of 1942, when the first rumors of labor camps came up, we decided to give our little daughter away, for her own protection. Through the Hachsharah we had gotten an address for her, and the woman came to our house and took Susie, still in diapers, away in her baby-carriage. In the summer of '42, Werner got new "protection papers," and we felt safe again for a short spell and asked for and got our baby back. In January of 1943, the Jews from all over Holland had to move to Amsterdam, where they were concentrated in several special neighborhoods—for easier rounding-up. But Dutch Nazi spies were left living there among the Jews.

Werner still worked for the Hachsharah and we still had those papers "exempting [him] temporarily from deportation." But now the razzias got bigger and more frequent and included the entire family—whole neighborhoods were emptied of their Jews in one large "action." That was when we finally made up our mind to part with Susie permanently—till the end of the war. Werner had a cousin whose wife was Christian. She became the go-between, as it was now much too dangerous to have the child picked up from our apartment by the foster-mother herself. Our only request was—if we should not come back—our little daughter would be sent to our family in Palestine. Then, one morning in May 1943, I went out with Susie in her stroller, and, as if by chance—I met our cousin's wife in the street; we talked with each other, walked around some street-corners, she took Susie out of her stroller, hugged her, talked to her; we turned another corner—she put her back in the stroller—then *she* took the handlebar and *I* went alongside—another corner and we said goodbye. To anyone, seeing this scene, *she* was the mother of the little girl. We went in opposite directions—and I did not dare to look back. We still heard that Susie was safely delivered to the Dutch Christian family, and then for more than two years we did not know anything about her at all. Any contact would have been much too dangerous for all concerned. Luckily, she could not speak very much yet then, and could not betray herself or the family.

On Erev Rosh Hashonoh 1943, in one of the last razzias, we were picked up and sent first to a Dutch concentration camp. Later, when we were already in Bergen-Belsen, there arrived regularly so-called "children's transports"—children who had been hidden and were found by the Nazis and sent to certain death. Every time we were afraid that our Susie might be among them. We tried to catch a glimpse of them—but then, we wouldn't even know how she looked. After all, at that age, she would have changed so much that we might not recognize her. Years later we heard that there had indeed been many tight moments when her foster-father went in hiding, taking her with him, as he considered her as a sacred trust.

When we came back to Holland after the war, we were given an address where to find Susie, which was unknown to us, and we feared she might be in an orphanage. As it turned out, Susie's foster-parents had heard through the Red Cross that we were alive, and as a transition from them to us, they had brought Susie to our cousin—who had moved to a new house. It took another month till we could get to Amsterdam in those troubled first months after the war. Werner has written a story about how we got Susie back—how we saw her first on the street among a group of children—without knowing whether she was out there—a little girl with brown, curly hair among all those light straight-haired Dutch ones. We did not know her, and she did not pay any attention to us as we passed. When she was finally called to come up, she asked matter-of-factly—in Dutch—"is this lady my mother?" And—after an affirmative answer—climbed on my lap—kissed me, then repeated the procedure with her daddy— and everything was alright with her. She had been "prepared" wonderfully. Together with her, we received a long "letter of instruction" on all we should know about her in those almost two and a half years of separation: her illnesses, tastes, likes and dislikes, habits, character-traits—and some special anecdotes about her outgoing way of making friends of all around her.

Susie had just turned four—and she had a lot of adjusting to do—from one pair of parents to another; from four brothers and a sister of almost the same age—to being the only child. And she came through with flying colours. But, when she heard an airplane overhead, she clasped her hands over her ears. Still years later, when we were already in America, she saw an airplane in a movie where we had gone together and she started to vomit vehemently. From this developed a fear of movies—even the most harmless children's movies—and it took years for her to overcome that trauma. She simply outgrew it and later on loved to "go to the movies" with her friends. It seemed to us that the unending air raids over that part of Holland where she was hidden must have affected her most—in an otherwise, to her, seemingly normal life.

Her foster-father, who was an engineer with the Dutch firm of Phillips, came in that capacity to America in 1947, and the family lived in Dobbs Ferry, north of Yonkers, when we immigrated in 1948. They were the ones who met us at the boat and we stayed with them for the first few days, and our now almost seven-year-old Susie had another jolt: two sets of parents—but again, she mastered the situation perfectly and had no regrets. She went to summer camp that year speaking only Dutch and came out after eight weeks—speaking English. We stayed then in Washington Heights [New York]—and I will never forget how she said one day to me: "All people here speak such a funny English!"

That fall, we settled in Grand Rapids, Michigan, and after a few weeks in Grade 1, she could skip to second grade, where she was right with her own age group. She was the only immigrant child in that school and she was made welcome there and felt at home. We changed cities several times till we finally settled permanently in Cincinnati. Our Susie made friends in each place and kept many of those contacts long after leaving. She was the normal American-Jewish child with the same problems as any other teen-ager; but she was always self-reliant and outgoing, which made her a very sought-after baby-sitter and youth-leader. As such, she went to Israel for one year after finishing high school. And when she came back home, her boyfriend from Louisville, Kentucky, who had waited for her through that whole Israel-year, was there at the boat to bring her home. On homecoming weekend of that year at Ohio University, they got engaged, and in 1961, after transferring to the University of Kentucky, she married, not quite twenty years old. She continued her studies even after she had her first baby, and finished them years later in evening school when both her children were older. She, too, is a teacher by profession.

For the last ten years she has lived again in Grand Rapids and is a very active member of her community, her congregation, the

P.T.A., and every other worthwhile cause. She has been teaching Sunday School, Hebrew School, Bas Mitzvah classes, and Adult Hebrew classes. She also prepared her own daughter for Bat Mitzvah three years ago and her son for his Bar Mitzvah this coming September. She is well beloved by her students and has numerous good friends. She has not forgotten her past, though. In one of her Sunday School classes when the children learned about Anne Frank, they all sat huddled in some Temple-member's empty attic, trying to recapture her feelings and fears. In a Hadassah program she represented the Dutch Jews, reliving with other European immigrants the dark past. When she prepared herself for that program, she asked us many questions for clarification—but we could clearly sense a certain shyness and reluctance concerning specifics, as if she did not want to open healed wounds. Our granddaughter, however, has shown a deep interest in that period and reads everything about it she can get hold of. She feels at one and the same time an objective observer but also—through us and her mother—emotionally deeply involved and searching for an explanation and a meaning. When our grandson had a school assignment about his "roots," he was much more interested in the European part of them than in the American, and he felt *that* to be *his* "specialty."

To speak now of our daughter's reaction to us: there were different aspects to that. When we started out in Grand Rapids, we were the first "witnesses" of the holocaust in both the general and the Jewish community. As principal and teacher, respectively, of the Hebrew School, Werner and I stood in the center of attention: both of us were often asked to talk to various groups and were, so to speak, given a special status, which rubbed off on Susie and made her feel important. Later on, when she was a teen-ager, she rather felt hindered by her parents being the "authorities" in Hebrew School and youth work, than by our "different" background. Many years later, she told us that she had felt "disadvantaged" at times by our stricter European education code and that she sometimes envied her American friends whose parents were far away from anything having to do with education.

Now, however, she appreciates it and told us so. There is an unexpressed closeness between us, which leaves us with the feeling that we did not do too bad with regard to her and that she came out of those terrible first years, hopefully, without any lasting scars.

There is one final note to this story. Susie's foster-mother visited her several times during the last years. She knows the whole family and has told our grandchildren many stories from their mother's early childhood. Last year, we applied at Yad Vashem in Jerusalem for recognition of this wonderful Dutch couple. Following extensive research, we located two more girls—they were teen-agers then—who were saved by the van Heeckerens.

With one of them, Susie had a reunion in Los Angeles this January (1978). And just one week ago we received the following letter from *Yad Vashem*:

"We are happy to inform you that at its last meeting on 28.5.78 the Commission for the Designation of the Righteous decided to confer upon Wim and Jenny van Heeckeren its highest expression of honour, a medal of honour with the right to plant a tree in the Avenue of the Righteous, on the Mount of Remembrance in Jerusalem, if and when they happen to visit Israel. . . .

> Yours sincerely,
> Vera Prausnitz
> Head of the Department
> for the Righteous"

140

SISTER DOROTHY JACOBS BELLANCA, UNION LEADER, MAKES A REPORT
1940

At the 1940 biennial convention of the Amalgamated Clothing Workers of America, Dorothy Jacobs Bellanca (1894–1946) reported on the progress that the union had made since its founding in 1914. She stressed the achievements of the women organizers, who by that time had obtained a measure of recognition. The union's success was due, in no small degree, to Sister Dorothy, who may be ranked with Bessie Abramowitz Hillman and Rose Schneiderman for the work she did bringing women into the labor movement and improving their lot.

Hers was indeed a notable career. Born in Latvia, she came to this country at the age of six and went to work as a buttonhole maker when she was thirteen. The first four weeks, while still an apprentice, she worked for nothing; her pay after that was $3.00 a week. At twenty, she headed a local which she had organized; in 1916, at twenty-two, she was already on the executive board of the Amalgamated; in 1934 she became its first female vice-president. That was only a beginning. National recognition was accorded her during Franklin D. Roosevelt's administration. Named to an advisory committee for maternal and child care, she subsequently attended White House conferences on national health, served as an advisor to the Department of Labor, helped found the American Labor Party, and even ran for Congress.

In her own day, she was called the "Joan of Arc" of the labor movement because she battled to emancipate women from industrial slavery. Thousands of children between the ages of ten and sixteen were in the textile mills and the cotton fields; some went to work at the age of seven. Sister Dorothy faced obstacles even from the men in her own union, but she surmounted them. She forced the men to admit that women made good unionists. Dorothy Bellanca, probably the outstanding female organizer in American labor, accomplished what she did because she was a woman of superb ability, an excellent organizer, and—above all—an indefatigable worker.

Her report to the Amalgamated Clothing Workers of America convention follows.

———

Sister Dorothy Bellanca: Mr. Chairman and Delegates: . . . I think it is only fitting that at this convention of our 25th anniversary, we ought to get a bird's eye view of what has been done in a quarter of a century of activity in the field of organization work in the Amalgamated family in our industry of clothing and allied trades connected with our organization at this time.

When we came to the convention in 1914 in New York, there was a strike that had already begun before the Amalgamated was born, and that was the first strike of the Amalgamated in the city of Baltimore. It was my home. *(Applause.)* It still is my home.

There were 3000 people out on strike in the factory of Henry Sonnenborn & Co. We did not have a strong organization to back us up; we were not sure of the kind of leadership and the direction we would get. But the people were determined with the new vision that was given them and the new hope that they had, that ultimately an organization would be established.

So, when we came back from New York with the name of the Amalgamated to carry to the 3000 strikers in Baltimore, we started with new vigor and new hope. This strike went on for 14 long weeks, in the middle of the bitter cold winter, without any financial support. We did not have as many members in the entire city of Baltimore as we have gathered here as delegates from 32 states of our nation. *(Applause.)* We were bankrupt financially, but we were rich morally in spirit.

And when the national organization of the young Amalgamated came forth with its leadership and its advice, and when we received a large contribution from the national office of $500 to support the 3000 strikers in the city of Baltimore, we thought that it was a great sum of money. We did the best we could to help the struggling, down-trodden tailors who made the first fight in the Amalgamated family to establish their right to organize and bargain collectively.

Some of us are here today at the convention of our 25th

Anniversary. All of us were very young. We did not know just how far we could go, but here we are celebrating the achievements of a quarter of a century. Here is the delegation from the city of Baltimore, the old and the young, testifying to its strength and ability to carry on. *(Applause.)*

I am not going to mention the names of the leaders in that strike, and through the period of our organization campaigns in that city, because there are so many and I do not want to miss one person. But it was the whole membership, the whole membership, that was tried and tested and that established one of the outstanding groups in the Amalgamated family. From then on we went along with our organization campaigns, from city to city, wherever clothing was being made. And we were received in the same spirit of cooperation, with the great desire to establish a real organization of clothing workers, to give service and security to the thousands of men and women working in that industry.

It was not an easy road that we travelled. It is very simple now to gather together here and celebrate, but we must not forget for one moment the struggle that has been made in this quarter of a century of our life, and the sacrifices that the old timers have made and contributed to the strength and the power of this organization.

Then, in 1931, we began to organize the cotton garment workers. Just as miserable as the conditions of the clothing workers were in 1914, just as long as the hours were then and the sweated wages, the low earnings and the exploitations, so were the conditions of the cotton garment workers in the year 1931. None of us will forget the dramatic and colorful struggle that was carried on during those years of organization among the shirt workers in Pennsylvania, the shirt workers in Connecticut and New Jersey, and the State of Maryland.

And now, we can boast of a membership of over 40,000 in the shirt and cotton garment industry. *(Applause.)* And we have there developed splendid leadership among the young members of our organization. In that industry most of the workers, the greatest majority of them, are women. And I am happy to tell that to those old timers here, who years ago questioned whether it was worth while to organize women in the clothing industry, or whether they would remain in the clothing industry, and whether they would be able to make their contribution as organized workers.

You know now that they have made their contribution in the clothing industry and they have made their splendid contribution in our cotton garment organization. Most of our business agents, I believe, in the State of Pennsylvania are women. *(Applause.)* The greatest majority of our Chairmen and Shop Committees are women. *(Applause.)* And the mere fact that through these trying years we have been able to keep this organization together, which was so questionable in 1931, and make steady progress in the organization of that industry, is an illustrious testimony to the ability of women to organize, *(applause)* and to deal with the industrial problems of their factories and their shops and their organizations.

I do not want to take up too much of your time. I can report to you that we have made a great deal of progress in a quarter of a century. I am not satisfied with the complete report that we have given at this convention. It has been difficult, in many places, to organize. We have had to plow our way through and fight our way through in many of the small communities of our nation, where we were not wanted, where we were not welcome, and where we were even put out of town.

But, we are keeping on and we are carrying on the banner and the message and the missionary work of organization among our industries, through the splendid organization staff in our national office.

We began in 1914 with clothing workers. We can report to this convention with a great deal of pride that 95 percent of that industry is organized. But, since then we have gathered into the Amalgamated family, along with the clothing workers, shirt workers, cotton garment workers, taking in underwear and overalls, leather garment workers and mackinaws, neckwear workers, and glove workers, children's washables and white ducks, the service industry of cleaners and dyers, and laundry workers, and the button workers who kept the pants and vests and the coats together. *(Applause.)*

And so, while these groups may not be as large as we would like to have them, and while these industries that I have mentioned, after clothing, are not 95 percent organized, I can assure this convention that with the cooperation of every unit of our membership throughout the country from coast to coast, we will go on with our organization work to greater achievement and that in 1942 we will be able to report not only 50,000 organized in the last two years and 40 charters issued to new unions, but that we hope to report at least 75 percent of the shirt workers organized, and a greater proportion of all the allied trades within the Amalgamated family. Thank you. *(Applause.)*

141

TRUDIE ROSENTHAL: "I AM PROUD TO BE A JEWISH WOMAN"
1945

One wonders sometimes what happened to the refugees who came to this country after having been liberated from German concentration camps. The following memoir briefly recounts the life of a rabbi's wife who survived the Holocaust. Arriving on these shores in 1945, she was already in her fifties. Starting life over again on coming to this land of refuge, she and her husband amassed a substantial estate. Most of it was willed to their Wilmington, North Carolina, congregation.

THE LONG NIGHT OF ANGUISH ENDS IN A MORNING OF JOY
by Doris Bryson

Life began for Trudie Rosenthal [1891–1979] over 80 years ago in the coal district of Westphalia, Germany. Since then she has lived in other countries, and in Nazi concentration camps, and has probably seen more of America than most Americans have, she says.

Mrs. Rosenthal graduated from college in Detmold as a teacher. In addition to her native language, she speaks English, French and Dutch and has taught languages to students in Germany and the United States.

She arrived in the United States in 1945 on a freighter from Portugal in a December storm, she recalls, after spending over three years in concentration camps.

"My husband and I had been separated seven years when I came here," she recalls.

The Rosenthals lived in Philadelphia, then Fredricksburg, Va., and Springfield, Ill., before coming to Wilmington where Karl Rosenthal became rabbi of Temple of Israel. He died in 1952 while on vacation.

Though left alone in the world, Mrs. Rosenthal says she has much to be thankful for: "I taught religion for eight years, and I still see some of my students. They talk about the influence I had on them.

"Wilmington has been a lifesaver for me, because I have so many people who are interested in me. I am surrounded by people who are wonderful friends and love me—not just older people, but also middle-aged and young ones."

Her life in Wilmington includes volunteer work. She had planned to teach, she explains, but found she would have to start from scratch in her education, so she tutored instead.

"German is difficult to teach Americans," says Mrs. Rosenthal. "English is much easier to learn, and French is a beautiful language. I think more languages should be taught in the public schools here."

Though she came to this country with only $10 and the clothes on her back, she says, money was never discussed in her family when she was a child: "There was always enough of it.

"Life was nice in Germany before Hitler began to rule; then all we could think of was getting out of the country. We sent our older son to this country, and I went to Holland with my husband and younger son.

"My husband then went to England to study. Later they came to get my son, and I knew I would never see him again. He was murdered in a concentration camp at 19. Our older son died later of a disease he got while he was in the war.

"When your husband dies, at least he may have had the chance to reach some of his goals, but it's different when you lose your children who are still looking forward to life. I almost could not accept it."

Mrs. Rosenthal describes her experience in the Nazi camps as "hell." The people were starved to death, she says, and the women on both sides of her died. She had given herself two weeks to survive, she recalls, when she was freed.

"My feet are deformed as a result of the cold winters when I had no shoes," she says.

She was liberated before the war ended, and weighing 85 pounds, was taken to a rehabilitation camp in Algeria.

"It was there that I had my first connection with Americans," she points out. "I was the sickest one there, and I stayed for about three months. While I was there, I translated for the nurses and doctors. At first I thought the nurses were disrespectful because they came in every morning and said, 'Good morning, girls.' "

She stayed in Algeria for a year waiting for transportation to America, she goes on, and then went to Portugal, where she got a freighter that carried 12 passengers. Twenty-five days later she reached the end of her journey and was reunited with her husband.

"Even though I was six years younger than my husband, I was worried that I looked too old," says Mrs. Rosenthal. "My hair had turned white by then, but we both looked older."

As the wife of a leader of Reform Judaism in Germany, Mrs. Rosenthal says, she encountered no special problems being married to a rabbi. The members of a congregation don't count on her, and she had no obligations.

"But in this country, the wife of a rabbi plays an important role," she explains. "The congregation counts on her and sees her as a partner in her husband's work."

She has integrated herself into this country, she says, that gave her citizenship, something she had not had for 10 years, since Hitler took it away: "We lost our German citizenship because we weren't good enough there.

"I love Germany and grew up to respect the Kaiser. When I became an American citizen, it was my finest hour."

She has felt no discrimination here against the Jews, she says, but feels that it does exist, even though people don't always show it. There is discrimination everywhere, she believes.

"I am proud to be a Jewish woman. The religion satisfies me in every way," Mrs. Rosenthal says.

"We have modernized our religion to today's life. I would not have married a man who was not a liberal."

She has made herself strong in order to endure her traumatic experiences, she says. It was the only way to survive, but she does not feel bitter, Mrs. Rosenthal adds.

She expresses her philosophy as one of acceptance of things

that cannot be changed in her life: "That makes my life better. I feel I have been successful in making the best of everything. "I have to be prepared for death, and I'm not afraid," says Mrs. Rosenthal. "But as long as my mind is straight, I hope life will last a little longer. You have to make the most of every day."

142

WOMEN IN THE CONSERVATIVE SYNAGOGUE*
1950's

Back in Europe, particularly in the lands east of the Oder River, religion was primarily a man's job. The woman's domain was the home. Here in the United States, immigrants found it advisable to change their synagogal way of life. Christians—and Reform Jews too—assigned women an honored role in their houses of worship; middle-class amenities demanded that wives and daughters have some place in the service. Tradition-minded Jews, eager to be accepted as "Americans," conformed to the prevailing religious mores; women were brought down from the latticed galleries to share and fill the pews, often empty because their husbands refused to leave their businesses on the Sabbath. To a degree, but only to a degree, the synagogue was now being feminized. As surrogates for their husbands, women were now to become an integral link in the chain of tradition.

Such minor social and religious changes in the lives of American Jewish women of traditional bent are clarified in the following selection by the sociologist Marshall Sklare. A generation later, many women are no longer content with the recognition accorded them; they have begun to insist on religious parity with their husbands in the Conservative houses of worship.

THE FORM OF WORSHIP

The forms of worship characteristic of Orthodox Judaism differ widely from those common in Western countries, particularly in Protestant lands. In addition to this overall factor, it is notable that behavior during Orthodox worship is not in keeping with the particular cultural norms observed by the *American middle class.* Among Jewry, extreme informality in the religious setting and the continuance of "secular" behavior in "sacred"

*Reprinted with permission of Macmillan Publishing Co., Inc. from *The Jews: Social Patterns of an American Group* by Marshall Sklare. Copyright © 1958 by The Free Press, Glencoe, Ill.

situations . . . were exhibited by members of all classes in Eastern Europe. In the United States, however, with former lower- and lower-middle-class Jews adopting middle-class ways, and with the Jewish upper class no longer adhering to tradition, the old deportment comes to be thought of as *characteristic* of Orthodoxy as a system. Consequently, the individual is motivated to break with previous patterns not only because of possible theological objections, but by the very fact that his mobility has served to stigmatize much of his previous behavior—including that in the field of religion—as lower class and hence inappropriate to his new station.

Furthermore, since traditional Jewish worship is *actually* characterized by so many patterns which are, according to American norms, typed as being lower-class, the identification of Orthodoxy and social inferiority has been especially pronounced. While the ends of Jewish worship are approved by the general community inasmuch as they are considered to be identical with the goals of Christian devotion, some of the *means*—or devotional practices—used to attain them do violence to the conventional norms and aesthetic standards observed by middle-class persons. Were the traditional patterns of worship continued, middle-class Jews would be alone among middle-class people generally in practicing rites of a lower-class character. This disparity, then, introduces a strain in the institution and a readjustment becomes necessary. If the synagogue is to retain its middle class, standards during worship must at least approach those in general use. Essentially, new means must be devised or appropriated to enable old ends to be served. The following quotation illustrates the way in which Conservative Jews themselves have conceptualized this problem:

> When the Conservative Movement was organized, the Rabbis and the laymen, in order to build a Synagogue which would attract the young American Jew, were confronted with the problems of developing a service which would be traditional and at the same time modern so that the American Jew would find himself at home.

The form of worship may be studied under three headings: (1) changes in the status of *woman*, (2) introduction of *decorum* at services, and (3) reduction in "*commercialism*" during worship. Our analysis of these factors will highlight the view that the changes introduced by Conservatism constitutes a Western, bourgeois version of Jewish tradition necessitated by rapid upward social mobility and acculturation, and that furthermore the development of Conservatism has aided in the maintenance of some measure of equilibrium in the sub-community.

1. THE STATUS OF WOMAN. Perhaps the single most disruptive force, or "strain," to American-Jewish Orthodoxy has been the position of woman. Female subordination constitutes an important violation of Western norms. Furthermore, there is the consideration that the inferior position of woman is not only alarming when considered strictly normatively, but—viewed from the standpoint of institutional survivalism—it also presents a vital *organizational threat*. This is a consequence of the fact that males do not evince the same degree of religious interest as of old. Were they actively participating in worship and religious study, female subordination might constitute a serious annoyance, but it would hardly threaten institutional integrity. The gradual withdrawal from worship and religious study on the part of the male creates a void which must somehow be filled; women represent the logical group which can bridge the gap. To encourage their participation, the norms of Judaism must be modified. Considered technically, the subordination of woman, inasmuch as it contributes to institutional instability, constitutes a "dysfunctional" element in the traditional system. Even though change will entail a serious violation of the religious code and the overcoming of much resistance, a *status quo* position would mean organizational suicide.

It is highly significant to note that varying with class and other factors, religion in Western culture is predominantly an activity of *females*. For example, Robert and Helen Lynd found that women tend to take religion more seriously than men. Some 62 per cent of the membership of Middletown's largest church, they discovered, was female. Leiffer has estimated that ". . . the average [Protestant] church has about 50 per cent more women than men in its membership." Fichter suggests that the same situation is found among Catholics: women outnumber men by approximately seven to three in partaking of the spiritual activities of the parish.

Unlike Christianity, Orthodox Judaism has not been able to make much use of the tendency in our culture for religion to maintain itself by appealing to a female public. While second settlement [the first remove from the ghetto] Orthodox synagogues may accept some financial assistance proffered by their ladies' auxiliaries, institutional rigidity prevents the utilization of any really large-scale reinforcement. It may well be that by the second settlement the Jewish woman is already more faithful in complying with the requirements of the sacred system than is her spouse. One may observe in such areas that, unlike their husbands, some Orthodox women are reciting prayers or reading devotional literature faithfully each day (as females they are not under any religious obligation to do so). Indeed they receive no encouragement—formally or informally—for participating in such spiritual exercises. Their devotions are held in private and if not practiced on what could be described as a secretive basis, certainly the prayers are said in real seclusion. The same rituals are being performed concurrently at the synagogue by a diminishing group of males. It seems safe to say that the inability of Orthodoxy to use this "spiritual reserve" for the strengthening of its institutions, rather than permitting the effect of the activity of women to be dissipated because of highly informal structuring, has helped contribute to its own decline.

Against this background, the importance of the following observation is manifest: the overwhelming majority of Conservative synagogues seats men and women together. This is known as "mixed seating," or the family pew system. The adjustment of woman's position is an outstanding feature of the Conservative synagogue as well as the most commonly accepted yardstick for differentiating Conservatism from Orthodoxy. This change is taken by the woman as symbolic of her new status, and was regarded by both sexes at the time of its adoption as a concession of crucial significance.

We are interested in some of the effects of this shift. Since the

Friday evening service forms the backbone of the year-round worship program in Conservatism, the sex distribution at these services can be taken as a measuring rod. According to the figures submitted by local synagogue officials, women already predominate among the worshipers. In 39 per cent of Conservative institutions women now form between 25 per cent and 49 per cent of the congregation on Friday night, while in 54 per cent of the congregations they constitute from 50 per cent to 74 per cent of those attending. Although it is admittedly difficult to measure whether or not the revision in woman's status has had real "functional" value—and if so to what degree—we suggest that it *is* helping in institutional maintenance. Women in the Conservative synagogue are taking up the slack produced by the male, whose decrease in attendance may well represent his acceptance of the general American pattern in the field of religious behavior. The sex distribution during worship in Conservative synagogues may soon approach Western standards. The new norms, responsible as they are for the destruction of the unity of the Jewish sacred system, have provided a compensating factor. Jews are beginning to follow a pattern new to their group but implicit in the *American* system: much concern on the part of women for religion—an interest for which they are presumed to have a special affinity.

It is notable that as the Jewish woman reaches a new class level and becomes acculturated, she can turn to religion (or, more exactly, to attendance at public worship and participation in synagogue activities) as a leisure-time interest and as a symbol of newly won status. Under these conditions, the synagogue may serve as the focus for "deflected achievement" on the part of its female public. However, at the same time that this participation is taking place, the woman is neglecting the performance of many of the prescribed rituals (such as certain laws relating to the food taboos, or to Sabbath observance) which are incidental to her activities. Paradoxically, the strength of organized religion is augmented while personal behavior becomes increasingly secularized.

It should not be inferred that women in Conservatism are accorded perfect equality with their spouses. Although the sexes do sit side-by-side during worship and the women take part in all the responses indicated in the liturgy, they are still excluded from certain worship activities. To take the most significant instance, the ritual surrounding the handling and reading of the Torah scrolls is still generally reserved for males. This varies, however, according to the sanctity of the service. During the High Holidays the exclusion of females from the pulpit is almost complete. The procedure is modified at times during the less awesome Sabbath morning service. Women are frequently allowed considerable freedom at Friday evening worship, for the Torah scrolls are not particularly important in this service.

Thoughtful laymen have maintained that these variations indicate an inconsistency in the Conservative approach. For example, a leading Conservative figure in the Midwest has stated that:

> A generation ago the young architect, the young engineer, the young doctor, the young lawyer, the young business man saw in Conservative Judaism a chance for genuine religious self-expression integrated with the best of thinking in the world at large. We saw the opportunity of giving equality to the women within the framework of our religious life. We gave them seats beside us, and since then, we have spent most of our time wondering about how we ever dared to be guilty of such a deviation. Our congregations still argue about the question of a mixed choir, not to speak of . . . calling a woman to the Torah. In this instance and in so many others, we feel that the past twenty-five years have not brought the fruition . . . to which we looked forward with such eager expectancy.

But there has been no widespread agitation for perfect equality. Conservative women have generally been satisfied with their limited status—a great advance over the age-old segregation. Furthermore, the pattern of formal equality coupled with limited participation follows the model of many Christian denominations where the rites central to worship are also performed largely by males.

143

TEENAGERS' TESTAMENTS
1958

At the conclusion of the academic year 1957–58, the Reverend Dr. Victor E. Reichert of the Rockdale Avenue Temple in Cincinnati executed a pedagogical tour de force. He asked the boys and girls in his confirmation class to write "ethical wills," as if they were parents instructing their children how to conduct themselves as they faced the challenge of the world about them. Older readers of these wills who grew up in the pre-radio and pre-television decades cannot help but be impressed by the maturity, the high intelligence, the literary skills of these youngsters. In a foreword to these published documents, Dr. Reichert wrote:

These testaments speak eloquently of the ethical idealism and religious faith of the coming generation. In a day when there is so much pessimistic talk about juvenile delinquency and the waywardness of our youth, it is refreshing to behold here a group of young men and women on the threshold of maturity who already display keen insight into the mystery of life and high resolve to add to the richness of the human adventure.

The following two testaments are by girls in their mid-teens.

A

I wear lipstick, heels, and chemise dresses, but I am still a child. I go to formals, read historical novels and current affairs, but the thought of snow and water pistols still produces a happy, impish feeling. I know that my heart is divided into many rooms; the first contains goodness; the second, selfishness, thoughtlessness; the third, sadness. And as the delicate lilac absorbs from its growing place the tiny drops of dew and gives forth fragrance, so does my heart admit and release those qualities of goodness, thoughtlessness and sadness. This has been my year of learning. Through happy and disappointing experiences, I think that I have become a little more tolerant and understanding of people. I mention these facts about myself because I wonder if I am mature enough to make an ethical will.

The dictionary defines ethical as "relating to moral action, motive or character." I bequeath the qualities of character or motive which I think help produce moral action. The first is sympathy and understanding for the feelings of others. Although parents seem to perceive their child's dreams and emotions, they say to a friend, "How lucky she is, not having anything to worry about. Little does my child know of the harsh world." How little do the parents remember the agitation and uncertainty of childhood, unless they can relive their own, the little things . . . the broken doll, the yearning for a sled, the feeling of a left out child.

To all young people I bequeath a sense of justice. To see another viewpoint than your own is the hardest work in the world. To be fair in your dealings with others, you must be honest with yourself. When I argue with my best friend, I try to remember that she thinks she is right, too. This is very difficult. Not so hard is seeing injustice when it doesn't concern you. When I see a little child overpowered by a bigger one, I grow angry. When I see someone persecuted who cannot help himself, I do not like it. I try to help. Trying to make fair the unjust is one quality I believe makes a better person.

To all young people I bequeath tolerance. If a child goes to a foreign school and dresses oddly and speaks with an accent, I think she should not be laughed at. Even if a child is American, but behaves differently from his schoolmates, I don't think he should be ridiculed. A little kindness will help the one who receives and the one who gives.

To all young people, I bequeath a love of learning. Learn, always learn, for learning is life. Learning blooms at sunrise and fades away at dusk. Learning is like sewing. One takes one stitch, then another. It is not always easy. Sometimes the light grows dim, but the finished dress makes the struggle worthwhile.

To all young people, I bequeath high standards, the strength to do what is right, because it is right.

To all young people, I bequeath courage. Courage is one of the hardest qualities to develop. President [Franklin D.] Roosevelt who conquered polio, said during a time of great fear, "the only thing to fear is fear itself." Fear paralyzes; courage makes one able to do the things that are necessary in moments of unhappiness and crisis.

To all young people, I bequeath gallantry so that they can meet disappointment with good grace. Gallantry which flourished in the Middle Ages is little valued in the rocket age, but the sportsmanship and consideration it represents can make a person more valuable.

One of the greatest qualities I bequeath is love, of people, animals, nature. The gift of love returns a hundred times to the giver.

Last of all, to all young people, I bequeath faith, faith in God, their fellowmen, and faith in themselves, to learn "To do justice, to love mercy, to walk humbly with thy God."

B

To my children:

To you, my children, I would like to pass on some of my thoughts and beliefs which I have gained through experiences both happy and sorrowful.

I hope that through my efforts and those of your father, that you have come to love and revere the Lord and have found a place in your heart for Judaism. Your father and I have tried to give you a home that made you feel that it and its inhabitants belonged to the Jewish faith. I hope that you have truly felt that attachment for your religion that I have felt.

Though at the time you may have felt greatly taxed at being forced to go to Sunday School, I do hope that you will send your children. I also hope that you yourselves will take an interest in the Sunday School while your children are attending there. From experience, I know that there is possibly the feeling that you would not want to "force" your children to go, because of your distaste for it (if you hold such a distaste). But I would like to recall to you that I felt that I lacked a sufficient knowledge of Judaism because I did not attend Sunday School regularly until eighth grade.

The most important phase of religion is living it. You must not let your religion become mechanical, but make it a part of your daily life and give it its true merit. Attend services as much as possible and set an example for your children. Do not go if you do not feel the urge within you. Do not go just to be "one of the crowd" or just out of habit.

Do not think that once you are confirmed that you know all that there is to know. Continue to study as much as possible even when you are adults. I have often heard and have noticed how uninformed some Jews are concerning their religion. Be sure to learn all you can about it. But on the other hand, do not become bigoted; become well-rounded and as proficient as possible in all fields.

If you ever feel that things are dark for you, there is one sure way to help yourselves. Do not feel sorry for yourself and be a burden to others. Do the exact opposite. Get out and do something to help others. By getting out to help these people, and out from below your own difficulties, you will realize there are many people in much worse conditions than you are. By helping others you will also be helping yourself. Never succumb to letting your difficulties mushroom out of proportion, for you will not only be doing yourself an injustice but you may get to the point where you can not see over the top.

I realize some of the requests I have asked will be hard to uphold, but I hope your lives can be as profitable and as happy as possible. These are the things which I have experienced throughout my life, and I hope you can learn something from them. I believe one important thing to always remember is to keep your opinion of yourself on par with your actual person.

· 144 ·
SEPARATE PEWS FOR WOMEN IN THE SYNAGOGUE
1959

The sexes are seated separately in all Orthodox synagogues and in some Conservative sanctuaries. The Reformers have no separate pews; they are all "mixed," men and women sit together. The whole question of seating men and women together or keeping them apart during religious services plays an important part in the ideology of American Jewish religious denominations. It is a sensitive subject, for apparently it concerns itself with the place of women in Judaism.

The following article is addressed to this issue. It was written by Norman Lamm (b. 1927), an Orthodox rabbi, who in 1959 was the editor of the Orthodox journal Tradition. *In later years, he was elevated to the presidency of Yeshiva University.*

SEPARATE PEWS IN THE SYNAGOGUE
A SOCIAL AND PSYCHOLOGICAL APPROACH
by Norman Lamm

The problem of "mixed pews" versus "separate pews" in the synagogue is one which has engaged the attention of the Jewish public for a number of years. It has been the focus of much controversy and agitation. More often than not, the real issues have been obscured by the strong emotions aroused. Perhaps if the reader is uninitiated in the history and dialectic of Jewish religious debate in mid-twentieth century America, he will be puzzled and amused by such serious concern and sharp polemics on what to him may seem to be a trivial issue. If the reader is thus perplexed, he is asked to consider that "trivialities" are often the symbols of issues of far greater moment. Their significance often transcends what is formally apparent, for especially in Judaism they may be clues to matters of principle that have far-reaching philosophic consequences. In our case, the *mechitzah* (the physical partition between the men's and women's pews) has become, in effect, a symbol in the struggle between two competing ideological groups. It has become a *cause célèbre* in the debate on the validity of the Jewish tradition itself and its survival intact in the modern world. The *mechitzah* was meant to divide physically the men from the women in the synagogue. In our day it has served also to divide spiritually synagogue from synagogue, community from community, and often rabbi from layman. This division has become a wide struggle, in which one faction attempts to impose contemporary standards—whatever their quality or worth— upon the inherited corpus of Jewish tradition which it does not regard as being of divine origin, and in which the other side seeks to preserve the integrity of Jewish law and tradition from an abject capitulation to alien concepts whose only virtue is, frequently, that they are declared "modern" by their proponents. The purpose of this essay is to demonstrate the validity of the Jewish tradition in its view that separate seating for men and women ought to prevail in the synagogue.

The Law

The separation of the sexes at services, is not a "mere custom reflecting the mores of a bygone age." It is a law, a *halakhah*, and according to our outstanding talmudic scholars an extremely important one. Its origin is in the Talmud [Sukkah 51b], where we are told that at certain festive occasions which took place at the Temple in Jerusalem great crowds gathered to witness the service. The Sages were concerned lest there occur a commingling of the sexes, for the solemnity and sanctity of the services could not be maintained in such environment. . . .

Our main concern in this essay is to demonstrate that the separation of the sexes at religious services makes good sense even—or perhaps especially—in America, where woman has reached her highest degree of "emancipation." What we will attempt to show is that if there were no law requiring a *mechitzah*, we should have to propose such a law—for good, cogent reasons. These reasons are in the tradition of *taamey ha-mitzvot*, the rationale ascribed to existing laws, rationales which may or may not be identical with the original motive of the commandment (assuming we *can* know it), but which serve to make immutable laws relevant to every new historical period. . . .

Those who want to reform the Tradition and introduce mixed pews at religious services present two main arguments. One is that separate seating is an insult to womanhood, a relic of the days when our ancestors held woman to be inferior to man, and hence untenable in this era when we unquestioningly accept the equality of the sexes. The second is the domestic argument: the experience of husbands and wives worshipping next to each other makes for happier homes. The slogan for this argument is the well-known "families that pray together stay together." These arguments deserve detailed analysis and investigation to see whether or not they are sufficiently valid premises upon which to base the mass reform of our synagogues.

THE EQUALITY OF THE SEXES

. . . It is simply untrue that separate seating in a synagogue, or elsewhere, has anything at all to do with equality or inequality. And Judaism—the same Judaism which always has and always will insist upon separate seating—needs no defense in its attitude towards womanhood. For in our Tradition men and women are considered equal in *value*—one is as good as the other. But equality in *value* does not imply identity of *functions* in all phases of life. And our Tradition's estimation of woman's *value* transcends anything that the modern world can contribute. . . . In the eyes of God, in the eyes of Torah, in the eyes of Jews, woman was invested with the full dignity accorded to man. Equality of value there certainly was. . . .

There is a far more basic criterion than isolated quotations or fine legal points by which to judge the traditional Jewish attitude to woman. And that is, the historic role of the Jewess—her exalted position in the home, her traditional standing and stature in the family, her aristocratic dignity as wife and mother and individual. By this standard, any talk of her inferiority is a ridiculous canard, and the chivalry of those who today seek so militantly to "liberate" her by mixing pews in the synagogue is a ludicrous posture of misguided gallantry. . . .

The blessing recited as part of the morning service ". . . Who hast not made me a woman," is to be understood in the light of what we have written. This is not a value-judgment, not an assertion of woman's inferiority, any more than the accompanying blessing ". . . Who hast not made me a heathen" imputes racial inferiority to the non-Jew. Both blessings refer to the comparative *roles* of Jew and non-Jew, male and female, in the religious universe of Torah, in which a greater number of religious duties are declared obligatory upon males than females and Jews than gentiles. The worshipper thanks God for the opportunity to perform a larger number of commandments. The woman, who in general is excused by the Halakhah from positive commandments the observance of which is restricted to specific times, therefore recites a blessing referring to *value* instead of *function* or *role*: ". . . Who has made me according to His will." The latter blessing is, if anything, more profoundly spiritual— gratitude to God for having created me a woman who, despite a more passive role, is, as a daughter of God, created in His image no less than man. . . .

FAMILIES THAT PRAY TOGETHER

The second line of reasoning presented in favor of mixed pews in the synagogue is that of family solidarity. "Families that pray together stay together," we are told day in, day out, from billboards and bulletin boards and literature mailed out both by churches and non-Orthodox synagogues. Family pews makes for family cohesion, for "togetherness," and the experience of worshipping together gives the family unit added strength which it badly needs in these troubled times. . . .

And yet it is because of our very concern for the traditional togetherness of the Jewish family that we are so skeptical of the efficacy of the mixed pew synagogue in this regard. If there is any place at all where the togetherness of a family must be fashioned and practiced and lived—that place is the home, not the synagogue. If a family goes to the theater together and goes to a service together and goes on vacation together, but is never *home* together—then all this togetherness is a hollow joke. That is the tragedy of our society. During the week each member of the family leads a completely separate and independent existence, the home being merely a convenient base of operations. During the day Father is at the office or on the road, Mother is shopping, and the children are at school. At night, Father is with "the boys," Mother is with "the girls," and the children dispersed all over the city—or else they are all bickering over which television program to watch. And then they expect this separateness, this lack of cohesion in the home, to be remedied by one hour of sitting together and responding to a Rabbi's readings at a Late Friday Service! The brutal fact is that the Synagogue is not capable of performing such magic. One evening of family pews will not cure the basic ills of modern family life. "Mixed pews" is no solution for mixed-up homes. . . .

So that just "doing things together," including worshipping together, is no panacea for the very real domestic problems of modern Jews. "Li'l Abner," the famous comic-strip character, recently refused to give his son a separate comb for his own use because, he said in his inimitable dialect, "th' fambly whut combs together stays together." We shall have to do more than comb together or pray together or play baseball together. We shall have to build homes, Jewish homes, where Torah and Tradition will be welcome guests, where a Jewish book will be read and intellectual achievements reverenced, where parents will be respected, where the table will be an altar and the food will be blessed, where prayer will be heard and where Torah will be discussed in all seriousness. Madison Avenue slogans may increase the attendance at the synagogues and Temples; they will not keep families together. . . .

On the Positive Side

Thus far the arguments of those who would do violence to our Tradition and institute mixed pews. What now are the reasons why the Halakhah is so firm on separating the sexes at every service? What, on the positive side, are the Tradition's motives for keeping the *mechitzah* and the separate seating arrangement? The answer to this and every similar question must be studied in one frame of reference only. And that is the issue of prayer. We begin with one unalterable premise: *the only function of a religious service is prayer*, and that prayer is a religious experience and *not* a social exercise. If a synagogue is a place to meet friends, and a service the occasion for displaying the latest fashions, then we must agree that "if I can sit next to my wife in the movies, I can sit next to her in the Temple." But if a synagogue is a *makom kadosh*, a holy place reserved for prayer, and if prayer is the worship of God, then the issue of mixed pews or separate pews can be resolved only by referring to this more basic question: *does the contemplated change add to or detract from our religious experience?* Our question then is: does the family pew enhance the religious depth of prayer? If it does, then let us accept it. If it does not, let us stamp it once and for all as an alien intrusion into the synagogue, one which destroys its very essence.

THE JEWISH CONCEPT OF PRAYER

. . . This complete concentration on God, this awareness only of Him and nothing or no one else, is called *kavvanah*; and the direction of one's mind to God in utter and complete concentration upon Him, is indispensable for prayer. Without *kavvanah*, prayer becomes just a senseless repetition of words.

DISTRACTION

For *kavvanah* to be present in prayer, it is necessary to eliminate every source of distraction. When the mind is distracted, *kavvanah* is impossible, for then we cannot concentrate on and understand and mean the words our lips pronounce. And as long as men will be men and women will be women, there is nothing more distracting in prayer than mixed company.

Orthodox Jews have a high regard for the pulchritude of Jewish women. As a rule, we believe, a Jewess is beautiful. Her comeliness is so attractive, that it is distractive; *kavvanah* in her presence is extremely difficult. It is too much to expect of a man, sitting in feminine company, to concentrate fully upon the sacred words of the Siddur [prayer book] and submit completely to God. . . . (And what woman can concentrate on the ultimate issues of life and feel the presence of God, when she is far more interested in exhibiting a new dress or new chapeau? How can she try to attract the attention of God when she may be trying much harder to attract the attention of some man?) When the sexes are separated, the chances for such distraction are greatly reduced.

FRIVOLITY

And it is not only that what one *sees* prevents one from experiencing *kavvanah*, but that mixed company in general, in the relaxed and non-business-like atmosphere of the synagogue, is conducive to a kind of frivolity—not disrespectful, but levity nonetheless. And if a synagogue is to retain its character as a holy place, it must possess *kedushah*, or holiness. . . .

BASHFULNESS

In addition to distraction and frivolousness, there is yet another aspect of mixed seating which makes it undesirable for an authentically Jewish synagogue. And that is the matter of bashfulness. . . . Note that the inner experience of prayer results in an outward physical expression as well. And in the mixed company of a family-pew-Temple, who is not going to be bashful? Who will tremble just a bit, and give vent to a sigh, and shed a tear, and glance upward with a pleading eye? Who is brave enough and unbashful enough to risk looking ludicrous by becoming absorbed in prayer and letting the innermost thoughts and feelings show outwardly, without any inhibition? Bashfulness presents enough of a problem as is, without the added complication of mixed seating which takes *kavvanah* out of the level of the difficult and into the realm of the highly improbable.

THE SENSE OF INSECURITY

To understand the next point in favor of *mechitzah*, we must mention yet one other argument in favor of family pews that merits our serious attention—the desire of a wife to sit next to her husband because of the feeling of strength and protection and security that his presence gives her. . . . There must be a recognition that without God none of us has any security at all, that my husband's life is dependent on God's will, his strength on God's favor, his health on God's goodness. Standing before God there is no other source of safety. It is only when we do not have that feeling of reliance on others that we can achieve faith in God. When we leave His presence—then we may feel a sense of security and safety in life . . . and finally, when Orthodoxy tells the modern woman not to worship at the side of her husband in whom she so trusts, it reveals an appreciation of her spiritual competence much greater than that of the Reformers and half-Reformers who offer mixed pews for this very reason. Torah tells her that she need not rely upon a strong, superior male. It tells her that she is his spiritual equal and is as worthy of approaching God by herself as he is. . . .

MIMICRY

The final reason we offer in favor of the age-old system of separate seating at all religious services is that of religious mimicry, of copying from other faiths. The principle of Jewish separateness is fundamental to our people and our religion. We are different and we are unique. . . . And it is this separateness, this anti-assimilation principle, which has kept us alive and distinct throughout the ages in all lands and societies and civilizations.

The source of this principle in the Bible is the verse "Neither shall ye walk in their ordinances," and similar verses, such as "And ye shall not walk in the customs of the nations" [Lev. 18:3, 20:23]. Our Tradition understood this prohibition against imitating others to refer especially to the borrowing from gentile cults and forms of worship. . . .

We can now see why from this point of view the whole idea of mixed seating in the synagogue is thoroughly objectionable. It is an unambiguous case of religious mimicry. The alien model in this case is Christianity; worse yet, the specifically *pagan* root of Christianity. . . .

Mixed seating thus represents a desire by Jews to Christianize their synagogues by imitating the practices of contemporary Christian churches. And this kind of mimicry is, as we pointed out, a violation not only of a specific law of the Torah, but an offense against the whole spirit of Torah. . . .

We thus have only one conclusion as far as this is concerned—that those who have favored family pews have unwittingly advanced the cause of the paganization and Christianization of our Synagogues. . . .

CONCLUSION

What we did want to accomplish—and if we have failed it is the fault of the author, not of Orthodox Judaism—is to show that even without the specific and clear judgment of the Halakhah, separate seating ought to be the only arrangement acceptable to serious-minded modern Jews; for it is consistent not only with the whole tradition of Jewish morality and the philosophy of Jewish prayer, but also with the enlightened self-interest of modern Jewish men *and* women—and children—from a social and psychological point of view.

145

A YOUNG TRADITIONALIST TURNS TO REFORM
1959

In its pursuit of acculturation, Reform Judaism adapted for its own needs the Christian ceremony of confirmation. In Judaism, confirmation became the public act whereby young Jews proclaimed their adherence to the faith. The first Jewish boy was confirmed in Germany in 1810; girls, no later than 1818. Confirmation for Jewish youngsters was introduced here in the United States in the 1840's and soon became an integral part of Reform practice. A 1950 survey made by the Union of American Hebrew Congregations revealed that boys and girls belonging to Reform synagogues were being confirmed between the ages of thirteen and sixteen, most of them at fifteen. In 1959, a girl in a confirmation class wrote the following essay describing the appeal that Reform had for her. Originally her sympathies had been traditionalist.

WHAT REFORM JUDAISM NOW MEANS TO ME

Now that I am in the Confirmation Class, I am learning to understand and accept Reform Judaism.

Up until this year, I really had my doubts about some customs associated with Reform Judaism. I just could not accept the fact that the yarmulka [skullcap] and talis [prayer shawl] were not worn; that there was an organ, of all things, in a synagogue. I had also heard Temple Israel referred to as a "church."

Truthfully, I felt skeptical about the temple, since my grandparents are devout Orthodox Jews, and my earlier training was along traditional lines.

Coming to temple for my Jewish education made me suspicious of what my teachers were trying to teach, and I did not give Reform Judaism a fair chance.

The critics tend to think of Reform Judaism as the creed of the uninformed, disinterested, and lukewarm Jews.

Actually, Reform Judaism is the outgrowth of Orthodoxy. In a changing age, men of reason questioned the necessity of following practices which originated in the distant past, many of them superstitious.

Reform Judaism discarded many such beliefs and practices, but held to what is basic and meaningful in Judaism. Reform modified and "reformed" some of the observances and practices to adjust them to the times and to assure them of continuity.

Actually, there is no biblical commandment pertaining to the wearing of a hat at worship. It is merely a custom dating back to the Babylonian captivity. Originally, in Palestine, Jews did not worship with their heads covered. Only the priests did so.

The organ enhances the beauty of our services. There is a passage in the Bible explaining that piped music accompanied the service.

Yes, and what about our temple being a "church"?

Such remarks are made in jest or ignorance. We must learn to tolerate them and keep in mind that those making the remarks are uninformed about Judaism in general, and of our branch of Judaism in particular. Such may sound off with: "Why, there's hardly any Hebrew!" and: "Of all things the pages in your prayerbook run in the non-Jewish way [left to right]!" But our way of Judaism is modern in practice and thinking. We feel that it is far better to understand our prayers than just to recite Hebrew without any understanding of the content.

Oh, yes, and as for men and women sitting together, we prefer the Western way in our Western world to the Eastern fashion of men and women sitting apart.

An aspect of Reform Judaism that particularly appeals to me is the fact that we are presented with facts and permitted the freedom to decide for ourselves what can reasonably be accepted.

In my earlier years at Sunday School, I can recall being told that Reform Judaism was a result of the Jew, after being free from the ghettos, wanting to be more like his Christian neighbors. This left me with an entirely wrong impression. Somehow to me this implied that Reform Jews were trying to get as far away as possible from their Judaism without losing complete identity.

Today, however, I realize that this is not the case. Ours is the modern way of Judaism which fits our needs and times. Yet we need also to make clear to our friends, Jewish and non-Jewish, that we do believe and accept Judaism as our creed.

To sum it all up, let us all be proud as we say, "We are American Reform Jews."

Jacqueline Friedman, Confirmation Class, Temple Israel, Akron, Ohio.

146

JANICE BERNSTEIN TRIES TO INTEGRATE
MATTAPAN*
1960's

Janice Bernstein (b. 1931), of Boston, went to work early, got a good job at Filene's department store, married the man she loved, and raised a small but happy family. She never made money, but somehow or other managed to live "respectably" and furnished her home with all the conveniences so prized by aspiring American families.

The following memoir recounts the story of this vigorous, able woman, a "doer" who assumed leadership in her community, always trying to help others. The burden of her narrative is the attempt to save the Boston neighborhood of Mattapan from real estate blockbusters who frightened off the whites and made impossible the peaceful integration of what had once been a fine community. It is a chronicle of the magnificent failure of a courageous woman.

———————

I was born in Dorchester on May 1, 1931. I lived in Dorchester-Mattapan all my life. Born there, bred there and lived there till only four years ago [1972?].

My mother was divorced when I was fourteen months old. She had to go out to work, so I was raised by my grandparents. I was an only child and they spoiled me rotten. They didn't want anything to happen to the little baby, you know? I wasn't even allowed to go out in the street without an escort until I was in my early teens. . . .

When my mother and father got divorced, my father left, and my mother had to support us. She worked for twenty-two years as a salesgirl. She got married again twenty-two years later to a cousin of my husband's. The year after I got married, my husband and I fixed them up. He was a very kind, wonderful man whose wife had passed away. My mother lived nine years of

*Reprinted by permission of Simon & Schuster, a Division of Gulf & Western Corporation.

delirious happiness with this man who when they made him they threw away the mold. He was the only father I ever knew.

Funny thing is, about ten years ago I got a very strange note in the mail with forty dollars in it from Denver, Colorado. No name on it, but I knew it was from my father. So I wrote him a letter and I said, "For God's sake, you could at least sign your name. I know who it's from." After that we started corresponding.

When I was a kid, every once in a while my father's mother would send me a gift. I knew her name but I had never seen her. I had heard that she was the head salesgirl in the fur department at Chandler's [in downtown Boston]. So one day when I was about thirteen, I went into town with my girlfriend for the first time and we happened to go right by Chandler's. I said to myself, I want to go see what my grandmother looks like.

I was a little nervous, but I was curious and something sort of pulled me up there. I asked somebody who she was and then I went over to her and I asked her if she knew who I was. She said, "No." So I said, "I'm your granddaughter." Well, she was so thunderstruck I thought she was going to have a heart attack. We got very close after that and I saw her quite a bit. She could never explain her son. . . .

My husband's a very devoted father. He loves kids and he would have liked to have a dozen. I had a miscarriage after Karen, so then I said that's it for me. But he took over from the time I came home from the hospital. He never had any qualms about picking up the children like some fathers have, or feeding them at night. Once a week I'd go out with my card group or Mah-Jongg group and he'd think nothing of feeding the baby and putting it to sleep.

My husband is the kindest most easy-going person. We made a vow not to argue in front of the children and if he sees I'm upset he knows just what to do. He walks out of the room! I get over it, because who am I going to argue with? He gets along with everybody. He always sees the good side. I used to be hard on people and hold grudges like my mother, and my grandfather was like that too, but my husband's influence really changed me.

I was absolutely happy just being a housewife. I loved it. The only thing I hate to do is shop for food, but I love to bake and I love to cook. I love to take care of my family and have company over. I was never dissatisfied with my life. . . .

One day I was hanging out clothes on the line, and I happened to hear a neighbor in the back asking another neighbor to come to a meeting at his house. It struck me kind of funny, so I kept listening, but I could only get dribs and drabs about people getting frightened, rumors. So then I yelled over to him and I said, "Jack, I didn't mean to overhear, but are you having some sort of a neighborhood meeting?" . . .

What had happened was, they had heard rumors that the crime rate had gone up 33 percent in one year in Dorchester and that the neighborhood was turning black. People were panicking so, that they were underselling their houses to get out. . . .

In the meantime, we had meeting upon meeting and we decided to form an organization. Dorchester had the bulk of the Jews and Mattapan was more of an integrated community religious-wise, but we decided to call it the Mattapan Organization. By the time we got the organization off the ground, we realized that there was nothing we could do to save Dorchester, but we could save Mattapan. Not by keeping blacks out, but to make sure that it was truly integrated. Because we all wanted to live there till we died. I thought we'd marry our kids out of there. My in-laws thought they'd be carried out in coffins from there. The organization started in 1967. . . .

The summer of 1968 I ran the program in Mattapan with a limited budget. I got paid very little but I was just happy to try to keep the neighborhood together. It was really such a terrific summer that I thought maybe things might turn back a little bit. You know, that people would begin to trust each other again.

I ran classes for the children, arts and crafts, and guitar lessons and dancing lessons and photography. And they opened the school for me so the kids could have classes there. Then we had nighttime programing so the adults could come too. The Boston Ballet came down to the playground and rock 'n' roll bands. Then there was all kinds of ethnic dancing, I had square dancing, we showed first-rate movies outdoors. It was really a terrific year. And it was really a mixed group. A good number of blacks participated too.

The second year was even better than the first, because I had more money to work with so I was able to bring in more entertainment, and I could have workshops for some of the older people as well as the youngsters. The third year was devastating. Nineteen-seventy was worse than I could have imagined. By then, a great many black people had moved in and it was already tipping the scales. And some of them would do anything in their power, unfortunately, to disrupt the performances. And we couldn't leave anything in the playground without a guard anymore. It was always stolen.

We started to get kids in there that were just out to get whitey, no matter what. We never had this before that summer, but every other word out of their mouths was "mother fucker," "honky," "white trash." They just hated the whites and that was it. It was a group of real southern blacks. You could tell from their accent.

We really tried. I brought in soul singing and the Graham rock 'n' roll gospel singers to try to bring about a compatibility, for people to learn about other cultures. But then our equipment from the photography workshop was stolen. I used to have so much equipment left over that I would save it for the following year. Then I had things stolen out of my garage. It was incredible. Something we never anticipated before.

I had worked so hard to make it a good program. The long hours. I was at every performance and every workshop to make sure that things went well. I hired teachers who I thought could really handle all kinds of kids and we had no problems the first two years. But that third year, I never experienced things like that in my life. And that's what I think happened to the Jewish community that caused this huge exodus. They had never experienced the problems that they had then. Some with their children in school, some with their homes, and then the businessmen.

People couldn't stay in business anymore. I remember going up to one couple who were robbed at least a dozen times. It was a shop where they sold fabrics and items for sewing, like a five and ten. They had been in that block for forty years. My family did business with them and over the years they had increased it. But they couldn't keep up with the thievery so they decided to close it.

The husband said, "You know, we knew everybody on this block at one time. Now they're all strangers to us." They always dealt with black people and he says, "What did we ever do to them that would cause them to act this way?" His insurance was canceled. He couldn't get any more, so he boarded up the store. Blue Hill Avenue has become plywood city. If it wasn't burned out, it was rock-infested. Windows were smashed. It was just unbelievable.

It was a tough neighborhood. Here we had a drugstore on the corner of our street and my son could not walk to that drugstore anymore. I often wondered what would happen if I ever saw my kid or somebody else's kid being attacked. Would I run for the police? Would I not get involved? What would I do? And then it happened.

My kid was only twelve years old and at the corner of our street there was a place where you could get hamburgers and soft drinks. By that time we had a car pool because we couldn't let our kids come home by bus anymore. Children were constantly being attacked up and down the street. No child was safe, black or white. So it was my day for the car pool and when we got to the corner of our street, my son said he wanted a milkshake. So I said, "Okay, I'll drop you off here."

I kept a baseball bat in my car. To this day, I'm still referred to as the lady with the bat. It's a lousy reputation to have, but it really got to the point where you could not go out in the street without some sort of a weapon, and I felt that was the safest for me to carry. You couldn't even stop at a traffic light, that's how bad it was.

He went in to get his milkshake and he came out wedged between two black kids, pushing him from both sides. The kids were huge compared to his size and there was a third one in back, kicking him in the behind. My kid was shaking so that the milkshake was spilling all over and he looked like he was in shock. All I could think of was three against one, and I just took that baseball bat out of my car and started chasing those kids.

It's more than likely that a group of them could have gotten together and beaten me up, but I never thought of that. I just ran after them with that bat and I could feel my heart pounding. I almost lost all my equilibrium, but I was swinging that bat and my face must have showed rage because they ran like hell. Everybody was standing around watching, but nobody did anything. Well finally I put my son in the car and a policeman came by.

Of course, after that we had to have the place patrolled with police inside and out. It became a police school and we had to have buses take those kids from Roxbury directly home, with a police car following to make sure that the kids did not get off at any other bus stop. Then businesses were closed from 2:30 to 3:30 every day. There was so much pilferage they refused to stay open until the kids went home. And a police car was stationed at the bottom of that hill, every single day.

I used to really feel bad for my neighbors who were black. They were the nicest people. They were good friends and they really wanted to live in harmony with us. And they could have very easily. All of this is such a tragic thing. In fact right after that incident, the niece of my neighbor next door who was black called me on the phone and she said, "Mrs. Bernstein, I saw what happened and I know those three kids." And she said, "If you promise not to tell my name, I'll give you their names so you can go up to the school and report them." I said to her, "I won't say a word."

She gave me their names and the next day I went traipsing up to the school. We happened to get a new principal up at the [Solomon] Lewenberg School that wasn't going to stand for any nonsense, so he was delighted to see me. He said, "If more parents would just come up, we could get rid of these troublemakers, but they're afraid." He says, "These three kids that you named are some of the worst troublemakers in school, but I have no evidence."

Then he said, "You sit out in that front office and I'm going to call them in. You just nod and tell me if it's them." Well they saw me sitting there, they recognized me, and they turned pale. The principal suspended them for three days, until the parents came. Then they were transferred to another school. I refused to prosecute them because actually my kid wasn't hurt, but let that be a lesson to them. The NAACP [National Association for the

Advancement of Colored People] came running up there with a lawyer, but the principal said, "Now, look, I have a witness and I don't want to keep troublemakers at this school." You wouldn't believe the vandalism in that school. You walk in there now and there's a policeman with a walkie-talkie at the door.

I'll tell you something. Kids reflect what their parents are. As I said, it wasn't the northern blacks. Here we had a bunch of low-class people and there's low-class in every religion and race and every ethnic group, I don't care who you are. But some of these people are really emotionally disturbed. They come from parents who hate. They don't teach those kids respect for people—their teachers or people who live on their street. Or respect for property. You don't piss out the window. And don't throw garbage in the backyard. Because I've seen that. I don't understand. It's emotionally disturbed people and I don't know what can be done to help them.

You have a group of people that were persecuted for four hundred years. Now I'm so sick of hearing about that that I feel like throwing up. Say listen, there isn't one religion or ethnic group that hasn't gone through persecution at one time or another. Especially the Jews, who were supposed to be the "chosen people." I don't know what the hell they were chosen for except to suffer all their lives. But you talk about the potato famine with the Irish, and what went on with the Crusaders, and the Protestants hated everybody, and then you've got the Ku Klux Klan. So I mean there hasn't been one group that hasn't gone through it. So all right.

In my family, we had many relatives that were killed in the concentration camps. If I spent the rest of my life hating every German and telling them they're no goddamned good and I don't trust any of them, and I keep looking back to the past, then I have no future. I have to look toward the future and try to better things so that something like this will never happen again. So I'm sick and tired of being blamed by the blacks. First of all, my grandparents weren't even born here and they had nothing to do with their persecution!

I really had respect for Martin Luther King because he spoke out and he really got his people aroused. The only thing I regretted was that, as peaceful a man as he was supposed to be, no matter where he went violence followed him. But his was a very untimely death and a useless death, as was Bobby Kennedy's and Jack Kennedy's. I think he really led his people the right way. It's just what happened afterward. There is such a movement of hatred against white people and I don't know where it's going to end. . . .

Do you know that out of 141 families, there were only seven white families left on my street in two years? My neighbors were all gone and my friends would say to me, "Janice, give up. You're fighting a losing battle. You're fighting powers-that-be that you're not powerful enough to fight." But I just was not a giver-upper. The Mattapan Organization had finally opened up an office on Blue Hill Avenue and there were only twelve of us left, and my husband and I were two of them. We fought to the very end.

In fact, the day we closed our office in June 1970, I was in shock. I couldn't believe this had happened. By that time, more than half of Mattapan was already black. I knew it was hopeless. But you know it's a funny thing. You'd think that I would have given up, wouldn't you?

Within six months Ormond Street cleared out. I never saw so many moving trucks in all my life on one street like mine. I guess the final straw that made us move was when my in-laws were driving up the street one day and the kids from the Lewenberg School jumped on their car and tried to open the door. My mother-in-law said, "That's it. We've got to get out of here." We owned the house together, so we decided to sell. It took nine months to get a buyer approved by the Association for Better Housing and we lost our shirts.

If we'd sold our house in normal times, we would have gotten twice as much back on it as we paid. We had put five thousand dollars in modernizing it when we moved in and we had to sell it for less than we bought it for. We lost our life savings in Mattapan. When we came into this house we had nothing. But nothing! Not even a pot to piss in, pardon the expression. . . .

Despite all that's happened, I really enjoy life. I'm awfully glad I'm up here and not six feet under. I'm a free woman. I can go where I want, do whatever I want, within reason, of course. I like living and I love to be with people. I enjoy gardening, my vegetable garden and flowers. And I don't really have to account to anyone. My husband and I have a terrific relationship and the communication is great. Don't think we're a perfect couple. We have our ups and downs, but I think it's a damn good marriage. If I had it to do over again, I think I'd marry the same guy, have the same kids and do the same things mostly that I did before. So I really can't complain. . . .

I don't want to be rich, I just want to have a little money in the bank for a rainy day, and enough to pay my bills. I'd like to pay cash for something once in a while. If I need a new TV set, not to charge it or have to say, "Send me three payments." No creditors at my door, thank God, although sometimes I get a warning letter if I don't pay it for two months. But you know it could always be a heck of a lot worse. Instead of being here, I could be in some two-by-four apartment collecting a welfare check. So I say, "Accept what you have, hope that it might be better, and thank God it's not worse."

147

A WOMAN'S STRUGGLE FOR A CAREER IN SCIENCE
1960's–1970's

The following article describes with clarity the problems of a woman who set out to make a career for herself in the natural sciences. With rare exceptions, the colleges and universities of the mid-twentieth century were unsympathetic to women who aspired to become scientists. Dr. Ruth Weiner, the author of the memoir reprinted here, was the daughter of cultured Viennese Jewish émigrés who had been professionals for generations. Her narrative takes on added significance because it underscores the difficulties of maintaining a normal family life when both husband and wife are professionals. What happens to this household when one member leaves town to accept a better position? Does the remaining employed spouse go along or stay behind and build a new life as a "single"? What happens to the children? These are serious problems and undoubtedly will plague many a home in the years that lie ahead.

CHEMIST AND "ECO-FREAK"
by Ruth Weiner

My family background was probably more conducive than most to pursuit of a professional career. I was born in Vienna, Austria; my father holds both an M.D. and a Ph.D. in zoology, and my mother was one of the first women to receive a Ph.D. from the University of Vienna in a science (biology). My two grandfathers were both physicians (my father's father was Mrs. Freud's obstetrician!). In general, my family belonged to the upper-income Jewish society of Vienna; indeed, my paternal grandmother was extremely wealthy. My parents were religious freethinkers, to the extent that they formally disaffiliated with Judaism, and were political liberals. My mother was, until the Anschluss [annexation of Austria to Germany, 1938], a Social-Democrat member of the Vienna City Council.

I am the younger of two half-sibs: my brother is the child of my father's first marriage. It was always assumed that he and I would (1) pursue our education through some graduate degree (preferably in a science), (2) speak at least three languages fluently, and (3) play at least one musical instrument quite well. These, I might add, were the normal expectations for children of the social subgroup into which we were born. Our subsequent forced emigration to the U.S., and life there in moderate poverty for the first decade after immigration, made no difference in these expectations. In fact, we lived up to them. My brother is Dean of the College of Humanities at Montclair State College, New Jersey, and was for several years Chairman of the Department of Comparative Literature at the University of Massachusetts.

It was always assumed that I would pursue a scientific career, since I showed some talent in that direction, and I was strongly pressed to go into my father's field: medicine. I cannot say that I was *encouraged* to have professional aspirations, as much as that it was *assumed* that I would fulfill them. Indeed, throughout childhood I was quite strictly punished for less than superior academic achievement. I was simply too old to change my basic aspirations when I learned that American girls did not, for the most part, share them.

I am a product of the Baltimore, Maryland, public school system, and my recollections are that I fought it every inch of the way. My high school (interestingly, a girls' public high school, one of two such in Baltimore, and with the best academic reputation in the city) discouraged pursuit of scientific professional careers: "Don't you want to go into nursing, instead?" Since I was already on the principal's blacklist because of various political views and general intellectual snobbery and nastiness, this attitude only encouraged me. At the University of Illinois, I was neither encouraged nor discouraged. I chose physics mainly because it was difficult and challenging, rather than out of any great interest. It never occurred to me until much, much later in life that one could enjoy intellectual pursuits and endeavors that *weren't* difficult.

I married at 18, so that almost all adult professional and social interactions came after marriage for me. My husband also always assumed that I would pursue a professional career, along with him. The question "Was your profession a handicap to love and marriage?" is meaningless for me. I would, however, agree wholeheartedly that marriage has been a handicap to my professional career. The one person who crystallized what is my present professional life is my husband's (and later, my) preceptor for the doctorate, who urged me to do what I wanted and go to graduate school.

The doors began to close to me after graduate school. I am now aware that there is considerable discrimination against women in chemistry at the point of graduate school admissions. I suppose that, at that time, in graduate school, I didn't think about it and accepted it as a normal state of affairs. In my last graduate school year, I did become aware that the reasons given for sex discrimination (girls marry and don't finish; girls don't use their degree even if they do finish; girls have babies and quit) were part of a vicious circle that included inadequate child care and enormous social pressures. I suggested a counseling service for female graduate students—a suggestion that caused considerable hilarity among my colleagues and professors.

My first child was born six months before I began graduate school; my fourth, one year after the Ph.D. Two of my children were contraceptive accidents, and would not have been born had there been any legal abortion available to me. If we can render one service to all women, everywhere, and especially those with professional aspirations, it is to legalize abortion on request by the pregnant woman. As long as the burden of contraception rests primarily on women, this is especially necessary.

Child care was difficult, and enormously expensive. Johns Hopkins University had a good day care center for children from 18 months on, which was my best experience with child care altogether. Other than this one experience, I always employed housekeepers, and was paying, in the last year of graduate school, 75% of my income for child care. Since my youngest child started first grade, I have employed no one for either child care or housekeeping, nor does my husband, now that we live apart. I did experience a great deal of guilt leaving my children to go to work, most of it, I now realize, brought on by comments of nonworking mothers such as those at nursery school: "Don't you think you are ruining your children's lives?" From my present perspective, now that they are eight through fourteen years old, they seem to be normal children, with a normal relationship toward me and their father. They are, perhaps, more independent and self-sufficient; for example, my thirteen-year-old bicycles to the orthodontist and they *always* walk to school.

As girls, they have perhaps one unique advantage: their father assumes that they have the same aspirations as do boys and that they would undertake no greater household responsibility than nor exhibit markedly different behavior from boys their age. Their attitude toward a professional mother is that this is the normal state of affairs for them. Their behavior and attitudes truly seem to be shaped more by their individual personalities and the way the six of us interact than by whether or not I have a full-time professional job. The two elder ones are extremely "liberated" young women, and are both explicit and vociferous about any sex discrimination that they observe at school or among their friends. I have perhaps been lucky in that they are all sound constitutionally, and are almost never ill. On the other hand, I also encourage them to ignore minor ailments. They have also been, of course, saddled with a mother who could never be "Room Mother," who could not always attend the school Christmas Play, who never made cookies for the bake sale, but does any of this matter in the long run?

I have never made a conscious effort to spend my spare time with my children, but both my husband and I generally do so. We are a close family, and we like to do things such as skiing and traveling as a family. I certainly enjoy my children's company, and this may, in part, be because I have not ever had it for 24 hours a day, day after day after day. Our social life, rather than our children's, is different from that of our colleagues. Because there is little time for household chores (and less inclination to do them) and little interest on either my own or my husband's part in the house and its setting, we live simply and somewhat shabbily. The place is generally a mess; we almost never entertain in the formal sense. Now that we have separate households, this is even more true. Both domiciles are still furnished in "early Salvation

Army," and the sum of the two housing payments are about 12% of our combined incomes. If my children could point to one distinguishing feature of their lives as children of professional parents, it is that our housing and life style are well below the expectations in our income level.

When I had completed a year of postdoctoral fellowship, I went with my husband to Denver, where he had found a position at the University of Denver. We had decided that *he* should look for a job, but, if possible, should take one in a place where I would have opportunities also, and Denver seemed like such a place. In looking for an academic position in the Denver-Boulder-Colorado Springs area, I came on very restrictive and very overt sex discrimination. The University of Denver, where my husband was, would not even consider my application (nepotism, although a father and son had been department members in the recent past). The Colorado School of Mines wrote (although their policy has since changed), "We never hire women in the sciences." In general, the attitude toward a person seeking an academic job in a given place because her family is in that place is very negative. I finally got a position at the University of Colorado School of Medicine as a research associate, paid from grant funds. I really got this only because both the chairman and my subsequent coauthor were Johns Hopkins men themselves. After three years, by a stroke of luck, a position as assistant professor of chemistry at Temple Buell College, a woman's college in Denver, opened up. Since CU [Colorado University] would not put me on hard money or a tenure track, I went to Temple Buell. I was considered by my preceptor at Hopkins to be a great success, because I had a tenure-track teaching position at a small college for women, one that is not, in my opinion, first-rate.

My experience at both the Medical School and Temple Buell demonstrated to me that fulfillment involved more interaction with people than was possible in a purely research position and a larger role in policy-making than was possible as a very junior faculty member. At TBC I was, fortunately, able to have positive power in making decisions about curriculum, new faculty, budget, and so on. It is a small college, and a faculty member's role in decision making depends rather heavily on his or her own initiative. The structure of the chemistry major program there is primarily my creation; there was no chemistry major when I went on the faculty.

My experience at TBC demonstrates the enormous importance of women as role models for women students. Prior to my appointment, all the physics, chemistry, and mathematics faculty had been men. The highest professional aspiration voiced by any student then was to become a laboratory technician! Not only was I able to encourage the girls to go on toward a professional career, but I convinced my closest colleague in the Department that encouragement was both necessary and worthwhile. Although he was not himself prejudiced in any way, he had failed to realize that most girls need encouragement to overcome the tremendous internal pressures that have been built up in them.

Shortly after we moved to Colorado, and because I really felt somewhat unfulfilled in my work, I became active in what was then called the conservation movement. We are very active, out-of-doors people and enjoy all sorts of wilderness experiences, and in this sphere, I have developed a deep sense of responsibility of man toward the earth, and see a need to change some fundamental human attitudes. I also saw where, as a scientist, I could render some valuable services to the "lay" citizenry concerned about conservation.

In 1965, a group of us founded the Colorado Open Space Council. I have been on the board since its inception, and have served both as secretary (1966–67) and as vice-president (1970–71). In 1969 I became one of the founders and chairman of Colorado Citizens for Clean Air, and held this post until leaving Colorado in 1971. I served for two years as legislative chairman for the Open Space Council, and was appointed by the Governor of Colorado to the Executive Committee of the Colorado Environment Commission 1970 (one of two women on the 56-member Commission and the 11-member Executive Committee). I have given technical testimony on air- and water-resource problems before innumerable state legislative committees, and five times—twice by invitation—before committees of the United States Congress. I have helped write several laws, including the

Colorado Air Pollution Control Act, and have received several state awards for my activity in the field of conservation.

In spring of 1970, while on a speaking tour for the Conservation Foundation, I spoke at a luncheon for a citizens' clean-air group in Miami. One member of the audience (whom I did not meet at the time) was Dean of the College of Arts and Sciences at my present institution—Florida International University. As a result of the speech, I was offered a deanship (which I turned down), and then the chairmanship of the Department of Chemistry, which I ultimately accepted. FIU has made a deliberate effort to hire women for upper-level administrative positions. For this reason, and because of my work in environmental concerns, they wanted me as chairman. My offer from FIU was totally unsolicited by me and came, I might add, as such a complete surprise that I never connected it with the speech I had given there.

What has happened to my family life as a result of my move to Miami has caused a great deal of private and public comment. Having myself been in the position of looking for an academic job while tied to a given geographic location, I did not want to put my husband, now professor of chemistry at the University of Denver, in that position. FIU has no nepotism rule, except that the case where one spouse has direct administrative authority over the other must be considered specially. I felt then, however, and I still feel, that insistence on a "package deal" would be unwise, would set a bad precedent, and would make everyone unhappy. Moreover, we were not sure that we were ready to transfer the entire family permanently from Colorado. Thus, we decided that, for the present, he would remain in Denver with two children, and I would take two with me to Miami.

Our situation certainly focuses a major problem for women (or perhaps one ought to say for married couples) pursuing professional careers. Unless we initiate jobs that are filled by a married couple rather than by a single person, we cannot guarantee a husband and wife equally satisfying professional appointments in the same geographic location, because there are so few positions available. Elimination of nepotism rules is vitally necessary, and will go a long way toward alleviating this situation, but it is no guarantee of good positions for a married couple.

The choice I made is one which a married woman (or man) would make only after many years of marriage, or when contemplating a permanent separation anyway. It has taught me much about the relative roles of married and single people in our society. I am very lonely, but that is largely because almost all social life takes place for couples. In a married society, the woman alone is a social outcast. If we adapted more naturally to the presence of unmarried, mature adults in our social gatherings, they would not be so lonely, and, I am convinced, the present pressure to be married would be greatly alleviated.

I achieved my present position by a fluke, but in part because I had sought and found fulfilment in an area that is now booming: environmental studies. I became an active leader in the conservation movement because opportunities in my chosen professional area—chemistry—were so severely curtailed by sex discrimination. This is the first time since graduate school that I have felt challenged by my job; I enjoy it very much.

The primary advice I would give girls contemplating a professional career is:

1. Be well prepared, but stay flexible. Few women or men end up doing what they had planned while in graduate school.
2. Maintain your humanity in dealing with people and follow your natural instincts, even though some things you do may be labeled "feminine."
3. Be prepared to work very hard, if you plan to have children. Equality in housekeeping roles is something we are still working to attain.
4. Don't sacrifice your ambition, aggressiveness, or intelligence for any of the standard feminine rewards like marriage.
5. Learn to deal casually with, or to ignore, sexism and discrimination.
6. Set high goals for yourself, and set them independently of your sex.
7. If you marry, marry someone in sympathy with those goals.

148

THE ORTHODOX JEWESS
1960–1974

The Hasidim are the most colorful of the Orthodox Jewish groups. The Lubavitch Hasidim are also known as the Chabad people because they emphasize learning: Chabad is a Hebrew acronym for three words meaning wisdom, understanding, and knowledge. They have a women's auxiliary called Wives and Daughters of Chabad (Neshei Ubnos Chabad). These women adopted a series of resolutions at a convention they held in 1960. Four are reprinted below in selection A.

In 1972, Congress adopted the proposed twenty-seventh amendment to the Constitution, one specifying equal rights for women. It was to come into force when ratified by thirty-eight states. Right-wing Orthodox Jews in America are opposed to it; they want it discarded or revised to protect their religious practices and beliefs. "Torah-true" Jews require the separation of the sexes in synagogues and schools. The attitude of these Orthodox remonstrants is reflected in an article from the New York Times of April 4, 1972 (item B).

Most tradition-observing Jews in the United States are affiliated with the Union of Orthodox Jewish Congregations of America. At their seventy-sixth anniversary convention in November–December 1974, they passed a series of resolutions expressing their attitude to women. The resolutions are reprinted below (C). One resolution urged that women be permitted to hold office in the synagogue. Actually, the sponsors had their doubts as to whether the ladies could halakically, legally, serve as synagogal officers, but they seem to have resolved the doubts affirmatively, for two years later they again went on record recommending the election of women to important posts in congregations. Whether the resolution was ever implemented is unclear.

Though the Orthodox leaders insist on the retention of traditional religious differences between males and females, they are in agreement with all other Jews that women must be accorded parity, particularly in the economic sphere. This is a realistic concession to modernity. New also for most of them is the emphasis on intensive religious study for females—a marked twentieth-century departure from past norms.

Selection D deals with abortion and reflects the present-day Orthodox point of view (1974). Seven years earlier, in 1967, the Reform-minded Central Conference of American Rabbis and the General Assembly of the Union of American Hebrew Congregations had asked for more humane, liberal legislation in the area of abortion. On this issue, the two Jewish denominations, so often polar opposites, are not too far apart.

A

RESOLUTIONS OF THE 1960 CONVENTION OF NESHEI UBNOS CHABAD

BAAL SHEM TOV'S TEACHING

WHEREAS this coming Shavouos [Pentecost] is the 200th Yahrzeit [anniversary] of the holy Baal Shem Tov [the Master of the Good Name, Israel ben Eliezer, the founder of Hasidism, who died in 1760], the convention therefore
RESOLVES to strengthen by word and deed, the virtues *(midos)* of peace, friendship and harmony that he fostered among ourselves and in our communities.

MODESTY AND DECENT DRESS

WHEREAS the moral standards of our youth, and the restoration of the high standards of modesty of Jewish womanhood, are two of our chief concerns, the convention therefore
DIRECTS the attention of all Jewish women to the sorry state of modesty in our present society, and particularly to the immodest dress that is so common, with its consequent demoralizing effect on our youth.
CALLS on the responsible members of our community, such as rabbis, educators, parents, etc., to restore to its proper importance that exemplary modesty which has always been the badge of honor of Jewish womanhood.

Education of Jewish Girls

MOVED by our concern for our youth, the convention
RESOLVES to initiate an intensive campaign to plan for the
education of our daughters, especially those of high school age, in
those communities where suitable facilities do not as yet exist.

Supporting 'Di Yiddishe Heim'

WHEREAS we are proud of our quarterly magazine, 'Di
Yiddishe Heim' [*The Jewish Home*], and its successful efforts to
bring knowledge and Chassidic warmth to Jewish women, the
convention
RESOLVES that every member of Neshei Ubnos Chabad subscribe to 'Di Yiddishe Heim', and do all she can to increase its
circulation among others.

Our Resources

WHEREAS we are humbly aware of the great responsibility that
we bear in these times to strengthen Torah and Yiddishkeit
[traditional Jewish learning and Jewishness], the convention
CALLS on every branch of Neshei Ubnos Chabad to mobilize the
talents and resources of every member to achieve the maximum
lasting results for Torah.

B

Rabbis See Women's Rights Measure as Threatening Orthodox Practices
by Eleanor Blau
1972

A coalition of Orthodox rabbinical organizations charged
yesterday [April 3, 1972] that the proposed constitutional
amendment guaranteeing equal rights to women would threaten
the Jewish Orthodox practice of separating the sexes in

synagogues and parochial schools. The rabbis said it also could threaten morality through the country.

"A central tenet of our faith is the uniqueness of the respective roles of men and women," said Rabbi Abraham Gross, president of the Rabbinical Alliance of America. "This amendment directly threatens our rights to continue practicing our faith as we have for the past three centuries in America."

The coalition, which represents more than half of the 2,500 Orthodox rabbis in the United States, is made up of the Alliance, the Union of Orthodox Rabbis of the United States and Canada, the Rabbinical Council of the Sephardic Syrian and Near Eastern Jewish Community in America, the Central Congress of Rabbis, and the Metropolitan Board of Orthodox Rabbis.

The 900-member Rabbinical Council of America has not yet taken a position on the amendment measure.

In a news conference at the Alliance's offices, 156 Fifth Avenue, and in an interview afterward, Rabbi Gross said the First Amendment guarantee of religious freedom would not protect Orthodox synagogues from feminist lawsuits and might not prevent the Government from ending their tax exemption and school funds.

He urged a rewording of the amendment so that it would specifically guarantee religious rights.

The amendment was adopted by Congress last month. It needs the ratification of 38 states to become law.

The rabbis stressed that they believed in equal pay for equal work and in not regarding women as inferior to men. Rabbi Gross said women throughout Jewish history had played leading roles in government.

Nevertheless, Orthodox Judaism, the most conservative of the three branches of Judaism, draws many distinctions between the roles of the sexes. Women hold an honored position in the home, while men assume the major religious responsibility.

Rabbi David B. Hollander, vice president of the Alliance, said boys in Orthodox Hebrew day schools received "deeper academic study," while girls focused on subjects such as typing, stenography and home observance of dietary laws.

Rabbi Hollander said he knew of no move by any Orthodox

women to counter the traditional barriers. The rabbi, who teaches sociology at Long Island University, also remarked that "women should be feminine in appearance and philosophy, not brazen or arrogant."

Asked whether he regarded Betty Friedan and Gloria Steinem of the women's liberation movement as arrogant and brazen, he replied, "If they claim that American women are oppressed, that's arrogance."

Both Rabbis Hollander and Gross expressed concern that the amendment might produce a climate that would jeopardize sexual morality. Rabbi Gross cited the trend toward coeducational college dormitories as an example of the way in which changing rules could affect morals.

C

THE ORTHODOX WOMAN IN CONTEMPORARY SOCIETY

1974

The Orthodox community can ill afford to squander any of its resources—least of all the vitality, creativity, and contributions of our women. In the battle for Jewish survival in North America, the Orthodox woman is, as she has been throughout history, on the front lines. In home and school, in synagogue and communal affairs, in *tzedakah* [charity] projects, and in efforts to rally support for Torah causes, women play a vital and irreplaceable role. The Orthodox woman is an involved woman. This is true both of the single woman as well as of those who have accepted the added responsibilities of marriage and motherhood.

While insisting that the Halachic [Jewish law] differentiation of sex roles remains inviolate, we reaffirm our commitment to the principles of equal opportunity, recompense, and recognition.

The incoming administration is mandated to take decisive measures to ensure the public dissemination of the [Orthodox] Torah community's position on issues relating to women, and to assuring that women have every opportunity to participate fully in our community's endeavors.

Accordingly:

The Orthodox Union is called upon to expand the number of women on its Board of Directors and National Commissions.

The President of the Orthodox Union is mandated to appoint a study commission of Rabbinic figures and men and women lay leaders to examine the question of women serving as officers and on the Boards of Directors of Orthodox synagogues. This study commission is to report to the UOJCA Board of Directors by no later than July 1, 1975.

The Orthodox Union is mandated to help local communities develop meaningful quality Torah education programs for women—on the teen, post–high school, and adult levels.

Every effort must be made to increase the participation of women in synagogue Torah Study programs. Special shieurim [lectures] should be organized for women wherever possible.

Synagogues should investigate the feasibility of securing an *eruv* around their communities in order that women with young children may attend Shabbat services. Any such steps should, of course, be taken in consultation with appropriate Halachic authorities. [An *eruv* is a symbolic device to permit Jews to move about freely on the Sabbath.]

The purpose of the *mechitza* [partition] is to create sanctity through separation.

It is only through such separation during the synagogue service that true *Kedusha* [holiness] can be achieved during Tefila [prayer]. We call upon the synagogues to take every step to insure that their *mechitzot* fulfill all Halachic requirements while enabling women congregants to hear the entire service. The proper Halachic authorities should work with architects to determine a series of Halachically valid seating options for Orthodox synagogues.

The Orthodox Union will fight efforts to discriminate against women in terms of compensation, credit, and public policy.

We will remain vigilant, however, against any efforts to "legislate away" the basic sex-role differentiation that is so fundamental to the Halachic approach. It is for this reason that we continue to oppose the proposed twenty-seventh amendment. The problem with the 27th Amendment is that it would also make discrimination against men illegal and thus might render unconstitutional certain legislation benefiting women that society today takes for granted—such as exemption from the draft, protective labor legislation, alimony, and support laws. Fears in this respect are not far-fetched. The proponents of this Amendment loudly proclaim that it would and indeed properly should eliminate "discriminations" against men. In addition, the Amendment might threaten the right of an institution that is not coeducational to receive government funds.

We call for the redrafting of this amendment in a fashion that will not allow it to be used as a vehicle for attacking the very structure of the family unit and the prerogatives of the Halachah. We would strongly support a redrafted amendment that recognized these reservations.

D

Abortion

1974

Judaism regards all life—including fetal life—as inviolate. Abortion is not a private matter between a woman and her physician. It infringes upon the most fundamental right of a third party—that of the unborn child. . . .

For Jews, fetal life is inviolate unless continuation of pregnancy poses a serious threat to the life of the mother. The life of the mother takes precedence over that of the unborn child. Situations in which maternal health, rather than maternal life, are involved, pose complex problems requiring rabbinic adjudication. Similarly, situations involving the psychiatric components require authoritative determination in each individual case. Performance of an abortion cannot be sanctioned unless the relevant medical facts are submitted to a competent rabbinic authority who will review the medical data and render advice in accordance with Jewish law.

The incoming administration of the Orthodox Union is mandated to undertake steps to develop a program dealing with the Torah community's response to the abortion issue.

149

THE MADONNA OF THE FEMINIST MOVEMENT, BETTY FRIEDAN
1963–1976

In 1963, Betty Friedan (Naomi Goldstein, of Peoria, b. 1921) triggered a real revolution. She, perhaps more than anyone else, has helped emancipate women in the home and in the office. The feminist uprising of the 1960's and 1970's has been an ongoing middle-class bouleversement. To be sure, females in the United States were given the vote in 1920, but rather little happened after that. Over forty years later, Betty Friedan, a free-lance writer and a housewife, wrote The Feminine Mystique, *a book which made an anguished plea for freedom for American womankind—genuine freedom, cultural, sexual, political, and social. Women, she argued, had to be as free as men in every sense of the word. Because of this rebellion, women today are beginning to enjoy all the liberties and immunities that men enjoy; they are daring to live as they see fit and to do what seems right in their own eyes. Five thousand years of recorded patriarchal culture have been shaken to their very foundations. The position of women has been immeasurably improved.*

Why did feminism achieve such success in the 1960's? Posteventum explanations are always at hand, but it is impossible to prove their correctness. Were the 1960's a propitious decade because youth was in revolt, because women had already begun to move in massive numbers into factories and offices, because national statutes covered their advance, because they had aggressive leaders, among them many Jews? Why were Jewish women in the forefront among the country's females, a population of which they formed but 1.4 percent? It is not improbable that these Jewesses assumed leadership because they were well-educated, aggressive, competent, and ambitious. Because Jews as a group have always been frowned upon, their tacit relegation to secondary status has only served to incite them to prove themselves, and when opportunity opened doors for them, the Jewish women rushed in.

In selection A, below, Betty Friedan defines the feminine mystique, attacks it, and, somewhat vaguely to be sure, lays out a plan whereby women can become the authors of their own salvation. In the second passage, B, she triumphantly apostrophizes what may possibly be "the most far-reaching revolution of all time," the liberation of her sex. By 1976, The Feminine Mystique had sold over two million copies and Friedan had helped found both the National Organization for Women (1966) and the Women's National Political Caucus (1971). The feminist movement has flourished mightily; the National Organization for Women and the Women's National Political Caucus have not.

A

THE FEMININE MYSTIQUE*
1963

The feminine mystique says that the highest value and the only commitment for women is the fulfillment of their own femininity. It says that the great mistake of Western culture, through most of its history, has been the undervaluation of this feminity. It says this femininity is so mysterious and intuitive and close to the creation and origin of life that man-made science may never be able to understand it. But however special and different, it is in no way inferior to the nature of man; it may even in certain respects be superior. The mistake, says the mystique, the root of women's troubles in the past is that women envied men, women tried to be like men, instead of accepting their own nature, which can find fulfillment only in sexual passivity, male domination, and nurturing maternal love.

But the new image this mystique gives to American women is the old image: "Occupation: housewife." The new mystique makes the housewife-mothers, who never had a chance to be anything else, the model for all women; it presupposes that history has reached a final and glorious end in the here and now, as far as women are concerned. Beneath the sophisticated trappings, it simply makes certain concrete, finite, domestic aspects of feminine existence—as it was lived by women whose lives were confined, by necessity, to cooking, cleaning, washing, bearing children—into a religion, a pattern by which all women must now live or deny their feminity.

Fulfillment as a woman had only one definition for American women after 1949—the housewife-mother. As swiftly as in a dream, the image of the American woman as a changing, growing individual in a changing world was shattered. Her solo flight to find her own identity was forgotten in the rush for the security of togetherness. Her limitless world shrunk to the cozy walls of home. . . .

There are no easy answers in America today; it is difficult, painful, and takes perhaps a long time for each woman to find her own answer. First, she must unequivocally say "no" to the housewife image. This does not mean, of course, that she must divorce her husband, abandon her children, give up her home. She does not have to choose between marriage and career; that was the mistaken choice of the feminine mystique. In actual fact, it is not as difficult as the feminine mystique implies to combine marriage and motherhood and even the kind of lifelong personal purpose that once was called "career." . . .

Ironically, the only kind of work which permits an able woman to realize her abilities fully, to achieve identity in society in a life plan that can encompass marriage and motherhood, is the kind that was forbidden by the feminine mystique; the lifelong commitment to an art or science, to politics or profession. Such a commitment is not tied to a specific job or locality. It permits year-to-year variation—a full-time paid job in one community, part-time in another, exercise of the professional skill in serious volunteer work or a period of study during pregnancy or early motherhood when a full-time job is not feasible. It is a continuous thread, kept alive by work and study and contacts in the field, in any part of the country. . . .

The women I interviewed who had suffered and solved the problem that has no name, to fulfill an ambition of their own, long buried or brand new, to work at top capacity, to have a sense of achievement, was like finding a missing piece in the puzzle of their lives. The money they earned often made life easier for the whole family, but none of them pretended this was the only reason they worked, or the main thing they got out of it. That sense of being complete and fully a part of the world—"no longer an island, part of the mainland"—had come back. They knew that it did not come from the work alone, but from the whole—their marriage, homes, children, work, their changing, growing links with the community. They were once again human beings, not "just housewives." . . .

The problem that has no name—which is simply the fact that American women are kept from growing to their full human capacities—is taking a far greater toll on the physical and mental health of our country than any known disease. Consider the high incidence of emotional breakdown of women in the "role crises" of their twenties and thirties; the alcoholism and suicides in their forties and fifties; the housewives' monopolization of all doctors' time. Consider the prevalence of teenage marriages, the growing rate of illegitimate pregnancies, and even more seriously, the pathology of mother-child symbiosis. Consider the alarming passivity of American teenagers. If we continue to produce millions of young mothers who stop their growth and education short of identity, without a strong core of human values to pass on to their children, we are committing, quite simply, genocide, starting with the mass burial of American women and ending with the progressive dehumanization of their sons and daughters.

These problems cannot be solved by medicine, or even by psychotherapy. We need a drastic reshaping of the cultural image of femininity that will permit women to reach maturity, identity, completeness of self, without conflict with sexual fulfillment. A massive attempt must be made by educators and parents—and ministers, magazine editors, manipulators, guidance counselors—to stop the early-marriage movement, stop girls from growing up wanting to be "just a housewife," stop it by insisting, with the same attention from childhood on that parents and educators give to boys, that girls develop the resources of self, goals that will permit them to find their own identity. . . .

Educators at every women's college, at every university, junior college, and community college, must see to it that women make a lifetime commitment (call it a "life plan," a "vocation," a "life purpose" if that dirty word *career* has too many celibate connotations) to a field of thought, to work of serious importance to society. They must expect the girl as well as the boy to take some field seriously enough to want to pursue it for life. This does not mean abandoning liberal education for women in favor of "how to" vocational courses. Liberal education, as it is given at the best of colleges and universities, not only trains the mind but provides an ineradicable core of human values. But liberal education must be planned for serious use, not merely dilettantism or passive appreciation. As boys at Harvard or Yale or Columbia or Chicago go on from the liberal arts core to study architecture, medicine, law, science, girls must be encouraged to go on, to make a life plan. It has been shown that girls with this kind of a commitment are less eager to rush into early marriage, less panicky about finding a man, more responsible for their sexual behavior. Most of them marry, of course, but on a much more mature basis. Their marriages then are not an escape but a commitment shared by two people that becomes part of their commitment to themselves and society. If, in fact, girls are educated to make such commitments, the question of sex and when they marry will lose its overwhelming importance. It is the fact that women have no identity of their own that makes sex, love, marriage, and children seem the only and essential facts of women's life. . . .

When enough women make life plans geared to their real abilities, and speak out for maternity leaves or even maternity sabbaticals, professionally run nurseries, and the other changes in the rules that may be necessary, they will not have to sacrifice the right to honorable competition and contribution any more than they will have to sacrifice marriage and motherhood. It is wrong to keep spelling out unnecessary choices that make women unconsciously resist either commitment or motherhood—and that hold back recognition of the needed social changes. It is not a question of women having their cake and eating it, too. A woman is handicapped by her sex, and handicaps society, either by slavishly copying the pattern of man's advance in the professions, or by refusing to compete with man at all. But with the vision to make a new life plan of her own, she can fulfill a commitment to profession and politics, and to marriage and motherhood with equal seriousness. . . .

Who knows what women can be when they are finally free to become themselves? Who knows what women's intelligence will contribute when it can be nourished without denying love? Who knows of the possibilities of love when men and women share not only children, home, and garden, not only the fulfillment of their biological roles, but the responsibilities and passions of the work that creates the human future and the full human knowledge of who they are? It has barely begun, the search of women for themselves. But the time is at hand when the voices of the feminine mystique can no longer drown out the inner voice that is driving women on to become complete.

B

IT CHANGED MY LIFE

1976

Today, in 1976, the women's movement for equality, human freedom and human dignity—for her own participation in the actions and decisions of human destiny and her own identity in the family of man—clearly emerges as the major movement for basic social change in this decade and possibly the most far-reaching revolution of all time. It affects our daily personal lives immediately, women, men, children; pervades all our institutions, office and home; confronts the economy, politics of right and left, theology, sexuality itself, in unpredictable ways. . . .

For the reality of this revolution is that we—the middle-class women who started it—did it for ourselves. Other revolutions, despite the clichés of radical rhetoric, were also started by middle-class intellectuals (the only ones with education to put it into words), but they were always doing it for someone else: the poor, the working class, "them." Liberal whites used to tell blacks what they needed (and middle-class intellectual blacks still prescribe abstract doctrines for "them"). Doing it for *ourselves* is the essence of the women's movement: it keeps us honest, keeps us real, keeps us concrete. And it is that *doing*—not just being, feeling, or sweeping the floor that gets dirty again—which brings women into history. It is *new* for women to be making history— not just a few queens, empresses or exceptional geniuses, but hundreds, thousands, millions of women now entering history, knowing we have made history—by changing our own lives. The most superficial view of the daily paper—front page, sports page, financial page, want ads—shows not only the entrance of women into the actions and professions from which they were barred (the Little League, the police and fire departments, submarines, governor, mayor, Episcopal priest, Conservative rabbi, radical terrorist, orchestra conductor, Wall Street broker), but the transformation of the political, economic, theological and cultural agenda (the very language, the style, the questions addressed) and also the transformation of the women's page: lifestyle, of importance to men. [As of 1980, there were no female Conservative rabbis.]

We otherwise ordinary American women, finding the power to change our own lives, changed the face of history. We have thus known and experienced the unique human passion as not many men, and almost no women, have known it before. As the men who made the American Revolution knew two hundred years ago—it was the *doing* of it, the process, the participation in the making of our own history that brought us to a new level of human aliveness. For us who made the leap, herstory itself is the reward.

But women from now on will move in history in a new way: it is a qualitative change, that history will be made by women now as well as men. The history of these dozen years already has a different kind of agenda, style, texture from previous history created solely by men. Unlike the linear history of the past, our herstory inevitably deals with the stuff of daily life—in the total, circular, irregular, spontaneously changing flexible gestalt life comes in. As women begin moving into public, professional life—and as men begin to share child care, cooking, cleaning—the whole story is clearly more than a few women reversing roles with men or having a piece of the action, a chance at the jobs only men had before. Something else begins to happen—a bridging, a transcending of the polarization between masculine and feminine, between the abstract and concrete, between eternal values and grubby, sweaty, everyday realities. It will not be a eparate story very long. The rights were won after a century of truggle, and then there was a half-century of sleep, and now the omen's movement is changing society so women can use those ights. And then it will be human liberation: the next chapter of he human story. After we turn that corner.

150

THE FEMALE HOMOSEXUAL
1970's

The 1960's witnessed the revolt of the individual, the right of every man and woman to be himself or herself. People, particularly young people began to say what they wanted and to act as the spirit moved them. Man ceased to conform or slavishly adhere to the amenities. By the 1970's, man lesbians "came out of the closet," publicly avowing their homosexuality One Jewish lesbian ventured the opinion that at least 10 percent of al Jewish women share her sexual proclivities. This of course is only a guess Some gay women have broken with traditional Judaism because i tolerates only heterosexuality; others, loyal to their people and its religiou way of life, are proud and zealous Jews.

The following document reflects the problem of a young woman who ha not "come out of the closet."

DILEMMA OF A JEWISH LESBIAN

1977

My parents are driving me to the airport after one of my semiannual visits. The radio newscaster reports that the Ameri can Psychiatric Association has voted to remove homosexuality from its list of "diseases." My father is appalled: "Who wil protect us from the perverts who molest little children?" My mother mentions there is a gay synagogue. This further inflames my father who points out that Biblical law punished homo sexuality by death. I, very alone in the back seat, am thankful that the topic came up this late in my visit, and that I will soon be back in the city I chose to live in partly to minimize the number of experiences like this.

This story epitomizes the estrangement I feel from my family from Judaism and the Jewish community because I am lesbian True, the Biblical law condemns only male homosexuality, but his only increases my alienation since it illustrates that in our atriarchial religion the activities of women were not considered nportant enough to rate regulation. Besides, this law can be used o deny both female and male gay Jews Israeli citizenship under he Law of Return.

Yes, it has been a very long time since any Jew has been put to eath for homosexuality. But the Biblical law symbolizes the istoric and current overwhelming orientation of the Jewish eople toward family and procreation which effectively pushes ne and all homosexuals away from the community.

Being a single and childless Jew carries a stigma. *Life Is With eople* [by M. Zborowski and E. Herzog], the classic sociological tudy of the Jews of the shtetl (Jewish ghetto in Eastern Europe), lescribes a culture and world view very much like the one in vhich I was raised. It requires that "a person is part of a family. There is no fulfillment of one's duties or one's pleasures as an solated individual. If a man is not a husband and father 'he is iothing.' A woman who is not a wife and mother is not a 'real' voman. To be an old maid or a bachelor is not only a shame but a in against the will of God, who has commanded every Jew to narry and beget offspring."

It is not my mother alone who regards me, past thirty, as still a hild. Probably every Jewish mother of a "child," who for vhatever reasons has chosen not to marry, feels the same way. Perhaps my Catholic gay friends feel no less estranged from their amilies than I do, but I think it must be easier to be unmarried in tradition which honors at least certain groups of unmarried people. My being single is a constant embarrassment to my parents. Marrying me off was one of the most basic obligations hey undertook when they brought me into the world. Again rom *Life Is With People*, "the development of the child is a direct ;ratification for the parent and what happens to the child in an .lmost literal sense happens to the parent. His marriage and his chievements reflect honor of the parents, his failure or disgrace is . direct reflection on them." So how can my parents *shep naches* take pride) as they are entitled to? They derive some pleasure rom their daughter the doctor, but it is clear that they would get nuch more pleasure were I their daughter, the wife and mother.

It is my impression that Jewish lesbians who marry and hav children before they come out are likely to have better relation ships with their parents than those of us who discovered ou sexuality earlier. Sometimes I wonder, bitterly, if my parents eagerness for grandchildren would be satisfied if I, unmarried were to produce children. There was a period during my lat twenties when they seemed to be saying, "Better a *shayget* (gentile man) than no husband at all," so anything is possible.

Hope springs eternal. When I leave my parents' house twic each year to return to my own life my mother wishes m "everything you want for yourself and one thing I want for you," as if to say, "I want so little from you, how can you deny me?" Sh even whispers to me that I could learn to like "it"! I think my mother knows, but does not want to know that she knows, that am lesbian. Even direct confrontation might not be enough t deter a Jewish mother. The mother of a friend of mine still tries t fix her up with nice Jewish boys even though my friend has beer very open about how she is choosing to live her life. And confrontation is not recommended in a culture in which a child i under a deep obligation not to shame her parents. Indeed, I dar not sign my name to this article.

Though I have focused so far on problems with my parents there are other ways I feel the pain of being lesbian and Jewish My sister was astonished when I mentioned that I went to the wake of my lover's father: she had never expected me to have a non-Jewish lover. I cannot conceive of myself having a non Jewish male lover; but since I, too, devalue the childless home I could make with a woman lover, it seems unimportant that we do not share a common background and practices. Besides, there seem to be so few lesbian Jews, that I cannot expect to always find a Jewish lover.

Sometimes I yearn for a more Jewish life and think about going to Israel. But I know that things are only worse there; in additior to the historical Jewish concern with procreation, there is the pressing concern for replacing the war dead and for not being numerically overwhelmed by Arabs within the State. The only place in Israel I know where one can go to meet lesbians is Te

viv, and only on Wednesdays and Saturdays which are wo-
en's nights. A Danish Jewish lesbian I know considered *aliyah*
mmigration to Israel), but the anti-gay feeling in Israel soon
scouraged her. "I'm used to *galut* (exile) in Denmark," she said.
t was more than I could bear to be in *galut* in Israel."
The picture I have painted seems quite grim. But there are
me ways in which things are bound to change for the better—if
e Jews are to survive at all. I am reminded of the indignation of a
iend of mine when the Rabbi sought to console her during *shiva*
nourning) for her father with the wish that she would soon be
arried. While my friend, being lesbian, may have felt more
ienated by this than most single Jewish women, the fact that she
a distinguished academic is the reason why the Rabbi's
mment was negatively received. The American zeitgeist in-
easingly favors individual identity rather than family
entification for women as well as men. If the Jewish community
ntinues in its traditional ways without allowing for this,
owing numbers of singles, whether divorced or never married,
ill be increasingly alienated from the community. Since Jews
ave historically been very successful at adapting in order to
rvive, I am optimistic that at least some of the discomfort I feel
a single person will be mitigated. I have other reasons to be
opeful.

Having lunch with half a dozen lesbians at an American
sychological Association conference we suddenly realized we
ere all Jewish. We poured out stories of family problems,
lations with Jewish and non-Jewish lovers, hopes for the future.
e felt a real camaraderie.

On a more formal basis, there are at least fifteen ongoing gay
wish groups in the United States, Canada, Bermuda, England,
d Israel. Showing great courage, the Tel Aviv–based Society
r the Protection of Personal Rights will host the third interna-
onal conference of gay Jewish organizations in 1979.

I have been invited by a sympathetic rabbi to speak at a local
illel house, and other houses and Jewish students in the United
ates have challenged Jewish anti-gay attitudes. Several Jewish
urnals have printed articles by gay Jews.

I am not holding my breath in anticipation of my paren
accepting my remaining unmarried, much less their relating
my lesbianism. But I sense more openness on these issues amon
Jews, and the seeds of a community that supports my indepen
dent womanhood and my lesbianism. One that lets me feel m
Jewishness not as a burden, but rather, as a joy and strength.

151

JEWISH WOMEN'S GROUPS: SEPARATE—BUT UNEQUAL?
1970

n the provocative article that follows, Doris Gold raises some interesting uestions. If women do not lead national organizations of men and omen—and they rarely do—is it because they have been bypassed or is it ecause they are happy in their own female organizations? Are they xually ghettoized, separate and unequal? Does the typical Hadassah ember feel that any man in any organized male group is superior to her accomplishes more? If confronted with any such claim, would she not nile derisively?

A great many women today believe that they are equal to their lords nd masters in almost all things; they know that they are efficient; they ten pride themselves on doing a better job than their consorts. Ms. Gold entures the thought that women need greater self-esteem. This is rguable. Most organization Jewesses of the fourth quarter of the wentieth century have no lack of self-confidence; they believe in them- lves. Discretion is always the better part of valor. It may well be that omen will not seriously vie for communal power, for they intuitively nse that, even should they hold the highest office, they will not exercise eal authority. Under the normal order of things, they will rarely be the ig givers; ultimately control rests with the rich, mostly men.

JEWISH WOMEN'S GROUPS: SEPARATE—BUT EQUAL?
by Doris B. Gold

A public bus on New York City's Fifth Avenue moves by, earing a brightly lit blue and white arrow advertising HADAS-SAH. We think about being a Jewish woman on our way to a omen's organization event at midday. While there is a burst of ride in our visibility, we wonder whether the phenomenon of lmost a million women members in 18 to 25 separate Jewish women's groups is appropriate at a time when there is again female emancipatory trend in the land.

It was in this mood that we talked and corresponded wit several national Jewish women's organization leaders, a woma editor of a Jewish publication, some Jewish women "actives," an queried a rabbi and some Jewish male professionals for balance We asked all of them for an opinion on a key question: whethe the existence of Jewish women's organizations, both independen and "divisions" of male-dominated organizations, indicated tha women lacked equal status in Jewish community life? Othe questions dealt with the possible barriers experienced by wome in working together with men in the Jewish Establishment; th preference of Jewish women for voluntary rather than pai professional jobs in the Jewish community; the "feminizing" c synagogue life, and last, what seemed to be the future trend c Jewish women's organizations.

Most of the women's leaders were emphatic in their contentio that their separation in no way indicated that they were second class citizens of the Jewish community. . . .

Even if one does accept the view that Jewish women's organi zational separatism may be a stage in the transitional process c her greater emancipation in Jewish life, it is this writer's observa tion after many years in and out of the Jewish Establishment, tha it is more possible to buck the resistance to her intellectua acceptance, her personal worth, in fact, through having, a Virginia Woolf put it, "a room of one's own." It seems to us tha the force of male authority and patriarchy is still very strong i the institutional life of the Jewish community, and one which ha originally assigned certain tasks to Jewish women to do it "housekeeping."

We believe there are other reasons to be found for th proliferating separatism of the women and the concomitan increased duplication and fragmentation of Jewish communit life. It seems to us that somewhere along the way in thei American advance, Jewish women took a more comfortabl detour (as did non-Jewish women, cited by Dr. Jessie Bernard, sociologist) from self-awareness or serious vocational prepara tion. They opted for the role of "organization woman" who coul attain status and *yichus* [importance] in the eyes of the men, even incidentally "beating them at their own game" in being as good or better money-raisers and becoming their own "power elite," albeit as "sorority sisters." It is evident that even those many women who are Jewishly educated and highly competent do not seriously vie for a place in the Jewish community, with the exception of some in Zionist circles and among Yiddishists.

All this does not imply that the many outstanding leaders of national Jewish women's organizations who labor mightily in their vineyards, exhibiting sophisticated Jewish identity and humanistic scope, are not "achievers." But their very stance of modesty, reticence and moral concern may be too much of a good thing for their own self-development and for greater maturity in male-female relationships in the American Jewish community.

The most striking example of the reticence of Jewish women to take up cudgels in their own behalf is the fact that only two independent women's groups are represented in the Conference of Presidents of Major Jewish Organizations. The others are represented via their male parent sponsors, or not at all. Mrs. Virginia Snitow, American Jewish Congress' Women's Division President, told us of movements afoot to consolidate Jewish women leaders at least into a consultative group, and remarked that ". . . the whole idea of standing up to be counted," of "feminism as the women see it, makes them timid of expressing themselves. They seem to feel that when they have an idea or want to raise an issue they must look for a man to 'represent' them, to give it 'legitimacy.' " . . .

It is clear that Jewish women's groups have already created a mass Jewish women's culture and style. In meeting the warm, gracious and often compelling personalities of the women leaders, one sees the blending of the "suburban ideal" and Jewish morality in word and deed. It is probable that the women's divisions or auxiliaries will become more like the large independent women's groups, with their already enlarged smorgasbord of activities to please every woman's palate (and also to retain the new younger members).

While there is no doubt of the good works that will be achieved for Jewry through giant efforts such as these, there persists the feeling that what the Jewish woman may also need is greater self-esteem and individuation. Will organized Jewish women turn to themselves for self-discovery, for doubting their best-of-all-possible-worlds stance? Will the Jewish "organization woman" provide a wider choice to the Jewish women of the "emerging seventies" beyond fund-raising or community service? Will she become a truly equal partner in American Jewish community life?

152

EMANCIPATION FOR THE CHAINED JEWESS
1970

One of the great problems faced by women who adhere to the halakah, Jewish law, is that from a modern Western point of view they suffer severe disabilities. The halakic status of females, the prescriptions and statutes governing relations between husbands and wives, were all determined well over a thousand years ago when women were not deemed equal to men. In the following article, Trude Weiss-Rosmarin, editor of the Jewish Spectator, describes these disabilities and passionately deplores their inequities.

Dr. Weiss-Rosmarin, a native of Germany (b. 1908), was trained as a scholar in Semitic and Judaic fields. In a way, she is a prototype of the new breed of women now engaged in serious Jewish study and research here in the United States.

THE UNFREEDOM OF JEWISH WOMEN
by Trude Weiss-Rosmarin

Equality is not, and must not be confused with, selfsameness. Emancipation must not be misinterpreted to imply that those who are to be accepted as equals are required to divest themselves of their identity. The notion that the premise of equality is selfsameness in the monolithic structure of a society which does not tolerate differentness is at the root of the dilemma of the modern Jew. . . .

The confused identification of equality with selfsameness has troubled, and continues to confound, also the Feminist Movement. It did not, and still does not, demand equal rights and opportunities for women *as women*. The Women's Liberation Movement fights for equality on the strength of the argument that women can, and do, as featly [well] as men in occupations regarded typically and exclusively "masculine."

Women have proved themselves to be as capable as men are in the "masculine" occupations and professions they were "permitted" to enter. In fact, some types of work, such as elementary school teaching and office work, which once upon a time were regarded as "masculine" work, now are typically and almost exclusively "feminine" occupations. But, as some of the ideologists of the Women's Liberation Movement have said, "only the development of an artificial uterus will truly liberate women, for it will free them from the oppression of pregnancy and childbirth." . . .

Until "the development of an artificial uterus" (and "artificial mothers") most women will spend their best and most active years as wives, mothers and home-makers. And most women will find fulfilment in this *natural* role and occupation. The real challenge of Women's Liberation is not taking women out of the home but emancipating *the home-maker as home-maker* and *housewife* by bestowing *dignity* upon her work instead of derogating it, as most men and "creative women" do.

As all revolutionary movements, Women's Liberation was conceived and is led by intellectuals and professionals. But unlike the social revolution which ideally but futilely aims at "taking from everyone according to his ability and giving to everyone according to his needs" [Karl Marx], the radical women liberators would deprive women of their *innate* ability as mothers and home-makers. They disregard that the vast majority of women find fulfillment in being mothers and home-makers, to the same extent as the vast majority of men find fulfillment in occupations which would thwart and frustrate the minority of the creative and highly gifted.

Of course, *all* women should be free to choose the work they want to do and they should have equal opportunities in employment and remuneration. But to denigrate housewifery and motherhood as "oppression" is not a service to Women's Liberation! It is the snobbism of a small exclusivist group and is as provincially narrowminded as the superciliousness of some men in the "status professions." The notion that a writer is "more important" than a factory worker and that a woman executive is on a higher level than a housewife is the result of a status-oriented society with a false scale of values and, hence, false value judgments. In the economy and balance of nature, the fly is as important and indispensable as the lion. And in the human economy the street cleaner is as indispensable as the city planner and road engineer. Some of the Sages of Yavneh penetrated to the core of the *real* problem of democracy and liberation when they said: "I am human and so is my fellowman. I work in the city and he works in the field. I rise early for my work and he for his. As he does not consider his work superior to mine, so I do not regard mine as superior to his. Lest you say that I achieve much and he little, we have learned: 'It does not matter whether one does much or little, provided one does it for the sake of heaven' " (Berakhot 17a). "For the sake of heaven" means in this context "wholeheartedly" and with the right motivation.

Women's Liberation should demand equality of "woman's work" and not its abolition, which is an impossibility. Homemaking and mothering must be raised to the status of a "profession," a *respected* profession with recognized status and with government provisions for economic security, not linked with or contingent upon the social security benefits of the husband. The notion that home-making and child-care is "unskilled" work is a male prejudice which is controverted by *all* psychological schools. Even those who do not agree with the Freudian thesis of the deterministic importance of infancy, acknowledge that this period is of crucial importance for adult adjustment to the demands of life. It is no small matter and it is a great responsibility to be entrusted with the care of the children who are *the future of mankind*.

There is no more "creative" work than guiding children to become *human*. That society celebrates the "creative" artist who makes statues and pictures which are imitations of life, while ignoring the *true* creativeness of women who *grow*, give birth and shape and determine the personality of their children, is a fatal aberration of male-dominated civilization.

Women must be liberated as WOMEN, even as blacks must be liberated as BLACKS and Jews as JEWS. They must be liberated in their selfhood as women and in fulfillment of their femininity—not by assimilation and imitation of men. . . .

Jewish women are especially disadvantaged because Jewish family law is revered as divinely revealed Torah and, thus, beyond change. Indeed, Jewish family law has been reinterpreted by the Sages of the Talmud and their successors. But its basic conviction of woman being the possession of man still prevails in contemporary Jewish legal theory and practice, also in Conservative Judaism. Thus, the late Boaz Cohen, Professor of Codes at the Jewish Theological Seminary of America, told the Joint Law Conference of the Rabbinical Assembly, in 1953: "We cannot engraft upon the tree of Jewish law a foreign branch, such as the principle of granting to women equal rights with the husband to *issue* a divorce." In another context, Cohen explained that, in Jewish law, betrothal and marriage are acts of acquisition with formalities which also "were recognized as valid in the acquisition of slaves and real estate" (*Jewish and Roman Law*, Vol. I, p. 290). Men (and literature) still speak of "possessing" women, although modern codes of law have abrogated this hoary male prerogative legislated also by the ancient Romans. Some wedding customs, however, still preserve the memory of the bride's "acquisition" by one male from another male, to wit, the custom that the father or another relative male "gives the bride away."

In Jewish law, however, the bride does become the legal possession of the husband and, consequently, only he can relinquish the proprietor's right. This means that *only the husband* can issue a divorce decree (*get*). The legal reasoning is that marriage is an act of acquisition (*kinyan*, literally "purchase") and thus the owner of "the possession" cannot be dispossessed by court action. He, and only he, can issue the writ of divorcement.

The wife may petition for divorce but if he refuses to set her free, even after abandoning her for years or decades, she remains bound to him as an *Agunah* (chained woman). She cannot free herself from the marriage, nor can the Rabbinical Court do so. . . .

In Jewish law many types of unfortunate women are classified under the heading *Agunah*. There is the "deserted wife," whose husband spitefully refuses her a divorce; there is the wife whose husband has wilfully or accidentally disappeared and whose fate cannot be ascertained. Medieval and modern Rabbinic literature is filled with expressions of compassion for the plight of the *Agunot*, whose husbands disappeared in pogroms, expulsions and wars, and whose death is presumptive but unwitnessed. Jewish law does not recognize "legal death," that is, the presumption of death after a stated period of absence. For the wife to secure her freedom and the right to remarry, there must be concrete proof of the husband's death—mere legal probability is not acceptable. There are thousands of cases where no such proof can be furnished. The rabbis hold conferences on the problems of these women and weighty tomes have been written on their plight—but they are agreed (and bewail the fact) that nothing can be done about their misfortune. The hapless women are admonished to bear their loneliness with the solace that their fortitude helps to strengthen the fortress of the Torah. . . .

The laws of *yibboom* (levirate marriage) and *halitzah* are utterly insensitive to the dignity and personal rights of women. *Halitzah* is Hebrew for "pulling off." In this context it means pulling off the shoes of the brother-in-law who refuses to fulfill the biblical law commanding that he marry his childless brother's widow so as to beget an heir for the deceased, lest his name be blotted out in Israel. In addition to pulling off his shoes, regarded as an indignity in biblical times, the widow is "to spit in his face, and make this declaration: Thus shall be done to the man who will not build up his brother's house" (Deuteronomy 25:5ff.). That the levir (Latin for brother) may have been married was not an obstacle in biblical and talmudic times when polygamy was permitted. But after Rabbi Gershom of Mayence prohibited polygamy for Ashkenazi Jews, *halitzah* became the rule.

As the *halitzah* procedure requires pulling off the shoes and a token spitting in the face of the brother-in-law—moreover various superstitions are associated with the ceremony—childless widows frequently encounter difficulties in being set free by their brothers-in-law. If they do not succeed in obtaining *halitzah*, they remain *agunot*—chained women. Childless widows, too, are victims of extortion and many have been abandoned to perpetual widowhood by spiteful or superstitious brothers-in-law. . . .

Jewish law is *male*-made and it protects the rights and advantages of men. Under Jewish law, women can neither vote nor be voted for. They are disqualified to serve as witnesses. They are not counted in the prayer quorum of the *minyan* and they are not to participate in the Grace after Meals (*birkat hamazon*) together with men.

According to Jewish law, the wife cannot own property nor is she permitted to engage in business without the husband's consent. Even for giving charity, she must have his permission. As she is his "possession," everything she owns, acquires or earns belongs to him. The sons—not the wife—are the husband's legal heirs. However, the sons are obliged to support their mother from the capital and earnings of their father's estate.

Judaism and Jewish law are "chivalrous." The Bible, the Talmud and Rabbinic literature abound in beautiful tributes to the *esh'et chayil*—the woman of valor who looks well and diligently after her husband and children. Jewish law secures the rights of the wife and Jewish ethics has much to say on how the husband is to honor and cherish her. But "chivalry" is not enough for today's Jewish women! They resent the legal inferiority and disabilities to which Jewish law subjects them. They want *legal equality*, especially with respect to the laws of marriage and divorce. It is intolerable and degrading for a woman to be reduced to the legal status of a "possession," that has no say about how the "owner" is to dispose of her. It is disgraceful that Jewish law leaves women totally and helplessly at the mercy of estranged husbands and spiteful brothers-in-law. It is insufferable and insulting to be "chained" to a man who has discarded the bonds of matrimony and is married and yet refuses to make it possible for his first wife or his deceased brother's childless widow to remarry.

The Orthodox consensus, which is shared by most Conservative rabbis, that legal equality for Jewish women in the context of *Halakha* is not possible is as typically "male" as is the *Halakha* which is declared to be "divine" and therefore not to be "changed." As a matter of fact and record, *Halakha* has never been static. Biblical laws were changed and rescinded by the Rabbis of the Talmud and talmudic laws (this also includes Mishnah laws) were changed and rescinded by the rabbinic successors of the Rabbis of the Talmud. In the context of law, "change" is taboo. The legal mind thinks in terms of "reinterpretation" and "amendment." There are *scores* of reinterpretations and amendments of biblical and talmudic law which are much more radical than would be a *real* and *realistic* "reinterpretation" and "amendment" of Jewish family law giving women equality and freeing them from the "chains" which hold captive so many *agunot*. . . . I am not a militant feminist to the extent where Women's Liberation would be my only concern. But I do "identify" as a woman and "The Unfreedom of Jewish Women" fills me with shame and anger.

153

BELLA ABZUG: NEW YORK CITY
CONGRESSWOMAN
1971–1975

Bella Savitsky Abzug (b. 1920) was the second Jewess to sit in Congress; the first was Florence Prag Kahn. Politically, they had little in common. Mrs. Kahn, who began to serve in 1925, was a conservative Republican; Bella Abzug is a fervent liberal Democrat. When she went to Washington in January 1971 to represent the citizens of her native New York, Congress did not accord her a very warm welcome. She was lonely, for she was a woman, a feminist, a New Yorker, a Jewess, a liberal, and a vigorous opponent of the Vietnam War. There was never any doubt as to where she stood, and her radical views were not calculated to make friends for her. She was often belligerent and abrasive—no doubt egotistic too—unwilling to make deals with her colleagues. But she was a shrewd lawyer, an amazing, buoyant, ebullient personality, a courageous leader. This was no wallflower; Bella had been the president of her class at Hunter College and an editor of the Columbia Law Review; *she was a spunky woman who dared to run for the United States Senate and for mayor of New York City. She had no hesitation in berating President Jimmy Carter because, she said, his administration was insensitive to the needs of America's women.*

The following autobiographical fragment sheds a great deal of light on her relationship to Jews and Judaism. Her identification with her people, their hopes and their problems, is unequivocal.

BELLA ON BELLA

When I was elected to the House in 1970, I was only the second Jewish woman in the history of our nation to serve in Congress. [The first was Florence Kahn, a Republican from California, who filled her husband's Congressional term after he died in 1925 (1924), then was reelected in her own right.] I was lonely at first, an oddity—a woman, a Jew, a New York lawyer, a feminist, a

Nixon opponent from way back, a peace activist who passionately opposed American involvement in Indochina and just as strongly favored aid to democratic Israel. And I was past 50.

In my third term, I no longer feel lonely. The Congress is changing. It is younger, livelier, more independent. There are more women, more Jews, more minorities.

A theory has developed that while women were deliberately excluded from the political process, particularly elective office, Jews excluded *themselves*, preferring the anonymity of behind-the-scenes power to the public vulnerability of office-holding. It isn't true. We now have 21 Jews in the House, compared with 12 last year; three of us are women. But while the number of Jews has almost doubled and now reflects our percentage of the population, women remain scandalously underrepresented—only 19 out of 435 members of the House, none out of 100 in the Senate. [1976]

Sometimes I'm asked when I became a feminist, and I usually answer, "The day I was born." If I was born a rebel, I attribute it to my family heritage. My father, Emanuel Savitzky, fled to the United States from Czarist Russia when the Russo-Japanese War of 1905 broke out [1904–1905]. He hated war. Once he told me how depressed he felt when America entered World War I. While President Wilson was proclaiming his 14-point peace settlement, my father painted his own one-point peace plank outside his butcher shop on Ninth Avenue in Manhattan. He renamed it "The Live and Let Live Meat Market."

My father did not do very well in business: "Live and Let Live" is not exactly a formula for commercial success. An extraordinarily sweet-tempered man, his real love was music. On Friday nights, after the big traditional Sabbath meal, he would sing Yiddish and Russian folk songs for us in his fine tenor. My sister, Helene, would play the piano. I scraped bravely away at the violin. (An interviewer once asked my mother what she thought of my political career. "Oh, I knew Bella would be a success," she said, "because she always did her homework and practiced her violin.")

When my father wasn't singing, his favorite Caruso records

were on the victrola. Our seven-room railroad flat would be filled with the plaintive melody of the "Pearl Fisher's Lament." We weren't rich; but we never lacked for anything essential.

My father and mother, who remembered the East European ghettos, considered themselves incredibly lucky to be living in the South Bronx, now one of the worst urban disaster areas in the country, but then a pleasant, almost rural neighborhood, paradise compared to the unspeakable (then and now) immigrant slums of the Lower East Side.

In my childhood fantasies, God and my grandfather were indistinguishable. Wolf Tanklefsky was my mother's father; three times a day, he went to shul, and, when I wasn't in school, he would take me along. I learned the prayers by heart, and my grandfather delighted in standing me on a table and having me demonstrate to his cronies my precocity in Hebrew. Then I would be sent to sit in the balcony with the women. When I asked why, I was told: "That's the way it is." I couldn't accept that.

We were living in the Kingsbridge section of The Bronx when my father's weak heart gave out, and he was dead at 52. I was almost 13, and every morning before school for the following year, I went to our synagogue to say *Kaddish* for him. In retrospect, I could describe that as one of the early blows for the liberation of Jewish women. But in fact, no one could have stopped me from performing the duty traditionally reserved for a son, from honoring the man who had taught me to love peace, who had educated me in Jewish values.

So it was lucky that no one ever tried.

When I was 12, I joined Hashomer Hatzair [The Young Guard], a Zionist youth organization. From then on, I was an enthusiastic Zionist who dreamed of working in a kibbutz, helping to build a Jewish national home in what was then called Palestine. Dressed in brown uniforms and ties, my friends and I rode the subways and stood in the cold on street corners, collecting pennies for our cause. It was my first venture into political campaigning, and also my first experience as a leader.

I'm not sure whether my leadership was based on ability, or on my friends' awe at what they regarded as my superior economic status. My family was lower middle class. The others in

Hashomer were *really* poor. When they talked about migrating to Israel, they envisioned a land where they would be better off economically. My approach was more romantic. I had never missed a meal or worked really hard; for me, going to [a] kibbutz would be roughing it. I felt drawn to Hashomer Hatzair because of its moral fervor, social idealism and pioneering militancy. Years later, when I read that the Warsaw Ghetto uprising was commanded by a young Hashomer Hatzair leader, I was not surprised. I would not have expected anything else.

Franklin Delano Roosevelt and his New Deal were already shaping my social consciousness when I entered Walton High, an all-girls school rated among the best academic public schools in the city. My mother, always a good manager, supported us by working as a cashier or saleswoman in department stores to augment the insurance my father had left. Helene became a piano teacher; I did *not* become a violin teacher. I worked summers as a sports counselor in camps, and on weekends as a Hebrew teacher at the Kingsbridge Heights Jewish Center. I became friends with our new young rabbi, Israel Miller, who is now Chairman of the Conference of Presidents of Major Jewish Organizations, and still a friend.

When I got to Hunter College, the tuition-free, all-women's division of the City University, the Hitler regime and persecution of the Jews were on the rise. I was also taking courses at the Jewish Theological Seminary. For the students of my generation, the war in Spain, the need for collective action to oppose the threat of Nazism and the persecution of the Jews, were the searing issues of the day. We had demonstrations, marches, campus strikes; we swapped our silk stockings for lisle in protest against the sale of the Sixth Avenue El as scrap iron for Japan. I transferred much of the intensity I had learned in Hashomer Hatzair to the political campaign to save democratic Spain from the Fascists, who were being openly supported by Hitler and Mussolini while our government and the rest of the western democracies remained neutral. I still remember the gloom, the foreboding we felt in 1939 when the Spanish Republican Army finally collapsed and World War II followed within months. I remember our outrage when, the morning after the Japanese bombed Pearl Harbor, we went to school to find our professors calmly discussing the English Romantic poets while President Roosevelt was coming before Congress to get a declaration of war.

My class graduated into an America at war, and for the next few years, all our thoughts and activities were bound up in helping to win that struggle. I worked for a defense contractor for a while, and then enrolled at Columbia Law School. By the time the war ended, I had met and married Martin Abzug, a young businessman who sat up nights working on his novels. Soon we were raising a family and at the same time I was trying to make my way in the legal profession.

Many of my Columbia classmates went into Wall Street firms or government. I specialized in labor law and later opened my own office, handling mostly tenants' rights and civil liberties cases. In the years that followed, I became active in Reform Democratic politics and in the women's movement to halt nuclear testing and the proliferation of nuclear weapons. Finally, I was elected to Congress.

I have moved from Orthodoxy to a Conservative synagogue affiliation; I no longer eat only kosher food; usually I'm in shul only on holidays—and for speaking engagements, which I can never resist because my grandfather would be so proud to see me in a pulpit. I've visited Israel several times, but I'm not going to settle there on [a] kibbutz [a collective settlement]. Yet it was a dream worth every minute of the dreaming, because it made me a Zionist, it made me a political activist, it kept me a rebel.

Sometimes, in Congress, I get pressure from Jewish constituents who take a narrow view of American foreign policy.

A few people asked me to modify my stand against the Vietnam war, to go along with State Department policy in Southeast Asia so as not to jeopardize American support for Israel. Secretary Kissinger tried to play on these fears when, in the final days of the conflict, he raised the same argument in a hopeless attempt to gather support for military aid to the crumbling regime of President Thieu. I always thought it was insulting to link Israel, a unified and courageous democracy, to a corrupt dictatorial regime like Thieu's, and I never accepted this view, nor did most supporters of Israel.

Similarly, during the height of the impeachment crisis, I received some telegrams from Jewish constituents, sternly advising me not to dare say a word against President Nixon for fear it might hurt the U.S. relationship with Israel. Again, I could not accept that. And I was glad to see that the vast majority of America's Jews never allowed their fears for Israel to overwhelm their sense of what was the right behavior for our country on other issues. (I've always wondered how Rabbi Korff felt when he read Nixon's anti-Semitic remarks in the tape transcripts.) [Rabbi Baruch Korff was a devoted friend of Nixon.] How could it possibly help Israel to tie our relationship with her to the fate of a discredited President or to the continuation of a discredited war?

We have to fight for what we believe in, no matter what the pressure against us. As Congressional adviser to our delegation at the International Women's Year Conference in Mexico City last June [1975], I urged our delegates to reject the totally unacceptable statement that Zionism must be eliminated along with colonialism and apartheid. The attack on Israel was not what we women came to Mexico for. We should have been contributing to a global dialogue on the subject of peace; instead, the anti-Israel bloc manipulated the women, utilizing the women's conference for political purposes, and we got the Declaration of Mexico, tainted with the UN anti-Zionist rhetoric that set the stage later for adoption of the outrageous General Assembly resolution. [November 10, 1975, the United Nations General Assembly adopted an Arab-backed resolution that Zionism was "a form of racism and racial discrimination."]

I am proud that the United States delegations voted against both statements. As a member of Congress, I was even prouder when both the House and Senate, in an action of solidarity with Israel and the Jewish people, unanimously voted to condemn the Assembly action and when women members of Congress joined me in an appeal to the Assembly not to approve the Declaration of Mexico.

I have never enjoyed a speaking engagement so much as my appearance before the First National Conference on the Role of Women in Jewish Life, in New York, February, 1973. The organizers felt the time had come to examine Jewish law and custom through the sensitized eyes of feminist consciousness, to adapt Jewish traditions to a contemporary society in which women sought equality with men in all aspects of their lives.

It was all very new at the time—but in the ensuing years, there has been a significant shifting of attitudes, a shake-up in the traditional feminine roles in the Jewish community. "That's the way it is" no longer is an adequate answer.

For me, the new consciousness in the Jewish community and throughout the country was perfectly expressed the day I arranged for Rabbi Sally Priesand to deliver the opening prayer at the House of Representatives.

She was the first Jewish woman to do so.

She was the first *woman* to do so.

At that moment, I felt that two movements for social progress had merged and come of age. And I really felt at home in Washington.

154

THE FEMALE RABBI: WHIMSY OR MALE CHAUVINISM?
1971

Davka, *a magazine representing the thinking of the Jewish New Youth of the early 1970's, was published by the Los Angeles Hillel Council at the University of California, Los Angeles, and subsidized by the Jewish Federation–Council of Greater Los Angeles. It was intended to be provocative, and it was. In 1971, an article appeared under the title "Fruma Buber—Girl Rabbi." The author's obvious object was to hold up to ridicule the very thought of a woman as a rabbi. A brief glossary will be helpful to the uninitiated, who may not understand the many tongue-in-cheek references.*

Fruma: the pious one
Buber: Martin Buber was the spiritual father of "Neo-Hasidism"
Christopher and Mary: Christopher is "Christ-bearing"; Mary, mother of Jesus
Steinem: Gloria Steinem is a well-known feminist
rebbitzin: the rabbi's wife
mandlen: Jewish cookies made with almonds
613: tradition has it that there are 613 affirmative and prohibitive precepts in Judaism
goy: the Hebrew-Yiddish word for Gentile

The homosexual congregation referred to in the text as a witty aside, "Congregation B'nai Gay," is now a reality in that city; a synagogue of homosexuals has been organized. The segregation of men is a reminder that, in Orthodox synagogues, women were not seated with the men.

In all probability, this article was prompted by the fact that Sally Priesand was about to be ordained a rabbi at the Hebrew Union College in Cincinnati. The question that might well be put is: Did this lampoon reflect male chauvinism or was it—what it seems to be—a whimsical exaggeration? The author is a comedian-satirist and an Orthodox Jew.

FRUMA BUBER—GIRL RABBI

by Bob Elias

In keeping with our policy of bringing you the news as it happens, we have procured an exclusive interview with the world's first woman rabbi. I was invited to Rabbi Fruma Buber's house, immediately after she was ordained from the Immaculate Delivery Jewish Theological Seminary (a new conception in modern Jewish thought).

Rabbi Buber lives in a homey apartment overlooking the burgeoning metropolis of Williamsburg. She lives with her husband, who is a stewardess for TWA, her two children, Christopher and Mary, and her pet gelding, Steinem.

Adorning the walls of the apartment were numerous stuffed snakes. Puzzled, I asked the rabbi about the reptiles.

"Oh, those? They're symbolic of women's original conflict with the forces of sin." She smiled, pausing to jab one of the specimens with a letter opener.

Rabbi Buber began by making the introductions.

"Good evening, I'm Fruma Buber, and this is my husband, the rebbitzin."

"Congratulations upon being the first woman to be ordained in the Jewish faith."

"Thank you. This is just one small step for woman, but one giant step for womankind.

"That's quite pithy and original, rabbi. What steps are you going to take to win the respect of your congregation?"

"I'm going to grow a beard," smiled Rabbi Buber, "nothing commands respect more than a traditional, rabbinic beard."

"And what if that fails?"

"I can always get a job with Barnum and Bailey. . ."

At this point in the interview, Hank, the rebbitzin, brought in some fresh baked mandlen, honeycake and tea. "Eat, eat," his baritone sounded sonorously. "I just baked these." He winked seductively and loped out of the room.

"The congregation loves Hank," said the rabbi, smoothing the pleats on her black midirobes. "He's an excellent cook and a charming host."

"What difficulties do you anticipate in your new post as spitirual leader?"

"I haven't been able to buy any really right outfits. This black affair from Bonwit Teller is just perfect for Shabbat, and I have something in voile in mind for the High Holy days, but besides that, I haven't found anything to really say *me*. Hank did crochet me a darling little halter with six hundred and thirteen sequins and the words Rabbi Buber emblazoned across each breast, but, in general, it's so infuriating!"

"During your officiating at Jewish ceremonies have you come across anything unusual?"

"Yes. When I perform marriages, I'm the only rabbi to cry at the ceremony."

"You've opened up a door, a virtual cornucopia of opportunities. What do you see in the way of future trends in modern Judaism?"

"Well, at the seminary, they're already preparing to ordain homosexuals. The first candidate is Lance Klein. He's slated to take over a new congregation on Hollywood and Gower, B'nai Gay. It's very orthodox. The men sit in the women's section."

"Who sits in the men's section."

"Transvestites."

"You mean transvestites are also active in Judaism?"

"Certainly. They make up most of the active members of B'nai Gay's sisterhood."

"Are there any other innovations that you might be able to enlighten us about?"

"Yes, as a matter of fact. The seminary plans to ordain a gentile, next week. They anticipate problems, so they've hired an ad firm to sell the idea. They've come upwith two slogans, so far, 'You don't have to be Jewish to be Jewish' and 'Employ a Goy'."

"Well, rabbi, what aspect of Judaism do you consider the most significant?"

"Definitely the circumcision ceremony. I plan to circumcize women in my congregation."

"You can't circumcize women! It's biologically impossible!"

"You can't kill a girl for trying," sighed Rabbi Buber.

"Thank you, rabbi, for the interview."

"Thank you. I've got to be going now to see about Hank. He's six months pregnant."

39. Sally Priesand

Courtesy, Garrett Cope, Jackson, Michigan

155

RABBI SALLY: THE FIRST WOMAN RABBI
1972–1975

On June 3, 1972, Sally J. Priesand was ordained a rabbi in the historic Isaac M. Wise (Plum Street) Temple in Cincinnati and shortly thereafter began her work as assistant rabbi of New York City's Stephen S. Wise Free Synagogue. Asked once why she wanted to be a rabbi, she answered:

I believe basically in four things: in God, in the worth of the individual, in Judaism as a way of life, and that Judaism is worth preserving for the future. Being a rabbi, in my opinion, is the best way I can perpetuate these beliefs.

Did she have any trouble securing the right to be ordained? Apparently none whatsoever. The decades that followed World War II with their egalitarian permissiveness smoothed the path for her. In the 1950's—and even earlier, in 1922–23—many Reform rabbis and the Faculty of the Hebrew Union College had already gone on record favoring ordination for women. The Board of the College—who possessed the ultimate authority—had expressed their unwillingness in 1923 to grant a rabbinical diploma to a woman.

The College Board's cavil notwithstanding, the Reform movement had always insisted—at least in theory—on equal religious rights for women. The very month Isaac M. Wise opened the Hebrew Union College, he declared quite unequivocally that he was ready and eager to train and ordain women for the rabbinate. And before Wise? For centuries, Orthodoxy, following its sacrosanct traditions, considered the ordination of women unthinkable, although it was fully aware that there were individual women learned in the Law and that on occasion women had even rendered judicial decisions, a prerogative generally reserved to learned men alone.

The following statement on women rabbis was issued as a news release by the American Jewish Archives in February 1972, before Sally Priesand was ordained (A). Document B, the rabbi's own chronicle of her student days, includes a brief description of her goals as a Jewish woman and as a leader of her people.

A

1972

On Saturday, June 3, 1972, the first woman rabbi will be ordained by a theological school, on the Cincinnati campus of the Hebrew Union College–Jewish Institute of Religion. On that date, Sally J. Priesand, now serving as Student-Rabbi at the Isaac M. Wise Temple in Cincinnati, will be ordained by President Alfred Gottschalk. Is "Rabbi Sally" the first woman ever to study for the rabbinate? When graduated, will she be the first ordained woman rabbi in the United States? In the world? As every historian knows, it is dangerous to postulate "firsts." There is no "first" Jew anywhere; there has always been one before. Is this true of Rabbi Sally?

The Isaac M. Wise Temple is named after the nineteenth-century rabbi who created the basic institutions of American Liberal Judaism. Wise died over seventy years ago. Were he to return to Cincinnati on June 3rd, would he be shocked? Not in the least, for within weeks after he opened his college in October, 1875, he welcomed a young girl as a student. She was eleven years of age and was in the seventh grade of public school. She should have been playing with jacks instead of juggling Hebrew verbs. There has never been a decade at this school in which there has not been at least one woman student. Some of them stayed on long enough to earn a Bachelor of Hebrew Letters degree, but they rarely went farther. Often a girl student ended up feeling sorry enough for a boy student to put him out of his misery by marrying him.

Sally is different. She means business—rabbinical business. She is determined to be a rabbi, and by the grace of God and the faculty she will be ordained. She is attractive, but at this juncture she seems not to be interested in marriage. . . .

Will Sally set a precedent for other women? She already has. The New York School of the College-Institute has two female candidates for the rabbinate and two for the cantorate. This is a radical innovation for Jews—though not for Christians. The first female Protestant clergyman finished her theological studies at Oberlin in 1850, but she was not licensed by a Congregational Church till 1853. Her name was Antoinette Louisa Brown Blackwell. Four years earlier, her sister-in-law to be, Elizabeth Blackwell, had become the first American woman to graduate from a medical school and to receive the degree of Doctor of Medicine.

We still have to answer the question: Will Sally be the first female ordained rabbi in America? In the world? In America, yes; in the world, no. Regina Jonas finished her theological studies at the Berlin Academy for the Science of Judaism in the middle 1930's. Her thesis subject was: *Can a Woman Become a Rabbi?* Of course she set out to prove the affirmative. The faculty accepted her dissertation, but the professor of Talmud, the licensing authority, refused to ordain her. The Rev. Dr. Max Dienemann, of Offenbach, however, did ordain her, and she practiced till 1940, primarily in homes for the aged. The Germans then dispatched her to the Theresienstadt Concentration Camp where she either died of natural causes or was sent to the gas chambers.

Will Rabbi Sally get a job, and will she be successful? There is not the slightest doubt that there will be no trouble in placing her. She is competent and unpretentious, a good speaker and a fine human being. The congregation will admire and respect her; the children will love her.

It is sad to think that American Jewry has had to wait so long for a woman to be ordained a rabbi. The American Republic began with a political, if not a social, revolution. The impact of that revolution throughout the world was tremendous. The generation of 1776 knew that it was ushering in a new world. Look at the back of the dollar bill, at the Latin phrase under the pyramid: "The new order of the ages." Some seventy-five years later there was a religious "breakthrough": the Protestants ordained a woman. Now, a hundred and nineteen years later, the Reform Jews are about to see Sally Priesand ordained a rabbi. Galileo was right: the earth *does* move—but sometimes it moves very, very slowly.

B

1975

PREFACE

On June 3, 1972 I was ordained rabbi by Hebrew Union College–Jewish Institute of Religion in Cincinnati, Ohio. As I sat in the historic Plum Street Temple, waiting to accept the ancient rite of *s'micha* (ordination), I couldn't help but reflect on the implications of what was about to happen. For thousands of years women in Judaism had been second-class citizens. They were not permitted to own property. They could not serve as witnesses. They did not have the right to initiate divorce proceedings. They were not counted in the *minyan* [quorum]. Even in Reform Judaism, they were not permitted to participate fully in the life of the synagogue. With my ordination all that was going to change; one more barrier was about to be broken.

When I entered HUC-JIR, I did not think very much about being a pioneer. I knew only that I wanted to be a rabbi. With the encouragement and support of my parents, I was ready to spend eight years of my life studying for a profession that no woman had yet entered. My decision was an affirmation of my belief in God, in the worth of each individual, and in Judaism as a way of life. It was a tangible action declaring my commitment to the preservation and renewal of our tradition.

As one would expect, there were problems even as I worked toward ordination. Though Reform Judaism had long before declared an official religious equality between men and women, Reform Jews still believed that a woman's place was in the home. They no longer insisted that men and women sit separately during worship services. They allowed women to be counted in the *minyan* to conduct the service, to serve as witnesses in ritual matters. They demanded that girls receive a religious education equivalent to that provided for boys. They allowed women to become members of the congregation with the privilege of voting and they even permitted them to be elected to offices on synagogue boards. But they were not yet ready for the spiritual leadership of a woman.

Undoubtedly, many believed that I was studying at HUC-JIR to become a *rebbetzin* rather than a rabbi, to marry rather than to officiate. Four years passed (while I concentrated on my studies at the University of Cincinnati) before people began to realize that I was serious about entering the rabbinate. During that time, I felt that I had to do better than my classmates so that my academic ability would not be questioned. Professors were fair, but occasionally I sensed that some of them would not be overly upset if I failed. And when, in my fifth year, I was ready to serve my first congregation as student rabbi, some congregations refused to accept my services. Still the members of Sinai Temple in Champaign, Illinois, received me warmly.

My sixth year of study brought the beginning of a tremendous amount of publicity. When you are a "first," you are expected to be an expert in everything. Personal appearances, interviews, statements on contemporary issues—all are expected. Surprisingly enough, though I have always considered myself an introvert, I somehow managed to cope with these new pressures. It helped to know that by this time I had the support, or at least the respect, of most of the members of the college community. Dr. Nelson Glueck, the late president of HUC-JIR, was a particular source of strength. His courage in accepting me as a rabbinic student made possible my eventual ordination.

As my eighth and final year drew to a close, I was faced with finding a job. Some congregations refused to interview me. I was disappointed and somewhat discouraged by these refusals. But since I had not expected everyone to welcome me with open arms, I had prepared myself for this possibility. I knew that I needed only one acceptance and I never really doubted that I would find one synagogue ready to accept me.

The offer of a position as assistant rabbi at the Stephen Wise Free Synagogue in New York City was a blessing in the true sense of the word. I have been extremely well-received by the members of the congregation, and it has been my privilege to work with and to learn from Rabbi Edward E. Klein, the senior rabbi. My activities have not been limited to one area of the Synagogue. My duties include conducting worship services, preaching on Shabbat, teaching both in the Adult Institute and in the Religious School, supervising the youth program, advising a biweekly study group, lecturing to the Golden Age Club, counseling, officiating at life-cycle events, and attending all committee meetings. The only area in which people have shown any real hesitancy has been that of my officiating at funerals.

In addition to my congregational responsibilities, I have lectured extensively throughout the country—an activity which has shown me that congregations and rabbis are ready for change. Ten years ago, women were much more opposed to the idea of a woman rabbi than were men. Since then, however, the feminist movement has made a tremendous contribution in terms of consciousness-raising, and women now demand complete and full participation in synagogue life. This is a significant development because changes will not be made until we change the attitudes of people.

Men and women must learn to overcome their own psychological and emotional objections and regard every human being as a real person with talents and skills and with the option of fulfilling his or her creative potential in any way he or she finds meaningful. Women can aid this process—not by arguing but by doing and becoming, for accomplishments bring respect and respect leads to acceptance. Women must now take the initiative. They should seek and willingly accept new positions of authority in synagogue life.

It is still too soon to assess the impact of my ordination, but I would hope that it would at least mark a transition in our congregations, that sole involvement on the part of women in the synagogue kitchen and the classroom should move toward complete and full participation on the pulpit and in the boardroom as well.

When I accepted ordination on June 3, 1972, I affirmed my belief in Judaism and publicly committed myself to the survival of Jewish tradition. I did so knowing that Judaism had traditionally discriminated against women; that it had not always been sensitive to the problems of total equality. I know that there has been a tremendous flexibility in our tradition—it enabled our survival. Therefore, I chose to work for change through constructive criticism. The principles and ideals for which our ancestors have lived and died are much too important to be cast aside. Instead we must accept the responsibilities of the covenant upon ourselves, learn as much as possible of our heritage, and make the necessary changes which will grant women total equality within the Jewish community.

156

JEWISH WOMEN CALL FOR A CHANGE
1972

Ever since the second decade of the twentieth century, the Conservative Movement has accorded its women a degree of recognition in its administrative structure. By the 1950's, some Conservative congregations permitted women to mount the rostrum and participate in the reading of Scripture. Eventually, the demands of the New Left pushed Conservatives into the parameters of liberalism. By that time—the late 1960's—a generation of "new" young Jewish women made their appearance. They were observant, religious, devoted, Jewishly knowledgeable, secularly cultured—and feminists.

It was as feminists that they made their demands. In 1971, they organized themselves into Ezrat Nashim, "Help (or "Support") for Women." In March 1972, they appeared at a Conservative rabbis' convention, the Rabbinical Assembly, and presented the following document, entitled "Jewish Women Call for Change." They wanted nothing less than religious equality with men. They did, however, stop short of demanding the ordination of women as Conservative rabbis. Ultimately, their appeal was met with sympathy by most agencies in the Conservative Movement.

Inasmuch as many of the words and phrases they employ are technical, a glossary is subjoined:

nerot: *lights; lighting candles on Sabbath Eve*
challah: *loaf; burning of a piece of dough, once a portion reserved for the priest*
taharat ha mishpachah: *"family purity," ritual bathing after menstruation*
LTF: *Leaders Training Fellowship*
USY: *United Synagogue Youth*
Seminary: *Jewish Theological Seminary*
eshet hayil: *the "woman of virtue" in Proverbs 31:10*
minyan: *a quorum of ten required for Jewish prayer*
Bruria: *the learned, heroic wife of the second century rabbi, Meir*

Dvorah: Deborah, the biblical *"Judge"*
aliyot: *call to ascend and "read" the Torah*
baalot keriah: *female, skilled Torah readers*
shelihot zibbur: *female leaders in communal prayer*
mitzvot: *meritorious deeds; divine commandments*

March 1972

JEWISH WOMEN CALL FOR CHANGE

The Jewish tradition regarding women, once far ahead of other cultures, has now fallen disgracefully behind in failing to come to terms with developments of the past century.

Accepting the age-old concept of role differentiation on the basis of sex, Judaism saw woman's role as that of wife, mother, and home-maker. Her ritual obligations were domestic and familial: *nerot, challah,* and *taharat ha-mishpachah.* Although the woman was extolled for her domestic achievements, and respected as the foundation of the Jewish family, she was never permitted an active role in the synagogue, court, or house of study. These limitations on the life-patterns open to women, appropriate or even progressive for the rabbinic and medieval periods, are entirely unacceptable to us today.

The social position and self-image of women have changed radically in recent years. It is now universally accepted that women are equal to men in intellectual capacity, leadership ability and spiritual depth. The Conservative movement has tacitly acknowledged this fact by demanding that their female children be educated alongside the males—up to the level of rabbinical school. To educate women and deny them the opportunity to act from this knowledge is an affront to their intelligence, talents and integrity.

As products of Conservative congregations, religious schools, the Ramah Camps, LTF, USY, and the Seminary, we feel this tension acutely. We are deeply committed to Judaism, but cannot find adequate expression for our total needs and concerns in existing women's social and charitable organizations, such as

Sisterhood, Hadassah, etc. Furthermore, the single woman—a new reality in Jewish life—is almost totally excluded from the organized Jewish community, which views women solely as daughters, wives, and mothers. The educational institutions of the Conservative movement have helped women recognize their intellectual, social and spiritual potential. If the movement then denies women opportunities to demonstrate these capacities as adults, it will force them to turn from the synagogue, and to find fulfillment elsewhere.

It is not enough to say that Judaism views women as separate but equal, nor to point to Judaism's past superiority over other cultures in its treatment of women. We've had enough of apologetics: enough of Bruria, Dvorah, and Esther; enough of *eshet hayil.*

It is time that:

women be granted membership in synagogues
women be counted in the minyan
women be allowed full participation in religious observ-
    ances—*aliyot, baalot keriah, shelihot zibbur*
women be recognized as witnesses before Jewish law
women be allowed to initiate divorce
women be permitted and encouraged to attend Rabbinical and
    Cantorial schools, and to perform Rabbinical and Cantorial
    functions in synagogues
women be encouraged to join decision-making bodies, and to
    assume professional leadership roles, in synagogues and in
    the general Jewish community
women be considered as bound to fulfill all *mitzvot* equally with
    men.

For three thousand years, one-half the Jewish people have been excluded from full participation in Jewish communal life. We call for an end to the second-class status of women in Jewish life.

EZRAT NASHIM

157

THE WOMAN WHO FOUND FULFILLMENT IN ORTHODOXY
1972

"Leah Cohen"—a pseudonym—is a girl from a nonobservant home. Invited to spend a few days with a Lubavitch Hasidic family in Williamsburg, Brooklyn, she came as a sort of sightseer, but ultimately "remained to pray." (The Lubavitch Hasidim are a special group of pietists who emphasize learning.) In the following account, Leah chronicles her rebirth.

A WOMAN REBORN
by "Leah Cohen"

1972

"Crazy, I must be crazy," I thought, "to use my precious few days of winter vacation to spend a 'real *Shabbos*' with 'real *Chasidim*.' " Yet there I was on a bus headed from my hometown for the Lubavitcher community in Brooklyn.

Of course I had all my preconceived notions packed with me in my luggage. I was sure they were facts, culled from reliable sources: the book *The Chosen*, Martin Buber, the play *Fiddler on the Roof.*

How I pitied the women and girls of the Lubavitcher community—*before* I got there. For weren't they doomed to a life built around an "arranged" marriage at an early age, a house full of kids—an endless battle against time, fighting to get the laundry done and the table set before their husbands came home from work? "In their hearts," I thought to myself, "they must envy girls like myself, a liberated modern woman!"

I was rather apprehensive when I arrived at my assigned Lubavitcher "home" for the weekend. What would I say to Sara, my hostess? What could we possibly talk about? How could I help her and educate her in the ways and advantages of the modern world?

SHABBOS WITH A FAMILY

I was given a warm welcome. After I settled down in the guest room set aside for their frequent visitors, I was invited to join in the lighting of the *Shabbos* candles to welcome the Sabbath Queen.

That Friday night, at the special meal and later when we sat around "just talking," I was struck by several factors: the peaceful quality that the burning candles seemed to bring, the delicious, special food, the pleasant conversation. Above all, this group of people was so clearly, so contentedly, a real family. I had rarely seen families, whole and functioning, before. At our house, my family never did anything together, and certainly not on Saturdays. No one was home then, all busy with private errands and such. There at the G's, though, it certainly seemed that everybody's life centered on home and family, even Mr. G's.

Throughout that first *Shabbos* two years ago, I kept observing and making mental notes. I talked to Mr. G. and to Mrs. G., to their teen-age daughter, to her friends. I think I asked a million questions.

DATING AMONG YOUNG

Many of them were about marriage and dating. The girls as well as the boys of that community are genuinely involved in learning Torah and related subjects and other time- and mind-consuming activities. Girls and women are not regarded as sex objects, and there is no dating until the time both boy and girl are sincerely interested in finding a lifelong partner. Both boys and girls are aware that marriage is a serious business and, when ready, they are introduced to likely partners by family, friends, teachers, etc., in the community. Their dating is serious, marked by earnest discussion of things like goals in life, values, ideology, Judaism.

Otherwise, there is minimal social contact between boys and girls and I, the liberated woman so to speak, found this setup very effective. Our superficial status symbol, the fun date—movies, skating, bowling—seemed silly and empty in contrast. And the girls here seemed so free of the pressures I had taken for granted: which boy likes me, who will escort me to the prom, etc. Marriage was far from my mind, so why really waste so much time on meaningless social interaction, I began to wonder. When I really thought about it, it seemed to me that the social activity I had always known—activity supposed to lead to poise, maturity, and knowledge of the opposite sex in preparation for successful marriage—did not work as advertised, at least among most of the couples I knew.

Here marriages last. Divorces or separations are really rare phenomena, which seems to indicate that something is right somewhere.

ROLE OF WOMEN

We also talked a lot about the role of the woman and the girl, which was uppermost in my mind at that time. The G's daughter pointed out that a woman clamors for liberation from household drudgery, for a career, and for equal rights only if she feels enslaved. In her community, on the other hand, the home, the family unit, is the single most important entity in everyone's life. This holds true even for the men, the more outstanding of whom may feel rather enslaved by their jobs and business activity which leave them too little time for the more rewarding pursuit of Torah scholarship and personal spiritual growth. And to the women who have careers—and there are many—home always precedes the job in importance. For it is in the home that the Torah and its precepts are practiced, its values reflected; the home surpasses the synagogue by far as the central focus of the community.

Consequently, the person entrusted with running the home and raising the children in their beloved tradition is highly respected. Women here know they are important, needed; their contribution basic and its value primary.

In the course of that *Shabbos*, something else became very clear to me. The people were very aware, very knowledgeable about everything going on in the world. Their indifference to Women's Lib, for example, stemmed from lack of interest in and identification with the plight of the enslaved housewife rather than from any kind of ignorance. The girls answered all my questions intelligently and well. How muddled was the picture I had harbored of the naive, old-fashioned, sheltered *Chasid!* I found these chasidic women, in a unique way, to be part of the 20th century, yet simultaneously part of the age-old world of Torah.

Everyone, and especially the girls and women, seemed involved in the community project *"Kiruv halevovos"* ["bringing hearts together"], which was explained as "bringing other Jews closer to G-d and the Torah." People like myself are frequent guests, and community members visit various universities and organizations for the purpose of spreading "true Judaism."

So there was something to this different society, after all. I thought about it for a long time after returning home. The contrast between my world and theirs seemed infinite. My dissatisfaction with my "good life" kept growing, and the inevitable happened.

EDUCATION FOR WOMEN

Now, it's two years later. I attend the Lubavitcher Beth Rivka Mechina [preparatory class]—a section of the movement's girls' high school and seminary program tailored for the many girls like myself with a very limited background in Jewish studies. It is located in Brooklyn.

The school curriculum is tough. The post-high school seminary program includes: Bible, Prophets, code of Jewish laws, *Chasidus* [the esoteric part of the Torah—the formal philosophy of their movement], Hebrew literature and grammar, philosophy, psychology, methodology of teaching, history, ethics, and more. The girls have a positive attitude towards learning, which continues after marriage. There are formal classes for married women every week in subjects such as *Chasidus* and Jewish law.

Yet there is more involved than just hard work. Interesting activities for leisure time are arranged by *B'nos Chabad* [Lubavitch Hasidic girls], an organization run by teenagers. Besides monthly *Melave Malkas* (festive meals honoring the departing Sabbath

Queen) and the usual clubs, the girls go on a trip every winter to another state for a convention sponsored by the Lubavitcher women's organization. Last year the trip was to Cleveland and we were greatly excited by the prospect. We enjoyed meeting people and having fun as a group but, of course, the best time was that which we spent together on the bus. We sang to the rhythm of guitars, and it was a lively night's riding. Despite the many serious talks and speeches, we girls had plenty of time to display our talents in a dramatic presentation. All in all, the seventy of us Lubavitcher teenagers from New York—dancing and singing with all our might—left a lasting impact—we hope!—on the Jewish community of Cleveland.

In addition to these special events, we have meetings for the sake of "the purpose"; nonreligious Jewish youths are invited to attend these events every weekend during which we have discussions, hospitality, entertainment.

I now live in an apartment with two other girls from irreligious Jewish backgrounds who have made the same choice as I have. Every *Shabbos* I continue to enjoy the hospitality of the G home. I've gained a whole new perspective into the role of marriage and women and life. Actually, I've gained a whole new perspective on life and am much happier now than I used to be.

How can I put it? Becoming a Lubavitcher was the best thing that happened in my life. Not everyone gets a chance to be reborn while still alive!

158

AN APPEAL TO ADMIT WOMEN INTO THE
HIERARCHY OF DECISION-MAKERS
1972

In 1972, Jacqueline K. Levine was president of the Women's Division of the American Jewish Congress and a vice-president of the Council of Jewish Federations and Welfare Funds. That year she addressed the General Assembly of the Council. In her talk, reprinted in part below, she pointed out that women were not accorded equality in the governing communal structure, and she appealed to the Council, the country's most influential Jewish organization, to permit women to exercise the role of decision-makers equally with men. It was her contention that Jewesses engaged in communal work had earned this right by virtue of their intelligence, their competence, and their achievements.

THE CHANGING ROLE OF WOMEN IN THE JEWISH COMMUNITY
by Jacqueline K. Levine

One certainly could have predicted that we would arrive at this point in time, and that Jewish life, far from being exempt from question of its attitudes towards women, would be forced to focus on them. For one thing, everyone is questioning his identity. We in the Jewish community have had probably the longest tradition of self-questioning, one which harks back over the millennia. Today our literature and philosophy are replete with new attempts to identify "who is a Jew" and "what is a Jew." Now we superimpose upon this general search for identity and its Jewish aspects the remarkable re-burgeoning of the Women's Movement from the mid-nineteen-sixties on. Women are stating, in clear and resounding cadences, that they will no longer be second-class citizens. And the result of all of these varying confluences is our discussion today. Certainly the Jewish community, so long in the vanguard of social change, must now come to grips with this issue. . . .

It is undeniable that Judaism, millennially old, contains within its tradition many practices which are incompatible with its own prophetic mandate for equality. Historically and traditionally women are not counted, cannot actively participate in religious services, and must even have their husbands' permission to give charity. If nothing else, this is an excellent example of the objectionable concept—I hope rejected—of separate but equal. The equality presumably resides in women's pre-eminent role in the home and in child-rearing. Today, however, any imposed definition of what is a male's role and what is a female's is becoming inappropriate. Men and women alike are now seeking to uncover and express their common humanity and their individual uniqueness as human beings.

At this point I believe that the results of the Council's [Council of Federations] survey will be extremely instructive. Thirty cities have thus far responded to the questionnaires which were distributed among 40,000 and over cities, 10 to 40,000 and under 10,000 population. We asked, among other things, for data on the numbers of women holding committee positions on Federation agency Boards, and of women holding Federation officerships, both in 1965 and now in 1972. Three of the top ten cities reported that 12.9% of the combined total of the Board of Directors were women in 1972, compared with 11.4% in 1965. In the middle population group, the respective women serving were 14.8% in 1972, 12.5% in 1965, and in the smaller communities 21.8% in 1972 and 16.5% in 1965. In all cases, interestingly enough, the actual number of women increased by 50% over the seven-year span.

The number of women serving on all Federation committees as well as serving as officers, showed a somewhat greater increase. In 1972 the large cities reported that 16.2% were women; with the intermediate cities at 22.1%, and the small cities at 28.4%. In 1965 the percentages were only 10.2%, 20.3%, and 19.5% respectively for women serving on any and all Federation committees. In all three categories, we do see a considerable percentage increase from 1965 to 1972 but obviously when the base used is so low, this kind of increase loses any real significance. . . .

In severely limiting the numbers of women who participate

actively on our Federation Boards, on local community institution boards or on any Jewish communal boards, in decision-making roles, the Jewish community is severely limiting the fullness and richness of its response to these overwhelming demands of concern for our fellow man. American Jewry prides itself, as well it should, on its sense of community. And yet a major voice in the Jewish apparatus, though it is being heard, comes through oh-so-faintly, although women in their own organizations have refused to be confined to previously defined boundaries. Community means totality. Federations have striven to reflect diverse interests knowing how important it is to hear the beat of that different drummer. We are all deprived when we do not all participate. Certainly our focus becomes distorted, and sometimes even warped when we do not give heed to all of our parts, to the gestalt. In many instances a most important part of the whole has been denied access to the highest levels of decision and policy making. Of course, I mean women. . . .

There is a very important reason, not often adduced, for utilizing women at top leadership levels, a reason which I want to be very careful in expressing. Were I to say that women are more compassionate or more sensitive or more caring than men, I would be told that I was engaging in sexist rhetoric and so would I be. However, it is a demonstrable fact that women in Jewish voluntary life are far more involved, on a daily basis, with the broader community than are men.

Women's communal activism has become so overwhelming that a woman luncheon speaker recently proposed that, rather than calling ourselves professional volunteers, we women might more appropriately be referred to as volunteer professionals. I assent to this suggestion. For, volunteer professionals that we are, we perform a dizzying catalogue of assignments without pay; and, to judge by the number of social experiments which have derived from women's voluntary organizations, most productively. Progressive child education programs, Head Start, the provision of sheltered workshops for handicapped workers, recreation for the aged; *all* were begun by women. Should not the Jewish women volunteers give their expertise and understanding where most needed? At the top. We wish to share, not glory, but responsibility. We wish to offer the independence of our thinking.

I offer to you another, and I believe, completely pragmatic reason for utilizing Jewish women at major levels of responsibility. We may otherwise, and many of us already are, resort to taking second-class jobs elsewhere. When someone has worked hard and successfully in a Welfare Fund campaign, on a Y board, or in Women's Leadership Development and yet is locked out at the level where her decision may mean something, namely, as it is put, "with the men," why should she not seek a role where her contributions will be appreciated? . . . .

Before going any farther, I must put to rest an obvious problem which may be troubling many of you: the overriding concern which all Federations have, and rightly must have, for their leaders' financial contributions to a campaign and concomitantly, as one executive director phrased it, their own "spheres of business influence." Of course, it is not only important, it is essential that contributing potential and actuality be prime criteria for the appointment of some Board members. But when this is an exclusive, or overriding consideration for the appointment of every Board member, the balance of the community is lost. Yes, there must always be members who are large contributors. There must also be Board members who are involved, who are activists, who are committed community leaders able to inspire others. Women may be any and all of these—big givers, activists, committed community leaders. Women are often married to men who are potential contributors but who need the catalyzing effect of their wives' involvement to convert their potential into actuality. And, until women are able to gain an equal economic footing with men, or able to be equivalent wage-earners, their appointment to Boards will have to take place for all of the other reasons I have offered. . . .

May I offer to you, then, a program for action which will, I hope, be undertaken by individual Welfare Federations. I am sure that it is understood that I am in no way suggesting that we now abandon [separate] Women's Divisions. If, however, you have agreed with my thesis that change is necessary for at least some, if not all, of the reasons I have offered, then we must be prepared for action within our total structure.

First, a Federation, utilizing either its own Executive Committee augmented, of course, with women, or using an entirely new appointed committee should ascertain the facts. A questionnaire is as good a starting tool as any in discovering what's what, and who is who on boards in leadership positions and in all community roles.

Second, there must be honest ventilation and understanding of individual personal attitudes. How do I feel about myself, as man or as woman? How do I feel about working with men, and with women? Will I be uncomfortable if there is a change?

Third, if agreement has been reached, as a result of analysis of both facts and attitudes, that the numbers of women in the community structure must be elevated, this goal must be approached through affirmative action on many levels:

    (a) on nominating committees themselves

    (b) on local agency boards

    (c) in the campaign structure

    (d) in all other community and committee positions

And finally, and of course, this must be only the beginning of a continuing and constant vigilance and concern. For if we stop before we have really begun it will be worse than not beginning at all. And we will all be the losers—men, women, community.

Seven years ago last March I participated in the glorious March from Selma to Montgomery, a march undertaken for the purpose of securing voting rights for all Americans. I stood, one balmy Alabama night, under a starry Alabama sky, and I heard the never-to-be forgotten voice of Martin Luther King ring out in his never-to-be heard again prophetic cadences as he said, "We are all witnesses together." He did not mean witness as onlooker, witness as voyeur. He meant witness—participant. And so are we women, when we ask to share in communal responsibility, asking to be witnesses, participants, in our own Jewish community. We are asking that there be developed a real community. We are asking that our talents of maintaining Jewish life through the centuries—of caring for our children, of developing a volunteer cadre capable of remarkable achievement, of welding realism with compassion, of developing an understanding of the real priorities a society should have—not be set aside any longer on the grounds of a prefabricated sexual role difference. We are asking, in short, to be treated only as human beings, so that we may be witness to and participants in the exciting challenge of creating a new and open and total Jewish community.

159

A CULTURED CONSERVATIVE JEWESS SEEKS EMANCIPATION
1972

Paula Hyman, a Conservative Jewess, wants to remain well within the ambit of a traditional Judaism that will grant complete equality to women. In some areas of Jewish law, such as court testimony, divorce rights, and the like, women are Jewishly second-class citizens. This she deeply resents; she is a full-fledged feminist. In 1972, when she wrote the following critique on the status of the Jewish woman in tradition, she asked that they be counted in a religious quorum, that they be called up to the altar for the reading of the Torah, and that they be certified as cantors and ordained as rabbis. In short, she insisted, women had to be accepted as first-class citizens and as legal entities in all areas. Undoubtedly, the impending ordination of a woman at the Hebrew Union College in 1972 moved cultured Conservative Jewesses to demand changes in their own denomination.

In the same decade of the 1970's, Dr. Hyman, who had taught at the Teachers' Institute of the Jewish Theological Seminary, was appointed to the staff of Columbia University, where she now teaches modern Jewish history (1979).

The Other Half: Women in the Jewish Tradition
by Paula E. Hyman

It has become fashionable in certain circles to label the more outspoken, and most often young, critics of Jewish life as self-haters. When those critics are also women, and their critique a feminist one, they can be written off as doubly self-hating, both as women and as Jews. This approach, however, has led to wasted opportunities. The first feminist articles published, some of them admittedly shrill and polemical, called forth from the educated, articulate, and (not unexpectedly) male leadership of American Jewry a stream of apologetic writing in defense of the faith. Instead of being considered a provocative challenge and an opportunity for examination of the tradition in a new light, the feminist critique of Judaism has evoked responses which distort the role of women in Judaism as radically as the sharpest feminist attack. What is most striking, though, is their insensitivity to the basic premise of feminist analysis.

Jewish feminists have not rejected Judaism; we are struggling with it in our desire to find a way to fulfill ourselves as Jews and as women. Had we rejected Judaism, we would hardly be spending so much of our time living, studying, discussing and thinking about it. . . .

It is spurious to argue . . . that for the Jewish woman who truly wanted it, success in the man's world was a real possibility. The processes of socialization being what they are, and the socio-economic conditions under which Jews have lived until the most recent times what they were, it is unlikely that large numbers of Jewish women longed for an equitable place in male society. Our expectations and desires alike are shaped by our vision of the possible, and until modern times equality of men and women within Judaism would not have been encompassed by that vision. Yet, even if the vast majority of Jewish women throughout history have been satisfied with their role, this alters neither the objective position of women in Judaism nor our modern percep-tion of that position as one of second-class status.

According to the apologists, however, within the Jewish tradition women enjoyed a position of respect and honor. The virtuous woman was extolled: for her the *Eshet Hayil* was recited every Sabbath evening [Prov. 31:10–31: the Virtuous Woman panegyric]. Within her sphere, the home, the Jewish woman was placed on a pedestal. Her role was different from the Jewish male's but no less regarded. In fact, however, separate but equal, in this as in other areas, remains an ideal most difficult to realize. Generally it has resulted in the dominant group's defining both the separateness and the equality of the second group, and justifying that separateness by projecting upon the group being defined a radical otherness. What this has meant in male-female relations is that the qualities of femininity have been defined by male culture in polar opposition to masculine traits. And uniquely female biological characteristics, in particular menstruation and child-bearing, have been perceived by men as both frightening and awesome, in no small measure because they are alien to male experience.

SPIRITUAL INEQUALITY

Within Judaism these attitudes have not precluded treating women with a full measure of humanity in familial relations, but they have given rise to the most rigid of stereotypes regarding the nature and duties of women. Thus, the Jewish woman, we are told, is responsible for the moral development of the family, being endowed with an exceptional capacity for moral persuasion. At the same time, however, the female in Judaism is regarded as inherently close to the physical, material world, while the Jewish male is immersed in the spiritual. Thus, conveniently, the male-female role division is perceived in the Jewish tradition as a most natural one, based as it is on the fundamental polarity of the male and female characters. The Jewish woman, therefore, is not spiritually deprived by her virtual exclusion from synagogue and study, for her spiritual capacity is inferior to the man's. Better for her to supply his and his children's needs, while he supplied her spiritual wants. A most efficient division of labor! And one which explains the tendency which existed among Eastern European Jewry to relinquish responsibility for the physical support of the family to wives, while the husbands withdrew to the *beit midrash* [the synagogue as a house of learning] to study and acquire spiritual merit for the entire family.

These imposed definitions of male and female, however, seem constraining today, when men and women alike seek to uncover and express both their common humanity and their individual uniqueness. And, within Judaism, they are particularly restrictive for women. It can be argued that there are few halakhic barriers to women taking upon themselves an ever greater role in Jewish religious life. Girls can, and do, study much the same curriculum as boys in institutions of Jewish learning, except for rabbinical schools. There is no halakhic rule barring women from laying *tefillin* [donning phylacteries at prayer]. Yet the psychological effects of tradition and upbringing are difficult to overcome. A woman who has, throughout her life, come in contact with a synagogue whose ritual is reserved for men gets the message: she is not needed there. Quite literally, she does not count. And if she chances or chooses to be there, she must not disturb the proceedings but merely observe them. Even should she begin to feel the first stirrings of discontent, there is no easy way for her to chart her own course. Within the synagogue she has few role models, and mechanisms for change do not lie within her hands. Thus, the most educated and progressive Jewish woman—who knows full well that her mastery of Hebrew and Jewish knowledge exceed that of the vast majority of Jewish men—feels ill-at-ease the first time she has an *aliya* [mounts the rostrum to recite the blessings as the Pentateuch is read]. If the synagogue is to be open to men and women on a basis of equality, then women must take a regular, rather than occasional, part in services as laymen as well as rabbis and cantors, and their participation must ultimately become both normal and normative. Only then will women truly have the freedom to choose, as men do, to participate or not.

LAWS OF FAMILY PURITY

Much has been made of the fact, and rightly so, that the Jewish tradition respects female sexuality and accords the right to sexual fulfillment to male and female alike. While it is well to distinguish the Jewish attitude to sexuality from the negative Christian attitude with which it is often wrongly identified, it is precisely in this area that the second-class status of women within Judaism is highlighted. . . .

According to halakhic prescriptions, the menstruating woman, or *niddah*, is to have no physical contact whatsoever with a man. Like the person suffering from a gonorrheal discharge, she is impure. Contact with her is permitted only after she has been free of her "discharge" for seven days and has undergone ritual purification in a *mikvah* [a ritual bathhouse]. During her period of impurity anything she touches becomes impure. While this state of impurity is a legal rather than a hygienic concept and, according to rabbinic authorities, does not imply that the *niddah* is physically unclean or repugnant, it is not clear that simple Jewish men and women throughout the ages have interpreted the laws of Family Purity in such a disinterested manner. Even the mere fact of legal impurity for two weeks of every month has involved many disabilities for a woman. And the psychological impact of the institution, especially in its strictest interpretation, upon a woman's self-esteem and attitude to her own body would seem to be harmful. . . .

What Jewish [religious] feminists are seeking, then, is not more apologetics but change, based on acknowledgement of the ways in which the Jewish tradition has excluded women from entire spheres of Jewish experience and has considered them intellectually and spiritually inferior to men. Realizing the historical, social, and biological factors which contributed in all generations to Jewish attitudes towards women, we must try to examine the Jewish tradition within its own context and refrain from pointlessly blaming our ancestors for lacking our own insights. But until we all recognize that a problem exists—that the conflict between the objective reality of women's lives, self-concept, and education and their position within Jewish tradition is a most significant one for all of Judaism—we cannot begin to take steps to attain equality for women, both in Jewish law and in Jewish attitudes.

Much of the strength of the Jewish tradition has derived from its flexibility and responsiveness to the successive challenges of the environments in which it has been destined to live. In an age when the alienation of young Jews from Judaism is of major concern to the Jewish community, we can hardly afford to ignore fully one-half of young Jews. Thus, the challenge of feminism, if answered, and not dismissed as the whining of a few misguided malcontents, can only strengthen Judaism.

160

ORGANIZING AMERICAN JEWISH FEMINISTS NATIONALLY
1973–1974

In February 1973, Jewish women gathered in New York City from all parts of the country to create the National Conference on Jewish Women; the following year they met again as the National Conference on Jewish Women and Men. At this second conclave, the Jewish Feminist Organization was established. The prime purpose of all of these meetings was to coordinate the activities of feminists as Jewesses and to achieve complete religious equality between Jewish men and women. It was a good beginning these women made—but for reasons that are not easy to fathom they have accomplished very little.

The National Conference assemblies of 1973 and 1974 are described in the article that follows. It was published in the Pioneer Woman, *the organ of Pioneer Women, the Women's Labor Zionist Organization of America, whose social and educational efforts include programs for Israeli women, youth, and children.*

NATIONAL CONFERENCE ON JEWISH WOMEN AND MEN
A REPORT
by Ethel C. Fenig

By now everyone has heard of the women's liberation movement and is familiar with its major goals, e.g., equal rights for all before the law, equal pay for equal work, men sharing household and child care responsibilities, to mention a few. Jewish women are disproportionately active in this movement as theoreticians, leaders and writers although for many of them, their concept of themselves as Jewish women is marginal at best.

What is not as well known is that paralleling the rise of the general women's movement has been a Jewish women's liberation movement which seeks to improve the status of Jewish women *as Jews* within a Jewish framework—both religious and secular.

Small Jewish women's groups have sprung up around the country to discuss their grievances and suggest remedies. They want changes in *halacha* (Jewish laws) which deny women independent status, such as inability to sue for divorce.

With rights come responsibilities which Jewish women are eager to assume. Religious women have expressed the desire to participate more actively in services. Two years ago a group of Jewish women confronted the Conservative rabbis at their convention, demanding to be counted in a *minyan*. Last year the Conservative rabbis ruled in favor of this. The Reform, who do not follow *halacha*, have always allowed this. Women are also experimenting with all women *minyans* which some Orthodox rabbis feel are permissible.

Already there are three female rabbis and more are on the way.

Women are tired of being confined to the women's auxiliary of such institutions as the synagogue and U.J.A. [United Jewish Appeal to raise money for overseas Jews] and are now demanding opportunities to work in the mainstream of Jewish communal life. At the moment, only a handful of women hold offices in national Jewish organizations that are not specifically for women. They are all dominated by men.

In February of 1973 over 400 Jewish women from the United States and Canada met in New York for the first National Conference on Jewish Women (sponsored by the North American Jewish Students' Network) to coordinate their activities and plan future actions for the rights of Jewish women. These women (and a few men) spent a heady week-end in discussions and small groups listening to reports and lectures on women and Judaism. Inspired by the conference, women in Chicago and Boston have since held regional meetings on Jewish women and in April of this year Network sponsored another national conference [1974].

Last year's conference was for women only, although men could and did attend the lectures. Men felt excluded, complaining about reverse discrimination. In acknowledgment, this year's conference, entitled the National Conference on Jewish Women and Men with the theme of Changing Sex Roles: Implications for the Future of Jewish Life, included men. "Jewish men have an equal stake in the Jewish women's movement and it's time for them to get together discussing their roles and conflicts," explained Leora Fishman, conference coordinator, justifying the controversial decision. About 275 women and 75 men attended the conference, a melange of lectures, panel discussions, workshops and rap groups.

Some women resented the men's presence. "I'm stuck in the house with my baby all week and this is the first chance I've had in a long time to be with women. The men will spoil everything by trying to take over," complained a young Orthodox woman who came without her husband.

The conference organizers aimed for a mix among generations, classes and backgrounds but only partially succeeded. As was to be expected, a majority of those present were from the New York metropolitan region with large contingents from Canada, Boston, Los Angeles and Chicago. Many of the participants were college age or in their 20's and single. There was a sprinkling of older women and about three older men. A few men accompanied their wives; most wives left their husbands at home. Their religious backgrounds varied but leaned towards the traditional.

Indicative of their diversity and openess to change were the three types of services conducted *erev* Shabbat and Shabbat morning. In the traditional but equal service, as implied, women and men participated equally. Needless to say, there was no *mechitza* [partition separating the sexes]. There was a women's traditional service conducted entirely by and for women. Those of an experimental nature attended a mixed creative service where men and women also participated equally, sang songs, looked at filmstrips and gave readings.

To avoid domination by the male minority, women and men ate separately and had separate workshops for the first day of the conference, coming together only for the large panel discussions. The purpose of this was to enable women and men to interact while giving them the opportunity to explore their own needs. Men discussed such topics as the Jewish American prince: fact or fiction (fact, they decided. Interestingly enough, there was no corresponding workshop on the Jewish American princess), male competition and fatherhood. Women discussed their sexuality, raising children, non-sexist Jewish education and changing *halacha* [Jewish laws]. Some of these sessions were useful, many were not, consisting merely of personal experiences that often weren't too helpful in solving broader problems. Since many of these workshops only lasted a couple of hours with little opportunity for continuation, such superficiality was regretfully to be expected.

Should women imitate men or should they develop separate practices associated with being female? This question remains unresolved within the general women's movement. Jewish women in Boston designed their own *tallit* [prayer shawl] rather than wear the men's because "it reminded me of my grandfather," said one of the designers.

It also emerged at a workshop on rituals for girls from birth to puberty. Women feel that the dearth of ceremony at the birth of a girl compared with that of a boy reflects which sex is more favored in Judaism. A naming ceremony followed by a kiddush for the birth of a girl can't compare with the celebrations associated with a *brit* [circumcision], a *pidyaon haben* (redemption of the first born son) or a *sholom zochor* (welcoming a male at a festive meal the first Friday after birth) which some celebrate.

To elevate the status of a girl baby a few women seriously suggested some form of female circumcision, others a *pidyaon habat* [redemption of a daughter]. Still others have substituted a common ceremony to be used following the birth of either a girl or a boy.

Bella Abzug's unexpected appearance caused waves of excitement. "It's she! She's really here!" Formidable as she is, even she has not been immune to discrimination by the male dominated Jewish hierarchy. Sometimes questioned for her absence at a rally for Israel or a demonstration for Soviet Jewry, she explained that she often isn't invited to them although her male colleagues are. However, she has patience with these groups and their leaders because they are Jews—her people.

What about Israel? They've had a female prime minister, women are drafted into the army—certainly there is no sexual discrimination there. But there is much to be desired in that area in Israel as Shulamit Aloni, newly elected member of the Knesset and head of the Civil Rights Party, outlined in her address. The early pioneers to Palestine were rebelling against European society and so shared responsibilities. This attitude of equality gradually changed as large numbers of Jews from Moslem countries, where women are subservient, entered the country. Compounding the problem of women in Israel is rabbinic control over many aspects of Israeli life. Women are not allowed to be witnesses. There is no civil marriage or divorce, only religious ones.

Shulamit Aloni deplored the tendency of Israeli leaders who cry for equality during times of emergency but then tell women to go home during times of depression. Women should be trained to do more than knit and bake during emergencies, she maintains. Even if women do work, their average salary is 40% of what men earn and they have trouble making adequate child care arrangements. Israeli day care centers and nursery schools are charitable institutions for women who are poor and/or have many children, she feels. They are not geared for women who want to work. To be more effective, she would like to see them change from charity to justice and admit children from all backgrounds.

Ms. Aloni does not think that women should form separate organizations to solve their problems but rather should work together with men towards their common goals.

The women at the conference formed the Jewish Feminist Organization to help women participate in all levels of Jewish life. Open to Jewish women of all ages, interests and backgrounds in the U.S. and Canada it will concern itself with their religious and secular problems both from within and without the community.

Is there a need for an annual national Jewish women's conference? For the time being, many women think there is. "It's nice to know I'm not alone. The Jewish women's movement fills the gap in the general women's movement for me," commented a young Chicagoan, summarizing the attitude of many. The men agreed. Initially uneasy, they felt the conference in particular and the Jewish women's movement in general is forcing them to reexamine Jewish tradition which could be the beginning of liberation for men and women.

161

THE UNITED SYNAGOGUE ACCORDS WOMEN
RELIGIOUS EQUALITY
1973

As a structured and organized movement, Conservative Judaism did not make its appearance on the American scene till 1886. Actually, this form of Judaism may claim to be almost as old as the first Jewish settlement on the continent, for in essence Conservatism is the adaptation of European Orthodoxy to the secular cultural demands of the New World. The differences between Reform, Conservatism, and Orthodoxy lie in the degree to which each group has adapted itself to the prevailing life-style of the Gentile majority. For Conservatives, the acculturational pace accelerated in the mid-twentieth century under the influence of the Jewish Reformers, the impact of the new feminism, the increasing participation of women in commerce and industry, and their corresponding emancipation. The Civil Rights Act of 1964 frowned on any aspect of sex discrimination. It was inevitable, therefore, that the dominant Conservative male elite would have no choice but to improve the religious status of their womenfolk.

The protests of the Ezrat Nashim in March 1972 were timely, for the governing body of the Conservative synagogues, meeting in convention in 1973, exhibited a readiness to accord women a substantial role in the service. Women were even urged to study at the rabbinical seminary— although, discreetly, nothing was said about ordination.

The following resolutions, therefore, reflect the willingness of the men to accede to the wishes of the women. It should be pointed out, however, that the final authority in matters religious lies in the hands of the Jewish Theological Seminary faculty, not in the lay synagogal body.

RESOLUTIONS

The Role of Women

THE PLACE OF JEWISH WOMEN IN SYNAGOGUE LIFE TODAY

Whereas, it is demonstrably evident that women have the same concerns and commitment to their synagogue as do men; and

Whereas, it is also demonstrably evident that women have not, generally, been accorded equal opportunity commensurate with their ability to serve as officers and trustees and members of congregational committees; and

Whereas, we recognize the justice of extending equality of opportunity to Jewish women in synagogue life; therefore

Be it resolved that the United Synagogue calls upon its member congregations to take such action as will insure equal opportunity for its women congregants to assume positions of leadership, authority and responsibility in all phases of congregational activity.

THE ROLE OF WOMEN IN RITUAL

Whereas, the United Synagogue of America desires to encourage and foster the availability of creative Jewish identity and experience to all members of the Jewish community; and

Whereas, women are, and have been, an integral part of synagogue life, generously contributing their energies and resources to its growth and development; and

Whereas, the Committee on Jewish Law and Standards of the Rabbinical Assembly has determined it is halachically permissible for women to participate in synagogue ritual; and

Whereas, the United Synagogue of America believes that the concept of full and equal opportunity and participation by women in religious as well as secular roles is an idea whose time has come; therefore

Be it resolved that the United Synagogue of America looks with favor upon the inclusion of women in ritual participation, including but not limited to participation in the *minyan* and *aliyot*, and looks with favor upon its member congregations adopting such programs as will meaningfully implement this resolution. [Women are to be included in a prayer quorum and to be "called up" to participate in the reading of the Law.]

ADMISSION OF WOMEN IN THE RABBINICAL SCHOOL OF THE JEWISH THEOLOGICAL SEMINARY OF AMERICA

Recognizing the growing role of women in the life of our congregations, the United Synagogue of America, in convention assembled, wishes to note that it looks with favor on the admission of qualified women to the Rabbinical School of The Jewish Theological Seminary of America.

162

THE ROLE OF THE JEWESS IN THE LOCAL COMMUNITY
1973

Daniel Judah Elazar (b. 1934), author of the following article on the American Jewess, is professor of political studies at Bar-Ilan University in Israel and director of the Center for the Study of Federalism at Temple University, Philadelphia.

Dr. Elazar is a gifted political scientist with a strong interest in history and sociology. His analysis of the status, work, and achievements of women in American Jewish life is thoughtful and illuminating. As he points out, they are not the elite decision-makers in any community, but it is equally true that they exert a profound influence at the local level. Disregarding for the moment the work done by Hadassah and Women's American ORT abroad, who will gainsay the contention that the accomplishments of Jewesses here in the United States are at least as significant as those of men! These women are doing as much for the survival of Jewry as their male counterparts.

WOMEN IN
AMERICAN JEWISH LIFE
by Daniel J. Elazar

The impact of the "women's lib" movement on American Jewry is just beginning to be felt but the usual high percentage of Jews involved in this movement as in others possessing radical chic means that it is likely to be great. In that connection, it is useful to pause at the threshold of change to see where women now stand within organized life of the American Jewish community and where their new involvement may take them.

With some exceptions, women function in environments

segregated from male decision-makers within the Jewish community. The exceptions are significant for what they reveal. Very wealthy women who have a record of activity in their own right, often in conjunction with their husbands but sometimes even without them, are admitted to the governing councils of major Jewish institutions and organizations. So, too, are the top leaders of the women's groups in an *ex officio* capacity which is sometimes translated into meaningful participation but frequently remains simply *ex officio*.

This is not to say that women's role in American Jewish life is insignificant. Quite the contrary; not only are these women to be evaluated as figures of greater or lesser importance in their own right, but the women's organizations play a significant if subordinate role in the constellation of Jewish communal institutions. The most powerful women's organization is Hadassah. Its leaders are also those taken most seriously in the community as a whole and its work has the greatest impact within the various segments of the community. The other women's Zionist organizations plus the National Council of Jewish Women play similar if slightly less visible roles because they are smaller in size. Probably the least important of the women's organizations devoted to public purposes are the sisterhoods, whose functions are clearly auxiliary and ancillary to the men's groups in the synagogues.

Women have been given custody of much of the direct social welfare and popular cultural activity of the community. This parallels developments in American society as a whole where these have come to be considered to be women's responsibilities. From the beginning of organized Jewish life in the United States, women have provided much of the "manpower" for fund-raising, for specific health and welfare institutions (except those that are linked to the federation "drive") and energy for developing the popular cultural programs provided by synagogues and similar organizations. In recent decades, the rising costs of social welfare activities have led to a reduced role for women in that field since they cannot raise the kind of money that is needed to make a significant difference to more than a few institutions. They now raise money to provide subsidiary or needed fringe benefits for the institutions to which they are committed.

In the popular cultural realm, on the other hand, women have gained in importance so that today they, in effect, determine what will be of cultural interest to the bulk of American Jewry. They buy the books and theater tickets that make Jewish books "bestsellers" and plays like *Fiddler on the Roof* "hits." They invite the authors to lecture to the congregations. They determine much of the content of the adult education programs. Since these popular cultural activities probably contribute more to determining the level of literacy of the American Jewish population than any other factor, their role in the community is a very important one.

The central role of women in the cultural sphere is due to the fact that "culture" is defined as a leisure-time activity in American society and hence the province of women, to be handled by them while men are doing the "serious" work of the world. To the extent that living Jewishly as a whole is increasingly being defined as a leisure-time activity, the role of women in other spheres of Jewish life is also growing. Women are becoming more visible among the leadership of synagogues, especially in the smaller Jewish communities where the pool of available leadership talent is limited. Only residues of a traditional outlook that viewed such activities as serious and hence the province of men coupled with the few traditional limitations on women as participants in synagogue rituals have prevented a great shift of decision-making power in the domestic functional spheres into the hands of women.

This latter situation poses an unanticipated problem, particularly as the barriers to expanded roles for women in the synagogue diminish. The increase in opportunities for women is likely to further reduce the presence of men in synagogue activities. While, on one hand, this will represent a voluntary choice to abdicate [on] the part of the men, it could further enhance the image of Judaism as "women's work," i.e., less important. Since the men will be replaced by women with "leisure time," that is to say, those who do not pursue careers in the world of "work," this image will be further enhanced even in light of the thrust toward greater acceptance of women as equals.

There are some communities where this has already become the case, where the voluntary leadership and lower echelon professions of the synagogues, organizations and agencies of the communities are predominantly women and only the rabbis, cantors and top federation executives are men. Without attempting to determine the cause and effect relationship, those communities are also among the weakest in the United States. Jewish life in them has become so much a leisure-time activity that commitment to Jewishness is as casual as befits a "hobby."

At present, women in large numbers "man" the lower echelons of Jewish communal life, both as professionals and volunteers, in most communities. They do so through their women's groups, as religious school teachers, or as the secretarial "top sergeants" in the offices of Jewish organizations and institutions, where their impact is great. But there are many signs that they will no longer be content with the limits heretofore placed on them. If conditions lead to their assumption of roles similar to the models that have heretofore developed, the entire Jewish community will undergo unanticipated changes of a radical nature that go far beyond the sheer presence of a woman rabbi on a pulpit.

163

A HASIDIC SPIRITUAL HOSPICE
1974

A great deal has been written about the Lubavitch movement in the United States. The American followers of the learned Russian Hasid, Shneor Zalman (1747–1812) are adept at public relations; they are brilliant and devoted propagandists. Their high visibility tempts one to surmise that they are very numerous; actually all the Hasidic groups in this country lumped together constitute a very small percentage of America's Jews. In some cities they work with young people who are lost souls, who need help desperately. The Lubavitchers offer them a home, a hospice, where they can find themselves spiritually, emotionally, even intellectually. The following article describes such a refuge for women in St. Paul.

WHERE WOMEN GO TO FIND JUDAISM—AND THEMSELVES
by Irving Spiegel

ST. PAUL—Friday at sundown. The Sabbath comes in cold and clear during early spring in Minnesota. In the warm shelter of the Chabad House, the young women greet it with flickering Shabbes candles set on glistening white tablecloths.

Silently, they intone the ancient Hebrew prayer: "Blessed art thou, O Lord our God, King of the Universe, who has sanctified us by his commandments and has commanded us to kindle the lights of the Holy Sabbath."

The moment had once been meaningless in their lives. Now it is a precious experience. They are "baelei t'shuva"—returnees to tradition.

These are young women rediscovering religious faith—and themselves. Their backgrounds are as diverse as their past life-styles. Some are college graduates, Ph.D.'s among them. Some were high school dropouts. Some had been involved with drugs. Others had flirted with the mystical beliefs of the Orient, the political tumults of the New Left and similar probings of the younger generation.

But all had shared in a sense of aimlessness, a search for personal identity.

'Existence by Escapism'

Here, under the sensitive guidance of the worldwide Lubavitcher Movement, which expounds the religious-intellectual philosophy of Orthodox Hasidic Jews, they are finding personal dignity, their own sense of worth.

They live in a converted 30-room mansion set on four and a half wooded acres in the fashionable Highland Park section of this city. Their number fluctuates. At times, the group is 80 or more.

Barbara is one of them. She is 20 years old, blue-eyed, blond. She is from Los Angeles, the product of a broken home and a half-dozen private schools.

"I had the whole cycle," she explains, matter-of-factly. "Drugs, sex, alienation. I couldn't stand being alone, or not being high. It was existence by escapism. Until a bitter realization that I was still alone—and traveling a horrible road."

Barbara surveys her new surroundings. "I've found peace here," she says, "and purpose."

To Barbara and her companions, the principles of Chabad have been a path to personal serenity. Chabad is the Lubavitcher philosophy. The term itself is an acrostic for the Hebrew words "chochma" (wisdom), "bina" (knowledge) and "daat" (understanding).

Behind the network of Chabad Houses in this country—and in London, Paris, Johannesburg, Milan, Melbourne and Jerusalem—is the pervasive influence of 72-year-old Rabbi Menachem Mendel Schneerson, a renowned Talmudic scholar and the spiritual leader of the Lubavitcher Movement. His international headquarters are in the Crown Heights section of Brooklyn, and his judgments are unquestioned.

Chabad Houses are not proselytizing centers. None of their enrollees is required to adopt the esoteric Hasidic life-style. Rabbi Schneerson's intent is to provide a traditional setting, together with instructions in classical Jewish studies for the wayward and untutored among Jewish youth.

The Chabad Houses here—formally known as the Women's Institute of Jewish Studies (another name is Bait Chana—House of Chana—in memory of the Rabbi's mother)—is unique in that it is the only one exclusively for young women.

The building, constructed in 1946 as the home of the banker and beer magnate, Otto Bremeras, includes two 40-by-25-foot rooms, one of which serves as a dining room–auditorium, the other as a chapel and lecture hall.

The basement has been converted into a dormitory to augment the mansion's 12 bedrooms. There is housing for 60 students and three staff families.

The institute offers spring, summer and winter sessions of two, twelve and six weeks, respectively.

Arlene, 28, attended a summer session. She is a well-paid computer programer, holds a master's degree in mathematics, and, in her words, "had everything: a busy social life, a spacious West Side apartment in Manhattan, summers at Fire Island . . ." and "a gnawing feeling about the purposelessness of it all."

"When I first encountered Lubavitch people, Orthodox Judaism was the farthest thing from my mind," Arlene said. "The Sabbath and Kashruth [dietary laws] were a joke to me. But I noticed how graceful and sincere the life-style of the Hasidim was. These people with beards and black hats were genuinely happy. They won my admiration."

Today, Arlene regularly addresses young women who attend Chabad meetings. "It was not just the study of Jewish laws or Bible or history that made me change," she recalls. "It was the emotional and intellectual experiences that helped me during my stay at the institute."

The girls who come here are generally sent by Lubavitcher centers in other cities. "It means," said 18-year-old Lynn, whose home is in South Africa, "that we are sent by friends to be cared for by friends."

"When a girl is referred to us by a Lubavitcher office, that office still feels responsible for her," observed Rabbi Moshe Feller, director of the Lubavitch's Upper Midwest regional office, which supervises Chabad House.

"They follow her progress here," Rabbi Feller said. "They pay the hospital bills for girls on drug withdrawal programs whose parents can't afford it. This feeling of responsibility is to see the girl all the way through—not just to start her out. They'll even help her find a suitable partner in marriage."

MARRIED TRADITIONALISTS

They have done that. A number of girls who attended the Chabad House here have since married young men who had also been introduced to a traditional Jewish life-style through the Lubavitcher Movement.

The rap sessions, guided by Rabbi Feller and his colleagues, are lively and spirited: "What am I as a Jew? What does being a Jew mean? What relevance does a heritage thousands of years old have today?" Patiently, the girls are guided to find the answers within themselves.

"These youngsters," Rabbi Feller said, "cry out for an uncompromising approach to their heritage, a cry that so often goes unheeded. For many of these girls, it is the first time in their lives that someone has listened to them at great length, trying to relate to them."

Rabbi Feller is one of the listeners. Another is his wife, Mindelle, a Phi Beta Kappa from Hunter College, the institute's dean of women. She lectures on the Bible and on practical aspects of the Jewish woman's life, coordinates the cooking program and strums a guitar whenever the girls break into a sing-along.

Rabbi Manis Friedman, Chabad House's principal, uses humble humor to articulate Jewish concepts and attitudes in sessions with the girls that often last more than five hours.

More than 300 young women have attended Chabad House since its start in the summer of 1971.

An indication of the program's effect, says Rabbi Feller, is that some 60 per cent have become totally committed to "Torah

Judaism"—strict observance of religious laws and traditional Jewish life.

And more: About one of every three, accepting Hasidic ways for herself, has gone to live in the Lubavitcher community in Crown Heights, Brooklyn.

164

JUDAISM AND THE FEMALE SINGLE
1974

Is Judaism so emphatically a family religion that it has very little to offer the unmarried woman, particularly the professional who has no time to attend afternoon meetings of female auxiliaries? The following apologia of a physician who has drifted away from the older traditions is well worth reading and studying. She poses some important questions; the answers are not obvious.

EXODUS FROM EDEN: ONE WOMAN'S EXPERIENCE
by Naomi Bluestone

I have been what you would call a "nice Jewish girl." I was born, bred and nurtured that way, happily at home with 3000 years of Jewish history even as a preverbal toddler. Our home was kosher, all holidays were observed, and a strong sense of identity shielded us from the mild anti-Semitism which occasionally flared around us. Both my parents were professionals working in the field of Jewish education and welfare, my mother as a Hebrew teacher, my father as a Jewish communal worker. I had a Conservative Hebrew School education, amplified by private studies with an eminent Hebrew scholar, and attended Hebrew-speaking camps.

My own brand of Judaism began to crystalize at the age of eleven, when the State of Israel was declared, and I joined the Labor Zionist Youth Movement (*Habonim*), an affiliation I still cherish. Quite unlike my parents' own more traditional Zionist leaning, the movement was one of the molding forces of my adolescence, for many years the most important focus in my life.

I worked in high school as a Sunday School teacher (Reform), and later earned my way through much of college by this means. I maintained my identity, including *kashrut* [Jewish dietary laws], through college, graduate school and medical school, despite great hardship and, surprisingly, despite membership in the liberal, intellectual segment of the predominantly non-Jewish campus community. It was clearly a double life. I have always been an intellectual sort of person, liberal politically and socially; and for a number of years people were surprised, even shocked, to discover that I took Judaism seriously, and practiced it. Although my friends were not restricted to Jews, I made efforts to seek them out, even organizing a social group for Jewish students in graduate school where none existed, despite a student enrollment of over 25,000.

At the age of twenty-three, while a medical student, I made my first trip to Israel, working, speaking the language, exploring the country, and making friendships which have endured. This visit, which had been so long deferred, was a deeply satisfying experience, and only the need to continue my education propelled me back to the United States.

The present writing finds me a very busy person, a public health physician, a single woman, living and practicing in New York City for the multiplex reasons that all people like me come to New York. It also finds me sadly aware that my Jewish traditionalism is, to a great extent, a thing of the past, having long ceased to be a dynamic force in my life. I no longer find it imperative to search for a Jewish husband, nor would I want to give my children the kind of Jewish education I had.

This awareness, though long in developing, broke through suddenly. A few months ago, while staring at the Late, Late Show long after it had flickered off, I realized that religion, if it works, is good for many things: spiritual sustenance, a feeling of community, a sense of history and self-pride, shared customs and ceremonies giving an aura of stability and continuity to life, etc. And I appraised just what Judaism and I had given to each other. It appeared that the pursuit of my own personal development away from traditional roles had cost me my place in the fellowship. I realized that *there is virtually no place in my Judaism for an unmarried woman over twenty-five.*

Superficially, over the next few months, this direct confrontation made no difference in my life. I still gave liberally to all the formal Jewish philanthropies (and, in good Jewish tradition, to many others as well). I have not removed the Mezuzah from the door [encapsulated Hebrew verses from the Bible], and the Hebrew and Jewish books rest undisturbed with the others on my shelves. The photograph of Bialik [H. N. Bialik, modern Hebrew poet, d. 1934] still hangs, and the Persian drawings of Moses and the bulrushes. Even the kosher kitchen has not been officially dismantled, although it has gotten messed up a bit since I started importing chicken sandwiches from the non-kosher deli.

But there was no denying what I had discovered. The realization that unless you fit into the mold, unless you have a family to feed *rozhinkes mit mandlen* [raisins and almonds, i.e. "Jewish" foods], unless you have children to send to Hebrew school, unless you have a husband to escort you to the annual dinner-dance, unless you have time for society meetings, unless you have appetite for sisterhood luncheons, unless you do all that your mother did, and her mother before her . . . Judaism offers nothing. For Judaism is fixated in a world of forty years ago. I'm younger than that and my whole life has been passing by.

But now let's consider the experiences which led to the revelations of the post-Late-Late Show. We'll start with the Synagogue. When I came to this city a few years ago, I went straightaway to the Synagogue, finding a beautiful Conservative temple not far away which boasted to be one of the oldest in the city. The congregation consisted of about 25 aged men (not unlike a pathetic congregation I saw several years ago in Riga), who assured me that the new young Rabbi was soon to be building a congregation from the young couples moving into the restored neighborhood. I promptly sent in a check for membership and received a rather puzzled letter in return. I was, apparently, the first woman in one hundred odd years to request membership for herself, and what were they to do with me? They decided to let me join, but they withheld voting and Board membership rights. I accepted, and never challenged it, with a passivity which seems shocking now in the light of Women's Lib.

However, it soon became evident that, despite a friendly environment I was a fish out of water. Between the old men *davening* [praying in Hebrew] in one corner, and the Purim *groggers* [noisemakers] in the other, I felt caught between two worlds. The Synagogue's adult education classes conflicted with my professional responsibilities and didn't interest me particularly, anyway. It seemed inappropriate for me to have a turn at making an *Oneg Shabbat* [Sabbath collation]. I had no little anniversaries or remembrances in my family to contribute to the Newsletter. I had no children for the nursery school, and no sisters for the Sisterhood. Heaven knows, the Synagogue was no place to go to meet eligible men. As a matter of fact, I felt self-conscious; a woman walking alone to Holiday services is the rough equivalent of a woman going alone to a Broadway opening. Not a widow, and not a schoolgirl, after several years I just gave up. Although Jews are not supposed to pray alone, I read my (autographed) *Mahzor* [prayer book for the holidays] in my living room.

As the synagogue receded in my life, so did customs and ceremonies. I stopped going home for any of the holidays except Pesaḥ [Passover], because after the age of thirty it becomes uncomfortable, embarrassing, and inconvenient. Just as the holidays were no longer observed, the Sabbath passed away. I felt foolish and awkward lighting candles; it seemed a childish attempt to recapture happy memories of a long dead past. Did I learn to cook Jewish? For whom? Does a woman make chicken soup for one, and freeze the rest? *Latkes? Dreidels? Esrog?* [Jewish pancakes; toy tops; a festive citron for Sukkot.] These are the toys of childhood, resurrected for each generation only when the generations continue, otherwise of no value!

Kashrut? Is the Jewish community aware of what happens to a kosher girl when a man asks her out on their first dinner date? I am an expert at lies: I *like* fish, I *adore* dry cheese sandwiches, I prefer tuna on rye to a steak *any* day! I am also an expert at telling the truth with a firm voice and a clear eye . . . and picking up the inevitable, usually unverbalized response: "Oy, I had to pick a religious nut." After thirty years of trying to convince men that "Yes, I am kosher but, no, I'm not a fanatic," I bit into my first deli hamburger, medium rare. It was delicious. The ghosts of all those rejected frankfurters at all those high school football games didn't even rise up to haunt me. Best hamburger I ever had. I eat a lot of them now; they console me for the loss of my illusions.

The question of *kashrut* raises the issue of traditionalism in general. I learned a long time ago that I *had* to go out on Friday nights, I *had* to cook, shop and clean on Saturday . . . because I had no other time to perform these necessary functions. I am a professional woman, not a housewife, and, therefore, not an observant Jew, by choice. This concession to reality has never upset me, and does not constitute a valid argument concerning the value of Judaism to the modern woman.

The discrepancy between the much-loved customs of Judaism, and the ways of the outside world did, for a time, propel me towards Jews with whom I might be able to "make it," observant Jews. On the Upper West Side of New York I found some *yarmulked* [wearing skullcaps] but wholly unsavory types, from whom I was soon pleased to flee, back to the more assimilated Jews with whom, I confess, I felt more comfortable. It is an interesting dilemma, to be caught between intellectual companions who know nothing of Judaism, and intolerant Jews who know ritual . . . but little else. I opted for the former; it was a purely personal decision. And it pushed me one step further away from Judaism.

Where, then, might I find some other Jews, perhaps affiliate with Jewish organizations, to remind me that I am still a Jew? The Synagogue is gone, the ceremonials of the home are memories, the holidays are not observed. Jewish dating is problematic; what then? Well, my name is on the lists, that's one thing. The Israel Bond people know me well. Once a year, three very nice gentlemen from the U.J.A. [United Jewish Appeal] call me up, each in turn, to request that I send my check to *his* particular affiliation for credit. (I give to whoever calls first.) Then, I'm on the mailing lists for all the dinners honoring rich, older, generous men, whom I have never met. I don't mind the $25.00 couvert; my trouble is finding someone crazy enough to go even to please me (which it doesn't). But I mention this Jewish contact for completeness' sake. It sort of makes me feel like I'm my father; *he* gets invitations like that.

Other affiliations? I am most sympathetic to the problems of young Jewish students on the campuses, what with the anti-Zionist focus of the radical new left, but I don't know many students, nor do I have access to them. I am similarly concerned with the plight of Russian Jewry, but don't really know the best way to help. I would like to attend lectures, as keen as the competition is for my time. I have long been meaning to try the Educational Alliance. I have attended the very interesting-sounding lectures at the Herzl Institute and, on the last occasion, found both speaker and moderator to be so rude, biased, and narrow-minded, I am now permanently "turned off."

Well, then, what of the women's organizations? Would you believe that I am the only Jewish woman in America never tapped by Hadassah? Incredible, but true. I don't know whether to laugh or cry. But I have never had my Jewish social vacuum penetrated by the good ladies of Hadassah. Have they discerned already that we apparently have very little in common? I think they are losing a good bet, myself. After all, I enjoy the kind of income which permits me to buy raffle books without consulting my husband first, and as to donating a cake, I could even afford to send one over from Rumplemeyer's (Or wouldn't that be kosher?). At any rate, I read my mother's copies of the Hadassah Newsletter, which I genuinely enjoy. After all, if I requested my *own* subscription, they might *find* me! I am, by the way, as unknown to ORT, Mizrachi, Farband, etc. [national organizations with female auxiliaries], as I am to Hadassah. Where do they get their membership lists . . . from the bridal columns?

I *do* belong to the "Alumni" group of my Zionist days. I cannot accuse them of re-hashing the glorious past, or of being senti-mental. They are truly, intelligently activist in Jewish causes, in America and Israel, and I support them, and even join them occasionally. *Very* occasionally. They are, inevitably, wrapped up in their children. I don't blame them; but I can't join them.

As I look back over my increasing isolation from all nostalgic remembrances of Judaism, or any modern replacements, it seems pointless to search for any one cause. It is also a moot point whether I have been abandoning the cultural and religious foci of Judaism . . . or whether they have abandoned me. One must still come to grips with the central premise of the religion: Do I believe, nevertheless, in God? Alas, readers, I no longer do.

Several years ago I was fated (or should I say privileged?) to have an opportunity to have my faith tested. Caught in a vortex of prolonged illness and depression, brought quite literally to my knees, *min ha-meẓar* ["in my distress," Ps. 118:5] as it were, I cried out . . . and got no answer. I am still trying to deal with that silence. I shall not dwell on it. Man's loss of faith has been dealt with sufficiently by others more eloquent. I would simply say: in my experience, Jewish religious education is incompatible with the needs of the adult individual. The God of children still prevails, apparently.

I can in no way fault the ethical and moral precepts of Judaism. I just rather suspect that Judaism does not corner the world's market on righteousness, and I suppose that's what some of the other modern (and competitive) new religious forms are all about. I feel no particular need to investigate them. I would not be surprised, however, if Jewish teenagers did. Judaism has been short-changing them, too.

Judaism needs an overhaul from the bottom up. I offer myself as evidence. If I can defect . . . anyone can.

165

WOMEN AS FEDERATION CAMPAIGN HEADS
1974–1975

The local federation of Jewish charities invariably dominates the Jewish community. It is controlled in one form or another by the local community's male elite. Its most important annual function is a campaign to secure the funds for local needs and for dependent Jewries abroad. This annual fund-raising campaign is carried on in conjunction with a nationwide organization, the United Jewish Appeal (UJA); the local leaders are, of course, responsible for the success or failure of the UJA drive. It is indicative of the growing influence of women that in 1975 they led campaigns in six American communities. To be sure, this was only a beginning, but it did indicate that women were making their way in the communal obligarchy.

Reprinted below are the reports of two women campaign heads. These female leaders describe in some detail the spirit with which their male coworkers received them. Inasmuch as Jewish giving is nearly always crisis giving, the women were "fortunate" that fate provided the crises to stimulate the contributors. The United Nations General Assembly, in November 1974, gave the Palestinian guerilla leader Yasir Arafat an ovation, accorded observer status to the Palestine Liberation Organization, and passed resolutions supporting PLO demands for a separate Palestinian state. That same month the Washington Post *published fragments of an address made at Duke University Law School the preceding month by the late General George S. Brown, Chairman of the Joint Chiefs of Staff. His rambling talk rehashed the accusations which have long been the stock-in-trade of anti-Semites. These two events moved the Jews solicited to give liberally to the UJA.*

The following reports from Nashville, Tennessee, and Binghamton, New York, attest that the men cooperated fully with these two women and that the women successfully met the challenge which confronted them.

NASHVILLE, TENNESSEE
by Lois Fox

In January, 1974, about the time the leadership was to be chosen for the new Federation campaign, I wondered why I was about to receive a visit from two male Jewish community leaders. I was Chairperson of our Federation Jewish Education Services Committee and I had been totally involved as an advisor (and solicitor) to our '74 Nashville Jewish Welfare Fund Campaign because of my experience as Chairperson of the Women's Division twice. Through the years two women had served as Federation President, but a woman as General Chairman of the campaign?

When the offer came, I had to consider my decision carefully. It was first important for me to accept my own role before I could expect the community to accept me as General Chairperson. Support and encouragement came from my husband, family, and close associates. I was completely comfortable with the job requirements in campaign structures; I could devote additional time to leadership development; I could count on cooperation from the Federation leadership I had worked with for years. But what about the men I would ask to work and the men I would be soliciting? I was assured that I would get cooperation, but knew that only time would tell.

Using the best skills I had learned in my women's campaign experience, I approached the structure of Campaign '75. Between leadership identification and the establishment of a cabinet structure, there were many phone calls, office visits, and lunches (for which my male guest always seemed to pay the check). My appointment as General Chairperson was announced to the community; I received many congratulations, but was often asked, "Who is the men's chairman?" The surprise on my questioners' faces as I answered that I was demonstrated that everyone wasn't prepared for a woman chairperson.

One of my greatest joys was leading the U.J.A. Israel mission with 27 other Nashvillians (twenty of them first-timers)—a mission we all saw as crucial for the '75 campaign and which turned out to be a great resource in leadership and fund raising in our community.

GAINING EXPERIENCE UNDER PRESSURE

In the fall our community had to face an unexpected blow, when our Federation Executive Director accepted a position in another city. Many questions were raised. Who would be in the office to keep the administrative machinery rolling? What about public relations? Who was liaison with National U.J.A.? We have a very slim Federation staff and no one else who was experienced with a campaign. We brought in a retired staff person to assist, and I began a fulltime job.

In the many months involved, I found that my commitment and enthusiasm opened all doors for me, whether in cabinet building, presenting the needs, or in soliciting. Our '75 goal was set very high, because Nashville had answered the needs in the Emergency of the [1973] Yom Kippur War and the 1974 campaign in unprecedented dollar giving. Faced with a sagging economy and the absence of the stimulus of gunfire, we raised 36% more than we had in our largest previous campaign in 1973 and 20% less than '74.

As a result of being campaign chairperson I feel that I am better prepared to become President of our Federation in May 1976. I can approach budgets, since I know the difficulty of raising the dollars; I can broaden the pool of prospective leaders because of my association with such a broad spectrum of people in the campaign; I can encourage innovative programming, for I have demonstrated that there can be new ways to approach old procedures.

The Jewish women across the country who have been involved in organizational life—campaigns, religious programs, human services, and other areas—are an untapped source of experience in communities. I, with my few counterparts across the country, have demonstrated that women can add a needed ingredient.

BINGHAMTON, NEW YORK
by Helen G. Pierson

When I accepted the chairmanship of the 1975 U.J.A.–Federated Campaign, I did so with some hesitation. I knew I could do the job, but wondered whether the men would work with me or would resent a woman as chairman? I knew I had a tough road to hoe—the economy, no apparent crisis situation, and a woman chairman to complicate matters. However, I was determined to do the very best I could, to get the campaign organized and set up in such a way that it could easily be followed from year to year.

My first step was to contact four men and extract a promise from them to take the chairmanship for the next four years, thus assuring our community of a continuity of leadership. Next I held a meeting of 25 key men who promised to work with me and supported the concept of a woman as campaign chairman. (These two factors were a prerequisite to my accepting the chairmanship.) From that point on, it was clear sailing. Every man I called to be a member of my cabinet accepted graciously, which pleased and encouraged me.

Unfortunately, General Brown's remarks and Arafat's standing ovation at the U.N. gave me my crisis, and strengthened my determination to do an even better job. What I once thought had been total commitment on my part was growing and growing. I found myself going out on solicitations all by myself and enjoying it. I also enjoyed my success; out of all the men I solicited, there were only two who did not go along with my requested pledge. And my campaign was a good one in general; the cooperation I received from everyone went far beyond my expectations.

Battling the U.J.A. Bureaucracy

Strangely enough, my one frustration came from the U.J.A. office itself. Four days before my major fund raising event (a $1,000.00 dinner), our new U.J.A. field man came to Binghamton to tell me I was doing it all wrong, and that he was going to re-solicit the entire community before the affair. When he realized that I was not going to back down, he approached a few men in the community to try "to reason with me." When this, too, failed, his superior in the U.J.A. office called to tell me "with all candor" that my campaign was in big trouble, and he assured me once again that I was doing it all wrong. My reply was that if he didn't like the way I was running the campaign, he should come down here and do it himself, and that "in all candor" I was about to hang up! This was the only time that I felt my ability as a woman campaign chairman was being questioned. I also feel that a man would never have had to cope with this type of conversation or treatment.

I believe that U.J.A. fails to recognize that competent and experienced leaders in each community know their peers and how to handle them better than anyone else, that each community is different and what works in one community will not necessarily be successful in another, and that competent and experienced volunteer leaders *can* do the job. Our campaign did fall 2½% short of the previous year. There were a few large cuts at the top that could not be overcome despite the many increases we got. The economy was a definite factor last year.

I would definitely take this job again, and I would probably do it in much the same way. Despite our not reaching our goal, I feel we accomplished much. I personally feel that I partially paid my debt to the 6 million killed in the holocaust. I feel that as a grown, knowledgeable woman in 1975, I was able to do what I could not do in the early 1940's as an unknowing teenager. I know my pride in being a Jew grew and grew every day of the campaign; I would like to feel that aside from the responsibility and privilege of serving, I helped assure the survival of Israel and Judaism.

166

THE AMERICAN JEWESS IN A LEADERSHIP ROLE
1975

Ann G. Wolfe, the head of the American Jewish Committee's programs on the status of women in the Jewish community, gave the following talk at a joint program institute of the National Council of Jewish Women in October 1975. Mrs. Wolfe makes the point that there are, as yet, few women decision-makers in the Jewish community. This is a fact that cannot be disputed. Additionally, she raises an important question: should these Jewesses continue to work in their all-female organizations, or should they seek to find fulfillment in a male-female setting, both locally and nationally? One might well ask too whether the average Jewish woman even has the desire to leave her own female association to work in groups of men and women. It is very probable that most women would resolutely refuse to desert ladies' societies and sections because they find them emotionally, culturally, and socially satisfying. Still another question: if women throw themselves wholeheartedly into local and national Jewish work and rise to the top through sheer ability—this is well within the realm of probability—will the men of tomorrow be psychically ready to take orders from women? Will these males, thinking only in terms of anthropocracy, submit to any form of gynecocracy where the real, ultimate authority is exercised by a woman?

No Room At The Top
by Ann G. Wolfe

In my view, women's role in the Jewish community today is what it has always been; there has been much talk but little action in the broad community to move us closer to the centers of decision-making or power. We are still separate and *un*equal. But something is brewing.

I do not mean to suggest that all Jewish women are unhappy and unfulfilled, nor do I believe that Jewish women are more oppressed than other women. I speak here about *community*—that entity that is the matrix in which individuals are likely to find their satisfactions and I speak for myself, and for many Jewish women with whom I've talked—committed Jews who look to our future with the realization that the place traditionally assigned to us and to our daughters in Jewish life is restricting.

The conscious movement toward equality for women within Jewish life started late in 1971. . . . In connection with a Task Force on the Future of the Jewish Community, organized by the American Jewish Committee, we commissioned a number of papers on various aspects of Jewish communal life. A serendipitous insight came to us in a paper prepared by Daniel J. Elazar of Temple University on the "Structure of the Jewish Community"—in a short section on the role of women in Jewish life. Professor Elazar's basic observation was correct—that women function in environments segregated from male decision-makers within the Jewish community.

Jewish community decision-makers are those who participate in setting the tasks, and evaluating the priorities to be set for the use of resources available to the Jewish community in fulfilling the tasks which the community has set for itself.

Decision-making, in my view, also includes the participation in the discussion of problems, and the appraisals which the whole Jewish community must make from time to time: for example, the use of resources, in explaining to the American people the American Jewish commitment to Israel, or our concern with the current Arab economic warfare. I am not suggesting that every Jewish organization and the people who speak for it should speak with one voice, or that we take our marching orders from one body. I am clearly suggesting that not all organizations nor segments of the Jewish population are invited or encouraged to participate in the important decisions made in the name of the Jewish community, including the allocation of funds for domestic programs. Your own emphases, described so well in your [National Council of Jewish Women] literature, are unfortunately not high in Jewish community priorities.

I could give you statistics on how many women go into the fields of Jewish education, social work, community relations, or fund raising. Where do they end up? How many ever get to be the executive of an agency, or the principal of the school, or the head of the department? The role models we use encourage our women to be teachers, not supervisors or principals; case workers, but rarely the executive of the child care or family agency; program specialists, but almost never the executive of the Jewish community center; the organizer of the women's luncheon to raise money, but not the chief fund raiser. We remain the helpers, the do-ers, the devoted and loyal assistants, but for us, there seems to be no room at the top. We see this in our national organizations as well as in our local community agencies.

The greater part of what I've had to say so far comes out of my assessment that the male domination in Jewish communal structure has deprived women of the opportunity to share leadership at the top—leadership in the mainstream of Jewish life. Which leads me to the touchy subject of women's organizations, sisterhoods, and other all-women activities.

This audience needs no lesson from me on the value of the program that women's organizations maintain, nor the service they have rendered to the Jewish and general communities. But I do think it is important to ask ourselves whether the focus of activity and the structure of women's organizations are adequate for today's needs or the future of the Jewish community. Will these all-women's groups continue to attract the younger women who seek a place to express themselves as complete personalities?

My own observation through visits to communities across the country is that younger women and men, those who are looking for some affiliation with Jewish communal life, seek a more integrated setting. What these younger people argue is that they do not see the issues that need to be addressed as dividing into female and male areas. Certainly, the issues on your own agenda—juvenile crime and the criminal justice system, gun control, health insurance, income maintenance, Soviet Jewry—are not specially feminine. Is a concern with Arab propaganda more male? Why should that be? And is Jewish family life only for the mother? What is the father's role?

On the other hand, I have noted the views of middle-aged and older women who have found great satisfaction through their work as members of women's organizations. This is particularly true for women who have achieved leadership positions in women's organizations and who treasure the autonomy of an all-women's group. They maintain that women's groups actually serve to multiply opportunities for leadership and mobilize a source of energy and power that move the over-all aims of the larger Jewish community. There may well be some truth to this argument.

I think that the future will see less separation between male and female participation in Jewish life but the time for abandoning women's groups, if that is to be, is not now. The larger women's movement is one of the most significant social forces of the century, and whether one regrets this force or not, one should see it, I think, as the reality we will live with. Simply, a person's *role* is the part he or she plays, and our social roles are based in the culture of our society. The images of women in the past were as the mothers and saviors of men; the evil women were the temptresses and destroyers of men. "Women," said Phyllis Bird in an article on the "Images of Women in the Old Testament," are necessary to the drama, and may even steal the spotlight occasionally; but the story is rarely about them."

The image that the Jewish woman is creating today is of a free human being, demanding the same options open to men, and participating equally on all fronts—so that the story *will* be about them as well.

167

JEWISH WOMEN IN POLITICS
1976

*Not many Jewesses go to Congress. Actually, in view of the fact that about
50 percent of all potential voters in the United States are females, it is
somewhat surprising to note how few women are elected to office two
generations after being accorded the franchise. The feminist revolt of the
1960's has thus far done very little for women politically. Many Jewesses
are in a strategic profession, the law, certainly an advantage if they seek
office. On the other hand, they are disadvantaged because they are Jewish;
anti-Jewish prejudice is a constant in American thinking. Most Jewish
males continue to harbor the conviction that woman's place is in the home,
that politics is a dirty business. Nevertheless, Jewish women are slowly
making their way in politics. Jewish men are beginning to realize that
their sisters, wives, and daughters are bent on seeking careers.*

*The following article was written by Sarah Davis, associate professor of
political science at Oakland Community College, Oakland County,
Michigan. She has been active in furthering the legislative goals of the
National Council of Jewish Women.*

JEWS IN POLITICS: WHERE ARE THE WOMEN?
by Sarah Davis

*"The pursuit of salvation through politics is a modern disease. And a lot
of Jews are infected with it."—Norman Podhoretz*
   The past decade has seen an impressive increase in the political
activity of women in the United States. The recent prominence in
American political life of such figures as Bella Abzug and Elizabeth
Holtzman may give the impression that Jewish women have
become especially active in politics. Is that impression borne out
by the facts? How politically aware and active is the American
Jewish woman? Is there a genuine interest in politics on her part?
Is her political activity in any way related to her religious

background and level of assimilation into the American mainstream? . . .

Now what of the political activity of American women in general? After a flurry of political activity in the late nineteenth century, the Nineteenth Amendment in 1920 seemed to be the signal for American women as a group to virtually withdraw from the political arena. But the civil rights, anti-war, and feminist movements of the 1960's began changing the patterns of political behavior for all women in America. Women have been moving out of the home and expanding their interests in activities, becoming aware of their own capabilities and skills and seeking satisfaction by finding productive communal uses for them. More women are speaking out and organizing to seek full equality of legal rights and job opportunities. . . .

Recalling the Jewish community's heavy involvement in politics, and the recent upsurge in political activity among women, we would expect to find Jewish women very active in politics. That, however, does not seem to be the case.

As partial explanation, we might recall that historically Jewish women have never been very active in politics. Several theories have been proposed to explain this political inactivity, but perhaps the most important of them is the explanation that Jewish women have had a key role in the home and an important influence as motivators of their families. Generally, Jewish mothers were and still are satisfied with their positions in the home and behind the scenes, encouraging the children, especially the sons, to aspire to community service careers.

Jewish women may have organized at synagogues to engage in activities that were extensions of their social functions within the traditional Jewish home, planning holiday suppers, and Bar Mitzvah and wedding receptions. They may occasionally have organized local clubs to aid the less fortunate among their own. But that seems to be the extent of communal involvement for the majority.

It is fair to say that the more traditional the religious background, the less likely a Jewish woman was, and is, to participate outside the home. In other words, the more Orthodox the religious background, the *less* political the woman. Those

Jewish women who have become active in politics, as lobbyists for social welfare causes or workers for candidates, tended to come from families of more assimilationist background.

Jewish women who do want to pursue an active political career find the difficulties they encounter as women magnified by the difficulties they encounter as Jews. A few Jewish women have been elected to university boards of regents . . . , to local judgeships, to state legislatures. But there are barely any at the highest levels of American government. No Jewish female has ever served in the U.S. Senate, on the U.S. Supreme Court (no woman has), in a president's cabinet. Only 4 percent of the membership of the U.S. House of Representatives is female (18 in number) but only .007 is female and Jewish (three). Elizabeth Holtzman (D., N.Y.), Bella Abzug (D., N.Y.) and Gladys Noon Spellman (D., Md.) are only the second, third, and fourth Jewish women ever to serve in the House. [The first Jewess in the House of Representatives was Florence Prag Kahn, who served 1925–1937.]

These three women represent both the "old" and the "new" look for American women—and Jewish women—in politics. The old look is characterized by the typical profile of women who have run for political office in the past—women in their mid- to late-forties. They have a couple of nearly grown children. They have come up "through the ranks" of a political party to run for office. They have had strong support from their husbands. They have looked upon their election to office as a positive contribution to society and as an end in itself, not as a stepping stone to something else, as men in elective office tend to see it.

This is the model represented by Mrs. Spellman, a fifty-six year old grandmother who began her political career with the neighborhood PTA. . . .

In many ways Ms. Holtzman and Ms. Abzug represent the "new" look for women in politics. They are well educated (both are lawyers). Both women are career-oriented, independent. They are both activists, and outspoken. Ms. Holtzman was barely 30 [31] when first elected to Congress in 1972. She was active in the anti-war movement and brought a lawsuit in federal courts questioning the constitutionality of American involvement in Vietnam. Ms. Abzug's age is *not* what qualifies her as the new political woman. (She was born in 1920.) But she had been visibly involved in the women's movement and is a founding sparkplug of the National Women's Political Caucus.

Despite the visibility of these women, the latest research as reported at Adelphi University in September indicates that politics is still considered a nontraditional activity for women, and more so for Jewish women.

For example, Mrs. Spellman was elected to the House in 1974 after a campaign laced with anti-Semitism. And Gloria Schaffer, Connecticut's Secretary of State and the Democrats' leading vote getter there in 1972, who is thinking of running against Lowell Weicker for a U.S. Senate seat next year, faces problems because of her religion.

Newsweek magazine has reported Ms. Schaffer's possible candidacy, but in evaluating it, made the point that not only is she a woman, but in addition, she is Jewish. The magazine then stated that Connecticut already has one Jewish senator (Abraham Ribicoff).

What can we conclude from our discussion? First, although political activity is increasing among women, it still remains largely in the male's domain. There is resistance in the society to women taking an active part in American political life, especially Jewish women. In addition to this resistance from the society at large, Jewish women have to contend with resistance from within the Jewish community, in its expectation that women will fulfill their historically traditional role in the home. Furthermore, they may have internalized that expectation, so that increased communal and political involvement may come only after a difficult inner struggle.

But there are hopeful signs. First, considering the enormity of the obstacles to participation that Jewish women face, even a small increase in the amount of participation is encouraging. Second, we should remember the recent research findings . . . that girls whose mothers hold high-status jobs are more likely than other girls to be actively interested in politics. Since more

Jewish women are moving out into better jobs and more Jewish women are going to law school and entering the legal profession, the prognosis for political participation among the next generation of Jewish women is good. In short, while the movement into politics may be slow, there is some potential for increasing political involvement among Jewish women.

168

A MOVE TO THE LEFT IN A GRASS-ROOTS
CONSERVATIVE CONGREGATION
1976

Conservative Jews, moderates in their adherence to Orthodox tradition, started patiently moving to the left no later than the middle decades of the twentieth century. Women were then assigned a larger role in the worship service. Originally modifications in ritual were made from the top down, but they have never been mandatory; individual congregations have had the right to accept or to reject them. Concessions have had to be made in order to cope with the threat of assimilation and to counter the appeal of the more liberal Reformers; later, by the 1960's and 1970's, the impact of feminism forced synagogues to make more liberal provisions for women. Wives and daughters insisted upon being heard; they could no longer be ignored.

The following newspaper dispatch recounts what happened in a grass-roots Conservative congregation in Wilkes-Barre, Pennsylvania, where a bitter battle over the question of according additional religious privileges to women resulted in a victory for the liberals.

SYNAGOGUE IN PENNSYLVANIA DIVIDED OVER ROLE OF WOMEN
by Kenneth A. Briggs

WILKES-BARRE, PA.—Joseph Kluger's bar mitzvah drew 500 well-wishers to Temple Israel here on a sunny, crisp day last Saturday. It was the second day of Hanukkah, and the combined effect of the two occasions engendered a festive mood in the congregation.

From the pulpit, Rabbi Abraham D. Barras reminded the onlookers of yet another milestone that belonged to the day. "This marks the last bar mitzvah," the rabbi said, "when a woman will not share in the honors."

Rabbi Barras referred to the decision earlier this month by official vote of the congregation to extend to women all religious rights hitherto reserved for men, including the honor of being called to read a portion of the Torah to the congregation, the status of being counted for the minyan—the quorum of 10 needed for a prayer service—and the responsibility for leading services.

The outcome of the vote, two-to-one in favor of change, followed months of emotional, sometimes bitter debate that continues to shake the 52-year-old congregation.

REACTIONS TO CHANGE

Some, including the rabbi, pushed hard for changes and welcome the results as an exciting departure, a new lease on life symbolized in the story of Hanukkah. Many moderates, describing themselves as traditionalists, backed the proposal but have deep reservations. The opponents, meanwhile, are split between those who will try to abide the innovations and those who threaten to quit.

The broadest consensus is that the old, established synagogue, made up of many families who helped organize the temple 52 years ago, can withstand the stress that accompanies the decision to embark on a new path.

"There was sufficient pre-education," noted Federal District Judge Max Rosenn, a member, "and it was done on a democratic basis. Those who lost are disappointed, but not embittered."

Temple Israel's struggle is mirrored in Conservative congregations across the nation that are assessing women's roles. By choosing to discard traditional barriers, moreover, the temple sided with a growing number of Conservative bodies that have begun to open doors to women, particularly since the umbrella United Synagogue of America organization urged such action three years ago.

SURVEY ON THE TREND

One survey earlier this year by Rabbi Stephen C. Lerner and his wife, Anne Lapidus Lerner, an instructor at Jewish Theological Seminary indicates the trend is well along. Of a total of 700

Conservative temples polled, 229 responded, 114 of which showed an expanded role for women in the past few years.

"These figures clearly show that significant changes in religious practice have taken place in our movement in the past two to three years," Rabbi Lerner concludes.

The pattern has not evolved without serious resistance. A group of 150 Conservative rabbis, many of them in Queens, have banded together in order to, in the words of one rabbi, "slow down the whole movement toward equality."

Particularly for congregations such as Temple Israel, the largest synagogue in an area where Jews account for 4,700 persons in an overall population of a quarter-million, the controversy involves a threat to the cohesion that has provided a spiritual anchor for generations.

FLOOD'S IMPACT FELT

Adversity of a different kind struck the temple four years ago when rampaging Susquehanna flood waters overflowed dikes and deposited a thick layer of mud on the sanctuary floor. Members pitched in, borrowed $600,000 for restoring the handsome brick edifice and, in the view of many, emerged with a stronger sense of pride in the congregation.

The drive to enhance women's religious rights tested this fiber. For several years, girls have received the same religious schooling as boys and have been tendered the bas mitzvah, the equivalent to the boys' bar mitzvah.

"We did encourage them to be bas mitzvah," said Shirle Gray, a member, "and that was marvelous. But the inequality was that we never allowed them to ascend that pulpit. That wasn't fair."

Similar signs of discontent have been growing. This past summer a special commission on ritual and custom was appointed to study the question of broadening women's prerogatives.

STRONGLY WORDED SERMON

The rabbi placed his weight behind proposed reforms in a strongly worded sermon during the High Holy Days. Shortly thereafter, a letter to the rabbi from the girls' confirmation class declared, "We believe that we are outcasts of Temple Israel's congregation because of this participation."

Debate raged for weeks in homes, on street corners and at the temple. On Nov. 24, ballots were mailed to congregants. Seventy-five percent voted. Every age category of each sex approved the change, though with varying margins. Least supportive were men over 60.

Minds changed in the process. Others hardened past positions. Many women said they did not want the new privileges for themselves but believed younger women should be entitled to them.

"I consider myself a traditionalist," said Herbert Rittenberg, "and for years I was against this. I wouldn't allow my daughter to be bas mitzvah and I didn't feel women should be on the pulpit."

An Optimistic View

"But now I've thought about it," he continued, "and I feel that in the long range view the strengthening of Judaism depends on greater participation by women."

On the other hand, Dr. Milton Burnat, a retired dentist, is convinced the temple is making a tragic mistake. "This is a very serious matter, and I disagree completely," he said. "It has divided the congregation, and I don't think I'll worship here any more."

Mrs. Isadore Goldstein insisted that women have been honored in the past and should not take over duties traditionally performed by men. "When I come to temple and walk in the door I feel that I count," she said, "Maybe I don't count in a minyan, but I'm there to worship with my husband. I'm very satisfied when my husband and my sons get an honor."

Rabbi Barras, who has served in this synagogue for 25 years, argues against the objection that tradition is offended by giving women full responsibilities. "It is equally offensive to deny women," he says.

'THE TIME HAS COME'

Why the overwhelming vote of approval for change? Morris Perloff, who describes himself as a "senior citizen" of the temple, summarizes the opinion of many members. "The time had come," he said, "for this idea to bear fruit. A half-dozen years ago, the margin would not have been so large. Six years from now it would have been larger."

For many in attendance at Joseph Kluger's bar mitzvah, the observance was the most impressive show of solidarity since the vote was counted on December 6.

The sparkle and charm of the boy became a striking focal point. Seated on long dark wooden pews, congregants smiled affectionately when Allan Kluger placed a handwoven prayer shawl around his son's shoulders and kissed the boy's cheek.

When the boy adeptly chanted his portion of Torah, the congregants exchanged looks of approval and admiration.

And after the final blessing, they filed into a room below, greeting one another with handshakes and embraces. Reaching for a miniature bagel with lox, one woman said, "We have our difficult moments, but this is a great place to be."

169

WOMEN IN THE SYNAGOGUE*
1977

In the following genre-like sketch, Lucy Dawidowicz discourses on women in the synagogue. For the most part, she writes about those of her fellow-Jewesses who, like her, prefer the Orthodox shul. She has little sympathy for the Reform service and its abbreviated prayer book. (Actually, Gates of Prayer: The New Union Prayer Book *is now just about 800 pages in length.) In the synagogue, this distinguished scholarly woman prefers "ignorant piety to literate brevity." Lucy Dawidowicz is devoted to the traditional way of life; it satisfies and fulfills her spiritually, emotionally.*

Lucy (Mrs. S. M.) Dawidowicz (b. 1915) is a notable writer and researcher who has worked in different fields. She was a member of the American Jewish Committee staff before she began to teach at Yeshiva University. A specialist in Holocaust studies, Mrs. Dawidowicz is the author of The War Against the Jews, 1933–1945.

My shul is better than most, I think, partly because it has only a modest share in the affluence that many American Jews enjoy. It is an Orthodox shul in the middle-middle-class community of Jackson Heights in Queens. . . . Most of its congregants are native Europeans who fled to the United States from Poland, Hungary, Austria, and Germany, some by way of Auschwitz and displaced-persons camps. Neither rich nor poor, they are small businessmen, retailers, accountants, salesmen, a few professionals.

The women, for the most part, are not prosperous enough to own the embroidered garments that the Vilna Gaon warned against or the mink habiliments that are de rigueur for bar mitzvahs. Their mode of dress and adornment would hardly necessitate any such sumptuary legislation as that enacted by

Jewish communal officials in Poznan (for example) in 1629, forbidding tailors, under penalty of a fine, to accept orders "for a garment of satin or damask even from the leading families of the province." Besides, being Orthodox (more or less), the women in my shul are by nature, as it were, decorous in their dress: the vagaries or vulgarities of individual taste are curbed by the insistence of tradition on modesty and propriety. . . .

This shul is, above all, a place where people come to pray. When there is a bar mitzvah ceremony, it does not usurp the service. The boy reads the haftarah; the rabbi acknowledges the occasion in his sermon and bestows upon the celebrant the sisterhood's gift of a *siddur;* then the service goes on as usual. The women, too, come to pray. Whenever they arrive—no matter how late—they recite the Shemoneh Esreh. Then they catch up with the rest of the congregation. Even behind the partition of lattice and scrollwork, the women of this shul can find their place in the prayerbook, without assistance from their menfolk.

To my astonishment—for I consider myself modern—I find I like the partition. Because of it, men are more intent on the liturgy (and, for that matter, women are too) than they might otherwise be. The original reason for separating the sexes, a practice which dates all the way back to the Temple, when women were assigned to the *ezrat nashim* [the women's area], was, presumably, to discourage amorous thoughts. Later, to ensure the same purpose, rabbinic leaders prescribed special galleries for women in the synagogue so that they "should look down from above and men look from below." (This was not a uniquely Jewish problem. Some English churches in the Middle Ages separated the sexes to discourage philanderers who, as John Gower put it, "in churches and in minstres eke, / That gon the women for to seke." The Duke of Mantua, a notorious operatic seducer second only to Don Giovanni, used to go to church to find girls when things got dull at his court.)

Separation by partition or gallery does, as a matter of fact, help the congregants concentrate on prayer. Separation also ensures that the service remains a men's service, that women do not usurp it. Judaism has always depended on its males to maintain the congregation. That is their prime responsibility. Because women do not share this responsibility, we are told again and again that Judaism regards women as inferior creatures. Every Jewish male, on arising, recites these benedictions:

> Blessed art thou, O Lord our God, King of the universe, who hast not made me a heathen.
> Blessed art thou, O Lord our God, King of the universe, who hast not made me a slave.
> Blessed art thou, O Lord our God, King of the universe, who hast not made me a woman.

Christians who like to argue the relative merits of religions often adduce Paul's annulment of these discriminatory distinctions as evidence of Christianity's greater tolerance for women: "There is neither Greek nor Jew, there is neither bond nor free, there is neither male nor female, for ye are all one in Christ Jesus" (Gal. 3:28). To propagandize his new religion, Paul promised equality both here and in the hereafter to heathens, slaves, and women. But on those women who were already committed to Christianity, he imposed total subservience. "*Mulieres in ecclesiis taceant,*" he wrote: "Let your women keep silence in the churches: for it is not permitted unto them to speak; but they are commanded to be under obedience, as also saith the law" (1 Cor. 14:34). And he commanded them also to dress and act modestly, and to pray in silence and subjection. For their sins, and Eve's original sin, they could be saved only by childbearing and "faith and charity and holiness with sobriety" (1 Tim. 2:9–15). What an easy argument for a Jewish polemicist to rebut: Compare the honor accorded the woman of valor in the Book of Proverbs [Chap. 31:10–13]. . . .

On Simhat Torah morning once, I attended services at a Reconstructionist synagogue, where I had been urged to come because the Torah reading was said to be beautiful. It was indeed, but Reconstructionists are much too rationalistic to observe Simhat Torah as it ought to be observed, and Simhat Torah is too transcendental, too supernatural for the Reconstructionists to assimilate. But I did not mind the dry-as-dust service so much as I did the feminist spirit which informed it. Women have equal rights in this synagogue all year round, and Simhat Torah was no exception. Not only were women called up to the Torah for *aliyot* (that is an ordinary Sabbath routine here), but they were also given the privilege of *Hatan Torah* [Bridegroom of the Law], which, Reconstructionists being strict rationalists, was renamed *Kallat Torah* [Bride of the Law]. Watching these women embrace the Torah, I found myself seized by wicked and perverse thoughts. Wicked: how insensible was this movement to the festival's symbolism, to its music and poetry. Perverse: only here could transvestitism appear as innocent farce.

If ever men abdicate their synagogal responsibilities to women, the synagogue will, I fear, succumb either to Italianization or to Hadassah-ization. Women, when passive, can turn the synagogue into something like a provincial Italian Catholic church. The rabbi assumes all sacerdotal functions: the women become his dutiful parishioners whose religion is part devotion, part ignorance, and part superstition. Religion, then, becomes a womanish thing. Men stay away out of contempt. But even more forbidding—to me at least—is the threat of female power, female usurpation of the synagogue. Women are efficient: they can organize, raise funds, bring order out of chaos. They can turn the shul into a Hadassah chapter. Not that I disapprove of Hadassah, its activities, or its ladies. But I do not like the idea of their taking over the synagogue. To my mind, the assumption by a woman of a rabbinic or priestly function in the synagogue undermines the very essence of Jewish tradition. To say that the "Jewish women's movement" is inherently antitraditionalist and implicitly antinomian is only to speak tautologically. . . .

That there is too much talking in shul is a criticism Jewish universalists are prone to make of Jewish particularists, as if idle conversation during services were unique to Jews or to Jewish women. But the complaint is more universal than the universalists may care to concede, because they are so particularist in their criticism of particularism. Bertold of Regensburg, a thirteenth-century Franciscan preacher, used to grumble at churchgoers who,

> while God is being served with singing or reading . . . laugh and chatter as if they were at a fair. . . . And ye women, ye never give your tongues rest from useless talk! One tells the

other how glad the maidservant is to sleep and how loth to work; another tells of her husband; a third complains that her children are troublesome and sickly!

One reason why women gossip in shul is, of course, that they have an innate feminine proclivity for it: "Of ten measures of talk that came down to the world, women took nine" [Talmud Bavli, Kedushin 49b]. Another reason is that they simply do not understand what is going on. I have discovered that many women in my shul, who can recite the prayers more fluently than I, seldom know their meaning, although they can locate them immediately in the *siddur*. Least of all do they understand the Torah reading. This, too, was not always the case. When Ezra first read the Torah, everyone knew what was going on: "And they read in the book, in the Law of God, distinctly; and they gave the sense, and caused them to understand the reading" (Neh. 8:8).

The Hasidim of medieval Germany believed that understanding the liturgy was the key to *kavanah*, the mystical meditation on the meaning and words of the prayers, inducing communion with God. The *Sefer Hasidim* (Book of the Devout) counseled God-fearing men who knew no Hebrew and women, "who certainly do not understand Hebrew" but who wanted to pray with *kavanah*, to pray in the language they understood: "For prayer is the heart's pleading. If the heart understands not what the lips utter, what good is such prayer?" Presumably, the Reform movement solved this problem with the Union Prayer Book. Reform women can understand the prayers; but if they don't gossip, or gossip less, in Reform Temple, it may be because the service is too short for social intercourse. The *Shema* and the *Shemoneh Esreh* have been so truncated that there is little left of the original liturgy either to understand or to misunderstand. And since hardly any Torah is read, that problem, too, has been solved by being done away with. I, for one, prefer ignorant piety to literate brevity. Besides, I find decorum more unnerving than talk.

Nevertheless, in my shul the hubbub of conversation during Torah reading often annoys me. But then, too, I can afford to be self-righteous because I have no one to talk to. Though I pay my way, I am an anonymous creature there. Sometimes, when I get lonesome, I daydream about my ideal *ezrat nashim*, about shul-going women I would like to talk to. When I come back to reality, I find I like things pretty much as they are. Still, it would be nice to have a friend with me once in a while so that I, too, could talk and be like other women in shul.

170

ROSALYN SUSSMAN YALOW, NOBEL PRIZE WINNER
1977–1978

In 1977, Rosalyn Yalow was awarded the Nobel Prize for medicine and physiology. In the autobiography which follows, selection A, she tells the story of her life. She was fortunate in that she sought to do graduate work in the early days of World War II, at a time when young male scientists were being called into government service. Despite the fact that she was a woman, she managed to crawl into the interstitial spaces in the science laboratories of graduate schools. Though exposed to some discrimination because she was a woman, she pursued her studies and eventually became the "first American-trained woman to be the recipient of a Nobel Prize in any of the sciences."

The year after she was honored by the Nobel Committee, the Ladies' Home Journal *informed her that she was to receive a special woman's award; she politely but firmly rejected the* Journal's *offer, which she saw as a "ghetto" citation given her because she was a brilliant woman, not a brilliant scientist. As a feminist, she was an egalitarian. In selection B, she describes in detail her reasons for refusing to accept the honor which the* Journal *was prepared to accord her.*

A

ROSALYN S. YALOW
1977

I was born on July 19, 1921 in New York City and have always resided and worked there except for 3½ years when I was a graduate student at the University of Illinois.

Perhaps the earliest memories I have are of being a stubborn, determined child. Through the years my mother has told me that it was fortunate that I chose to do acceptable things, for if I had chosen otherwise no one could have deflected me from my path.

My mother, nee Clara Zipper, came to America from Germany at the age of four. My father, Simon Sussman, was born on the Lower East Side of New York, the Melting Pot for Eastern European immigrants. Neither had the advantage of a high school education but there was never a doubt that their two children would make it through college. I was an early reader, reading even before kindergarten, and since we did not have books in my home, my older brother, Alexander, was responsible for our trip every week to the Public Library to exchange books already read for new one to be read.

By seventh grade I was committed to mathematics. A great chemistry teacher at Walton High School, Mr. Mondzak, excited my interest in chemistry, but when I went to Hunter, the college for women in New York City's college system (now the City University of New York [CUNY]), my interest was diverted to physics, especially by Professors Herbert N. Otis and Duane Roller. In the late '30's when I was in college, physics, and in particular nuclear physics, was the most exciting field in the world. It seemed as if every major experiment brought a Nobel Prize. Eve Curie had just published the biography of her mother, Madame Marie Curie, which should be a must on the reading list of every young aspiring female scientist. As a Junior at college, I was hanging from the rafters in Room 301 of Pupin Laboratories (a physics lecture room at Columbia University) when Enrico Fermi gave a colloquium in January 1939 on the newly discovered nuclear fission—which has resulted not only in the terror and threat of nuclear warfare but also in the ready availability of radioisotopes for medical investigation and in hosts of other peaceful applications.

I was excited about achieving a career in physics. My family, being more practical, thought the most desirable position for me would be as an elementary school teacher. Furthermore, it seemed most unlikely that good graduate schools would accept and offer financial support for a woman in physics. However my physics professors encouraged me and I persisted. As I entered the last half of my senior year at Hunter in September 1940 I was offered what seemed like a good opportunity. Since I could type, another of my physics professors, Dr. Jerrold Zacharias, now at

Massachusetts Institute of Technology, obtained a part time position for me as a secretary to Dr. Rudolf Schoenheimer, a leading biochemist at Columbia University's College of Physicians and Surgeons (P&S). This position was supposed to provide an entree for me into graduate courses, via the backdoor, but I had to agree to take stenography. On my graduation from Hunter in January 1941, I went to business school. Fortunately I did not stay there too long. In mid-February I received an offer of a teaching assistantship in physics at the University of Illinois, the most prestigious of the schools to which I had applied. It was an achievement beyond belief. I tore up my stenography books, stayed on as secretary until June, and during the summer took two tuition-free physics courses under government auspices at New York University.

In September I went to Champaign-Urbana, the home of the University of Illinois. At the first meeting of the Faculty of the College of Engineering I discovered I was the only woman among its 400 members. The Dean of the Faculty congratulated me on my achievement and told me I was the first woman there since 1917. It is evident that the draft of young men into the armed forces, even prior to American entry into the World War, had made possible my entrance into graduate school.

On the first day of graduate school I met Aaron Yalow, who was also beginning graduate study in physics at Illinois and who in 1943 was to become my husband. The first year was not easy. From junior high school through Hunter College, I had never had boys in my classes, except for a thermodynamics course which I took at City College at night and the two summer courses at NYU [New York University]. Hunter had offered a physics major for the first time in September, 1940, when I was an upper senior. As a result my course work in physics had been minimal for a major—less than that of the other first year graduate students. Therefore at Illinois I sat in on two undergraduate courses without credit, took three graduate courses and was a half-time assistant teaching the freshman course in physics. Like nearly all first-year teaching assistants, I had never taught before—but unlike the others I also undertook to observe in the classroom of a young instructor with an excellent reputation so that I could learn how it should be done.

It was a busy time. I was delighted to receive a straight A in two of the courses, an A in the lecture half of the course in Optics and an A- in its laboratory. The Chairman of the Physics Department, looking at this record, could only say "That A- confirms that women do not do well at laboratory work." But I was no longer a stubborn, determined child, but rather a stubborn, determined graduate student. The hard work and subtle discrimination were of no moment.

Pearl Harbor on December 7, 1941 brought our country into the war. The Physics Department was becoming decimated by loss of junior and senior faculty to secret scientific work elsewhere. The campus was filled with young Army and Navy students sent to the campus by their respective services for training. There was a heavy teaching load, graduate courses, an experimental thesis requiring long hours in the laboratory, marriage in 1943, war-time housekeeping with its shortages and rationing, and in January 1945 a Ph.D. in nuclear physics. My thesis director was Dr. Maurice Goldhaber, later to become director of Brookhaven National Laboratories. Support and encouragement came from the Goldhabers. Dr. Gertrude Goldhaber, his wife, was a distinguished physicist in her own right, but with no university position because of nepotism rules. Since my research was in nuclear physics I became skilled in making and using apparatus for the measurement of radioactive substances. The war was continuing. I returned to New York without my husband in January, 1945, since completion of his thesis was delayed and I accepted a position as assistant engineer at Federal Telecommunications Laboratory, a research laboratory for ITT [International Telephone and Telegraph Corporation]—the only woman engineer. When the research group in which I was working left New York in 1946, I returned to Hunter College to teach physics, not to women but to returning veterans in a pre-engineering program.

My husband had come to New York in September, 1945. We established our home in an apartment in Manhattan, then in a small house in the Bronx. It and a full-time teaching position at Hunter were hardly enough to occupy my time fully. By this time my husband was in Medical Physics at Montefiore Hospital in the Bronx. Through him I met Dr. Edith Quimby, a leading medical physicist at P&S. I volunteered to work in her laboratory to gain research experience in the medical applications of radioisotopes. She took me to see "The Chief," Dr. G. Failla, Dean of American medical physicists. After talking to me for a while, he picked up the phone, dialed, and I heard him say "Bernie, if you want to set up a radioisotope service, I have someone here you must hire." Dr. Bernard Roswit, Chief of the Radiotherapy Service at the Bronx Veterans Administration Hospital, and I appeared to have no choice; Dr. Failla had spoken.

I joined the Bronx VA as a part time consultant in December, 1947, keeping my position at Hunter until the Spring Semester of 1950. During those years while I was teaching full-time, I equipped and developed the Radioisotope Service and started research projects together with Dr. Roswit and other physicians in the hospital in a number of clinical fields. Though we started with nothing more than a janitor's closet and a small grant to Dr. Roswit from a veterans' group, eight publications in different areas of clinical investigation resulted from this early work. The VA wisely made a commitment to set up Radioisotope Services in several of its hospitals around the country because of its appreciation that this was a new field in which research had to proceed pari passu with clinical application. Our hospital Radioisotope Service was one of the first supported under this plan.

In January, 1950 I chose to leave teaching and join the VA full time. That Spring when he was completing his residency in internal medicine at the Bronx VA, Dr. Solomon A. Berson and I met and in July he joined our Service. Thus was to begin a 22 year partnership that lasted until the day of his death, April 11, 1972. Unfortunately, he did not survive to share the Nobel Prize with me as he would have had he lived.

During that period Aaron and I had two children, Benjamin and Elanna. We bought a house in Riverdale, less than a mile from the VA. With sleep-in help until our son was 9, and part-time help of decreasing time thereafter, we managed to keep the house going and took pride in our growing children: Benjamin, now 25, is a systems programmer at the CUNY Computer Center; Elanna, now 23, is a third year doctoral candidate in Educational Psychology at Stanford University. She has just married Daniel Webb and is with us on part of her honeymoon.

But to return to the scientific aspects of my life, after Sol joined our Service, I soon gave up collaborative work with others and concentrated on our joint researches. Our first investigations together were in the application of radioisotopes in blood volume determination, clinical diagnosis of thyroid diseases and the kinetics of iodine metabolism. We extended these techniques to studies of the distribution of globin, which had been suggested for use as a plasma expander, and of serum proteins. It seemed obvious to apply these methods to smaller peptides, i.e., the hormones. Insulin was the hormone most readily available in a highly purified form. We soon deduced from the retarded rate of disappearance of insulin from the circulation of insulin-treated subjects that all these patients develop antibodies to the animal insulins. In studying the reaction of insulin with antibodies, we appreciated that we had developed a tool with the potential for measuring circulating insulin. It took several more years of work to transform the concept into the reality of its practical application to the measurement of plasma insulin in man. Thus the era of radioimmunoassay (RIA) can be said to have begun in 1959. RIA is now used to measure hundreds of substances of biologic interest in thousands of laboratories in our country and abroad, even in scientifically less advanced lands.

It is of interest from this brief history that neither Sol nor I had the advantage of specialized post-doctoral training in investigation. We learned from and disciplined each other and were probably each other's severest critic. I had the good fortune to learn medicine not in a formal medical school but directly from a master of physiology, anatomy and clinical medicine. This training was essential if I were to use my scientific background in areas in which I had no formal education.

Sol's leaving the laboratory in 1968 to assume the Chairman-ship of the Department of Medicine at the Mount Sinai School of Medicine and his premature death 4 years later were a great loss to investigative medicine. At my request the laboratory which we shared has been designated the Solomon A. Berson Research Laboratory so that his name will continue to be on my papers as long as I publish and so that his contributions to our Service will be memorialized. At present my major collaborator is a young, talented physician, Dr. Eugene Straus, who joined me in 1972, first as a Fellow, then as Research Associate and now as Clinical Investigator.

Through the years Sol and I together, and now I alone, have enjoyed the time spent with the "professional children," the young investigators who trained in our laboratory and who are now scattered throughout the world, many of whom are now leaders in clinical and investigative medicine. In the training in my laboratory the emphasis has been not only in learning our research techniques but also our philosophy. I have never aspired to have nor do I now want a laboratory or a cadre of investigators-in-training which is more extensive than I can personally interact with and supervise.

The laboratory since its inception has been supported solely by the Veterans Administration Medical Research Program and I acknowledge with gratitude its confidence in me and its encour-agement through the years. My hospital is now affiliated with The Mount Sinai School of Medicine where I hold the title of Distinguished Service Professor. I am a member of the National Academy of Sciences. Honors which I have received include, among others: Albert Lasker Basic Medical Research Award; The A. Cressy Morrison Award in Natural Sciences of the N.Y. Academy of Sciences; Scientific Achievement Award of the American Medical Association; The Koch Award of the Endo-crine Society; The Gairdner Foundation International Award; American College of Physicians Award for distinguished con-tributions in science as related to medicine; Eli Lilly Award of the American Diabetes Association; First William S. Middleton Medical Research Award of the VA and five honorary doctorates.

B

THANK YOU, BUT NO THANK YOU
by Rosalyn Yalow
1978

Following are excerpts from a letter written by Dr. Rosalyn Yalow, one of the recipients of the 1977 Nobel Prize in Physiology or Medicine, to Lenore Hershey, editor in chief of the Ladies' Home Journal. In it, Dr. Yalow, senior medical researcher at the Veterans Administration Hospital in the Bronx, explains her reasons for not accepting one of the Ladies' Home Journal 1978 "woman of the year" awards.

There is no doubt that women are disproportionately under-represented among the scientists, scholars and leaders of our world. The failure of women to have arrived at positions consistent with their potential has been due in large part to social and professional discriminatory attitudes.

Some women have felt the need to strengthen their own psyches by banding together in women's groups since they, quite properly, felt rejected by the leadership of the "male world." Others, recognizing the existence of the problem, thought that if we were ever to move upwards we must demonstrate competence, courage and determination to succeed and must be prepared to challenge and take our place in the Establishment.

In 1961 a Federal Woman's Award was established to honor outstanding women in the Federal Civil Service. This award was clearly in recognition of the fact that women were under-represented as recipients of other awards, presumably open to all in federal service, but generally given largely if not exclusively to men. I viewed this award as second-class and, when I was chosen to be one of the first six recipients, my initial reaction was to reject it.

I was prevailed upon to accept and did in fact use the recognition accorded me to point out that even more important to women than honors or super-grade positions was the requirement of equal pay for equal work. Women in Civil Service did not have many of the important fringe benefits given to men such as protection for their spouses and children in medical, pension and death benefits. In the succeeding years some of these benefits have been better equalized and women are moving up, though too slowly, to positions of greater responsibility in some, though not all, of the government services.

Increasingly women are beginning to receive a fairer share of recognition for their accomplishments. I was therefore delighted to learn last year that the Federal Woman's Award was to be discontinued; I hope permanently.

It is obvious that there are differences between men and women. There may be perhaps good reason for awards to an outstanding father or mother; or a great husband or wife; perhaps even for the best actor or the best actress—all these are clearly sex-related. We recognize that on the average men are taller and stronger than women, so that it might be reasonable to have sex-related awards for athletic prowess. However there are fields of athletics in which these physical differences may be irrelevant and for these there should be awards for the best athlete—with no modifying adjective.

It may well be that, taken as a group, men are more intelligent, imaginative and talented than women. I do not accept this hypothesis; certainly such differences are not manifest in the very young and the differences in apparent aptitude even in fields such as science which are demonstrable beginning in adolescent and young adult life are quite likely attributable to what I call social discrimination—the non-competitiveness shown by many or even most women because of social pressures.

However, even if this hypothesis were valid, there is sufficient overlap such that some women can and should be expected to be fully competitive with the most talented of men. I therefore deem it inconsistent and unwise to have awards restricted to women or to men in fields of endeavor where excellence is not inherently sex-related.

As the first American-trained woman to be the recipient of a Nobel Prize in any of the sciences I feel that I have a special responsibility. I know very well that this ultimate reward does not make me more competent, more knowledgeable or in any way more worthy than I was before this recognition. However it does make me more visible. Therefore I cannot conform to traditional stands with which I disagree even if it were easier for me to not "make waves."

I have decided not to accept the 1978 Woman of the Year Award in the category of New Scientific Community from the Ladies' Home Journal although it would perhaps have been more diplomatic to accept it. I think it more appropriate for me to take a positive stand by rejecting what Susan Jacoby would have called a "ghetto" award.

She stated, very wisely I believe, that "A ghetto job is a ghetto job as long as it is perceived by male executives—and by the woman they hire—as a job with a 'for women only' sign. It doesn't matter whether the salary is $50,000 or $7,500 a year. . . . The situation can only be changed by women who regard themselves and are regarded by others as being plain excellent—not excellent only in comparison to other women. . . . Women who have 'made it' are no longer pleased to be told that their achievements are remarkable for a woman."

To this statement those of us who are committed to full equality for women can only add, "Amen."

Women, and other groups who have been victims of discrimination, may yet have a long way to go before achieving full equality. There may remain the need for some among us to accept token jobs or token awards as a temporary expedient on the road upwards. But we must view these aberrations as being temporary, worthy only for self-destruction.

If we are to have a world in which all people regardless of sex, race or creed are considered equally worthy some must take a stand against such discrimination. I do—I am certain that many others have in the past and will in the future join me in this stand.

171

RAPE AND THE JEWISH LAW
1977

It is a sad commentary on late-twentieth-century American civilization that Solomon B. Freehof, the Reform rabbinate's well-known authority on Jewish law, was asked to write a responsum on the religiolegal status of a Jewess who had been raped. Beyond the answer of the learned respondent is the significant fact that many Reform Jews are turning to halakah, the Jewish legal tradition. In the past, Classical Reformers often denied the binding authority of much in biblical and rabbinical law. Today, liberals want to know at least the content of the rabbinic prescriptions and even to be guided by them, if they find them rational and in consonance with the times. Jews of this generation are turning to "authority"; there is always a flight to the past in an age of political and spiritual crisis. Jews have begun to huddle together for comfort, all this in the aftermath of the Holocaust.

MARITAL RIGHTS OF A RAPED WOMAN

QUESTION:

If a married woman is raped, is the husband required to divorce her? What, in general, is the status in Jewish law of a woman who is the victim of a rapist? (Asked by S.S.)

ANSWER:

The problems, marital and legal, involved in the crime of rape are being discussed nowadays quite frequently and heatedly. This is true partly because of the general laxity of present-day morals and also because many social-minded people, and especially advocates of women's rights, protest the present treatment by the civil authorities of a woman who declares that she is the victim of rape. The charge is often made that the police question the woman in such a way as to imply that she was not raped at all but had consented to, or even encouraged, the sexual encounter. For all these reasons, it becomes rather important nowadays to analyze the status in Jewish law of a woman who is raped or who says that she has been raped.

The laws on this matter go all through Jewish legal literature, beginning with the Bible, continuing in the Talmud, and finding permanent place in the Codes, such as the *Shulchan Aruch* [16th cent.] and Maimonides [12th cent.]. It becomes clear, even from a cursory reading of the material involved, that Jewish law has maintained an attitude which is precisely the opposite of that imputed to the legal authorities today. That is to say, Jewish law, from the very beginning, comes to the defense of the woman who is raped or who claims to be raped. The Bible, in Deuteronomy 22:29, says that if a man rapes an unmarried woman, he must pay a fine and then must marry her and may never divorce her. The Mishnah repeats this law in *Ketubos* 3:4. The Talmud, discussing the matter in *Ketubos* 39b, says that the rapist must pay for the pain and shame that he has caused, and must marry his victim even if she is blind or lame (or deformed). The *Shulchan Aruch*, in *Even Hoezer* 177:3, modifies this law as follows: The rapist must marry the girl provided the father and the girl both consent to the marriage. And the *Shulchan Aruch* continues that if he divorces her, he must be compelled to take her back again.

Of course, rabbinical courts today do not deal with such matters. They confine themselves to cases in civil law, such as contracts, debts, etc., but do not consider that they still have the right to deal with criminal law, such as murder, rape, etc. (see *Choshen Mishpot* #1). Nevertheless, it is the decision of the scholars that the rapist, while he can no longer be legally compelled to do so, should be pressured to marry her (of course, as the *Shulchan Aruch* says, if she consents to be married to him). (See article "Anussa" in *Ozar Yisroel*.)

All this applies to an unmarried girl who is the victim of rape. But what if the victim is a married woman? Is there any reason in the law for the husband to divorce her? The questioner has the impression that this is so. This impression has some logic since it is based upon a clear analogy, namely, that if a woman is voluntarily and definitely immoral, her husband must divorce her. The question asked here is therefore the following: Does this duty to divorce her apply to a woman who is the victim of rape?

Definitely not! The Talmud in *Ketubos* 51b, discusses the matter and clearly states that if a wife is the victim of rape, she is permitted to continue as wife to her husband. The ground for this permission is the general principle in rabbinic law that a person under compulsion is forgiven whatever sin he may have committed (*onus rachmona patray* [the Merciful One acquits the one who is forced]). In fact the Talmud says that if she is being raped but during the process yields and participates willingly, even then she is to be forgiven because her desire has overcome her.

So the *Shulchan Aruch*, in *Even Hoezer* 6:11, states as a law that a woman who is raped is permitted to remain married to her husband. See *Be'er Hetev*, ibid., who says it is *obvious* (*pashut*) that she is permitted to remain his wife. The *Encyclopedia Talmudis* (s.v. "Anussa") refers to some authorities who are in doubt as to whether the husband need divorce his wife. But actually their doubts concern only the question of whether the wife was really raped or not. Yet even as to such doubts, the presumption of the law is that her statement is generally to be accepted as true. Of course if it is certain that she had been raped, then all authorities agree that the husband may keep her as his wife.

The *Shulchan Aruch*, stating this law, adds, however, that if her husband is a priest, she is not permitted to remain married to him. This exception is due to the special laws of ritual sanctity that surround the priesthood. For example, it is not a sin for a woman to be a divorcee, yet a priest may not marry a divorcee. In other words, the priest must follow special laws of sanctity which do not necessarily reflect upon the character of a wife.

It is interesting that even with regard to a raped woman and a priestly husband, there is a variation of the law which indicates that the attitude of Jewish law is exactly opposite to that which is imputed to present-day authorities. This variation is found in *Even Hoezer* 6:13. If it is proved definitely that the woman was raped, then, as has been stated, the priest may not retain her as wife, just as he may not marry a divorced woman. But if there is no proof, but she declared that she has been raped, the priest *may* continue to keep her as a wife, although after the priest dies his widow may not marry any other priest because of doubt.

Also related to the above discussion is the question of a captive woman. Here, too, the question rises of Jewish women taken into captivity and the presumption that they are raped as helpless captives. May the husband keep a captive woman after she is ransomed? These questions are discussed in the *Shulchan Aruch*, *Even Hoezer* 7, and it is clear that the slightest proof that the woman has remained pure is accepted both for Israelite and priestly husband. See especially the famous responsum of Meir of Rothenburg in [S. B. Freehof] *Responsa Literature*, pp. 99 ff.

To sum up: Contrary to the alleged attitude of present-day civil authorities, Jewish law from the very beginning has always been on the side of the woman-victim. If she is unmarried, the rapist must marry her if she consents to the marriage. If she is a married woman, the husband may keep her, unless he is a priest, for priests are subject to special laws which do not reflect upon the character of the woman.

172

BAT MITZVAH ADDRESS OF A YOUNG
ARISTOCRAT
1977

On Saturday, June 11, 1977, Susan Brandeis Popkin, great-granddaughter of United States Supreme Court Justice Louis D. Brandeis, delivered a bat mitzvah address at the Washington Hebrew Congregation, in Washington, D.C. Because the portion from the Bible read in most synagogues that week was Numbers 13–15, Susan used it to emphasize the virtue of moral courage. Moses, Joshua, and Caleb of old and her ancestor, Justice Brandeis, had all fought for the right against great odds.

The very fact that Susan was bat mitzvah, confirmed in her religious identity at the age of thirteen, is significant. Justice Brandeis, son of a Bohemian forty-eighter, had not been a religionist; neither, as far as it is known, was his father, Adolph. Over a hundred years after the birth of Louis D. Brandeis, his great-granddaughter publicly affirmed her allegiance to Judaism, the religion. Assimilation, in the sense of defection, is not inevitable in American Jewish life. It is not easy to guess how the Justice would have reacted had he been privileged to see little Susan recite the Hebrew blessings at her bat mitzvah. One thing is sure: Brandeis' uncle Louis N. Dembitz, after whom he was named in 1856, would have gaped with astonishment, maybe even pride. He was an observant Orthodox Jew.

My torah portion helped me to understand the true message of courage. It tells how afraid the Israelites were to enter the promised land. Even after the spies who had scouted the land told the people how good it was, the Israelites were still afraid. Yet Moses found courage from the Lord which enables him to lead the Israelites out of Egypt to the Promised Land.

Moses was one of the most courageous men in Jewish history. He had the strength to keep his people's spirits up when they had lost faith. He was brave but his moral courage was more outstanding. Moses used this courage to stand up to the people when they turned against him. An example of this took place in my torah portion.

I admire people who are courageous when it comes to facing danger. I would like to be brave when it is needed, but I would also like to have moral courage.

Moral courage means doing things you believe in and know to be right. It means standing up strongly for a person or an idea, even if many others disagree. It is difficult to fight for an idea when others are arguing in opposition.

My great-grandfather, Justice Louis D. Brandeis, showed a great deal of moral courage on behalf of the people of this country. He was one of the earliest fighters for Zionism and the Jewish cause. He was known as the "people's attorney" because he frequently worked for causes of the people against big business. In one example, he fought for minimum wages and better working conditions for women. He became famous for his defense of the individual. He thought that "Courage" was "the secret of liberty" and that democracy must be based on the responsibility of each individual.

I would like to follow in my great-grandfather's tracks. I am very interested in law and the supreme court. I also am very interested in Zionism and the fight for Israel and the Jewish people.

I hope always to stand for what is right and to defend the rights of the individual.

I would like to thank my family for making this occasion special. It has made it even more special to have my friends share it with me.

173

POSTEVENTUM REFLECTIONS OF A CONVERT
1977

In 1972, Irma Bailey, an educator, became a convert to Judaism. Five years later she reviewed her decision; she had no regrets. Though Mrs. Bailey is black, it would seem that her racial background in no sense influenced her decision to embrace Conservative Judaism. In the following brief sketch, she describes some of her experiences and some of her thoughts since she turned to the Jewish religion.

Conversions to Judaism by women are relatively frequent today; thousands of Gentiles have taken this fateful step. Most of them have changed their faith in order to marry a Jew; how many are happy in their new religion is difficult to determine. Reform Jews in particular are not adverse to proselytism; they tend to be cordial to neophytes and strive to make them feel at home socially and religiously. This is, generally speaking, also true of the Conservatives. Mrs. Bailey is a vice-president of the Beth Israel sisterhood in Coatesville, Pennsylvania.

THOUGHTS OF A CONVERT FIVE YEARS LATER
by Irma Bailey

Since most of us go through life having to make decisions, when we finally make a choice it becomes a special event, particularly when that choice is to change one's entire life style. For those who find it difficult to choose what to wear each morning or what to select from a large, descriptive menu in a restaurant, the choice of converting to Judaism may well represent the one declarative statement the individual will make in his or her lifetime.

I believe that most of those of us who have made the decision and taken the option of converting to Judaism have not done so under stress. Whatever the circumstances surrounding an individual's ultimate decision, I believe it to have been made under conditions of absolute clarity of mind. Conversion should never be considered lightly by the convert—or by those in the community who may look on the convert as an oddity.

I suppose the question that comes to the minds and tongues of most people upon learning of my choice, is why? Quite honestly, I have asked myself that same question many times. The answer is, simply, that it seemed the natural thing for me to do. Most important, it was what I wanted. Having served as a volunteer with a Zionist organization, I developed strong feelings for the State of Israel and developed many solid Jewish friendships. The many role models who have evolved from those friendships have become people for whom I hold great admiration. They helped to reinforce my decision.

A few years ago, I was told by a Jewish friend, who was having some difficulty identifying with his heritage, that he could accept me as a Negress, but not as a Jew. My reply was, "That is your problem, since I have not asked for your acceptance in either area." A pretty brash statement but, nonetheless, true. Since acceptance by others does not come easily to any of us in any area, my task was to prove by my actions the strength of my commitment.

The choice is not, and has not been, a bed of roses. Making the decision and then living with it daily, sometimes proves to be difficult with family, friends and associates. Some refuse to believe; others seem to accept so overwhelmingly that it is sometimes frightening. I feel this temporary air of discomfort stems from people's innate and unchangeable mind sets. Fortunately, THEY are the minority.

Being a black mother of five is not immediately in consonance with modern conservative standards. Acceptance of my religious conversion in the very town in which I was born and raised was the more complex. My own mother, when she saw my photograph in the local paper recently, commented, "I saw your picture with all those Jews." A Jewish friend upon learning of my choice, quipped, "How's that? Why that would be like my wanting to become black!" Since I do take my conversion seriously, my reaction to this is with loving humor.

From the day I entered the Rabbinical Assembly's office in Philadelphia to inquire about Jewish studies to having been questioned by a *Bet Din*, to the immersion in the *Mikvah*, to publicly giving up my lifetime of Episcopalianism and pledging my loyalty to Judaism and the Jewish people, to finally reciting the *Shema* as my own personal declaration of faith, I knew I was doing the right thing. I have not regretted my decision once in the last five years.

Those who seemingly convert for reasons of marriage may satisfy, or give the easy answer to, the casual observer. If one examined the individual situation very closely, it would, in many instances, reveal a deep-seated desire to become Jewish and marriage becomes secondary to the happy motivating factor of making a choice. The choice becomes an individual matter entirely.

Most certainly, converts who wish to become members of an established community require both the community's verbal and non-verbal support, to help them with daily living.

Becoming an integral part of the community can only be achieved by total involvement on the part of the convert. The convert must attend Services and become as much a part of the general activity of the community as possible.

How can a community best help a convert? By accepting him on the faith of his choice. How can a convert prove the faith of his choice? By learning and following to the best of his knowledge the tenets of Judaism. In the words of a Negro Spiritual, "Let the Life You Lead, Speak for You."

174

WOMEN IN THE JOB MARKET
1978

Today a very substantial percentage of all employed persons in the United States are women. They are flocking into the job market in large numbers. A few, wives of high-salaried professionals, have time on their hands and desire to do something that has appeal for them. Most women who take jobs do so because they require more money to maintain a decent standard of living in an inflationary age or want to secure the funds to send a youngster through college.

In the following article, Walter Duckat, a psychologist and guidance counselor, describes his experience placing Jewish women and offers advice on the opportunities available to those who seek remunerative work.

SECOND CAREER—GUIDANCE FOR THE MATURE JEWISH WOMAN
by Walter Duckat

Recently, a trim, well-dressed matron came to my office. Her cultured accent and well-tailored clothes evidenced her good breeding and taste. Her husband was a successful surgeon, she explained, and she did not require vocational counseling because of economic need. Nevertheless, with two of her three children married and her youngest away at college, she was seeking fulfilling activities.

She enjoyed painting, was moderately active as a volunteer, but expressed interest in a paid job. She acknowledged apprehension with regard to the receptivity of employers to a woman in her late forties who had not worked since her marriage. Although she had no precise preference, she spoke vaguely about wishing to help others in some creative way. After taking psychological and aptitude tests, she declared her intention to become an occupational therapist aide, an activity which would afford her the opportunity to combine the desire to serve others and to utilize her artistic interests and talents.

Mrs. C.Z., age 43, was a tall, slender, intense woman who came with an urgent request. Obviously distraught, she dabbed her eyes frequently as she explained the circumstances. After 23 years of what she termed a ghastly marriage, she had separated from her husband. "Now that I have left him, the only way to keep my sanity and what's left of my self-esteem is to find a job." Prior to her marriage, she had worked as a secretary but now she wanted administrative work. She was advised of the courses to take that would facilitate entry to such positions.

Mrs. L.T., a petite, soft-spoken, woman of 40 had lost her husband a month previously, after a long illness which had drained their resources. Left with a boy of 14 and a girl of 11, she was torn between her desire to carve out a career to provide for her family and herself, and the wish to have sufficient time with her children. Becoming a medical technologist required expensive schooling. She was advised of financial aid to pursue the program. Since she was also an excellent typist, she was counseled on supplementing her income with part-time typing assignments.

These examples are typical of the situations which come to Jewish Vocational Services and similar facilities throughout the continent. Most mature women who come for vocational counseling do so because of economic need. But I have counseled the wives of physicians, research personnel, engineers, and other professionals who sought employment to meet the rising costs of their standard of living and of school tuition.

A substantial number indicated that the desire for greater self-fulfillment had motivated them. Some expressed their *malaise*, saying that they had lived for their husbands and children, but now wished to satisfy their own aspirations. A few were members of the Women's Liberation Movement.

Except among some European Jewish women whose husbands were scholars, the middle-aged, middle-class working woman is a relatively new phenomenon. During the time of her parents or grandparents, the average woman lived about 14 years after her youngest child was 21 years old. Today, she is likely to live 30 or more years after she has completed her custodial duties as a mother. She observes with increasing uneasiness that despite her efforts, her youthful appearance has begun to fade. With no small children who need her close personal care, her feeling of usefulness may also be declining. Even if he still remembers her birthdays and their anniversaries, her husband's ardor or attentiveness may also have declined. Frequently, she requires reassurance, but neither her husband nor her children, burdened with their own problems, are willing or able to meet her emotional needs.

Because employment allows her to be away from home, it may help to banish her frustration and reaffirm her individuality. But she frequently has to pay for these benefits. Unless she is a professionally trained woman, she is likely to find the jobs available to her are fairly routine, tiring and at best only moderately paid. After taxes, the additional expenditures for clothing, grooming, transportation and lunch, she may have little to show for her efforts. (If it is important that she find work for psychological reasons, these negative factors may be less significant.)

Whatever the reasons that impel mature women to reenter the labor market, their return is marked. Currently, women over 45 constitute about half of all women workers, almost double the percentage of 1940. Forty percent of all employed persons in the United States are women; 13 million of them have children; 74 percent of divorced women are employed.

During more than 30 years of counseling the returning mature woman, I have found certain common tendencies: marked feelings of self-doubt and anxiety, unrealistic aspirations, and unfamiliarity with the current labor market. Husbands who may ridicule their desire to work, rusty skills and a dearth of training facilities may account for some of their fears and doubts. The current bleak job market has discouraged many.

How a woman fares in her quest for employment hinges on such factors as the length of time that she has been away from the labor market, the nature of her training and experience, the demand for her skills, and her appearance and manner. Since she frequently is at a loss on how to proceed, she may find valuable assistance at Jewish Vocational Services found in principal cities of the United States and Canada. The offices of State Employment Services offer job counseling and placement. Private vocational service agencies approved by the National Vocational Guidance Association in Washington, D.C. provide counseling and testing.

Experienced counselors aid their clients to appraise their interests, abilities and personalities and provide important labor market information. Some aid in the preparation of a resumé, school information, job leads, suggestions as to how to respond to interviewers. Interestingly, the major sources for jobs are not employment agencies or newspaper ads, but rather friends and relatives. Of course, if this source is unproductive, one must turn to ads and agencies, apply directly to employers, school placement services and whatever other avenues may be available.

Many clients ask which fields presently offer good opportunities. A precise answer is difficult, because of regional variations and the current glut in a number of professional and other fields. Consider, for example, the shrinkage of jobs that until recently absorbed thousands of women in teaching, social work, and at all levels of City, State and Federal Civil Service. Experts believe well-trained mature women can find berths in such fields as occupational and physical therapy, pharmaceuticals, medical technology, accounting, engineering and dietetics. Opportunities are still plentiful in various phases of secretarial and business machine operation. Generally, the outlook for the mature woman will be best in those fields that have traditionally employed a preponderance of women, and poorest in those highly competitive, artistic or creative fields where emphasis is still on youth.

Many women reentering the labor market prefer to start with part-time jobs. This enables them to discharge their homemaking and community responsibilities more effectively and does not tax them as severely physically as full-time work. Many employers have learned that they can recruit superior staff by adjusting their work schedule to the schedules of some of their employees. But when there is an abundant supply of personnel, there is often resistance to hiring part-time employees because of the additional paper work this may require.

Extensive occupational information is available in the United States Government publication, the *Occupational Outlook Handbook* or this writer's *A Guide to Professional Careers*, both available in many public libraries.

175

A REFORM JEWESS TURNS TO ORTHODOXY
1978

The following brief memoir recounts the decision of a Reform Jewess to study Orthodoxy and, possibly, find a path to a new-old way of life which will bring her a sense of calm and inner peace. It describes a "conversion" in a state of becoming. There are many educated, sophisticated, unhappy women looking for a spiritual home. This search marked the lives of many in the troubled decades of the 1960's and 1970's. Whether these women—and men, too—will find the refuge they glimpse on the far horizon remains to be seen.

FINDING MY JEWISH SELF
by Judith Slawson

I slip into a seat at the back of the classroom of the beginners' Shavuot [Pentecost] study group. It is nearly midnight on a warm June evening and at Lincoln Square Synagogue, a large and popular Orthodox *shul* on Manhattan's West Side, everyone is settling down for the traditional night of study. The rabbi reads with us the story of the Jews receiving the Torah from God. His own feelings of awe and joy communicate themselves to this class of Jews from non-observant backgrounds who are drawn to Orthodox Judaism.

As the night wears on I find myself remembering how when I was a child in the 50's, on the High Holy Days my parents took me to Temple Emanu-el. In that cathedral-like bastion of Reform Judaism, the men were bareheaded while the women wore stylish hats set atop carefully coiffured hair. The service was entirely in English complete with organ, choir and a highly polished sermon. I always felt uncomfortable in the dressy clothes I was expected to wear, bored and fidgety in the chilly atmosphere of that half-world that had almost ceased to be Jewish in its slavish imitations of Christian worship.

I attended Temple Emanu-el's Sunday School; Shabbat didn't exist for me. In the first grade a spirited teacher captured my imagination by telling stories from Genesis as she illustrated them on the blackboard with colored pieces of chalk. I still remember the green pasture indicating the land of Canaan and the two black dots representing Sodom and Gemorrah. It was to be the last interesting learning experience in nine years of Sunday School. The first few were in Temple Emanu-el and the last several in Central Synagogue, after I told my parents I refused to go to Emanu-el any more. Central Synagogue was not quite as cold as Temple Emanu-el but its Sunday School was no improvement.

SULLEN BOREDOM

When I was 14 the Sunday School years ended with a meaningless ceremony called a confirmation. I spent those Sunday mornings in a state of sullen boredom. Except for a few token Hebrew lessons, classes were devoted to a study of Jewish history. But it was a strange kind of history which stopped at the second destruction of the Temple and started again with the contribution of Jews to American life. We learned about the handful of Jews in the American Revolution and the Civil War but I don't remember anything about immigrant life on the Lower East Side, Yiddish culture, life in the ghettos and *shtetls* of Eastern Europe, or of Jews in the Eastern tradition. The Holocaust was never mentioned, and minimal attention was given to the State of Israel. But this was in the 1950's, and I doubt if that self-consciousness about being Jewish, that frantic need to be more American than the Mayflower passengers is typical of Reform Jewish education today. But it did characterize my early religious education and came very close to robbing me forever of the chance for a meaningful Jewish religious experience. The process instilled in me a sense that my Jewishness was an unfortunate burden which was to be carried as unobtrusively as possible.

But every year my parents had a seder to which they invited some European friends. Seeing the joy of these people as they read from the Haggadah and sang the Passover songs gave me an inkling that there was something more to being a practicing Jew than I was given in my sterile Sunday School. My family was highly active in Jewish communal life and they did manage to convey to me a positive sense of being Jewish despite the negative influence of my Reform Jewish education.

After completing Sunday School I didn't set foot in a synagogue for years. I read Jewish history on my own, spent several months in Israel and was always aware of Jewish issues. But while I did have an affirmative sense of being Jewish I had no concrete means of expressing it. I taught in a Catholic school for several years and probably knew more about Catholic theology than about Jewish religious practices.

"LA VIE BOHEME"

Today, I've found a Jewish content to my life: and in the place I would least have expected it—in NYC's Greenwich Village. I had moved to the Village in search of "La Vie Boheme." I wanted to write and to meet artists and writers. The life I made for myself was free of constraints but it lacked warmth, caring, continuity. One day, luckily, I found them, in a small restaurant-delicatessen owned by an elderly couple, Holocaust survivors. A group of "regulars" frequent this restaurant; among them are European Jews, Israelis, and American Jews with an intense interest in Jewish issues. Over endless cups of tea and glasses of mineral water we talk about Jewish literature, history, and politics. There is much laughter, lively conversation and heated debate.

It was through an observant friend I made at the restaurant that I first went to *shul*. I was hesitant to go because I thought that while I had found a *cultural* expression for my Jewishness I would never be able to find a religious one. But at my friend's urging one Rosh Hashanah I did go, and I found a door which should never have been closed to me, beginning to open.

The *shul* is small and Orthodox, tucked way into a corner of a peaceful tree-lined street in Greenwich Village, just a block from where I live. I sit upstairs in the women's section. Although I consider myself a feminist, this does not trouble me because I am in search of the tradition of which this separation is an inherent part. It is a *shul* that takes a stand where deeply felt religious values are involved; it is not concerned with petty customs that have no spiritual significance. It has maintained the separation of the sexes out of conviction although it has cost them congregants; but they don't care what one wears to *shul*. Women can wear long dresses, or dressy suits and slacks or even jeans. Worship is taken seriously; it is not a fashion show.

From attending the little *shul* on the corner I have gotten a glimmer of the warmth and joyous comfort of Jewish religious life, but it has remained peripheral in my own life. My attendance is highly sporadic and still I don't observe Shabbat. The *shul* is a kind of stage setting for me where I play-act a part in a world I have never known. I remember the feeling I had walking through an early autumn misty drizzle to the Hudson River for *Tashlich* with the members of the *shul*. Throwing crumbs into the dirty waters of the Hudson, I understood that I was enjoying the moment for its drama of intensive personal reflection, but the religious symbolism of the crumbs as sins eluded me. [Tashlich is the symbolical casting of one's sins into the water on Rosh Hashanah afternoon.]

"It Will Take Work"

I have come to realize that if I want an authentically Jewish religious life, it will take work and not fantasies. I have begun to study Hebrew, exchanging lessons with Israeli friends to whom I am teaching English composition. The *shul* in the Village is not really for me until I can understand the prayers and the traditions behind them. But that *shul* has awakened in me a spiritual hunger that was lulled into dormancy by the experience of Reform Judaism I had as a child.

In search of knowledge and community I attended a session of a *Havurah* [association] that meets every Shabbat in Greenwich Village, where young Jews with backgrounds of varying degrees of religious observation come together to share prayer and discussion. I felt an earnest sweetness and seeking among the people there which I found heartening. But most of them didn't know that much more than I, and I feel as much a need for instruction as for shared experience.

So I find myself in the beginners' class of a bustling Orthodox *shul* on Shavuot. It is far larger than the *shul* in the Village and offers instruction to those like me who are discovering Orthodox Judaism as adults. This beginners' class meets every Shabbat and I am planning to attend it regularly this Fall. What is learned naturally as a child is learned only with an effort of will as an adult. Whether I have that will remains to be seen.

Dawn is breaking this Shavuot morning. In the room next door the advanced group is going downstairs to the Main Sanctuary for *davening* [praying in Hebrew]. The rabbi concludes the beginners' session by explaining that he has found that for those who come to study Orthodox Judaism as adults, "the crucial factor in whether or not they are going to make it is their commitment to studying Torah." For me this will require a discipline which will prove if my interest in Orthodoxy is solid or a passing phase.

I feel a sadness that my heritage was obscured for me by the sterile Jewish education I was exposed to as a child. It had not even the shadow of the vitality and beauty of the deep Jewish religious experience. As this New Year approaches, I hope it will be the first in which I will be able to follow the weekly Torah readings in *shul*. I am sure that if I am able to become an observant Jew, my religion will be that much more precious to me, for now I know how close I came to never having known it.

176

WOMEN RABBIS IN CONSERVATIVE JUDAISM
1979

The 1970's have found Conservative Jews debating the issue of accepting or rejecting women as rabbis. Inasmuch as the Conservatives have never formally denied the authoritative, binding character of biblical and rabbinical law, they confront what some take to be legal barriers. In important areas of practice, traditional Judaism is a man's religion; women rabbis would be seen as a circumvention of the Law. The opponents of ordination for women wish to preserve the age-old restraints; as traditionalists, they fear that putting women in the pulpit to talk down to men can only be divisive; 4,000 years of Jewish male religious leadership cannot be ignored. The proponents of ordination, cultured American women influenced by feminism, insist on religious equality; women must fulfill themselves; they are as able and dedicated as men; they cannot be urged to study Judaism and then be denied the right to serve as religious leaders. Many Conservatives have been willing to bypass the traditional prohibitions. Conservative Judaism has always favored a synthesis of tradition and modernism. With one exception, by 1979, all the major agencies of the Conservative Movement were ready to ordain females. Only the faculty of the Jewish Theological Seminary in New York City, the defenders of the faith, are not willing to ordain Jewish women as rabbis. As of 1980, they have refused to do so.

If the majority of the Seminary faculty do not opt for ordination, Conservative female devotees will continue to matriculate at the liberal Jewish theological schools and then seek out pulpits in Conservative congregations. And even if the Seminary does finally agree to ordain females, the problem will still remain. Vox populi vox dei. Will the men and women in the pews accept women as their religious leaders or will they relegate them to teaching jobs, assistantships, administrative posts? Time alone will tell. The record of women in Protestant churches over the last century or more suggests that the future for women rabbis is a bleak one. Apparently, the twentieth century is still a man's century.

Still there are men who feel otherwise. In the following document, a sermon preached by Rabbi Jack Segal (b. 1929) of the Beth Yeshurun

Congregation in Houston, Texas, Conservatives are urged to ordain women.

"SHOULD WE HAVE WOMEN IN THE CONSERVATIVE RABBINATE?"
by Rabbi Jack Segal

Several months ago I officiated at a unique wedding in our Chapel. During the 24 years that I have been a rabbi I have co-officiated with Orthodox, Conservative, and Reform rabbis and cantors. But this was the first time that I was co-officiating with a *female* cantor. Both Annette Sondock and I were conducting the wedding service together.

However, prior to the wedding Annette and I, the parents of the bride and groom, and the bride and groom assembled together in the Bride's Room in order to sign the *Ketubah*, the marriage document. As we were about to begin the ritual Annette said to me, "Rabbi, would you like me to sign the *Ketubah* as one of the witnesses?" She said this because she knew that Cantor Wagner always signs the *Ketubah* as a witness when he co-officiates at a wedding with me. She was merely trying to be helpful.

But I must admit that my face quickly turned red and with a forced smile I weakly said, "I'm sorry Annette. I would love to have you sign the *Ketubah* both in Hebrew and English but the Conservative movement has as yet not sanctioned women to be witnesses for such a ritual. It still follows the Orthodox tradition as stated in the Talmud (Yoma 6:1), *'En ha'ishah me'idah,'* 'A woman may not be a witness.' Whenever we receive official documents from the Seminary—conversions, divorces, marriages —you will always notice that the witnesses are men." However, in order to possibly make her feel better I concluded my statement by meekly saying, "I'm really sorry Annette—*maybe next year.*"

But, I still needed a second witness—one who was Jewish, male, older than 13, and not a blood relative of the bride or groom.

Finally, a man was brought into the Bride's Room and I was

told, "Rabbi, this is your second witness," and he proudly said, "Just show me where to sign it."

I showed him the line where he was supposed to sign as the second witness and I said to him, "Please also sign your name in Hebrew on the other line"—and I pointed to a line on the Hebrew side of the document. However, this second witness said, "I don't know my Hebrew name and I don't know how to write Hebrew."

Well, we asked several people and we finally came forth with his Hebrew name and his father's Hebrew name and solved that perplexing problem. However, I then asked him, "Are you a *Kohane, Levi,* or *Yisra'el?*" [priest, Levite, or Israelite]—but he merely hesitated for a moment and then finally said, "Neither . . . I'm a lawyer."

Well, to make a long story short I wrote his full Hebrew name on a piece of paper and he then copied it onto the *Ketubah.*

My friends, I bring this incident to your attention simply because it is not rare. It occurs very frequently.

I bring it to your attention because *he* was considered a legal and kosher witness but *Annette* who leads our Family Service on Rosh Hashanah and Yom Kippur, who teaches our school children how to chant the Haftorah, who conducts our ESP Youth Choir, who trained and led our Youth Choir for the Interfaith Service this year, and who does so many things at our synagogue . . . to *Annette* I was obliged to say, "Sorry, *you* cannot be a witness for a Jewish marriage. You are a woman . . . maybe next year."

My friends, I bring this entire subject to your attention this evening because the Seminary is presently studying a possible major innovation. The Seminary is presently being asked to ordain women as Conservative rabbis . . . which it has so far not done . . . and which it has, up to the present, *refused* to do.

Today, there are 75 girls studying for the rabbinate at the Reform and Reconstructionist Seminaries. In five years, one-third of all the rabbinic graduates of these two Seminaries will be women, but the closest we in the Conservative movement have come to that is the statement: "Our final decision will be made during the summer of 1979."

Until now the Conservative movement has merely stated,

"Yes, women may receive aliyot; they may read from the Torah; they may be considered part of a minyan; but the rabbinate is *verboten* and prohibited to them."

It should be noted that this really is a problem since within the last two or three years many young women have said: "I believe in *Conservative* Judaism; I am comfortable in *Conservative* Judaism; I want to be a religious leader in *our* movement; I want to be a *rabbi*."

However, until now the answer from the Seminary has always been the same: "We feel sympathy for you; we understand your wishes; but, unfortunately, there is no such thing as a 'woman rabbi' within the Conservative movement; there is no such thing as ordaining women within our religious persuasion."

But a week ago this became even more than a theoretical question for me. One of our own Beth Yeshurun girls, a junior in college, said to me, "Rabbi, how do you feel about women rabbis? *I* would like to enter the rabbinate. I have made my decision. I want to be a *rabbi* . . . not a *rebbetzin* [a rabbi's wife]. I want to be a Jewish *leader* . . . not a Jewish *follower*. I want to help *mold* Jewish religious minds . . . not merely have someone do it for me. I don't want to become a Reform or Reconstructionist rabbi . . . I want to be a *Conservative* rabbi. I want to remain within the religious movement in which I was raised and in which I feel comfortable."

My friends, frankly speaking, I agree with her 100%. I must admit that when I came to Beth Yeshurun some 13 years ago I was opposed to such so-called "wild" and "intemperate" ideas. But I have changed. I have matured.

I have changed not because I have been pressured into change but rather because I have given this subject much thought and the only conclusion that I could reach was . . . help open the Seminary and the Conservative rabbinate to those girls who want to become Conservative rabbis.

Before this young girl returned to Austin this week I said to her, "I am willing to make you a test case. I will personally back you, and sponsor you, and encourage you, and if we are successful and eventually you are ordained I will personally be happy to share this pulpit with you and have you become my assistant rabbi."

My friends, since that incident at the wedding several months ago I have taken the liberty of asking many of our members, men and women, young and old: "Are you in favor or are you opposed to having women in the Conservative rabbinate?"

To my surprise, my unofficial, and limited, and unscientific personal survey indicated that most people to whom I spoke were actually opposed to women in the Conservative rabbinate. As I listened to them I heard three major arguments articulated.

Firstly, "What is the next thing you are going to bring to our congregation, rabbi? First you gave women aliyot. Then you brought baby girls on the pulpit to be blessed. Where are we going? I am not used to all these *new* things. Are you trying to make women into men?"

Secondly, I heard others say: "If Moses would come back tomorrow he would not recognize the Judaism he gave us. We are doing away with our *traditions.* Women in the rabbinate is *not* traditional."

Thirdly, still others said to me: "Rabbi, you are taking us further and further away from the Orthodox movement. Our synagogue was always a synthesis of the Orthodox and the Conservative. That is the way we always felt comfortable. In fact, we even have an Orthodox Chapel and a Conservative Sanctuary. But, rabbi, you're trying to break that link. You're bringing us closer to Reform Judaism with your new idea of women rabbis."

My friends, these three statements are very good statements, but unfortunately they really dodge and ignore the major issue.

I am *not* interested in making women into men. I personally believe in *"Vive la différence."* However, I do believe that those women who want to be totally Jewish as *they understand it* should be given that opportunity . . . be it by signing a *Ketubah,* or becoming a rabbi, or performing *any* Jewish ritual that we have.

Yes, I realize that years ago these opportunities were not granted to women and the concept of women rabbis is a new and different concept, but I say that "times have changed." You cannot reattach to the calendar the pages of the months that have already been torn off. One must primarily live in the present and the future.

Do you remember the biblical story of the woman who wanted to live *only* in the past? Do you remember the story of Lot's wife and what happened to her when God destroyed Sodom and Gemorrah?

The Bible tells us that God told Lot and his wife (Gen. 19:17), "*Al tabit achareka,*" "Don't look behind you. (Stop talking about the beautiful parties *you used to have*. Stop referring to the expensive furniture *you used to have*. Stop making comments about the impressive garden *you planted several years ago*. *Stop living in the past*. Face reality. Run toward the mountain. Keep your eyes focused on that which is *before* you . . . the present and the future.)"

But Lot's wife refused to heed God's advice. "*Vatabet ishto me'acharav, vatehi netziv melach,*" (Gen. 19:26). She insisted on turning around, on concentrating on the past, on ignoring the present, and the Bible tells us that she became "*netziv melach,*" "a pillar of salt."

My friends, we, too, can no longer ignore the present and reality. Women, for better or for worse, no longer want to remain home simply sewing, cooking, knitting. Many want to be active in all fields of endeavor and some even want to enter the field of religion.

Frankly speaking, to *me* women in the Conservative rabbinate should not even be thought of as a unique experience by those who are members at Beth Yeshurun. Just think of it, at our synagogue women chant the Torah and Haftorah *regularly*. They chant the Kiddush [the incoming Sabbath or festival bread and wine ceremony] *regularly*. In fact, when the cantor was on vacation this summer who led our services? I'll tell you.

Annette Sondock led the Shabbat services the first week; Margie Burman led the Shabbat services the second week; Barbara Babchick led the Shabbat services the third week; Michelle Hite and Lisa Lewis led the Shabbat services the fourth week . . . and everyone loved each one of those four services.

In addition to this, this year on Rosh Hashanah in the Main Sanctuary the Haftorah will be chanted by Rosemary Pachter and Frances Kaplan . . . and I can assure you that they will do an excellent job.

I can go on and on but I think that there is no necessity for that. Hence, if we at Beth Yeshurun would take a female rabbi to be my assistant I do not think anyone here would be entitled to say, "This is something new at Beth Yeshurun. It is difficult to get used to."

The second argument that was used was that placing women in the rabbinate was not a "traditional" act. However, I say that that really depends on how one defines the word "traditional."

I remember about three years ago a young woman entered the Sanctuary on a Saturday morning and seated herself in the side section toward my left. As I looked at her I noticed something different . . . she had put on a *tallit* [praying shawl] just like the men.

Later, when I entered the Pulaski-Rauch Auditorium for the *Kiddush* several people approached me and said, "Did you see that young woman in the front wearing the *tallit?* Was she cold? Was there something wrong with her?"

Still another individual said, "She must be a leader in a women's liberation organization."

In fact, one woman even said, "It's sacrilegious."

You see, no one had ever previously seen a woman wearing a *tallit* . . . and neither had I . . . and because of that, they were shocked. "It isn't traditional" they said.

But it is interesting to note that even though throughout the centuries women have not worn the *tallit*, the Talmud (Menahot 43a) tells us that there were even some rabbis who felt that women were *obliged* to wear a *tallit*. In fact, the *Maharil* tells us of a certain rabbi's wife, Bruna, who *insisted* on wearing a *tallit*, but still none of the rabbis seemed to become terribly excited about it.

In addition to this, the Talmud tells us (Eruvin 96a) "*Michal bat kushi haitah manechet tephillin velo michu bah chakamin,*" "Michal, the daughter of Kushi (Saul) put on the tephillin every day . . . however, the rabbis did not protest." The rabbis of 2,000 years ago did not get excited and shout, "We protest. IT'S NOT TRADITIONAL." They allowed her to find personal fulfillment in Judaism as *she* thought it necessary. (In fact, Rabbi Aaron ha-Kohen of Lunel [early 14 Cent.] quotes the Rashba to the effect that women are allowed to put on tephillin [phylacteries]

[*Orchot Hayyim*, sec. on Tephillin, #3], and the Tosaphot state that Rabbenu Tam also ruled likewise [R.H. 33a, *s.v.* Ha Rebe Yehuda . . .].)

Similarly, the third argument . . . ordaining women in the Conservative movement will simply take us further away from the Orthodox . . . also does not bother me. We are already there . . . even if we do not want to admit it.

True, there are certain rituals that are important to both the Orthodox and Conservative movements but that is totally immaterial to the Orthodox movement today.

In Israel, and even in many places in the United States, the Orthodox rabbinate does *not* recognize or honor our Conservative conversions or divorces. It is as if we do not exist.

In fact, I remember, about eight or nine years ago when Rabbi Malev and I used to have our Jewish divorces written in New York by an Orthodox rabbi I called the Orthodox rabbi in New York and said, "I have a major problem. A woman approached me and said that she and her husband were divorced a year ago but, now, he refuses to give her a *Jewish* divorce. What can we do?"

I remember very vividly how he said, "Tell me, who officiated at the wedding?"

I replied, "A Conservative rabbi" . . . and I stated the specific city where the rabbi lived.

The Orthodox rabbi in New York then said, "Good, he probably used as witnesses people who do not observe the Shabbat according to Orthodox law. Therefore, *the marriage was never legal.* Hence, she does not need a Jewish divorce. You no longer have a problem."

Of course, that was the last time I consulted with that rabbi but I do believe that it is indicative of a trend that we in the Conservative movement are now experiencing.

My friends, I personally feel that the Conservative movement must now make a quantum move. The Conservative movement should issue a *takanah*, an amendment to our previous procedures, something that will be an improvement on the past, something that will take into consideration the present and the changes in society that have occurred during the last quarter of a century.

I personally think that this *takanah* should openly state:

1. The Jewish Theological Seminary will accept women in its rabbinic school;

2. These women will be ordained as rabbis upon completion of the complete rabbinic course of study;

3. These women will be offered rabbinic positions on the same basis as men are presently offered rabbinic positions.

Frankly speaking, I think that we at Beth Yeshurun will eventually get an assistant rabbi when the Seminary begins ordaining women into the Conservative rabbinate. I also believe that this *takanah* will enable many young Jewish women to achieve *personal* religious fulfillment, as they understand it.

I truly hope that next summer our movement will have the courage to take this quantum jump.

Amen!

177

SHE IS NOT A JEWESS IN THE FLESH
1980

A woman may not be Jewish "in the flesh," yet be Jewish in the finest, truest sense of the word. This does not mean that she will observe the Sabbath, follow the dietary laws, visit the synagogue. There are Christians—not many, to be sure—who love the Jewish way of life as the prophets have defined it. They are humanitarians, preaching the old-new gospel of love, kindness, justice, and good will to every man, woman, and child. Such a person is Mia Ingstad, who has written the letter that follows. She is the promise of that morrow yet to dawn when "The Lord shall be king over all the earth; in that day there shall be one Lord, with one name" (Zech. 14:9).

THE ADDED DIMENSION

Seeing my pictures in your October issue ("Convention '79") prompted me to take this opportunity to tell you a little about myself and what Hadassah means to me.

My name is Mia Ingstad, of Grand Forks—a fourth-generation North Dakotan. I'm 30 years old, married and the mother of a 4-year-old son. I spent the summer of 1968 in Kibbutz Maayan Barukh and 1969 at the Hebrew University in Jerusalem. I have a master's degree in history, and my thesis was on President Truman's decision to recognize the State of Israel in 1948.

I am not Jewish, nor is any member of my family: I am, however, a Zionist and a Hadassah Life Member. My mother wears a Magen David; my father went to the convention in Jerusalem with me and is a Hadassah Associate; my sister is a charter member of the Golda Meir Chapter of Hadassah in Minneapolis; my brother spent a summer in Israel.

Our Hadassah Chapter in Grand Forks is very small. We have 37 members, of whom maybe 12 are active. But we over-subscribe. We do whatever we can and then some. I have been a speaker at many service clubs throughout North Dakota whenever and wherever I can. Why?

First, because of what Israel means to me as an ideal and a living entity, and second, what Hadassah has become for me. There are few organizations that have touched so many with so much. Wherever there was a need, Hadassah reached out—is *still* reaching out—a vital, thriving movement which has made me feel as if I made a difference. The women I have met are bright, knowledgeable and involved. They are women whose husbands and children look up to them because they care enough to share themselves—the ultimate gift.

Hadassah members, as an Israeli from Haifa told me, have *nefesh*, soul. I want to thank Hadassah for the added dimension it has brought to the life of my family.

Mia Ingstad

Grand Forks, N. Dak.

ACKNOWLEDGMENTS

The following authors, editors, publishers, and institutions have permitted me to reprint copyrighted materials or documents subject to their control:

Document 1
American Jewish Historical Society: Leo Hershkowitz and Isidore S. Meyer (eds.), *Lee Max Friedman Collection of American Jewish Colonial Correspondence: Letters of the Franks Family, 1733–1748*. (American Jewish Historical Society, Waltham, Mass., 1968.)

Document 3, A and B
Historical Society of Pennsylvania, Philadelphia, Pa., Etting MSS.

Document 18
State Historical Society of Wisconsin, Madison. Rebecca Franks, Phila., to brother John, Montreal, Feb. 5, 1789. John Lawe Papers.

Documents 19, 22
Duke University Library, Jacob Mordecai Papers, Manuscript Department, William R. Perkins Library, Duke University, Durham, N.C.

Document 23
American Jewish Historical Society Library, Grace Nathan Papers.

Document 26, A, B, D, E
The Education of the Heart: The Correspondence of Rachel Mordecai Lazarus and Maria Edgeworth, edited by Edgar E. MacDonald. Copyright ©, 1977. The University of North Carolina Press, Chapel Hill, N.C. My special thanks to Professor MacDonald for his help.

Document 26, C
North Carolina Department of Cultural Resources, Division of Archives and History, Raleigh, N.C.

Document 27, C and I
American Jewish Historical Society Library, Gratz Papers.

Document 27, H
University of North Carolina at Chapel Hill Library. Letter, Rebecca Gratz to Miriam Gratz Cohen, March 29, 1841, in the Miriam Gratz Moses Papers, No. 2639, Southern Historical Collection.

Document 29
Historical Society of Pennsylvania, Etting MSS.

Document 43, C
My thanks to Morris U. Schappes and the publishers for permission to reprint excerpts from Morris U. Schappes, "Ernestine L. Rose: Her Address on the Anniversary of West Indian Emancipation," *Journal of Negro History* 34 (July 1949): 347 ff.

Document 51

I. J. Benjamin II, *Three Years in America, 1859–1862* (The Jewish Publication Society of America, Philadelphia, 1956), I, 85–88. This material is copyrighted and used through the courtesy of the Jewish Publication Society of America.

Document 60

Sefton D. Temkin, *The New World of Reform* (London, Leo Baeck College, 1971), pp. 117–19.

Document 65

By permission from *I Married Wyatt Earp: The Recollections of Josephine Sarah Marcus Earp*, collected and edited by Glenn G. Boyer, Tucson, University of Arizona Press. Copyright © 1976.

Document 66

My thanks to Mr. Paul Gerstley, Santa Monica, Calif., and Mrs. Margaret Benjamin, Chicago, Ill., for permission to publish excerpts from Jennie Gerstley's memoirs, a copy of which is housed in the American Jewish Archives, Cincinnati.

Documents 69 and 126

My thanks to Richard Lindheim for permission to publish excerpts from Irma L. Lindheim, *Parallel Quest: A Search of a Person and a People* (Thomas Yoseloff, New York, 1963), pp. 4–10, 51–59.

Document 71

My thanks to Sina Fosdick, Executive Vice-President of Nicholas Roerich Museum, for permission to publish excerpts from Florentine Scholle Sutro, *My First Seventy Years* (Roerich Museum Press, New York, 1935), pp. 24–32.

Document 73, B

Harper's Magazine, December 1934, pp. 52–58. Copyright © 1934 by *Harper's Magazine*. All rights reserved. Excerpted from the December 1934 issue by special permission [Copyright © renewed 1962].

Document 74, A

My thanks to the Regional Cultural History Project, Bancroft Library, University of California, Berkeley, Calif., for permission to publish excerpts from Amy Steinhart Braden, *Child Welfare and Community Service*, an oral interview by Edna T. Daniel (Berkeley, 1965), pp. 17–19, 34–35, 45–46, 53–54.

Document 74, C

From *920 O'Farrell Street* by Harriet Lane Levy, Copyright © 1937, 1947, pp. 235–40. Reprinted by permission of Doubleday & Company, Inc., Garden City, N.Y.

Document 75

My thanks to the Trustees of the Estate of Edna Ferber for permission to reprint excerpts from Edna Ferber, *A Peculiar Treasure* (Doubleday & Company, Inc., Garden City, N.Y., 1960), pp. 52–56, 313–14. Copyright ©, 1938, 1939 by Edna Ferber; copyright ©, 1960, by Morris L. Ernst, et

Document 81

Journal of the American Association of University Women, June 1938, pp. 226 ff. Reprinted by permission from the AAUW *Journal*, published by the American Association of University Women.

Document 84

My thanks to Paul S. Eriksson and the authors for permission to reprint excerpts from Rose Schneiderman with Lucy Goldthwaite, *All for One* (Paul S. Eriksson, Inc., New York, 1967), pp. 35–46.

Document 89

Reprinted from *The Maimie Papers*, pp. 191–96, Historical editor Ruth Rosen, Textual editor Sue Davidson, with an introduction by Ruth Rosen; copyright © 1977 by Radcliffe College; reprinted by permission of The Feminist Press, Old Westbury, N.Y.

Document 98

The Jewish Advocate: Tercentenary Magazine Supplement, Section A, January 27, 1955, p. 25-A. Reprinted by permission of the publishers.

Document 104

My thanks to Brandeis University, Waltham, Mass., and Washington University, St. Louis, Mo., for permission to publish excerpts from *Anatomy of Me: A Wonderer in Search of Herself* (Doubleday & Company, Inc., Garden City, N.Y., 1958), pp. 131–43.

Document 105

My thanks to Morris U. Schappes for permission to reprint Paula Scheier's article, "Clara Lemlich Shavelson: 50 Years in Labor's Front Line," from *Jewish Life*, November 1954, pp. 7–11.

Document 106

My thanks to the publishers of *Labor History* and to Alice Kessler-Harris for permission to reprint her article "Organizing the Unorganizable: Three Jewish Women and Their Union," *Labor History* 17, no. 1 (Winter, 1976): 5–23.

Document 109

My thanks to the publishers for permission to reprint excerpts from Goldie Stone, *My Caravan of Years: An Autobiography* (Bloch Publishing Company, New York, 1945), pp. 154–68.

Document 112, A and B

From *Henrietta Szold: Life and Letters* by Marvin Lowenthal, pp. 84–88, 191–96. Copyright © 1942, The Viking Press, Inc. Copyright © renewed, 1970, Herman C. Emer, Harry L. Shapiro, Executors for the Estate of Marvin Lowenthal. All rights reserved. Reprinted by permission of Viking Penguin, Inc., New York.

Document 114

My thanks to *Montana: The Magazine of Western History* 24 (July 1974), and to

Belle Fligelman Winestine, for permission to reprint her article "Mother Was Shocked," pp. 70–78.

Document 116

Reprinted from *Enterprising Women* by Caroline Bird, pp. 199–203, with the permission of W. W. Norton and Company, Inc., New York. Copyright © 1976 by Caroline Bird.

Document 117

My thanks to the authors Sydelle Kramer and Jenny Masur (eds.), *Jewish Grandmothers* (Boston, 1976, pp. 138–51) and to the publisher Beacon Press. Copyright © 1976 by Sydelle Kramer and Jenny Masur. Reprinted by permission of Beacon Press.

Document 120

My thanks to Grant Sanger, M.D. for permission to reprint excerpts from Margaret Sanger, *An Autobiography* (W. W. Norton & Company, Inc., New York, 1938), pp. 88–92.

Document 121

My thanks to the publishers Lyle Stuart, Inc., for permission to reprint excerpts from Mrs. Gustave Hartman, *I Gave My Heart* (The Citadel Press, New York, 1960), pp. 27–32, 240–43. Copyright © 1960 by Mrs. Gustave Hartman, published by arrangement with Lyle Stuart.

Document 122

My thanks to the publishers for permission to reprint excerpts from Polly Adler, *A House Is Not a Home* (Holt, Rinehart & Winston, New York, 1953), pp. 7–24.

Document 123

I am grateful to Ms. Elaine S. Anderson, Montgomery, Michigan, for sending me a copy of this statement of Mrs. Joseph Steinem.

Document 125

Excerpted from *Mother Is Minnie*, by Sophie Guggenheimer Untermeyer and Alix Williamson, pp. 15–20. Copyright © 1960 by Doubleday & Company, Inc. Reprinted by permission of the publishers.

Document 127

My thanks to The Quaker Oats Company for permission to reprint Frances Stern's article, "Dietetics and the Food Clinic Development," *Nutrition* 4 no. 5 (September–October 1941): 1, 3–4.

Document 129

My thanks to the Alschuler family for permission to publish Rose H. Alschuler, "I Believe—*Today*" from *Bits and Pieces of Family Lore* (Chicago[?], 1962).

Document 130

My thanks to Morris U. Schappes for permission to republish the article of Alice Citron, "An Answer to John F. Hatchett," *Jewish Currents*, September 1968, pp. 12–13.

Document 133

My thanks to the editors of *Women's American ORT Reporter* and to Irena Penzik Narell for permission to reprint the latter's "Florence Prag Kahn: The First Jewish Congresswoman," *Women's American ORT Reporter*, January–February 1978, pp. 5–6.

Document 135

Reprinted by permission of Atheneum Publishers, New York, from *They're Playing Our Song*, by Max Wilk, pp. 40–50. Copyright © 1973 by Max Wilk.

Document 136

My thanks to Jeane Westin for permission to reprint excerpts from her *Making Do: How Women Survived the '30's* (Follett Publishing Company, Chicago, 1976), pp. 142–44, 183–87, 275–77.

Document 138

My thanks to Louise L. Henriksen for permission to republish excerpts from Anzia Yezierska, *Red Ribbon on a White Horse* (Charles Scribner's Sons, New York, 1950), pp. 149–55.

Document 139

My thanks to Mrs. Werner Weinberg for permission to reprint "Susie's Story," Read at the Nuernberg-Fuerth Grand Reunion, July 7–9, 1978, at Grossinger's, Grossinger, N.Y.

Document 140

My thanks to the Amalgamated Clothing and Textile Workers Union for permission to reprint excerpts from the *Amalgamated Clothing Workers of America, Twenty-Fifth Anniversary Convention Report of the General Executive Board and Proceedings of the Thirteenth Biennial Convention, May 13–24, 1940*, pp. 476–78.

Document 142

Reprinted with permission of Macmillan Publishers Co., Inc., New York, from *The Jews: Social Patterns of an American Group*, by Marshall Sklare, pp. 357–61. Copyright © 1958 by The Free Press, Glencoe, Ill.

Document 144

My thanks to President Norman Lamm and to Rabbi Walter S. Wurzburger for permission to reprint excerpts from *Tradition* 1 (Spring 1959): 141–64.

Document 146

My thanks to the author and publishers for permission to reprint excerpts from "Janice Bernstein," in Nancy Seifer, *Nobody Speaks for Me! Self-Portraits of American Working Class Women* (Simon & Schuster, New York, 1976), pp. 90–131. Copyright © 1976 by Nancy Seifer. Reprinted by permission of Simon & Schuster, a Division of Gulf & Western Corporation.

Document 147

My thanks to the publishers of *Annals of the New York Academy of Sciences* and to Ruth F. Weiner for permission to reprint "Chemist and 'Eco-Freak,' " in *Annals of the New York Academy of Sciences* 208 (March 15, 1973): 52–56.

Document 149, A
Selections are reprinted from *The Feminine Mystique* by Betty Friedan with the permission of W. W. Norton & Company, Inc., New York. Copyright © 1974, 1963 by Betty Friedan, pp. 37–38, 330, 336, 343–44, 351, 353, 361–62, 364.

Document 149, B
My thanks to Betty Friedan and to Random House, Inc., New York, for permission to republish excerpts from *It Changed My Life: Writings on the Women's Movement* (New York, 1976), pp. 12, 18–19.

Document 150
My thanks to the editors of *Chutzpah: A Jewish Liberation Anthology* (New Glide Publications, Inc., San Francisco, 1977) for permission to reprint "Dilemma of a Jewish Lesbian." Copyright © by the Chutzpah Collective, 1977, pp. 30–31.

Document 151
My thanks to Doris B. Gold and to *Congress Bi-Weekly* for permission to reprint excerpts from "Jewish Women's Groups: Separate—But Unequal—" *Congress Bi-Weekly*, February 6, 1970, pp. 9–11.

Document 152
My thanks to Trude Weiss-Rosmarin for permission to reprint her article "The Unfreedom of Jewish Women," *Jewish Spectator* 35 (October 1970): 206.

Document 153
My thanks to Bella Abzug and the publishers for permission to reprint "Bella on Bella," *Moment* 1 (February 1976): 26–29.

Document 154
My thanks to Los Angeles Hillel Council for permission to reprint the article by Bob Elias, "Fruma Buber—Girl Rabbi," *Davka* 1, no. 4 (Summer 1971): 12–14.

Document 155, B
My thanks to Rabbi Sally Priesand and the publishers of the National Council of Jewish Women's *Council Woman* for permission to use material in Sally Priesand, *Judaism and the New Woman* (Behrman House, Inc., New York, 1975), Preface.

Document 156
My thanks to Professor Paula E. Hyman for providing me with a copy of "Jewish Women Call for Change," the manifesto of Ezrat Nashim.

Document 157
My thanks to the publishers of *Keeping Posted* and to "Leah Cohen" for permission to reprint "A Woman Reborn," *Keeping Posted*, April 1972, pp. 7–8.

Document 158
My thanks to Jacqueline K. Levine and to the publishers of *Response* for

permission to reprint excerpts of her article, "The Changing Role of Women in the Jewish Community," *Response* 7, no. 2 (Summer 1973): 59–65.

Document 159

My thanks to the Rabbinical Assembly, to the Jewish Theological Seminary of America, and to Professor Paula E. Hyman for permission to republish excerpts of her article, "The Other Half: Women in the Jewish Tradition," *Conservative Judaism* 26, no. 4 (Summer 1972): 14–21

Document 160

My thanks to the publishers of *Pioneer Woman* and to Ethel C. Fenig for permission to publish her article, "National Conference on Jewish Women and Men: A Report," *Pioneer Woman* 19 (June 1974): 7–8, 12.

Document 161

My thanks to the United Synagogue of America for permission to reprint excerpts from *Proceedings, the United Synagogue of America, 1973 Biennial Convention*, pp. 108–9.

Document 162

My thanks to *Congress Bi-Weekly* and to Professor Daniel J. Elazar for permission to reprint his article, "Women in American Jewish Life," *Congress Bi-Weekly* 40 (November 23, 1973): 10–11.

Document 164

My thanks to Dr. Robert Gordis, Editor of *Judaism*, and to Dr. Naomi Bluestone for permission to reprint her article, "Exodus from Eden: One Woman's Experience," *Judaism* 23 (Winter 1974): 95–99.

Document 165

My thanks to Dr. Eugene Borowitz, Editor of *Sh'ma*, for permission to reprint the following two articles: Helen G. Pierson, "Binghamton, New York," and Lois Fox, "Nashville, Tennessee," *Sh'ma*, February 1976, pp. 62–64.

Document 166

My thanks to the National Council of Jewish Women and to Anne G. Wolfe for permission to reprint her article, "No Room at the Top," *Council Woman* 38 (January 1976): 3–4.

Document 167

My thanks to the National Council of Jewish Women and to Professor Sarah Davis for permission to reprint excerpts from her article, "Jews in Politics: Where Are the Women," *Council Woman* 38 (January 1976), 5–7.

Document 169

My thanks to Holt, Rinehart and Winston and to Professor Lucy S. Dawidowicz for permission to reprint the latter's article, "On Being a Woman in Shul," *The Jewish Presence: Essays on Identity and History* (New York, 1977), pp. 47–57.

Document 170, A

My thanks to the Nobel Foundation and to Dr. Rosalyn S. Yalow for permission to reprint her copyrighted © 1978 autobiography.

Document 171
My thanks to the editors of the Hebrew Union College Press and to Dr. Solomon B. Freehof for permission to reprint pp. 216–20 from the latter's *Reform Responsa for Our Time* (Cincinnati, 1977).

Document 173
My thanks to the Women's League for Conservative Judaism, to the editors of their magazine, *Women's League Outlook*, and to Irma Bailey for permission to republish the latter's article, "Thoughts of a Convert—Five Years Later," *Women's League Outlook* 48 (Fall 1977): 12.

Document 174
My thanks to the Women's League for Conservative Judaism, to the editors of their magazine, *Women's League Outlook*, and to Walter Duckat for permission to reprint the latter's article, "Second Career—Guidance for the Mature Jewish Woman," *Women's League Outlook* 48 (Summer 1978): 7, 28–29.

Document 175
My thanks to the editors of *Women's American ORT Reporter* and to Judith Slawson for permission to reprint the latter's article, "Finding My Jewish Self," *Women's American ORT Reporter*, September–October 1978, p. 9.

Document 176
My thanks to Rabbi Jack Segal of Congregation Beth Yeshurun, Houston, to the editors of the synagogal *Message* (1978), and to Gabriel Cohen, Editor of the *Jewish Post and Opinion* (January 19, 1979), for permission to reprint a sermon of Rabbi Segal, "Should We Have Women in the Conservative Rabbinate?"

Document 177
My thanks to Mr. Jessie Lurie, the executive director of *Hadassah Magazine*, for permission to reprint the Mia Ingstad letter.

Illustrations
As far as possible, all photographs that require credit lines have been so marked. The publishers will be pleased to receive information concerning additional credit lines for all future printings of this volume.

NOTES

1. Leo Hershkowitz and Isidore S. Meyer, *The Lee Max Friedman Collection of American Jewish Correspondence: Letters of the Franks Family, 1733–1748* (Waltham, Mass., 1968), pp. 57 ff., 116 ff. These letters were first printed in Jacob Rader Marcus, *Early American Jewry: The Jews of New York, New England and Canada, 1649–1794* (Philadelphia, 1951), I, 58 ff., 68 ff.
2. The Henry Joseph Collection of Gratz Papers, American Jewish Archives, Cincinnati; Jacob Rader Marcus, *American Jewry—Documents—18th Century* (Cincinnati, 1959), pp. 358–59.
3. Etting MSS, Historical Society of Pennsylvania, Philadelphia.
   A. Marcus, *Early American Jewry: The Jews of Pennsylvania and the South, 1655–1790* (Philadelphia, 1955), II, 32–33.
   B. William Vincent Byars (ed.), *B. and M. Gratz: Merchants in Philadelphia 1754–1798* (Jefferson City, Mo., 1916), p. 164.
4. Lopez Papers, Newport Historical Society; Marcus, *Early American Jewry*, II, 254.
5. A. *The Pennsylvania Magazine of History and Biography*, XVI, 216–18.
   B. MS, Historical Society of Pennsylvania; Marcus, *Early American Jewry*, II, 113–17.
6. Lyons Collection, American Jewish Historical Society, Waltham, Mass.; *Publications of the American Jewish Historical Society*, XXVII, 171–72.
7. Etting MSS, Historical Society of Pennsylvania;
   A. Byars, p. 182.
   B. Marcus, *American Jewry—Documents*, pp. 55–56.
8. Allen D. Candler, *The Colonial Records of the State of Georgia* (Atlanta, Ga.), XII, 454–56.
9. Mr. and Mrs. B. H. Levy Collection of Sheftall Papers, Savannah, Ga.;
   A. Marcus, *American Jewry—Documents*, pp. 264–65.
   B. Marcus, *Early American Jewry*, II, 361–63.
10. College of William and Mary, Williamsburg, Va., British Headquarters Paper (Carleton Papers), No. 3427; Marcus, *American Jewry—Documents*, p. 274.
11. Archives of Congregation Mikveh Israel, Philadelphia; Marcus, *American Jewry—Documents*, pp. 134–36.
12. Reprinted by permission of the owner of the letter, Gordon A. Block, Jr.; *American Jewish Archives*, XXVII, 239–42.
13. Archives of Congregation Mikveh Israel, Philadelphia; Marcus, *American Jewry—Documents*, pp. 143–44.
14. The Henry Joseph Collection of Gratz Papers, American Jewish Archives; Marcus, *American Jewry—Documents*, pp. 51–54.
15. Jacob Mordecai Papers, Manuscript Department, William R. Perkins Library, Duke University, Durham, N.C.; Marcus, *American Jewry—Documents*, pp. 60–62.
16. A, B. Archives of Congregation Mikveh Israel, Philadelphia;
    B. Edwin Wolf 2nd and Maxwell Whiteman, *The History of the Jews of Philadelphia from Colonial Times to the Age of Jackson* (Philadelphia, 1956), p. 234.
17. Jacob Mordecai Papers, Manuscript Department, William R. Perkins Library, Duke University; Marcus, *American Jewry—Documents*, pp. 78–79.
18. John Lawe Papers, State Historical Society of Wisconsin, Madison; Marcus, *American Jewry—Documents*, pp. 83–85.
19. Jacob Mordecai Papers, Manuscript Department, William R. Perkins Library, Duke University.
20. Myer Moses, *An Oration, Delivered before the Hebrew Orphan Society, on the 15th Day of October, 1806* (Charleston, 1807), pp. 29–31.
21. Shearith Israel Trustee Book, II, 95 (second numbering), 1807. Hyman B. Grinstein, *The Rise of the Jewish Community of New York, 1654–1860* (Philadelphia, 1945), p. 26.
22. Jacob Mordecai Papers, Manuscript Department, William R. Perkins Library, Duke University.
23. Grace Nathan Papers, American Jewish Historical Society.
24. Barnett A. Elzas, *The Old Jewish Cemeteries at Charleston, S.C.* (Charleston, 1903), pp. 9, 12, 29, 76, 85, 91.

25. Charles J. Cohen Collection, American Jewish Archives; *American Jewish Archives*, VI, 13.
26. A, B, D, E. Edgar E. MacDonald (ed.), *The Education of the Heart: The Correspondence of Rachel Mordecai Lazarus and Maria Edgeworth* (Chapel Hill, N.C.), pp. 6, 111, 274, 305–7. Copyright © 1977, The University of North Carolina Press.
    C. Mordecai Papers, North Carolina Department of Archives and History, Raleigh. Printed in MacDonald, p. 212.
27. A. *The Constitution of the Female Hebrew Benevolent Society of Philadelphia* (Philadelphia, 1825).
    B. Jacob Rader Marcus, *Memoirs of American Jews, 1775–1865* (Philadelphia, 1955), I, 272 ff.
    C, I. Gratz Papers, American Jewish Historical Society.
    D, E, F, G, J. David Philipson (ed.), *Letters of Rebecca Gratz* (Philadelphia, 1929), pp. 145–46, 228, 244–45, 289–90, 341–42.
    H. Letter, Rebecca Gratz to Miriam Gratz Cohen, March 29, 1841, in the Miriam Gratz Moses Papers, No. 2639. Southern Historical Collection, Library of the University of North Carolina at Chapel Hill.
28. *Henry Luria; or, The Little Jewish Convert: Being Contained in the Memoir of Mrs. S. J. Cohen* (New York, 1960), pp. 77–92.
29. Etting MSS., Historical Society of Pennsylvania.
30. Will of Esther Sheftall, June 6, 1828, Court of Ordinary, Chatham County, Ga.
31. *Publications of the American Jewish Historical Society*, XXVII, 301.
32. A. Nathan Family Papers, American Jewish Archives.
    B. Mordecai Papers, Library of Congress.
    C. Copy in Jacob R. Marcus Papers.
33. A, C, D, E, F, G. *Secular and Religious Works of Penina Moïse, With Brief Sketch of Her Life.* Compiled and Published by Charleston Section, Council of Jewish Women (Charleston, S.C., 1911), pp. 37, 57, 177, 211–12, 289, 313.
34. Isaac Leeser, *Discourses on the Jewish Religion* (Philadelphia, 1866–67), II, 172–76.
35. Register of Mesne Conveyances and Judge of Probate, Charleston, S.C., Will Book, 45 (1845–1851), pp. 581–83.
36. "Recollections of the First Hebrew Sunday School," *The Hebrew Watchword and Instructor*, February–April (1897), No. 6, p. 5; No. 7, pp. 11–13; No. 8, pp. 4–5; Marcus, *Memoirs of American Jews, 1775–1865* (Philadelphia, 1955), I, 281 ff.; *PAJHS*, XLII, 397 ff.
37. Copy in Jacob R. Marcus Papers.
38. Mendes Cohen Collection, Maryland Historical Society, Baltimore, Md.
39. Minutes of Congregation Beth Elohim, October, 1841, Charleston, S.C., pp. 197–201.
40. *The Occident*, I, 162–66.
41. Marcus, *Memoirs*, III, 55 ff.
42. *The Occident*, IX, 79 ff.
43. A. *The Proceedings of the Woman's Rights Convention Held at Worcester, October 15th and 16th, 1851* (New York, 1852), pp. 36–37.
    B. *The Proceedings of the Woman's Rights Convention Held at Syracuse, September 8th, 9th, and 10th, 1852* (Syracuse, 1852), pp. 63–64.
    C. *Journal of Negro History*, XXXIV, 347 ff.
44. M. J. Raphall (ed.), *Ruhamah: Devotional Exercises for the Use of the Daughters of Israel* (New York, 1852), pp. 116–17, 129–30.
45. Rebekah Hyneman, *The Leper: and Other Poems* (Philadelphia, 1853), pp. 80, 149, 151.
46. *The Asmonean*, March 24, 1854, pp. 180–81.
47. Marcus, *Memoirs of American Jews, 1775–1865* (Philadelphia, 1955), II, 351 ff.
48. Octavia Harby Moses, *A Mother's Poems: A Collection of Verses* (n.p., 1915), pp. 24–25.
49. A. Morris Silverman, *Hartford Jews, 1659–1970* (Hartford, Conn., 1970), p. 24.
    B. Paper of Mrs. Leon Ullman read at the "Get Together" Meeting of the Sisterhood, February 1917, Anniston, Ala., Jacob R. Marcus Papers.
    C. MS Minutes of the Ladies Benevolent Society of Portsmouth, Ohio. Copy in American Jewish Archives.
    D. *Constitution and By-Laws of the Ladies Hebrew Benevolent Society of Galveston, Texas* (Galveston, 1903).
    E. *Constitution of the Sisterhood of Keneseth Israel [Philadelphia] Organized April, 1912.*
50. Copy of MS Letter in American Jewish Archives.
51. [I. J.] Benjamin II, *Three Years in America, 1859–1862* (Philadelphia, 1956), I, 85–88.

52. Sarah M. Wartcki, *My Mother's Memories of Her Childhood* (Cincinnati, 1976), pp. 3–7, 18–21.
53. Marcus, *Memoirs*, II, 268 ff.
54. A. *Sinai*, VI, 381–84; Morris U. Schappes (ed.), *A Documentary History of the Jews in the United States, 1654–1875* (New York, 1971), pp. 459 ff.
    B. Copy in the Bertram W. Korn Collection in the American Jewish Archives, apparently from the *Philadelphia Ledger*, June 26, 1863.
55. Phoebe Yates Levy Pember, *A Southern Woman's Story* (New York, 1879), pp. 36–44, 72–76; *American Jewish Archives*, XIII, 44–51.
56. [Clara Lowenburg Moses,] *Aunt Sister's Book* (New York, 1929), pp. 1–14; Marcus, *Memoirs*, I, 261 ff.
57. Marcus, *Memoirs*, III, 357–74.
58. Maud Nathan, *Once Upon a Time and Today* (New York, 1933), pp. 27–31.
59. Adah Isaacs Menken, *Infelicia* (Philadelphia, 1870), pp. 20–23, 47–50, 67–71, 82–86.
60. Sefton D. Temkin, *The New World of Reform* (London, 1971), pp. 117–19.
61. A. *American Israelite (AI)*, January 8, 1875, p. 4, c. 5.
    B. Ibid., January 22, 1875, p. 5, c. 3.
62. A. Ibid., September 8, 1876, p. 4, c. 3, 4.
    B. *Jewish Messenger (JM)*, September 9, 1881, p. 5, c. 3.
    C. *The American Jewess*, June 1895, p. 153.
    D. *Proceedings of the Union of American Hebrew Congregations* (Cincinnati, 1923), X, 9329–30.
63. *AI*, July 13, 1877, p. 4.
64. A. Ibid., January 10, 1879, p. 7, c. 1.
    B. Evelina Gleaves Cohen, *Family Facts and Fairy Tales* (Wynnewood, Pa., 1953), pp. 94–95.
65. Glenn G. Boyer (ed.), *I Married Wyatt Earp: The Recollections of Josephine Sarah Marcus Earp* (Tucson, Ariz., 1976), pp. 5–9, 13–15, 121–25.
66. Jennie R. Gerstley, "My Childhood in Early Chicago" (Chicago, 1937), pp. 129–37. MS copy in American Jewish Archives.
67. Liebman Adler, *Sabbath Hours Thoughts* (Philadelphia, 1893), pp. 37–41.
68. *The Poems of Emma Lazarus* (Boston, 1888), I, 202–3; II, 3–4, 14–15.
69. Irma L. Lindheim, *Parallel Quest: A Search of a Person and a People* (New York, 1962), pp. 4–10.
70. Copy of original German letter is in the American Jewish Archives.
71. Florentine Scholle Sutro, *My First Seventy Years* (New York, 1935), pp. 24–32.
72. A. *JM*, October 13, 1882, p. 4, c. 2.
    B. Ibid., January 12, 1883, pp. 4–5; January 19, 1883, pp. 4–5.
73. A. *The New York Times*, May 14, 1940, p. 23, c. 1–2.
    B. *Harper's Magazine*, December 1934, pp. 52–58.
74. A. Amy Steinhart Braden, *Child Welfare and Community Service: An Interview Conducted by Edna Tartaul Daniel*. University of California, Regional Cultural History Project (Berkeley, 1965), pp. 17–19, 34–35, 45–46, 53–54.
    B. *The American Jewess*, October 1896, pp. 10–12.
    C. Harriet Lane Levy, *920 O'Farrell Street* (Garden City, N.Y., 1947), pp. 235–40.
75. Edna Ferber, *A Peculiar Treasure* (Garden City, N.Y., 1960), pp. 52–56, 313–14.
76. *JM*, May 23, 1890.
77. Annie Nathan Meyer, *Woman's Work in America* (New York, 1891), pp. iii–vi.
78. A. *Year Book of the Central Conference of American Rabbis*, III, 40.
    B. Ibid., XXIII, 120, 133–34.
    C. Ibid., XXV, 133.
    D. Ibid., XXVII, 175–77.
    E. Joseph Krauskopf, *The Ascendency of Womanhood* (Farm School, Bucks County, Pa., 1917).
79. *The American Jews' Annual for 5653 A.M., January 1st, 1893 . . . January 1st, 1894* (Cincinnati, 1893), pp. 91–95. This article is a reprint from the *Ladies' Home Journal*.
80. A. Lillian D. Wald, *The House on Henry Street* (New York, 1915), pp. 4–8.
    B. Ibid., pp. 22–23.
81. *Journal of the American Association of University Women*, June 1938, pp. 226 ff.
82. A. *Papers of the Jewish Women's Congress. Held at Chicago, September 4, 5, 6, and 7, 1893* (Philadelphia, 1894), pp. 91 ff.
    B. Ibid., pp. 218 ff.
    C. Ibid., pp. 266–67.

    D. *The American Jewess*, April 1895, p. 30.

    E. *Proceedings of the First Convention of the National Council of Jewish Women Held at New York, November 15, 16, 17, 18 and 19, 1896* (Philadelphia, 1897), pp. 93–94.

    F. Ibid., pp. 73–74.

    G. Ibid., pp. 84–85.

    H. Hannah G. Solomon, *A Sheaf of Leaves* (Chicago, 1911), pp. 175 ff.

83. *The Menorah Journal*, Winter 1947, pp. 111 ff.

84. Rose Schneiderman with Lucy Goldthwaite, *All for One* (New York, 1967), pp. 35–46.

85. *The American Jewess*, I (1895), 10–11.

86. Ibid., I (1895), 67–70.

87. Ibid., I (1895), 262, 264.

88. *The New-York Daily Tribune. Illustrated Supplement*, January 15, 1898, p. 5; Allon Schoener (ed.), *Portal to America: The Lower East Side 1870–1925* (New York, 1967), pp. 118–19.

89. Ruth Rosen and Sue Davidson (eds.), *The Maimie Papers* (Cambridge, Mass., 1977), pp. 191–96.

90. Rebekah Kohut, *My Portion: An Autobiography* (New York, 1927), pp. 223–32.

91. A. Charles K. Harris, "A Rabbi's Daughter" (Milwaukee, 1899). Original in collection of Lester S. Levy of Baltimore.

    B. *The Jewish Daily News*, August 12, 1903, English Department page.

92. *The New York Times*, January 3, 1933, pp. 1, 24.

93. *New-York Tribune. Illustrated Supplement*, August 26, 1900, p. 13, c. 1–3; Schoener, pp. 120–22.

94. A. *New-York Tribune*, September 30, 1900, p. 4; Schoener, pp. 117–18.

    B. *New-York Tribune. Illustrated Supplement*, June 30, 1901, p. 4, c. 1–2; Schoener, p. 120.

95. A. Hutchins Hapgood, *The Spirit of the Ghetto: Studies of the Jewish Quarter in New York* (New York, 1909), pp. 71–89.

    B. Charles S. Bernheimer, *The Russian Jew in the United States: Studies of Social Conditions in New York, Philadelphia, and Chicago, with a Description of Rural Settlements* (Philadelphia, 1905), pp. 225–26, 231–32.

96. Mrs. Simon Kander and Mrs. Henry Schoenfeld (compilers), *The Way to a Man's Heart. Under the Auspices of "The Settlement"* (Milwaukee, 1903), pp. 4–5.

97. *The New York Times*, May 30, 1951.

98. *The Jewish Advocate. Tercentenary Magazine Supplement*, Section A, January 27, 1955, p. 25-A.

99. A. George M. D. Wolfe, *A Study in Immigrant Attitudes and Problems Based on an Analysis of Four Hundred Letters Printed in the "Bintel Brief" of the "Jewish Daily Forward"* (dissertation submitted to the Training School for Jewish Social Work, New York, 1929), pp. 31–32.

    B. Ibid., pp. 75–78.

    C. Ibid., pp. 106–8.

    D. Ibid., pp. 112–14.

    E. Ibid., p. 175.

    Copy in American Jewish Archives.

100. *Annals of the American Academy of Political and Social Science*, XXVII, 627–37.

101. *New-York Tribune*, June 28, 1906, p. 4; Schoener, p. 132.

102. Neil Kominsky, *Jennie Franklin Purvin: A Study in Womanpower* (Cincinnati, 1968) pp. 1 ff.

103. *The New York Times*, October 28, 1938, p. 23, c. 1.

104. Fannie Hurst, *Anatomy of Me: A Wonderer in Search of Herself* (Garden City, N.Y., 1958), pp. 131–43.

105. *Jewish Life*, November 1954, pp. 7–11.

106. *Labor History*, XVII, 5–23.

107. *The New York Times*, March 26, 1911, pp. 1 ff.

108. *American Jewish Year Book, 1924–1925*, XXVI (Philadelphia, 1924), 345–47.

109. Goldie Stone, *My Caravan of Years: An Autobiography* (New York, 1945), pp. 154–68.

110. Mary Antin, *The Promised Land* (Boston, 1912), pp. 197–98, 222–23, 244, 246–48.

111. *American Jewish Archives*, XXVI, 14–22.

112. A. Marvin Lowenthal, *Henrietta Szold: Life and Letters* (New York, 1942), pp. 84–88.

    B. Ibid., pp. 191–96.

    C. *Hadassah News Letter*, April 1934, pp. 3–5.

113. Works Progress Administration, Chicago Foreign Language Press Survey, reel 91-B, boxes 32–41, American Jewish Archives.

114. *Montana: The Magazine of Western History*, XXIV (July 1974), 70–78.
115. A. Sophie Irene Loeb, *Epigrams of Eve* (New York, 1913), pp. 32–36.
    B. *The American Hebrew*, September 10, 1915, pp. 458–59, 461, 534–35.
    C. *The Evening World*, January 19, 1929, p. 11.
116. Caroline Bird, *Enterprising Women* (New York, 1976), pp. 199–203.
117. Sydelle Kramer and Jenny Masur (eds.), *Jewish Grandmothers* (Boston, 1976), pp. 138–51.
118. A. David Philipson, *My Life as an American Jew: An Autobiography* (Cincinnati, 1941), pp. 234–37.
    B. *American Jewish Archives*, XXV, 97–98.
119. *The New York Times*, November 21, 1972, p. 1, c. 1–3; p. 46, c. 2–3.
120. Margaret Sanger, *An Autobiography* (New York, 1938), pp. 88–92.
121. Mrs. Gustave Hartman, *I Gave My Heart* (New York, 1960), pp. 27–32, 240–43.
122. Polly Adler, *A House Is Not a Home* (New York, 1953), pp. 7–24.
123. *Toledo Blade*, October 28, 1914, p. 9.
124. *The Menorah Journal*, II, 294–300.
125. Sophie Guggenheimer Untermeyer and Alix Williamson, *Mother Is Minnie* (Garden City, N.Y., 1960), pp. 15–20.
126. Irma L. Lindheim, *Parallel Quest: A Search of a Person and a People* (New York, 1962), pp. 51–59.
127. *Nutrition*, IV (Chicago, Ill., September–October 1941), 1, 3–4.
128. Jessie E. Sampter, *Around the Year in Rhymes for the Jewish Child* (New York, 1920), pp. 11, 36, 49.
129. Rose H. Alschuler, *Bits and Pieces of Family Lore* (Chicago[?], 1962).
130. A. *The Worker*, July 10, 1955, p. 11.
    B. *Jewish Currents*, September 1968, pp. 12–13.
131. *Year Book of the Central Conference of American Rabbis*, XXXII, 51, 156–64.
132. *The Jewish Woman*, III (October 1923), 6, 26–27.
133. *Women's American ORT Reporter*, January–February 1978, pp. 5–6.
134. "To My Mother on Her Seventy-Fifth Birthday, March 18th, 1928," by David A. Brown. Copy in American Jewish Archives.
135. Max Wilk, *They're Playing Our Song* (New York, 1973), pp. 40–50.
136. A. Jeane Westin, *Making Do: How Women Survived the '30's* (Chicago, 1976), pp. 142–44.
    B. *Ibid.*, pp. 183–87, 275–77.
137. A. Esther Bengis, *I Am a Rabbi's Wife* (Moodus, Conn., 1937), pp. 45–50.
    B. News release, Union of American Hebrew Congregations, September 1, 1954, copy in American Jewish Archives; *American Jewish Archives*, XXV, 66–67; *American Judaism*, III (January 1954), 11–12; IV (September 1954), 9.
138. Anzia Yezierska, *Red Ribbon on a White Horse* (New York, 1950), pp. 149–55.
139. Lisl Weinberg, "Susie's Story." Read at the Nuernberg-Fuerth Grand Reunion, July 7–9, 1978, at Grossinger's, Grossinger, New York. Typescript in American Jewish Archives.
140. *Amalgamated Clothing Workers of America. Twenty-Fifth Anniversary Convention. Report of the General Executive Board and Proceedings of the Thirteenth Biennial Convention, May 13–24, 1940*, pp. 476–78.
141. The Wilmington (N.C.) *Star-News*, November 10, 1974.
142. Marshall Sklare (ed.), *The Jews: Social Patterns of an American Group* (Glencoe, Ill., 1958), pp. 357–61.
143. *My Ethical Will: Teenagers' Testaments. Written by the Members of the Confirmation Class of May 25, 1958, of the Rockdale Avenue Temple, Congregation Bene Israel, Cincinnati, Ohio*, pp. 7–8, 26–27.
144. *Tradition*, I (Spring 1959), 141–64.
145. News release, Union of American Hebrew Congregations, September 1, 1954. Copy in American Jewish Archives; *American Jewish Archives*, XXV, 67–69.
146. Nancy Seifer, *Nobody Speaks for Me! Self-Portraits of American Working Class Women* (New York, 1976), pp. 90–131.
147. *Annals of the New York Academy of Sciences*, CCVIII (March 15, 1973), 52–56.
148. A. *The Jewish Home. Di Yiddishe Heim*, II, No. 3 (1960), 23.
    B. *The New York Times*, April 4, 1972.
    C. *Resolutions Adopted by the Union of Orthodox Jewish Congregations of America, 76th Anniversary*

Biennial [sic!] Convention, 13–17 Kislev, 5735, November 27–December 1, 1974 . . . Boca Raton, Florida, pp. 24–25.

    D. Ibid., p. 36.

149. A. Betty Friedan, *The Feminine Mystique* (New York, 1973), pp. 37–38, 330, 336, 343–44, 351, 353, 361–62, 364.

    B. Betty Friedan, *It Changed My Life: Writings on the Women's Movement* (New York, 1976), pp. 12, 18–19.

150. Stephen Lubet et al., *Chutzpah: A Jewish Liberation Anthology* (New Glide Publications, San Francisco, 1977), pp. 30–31.

151. *Congress Bi-Weekly,* February 6, 1970, pp. 9–11.

152. *Jewish Spectator,* XXXV (October 1970), 2–6.

153. *Moment,* I (February 1976), 26–29.

154. *Davka,* I (Summer 1971), 12–14.

155. A. *American Jewish Archives,* XXVI, 236–38. This release has been modified by its author, Jacob R. Marcus.

    B. Rabbi Sally Priesand, *Judaism and the New Woman* (New York, 1975), Preface.

156. "Jewish Women Call for Change," March 1972 (mimeo). This copy has been made available through the courtesy of Professor Paula E. Hyman of Columbia University.

157. *Keeping Posted,* April 1972, pp. 7–8.

158. *Response,* VII (Summer 1973), 59–65.

159. *Conservative Judaism,* XXVI (Summer 1972), 14–21.

160. *Pioneer Woman,* XIX (June 1974), 7–8, 12.

161. *Proceedings. The United Synagogue of America, 1973 Biennial Convention, Concord Hotel, Kiamesha Lake, N.Y., November 11–15, 1973,* pp. 108–9.

162. *Congress Bi-Weekly,* XL (November 23, 1973), 10–11.

163. *The New York Times,* April 17, 1974, p. 48.

164. *Judaism,* XXIII (Winter 1974), 95–99.

165. *Sh'ma,* February 20, 1976, pp. 62–64.

166. *Council Woman,* XXXVIII (January 1976), 3–4.

167. Ibid., 5–7.

168. *The New York Times,* December 24, 1976, p. A-8c.

169. Lucy S. Dawidowciz, *The Jewish Presence: Essays on Identity and History* (New York, 1977), pp. 47–57.

170. A. Rosalyn Yalow autobiography, submitted by her to the Nobel Prize Committee and published here with the consent of Mrs. Yalow and the Nobel Foundation.

    B. *The New York Times,* June 12, 1978, p. A–19.

171. Solomon B. Freehof, *Reform Responsa for Our Time* (Cincinnati, 1977), pp. 216–20.

172. Bat Mitzvah address of Susan Brandeis Popkin, Washington Hebrew Congregation, Washington, D.C., June 11, 1977. Copy in American Jewish Archives.

173. *Outlook,* XLVIII (Fall 1977), 12.

174. Ibid. (Summer 1978), 7, 28–29.

175. *Women's American ORT Reporter,* September–October 1978, p. 9.

176. *The Jewish Post and Opinion,* January 19, 1979, pp. 3–4. Originally in the *Message* of Congregation Beth Yeshurun, Houston, Texas, October 6, 1978, VI, No. 1 (1978), 5–6.

177. *Hadassah Magazine,* January 1980, p. 23.

INDEX
Compiled by Robert J. Milch, M.A.

*The index entry for "East European Jews" provides separate listings for the various nationality designations used by the many different writers of the selections in this volume. Users of the index should bear in mind, however, that some of the writers applied the term "Russian Jew" to all East European Jewish immigrants, and that in other cases the terms "Russian" and "Polish" have essentially the same geographical connotation.